A Companion to Chaucer

Blackwell Companions to Literature and Culture

PUBLISHED:

Companion to Victorian Literature and Culture *Edited by Herbert F. Tucker*
Companion to Romanticism *Edited by Duncan Wu*
Companion to Shakespeare *Edited by David Scott Kastan*
Companion to Gothic *Edited by David Punter*
A Feminist Companion to Shakespeare *Edited by Dympna Callaghan*
Companion to Postcolonial Studies *Edited by Henry Schwarz and Sangeeta Ray*
Companion to Film Theory *Edited by Toby Miller and Robert Stam*
Companion to Children's Literature and Culture *Edited by Peter Hunt*

FORTHCOMING:

Companion to Literary Theory *Edited by Terry Eagleton and Stephen Regan*
Companion to Art Theory *Edited by Paul Smith and Carolyn Wilde*
Companion to Shakespeare's Histories *Edited by Richard Dutton and Jean Howard*
Companion to Shakespeare's Early Comedies and Non-Dramatic Verse *Edited by Richard Dutton and Jean Howard*
Companion to Shakespeare's Tragedies *Edited by Richard Dutton and Jean Howard*
Companion to Shakespeare's Problem Comedies and Late Plays *Edited by Richard Dutton and Jean Howard*
Companion to Anglo-Saxon Literature *Edited by Phillip Pulsiano and Elaine M. Treharne*
Companion to Medieval Literature and Culture *Edited by Peter Brown*
Companion to Early Modern Women's Writing 1500–1700 *Edited by Anita Pacheco*
Companion to English Renaissance Literature *Edited by Michael Hattaway*
Companion to English Renaissance Drama *Edited by Arthur F. Kinney*
Companion to Milton *Edited by T. N. Corns*
Companion to Literature from Milton to Blake *Edited by David Womersley*
Companion to Restoration Drama *Edited by Sue Owen*
Companion to the Victorian Novel *Edited by Patrick Brantlinger and William Thesing*
Companion to Victorian Poetry *Edited by Richard Cronin, Alison Chapman and Anthony Harrison*
Companion to Modern Irish Literature *Edited by Stephen Regan*
Companion to Twentieth-century Poetry *Edited by Neil Roberts*
Companion to Modernism *Edited by Jeri Johnson and Andrew McNeillie*
Companion to American Literature *Edited by Paul Lauter*
Companion to African-American Literature *Edited by David L. Smith*
Companion to American Poetry *Edited by Albert Gelpi and Gareth Reeves*
Companion to the Modern American Novel 1900–1950 *Edited by John Matthews*
Companion to Post-war American Literature and Culture *Edited by Josephine Hendin*
Companion to Literature and Culture of the American South *Edited by Richard Gray*

A COMPANION TO
CHAUCER

EDITED BY **PETER BROWN**

Copyright © Blackwell Publishers Ltd 2000
Editorial matter, selection and arrangement copyright © Peter Brown 2000

First published 2000

2 4 6 8 10 9 7 5 3 1

Blackwell Publishers Ltd
108 Cowley Road
Oxford OX4 1JF
UK

Blackwell Publishers Inc.
350 Main Street
Malden, Massachusetts 02148
USA

British Library Cataloguing in Publication Data

A CIP catalogue record for this book is available from the British Library.

Library of Congress Cataloging-in-Publication Data

A companion to Chaucer / edited by Peter Brown.
p. cm. – (Blackwell anthologies)
Includes bibliographical references and index.
ISBN 0-631-21332-5 (alk. paper)
1. Chaucer, Geoffrey, d. 1400. 2. Chaucer, Geoffrey, d. 1400 – Knowledge and learning.
3. Civilization, Medieval, in literature. 4. Literature and society – England – History – To 1500. 5. England – Civilization – 1066–1485. 6. England – Intellectual life – 1066–1485. I. Brown, Peter, 1948– II. Series.

PR1906.5 C66 2001
821'.1 – dc21   00-039735

Typeset in 11 on 13 pt Garamond 3
by Best-set Typesetter Ltd., Hong Kong
Printed in Great Britain by TJ International, Padstow, Cornwall
This book is printed on acid-free paper

Contents

Illustrations

The Contributors

Malcolm Andrew is Professor of English Language and Literature at the Queen's University of Belfast, where he has become increasingly involved in management during the past few years. His main publications include *The Poems of the Pearl Manuscript* (with Ronald Waldron, 1978), an annotated bibliography of writings on the *Gawain*-poet (1979), *Two Early Renaissance Bird Poems* (1984) and the Variorum Edition of the General Prologue of the *Canterbury Tales* (with Charles Moorman and Daniel J. Ransom, 1993).

Alcuin Blamires is Reader in English at Goldsmiths College, University of London. He has specialized recently in research on the medieval debate about women, on which he has published articles, an anthology of texts and the monograph *The Case for Women in Medieval Culture* (1997). Another interest is coming to fruition in a co-authored book (with Gail Holian) on *Roman de la rose* manuscript illumination. His current project is a book on Chaucer, gender and ethics.

Derek Brewer is Emeritus Professor of English of Cambridge University and a Life Fellow of Emmanuel College, of which he was Master from 1977 to 1990. His latest book is *A New Introduction to Chaucer* (1998), a radically updated version of the book of the same title first published in 1984. He was a contributor to and joint editor of *A Companion to the* Gawain-*poet* (1997, repr. 1999) and has published books and many articles on medieval and other English literature, on which he continues to work.

Peter Brown is Senior Lecturer in the School of English and Director of the Canterbury Centre for Medieval & Tudor Studies at the University of Kent. His books include *The Age of Saturn: Literature and History in the* Canterbury Tales (with Andrew Butcher, 1991), *Chaucer at Work: The Making of the* Canterbury Tales (1994) and, as editor and contributor, *Reading Dreams: The Interpretation of Dreams from Chaucer to*

Shakespeare (1999). Present projects include the editorship of *The Cambridge Bibliography of English Literature*, i: *600–1500*.

David Burnley is Professor and Head of the Department of English Language and Linguistics at the University of Sheffield. He has published numerous articles on medieval language and literature as well as the history of English and is the author of *Chaucer's Language and the Philosophers' Tradition* (1979), *A Guide to Chaucer's Language* (1983) and (with M. Tajima) an annotated bibliography, *The Language of Middle English Literature* (1994). His most recent book is *Courtliness and Language in Medieval England* (1998). He has just completed a revised second edition of *The History of the English Language: A Source Book* and is working on a CD-ROM introduction to Old English.

Carolyn Collette is Professor of English Language and Literature on the Alumnae Foundation and a member of the Medieval Studies Program at Mount Holyoke College, Massachusetts. She is currently President of the North American Branch of the International Courtly Literature Society. Her current research is appearing in a series of articles on the ideal of the good wife in late medieval and early modern Anglo-French literature. She has just completed her most recent book, *Species, Phantasms and Images: Vision and Medieval Psychology in the* Canterbury Tales (2000).

Janette Dillon is Reader in Drama at the University of Nottingham, where she teaches and researches in medieval and Renaissance literature as well as drama. Her *Geoffrey Chaucer* was published in 1993, and her most recent books are *Language and Stage: Medieval and Renaissance Drama in England* (1998) and *Theatre, Court and City 1595–1610: Drama and Social Space in London* (2000).

Caroline D. Eckhardt is Professor of English and Comparative Literature at Pennsylvania State University, where she is also Head of the Department of Comparative Literature. She has written on the General Prologue to the *Canterbury Tales* and other Chaucerian topics, and on Arthurian literature, including the historical uses of the prophecies of Merlin. Her most recent book is a two-volume edition of *Castleford's Chronicle, or The Boke of Brut* (1996); she is presently at work on a third volume.

Robert R. Edwards is Distinguished Professor of English and Comparative Literature at Pennsylvania State University and a life member of Clare Hall, Cambridge. He is the author of *The Dream of Chaucer* (1989) and *Ratio and Invention* (1989), and editor of John Lydgate's *Siege of Thebes* (forthcoming), selections from *Troy Book* (1998) and *The Poetry of Guido Guinizelli* (1987). His current book project focuses on Chaucer's representation of antiquity and modernity.

Roger Ellis is Senior Lecturer in the School of English at the University of Cardiff. He has written on Chaucer, Hoccleve, the Middle English mystics, medieval translation and St Birgitta of Sweden; he has organized conferences on medieval translation and St Birgitta, and edited the proceedings of the former as *The Medieval Translator* (6 vols to date).

Susanna Fein is Professor of English at Kent State University. She writes on Middle English manuscripts, alliterative and devotional verse, and Chaucer. She is co-editor of *Rebels and Rivals* (1991), a collection of essays on the *Canterbury Tales*. A recent book, *Moral Love Songs and Laments* (1998), examines seven longer lyrics of the *Pearl* tradition. She is also a contributor to and editor of *Studies in the Harley Manuscript* (2000) and general editor of an in-progress edition and translation of MS Harley 2253's full contents.

John M. Fyler is Professor of English at Tufts University, Massachusetts. He edited the *House of Fame* for the *Riverside Chaucer*, and is the author of *Chaucer and Ovid* (1979) and a number of essays, most recently 'Froissart and Chaucer' in *Froissart across the Genres*, ed. Donald Maddox and Sara Sturm-Maddox (1998). He is currently completing two books, one a collection of essays on *Troilus and Criseyde*, the other a study of medieval ideas about the nature and origin of language, in particular as they appear in the poetry of Jean de Meun, Dante and Chaucer.

Andrew Galloway is Associate Professor of English and Medieval Studies at Cornell University. Currently editor of *The Yearbook of Langland Studies*, he has written most recently on medieval historical writing (in the *Cambridge History of Medieval English Literature* [1999]), textual scholarship of *Piers Plowman* (*Studies in Bibliography* [1999]), and eleventh-century Latin satire (*Medium Ævum* [1999]). He is collaborating in an annotation of *Piers Plowman* and, with Russell Peck, an edition of Gower's *Confessio Amantis*.

Nicky Hallett is Lecturer in the School of English at the University of Kent at Canterbury. She is a member of the Canterbury Centre for Medieval & Tudor Studies and teaches, among other subjects, courses on medieval women writers and readers and on women's auto/biography. Her research is in social ostentation in art and literature of the Middle Ages; her recent publications are on Anne Clifford (1590–1676) and Virginia Woolf, and a book, *Lesbian Lives: Identity and Auto/biography in the Twentieth Century* (1999).

Michael Hanly is Associate Professor of English at Washington State University and researcher in a medieval history unit, based in Paris, of the Centre Nationale de la Recherche Scientifique (CNRS-UMR 8589). His articles have appeared in *Romania*, *Traditio*, *Viator* and *Multilingua*, and his critical edition of the *Apparicion maistre Jehan de Meun* (1398) by Honorat Bovet will appear in 2001. He is working on a project examining literary transmission between Italy, France and England in the time of Chaucer.

Michael Hanrahan is Lecturer at St John's College in York. He has published articles on Chaucer and Thomas Usk and is presently completing a book on the cultural responses to treason and scandal at the court of Richard II.

Laura Kendrick is Professor of English at the Université de Versailles, where she directs the Department of Humanities. She has written two books about medieval literature and play, *Chaucerian Play: Comedy and Control in the* Canterbury Tales and *The Game of Love: Troubadour Wordplay.* Her latest book, *Animating the Letter: The Figurative Embodiment of Writing from Late Antiquity to the Renaissance* (1999), is on the image of medieval writing.

Tim William Machan is Professor and Chair of English at Marquette University, Milwaukee. He has published widely on medieval language, literature and manuscripts. His most recent book concerns the sociolinguistics of late medieval society.

Helen Phillips is Senior Lecturer in the Department of English Language and Literature at the University of Liverpool. Her latest books are *Chaucer's Dream Poetry*, co-edited with Nick Havely (1997) and *An Introduction to the* Canterbury Tales: *Reading, Fiction, Context* (2000). She is currently working on a study of fifteenth-century feminism.

John F. Plummer is Professor of English at Vanderbilt University in Nashville, Tennessee. He is the author of *The Summoner's Tale: A Variorum Edition of the Works of Geoffrey Chaucer* and of articles on Chaucer, Arthurian romance and medieval drama. At present he is working on a study of Chaucer's *Canterbury Tales* Host, Harry Bailly, and a book on the self in the Arthurian romances of France and England.

James Simpson is Professor of Medieval and Renaissance English at the University of Cambridge and a Professorial Fellow of Girton College, Cambridge. He has published widely in the field of medieval literature, with many articles and two books, *An Introduction to* Piers Plowman (1990), and *Sciences and the Self in Medieval Poetry: Alan of Lille's* Anticlaudianus *and John Gower's* Confessio Amantis (1995). He is currently working on a literary history of the period 1350–1550.

Lynn Staley is Harrington and Shirley Drake Professor in the Humanities at Colgate University, Hamilton, NY. She is the author of *The Powers of the Holy: Religion, Politics, and Gender in Late Medieval English Literature*, with David Aers (1996), *Margery Kempe's Dissenting Fictions* (1994), *The Shepheards Calender: An Introduction* (1990) and *The Voice of the* Gawain-*poet* (1984), and editor of *The Book of Margery Kempe* (complete text, modernized spelling and notes: 1996). She is presently working on a book on Ricardian court culture and completing a translation of *The Book of Margery Kempe* (2000).

Sarah Stanbury teaches in the English Department at the College of the Holy Cross, Worcester, Massachusetts. She is the author of *Seeing the* Gawain-*poet: Description and the Act of Perception* (1991) and co-editor of *Feminist Approaches to the Body in Medieval Literature* (1993), *Writing on the Body: Female Embodiment and Feminist Theory* (1997), and currently of the Web project, Mapping Margery Kempe <www.holycross.edu/kempe>.

Robert Swanson is Reader in Medieval Church History at the University of Birmingham. His books include *Church and Society in Late Medieval England* (1989) and *Religion and Devotion in Europe, c. 1215–c. 1515* (1995). His current work focuses on the place of indulgences in late medieval English religion, and on the economic impact and implications of the church and spirituality in pre-Reformation England.

Irma Taavitsainen is Senior Fellow of the Finnish Academy and Professor of English Philology at the University of Helsinki. She has compiled *Handlist X: Manuscripts in Scandinavian Collections* of *The Index of Middle English Prose* (1994). Her most recent book is *Writing in Nonstandard English* (1999, with Gunnel Melchers and Päivi Pahta). She is at present working, together with a research team, on a project on *Scientific Thought-styles: The Evolution of Medical Writing*. She is also an editor of the *Journal of Historical Pragmatics*.

Linda Ehrsam Voigts is Curators' Professor of English at the University of Missouri–Kansas City. She has produced with Patricia Deery Kurtz a CD-ROM database of information on more than 8,000 scientific and medical texts in Old English and Middle English: *Scientific and Medical Writings in Old and Middle English: An Electronic Reference* (2000). She has published editions and studies of many of these texts and is now working on an edition of the Middle English version of Bernard of Gordon's *De pronosticiis*.

David Wallace is Judith Rodin Professor of English and Comparative Literature at the University of Pennsylvania. His most recent book is *Chaucerian Polity: Absolutist Lineages and Associational Forms in England and Italy*; he has also edited *The Cambridge History of Medieval English Literature*.

Nicholas Watson is Professor of English at the University of Western Ontario. He is author of *Richard Rolle and the Invention of Authority* (1991) and numerous studies of medieval English religious writing. His most recent publication (with Jocelyn Wogan-Browne, Andrew Taylor and Ruth Evans) is *The Idea of the Vernacular: An Anthology of Middle English Literary Theory, 1280–1520* (1999). He is presently working on a book entitled *Balaam's Ass: Vernacular Theology in Medieval England*.

Scott D. Westrem is Associate Professor of English and of Comparative Literature at the Graduate Center and Lehman College of the City University of New York. His most recent work includes *Broader Horizons: Johannes Witte de Hese's* Itinerarius *and*

Medieval Travel Narratives (2000) and, with Charles Ryskamp, *The Works of John Chalkhill* (1999). He is one of four co-editors of *Travel, Trade and Exploration in the Middle Ages: An Encyclopedia* (2000). Projects nearing completion include books on the Hereford *mappamundi* and on an unstudied world map at the University of Minnesota, and a critical edition and translation of the pilgrimage narrative of William of Boldensele (1336).

Edward Wheatley is Associate Professor of English at Hamilton College, Clinton, NY, where he has also served as Chair of the Medieval and Renaissance Studies Program. He has published *Mastering Aesop: Medieval Education, Chaucer, and his Followers* (2000). He is currently working on a project on blindness in medieval literature and history.

Acknowledgements

My first thanks go to Andrew McNeillie for suggesting the project and for providing subsequent, highly congenial, encouragement. His colleagues at Blackwells, particularly Alison Dunnett and Jenny Lambert, have steered the typescript skilfully through the various stages of its production. The copy-editor, Gillian Bromley, a model of equanimity and efficiency, has introduced more clarity and consistency than the book would otherwise have. Norman Blake, Al David, Derek Pearsall and John Ganim were enthusiastic endorsers of the idea of a *Companion to Chaucer*, and they made many helpful suggestions about its direction, design and content. I have also come to rely on the good judgement of my colleague, Nicky Hallett. The brunt of a demanding schedule has been shared, and occasional bouts of editorial exasperation relieved, by my family—Helen, Oliver and Louisa, to whom I dedicate this book.

Canterbury
January 2000

The editor and publishers are grateful to Houghton Mifflin for their kind permission to reproduce extracts from the following edition, to which all line references refer:

Benson, Larry D. (editor), *The Riverside Chaucer*. Third edition. Copyright © 1987 by Houghton Mifflin Company. Used with permission.

Abbreviations of Chaucer's Works

MLT	Man of Law's Tale
NPP	Nun's Priest's Prologue
NPT	Nun's Priest's Tale
PardI	Introduction to the Pardoner's Tale
PardP	Pardoner's Prologue
PardT	Pardoner's Tale
ParsP	Parson's Prologue
ParsT	Parson's Tale
PF	*Parliament of Fowls*
Purse	Complaint of Chaucer to His Purse
Ret	Chaucer's Retraction
Rom	*Romaunt of the Rose*
RvP	Reeve's Prologue
RvT	Reeve's Tale
ShT	Shipman's Tale
SNP	Second Nun's Prologue
SNT	Second Nun's Tale
SqT	Squire's Tale
SumP	Summoner's Prologue
SumT	Summoner's Tale
TC	*Troilus and Criseyde*
Th	Tale of Sir Thopas
ThP	Prologue to the Tale of Sir Thopas
Ven	Complaint of Venus
WBP	Wife of Bath's Prologue
WBT	Wife of Bath's Tale

The Idea of a Chaucer Companion

Peter Brown

From his own reading, Chaucer was familiar with the notion of an authoritative companion providing direction to an individual otherwise lost and uncomprehending. In the *Somnium Scipionis*, which was, together with its commentary by Macrobius, a model for the *House of Fame*, Scipio's grandfather, Africanus, assumes the role of interlocutor. He appears within a dream to explain, from the vantage-point of the starry heavens, the political future of Carthage, Scipio's destiny as its conqueror and the insignificance of human ambition. The *Divine Comedy*, which influenced Chaucer throughout his writing career, shows how Virgil leads Dante through hell and purgatory, explaining the twists and turns of divine justice, keeping Dante to the path and gradually effecting his enlightenment. Appearing in a work Chaucer translated, the *Consolation of Philosophy*, Lady Philosophy uses scholastic discourse and force of logic to reason Boethius out of an abject acceptance of his state of imprisonment, and into a frame of mind in which an existential freedom becomes possible.

All three companions are the best imaginable, and yet they have considerable disadvantages and limitations. None is real, but instead a figment of a dream vision or an other-worldly experience. All of them emerge uninvited and unannounced (however welcome their arrival) to intrude on the narrator's consciousness and cause considerable mental and emotional disturbance. Even their beneficial effects can be felt for only so long: Africanus disappears with Scipio's dream; Virgil cannot enter paradise and must cede his place to Beatrice, leaving Dante momentarily bereft; and Philosophy can help Boethius only in so far as he is prepared to accept the harsh truth of her arguments. The point in each case is that the subject who benefits from a learned and didactic companion must at some point achieve an independence and intellectual growth that render the continued services of the companion otiose. The companion is not a substitute for personal knowledge, but a means whereby it is accessed, communicated, absorbed, internalized, applied.

In his own writing, Chaucer explored the limitations of companions yet further, expressing deep scepticism and ambivalence about their usefulness – a reflection of his complex negotiations with authority more generally, in both its written and social forms. Thus the *Book of the Duchess*, his first major work, omits a conventional companion or guide altogether, to focus instead on three figures (the dreamer, Alcyone, the man in black) tormented by mental states for which there is no obvious or immediate relief. Here, the work of companionable guide or therapist is displaced, by way of a distinctly unauthoritative narrator, to the reader, who must perforce make connections between the three figures according to the clues that Chaucer has left, and thereby devise knowledgeable explanations of the predicaments that face them. When Chaucer does introduce a more traditional companion into another of his dream visions, the *House of Fame*, it is not as a person but as an eagle. Although effective in securing the rescue of a lost and disoriented narrator, this companion is garrulous, exults in knowledge for its own sake, and is over-helpful on matters which, though they might be of great academic interest, are not of immediate concern to 'Geffrey' as he dangles, terrified, in the bird's claws. In other genres, too, companions are revealed as ridiculous, ineffectual, or both. The authority of Harry Bailly, self-appointed major-domo of the Canterbury pilgrims, is undermined on numerous occasions, notably by the Miller and Pardoner. The loquacious Pandarus, companion to Troilus, is silenced once the shallowness of his advice is exposed.[1]

It is to be hoped that the present book avoids some of the worst shortcomings of Chaucer's fictive companions. Nevertheless, it acknowledges the force of his misgivings about them. It does not seek to intrude as a declamatory 'last word' on any of the topics it covers, but rather to provide stimulating advice and guidance; to identify the terms of current debates, exploring their ramifications and applications; to demonstrate how, in practice, particular ideas and theories affect the interpretation of Chaucer's texts; and to suggest further routes of enquiry. In the manner both of the literary companions Chaucer read about and of the ones he created, it insists on strenuous engagement with the writings and ideas it discusses, offering its users models of approach and encouraging them to achieve independence of thought as rapidly as possible.

Students All

For all their best attempts to open up and make available the cultural contexts of medieval literature, books such as this can seem to intimidate by the very wealth of expertise on display. But it is as well to bear in mind that, whether the user be a professional academic steeped in specialist lore, a teacher in a college or school, a graduate researching a thesis, or an undergraduate or sixth-former working on an essay, we are all students and, the further advanced, the more aware of what we do not know. The present volume has been compiled with all such students of Chaucer in mind. It contains enough original research and new syntheses to interest long-established scholars. At the same time it provides accessible coverage of key contexts for those less well acquainted with Chaucer studies.

What can such students of Chaucer expect the *Companion* to provide? It is predicated on the reasonable assumption that the experience of reading Chaucer's works prompts numerous questions about the circumstances in which he lived and worked, and about the effects of those circumstances on what he wrote and how we now understand it. So each chapter strikes a balance between textual analysis and cultural context; but the kind of context varies. Some chapters stay within a literary frame of reference, exploring the genres or modes (such as comedy) available to Chaucer, or placing him in relation to other authors writing at the time, or discussing the production and circulation of texts in a manuscript culture, or emphasizing the importance of translation, or narrative, within late medieval literary practice, or looking at his linguistic or stylistic situation. Another, related, group of chapters covers broader cultural topics in order to account for some of the factors that sustained and conditioned him as a writer, such as structures of literary authority; kinds of social organization and their ethical principles, including those of chivalry; the range of audiences for which Chaucer wrote; and the political nature of London and the court, considered as literary milieux.

The largest group of chapters takes as its general area of interest the recovery of those medieval structures of thought, feeling and imagination, now lost or half-buried, that are subtly and sometimes radically different from our own, and that formed Chaucer's operating assumptions. Religious ideology in all its manifestations – including pilgrimage and Lollardy – is important here. But there are other explanatory systems, with which Christianity had an uneasy relationship, on which Chaucer draws extensively: those of faery, for example, or of the pagan world, or of astrology – the last of these underpinning accounts of the human body and of scientific procedures. One of the notable features of all of these systems is that they crossed cultural boundaries: they were not the quaint beliefs of a small society, but the general inheritance of the Latin West. Quite how wide Chaucer's cultural perspectives were is clear from underlying concepts of geography and travel, and from his own life history, especially his extensive first-hand experience of France and Italy.

Of course, narrative poetry – what Chaucer mainly wrote – is not cultural history but a multi-faceted account of individuals living within particular (if imagined) times and places. Thus it is that a further group of chapters draws attention to other expressions of social practice, including games, love, visualizing, concepts of personal identity and, in relation to these, the different aptitudes and sensibilities of men and women. Whether the student's curiosity focuses on language, Christianity, eroticism, astrology, concepts of the self, pilgrimage, violence, heresy, London, Europe or any of a host of other topics, this book will provide food for thought, and extend horizons.

Designs on Chaucer

Determining the structure of the *Companion*, and of the individual chapters, was no easy matter. Initially, my thoughts were much helped by existing guides and

companions to Chaucer's works, and it seemed sensible to organize the book according to Chaucer's individual compositions, partitioning the whole according to the
customary tripartite schema: *Canterbury Tales*; *Troilus and Criseyde*; dream visions and
minor poems.[2] To do so would have ensured a broad coverage of Chaucer's works, but
it risked alienating users with an over-familiar approach, and it would have entailed
ungainly repetition of key topics. 'Love', for example, or 'chivalry' might legitimately
have been discussed in relation to a number of different Chaucerian texts. On reflection it seemed better, more exciting, to foreground issues and themes rather than
named texts. The result is a novel and intriguing division of content that allows for
and encourages movement across different compositions, and beyond literary frames
of reference. To avoid the problem of repetition in the discussion of texts, contributors were asked to nominate, from the entire range of Chaucer's works, three passages
which they would be prepared to discuss in detail in relation to the chapter title.
Clashing choices were thereby identified early and renegotiated, ensuring a properly
varied coverage.

Arriving at a satisfactory list of chapter titles caused more headaches. The first step
was to draft a comprehensive list of all those topics on which a reader of Chaucer
might require discussion. Adding items to the list became a kind of parlour game
played with colleagues, students and, on one occasion, a casual acquaintance on a
railway journey from London to Canterbury. The opening gambit was: 'If you were
reading this or that work by Chaucer, what would you need to know more about in
order to make better sense of what he wrote?' The outcome was a list of well over one
hundred items. Some had natural affinities with others; some were more difficult to
group. Eventually, through a process of trial, error and re-sorting, the categories
emerged that now form the chapter titles. Thus 'community, church, estates, fellowship' were subsumed by the chapter on 'Social Structures', while 'faery, dreams, folklore' appear under 'Other Thought-worlds'. However, the titles are not mere flags
of convenience; on the contrary, they are viable terms of analysis, rooted in current
discussions about the nature and meaning of Chaucer's literary output. As authors
have developed their arguments, certain topics have been stressed at the expense of
others, but it has seemed more important to promote vigorous argument rather than
to attempt an unattainable ideal of complete coverage.

Armed with my highly condensed prospectus, I began to think of how best to
engage appropriate contributors – ones who would respond in authoritative but flexible and sympathetic ways to the aims of the volume. In this I was much helped by
well-placed colleagues in England and the United States, who put forward recommendations that otherwise, through my own ignorance, would not have arisen. By
this means the book has acquired a very strong field of essayists from Europe and
North America. Since many of the topics offered to them have been a little out of the
ordinary, either in content or scope, there is little in the *Companion to Chaucer* that can
be read as a routine treatment of a standard subject. There is much here that is fresh
and invigorating, and that makes new and significant contributions to matters of
concern among students of Chaucer.

Each contributor has produced an original essay that conforms to certain criteria designed to both ground and challenge the reader of Chaucer: an account of existing scholarship in a given area; a discussion of the key issues; an application of those issues to specific passages from Chaucer's works; and an annotated bibliography of some twenty items for reference and further reading. Every chapter subdivides into a number of distinct sections, and each section is signposted (as in this introduction) so that a user is directed quickly to the pages that are most relevant to a particular area of interest. Where the material covered by one contributor relates to that covered by another, cross-references are given at the end of the chapter. As such features indicate, the *Companion* repays browsing. And, just as it does not privilege one kind of user over another, so it attempts to secure a broad equality of treatment for the different chapter topics by placing them within that most levelling of classifications, the alphabet. Alternatively, a student focused on a particular topic, or a specific composition by Chaucer, can turn to the index to discover where to find useful discussions. All line references are to the *Riverside Chaucer*, cited in the Acknowledgements above (p. xv).

'I make for myself a picture of great detail'

The analogy urged earlier between Chaucer's fictive companions and this volume cannot be pressed too far. Chaucer and his works have themselves become the terrain – difficult and delightful in turn – in need of a mentored map. Nor, in this *Companion* at least, does any one contributor attempt to provide an *ex cathedra* reading of all the contours and features that constitute 'Chaucer' in the manner of an Africanus, a Virgil or a Lady Philosophy. Instead, various individuals, 'ful nine and twenty in a compaignye', offer their considered opinions. As in the case of Chaucer's Canterbury pilgrims, there are competing points of view, potential clashes of temperament and ideological differences – all of which increase the need and opportunity for informed and lively debate.

If there is a concept, lying deeper than the idea of a companion, that articulates the kind of essay found in this book, as well as the experience of compiling it, then it might be caught in the words of the subheading above, used by Milman Parry to describe the process of trying to understand Homeric poetry in its historical context.[3] At first glance the statement seems to reflect a straightforward concept of the literary historian as archaeologist, perhaps as restorer of a shattered mural, deferential to the inheritance of the past, dedicated to the accumulation of more and more fragments of evidence, and working with the aim of producing an intricate, objective account of a remote society and the place within it of a literary artefact.

But implicit in Parry's words are ideas that suggest a more complex model of enquiry. In the first place, the undertaking is highly reflexive, with a strong personal dimension. The relationship between past and present is effected by means of a subjective agent, 'I . . . myself', who contributes an individuated slant to the evaluation of empirical data. Then again, the enquirer's characteristic activity is fabrication, an act of making, an essentially artificial reinvention of the past from the available information. Finally, that reconstruction is itself a representation, a 'picture' betraying the hand of its maker, but also incorporating selection, foregrounding, emphasis and all the other artistic techniques that contribute to a convincing and effective portrayal.

Once made, the picture becomes the focus of the literary historian's interest, replacing the original object of enquiry, while at the same time providing an analytical frame in which to examine further configurations of text and context. Nor is the scrutiny only in one direction. The relationship between past and present is that of a dialogue whereby the modern enquirer asks questions of and through a carefully made picture only to find – disconcertingly – that the picture itself interrogates the very basis of her or his own presumptions. In the case of Chaucer, the exploration of half-forgotten belief systems, and the realization that they were valid working premises in a poetry that had wide appeal, alerts us to the relativity of our own assumptions and credos. As the next chapter shows, his reputation has changed its nature quite drastically as successive generations of readers have discovered in his writings features that have responded to their own cultural preoccupations.

Chaucer Stellified

This *Companion* is nothing if not an historical exercise, and an attentive user should take away an enlarged sense of the circumstances in which Chaucer wrote, of the literary possibilities open to him, of the extent to which he was actively engaged with many of the political and religious issues that beset his society. But as well as making Chaucer the occasion for cultural explorations of the past, it also highlights the extent to which what Chaucer wrote is itself a precious record of the thoughts and feelings that constituted human experience as he knew it. That record deserves our continuing respect, intellectual interest and enthusiasm because it is exceptionally rich, complex and innovative. Capable of sparking flashes of sympathy and recognition across six centuries, of being remarkably present to our reading consciousness, it is nevertheless the record of a culture only half familiar. The other half is alien, a foreign country, and all the more intriguing for that. This book will act as a Baedeker to its deeper exploration, and perhaps enable some to become explorers in their own right.

We should not imagine that relationship in linear terms, with Chaucer's works receding further and further into the past. On the contrary, thanks to the endeavours of all kinds of students, our familiarity with and understanding of what Chaucer wrote makes him seem closer than ever. As it happens, the year 2000 encourages us to celebrate Chaucer as a star in the literary firmament, and he would have enjoyed the compliment. Aware of the possibilities, as well as the pitfalls, of enduring literary fame, he imagined somewhat apprehensively (as that same companionable eagle bore 'Geffrey' aloft) what it might be like to be 'stellified' among the gods (*HF* 584–93).

Taking a cue from this conceit, the trajectory of our relationship with Chaucer might be that of an elliptical orbit, its shape governed by the alternating gravity and levity of his writings. As we move first towards him, then further away, now closer, now more distant, we glimpse features of his writings from new and often startling angles. The coincidence of the millennial year with the 600th anniversary of Chaucer's death prompts the hope that this exhilarating parallax will continue to provoke surprise, delight, and curiosity both in medieval Chaucer and in our postmodern selves.[4] This book is intended to aid and sustain that process.

NOTES

1   Cf. Peter Brown, *Chaucer at Work: The Making of the* Canterbury Tales (London and New York: Longman, 1994), 6–8.

2   As in the three *Oxford Guides to Chaucer* (Oxford: Clarendon), written by Helen Cooper (*The Canterbury Tales*, 1989), Barry Windeatt (*Troilus and Criseyde*, 1992) and Alastair Minnis (*The Shorter Poems*, 1995). As examples of earlier guide-companions, see *The Cambridge Chaucer Companion*, ed. Piero Boitani and Jill Mann (Cambridge: Cambridge University Press, 1986) and Beryl Rowland, ed., *Companion to Chaucer Studies*, rev. edn (New York: Oxford University Press, 1978).

3   Milman Parry, 'The historical method in literary criticism', *Harvard Alumni Bulletin* 38 (1936), 778–82 (p. 780), repr. in *The Making of Homeric Verse: The Collected Papers of Milman Parry*, ed. Adam Parry (Oxford: Clarendon, 1971), 408–13 (p. 411).

4   See the introduction to *Chaucer: The Canterbury Tales*, ed. Steve Ellis, Longman Critical Readers (London and New York: Longman, 1998), 1–22.

1
Afterlife
Carolyn Collette

Chaucer's afterlife constitutes a reputation virtually unique in the history of English literature. More than any other English writer, Chaucer has been constructed and deconstructed by successive generations of his readers. Beginning in the fifteenth century with a group of writers who felt themselves either directly connected to him through acquaintance, as did Thomas Hoccleve, or spiritually connected to him through admiration and literary aspiration, as did John Lydgate and the Scottish Chaucerians, Chaucer's reputation as an author has been founded in, but also quite separated from, his work. In reading the multiple volumes of allusions to Chaucer in the six hundred years since his death, one sees his reputation flourish and diminish. Within this pattern of change one fixed point stands out: Chaucer the man – his learning, temperament, disposition – is as much a centre of allusion and critical discussion as his works. Michel Foucault notwithstanding, the record shows that Chaucer the man has been central to the idea of Chaucer the author.

Thanks in large measure to the work of Martin Crow and Claire Olson in editing the *Chaucer Life-records* (1966), the outlines of Chaucer's life are now apparently clear: we know somewhat of where he travelled and when, what offices he held, whom he served; yet until very recently these facts, as well as the real substance of his life – his passions, hopes and fears – were unknown. As a result, over the centuries he has served as a useful cipher on to whom critics and editors could project their own ideas of what he must have thought, felt and been like, depending on the cultural circumstances in which they wrote. All this has made for a rather lively afterlife for this fourteenth-century writer of whose inner life we know for certain very little beyond the fact that it created a literary genius of the highest order .

Caroline Spurgeon's *Five Hundred Years of Chaucer Criticism and Allusion, 1357–1900* and Derek Brewer's later work, *Chaucer: The Critical Heritage*, both contain an extensive range of allusion, citation and reference, drawn largely from the comments

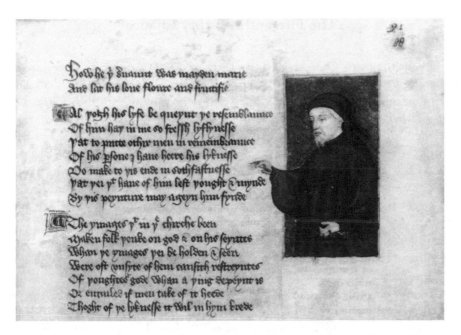

Figure 1.1   The 'Hoccleve Portrait' of Chaucer. From the *Regiment of Princes* by Thomas Hoccleve. London, British Library, MS Harley 4866, fo. 88 (1411–12). [By permission of the British Library.]

of writers and essayists. In addition, both scholars have contributed important summaries of the ebb and flow of Chaucer's reputation, Spurgeon in the extensive analytical introduction in the first volume of her three-volume work, and Brewer most notably in 'Images of Chaucer, 1386–1900'. Their research demonstrates that, for most of the time between the fifteenth century and the twentieth, Chaucer's literary reputation, the sense of what kind of a writer he was, sprang from a sense of who he was as a person – how he thought, what he knew, what he believed, how he was shaped by the age in which he lived. The fifteenth, sixteenth and nineteenth centuries are particularly rich periods for considering the phenomenon of high interest in Chaucer the man. Although each period produced a criticism distinctly related to its own peculiar historical circumstances, all three periods constructed Chaucer similarly as a figure of unusual intellectual *virtu*; in all three periods the record of allusions shows he appeared as a benign yet essentially distant figure of power and learning who showed a way to a better England. In many respects the early fifteenth-century Hoccleve portrait (figure 1.1) represents the continuity at the centre of the idea of Chaucer over time: a seemingly gentle and wise man, adorned with symbols of his craft and art, points towards something invisible to us, but visible to him as he focuses his eyes on the lower middle distance, on a plane we cannot access.

The Fifteenth-century Chaucer

The fifteenth-century Chaucer, as Seth Lerer and A. C. Spearing have argued, is a father figure to writers who see in him both the patriarch of their craft and, as Spearing argues, the source of their anxiety: 'The son wishes to inherit the authority of a father who has denied that any such inheritance is possible and has in any case ended his own fatherhood . . . As father, he made possible their very existence as English poets, yet, as his successors, they inevitably came too late' (Pinti 1998: 160). Lerer goes even further, asserting that Chaucer's fatherhood renders readers as well as writers childlike; he discusses 'the ways in which Chaucer's authority subjects his readers, subjugating them into childhood or incompetence' (Lerer 1993: 5).

But the records Spurgeon and Brewer have amassed reveal an even more complicated dimension to the fifteenth-century idea of Chaucer. At the same time that he is termed 'father' to the writers who followed him, he is also constructed as a benefactor to a larger posterity: all those who speak the English language. He is pictured as simultaneously writing within and standing outside of the language he used. In an image that several Renaissance critics later recall, John Lydgate in his *Fall of Princes* terms Chaucer the lodestar of English: 'Whom al this land sholde off right preferre, / Sithe off our language he was the lodesterre' (Brewer 1978: i, 52). Chaucer serves as a guide, a fixed point by which to navigate the possibilities of expression, a figure both dominating and yet external to the world of fifteenth-century poetry. From that vantage point he is able to exert his beneficent influence over the common tongue. The anonymous author of a *Book of Curtesye, c.*1477, suggests the same distant quality through a rich agricultural metaphor. He terms Chaucer and John Gower 'faders auncyente' who 'Repen the feldes fresshe of fulsomnes / The flours fresh they gadred vp & hente / Of siluer langage / the grete riches'. The metaphor of reaping a harvest implies the plenty of Chaucer's verbal imagination: he is the farmer who sows language and reaps a harvest of rhetoric. In contrast, the current generation of writers, coming after, must 'begge' the 'grete riches' of 'siluer langage' from them. But, at the same time that the writer acknowledges that Chaucer and Gower have dominated literary language, he also implies an important gift inherent in that dominance when he says, 'For of our tunge they were both lok & kaye.' This statement of despair about the father figure who pre-empts the opportunities of his literary heirs, barring their way to independence and innovation by the lock of his prevenient genius, also asserts Chaucer's gift to the speakers of 'oure tunge', for whom he provides the key of expression (Brewer 1978: i, 73).

In this period Chaucer is repeatedly figured as the poet of new beginnings, of potency and life. In *The Life of Our Lady*, Lydgate describes Chaucer as the one who first made 'to distille and rayne / The golde dewe dropes of speche and eloquence / Into our tunge, thurgh his excellence / And fonde the floures, firste of Retoryke, / Our Rude speche, only to enluymyne' (Brewer 1978: i, 46). For Lydgate, Chaucer is the father who has generated a new spring of linguistic possibility. William Caxton repeats this theme of potency and fertility in his epilogue to Chaucer's translation of Boethius, where he implies that Chaucer's fatherhood is realized by his relationship to the 'moder tonge': 'Therfore the worshipful fader & first foundeur & enbelissher of ornate eloquence in our englissh. I mene / Maister Geffrey Chaucer hath translated this sayd werke oute of latyn in to oure vsual and moder tonge' (Brewer 1978: i, 75). The result of this translation is aureate diction and 'ornate wrytyng' (76) located in the substance and power of his pithy style: 'For he wrytteth no voyde wordes / but alle hys mater is ful of hye and quycke sentence' (75).

The opinion that Chaucer's genius was realized in his ability to transform English appears frequently, as in this translated couplet from his fifteenth-century epitaph: 'By the verses [that he composed] in his [British] mother tongue he made it [as] illustrious as, alas, it had once been uncouth' (Brewer 1978: i, 79), as well as in John Shirley's 'Prologue to the Knight's Tale', c.1456: 'þe laureal and moste famous poete þat euer was to-fore him as in þemvellishing of oure rude moders englisshe tonge, clepid Chaucyer' (Spurgeon 1925: i, 54). Praise of Chaucer the author is thus praise of the man who was able to generate a literary language out of a previously unauthorized mother tongue. In this light the language of fifteenth-century allusions to Chaucer as a poet of the 'fresshe' and 'newe' is a language of fertility and generation, of the 'floure of Retoryke', generated by a father who may indeed have left his literary heirs crippled, but whose genius at the same time empowered all his other heirs, by showing them how to unlock the riches of their common tongue.

The Renaissance Chaucer

In the sixteenth century Chaucer's reputation as a master of literary expression slipped out of focus; as his language began to seem more and more distant, his achievement dimmed. Sir Philip Sidney seems to sum up the tenor of this vein of criticism when he praises the *Troilus*, but concludes, 'Yet had he great wants, fitte to be forgiuen, in so reuerent antiquity' (Spurgeon 1925: i, 122). At the same time that praise for Chaucer as a father of English poetic expression waned, another idea of Chaucer came forward: the Chaucer who is a man of learning, philosophy and occult science. The tradition that Chaucer was unusually learned and wise appears as early as Hoccleve's reference to Chaucer as a highly educated poet, 'vniuersal fadir in science', 'hier in philosophie / To Aristotle / in our tonge' (Brewer 1978: i, 63). A persistent but unfounded tradition that Chaucer attended university appears to have been widely accepted by sixteenth-century scholars. John Leland's biography of Chaucer (c.1540–5), which circulated widely in manuscript, reinforced this sense of him as highly learned, exerting a powerful and long-lived control over the shape of Chaucer's reputation. Leland built on the tradition of the wise Chaucer, constructing him as a universal scholar and an auto-didact in a description which other writers borrowed and helped disseminate:

He left the university an acute logician, a delightful orator, an elegant poet, a profound philosopher, and an able mathematician . . . Moreover, he left the university a devout theologian . . . while he so applied himself at Oxford, he also pursued his studies elsewhere, and by long devotion to learning added many things to the knowledge he had there accumulated. (Brewer 1978: i, 91)

Chaucer's reputation for learning made him an attractive figure to Reformation propagandists. For Protestants, Chaucer's reputation for wisdom indicated that he could see beyond the prejudices of his own age to anticipate a time when England would be free of the excesses of Romish superstition. John Foxe, anxious to appropriate Chaucer's reputation for wisdom to his own purposes, praised him in his 1570 *Ecclesiasticall history contaynyng the Actes and Monumentes of thynges passed in euery Kynges tyme in this Realme* as author of the *Jack Upland* (a Lollard attack on corrupt friars), and therefore a proto-Protestant sympathizer. Foxe melded Chaucer's learning with his supposed Protestant leanings, appropriating England's greatest poet to his cause as a faithful witness in the time of Wyclif (Brewer 1978: i, 107). Chaucer, like Gower, was 'notably learned, as the barbarous rudenes of that tyme did geue . . . so endeuoryng themselues, and employing their tyme, that they excelling many other in study and exercise of good letters, did passe forth their lyues here right worshipfully and godly, to the worthye fame and commendation of their name' (Spurgeon 1925: i, 105). Chaucer, says Foxe, 'saw in Religion as much almost, as euen we do now, and vttereth in hys works no lesse, and semeth to bee a right Wicleuian, or els was neuer any, and that all his workes almost, if they be throughly aduised, will testifie (albeit it bee done in myrth, and couertly)'. Chaucer was able 'vnder shadowes couertly, as vnder a visoure' to convey truth 'and yet not be espyed of the craftye aduersarie' (Spurgeon 1925: i, 106).

The idea of Chaucer's learning in this period seems at odds with the prevailing sense of his language as rough and rude. This dichotomy demonstrates the bifocal nature of his reputation: his poetry might be difficult to appreciate, but he had gained status as a venerable figure separate from his works. As Foxe noted, his works and Gower's were exempted from censorship in Henry VIII's *Acte for thaduauncement of true Religion and for thabolisshment of the contrarie* of 1542–3. (In this period Chaucer is paired with Gower in many allusions, suggesting that the sixteenth century thought of him as part of a literary tradition, not necessarily as the singular genius he seemed a hundred years earlier.) Richard Puttenham refers to him in *The Arte of English Poesie* (1589) as the most renowned of the early English poets, 'for the much learning appeareth to be in him aboue any of the rest' (Brewer 1978: i, 126). Gabriel Harvey's *Marginalia* emphasizes Chaucer's scientific learning: 'Notable Astronomical descriptions in Chawcer, & Lidgate; fine artists in manie kinds & much better learned then owre moderne poets. Chauwcers conclusions of the Astrolablie, still excellent, vnempeachable . . . A worthie man, that initiated his little sonne Lewis with such cunning & subtill conclusions, as sensibly, & plainly expressed, as he cowld deuise.'[1] in a much-quoted continuation of the same passage, Harvey went on to assert the Renaissance principle that great poetry springs from great learning:

Other [*sic*] commend Chawcer, & Lidgate for their witt, pleasant veine, varietie of poetical discourse, & all humanitie: I specially note their Astronomie, philosophie, & other parts of profound or cunning art. Wherein few of their time were more exactly learned. It is not sufficient for poets, to be superficial humanists: but they must be exquisite artists & curious vniuersal schollers. (160–1)

By the late sixteenth and early seventeenth centuries Chaucer's reputation for general wisdom accorded him the status of master of occult sciences. In his extensive response to Thomas Speght's 1598 edition of Chaucer, Francis Thynne corrected Speght's error in spelling the term *resalgor*, an alchemical term which Speght rendered *resagor*. Thynne objected to Speght's mistake first because of the error itself, and second because Speght had not properly or fully understood that Chaucer was a man of extensive learning: "This worde sholde rather be "resalgar": wherefore I will shew you what Resalgar ys in that abstruce scyence which Chawcer knewe full well, althoughe he enveye against the sophisticall abuse thereof in the chanons yeomans tale.'[2] Elias Ashmole's 1652 encyclopedia of alchemy, *Theatrum Chemicum Britannicum*, describes Chaucer, author of the Canon's Yeoman's Tale, as 'ranked amongst the *Hermetick Philosophers*' with Gower, his master; those who read the latter part of the tale, Ashmole asserts, 'wil easily perceive him to be a *Iudicious Philosopher*, and one that fully knew the *Mistery*' (Spurgeon 1925: i, 227). Robert Schuler has documented the extensive, if apocryphal, body of prophetical and alchemical works attributed to Chaucer, concluding that Chaucer was revered as magus as much as poet: 'if the Renaissance Chaucer was the "English Homer", he was being treated just as Homer had been by scholars and teachers in the fifth and sixth centuries B.C.: not primarily as a great poet, but as an encyclopedia of military strategy, history, geography, economy, and eloquence' (Schuler 1984: 316–17).

The Nineteenth-century Chaucer

After a period of comparative neglect in the seventeenth and early eighteenth centuries, Chaucer's reputation flowered once more in the nineteenth century. Like the fifteenth and sixteenth centuries, the nineteenth century was comparatively uninterested in discussing the intricacies of Chaucer's texts, more concerned with Chaucer the man and the time in which he lived. Matthew Arnold's 1880 criticism of Chaucer shows this bias quite clearly as it side-steps consideration of the dynamics of the text in favour of inferences about the mind that created it: 'If we ask ourselves wherein consists the immense superiority of Chaucer's poetry . . . we shall find that his superiority is both in the substance of his poetry and in the style of his poetry. His superiority in substance is given by his large, free, simple, clear yet kindly view of human life' (Brewer 1978: ii, 216–17).

The production of multiple popular editions of Chaucer's works, designed for the expanding and increasingly educated reading public, made Chaucer's name a familiar one among the educated classes in the nineteenth century. Chaucer became the father of English literature, the poet of the fresh green youth of England's greatness, and the poet of a time whose values and whose spirit held wisdom the modern world needed. Paradoxically, this sense of his ancient knowledge was bolstered by an awareness of Chaucer's freshness and rawness, his humour and coarseness, all traits deemed characteristic of the age in which he lived. He became thus a dual figure: a wise father leading the way in language and art, as well as a figure of English energy and power.

Brewer and Spurgeon's nineteenth-century allusions to Chaucer focus on his reception by major writers of the period and key figures of what would become the tradition of Chaucer criticism. Their work shows the Chaucer familiar to all of us – the somewhat coarse humorist (Brewer 1978: ii, 72, 125, 223, 280), the childlike, gay poet writing at the dawn of English literature (226) – as well as Chaucer the prototype of the nineteenth-century gentleman (88–9, 108). But the nineteenth century also produced an extensive range of parallel Chaucer criticism in the magazines and monthly periodicals that flourished from 1830 to 1880. In the pages of these journals we see shaped and reflected a popular conception of Chaucer that complements the more familiar one of the kindly poet of what Arnold called 'joy and strength'. This Chaucer, a wise poet, came from a culture that understood how to integrate art and science, poetry and life. Studying him might show the way to creating a modern equivalent of his achievement.

Many of these articles on the subject of Chaucer are reviews of recent editions, but virtually every one begins with Chaucer the man, moves on to consider the culture of his time, and eventually draws some contrast between his age and the Victorian age. For example, the Edinburgh *North British Review* for February 1849 begins its account of several editions by evoking both Chaucer's distance from and his relevance to contemporary issues: 'The name of Geoffrey or Geffray Chaucer, has a grateful sound to English ears, and the image which it conjures up, purified by time from every taint of ignoble association, looms large to us through the mists of the five centuries which intervene' (293). According to this reviewer, Chaucer felt none of the *Angst* typical of the poet in the nineteenth century: 'He was the "clear and conscious" man of his time. In his opinions there was nothing which others did not feel, but what they felt unconsciously he thought and expressed . . . There was no antagonism between him and his age' (314–15). A *London Review* article of 1859 assures us that Chaucer was 'well versed in philosophy and divinity and the scholastic learning, and displays an intimate acquaintance with most of the sciences, as then cultivated, especially astronomy' (285). More important, he was the poet of an age that revered and read poetry (292), an age very different from the writer's own:

our forefathers, with a tythe of our knowledge and experience, effected in art what lies beyond our power. The preceding observations will have thrown some light upon what the age of Chaucer possessed which we have lost, viz., a common poetical atmosphere, a common love of poetry, and desire to be instructed in a true way, that is, to be told of things by poets, and a common consent in the sort of thing that was to be looked for at their hands. (295)

Moreover, the author says, Chaucer's age was superior in the very area of logic and reason on which the nineteenth century prided itself (296). The article concludes with a sense of Chaucer's surpassing greatness and essential distance:

> Here we leave Chaucer. We have seen his majestic countenance, full of brooding light; his long life and ceaseless energy. His influence for centuries was unbounded, and probably wider than even that of Shakespeare. He created a language and a method of versification, which was followed by the poets both of England and Scotland. We have seen how exhaustless was his genius; how just his love and fixed his faith in human nature; how firm and true, and fearless his dealing with all things. We have seen how much of this was owing to the age which nurtured and understood the poet. Also, we have not failed to see how different, strangely different, the condition of poetry in an essentially scientific age has become. (303)

In yet another example of Chaucer criticism sprung from Victorian anxiety, the London *National Review* published in June 1862 ascribes Chaucer's genius to his ability to combine the imaginary and the real:

> The prominent qualities which modern critics have ascribed to Chaucer are, fancy, imagination, grace, delicacy, tenderness; and undoubtedly he possessed these and other cognate qualities in a great degree. But the essential characteristic of his genius seems to us to be a strong sense of the real. In the highest flights of his genius the actual is ever present to him, as if the *purely* imaginative was something alien to his nature. (12)

Not long after this was written, F. J. Furnivall founded the Early English Text Society (1864) and the Chaucer Society (1868), and attention shifted from Chaucer's character and age to Chaucer's actual works. But even Furnivall, romantic, inveterate and energetic editor that he was, located the centre of Chaucer's meaning in Chaucer the man. In a typically wide-ranging article for the London *Macmillans Magazine* (volume 27, 1872–3), Furnivall railed at the fact that only sixty men out of the millions of inhabitants of Great Britain were willing to support the Society with donations, and that the average person would say of Chaucer's works, 'How can one find time to read a man who makes "poore" two syllables? Life is not long enough for that' (383). Even as he discusses editions, manuscripts and the importance of chronology in understanding Chaucer, Furnivall asserts that the reader who wishes to understand Chaucer's poetry must know the man, 'must start with him in his sorrow, walk with him through it into the fresh sunshine of his later life, and then down to the chill and poverty of his old age' (388).

Ironically, Furnivall's efforts and energy helped move Chaucer for ever out of the realm of such romantic interpretation, as well as out of the realm of the average reader.

At the end of the nineteenth century the familiar features of Chaucer the man began to fade, just as the familiar father of fifteenth-century English had faded in the sixteenth. In the earlier instance he remained a respected figure associated with learning and philosophy. In the latter he disappeared into the academy to become the subject of professional study. What now dominated was an academic interest in studying Chaucer's works and texts systematically and according to fixed principles, an interest manifest in increasing pressure to publish a definitive edition of his works which, based on the best manuscripts available and the best modern principles of editorial decision, would prove worthy of the father of English poetry. W. W. Skeat's six-volume (ultimately seven-volume) edition of 1894–7 provided such a text. Heir to nineteenth-century popular interest in Chaucer (it was also available in a 'student's edition' presumably designed for the average educated reader), it proved to be a text for scholars, not for the educated public. The publication of Skeat's edition, coupled with the founding of the Chaucer Society to edit and propagate his works, had an unintended consequence: increasingly Chaucer and his writing became the province of scholars whose interest lay with text and manuscript.

Chaucer's Modern Reputation

The twentieth century produced an extensive scholarship of Chaucer's work, and a comparatively diminished interest in Chaucer the man. More than any other period after the fifteenth century, the twentieth century saw Chaucer's reputation tied to the critical assessment of his art. A series of editors has shaped the text of Chaucer's work to make it available to thousands of students who have in turn analysed, interpreted, constructed and deconstructed his meanings. Beginning with G. L. Kittredge and his assertion of the dramatic principle at the heart of the tales, twentieth-century Chaucer criticism was dominated by the *Canterbury Tales* and by successive fashions in twentieth-century academic literary criticism. A trend, first identifiable in the eighteenth century, towards reading Chaucer's works in light of the genre of the novel flowered in the middle third of the century, reaching its apogee in criticism of *Troilus and Criseyde*, often termed the first novel in English. The development and popularization of theories of human psychology in the twentieth century also focused critical attention on the characters of Chaucer's work, on the pilgrims and particularly on Criseyde, as Alice Kaminsky (1980) has shown. New criticism, with its emphasis on the text and its propensity to see irony lurking under every couplet, contributed to a sense that it is hopeless to try to know the man Chaucer, that his surrogate the pilgrim–narrator is all we can know, and that the latter is enigmatic and elvish, as E. Talbot Donaldson argued so persuasively in 1954.

In the most radical critical departure of the century, *A Preface to Chaucer* (1962), D. W. Robertson Jr attempted to redirect the focus of criticism from the dynamics of the text towards historicizing the text, albeit in one narrow channel. Ultimately, this served to diminish the idea of Chaucer the author; for his work, it could now be shown, was less a matter of unique inspiration and genius than a site in which cultural conventions and traditions were played out. Indeed, the criticism of the last thirty years of the twentieth century strove to defeat the idea of Chaucer as a unique individual and instead reinvented him as a conduit of the social *Angst* of his world, a writer bound by the misogyny of his period and mediated through his scribes. By the end of the twentieth century he no longer seemed to possess secret knowledge, or to show the way to a deeper understanding of what English is capable of. Rather, he seemed all too caught up in the pettinesses and intrigues of a dangerous, unstable court, itself a part of a destabilizing world founded on and yet anxious about the codes of chivalry, love and duty it expressed in its literature.

Chaucer's Retraction (ParsT 1081–92)

In his own work Chaucer seems to have demonstrated a remarkable prescience about many of the issues that would arise in response to his writing. In the Retraction at the end of the *Canterbury Tales,* in the *House of Fame* and in the lyric addressed to Adam Scriveyn, he identifies three topics that seem to cause him anxiety: concern with the tone and subject of his work, concern for the mutability of fame and the status of the great author, and concern about the faithful transmission of his text. In each instance, the history of Chaucer criticism has proven him right in his concern.

In the Retraction that follows the Parson's Tale Chaucer expresses anxiety about the reception of his work and apologizes for and 'withdraws' the great bulk of his literary production, terming it 'worldly vanitees'. Over the centuries Chaucer's earthy humour and 'broad' speaking have indeed occasioned frequent criticism. We see hints of this in the Renaissance comments on the rudeness and antique flavour of Chaucer's language: Beaumont addresses 'the inciuilitie *Chaucer* is charged withall' by responding, 'What Romane Poet hath lesse offended this way then hee?' (Brewer 1978: i, 137). Such criticism flowers in the early nineteenth century in statements like this one by Byron: 'Chaucer, notwithstanding the praises bestowed on him, I think obscene and contemptible' (Brewer 1978: i, 249). Leigh Hunt blames a change of manners for what might once have pleased the court and *gentils* but was, in the mid-nineteenth century, 'sometimes not only indecorous but revolting' (Brewer 1978: ii, 71). Matthew Arnold's charge that Chaucer lacked 'high seriousness' seems an uncanny echo, after nearly five hundred years, of Chaucer's own fears.

Imagining Fame (*HF* 1356–1519)

Chaucer represents the capricious nature of reputation and of fame throughout the *House of Fame*, focusing on literary reputation in lines 1356–1519. He images the 'godesse' Fame as a creature of multiple ears and tongues, swelling and shrinking. Her throne room is lined with 'many a peler' on which stand figures of such great writers as Josephus, Statius, Homer, Geoffrey of Monmouth, Virgil and Ovid, whose own fame was so great that it altered the size of the hall which 'Was woxen on highte, length, and brede, / Wel more be a thousand del / Than hyt was erst' (1494–6). In these lines, Chaucer imagines fame as the property of the author as individual, rather than an attribute of his work. We know that he desired such fame from the end of *Troilus*, where he presents his book to the tradition of such great writers, claiming the story of Troy as part of England's literary heritage, and positioning himself as a novice reverently following in the steps of the great writers of antiquity.

Chaucer did attain the kind of lasting fame he attributes to these great writers. From one generation to the next Chaucer has been likened to the predecessors he so clearly admired. As early as Hoccleve's praises, Chaucer was being constructed as an English equivalent of the great *auctores*: 'for vnto Tullius / Was neuer man so lyk amonges vs / Also who was hier in philosophie / To Aristotle / in our tonge but thow / The steppes of virgile in poesie / Thow filwedist' (Brewer 1978: i, 63). In the six-teenth century, Roger Ascham terms him the 'Englishe Homer', and Francis Beau-mont asserts that Chaucer is a philosophical writer of the highest order, as *Troilus* shows, imitating Virgil and Homer in the 'pith and sinewes of eloquence' (Brewer 1978: i, 100, 138). Dryden compares Chaucer to Ovid, one the last poet of the 'Golden Age of the Roman Tongue', the other the beginner of English poetry. Perhaps the highest praise of Chaucer is that offered by William Godwin in his 1803 biography, that Chaucer was the father of 'our language', the man who restored English to the Muses: 'No one man in the history of human intellect ever did more, than was effected by the single mind of Chaucer' (Brewer 1978: i, 238). Thus, although his reputation, like the form of the goddess of Fame, has grown and shrunk, Chaucer has laid claim to be one of the 'folk of digne reverence' in the *House of Fame*.

'Chaucer's wordes unto Adam, his owne scriveyn'

Perhaps the most intriguing instance of apparent Chaucerian prescience comes in the little lyric in which he excoriates his scribe Adam for mistakes arising from haste and inattention, charging him:

> . . . after my makyng thow wryte more trewe;
> So ofte adaye I mot thy werk renewe,
> It to correcte and eke to rubbe and scrape,
> And al is thorugh thy negligence and rape.
>   (4–7)

Given the history of Chaucer editions recounted by Ruggiers (1984), and more recently by Dane (1998), he was right to be concerned. The lyric to Adam (which itself is now accepted into the Chaucer canon, but on slender manuscript evidence) shows that Chaucer realized how difficult it was for an author to retain control of texts once they left the author's possession. Windeatt (1979) shows how generally an author's material was emended or altered in a culture in which reading a text commonly involved some sort of appropriation, often manifested as alteration. As early as Caxton's first printed edition of the *Tales* in 1478 the *mouvance* of Chaucer's text bedevilled his editor. Caxton struggled to produce an accurate text: in the Proheme, he tells of deferring to a gentleman who brought him a 'better' text, one closer to Chaucer's original. Caxton says, 'I fynde many of the sayd bookes / whyche wryters haue abrydgyd it and many thynges left out / And in somme place haue sette certayn versys / that he neuer made ne sette in hys booke' (Brewer 1978: i, 76). Walter Stevens, a sixteenth-century editor of a manuscript of Chaucer's *Treatise on the Astrolabe*, 'fownde the same corrupte and false in so many and sondrie places, that I dowbtede whether the rudenes of the worke weare not a gretter sclaunder to the authour, than trowble and offence to the readers' (Brewer 1978: i, 105). Speght writes that he undertook his edition at the request of gentlemen who wished to do 'some reparations on his [Chaucer's] works, which they iudged to be much decaied by iniurie of time, ignorance of writers, and negligence of Printers' (Brewer 1978: i, 141).

The history of modern Chaucer editions also suggests he was correct to worry, for here too the idea of the 'best text' has been central but elusive. A good deal of work in the past hundred years has been devoted to establishing the canon of Chaucer's work, and to establishing a central manuscript, the Ellesmere Manuscript, as an authoritative text. Thomas Tyrwhitt (1775) was the first editor really to look at Chaucer as an author whose work might have characteristic traits; he determined that a canon might therefore be determined on that basis, rather than historical tradition, and excised a lot of apocryphal material. Skeat continued the winnowing process Tyrwhitt began; as Edwards says, 'Skeat's final enduring achievement is a negative one. It consists in what he did *not* include in the Clarendon Chaucer. With Skeat's edition we approach very close to the final stabilization of the Chaucer canon, to the achievement of a complete works purged of the accretions of insubstantial attributions of earlier editors' (Ruggiers 1984: 188).

But the problem of establishing Chaucer's text continued throughout the twentieth century. The text produced by J. M. Manly and Margaret Rickert, which sought to provide definitive readings based on objective principles of manuscript collation and analysis, proved to be, in the words of George Kane, 'the product of an immensely complex system of contingent hypotheses which seldom account for all the data and are sustainable only by the constant exercise of that editorial judgment which the editors set out to exclude' (Ruggiers 1984: 210). Even the Robinson edition, arguably the most influential Chaucer edition ever printed, because of its wide dissemination and popularity, was, according to Reinecke, a monument to Ellesmere and to Robinson's desire to print a 'regularly scanned, craftsmanlike, artistically significant . . . [text] conforming to his already determined opinions about Chaucer's grammar and meter' (Ruggiers 1984: 250). Most recently, the Variorum Chaucer project has preferred the Hengwrt manuscript over the 'highly edited' Ellesmere because of its early date (1400–10), its unedited state and its similarity to the Manly–Rickert reconstruction. In his preface to the variorum edition of Hengwrt, Donald C. Baker describes the editors' intent to publish a text 'which is as near as it is possible to get to what Chaucer must have written' and concludes that for 'most of the Canterbury Tales' that text is the Hengwrt manuscript.[3] While there is no doubt that certain manuscripts, Ellesmere and Hengwrt most famously, are thought to be more reliable than others, the fact remains that we do not have any holograph texts of Chaucer's poetry. One could make the case that the state of Chaucer's texts is analogous to the state of his reputation: both have been highly subject to interpretation. In the case of the texts, we have a series of manuscripts, each of which acts like a unique set of binoculars, adjusted to somebody else's eyesight.

> Each set is focused differently in the fine detail of its account of the text. For the editor the medieval poem is accordingly something of an aspiration, a hardest idea, somewhere between, behind, or above the network of available scribal variations in any given line. Chaucer's poems survive for each line somewhere mid-way in a band of possible scribal variation on either side. (Windeatt 1979: 139)

See also AUTHORITY; CRISIS AND DISSENT; GEOGRAPHY AND TRAVEL; LANGUAGE; LIFE HISTORIES; LONDON; NARRATIVES; SCIENCE; TEXTS.

NOTES

1   *Gabriel Harvey's Marginalia* [c.1600], ed. G. C. Moore Smith (Stratford-upon-Avon: Shakespeare Head Press, 1913), 159.
2   *Chaucer: Animaduersions . . . 1598 sett downe by Francis Thynne*, ed. G. H. Kingsley, Early English Text Society, original series 9 (1865), 36.
3   *The Canterbury Tales: A Facsimile and Transcription of the Hengwrt Manuscript with Variants from the Ellesmere Manuscript*, ed. Paul G. Ruggiers (Norman, Okla.: University of Oklahoma Press, 1979), pp. xvii–xviii.

REFERENCES AND FURTHER READING

Brewer, Derek S. (1966) 'Images of Chaucer 1386–1900', in *Chaucer and Chaucerians: Critical Studies in Middle English Literature*, ed. Derek S. Brewer (University, Ala.: University of Alabama Press; London: Nelson), 240–70. A succinct and elegant overview of the history of Chaucer's reputation.

——(1997) 'Modernising the medieval eighteenth-century translations of Chaucer', in *The Middle Ages after the Middle Ages in the English-Speaking World*, ed. Marie-Françoise Alamichel and Derek Brewer (Cambridge: Brewer), 103–20. Brewer focuses on the eighteenth-century reception of a series of translations appearing after Dryden in an age which he describes as the beginning of modern criticism and textual scholarship of Chaucer.

——, ed. (1978) *Chaucer: The Critical Heritage, 1385–1933*, 2 vols (London: Routledge & Kegan Paul). Brewer confines this collection to the heritage of Chaucer criticism. It overlaps in the early period with Spurgeon's, but contains a much fuller record of nineteenth-century and twentieth-century criticism.

Cannon, Christopher (1998) *The Making of Chaucer's English: A Study of Words*, Cambridge Studies in Medieval Literature 39 (Cambridge and New York: Cambridge University Press).

Cannon sets out to offer a 'complete lexical history of Chaucer's English as well as an analysis of that history and its implications'. A useful text to read against fifteenth-century praise of Chaucer's shaping influence on English.

Collette, Carolyn P. (1989) 'Chaucer and Victorian medievalism: culture and society', *Poetica* 29–30, 115–25. An analysis of popular Victorian attitudes toward Chaucer fostered by periodicals which constructed him variously as a child poet, a poet of the English countryside and a poet–businessman.

Dane, Joseph A. (1998) *Who Is Buried in Chaucer's Tomb? Studies in the Reception of Chaucer's Book* (East Lansing, Mich.: Michigan State University Press). A provocative and somewhat polemical book that raises many questions about the tradition of editing Chaucer and the principles on which modern editions have been based.

Donaldson, E. Talbot (1954) 'Chaucer the pilgrim', *Proceedings of the Modern Language Association* 69, 928–36; repr. in *Speaking of Chaucer* (London: Athlone; New York: Norton, 1970), 1–12. In distinguishing Chaucer the poet from Chaucer the pilgrim–narrator, Donaldson opened the way for multiple new critical readings of the irony produced by the simultaneous *naïveté* of the pilgrim and the moral judgement of the author in the pilgrim portraits of the General Prologue.

Georgianna, Linda (1990) 'The Protestant Chaucer', in *Chaucer's Religious Tales*, ed. C. David Benson and Elizabeth Robertson (Cambridge: Brewer), 55–69. Georgianna argues that sixteenth-century assumptions of Chaucer's 'Protestant' leanings continue in contemporary attitudes towards Chaucer's religious beliefs and attitudes.

Kaminsky, Alice R. (1980) *Chaucer's* Troilus and Criseyde *and the Critics* (Athens, Ohio: Ohio University Press). A retrospective analysis of the various types of critical response to *Troilus and Criseyde* during the middle years of the twentieth century.

Lerer, Seth (1993) *Chaucer and his Readers* (Princeton: Princeton University Press). An extended and learned discussion of Chaucer's reception in the fifteenth century, an attempt to 'understand the quality of post-Chaucerian writing . . . to chart the forms and consequences of the reception and transmission of Chaucer's poetry by those admittedly unworthy of his mantle'.

Matthews, David (1999) *The Making of Middle English 1765–1910* (Minneapolis: University of Minnesota Press). Chapter 7, ' "Wise and gentle speech": from the Chaucer Society to the universities', is an account of the transformation of Chaucer's work from the subject of belletristic criticism to the subject of scholarship at the hands of late nineteenth- and early twentieth-century editors and scholars.

Miskimin, Alice (1975) *The Renaissance Chaucer* (New Haven: Yale University Press). Still the most extensive discussion of the reception of Chaucer in the sixteenth century. Addresses Chaucer's reputation for learning in this period.

Patterson, Lee (1987) *Negotiating the Past: The Historical Understanding of Medieval Literature* (Madison: University of Wisconsin Press). Chapter 4, 'Ambiguity and interpretation: a fifteenth-century reading of *Troilus and Criseyde*', explores how a fifteenth-century treatise for women religious draws on and refers to Chaucer's *Troilus*, combining moral instruction and literary appreciation.

Pinti, Daniel J., ed. (1998) *Writing after Chaucer: Essential Readings in Chaucer and the Fifteenth Century* (New York: Garland). A collection of articles by Partridge, Windeatt, Schibanoff, Fisher, Strohm, Boffey, Spearing, Fradenburg, Machan, Bowers, C. David Benson and Lerer, all on the subject of fifteenth-century reception of Chaucer's work.

Robertson, D. W., Jr (1962) *A Preface to Chaucer: Studies in Medieval Perspectives* (Princeton: Princeton University Press). A paradigm-shifting text for mid-century students of Chaucer. Robertson, in arguing an Augustinian religious context for much of Chaucer's work, opened the way to new historicist readings of Chaucer's art in its time.

Ruggiers, Paul G., ed. (1984) *Editing Chaucer: The Great Tradition* (Norman, Okla.: Pilgrim Books). Extensive and thoughtful analyses of the major editions of Chaucer's work by a variety of well-respected scholars and editors.

Schuler, Robert (1984) 'The Renaissance Chaucer as alchemist', *Viator* 53, 305–33. Schuler identifies and analyses a considerable but little-known series of Renaissance texts which accord Chaucer status as master-alchemist. He concludes that Chaucer's reputation as a magus was well known, that it had developed over the course of 200 years, and that it is essential to understanding the Renaissance idea of Chaucer.

Spearing, A. C. (1985) 'Father Chaucer', in *Medieval to Renaissance in English Poetry* (Cambridge: Cambridge University Press), 88–110; repr. in Pinti (1998: 145–66). A consideration of Chaucer's relationship to his literary predecessors and successors through Chaucer's own discourse of fathers and sons; Spearing constructs Chaucer in the centre of a web of influence and anxiety, standing between the *auctores* he admired and his literary heirs.

Spurgeon, Caroline F. E. (1925) 'Introduction', in *Five Hundred Years of Chaucer Criticism and Allusion, 1357–1900*, 3 vols (Cambridge: Cambridge University Press), pp. ix–cxliv. The three volumes of this work contain an encyclopedic record of allusions to Chaucer. The extensive introduction in volume 1 analyses and organizes the vast body of citation Spurgeon gathered.

Windeatt, Barry (1979) 'The scribes as Chaucer's early critics', *Studies in the Age of Chaucer* 1, 119–41. A study of fifteenth-century reception of Chaucer's work by reading scribal variation and alteration as products of understanding and criticism rather than as marks of confusion and error.

2
Authority
Andrew Galloway

In one form or another, notions of authority and Chaucer's demonstrations of negotiations with it can hardly be avoided in criticism from the mid-1980s through to the early 1990s, and are only somewhat less pervasive thereafter. These issues shape nearly every critical discussion of Chaucer launched in this period, from the gender implications of Chaucer's textual hermeneutics (Dinshaw 1989), to the situating of his notions of subjectivity in his negotiations with courtly and civic pressures and opportunities (Patterson 1991), to his characters' disillusioned negotiations with 'institutions', understood as any traditional or official discourse (Leicester 1990), to the social and ideological contexts of his dialectic between 'factional' and 'hierarchical' social visions (Strohm 1989; cf. Wallace 1997), and indeed to the large projects of collecting and elucidating explicit medieval discussions of authorship and authority (Minnis 1984; Minnis and Scott 1991; Wogan-Browne et al. 1999).

No doubt the initial focus on Chaucer's negotiations with authority, appearing from so many directions, may be traced, if partly and indirectly, to the work of Michel Foucault, whose arguments for the pervasiveness of social power, defining both artistic and 'natural' aspects of identity and social life via the comprehensive notion of 'discourse', and especially 'authorship', were widely influential on scholars of Renaissance literarature and helped put the topic of 'authority' in the air. John Guillory's stimulating *Poetic Authority: Spenser, Milton, and Literary History*, for example, with its assumption that 'canonical authors' defining their authority are much like 'their contemporary workers in the medium of power',[1] draws directly on the principles in the works of Foucault then being translated.

But the gap between this and medieval materials and scholarship is notable, as even a crude distinction shows. Guillory can proceed on the basis of *a* 'medium of power' because his data for Spenser's and Milton's self-authorizing are their respective manipulation of claims to origins in English literary authority, including their use of these as marks of failing to claim something more sacred than mere literary 'imagination'. Fourteenth-century English poets have not only little hope of vatic status, they have no 'literary tradition' to settle for: they rarely name immediate predecessors and sources, preferring to cite ancient and patristic *auctores* to authorize their writing (Chaucer's 'Lollius' is an example notable only for its flagrancy). A great deal more context than named indebtedness is necessary even to begin to assess negotiations with literary or any other kind of authority in and by Chaucer and his contemporaries. Indeed, recent important work focusing on Chaucer's modes of negotiating authority moves still further beyond 'literature' and even beyond England (Scanlon 1994; Gellrich 1995; Wallace 1997).

It is more appropriate to say that fourteenth-century writers in English had no given or single 'medium of power' at hand. The society they wrote in emphatically proclaimed clerical authority in learning, and aristocratic and royal status in political power. Assertions of clerical supremacy or even exclusivity in learning were expressed all the more polemically by those resisting either the lay access to translations of the Bible that the Lollards promoted, or the 'peasant' uses of documents and law that sought to overturn monastic landlord rights. Likewise, aristocratic and royal political supremacy was asserted all the more fiercely by some in a century that saw the deposition of two kings, the murder of at least one, and the emergence of the 'commons' – the county gentry in Parliament – as a force that the higher nobility continually had to confront and sometimes appease. Both kinds of assertion, and the corresponding implications about the base status of vernacular poetry, were extreme (on the last, see Wogan-Browne et al. 1999: esp. 8–10, 15–16).

As much of the scholarship on fourteenth-century literature and culture correctly asserts or implies, new social and intellectual structures of authority – to adapt Raymond Williams' sociological term 'structures of feeling'[2] – were fundamentally challenging the shop-worn claims of clerical and aristocratic dominance (in the old Gelasian formulation, clerical *auctoritas* and royal *potestas*) and the traditional interlocking structure of society presumed on these bases. Society as a whole had no one secure 'medium of power'. Non-aristocratic, non-clerical vernacular poets like Chaucer were engaged in a process not of manipulating a given medium, but of engaging multiple challenges in ways that gradually precipitated an authoritative medium for their own and their Renaissance followers' endeavours, even if Renaissance presumptions of literary and indeed political authority typically trimmed and provincialized Chaucer's full range of negotiations with authority – the 'Immodesty', 'Profanation' and 'trivial things' that Dryden disparages in his preface to his *Fables* (Wallace 1997: 64).

Social

Along with many demands for a return to a traditional hierarchical order, the period witnessed a splintering of traditional social authority by what can be called the 'politicizing' of various social spheres, often by those most vociferously demanding return to tradition: from the self-conscious identifications of the rural rebels of 1381, who called themselves the 'true commons', to the persistent efforts of the gentry to demand reform in royal administration, including the clash between knights and a group of courtiers in the Good Parliament of 1376, where for the first time a speaker for the commons was elected and where the circle around the old king was impeached. Later effects of this 'politicizing' include the continual pressures put on the king by petitions from the Commons, followed by the more savage conflicts between Richard's uncles and the royal group close to Richard culminating in 1388. Then, on the basis of their 'traditional' rights, Richard's uncles had many of the king's closest advisers hanged, including figures who knew Chaucer such as Thomas Usk and the London mayor Nicholas Brembre, as a result of an unprecedented summary trial at Parliament (the Merciless Parliament). Since this conflict ultimately led to Richard's 1397 reprisals against the higher nobility, and thence to his 1399 deposition by the Lancastrian party (Strohm 1992: 75–94, Saul 1997: 366–434), it might be said that the higher orders became politicized too, in the sense of more self-consciously defining their traditional rights and identity. Lineage hardened as a requirement for nobility; the king's novel creation of new peers deeply irked the higher caste.[3] Richard's personal law-book suggests he studied the century's legal challenges to kingship (Saul 1997: 237); his relation to traditional kingly rights was thus as strategic as other claims to traditional authority.

The period's schemes of social order reflect such unsettling (and what Leicester calls 'disenchantment'), as well as its underlying economic and cultural causes. Surveys of estates types in twelfth- and thirteenth-century Latin and French poetry already show progressive proliferation of the initial three estates, and Chaucer's contemporaries John Gower and William Langland show much greater flexibility still (Mann 1973). Chaucer's opening sequence in the General Prologue – of Knight (with son and servant), three religious figures of some power and economic substance, and then, less clearly, figures occupied in humbler modes of living (after the irascible Parson, most of the figures are explicitly beholden to some absent lord or 'maister'), ending with sheer hypocrites and rogues – superficially shows a more dutiful acceptance than Gower's or Langland's surveys of the customary ideal harmony of 'those who fought, those who prayed, those who worked'. But his view increasingly weakens any claim of that structure to be something in itself to revere (Leicester 1990: 383–417). The unexpected and slippery bases of authority in Chaucer's opening portraits are more unnerving than those of his fellow estates satirists': for example, the Knight's portrait is based on an increasingly economic sense of 'worthiness', and the Prioress's portrait on her faithful if not wholly successful efforts to emulate courtly style. Chaucer's principles slide alarmingly between traditional ideals of the estates' presupposed stability and legitimacy, and a marketplace ideology which undercuts that stability and legitimacy (Aers 1986: 14–20). As Mann showed, the only constant feature in his survey is each figure's self-sufficient professional competence and equally specialized morality (1973: xi, 187–202).

In some measure this slippage of principles for hierarchical authority is culture-wide. Novel parliamentary efforts at comprehensive social legislation from the 1350s to the end of Richard's reign – initially responses to the devastating changes of the Black Death, and the subsequent rise of scarce labourers' wages – also waver continually between nostalgic hopes of restoring people to their traditional 'places' and a market-oriented set of concerns which bespeaks the forces responsible for moving people out of their traditional 'places'. Chief among such legislative efforts (of which Chaucer, near the centre of government, would have known) was the Statute of Labourers and Artisans (1351, and again 1388). It sought to set wages at pre-plague levels and required that all workers and artisans take an oath before king's justices to obey the new (or 'old') wage and price rules (Musson and Ormrod 1999: 95–6). To impose central wage control and intervene in the traditional relationship between local landlords and their workers were stunning innovations, even on the grounds of recovering 'traditional order', making every labourer in effect a state-regulated worker. The required oath deserves contemplation too. It obviously publicized the new law, but also further transferred social allegiance from local landlords or civic entities to the central, administrative state. The re-issued 1388 statute went further: travelling labourers must carry documents issued by Chancery justifying their movements (Musson and Ormrod 1999: 94).[4]

Other statutes constitute or reveal similar paradoxes, in tradition's name replacing traditional social ties with a new ideal of central bureaucratic authority and an insistently monetary measure of status. The (soon retracted) ordinance of 1363 on diet and clothing, the first in England, denounces the collapse of traditional hierarchy – 'apprentice boys dress like masters, masters like valets, valets like squires, squires like knights, to the great destruction of the lords and commons' – but defines social rankings by yearly income. Clerks' and knights' clothing licences are interchangeable, if the clerics' income suffices.[5]

Religious

Professional religious authority was variously challenged throughout this period of expanding lay literacy. In a break with medieval administrative tradition, clerics were periodically purged from royal government, while proposals to disendow the monasteries were bandied about – and not just by Lollards.[6] The answering abundance of clerical claims for authority actually weakened their general credibility, possibly with general effects. The professional orders' pressure for historical primacy, and hence their revision of history, was constant. The Friar in the Summoner's Tale epitomizes this not just by parading his order's ludicrous claim to antiquity, but also by concocting a professionally self-serving account of his vision when he learns the wife's baby died: he cannot keep from revising history even on the most personal scale. Monks were similarly disposed: a treatise 'on the antiquity and authority of monks' circulated in the late fourteenth century among Benedictine chroniclers, and was copied (for example) by Thomas Walsingham after his narrative of his abbey's suppression of the rural tenants who rebelled in 1381.[7] Historical claims were always the currency of authority in medieval culture; but since the rebellious tenants themselves claimed ancient rights, the strategy could only produce further challenges, bringing attention to all manipulators of history seeking present authority.[8]

Official release from hierarchical authority existed, of course, but was of a different order from these political and social challenges, although they sometimes built on it. The 'ritual year' allowed an ebb and flow of indulgence and restraint, which probably helped make tolerable the permeating hierarchical scheme of society, somewhat transmuting social inequities into temporal inequities by which all were affected. From Advent (fourth Sunday before Christmas) to Christmas Eve food was restricted, making the feast of Christmas and the twelve days following a collective relief and, with their Lords of Misrule and boy bishops, collective transgression of workaday social 'place'.[9] The June Corpus Christi feast allowed similar festivity, but also, by the later fourteenth century, processions and public religious drama, displaying civic hierarchy as well as parodying it. Presumably it was the festival's licence for subversion and assertion of collective social identity that encouraged rural communities to choose Corpus Christi week in 1381 for the most organized popular rebellion England had ever seen.[10] Chaucer's Miller's Tale, with its scornful mockery of a rustic believer in the re-enactment of Noah's Flood, shows that Chaucer found much to ridicule in the feast's support of sacred drama (perhaps also commenting on and containing the implications of the rising, as Patterson argues [1991: 244–79]). But unlike the dramatists who included some burlesque in the Corpus Christi drama, Chaucer apparently did not need or seek an occasion from the national ritual year for revelry and liberation in his poetic themes: he built these rhythms into the sequence of the *Canterbury Tales* (as when the Miller interrupts after the Knight's Tale), just as he established internal seasonal and festival markings there and elsewhere, including idiosyncratic ones such as his mysterious 10 December and 3 May.

Literary

Such narrative incorporation of a larger cultural rhythm between authoritarian austerity and rebellion suggests a larger point about Chaucer's claims for literary authority. The right balance of mimicry and originality let vernacular literature bid for capacious, self-sufficient cultural authority in spite of its overt dependence on Latin, French and Italian sources, on mere reportage and on compilation. Naturally, the Latin commentary tradition, whose glosses of the Bible, law, grammar, classical and medieval standard texts (*auctores*) presented most explicitly the discussion of authority, still commanded a primary claim to textual authority: what was glossed was authoritative, as was what or who did the glossing. A vernacular, courtly writer concerned with satire and secular love could hardly hope for either. Yet Chaucer's contemporary Gower sought in some sense the authority both of the commentary tradition and of what it glossed, by supplying extensive Latin glosses to his long English poem treating love, ethics and politics, the *Confessio Amantis*.

The manuscripts of Chaucer's *Canterbury Tales* also show signs of a programme (probably not wholly Chaucer's) for Latin glossing; the most intriguing are those that seem at odds with the vernacular narrator, as in the Wife of Bath's Prologue.[11] Ellesmere and other manuscripts of the *Canterbury Tales* even frequently mark 'auctor' in the margin; Ellesmere carefully restricts this to poetic apostrophes (e.g. 'O stormy peple! Unsad and evere untrewe!' by the narrator of the Clerk's Tale [995; fo. 99ᵛ], and many others). While an intriguing instance of literary self-consciousness by Chaucer's early scribes, and perhaps an early recognition that apostrophe is a narrative feature especially signifying 'poetry',[12] this Latin label of *auctor* – pedantically defined by commentators as an increaser of great deeds and thoughts from the past (from *augere*), more whimsically in the twelfth century by Walter Map as a writer sanctioned by death (Minnis 1984: 11–12) – grants Chaucer far more authority than the English colophon closing most manuscripts of the *Canterbury Tales* which is more likely from Chaucer's hand: 'Heere is ended the book of the tales of Caunterbury, compiled by Geffrey Chaucer.'

A compiler's role had by the fourteenth century been carefully defined as subordinate to an *auctor*'s (a Latin work on astrology written for King Richard II asserts the distinction, and Latin encyclopedists such as Vincent of Beauvais and historians such as Ranulph Higden imply it): yet it has a certain authority (Minnis 1984: 94–103, 190–210; Wogan-Browne et al. 1999: 61–72). Moses was said to have in part 'compiled' the Pentateuch; and Ranulph Higden presents his role as compiler in surprisingly grandiloquent terms. Higden, a northern monk writing in Latin for a national clerical audience in the 1330s–1340s, is worth noting as opening new possibilities for a compiler to claim both national and modern authority, different from but in some ways measurable against his past *auctores*. In John Trevisa's 1387 translation, Higden states he has 'y-kast and y-ordeyned, as I may, to make and to write a tretes, I-gadered of dyuerse bookes, of the staat of the ylonde of Britayne, to knowleche of men that cometh after us'; he presents such labour as merely entering 'into the feeldes of our forme fadres, and following the rype men [reapers], yif I may any wyse leese and gadre me som eres that rype men schedeth and skepeth of here hondes', but also as a declaration of his authority (via Isidore's quotation of Horace) – 'It were wel greet strengthe to wreste a mace oute of Hercules honde' – concluding with an equal if less vivid claim: 'And thei [even if] I take it of other menis, I clepe this storie [history] myn.'[13]

If the modern compiler was more obtrusive by the fourteenth century, so were the historical agents behind his sources; this too offered Chaucer both challenges and opportunities for redefining authority, particularly his own. *Auctoritas* in Latin has a reverential, supra-human aura and sense: it denotes a specific text or the prestige of a writer behind the text; the power of making rules or enforcing them. But increasingly in the thirteenth and fourteenth centuries the focus shifted to human *auctores*, even of the Bible: the authoritative text was approached via its human constructors, rather than as if it were unmediated divine truth (Minnis and Scott 1991: 1–11). Higden (again he is notable) constantly assesses his heaped-up *auctores* in terms of their historical accuracy and sometimes their historical contexts, using the symbol 'R' (Ranulphus) to identify his own comments. The Latin word cannot manage all this; but Middle English *auctoritee* can mean 'authority' in the personal sense of *auctor* as well as the impersonal senses of *auctoritas*. Perhaps helped by this, Chaucer invariably emphasizes the historical agent behind a text (his usual meaning, in fact, for *auctoritee*) rather than accepting any transcendently authoritative 'sentence'. Indeed, his sensitivity to human origins of knowledge is so great that encounters with 'olde bokes' usually involve some degree of crisis regarding their claims to authority, increased by his compilational tendency. Thus his presentation of Virgil's *Aeneid* persistently rewrites it through Ovid's Letter of Dido in the *Heroides*; by so turning Virgil's grand narrative of *pius Aeneas* into 'false Aneas', Chaucer implies that every story has another side, all narrative depends on perspective, and Virgil is no more omniscient a reporter than the Geffrey who is set down before the petitioners to Fame to witness the negotiations that have left them glorified or disgraced.

Chaucer's keen sense of the limited, human origins of texts does not, however, help him define a stable 'presence' behind them (for this as a general issue in the period, see Gellrich 1995); instead, the 'meaning' of any authority, indeed of any speaker – including the present pilgrims – retreats into ever-further uncertainties of conscious and unconscious subjectivity or *entente* (because of Chaucer's emphasis on its elusiveness, the scholastic category *intentio auctoris* is only a superficial parallel; cf. Minnis 1984: 191). Seeing the Pardoner's personal stake in his tale or the Wife of Bath's in hers does not simplify the meanings of either (which of course involve these personal stakes: see Dinshaw 1989, Leicester 1990, Patterson 1991 for whole chapters on these figures). Even the Parson's Tale has been well described as locating its authority in the teller, thus, it is claimed, providing Chaucer with 'an authorization of his own voice, an authorization so implicit it has gone unnoticed' (Scanlon 1994: 13).

However ultimately elusive such authorial 'presence' ever is – especially in a world where texts circulated far beyond the author's immediate circle – desire for it is like the desire for narrative authority beyond the constraints of circumstance or professional agenda (in the religious, medieval sense as well as the modern, secular sense), both of which, Chaucer continually shows, distort learning and govern textual 'interests' and production. Indeed, it may be that the professionalizing of knowledge – the blurring of learning's goals from theology to various administrative purposes in fourteenth-century universities, enhanced by the parasitical sprawl of less formal vocational schools and the general invasion of legal and documentary culture into social commerce of all kinds[14] – kindled a corresponding rise in the value of *non*-professionalized learning, of knowledge and reading purged of the social or professional interests loading it with strategic claims to authority. Anticlerical heretics and book-burning peasants express this desire acutely, if self-contradictorily (Gellrich 1995: 151–91). A subtler response is for a vernacular poet to find strategies emphasizing that he is neither institutionally constrained nor an obsequious princepleaser or professional versifier (one strategy was wittily to pretend to be, as in Thopas or the

Legend of Good Women; another was to satirize courtly flatterers, such as Placebo in the Merchant's Tale). His authority would lie in being an amateur, implicitly unconstrained by professionalized learning of the sort he satirized.

The rise in the late fourteenth century of such writers, like Chaucer whose salary came from more authoritative courtly and civil service obligations than poetry, explains the marked decline of 'professional' courtly poets, that is, the minstrels employed by kings or nobles (Green 1980). Their rise also explains why courtly and London writings in the period were often serious efforts at philosophical, ethical or social inquiry, unconstrained by a narrowly defined clerical or royal agenda. Boethius' *Consolation of Philosophy*, with its absence of overt Christian dogma, is a key text in this intellectually sophisticated and often factional and dangerous lay environment, where the kind of stoicism that Chaucer generally cultivates would be politically useful and emotionally attractive (Aers 1986: 59–61; Thomas Usk's *Testament of Love* also aspires to this[15]). Topical politics, or more general philosophy of politics, might be explored rather than partisanly declared (Strohm 1989: 144–51; Ferster 1996). Religious guidance could pass entirely from the professionals' hands: just as London provided a reservoir of Lollard books, and teachers or poets like Langland debated theology, so at court lay rather than clerically mediated forms of religious worship were cultivated: for example, the work of Chaucer's friend John Clanvowe, *The Two Ways*, while not distinctly Lollard, makes no reference to clerical guidance (but then, the reference to a 'preest' to hear the confession solicited by the Parson [ParsT 318] is a quite forgettable occasion for this do-it-yourself guide to penance and reform). Courtly funerals had for decades favoured austerity and eschewed clergy, but in the late fourteenth century Lollardy surrounded the court to the extent that reports circulated naming Richard's chamber knights responsible for nailing to the doors of Westminster the Lollard manifesto of 'twelve conclusions' in 1395.[16]

Richard helped persecute the Lollards; but his court, in spite – or because – of the king's own autocratic style, seems to have provided a kind of suspension or at least detached view of other kinds of authority: precisely an atmosphere where a group of royal 'favourites', lacking lineage, military prowess, family money or other traditional connections to aristocratic authority, might flourish. (The young Robert de Vere, elevated by Richard to the first marquisate in English history, then made Duke of Ireland, was a notorious example.) This ill-fated royal court with its autocratic challenges to traditional aristocratic dominance may have been a propitious context for a poetic exploration of authority that other factors, such as increasing lay literacy and rapidly increasing acceptance of English instead of French or Latin, were in any case generating – if, of course, a writer there could evade partisanship or dangerous topicality, the very features that Chaucer's short-lived contemporary, Usk, most cultivated (Strohm 1989: 24–46).[17] Just as propitious a context was the surrounding city, where a burgeoning vernacular book trade and conflux of mercantile, clerical, heretical, aristocratic, legal and other literate lay and clerical groups would constitute a ready audience and a vigorously dialectical setting for vernacular poetry measuring and negotiating structures of authority old and new. The fishbowl of Richard's autocratic court, and the sea-washed strands of the entrepôt London, together offered extraordinary opportunities for those pursuing these goals.

The Knight's Tale, 2987–3074

Theseus' speech on the 'Firste Moevere' at the end of the Knight's Tale is Chaucer's fullest presentation of authority as a comprehensive principle. But it has always generated a variety of interpretative complaints and debates. It opens with a vast perspective, funnelling down to the reasons for quietly accepting Arcite's death and Palamon's and Emelye's marriage:

> 'The Firste Moevere of the cause above,
> Whan he first made the faire cheyne of love,
> Greet was th'effect, and heigh was his entente.
> Wel wiste he why, and what thereof he mente,
> For with that faire cheyne of love he bond
> The fyr, the eyr, the water, and the lond
> In certeyn boundes, that they may nat flee.
> That same Prince and that Moevere', quod he,
> 'Hath stablissed in this wrecched world adoun
> Certeyne dayes and duracioun
> To al that is engendred in this place,
> Over the whiche day they may nat pace,
> Al mowe they yet tho dayes wel abregge.
> Ther nedeth noght noon auctoritee t'allegge,
> For it is preeved by experience . . .'
>
> (2987–3001)

The speech claims the self-evident authority of authority, as a natural, political and philosophical necessity; but such authority emerges as unpleasant, paradoxical and increasingly strained, under pressure alike from the energies of the confined elements and from the emotions and complaints of human beings, implicitly including the speaker's. The speech's dark features are obvious; life is 'this wrecched world', the only escape suicide ('Al mowe they yet tho dayes wel abregge').

The courtly taste for Boethian philosophy, as a way of standing above the vicissitudes of courtly 'fortune', is here put to its toughest test. For if Boethius in his paean to God, 'O qui perpetua' (*Consolation* III, metrum 9), a celebratory lyric recast by so many of the Latin authors Chaucer read, uses occasional metaphors of 'binding' to describe the order imposed by the 'creator of heaven and earth', Theseus presents such binding as an iron grip imposing a quasi-political autocracy on all creation, from the chained elements to the impulses of human beings to bewail death and loss, as his conclusion to his argument shows: 'And whoso gruccheth ought, he dooth folye, / And rebel is to hym that al may gye' (3045–6).

One response to the speech is to see it as imagining a pre-Christian philosophy, from which all sense of a 'loving god' is absent and in which the value of fame is supreme;[18] another, as a blatant instance of using the cosmos to justify political domination by the ruling class, hence part of Chaucer's criticism of such authority (Aers 1986: 29–32); another, as showing the speaker's discomfort with such a scheme but his disenchanted acceptance of the disorder and death he simultaneously reveals, while for practical reasons he strives to offer the less hardened listeners an illusion of order governing such challenges to social stability (Leicester 1991: 363–76).

All three interpretations have support. The speech's point – if it can be momentarily lifted from its dramatic moment and nesting narrative contexts, which are of considerable importance – is the Stoic one, 'To maken vertu of necessitee, / And take it weel that we may nat eschue' (3042–3); its pagan outlook is clear in the references to Jupiter and the omission of Boethius' view of the joyous self-sufficiency that his *Philosophia* stresses in contemplating divinity. Its point is also self-servingly political. What principle it defines is never named, but the 'contrarie of al this' is: 'wilfulnesse' (3057), manifested even in *grucchying* (complaint) and of course any other means of being 'rebel . . . to hym that al may gye'. The implied need, then, is for a *human* authority that the speech never mentions (apart from a narrow sense of the word when Theseus says there is no need for any textual 'auctoritee' to support his point), but which distinctly emerges by contrast to rebellion and *grucchying*. Theseus (and presumably the Knight) is taking charge in the human realm on the grounds of a transcendent order with which his own words show him to be less concerned than with how human beings control themselves or one another. Finally, its point is also the speaker's efforts at self-control, especially his self-denial of any transcendent comfort, pagan or other, although he cannot hide a variety of peculiar tones and implications, including his own simmering complaints at uncontrollable 'necessitee' and his sense of the inherent meaninglessness of the cosmos. For he emphasizes that such 'order' does not translate into any basis for the social hierarchy on earth (as the later elaborations of how everyone must die, the young and the old, 'the kyng as shal a page' [3030], suggest).

All these views usefully articulate the speech's negatives: its deficiencies and limitations in its presentation of universal principles of authority. In presenting pagan worldliness, cynical power politics and existential endurance, the speech hollows out the main principles of institutionalized, traditional authority that, in keeping with its genre, it should claim. A closer (more wholehearted?) translation of Boethius' neoplatonic passages, or of other works in the 'Dionysian' tradition (Minnis and Scott 1991: 165–96), would have yielded fewer internal conflicts. But against the cultural contexts mentioned above, more positive if oblique claims appear in it. The speech betrays the undermining everywhere in Chaucer's context of the principles of authority, particularly those that his self-authorizing depended on debunking: impermeable and fixed social hierarchy; clerical bookishness and clerical claims on transcendent meaning; and reliance on tradition. The claims for social hierarchy are contradicted by the gratuitous repeated emphases on the meaninglessness of human hierarchies in the face of death: 'heer-agayns no creature on lyve, / Of no degree, availleth for to stryve' (3039–40; see also 3027–30). The value of bookishness and clerical tradition, which should be implied by the speech's vast cosmic perspective as well as its learned traditions, is brusquely dismissed from the outset, in a voice that in a freer narrative context could expand into the Wife of Bath's (above, 3000–1).

The speech has other life-affirming tones that are not appreciable in readings stressing its darkness and sense of limitations: for example, sexuality is persistently affirmed – even in the grimmest moments of the overt argument. It first appears wrapped in Theseus' conclusion to his first long argument, where the speaker, about to discuss death and decay, approaches sexuality with awkward formality, in a reference to an 'engendering' that is 'corrumpable' (3010):

> And therefore, of his wise purveiaunce,
> He hath so wel biset his ordinaunce
> That speces of thynges and progressiouns
> Shullen enduren by successiouns . . .
> (3011–14)

'And therefore' makes it seem for a moment that the point of all this is not order but sexuality. Even lineage seems tonally subordinate here to the fair *means* of 'successiouns', as in 'He hath *so wel* biset his ordinaunce'. Affirmation of sexuality returns again as a meaningful second sense of the final lines: the speaker declares there should be no complaint about Arcite's death from Palamon and Emelye 'That both his soule and eek hemself offende, / And yet they mowe hir lustes nat amende' (3065–6) – they 'offende' him syntactically by mourning, but contextually by marrying one another. Syntactically, their 'lustes' are their 'desires to complain'; contextually, the amatory pleasures they cannot renounce. However oddly timed, these affirmations of sexuality expel the tone of clerical bookishness, and even of high politics. With sexuality so noticeable, this union is finally not (*pace* Aers 1986: 30) a grand aristocratic alliance (as Theseus makes clear in emphasizing Palamon's poverty [3085]), but a familial solution to a series of awkward situations, indeed an act of diplomacy and convenience more on a bourgeois than a stately scale.

Whether fully in the narrator's control or not, the speech can be read within the contexts above as de-authorizing old patterns of authority and implying positive, not yet nameable new structures of authority (in Williams's sense). The speech clearly does not support rebellion; its negotiations with traditional authority involve not undermining the supreme social power of the king, but showing he is a present manipulator of traditions and even an instigator of new principles – implied in disruptive tonalities and asides, in an argument that makes its points mostly by negation. These implied principles are secular, contemporary and as applicable to civic, non-clerical men well below lordly or aristocratic position as to the 'povre bacheler' Palamon (whose social standing Chaucer has carefully kept down but whose role he has elevated far above that of Boccaccio's Palemone). In such new principles, or tones, there is also an image of the interests of non-aristocratic, civic, non-clerical women, whom Emelye suddenly resembles in her rapid abandonment of a vow of celibacy, a vow that, as Chaucer has presented it, has mostly managed to keep her character decorously unlike that of Boccaccio's flirtatious Emilia. The implications of new structures and subtle disparagements of traditional authority indeed seem necessary to convince Palamon and Emelye to welcome their new 'bond'; the focus in the *Canterbury Tales* on bourgeois marriage as society's central institution begins here, amid the ruins of other kinds of social authority.

Finally, the new structures of authority also include the social power of narrative and its users, with implications beyond its immediate lordly speaker. For the story to end, there must be no more complaint that might cause yet more trouble and continue the plot (as Arcite's complaint in the woods led to all that follows). The silencing Theseus imposes collapses his role into the narrator's; thus it parallels those abrupt compressions by the narrator throughout the Tale. As that narrator acknowledges (especially through his use of *occupatio*) the pre-existing authority of the source but his present need to reduce it, so Theseus acknowledges the traditional structure of cosmic order but presses it noticeably into the service of solving his present problems: an end to complaint and his daughter's marriage.

Such expressions of present authority through manipulation of pre-existing materials implicate Chaucer too. What is a self-conflicted, rather tattered autocratic gesture in Athenian reality is socially and ideologically liberating in the context of the English poet's formulating new structures of non-clerical, non-aristocratic narrative authority, although that poet's social power derives not from curtailing *grucchyng* but from allowing new tones to emerge. Theseus' speech infuses the rest of the *Canterbury Tales* with a sense of how socially powerful narrative potentially is, even as it shows how thoroughly a ruler is limited to immediate contexts and personal, practical perspectives – and, of course, as the speech has emphasized, as subject to death and sexuality as anyone else.

The Prologue to the *Legend of Good Women*

The Prologue to the *Legend* directly presents the writer's authority, or subservience, before a king, and it too deserves a brief look to show how broader as well as more specific structures of authority are again implicated in the writer's negotiations. The legends are widely regarded as responses to the courtly pressures the narrator has suffered, with their incompleteness a final 'revenge upon authority' (Patterson 1991: 238); these are sometimes seen as the last 'courtly' literary endeavour before Chaucer turned to the more 'national' *Canterbury Tales*. But it is pertinent to note that the extant manuscripts of the *Legend of Good Women* are as far in quality from courtly milieux as any of Chaucer's work, and that the textual relationships of the manuscripts point to two large manuscript families, one of which evidently derives from a copying centre where two exemplars were used simultaneously and exchanged.[19] That is, a commercial London copying centre was probably near or even at the point of this 'courtly' work's first 'publication'.

Moreover, the scene of the royal imposition of the task of compilation and translation that forms the climax of the Prologue appears only after a 200-line rumination on the narrator's relation to books, his worship of a 'lady sovereyne', and springtime; and the conflict in the debate about the narrator's unflattering writings about love emerges because he has been already writing for others with other purposes, either as a thoughtless literary hack or the fearful servant to some other powerful patron. This uncertainty presents the clearest statement of the narrator's distance from courtly control, an uncertainty that Alceste urges the king to sustain:

> . . . peraunter, for this man ys nyce,
> He myghte doon yt, gessyng no malice,
> But for he useth thynges for to make;
> Hym rekketh noght of what matere he take.
> Or him was boden maken thilke tweye
> Of som persone, and durste yt nat withseye;
> Or him repenteth outrely of this.
>
> (F 362–8)

To be sure, the king's and queen's power is terrifying, their imperatives unappealable. The king, who has a general parallel to Richard II, specifically resembles him in his royal gaze, where the effect of his authority is concentrated, 'So that his loking dooth myn herte cold' (F 240): one contemporary chronicler claimed that 'whenever [Richard] performed kingly rituals, he would order a throne to be prepared for him in his chamber on which he liked to sit ostentatiously . . . talking to no one but watching everyone; and when his eye fell on anyone, regardless of rank, that person had to bend his knee towards the king'.[20]

But the narrator is extraordinarily free from royal autocratic authority in his usual self-indulgent relations with textual authority, grazing among old books and rewriting others' songs while worshipping a 'lady soveryne' that must be Queen Anne who died in 1394, since all references to her are absent from the G text. The F Prologue is not the work of a resentful courtier, but perhaps Chaucer's witty apology for no longer being in the court's ambit, yet emphasizing throughout his freedom from any patron's surveillance, especially the king's, thus refuting, for example, any culpability for the charges pressed in 1388 against others close to the king.

Whatever the topical politics of the F version, the wider importance of the Prologue's opening is that it enshrines from the outset a compiler's calculated uncertainty in an encounter with any authority – that is, precisely a model for the state of mind that Alceste later asks the king to emulate in avoiding 'tyrannye'. Chaucer's self-portrayal as a compiler opens (as does Higden's) with the importance of writing for capturing examples from the past; like Higden, he presents himself as merely a reaper gathering sheaves from others' works (F 66–83); later he asserts, as Higden does, that the works were 'his' (i.e. governed by his *entente*) even if taken from others: 'what so myn auctour mente, / Algate, God woot, yt was myn entente / To forthren trouthe in love' (470–2). Yet each of these gestures in Chaucer's *Legend* negotiates textual authority quite differently from Higden. Chaucer's belief in the value of writing is not assumed *a priori* (Higden takes it from John of Salisbury's *Policraticus*, with a minimum of logical justification);[21] rather, Chaucer starts with *objections* to faith in books ('ther nis noon dwellyng in this contree / That eyther hath in hevene or helle ybe' [F 5–6]), before offering arguments *in favour* of it ('thing is never the lasse sooth, / Thogh every wight ne may it nat ysee' [14–15]). The call for belief in 'olde appreved stories' in which this argument results ('Yeve credence') has no firm logical basis, but it is at least made into a more conscious, because lingering, *act of blind believing* than Higden's claims. The locus of authority thereby shifts from the uncertainty of the truth behind the text, to the equally uncertain *entente* which engages in such negotiation, finally to a simple contractual leap to accepting their authority on faith. If the king and queen do not precisely know Chaucer's *entente* behind his 'makyng', the leap of faith in books suggests that he would not fully know either.

His uncertain grazing among books at the outset defines the poet as bucolically pure of any professional agenda. But here this ideal has a larger point than his own authority. As Alceste renders this principle into politics, the fluid, personal, not professionalized negotiation between text and reader, involving a high degree of sheer faith, suggests a new structure for rulership and the entire political community. For she advises the king to maintain uncertain faith regarding the *entente* of *all* others': lords, 'poore folk' (390) or writers: 'This shoolde a ryghtwis lord have in his thoght, / And nat be lyk tirauntz of Lumbardye' (373–4). All should stand equal in his ignorance (rather than ranked by his piercing and paranoid gaze); the body politic would be allowed to move by its own processes, in a political version of what has been called Chaucer's 'skeptical fideism' as a reader.[22]

Uncertainty of anyone's *entente*, including his own, rules the amateur compiler's negotiation with authoritative books, allowing his reactions to guide him as he goes but treating those as personal reactions, not ultimate truth or professional authority; the same sceptical fideism, Alceste declares, and is left declaring even after Anne of Bohemia has died, would allow the king to 'compile' a nation without imposing tyrannical assumptions about its intentions. An ideal of national community emerges from an unnameable notion of unregulated, unjudged transactions, a free market of intellectual and other commerce that stands as a utopia against the period's self-defeating record of aristocratic, clerical and royal schemes for authority and control.

See also AFTERLIFE; BODIES; CHIVALRY; CHRISTIAN IDEOLOGIES; COMEDY; CONTEMPORARY ENGLISH WRITERS; CRISIS AND DISSENT; GAMES; LONDON; LOVE; MODES OF REPRESENTATION; PERSONAL IDENTITY; SCIENCE; SOCIAL STRUCTURES; STYLE; TEXTS; TRANSLATION; WOMEN.

NOTES

1 John Guillory, *Poetic Authority: Spenser, Milton, and Literary History* (New York: Columbia University Press, 1983), p. vii.

2 R. Williams, *Marxism and Literature* (New York: Oxford University Press, 1977), 133–4.

3   See generally C. Given-Wilson, *The English
    Nobility in the Late Middle Ages* (London and
    New York: Routledge, 1996).

4   See also Anne Middleton, 'Acts of vagrancy:
    the C version "autobiography" and the statute
    of 1388', in *Written Work: Langland, Labor,
    and Authorship*, ed. Steven Justice and
    Kathryn Kerby-Fulton (Philadelphia: Uni-
    versity of Pennsylvania Press, 1997),
    208–317.

5   *Rotuli Parliamentorum* (London: House of
    Lords, 1783), ii, 276–80.

6   A. Hudson, *The Premature Reformation: Wyclif-
    fite Texts and Lollard History* (Oxford: Claren-
    don, 1988), esp. 114–16, 338.

7   See W. A. Pantin, 'Some medieval
    English treatises on the origins of monasti-
    cism', in *Medieval Studies Presented to Rose
    Graham*, ed. V. Ruffer and A. J. Taylor
    (Oxford: Oxford University Press, 1950),
    189–215.

8   See R. Faith, 'The "great rumour" of
    1377 and peasant ideology', in *The English
    Rising of 1381*, ed R. H. Hilton and T. H.
    Aston (Cambridge: Cambridge University
    Press, 1987), 43–74; and A. Galloway,
    'Making history legal: *Piers Plowman* and
    the rebels of fourteenth-century England', in
    Piers Plowman: *New Essays*, ed. Kathleen
    Hewett-Smith (New York: Garland,
    forthcoming).

9   See R. Hutton, *The Rise and Fall of
    Merry England: The Ritual Year 1400–1700*
    (Oxford: Oxford University Press, 1996),
    7–68.

10 On the timing, see M. Aston, 'Corpus
    Christi and the corpus regni: heresy and
    the peasants' revolt', *Past and Present* 43
    (1994), 3–45; Paul Strohm, *Hochon's Arrow:
    The Social Imagination of Fourteenth-century
    Texts* (Princeton: Princeton University Press,
    1992), 53–6; and Steven Justice, *Writing
    and Rebellion: England in 1381*, The New
    Historicism 27 (Berkeley and Los Angeles:
    University of California Press, 1994), esp.
    153–76.

11 S. Schibanoff, 'The new reader and
    feminine textuality in two early com-
    mentaries on Chaucer', *Studies in the Age
    of Chaucer* 10 (1988), 71–108; *Jankyn's
    Book of Wikked Wyves*, ed. Ralph Hanna
    III and T. Lawler (Athens, Ga. and

    London: University of Georgia Press, 1997),
    84–7.

12 See J. D. Culler, 'Apostrophe', in *The Pursuit
    of Signs: Semiotics, Literature, Deconstruction*
    (Ithaca, NY: Cornell University Press, 1981),
    135–54.

13 *Polychronicon Ranulphi Higden Monachi
    Cestrensis . . .* , ed. C. Babington and J. R.
    Lumby, Rolls Series 41 (London: Longman,
    1865–86), i, 7–20. On Higden and
    Chaucer, see further A. Galloway, 'Chaucer's
    Legend of Lucrece and the critique of
    ideology in fourteenth-century England',
    ELH: English Literary History 60 (1993),
    813–32.

14 Starting points are J. I. Catto and T. A. R.
    Evans, *The History of the University of
    Oxford*, ii: *Late Medieval Oxford* (Oxford:
    Clarendon, 1992), and N. Orme, *English
    Schools in the Middle Ages* (London: Methuen,
    1973).

15 Thomas Usk, *Testament of Love*, ed. R. A. Shoaf
    (Kalamazoo, Mich.: Western Michigan Uni-
    versity, 1998).

16 London and Lollards: Hudson, *Premature
    Reformation*, 123–4; funerals: J. Catto, 'Reli-
    gion and the English nobility in the later
    fourteenth century', in *History and Imagina-
    tion*, ed. H. Lloyd-Jones, V. Pearl and B.
    Worden (London: Duckworth, 1981), 43–55;
    'Twelve Conclusions', in *Selections from English
    Wycliffite Writings*, ed. Anne Hudson (Cam-
    bridge: Cambridge University Press, 1978),
    24–9; Lollard knights: Nigel Saul, *Richard II*
    (New Haven: Yale University Press, 1997),
    297–303.

17 Usk, *Testament of Love*, ed. Shoaf.

18 Alastair J. Minnis, *Chaucer and Pagan An-
    tiquity*, Chaucer Studies 8 (Cambridge:
    Brewer, 1982), 125–31.

19 *The Legend of Good Women*, ed. J. Cowen and
    G. Kane (East Lansing, Mich.: Colleagues
    Press, 1995), 1–42.

20 C. Given-Wilson, ed. and trans., *Chronicles
    of the Revolution, 1397–1400: The Reign
    of Richard II* (New York: St Martin's, 1993),
    68.

21 *Polycratica*, Patrologia Latina, ed. J.-P. Migne
    (Paris: 1844–64), cxcix, 385a–b.

22 Sheila Delany, *Chaucer's* House of Fame: *The
    Poetics of Skeptical Fideism* (Chicago: Univer-
    sity of Chicago Press, 1972).

REFERENCES AND FURTHER READING

Aers, David (1986) *Chaucer* (Atlantic Highlands, NJ: Humanities; Brighton: Harvester). Broadly situates instances of how Chaucer's 'critical imagination' and 'neostoicism' generate critiques of oppressive social structures.

Dinshaw, Carolyn (1989) *Chaucer's Sexual Poetics* (Madison: University of Wisconsin Press). Gender implications of textual authority, in exegetical tradition and in Chaucer's presentations of textual interpretation.

Ferster, Judith (1996) *Fictions of Advice: The Literature and Politics of Counsel in Late Medieval England* (Philadelphia: University of Pennsylvania Press). Survey of 'advice to princes' writings joining self-authorizing to courtly flattery.

Gellrich, Jesse M. (1995) *Discourse and Dominion in the Fourteenth Century: Oral Contexts of Writing in Philosophy, Politics, and Poetry* (Princeton: Princeton University Press). Survey of ideas of political dominion in various genres striving (unsuccessfully) to sustain logocentric, 'oral' modality amidst increasingly textual modes of dominion and representation.

Green, Richard Firth (1980) *Poets and Princepleasers: Literature and the English Court in the Later Middle Ages* (Toronto: University of Toronto Press). Context and development of fourteenth-century courtly literature: the shifting of authority from minstrels to amateurs.

Hanna, Ralph, III and Lawler, Traugott, eds (1997) *Jankyn's Book of Wikked Wyves*, i (Athens, Ga. and London: University of Georgia Press). Introduction to the Latin misogynist texts (with edition; translation to follow in volume 2) and Chaucer's uses in the Wife of Bath's Prologue.

Leicester, H. Marshall, Jr (1990) *The Disenchanted Self: Representing the Subject in the* Canterbury Tales (Berkeley, Los Angeles and London: University of California Press). Scrutiny of some characters encountering and demystifying authoritative 'institutions', revealing Chaucerian perspectives comparable to modern theories (esp. those of Lacan) of consciousness as a 'text'.

Mann, Jill (1973) *Chaucer and Medieval Estates Satire: The Literature of Social Classes and the General Prologue to the* Canterbury Tales (Cambridge: Cambridge University Press). Funda-

mental survey of literary traditions and parallels to the General Prologue.

Minnis, Alastair J. (1984) *Medieval Theory of Authorship: Scholastic Literary Attitudes in the Later Middle Ages* (London: Scolar; Philadelphia: University of Pennsylvania Press; 2nd rev. edn 1988). Survey of medieval Latin discussions of authorship and authority from scholastic materials, concluding with Chaucer.

Minnis, Alastair J. and Scott, A. B., eds, with the assistance of David Wallace (1991) *Medieval Literary Theory and Criticism, c.1100–c.1375: The Commentary Tradition*, rev. edn (Oxford: Clarendon). Introductions to commentary genres, selected translations.

Musson, A. and Ormrod, W. M. (1999) *The Evolution of English Justice: Law, Politics and Society in the Fourteenth Century* (Basingstoke: Macmillan). Compact history emphasizing the growth of centralized law.

Patterson, Lee (1991) *Chaucer and the Subject of History* (London: Routledge; Madison: University of Wisconsin Press). Wide-ranging economic, social and literary contexts situating a variety of kinds of subjectivity in Chaucer as his negotiations with authority shifted from courtly to wider social ideologies.

Saul, Nigel (1997) *Richard II* (New Haven: Yale University Press). Extensive political and social contexts for Richard's reign.

Scanlon, Larry (1994) *Narrative, Authority, and Power: The Medieval Exemplum and the Chaucerian Tradition*, Cambridge Studies in Medieval Literature 20 (Cambridge: Cambridge University Press). Ideological and structural examination of the self-authorizing uses of exempla.

Strohm, Paul (1989) *Social Chaucer* (Cambridge, Mass.: Harvard University Press). Narrative properties of Chaucer's work as dissolving single authoritative voices, in social and intellectual contexts where factionalism of 'bastard feudalism' interacted with wider communitarian ideals.

——(1992) *Hochon's Arrow: The Social Imagination of Fourteenth-century Texts* (Princeton: Princeton University Press). Essays on historical and literary texts in terms of ideologies of authority and political and social contexts.

Wallace, David (1997) *Chaucerian Polity: Absolutist Lineages and Associational Forms in England and Italy* (Stanford: Stanford University Press). Studies of contexts, ideologies and political vision underlying and resulting from Chaucer's engagements with Italian literature and culture, especially his critical response to Petrarch's 'absolutist' ideology of politics and literature.

Wetherbee, Winthrop (1984) *Chaucer and the Poets: An Essay on* Troilus and Criseyde (Ithaca, NY: Cornell University Press). Chaucer's subtle self-authorizing in response to Dante's use of pagan poets.

Wogan-Browne, Jocelyn; Watson, Nicholas; Taylor, Andrew; and Evans, Ruth, eds (1999) *The Idea of the Vernacular: An Anthology of Middle English Literary Theory, 1280–1520* (University Park, Pa.: Pennsylvania State University Press; Exeter: Exeter University Press). English texts displaying vernacular authorship and authority, with discussions; brief mention only of Chaucer but important contemporary and later contexts, including others' self-authorizing use of him.

3
Bodies
Linda Ehrsam Voigts

When we describe someone as in a 'good humour', 'phlegmatic' or 'mercurial', or speak of 'Satur[ns]day', our words echo some of the understandings of the body that informed many of Chaucer's characters and that dominated Western thought from classical antiquity until the nineteenth century. Although much valuable recent historical and literary scholarship, drawing on the tradition called 'anthropology of the body', looks at aspects other than these medieval humoural and astrological assumptions,[1] this chapter concentrates on a basic grounding in fourteenth-century beliefs about the human body and its inseparable temperament. It focuses on the three most important of those assumptions for understanding and appreciating Chaucer's portrayals of bodies and their corresponding personalities: humoural physiology, planetary dominance and healthy habits.

Humours

For much of Western history, the body was seen as one pattern of fours in a tetralogical universe. The bodily tetrad, the four humours, corresponded to and expressed the four elements – earth, air, fire, water – and the four qualities – moistness, aridity, heat, cold. These elements and qualities had been understood as the building blocks of the terrestrial world since the fifth century BC in ancient Greece. In the Knight's Tale, Arcite describes the extent of his inconsolable plight when he says, 'there nys erthe, water, fir, ne eir, / Ne creature that of hem maked is, / That may me helpe or doon confort in this' (1246–8). The expertise of the Doctor of Physic is illustrated by his knowledge of qualities and humours:

> He knew the cause of everich maladye,
> Were it of hoot, or coold, or moyste, or drye,
> And where they engendred, and of what humour.
> (GP 419–21)

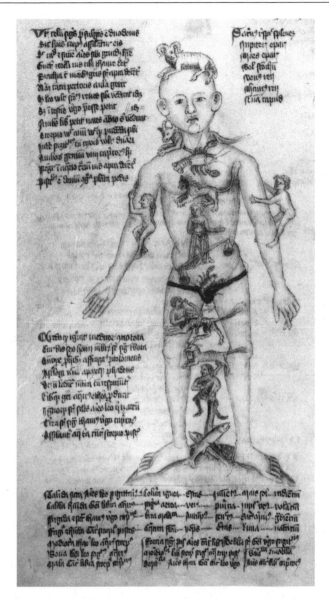

Figure 3.1 Zodiac man. From the Apocalypse of St John. London, Wellcome Library for the History and Understanding of Medicine, Western MS 49, fo. 43ᵛ (*c.* 1420?). [Wellcome Trust Medical Photographic Library.]

The four bodily equivalents of elements and qualities, the humours, were melancholy, choler, blood and phlegm. Choler was also known as bile or yellow bile, and melancholy as black bile. Humoural physiology linked the body to everything else in the universe, and over the centuries the humours and their cosmological connections were extensively written about and illustrated. A widely distributed table beneath the zodiac figure in figure 3.1 sets forth many of these connections. It lists correspondences of qualities, signs of the zodiac, complexions or temperaments, elements, seasons, ages of man and planets, as well as phases of the moon. For example, the terms in the first line link the qualities hot and dry; the signs of the zodiac Aries, Leo and Sagittarius; the choleric body and temperament; the element fire; the season summer; the stage of life youth; and the planets Mars and the Sun.

The implications of such correspondences for the human body were also presented in a discursive form in a considerable body of texts known to many, if not most, literate medieval people. They are set forth, for example, in the widely read pseudo-Aristotelian *Secreta secretorum* (Secret of secrets), a manual on statecraft that deals extensively with the human body; some 500 manuscripts of Latin versions are extant, and at least a dozen English translations from the fourteenth to the sixteenth centuries survive. In the version translated by James Yonge in 1422 the work sets forth the four kinds of *complexio* or *temperamentum*, that is, body types and personalities as they vary according to the dominance of one of the humours. A person has a melancholy complexion when dominated by black bile, cold and dry like the earth; a choleric complexion when dominated by yellow bile, hot and dry like fire; a sanguine complexion when dominated by blood, hot and moist like the air; and a phlegmatic complexion when dominated by phlegm, cold and moist like water (Steele 1898: 219–20).

Complexions were a model which assumed that psychological traits are physical in origin, a view not greatly different from scientific views at the beginning of the twenty-first century. A melancholy person was lean but gluttonous with a hearty appetite. By character or personality such a person was quiet, introspective and fearful. The choleric body was lean but of reasonable digestion and exceedingly lecherous. By temperament this person had a good memory and a sharp wit but was easily angered and vengeful. A sanguine person was physically attractive and healthy, fleshy but agile, of good digestion, a great sleeper, sexually active, easily wounded but quick to heal. In personality, the sanguine person was a sociable and generous extrovert. Texts describe the phlegmatic body as fat but frail, with weak digestion and little interest in sex. The phlegmatic temperament was serious, reticent and introverted.

These complexions were sometimes portrayed by artists as human bodies that illustrated physical characteristics of the body dominated by a specific humour as well as character traits associated with it. Figure 3.2 is a fifteenth-century portrait of a sanguine man. He is healthy-looking, ruddy and cheerful. Above him text is linked to picture with the relevant lines for the sanguine man from the popular Latin poem that begins 'Sanguineus: largus amans hilaris ridens rubeique coloris'.[2] One of the Middle English versions of this poem begins 'Sanguine: of giftis large, in love hathe great delite'. Another Middle English translation of the poem begins with the phlegmatic complexion:

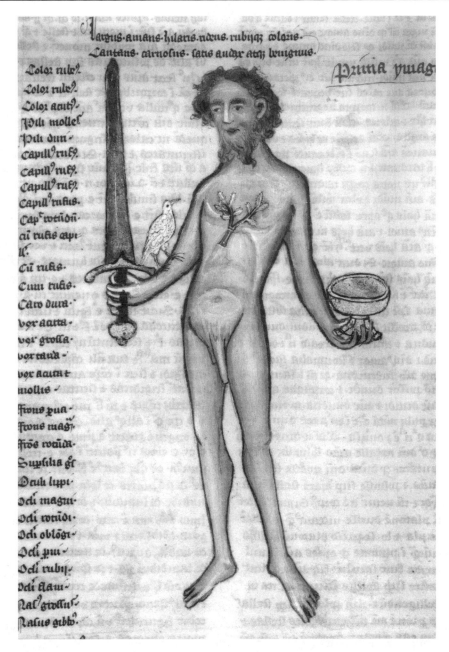

Figure 3.2 The sanguine body and personality. From the *Liber cosmographiae* of John de Foxton. Cambridge, Trinity College Library, MS R.15.21, fo. 12ᵛ (15th cent.). [By permission of the Master and Fellows of Trinity College Cambridge.]

Fleumaticus: Sluggy and slowe, in spetinge muiche,
Cold and moist, my natur is suche;
Dull of wit, and fat, of countenaunce strange,
Fleumatike, this complecion may not change.[3]

It is not surprising, then, that Chaucer conveyed to his medieval audience a great deal about the appearances and temperaments of characters simply by identifying their dominant humour. His listeners or readers knew what to expect of the appearance and character of the Franklin in the General Prologue from the opening lines of his description, 'of his complexioun he was sangwyn' (333). Similarly, the first information Chaucer gives us concerning the Reeve is that he was 'a sclendre colerik man' (GP 587). Echoes of these lost assumptions still survive in those adjectives 'sanguine' and 'choleric'.

Humours, which were believed to originate in the liver, were seen not only to determine body type and character; they also could have pathological manifestations. Texts for a general literate audience, like the encyclopedic treatise *De proprietatibus rerum* (On the properties of things) by the Franciscan Bartholomaeus Anglicus (*c*.1230), discussed pathological variations of the humours. Bartholomaeus' work was translated into English in the late fourteenth century by John Trevisa. This text explains how the liver turns foods of different qualities into the four humours and then discusses the ways in which a healthy humour can become pathological, either by mixture with other humours or by excessive heating in the body, called 'decoction'. Each humour could have pathological manifestations if inappropriately mixed with any of the other three humours or in some other way corrupted, as by its remoteness from bodily heat (Seymour et al. 1975: i, 148–62). This model for disease called for therapy directed at restoring humoural balance through diet, or by the application of medicines with compensating qualities; hence the importance of the Doctor of Physic's understanding of etiology in terms of qualities and humours.

In the Knight's Tale, Chaucer alludes to the humoural cause of disease in the case of Arcite's lovesickness, a real physical malady in medieval understanding. It is explained as resembling mania and originating from black bile in the front cell of the brain: 'lyk manye, / Engendred of humour malencolik / Biforen, in his celle fantastik' (1374–6). Chaucer also exploited humoural explanations for comic value. In Pertelote's analysis of both Chauntecleer's troubled dreams and his cowardice in the Nun's Priest's Tale, she sees the cause as 'compleccioun, / Whan humours been to habundant in a wight' (2924–5). In this episode (discussed below), after commenting on 'the humour of malencolie', the hen boasts, 'Of othere humours koude I telle also' (2933, 2937).

Heavens

Because all matter was seen to derive from four basic elements, the terrestrial corresponded to the celestial, as we have seen in the table beneath figure 3.1, where elements, qualities and complexions are linked to planets and signs of the zodiac. A popular late medieval plague treatise begins, 'As philosophers say, bodies upon earth beneath beith ruled and gendered by bodies above',[4] and in the Man of Law's Tale we are told:

> Paraventure in thilke large book
> Which that men clepe the hevene ywriten was
> With sterres, whan that he his birthe took,
> That he for love sholde han his deeth, allas!
> For in the sterres, clerer than is glas,
> Is writen, God woot, whoso koude it rede,
> The deeth of every man, withouten drede.
>
> (190–6)

Chaucer depicts the planets as the most powerful celestial forces affecting the body, often malignantly. For much of the pre-modern era, a geocentric view of the cosmos prevailed, and the 'planets' were identified, beginning with the most remote from earth, as Saturn; Jupiter or Jove; Mars; the sun; Venus; Mercury; and the moon. These planets influenced the body, particularly in the hours and days they were thought to control (for example, Monday for the moon, Saturday for Saturn), as well as in their dominance over particular parts of the body. Recovery from injury or surgery at a time controlled by a planet, especially on a body part dominated by that planet, could be affected by the celestial body. The Doctor of Physic's expertise was based not only on his understanding of humoural physiology, but also on his astronomical skills, his ability to calculate the planetary position of signs of the zodiac:

> For he was grounded in astronomye.
> He kepte his pacient a ful greet deel
> In houres by his magyk natureel.
> Wel koude he fortunen the ascendent
> Of his ymages for his pacient.
>
> (GP 414–18)

Near the left ear of the zodiac man in figure 3.1 is a typical list of body parts affected by planets; here, for example, the spleen and the head under the influence of Saturn. Many short Middle English texts also list body parts affected by the planets. One such bears the rubric, 'Places that Folk be Tormented in by the Planets', and goes on to identify Saturn as tormenting the breast, Jupiter the belly, Mars the head and so forth.[5] Chaucer identifies Saturn and Mars as 'wicked' planets in his *Treatise on the Astrolabe* (II, 4, line 35).

This belief in planetary dominance was represented in visual as well as literary traditions, sometimes cited with the later iconographic designation *Planetenkinder* (children of the planets). Figure 3.3 reproduces a fine example of a portrayal of Mars, illustrating the planet's influence, by the artist who created the sanguine

Figure 3.3 Personification of the planetary force of Mars. From the *Liber cosmographiae* of John de Foxton. Cambridge, Trinity College Library, MS R.15.21, fo. 44ᵛ (15th. cent.). [By permission of the Master and Fellows of Trinity College Cambridge.]

figure (figure 3.2). Here the power of the planet, especially on those born under its dominance, is illustrated by a warrior in armour bearing the zodiacal images for Aries and Scorpio. His bellicose nature is indicated by his raised sword and the slaughtered children beneath his feet. Echoes of the pervasiveness of belief in planetary control over body and temperament survive in the language in words like 'martial', 'jovial' and 'mercurial'. The role planetary control of the body plays in the character of the Wife of Bath and on events in the Knight's Tale will be discussed below.

The 'planet' that was considered to affect the body most forcefully was the moon, not surprisingly when one observes its control of tides or the correlation of lunar and menstrual cycles. The four phases of the moon were accorded significance for chances of recovery from illness, depending on the phase in which the malady began, and each day in a thirty-day lunar cycle was relevant as well. Lunar astrology – the relation of signs of the zodiac to the moon – was also often invoked as an explanation of unfortunate outcomes of illness or injury. The ubiquitous zodiac man (figure 3.1) was often accompanied in medieval illustrations by texts listing the zones of zodiacal dominance, as in the case of the text beside this figure's right ear. Scores of such texts also circulated in Middle English manuscripts, many of them emphasizing the importance of the moon among the other heavenly bodies. Some begin, 'If thow be syke in ony lyme whan the mone is in the signe of that lyme, do no medicyne.'[6] Others begin 'Aries hathe of mannes body heued and visage, Taurus hathe nek and throt.'[7]

This complex interrelationship of humours, planets and lunar astrology was woven together by assumptions about elements (earth, air, fire, water) and qualities (heat, cold, aridity, moistness) and required extensive knowledge. 'It is to be wist that of twelve signes three bien hoote and drie: Aries is hoote in the second and drie in the first degre, Leo is hoote and drie in the fourth degre.'[8] This text, titled *De XII signis*, goes on to discuss the relationship of planets to elements as well as all of these to seasons and humours, and the need for a physician to calculate all the connections in treating the sick, often with herbal medications that also were categorized by degrees of heat and cold so as to counteract the factors that affect illness and recovery. A typical example of a text dealing with such quantified therapy is the *Circa instans* of Platearius, a *receptarium* where every remedy was classified by its qualities.[9] Some twenty manuscripts survive containing Middle English versions of this text, which begins 'Aloe is hot and dry in the second degree' (Voigts and Kurtz 2000). We shall return to the idea of restoring health through such treatment of the body in the discussion of the Nun's Priest's Tale, below.

Healthy Habits

Humoural and celestial control of the body appear to the modern observer exotic and deterministic in the extreme, leaving the individual little control over body or personality, merely the calculation of forces that control the human body and the determination of when treatment is useless. Such a reaction would be completely valid if the pre-modern understanding of the body consisted only of humours and complexions, along with planetary and astrological domination. These aspects of the body were, however, only the first ('natural things') and part of the third ('things beyond nature') of three ways of viewing the body and health that developed out of the learned traditions of Galenism and of Aristotelian natural philosophy: _res naturales, res non-naturales_, and _res praeter naturam_. The third aspect, pathological things (_res praeter naturam_) was understood as illness in three facets: disease itself as a change in the body, especially in the humours; the etiology of the illness; and the symptoms or the way the illness could be observed in the body.[10]

It is, however, the second among these three components of health and disease in the pre-modern intellectual construct, the 'non-naturals' (_res nonnaturales_), that loomed large in everyday understanding and that resonates in our own era. The eleven non-natural things are facets of one's environment – physical, social and psychological – and of the way one conducts one's life. They include emotions, called 'passions of the mind', and five groups of pairs: air and environment; food and drink; sleep and waking; motion and rest; repletion and evacuation – all factors over which a physician might assist the individual in exercising some control. Lists of non-naturals varied somewhat, but Chaucer's contemporary Trevisa translated the typical list of Bartholomaeus, 'thingis that kindeliche kepith man in beinge, and beith . . . aier, busines and traueile, reste, mete and drinke, wakinge and slepinge, for withoute thuse manuce body is nought ikept' (Seymour et al. 1975: i, 320).

The non-naturals were explained and transmitted in the _Isagoge_, the popular introductory text to Galenic concepts by Hunayn ibn Ishaq that was the beginning medical text studied in the medieval university.[11] This tradition was further complemented in medieval universities by the study of natural philosophy requiring the reading of Aristotle's shorter scientific works, grouped together under the title _Parva naturalia_, a series of treatises addressing such subjects relating to the human body as physical motion, food and nutrition, sleep and waking, sense and sensation, and the mind and mental processes.[12]

Not attending to the non-naturals was perilous to health, as another version of the _Secreta secretorum_ emphasizes in the warning that the individual should avoid eating and drinking too much, excessive labour, overlong time in the sun, too much travelling, excessive sleep before dinner, despondent and pensive states of mind, salty foods and the like (Manzalaoui 1977: 352). Because the individual can in many cases exert some control over food and drink, exercise, sleep and stressful environments, an important function of the physician was to encourage healthy habits by writing out for patients specific plans for a healthy life.[13] Based on assumptions concerning the importance of the non-naturals to the body, such plans included recommendations on food and drink, exercise and rest, sleep and waking; sometimes they also regulated sexual activity and encouraged listening to music and poetry for the benefit of the emotions.[14] Physicians prepared regimens of health for specific patients, such as the one written for Humfrey, Duke of Gloucester, in the fifteenth century by the physician

Gilbert Kymer, Chancellor of Oxford University, or the dietary sent to Henry V by the Emperor Sigismund.[15]

Much more common, of course, were generic regimens, suitable for anyone. Perhaps the most widely disseminated of all medical texts (other than recipe collections) among the 8,000 or so surviving scientific and medical writings in Middle English were the *c.*250 Middle English regimens of health; the most popular of these was organized by the twelve months, and began, 'In January drink white wine fasting, and bloodletting forbear' (Voigts and Kurtz 2000). A much longer popular regimen was the thirteenth-century Latin verse *Regimen sanitatis Salernitanum*, deriving in part from the twelfth-century medical school at Salerno. This 'Rule of health' was translated and widely read into the seventeenth century and was summarized in the formula stating the keys to good health as 'Doctor Diet, Doctor Quiet, and Doctor Merryman'.[16]

A relatively lengthy Middle English regimen, called the *Governayle of Helthe*, circulated in manuscript from at least the early fifteenth century and was the first medical book printed in the English language, by William Caxton in 1489. Like other rules for health, it places little emphasis on the body as controlled by humours, planets or zodiacal signs. Rather, it presents the body as something that can be affected by leading a healthy life, that is, by exercising control over the non-naturals. It is organized in eight chapters, dealing respectively with (1) the nature of bodily health; (2) activities to undertake upon rising in the morning; (3) the nature of physical exercise and general guidelines for it; (4) specific kinds of recommended exercise for outdoors or indoors (rope-climbing and stone-lifting are recommended indoor exercise); (5) general and specific guidelines for food; (6) general and specific guidelines for drink; (7) appropriate behaviour after eating; and (8) the 'noyse of evil governance' or how one can rid oneself of unhealthy habits and acquire healthy ones.[17]

The significance to Chaucer of the widespread knowledge of these regimens of health in late fourteenth-century England is well illustrated by the exemplum with which the Nun's Priest's Tale begins. The description of the poor widow, which must of course be compared favourably to that of the teller's employer, the Prioress, in the General Prologue, and whose diet is more modest than that of the Prioress's dogs (GP 118–62), presents the widow as a model, not just of moral virtue, but also of the healthy body consequent upon a healthy lifestyle. In short, her diet, exercise, abstinence from alcohol and patient acceptance of her lot illustrate the health that results from following such regimens as the *Governayle of Helthe*.

> Of poynaunt sauce hir neded never a deel.
> No deyntee morsel passed thurgh hir throte;
> Hir diete was accordant to hir cote.
> Repleccioun ne made hire nevere sik;
> Attempree diete was al hir phisik,
> And exercise, and hertes sufficaunce.
> The goute lette hire nothyng for to daunce,

> N'apoplexie shente nat hir heed.
> No wyn ne drank she, neither whit ne reed;
> Hir bord was served moost with whit and blak –
> Milk and broun breed, in which she foond no lak,
> Seynd bacoun, and somtyme an ey or tweye.
>
> (2834–45)

This description illustrates well the perceived importance of healthy habits. Three other passages in the *Canterbury Tales* deserve closer analysis to examine Chaucer's use of humoural physiology to explain bodies and their personalities, and his depiction of planetary control over body and character.

Pertelote's Purges (NPT 2923–39, 2942–9, 2955–66)

When Chauntecleer communicates to Pertelote in the Nun's Priest's Tale his fear at his dream of the dog-like beast, Pertelote reproves him for not understanding the humoural causes of bad dreams.

> 'Swevenes engendren of replecciouns,
> And ofte of fume and of complecciouns,
> Whan humours been to habundant in a wight.
> Certes this dreem, which ye han met to-nyght,
> Cometh of the grete superfluytee
> Of youre rede colera, pardee,
> Which causeth folk to dreden in hir dremes
> Of arwes, and of fyr with rede lemes,
> Of rede beestes, that they wol hem byte,
> Of contek, and of whelpes, grete and lyte;
> Right as the humour of malencolie
> Causeth ful many a man in sleep to crie
> For feere of blake beres, or boles blake,
> Or elles blake develes wole hem take.
> Of othere humours koude I telle also
> That werken many a man sleep ful wo;
> But I wol passe as lightly as I kan.'
>
> (2923–39)

> 'Now sire,' quod she, 'whan we flee fro the bemes,
> For Goddes love, as taak som laxatyf.
> Up peril of my soule and of my lyf,
> I conseille yow the beste – I wol nat lye –
> That both of colere and of malencolye
> Ye purge yow; and for ye shal nat tarie,
> Though in this toun is noon apothecarie,

I shal myself to herbes techen yow.'

(2942–9)

'Ye been ful coleryk of compleccioun;
Ware the sonne in his ascencioun
Ne fynde yow nat repleet of humours hoote.
And if it do, I dar wel leye a grote,
That ye shul have a fevere terciane,
Or an agu that may be youre bane.
A day or two ye shul have digestyves
Of wormes, er ye take youre laxatyves
Of lawriol, centaure, and fumetere,
Or elles of ellebor, that groweth there,
Of katapuce, or of gaitres beryis,
Of herbe yve, growying in oure yerd, there mery is.'

(2955–66)

This speech by Pertelote sounds very much like a parody of the discussion of choler and melancholy, their properties and pathological permutations, especially when mixed with other humours, in chapters 10 and 11 of the fourth book of Bartholomaeus' *De proprietatibus rerum*. The treatment in the Nun's Priest's Tale is comic, I believe, because in Bartholomaeus 'rede colera' for the most part confers a healthy state, where other forms of the humours are dangerous. Pertelote's knowledge of the action of humours in the body appears commensurate with her mastery of Latin (Seymour et al. 1975: i, 157–62).

Alisoun's Character (WBP 609–26, 697–706)

In her prologue, the Wife of Bath explains her libido, her physical energy and her strength on the basis of dual planetary influence. She was born when Taurus, the mansion of Venus, was rising in the east and Mars was in that sign. She bears on her body birthmarks conferred by both planets, and both dominate her character, Venus in her lust, and Mars in her strength and fortitude.

For certes, I am al Venerien
In feelynge, and myn herte is Marcien.
Venus me yaf my lust, my likerousnesse,
And Mars yaf me my sturdy hardynesse;
Myn ascendent was Taur, and Mars therinne.
Allas, allas! That evere love was synne!
I folwed ay myn inclinacioun
By vertu of my constellacioun;
That made me I koude noght withdrawe
My chambre of Venus from a good felawe.

Yet have I Martes mark upon my face,
And also in another privee place.
For God so wys be my savacioun,
I ne loved nevere by no discrecioun,
But evere folwede myn apetit,
Al were he short, or long, or blak, or whit;
I took no kep, so that he liked me,
How poore he was, ne eek of what degree.

(609–26)

Conflict between incompatible _Planetenkinder_ is inevitable when martial, lusty Alisoun marries the 'joly clerk, Jankyn'. Clerks are children of Mercury, and the Wife of Bath explains the inevitable conflict between the _Planetenkinde_r of those two opposing planets.

The children of Mercurie and of Venus
Been in hir wirkyng ful contrarius;
Mercurie loveth wysdam and science,
And Venus loveth ryot and dispence.
And, for hire diverse disposicioun,
Each falleth in otheres exaltacioun.
And thus, God woot, Mercurie is desolat
In Pisces, wher Venus is exaltat,
And Venus falleth ther Mercurie is reysed.

(697–706)

Arcite's Fate (KnT 2684–91, 2743–60)

Of all the _Canterbury Tales_, the Knight's Tale arguably shows bodies and events most pervasively in thrall to planetary influence. Theseus is initially described as Mars (975), and Palamon attributes the imprisonment he and Arcite suffer to Saturn: 'Som wikke aspect or disposicioun / Of Saturne, by som constellacioun, / Hath yeven us this' (1087–9). The third part of the poem depicts in great detail the temples of Venus for Palamon, of Mars for Arcite, and of Diana for Emelye, all constructed at Theseus' command on the occasion of the tournament. Each temple is elaborately decorated with the conventional imagery of the planetary gods, more extensively than in Chaucer's source, _Il Teseide_. The portrait of Mars resembles the planetary figure in figure 3.3. In these temple descriptions Chaucer appears to be giving equal claim to each of the three planetary gods by expanding the description of the temple of Diana/Luna/Hecate beyond Bocaccio's to balance the triad (Kolve 1984: 114–26).

On the day of the tournament, Palamon, Arcite and Emelye go to the temples of their respective patrons, each during the hour of the morning dominated by the respective planet. Palamon's vow to Venus is rewarded with a sign that his prayer to have Emelye shall be granted after a delay. Emelye's prayer to the planetary goddess to remain chaste receives the reply that she will wed one of the two suitors. Arcite's sacrifice to Mars is rewarded with the promise of victory in the tournament.

Following the visits to the three temples, the action shifts to the celestial region, where the planetary gods dispute among themselves. Jupiter fails to stifle the conflict between Mars and Venus over the conflicting claims of their protégés; 'pale Saturnus the colde' intercedes to boast of his control over death, suffering and mayhem, and says that he will see that both the claims of Mars and Venus are met (2438–78).

In the fourth part of the poem, the tournament takes place, with Palamon entering under the gate of Venus and Arcite under that of Mars. Arcite is aided by Emetreus, who is also Martian, but Palamon is aided by Lygurge, who is Saturn's child rather than Venus', foreshadowing the role Saturn plays in the outcome. Ultimately Palamon is taken captive, and Theseus proclaims Arcite victor. The narrative then turns back to the planetary gods; Venus laments the outcome, and Saturn tells her, 'Doghter, hoold thy pees! / Mars hath his wille, his knyght hath al his boone, / And, by myn heed, thow shalt been esed soone' (2668–70).

The poem returns to the lists. Arcite rides past Emelye, and at that point Saturn intervenes.

> Out of the ground a furie infernal sterte,
> From Pluto sent at requeste of Saturne,
> For which his hors for fere gan to turne,
> And leep aside, and foundred as he leep;
> And er that Arcite may taken keep,
> He pight hym on the pomel of his heed,
> That in the place he lay as he were deed,
> His brest tobrosten with his sadel-bowe.
>
> (2684–91)

Saturn has caused Arcite's horse to stumble and fall, and the saddle-bow shatters his chest. As a consequence, Arcite dies from a purulent wound in the chest, the part of the body 'that folk be tormented in' by Saturn.[18] In the passage following, Arcite's slow and painful expiry is described. Saturn has caused the fatal wound, but the immediate cause of death is the corruption of the humour blood, which cannot be expelled, either by the natural powers of the body or by the medical actions of phlebotomy, cupping, emetics or laxatives.

> Swelleth the brest of Arcite, and the soore
> Encreesseth at his herte moore and moore.
> The clothered blood, for any lechecraft,
> Corrupteth, and is in his bouk ylaft,
> That neither veyne-blood, ne ventusynge,
> Ne drynke of herbes may ben his helpynge.
> The vertu expulsif, or animal,
> Fro thilke vertu cleped natural
> Ne may the venym voyden ne expelle.

> The pipes of his longes gonne to swelle,
> And every lacerte in his brest adoun
> Is shent with venym and corrupcioun.
> Hym gayneth neither, for to gete his lif,
> Vomyt upward, ne dounward laxatif.
> All is tobrosten thilke regioun;
> Nature hath now no dominacioun.
> And certeinly, ther Nature wol nat wirche,
> Fare wel phisik! Go ber the man to chirche!
> (2743–60)

Both the heavens, specifically the planetary god Saturn, and the humours, specifically corrupted blood, control Arcite's body and his destiny. We cannot know if Chaucer himself held these deterministic views at any point in his life, but in the Knight's Tale he exploits celestial and humoural determinism of the body and its fate to inform the plot and to provide occasion for philosophical meditation. Arcite's destiny is planetary. Even after he invokes Jupiter with his dying words (2786, 2792), he must in death go with his planet Mars: 'Arcite is coold, ther Mars his soule gye!' (2815).

Arcite's death allows the poet the opportunity to introduce Egeus' Boethian lines on mortality (2838–52). Then Theseus, having arranged the funeral and games, and after a suitable passage of time, sends for Palamon and Emelye, and offers in his lengthy Boethian speech a response to determinism. He argues a belief in a First Mover that 'stable is and eterne' (3004), and posits that humans have the possibility for action within a determined universe, 'Thanne is it wysdom, as it thynketh me, / To maken vertu of necessitee' (3041–2). The philosophical underpinnings of this tale are more fully discussed in the previous chapter; what is important in the present discussion is that Chaucer in the Knight's Tale not only effects the plot by exploiting the determinism of planetary control over bodies, he also uses that control as the occasion to raise philosophical questions.

See also AUTHORITY; CONTEMPORARY ENGLISH WRITERS; GEOGRAPHY AND TRAVEL; LIFE HISTORIES; LOVE; OTHER THOUGHT-WORLDS; PAGAN SURVIVALS; PERSONAL IDENTITY; SCIENCE; SOCIAL STRUCTURES.

NOTES

1 Studies representative of scholarship in the 'anthropology of the body' tradition can be found in C. W. Bynum, *Fragmentation and Redemption: Essays on Gender and the Human Body in Medieval Religion* (New York: Zone Books, 1992); *Framing Medieval Bodies*, ed. S. Kay and M. Rubin (Manchester: Manchester University Press, 1994); and *Bodies and Disciplines: Intersections of Literature and History in Fifteenth-century England*, ed. Barbara A. Hanawalt and David Wallace (Minneapolis: University of Minnesota Press, 1996).

2 L. Thorndike and P. Kibre, *Catalogue of Incipits of Mediaeval Scientific Writings in Latin*, rev. edn (Cambridge, Mass.: Mediaeval Academy of America, 1963), 811N, 1374D.

3   C. Brown and R. H. Robbins, *Index of Middle English Verse* (New York: Columbia University Press, 1943); R. H. Robbins and J. L. Cutler, *Supplement to the Index of Middle English Verse* (Lexington: University of Kentucky Press, 1965), 2624, 3157. For 3157, the poem beginning with 'Fleumaticus', see M. S. Luria, *Middle English Lyrics* (New York: Norton, 1974), 111.

4   Oxford, Bodleian Library, MS Ashmole 1443, pp. 376–93.

5   Oxford, Bodleian Library, MS Ashmole 210, fo. 29.

6   London, British Library, MS Egerton 848, fo. 18.

7   London, British Library, MS Additional 34111, fo. 36ᵛ.

8   P. Pahta, *Medieval Embryology in the Vernacular: The Case of De Spermate*, Mémoires de la Société Néophilologique de Helsinki 53 (Helsinki: Société Néophilologique, 1998), appendix 3, 320–4.

9   Thorndike and Kibre, *Catalogue of Incipits*, 211C.

10   L. J. Rather, 'The six things non-natural: a note on the origins and fate of a doctrine and a phrase', *Clio Medica* 3 (1968), 37–47; S. Jarcho, 'Galen's six non-naturals: a bibliographic note and translation', *Bulletin of the History of Medicine* 44 (1970), 372–7; P. Niebyl, 'The non-naturals', *Bulletin of the History of Medicine* 45 (1971), 486–94.

11   Hunayn ibn Ishaq, known in the West as Johannitius, was a Nestorian Christian who translated texts from Greek into Syriac and Arabic for Abbasid rulers. As a court physician he also wrote a number of texts, the most influential being the *Isagoge*, an introduction to Galenic thought that had pride of place in the *Articella*, the introductory medical compendium in medieval universities. See L. I. Conrad, 'The Arab-Islamic medical tradi-

tion', and V. Nutton, 'Medicine in medieval western Europe, 1000–1500', in *The Western Medical Tradition: 800 B.C. to A.D. 1800*, ed. L. I. Conrad, M. Neve, V. Nutton, R. Porter and A. Wear (Cambridge: Cambridge University Press, 1995), 103–10, 141–3.

12   Thorndike and Kibre list each of the texts in the *Parva naturalia* separately; see their index, s.v. 'Aristotle'. A typical requirement that students attend lectures on the *Parva naturalia* is found in M. B. Hackett, *The Original Statutes of Cambridge University* (Cambridge: Cambridge University Press, 1970), 277, 279.

13   On these consilia see Nutton, 'Medicine in medieval western Europe, 1000–1500', 141.

14   See Glending Olson, 'The hygienic justification', in *Literature as Recreation in the Later Middle Ages* (Ithaca, NY: Cornell University Press, 1982), 39–90.

15   K. H. Vickers, *Humphrey Duke of Gloucester* (London: Constable, 1907), 141, 300 1, 281; on the dietary sent by Sigismund to Henry V, see London, British Library, MS Harley 5086, fos 91–98ᵛ.

16   *Collectio Salernitana*, ed. S. de Renzi (repr. Bologna: Forni, 1967), i (1852), 445–516, v (1859), 1–104, 113–69; *Regimen Sanitatis Salerni: The English Version by Sir John Harrington* [1607] (repr. Salerno: Ente Provinciale per il Turismo, 1953). See also M. McVaugh, 'Regimen sanitatis Salernitanum', in *Dictionary of the Middle Ages*, ed. J. Strayer (New York: Scribner's, 1982–9), x, 289.

17   *In This Tretyse* (1489). Linda E. Voigts and P. D. Kurtz, *Scientific and Medical Writings in Old and Middle English: An Electronic Reference* (Ann Arbor: University of Michigan Press, 2000 [CD-ROM]) contains records for twelve manuscript versions of this text.

18   Oxford, Bodleian Library, MS Ashmole 210, fo. 29.

REFERENCES AND FURTHER READING

Cadden, J. (1993) *Meanings of Sex Difference in the Middle Ages: Medicine, Science, and Culture* (Cambridge: Cambridge University Press). A valuable study of the origins and development of learned medical thought concerning sex and gender; deals with the dualistic model of masculine vs feminine utilized for such operations as celestial phenomena.

Campbell, S. D., Hall, B. and Klausner, D., eds (1992) *Health, Disease and Healing in Medieval Culture* (New York: St Martin's). Includes a number of diverse approaches.

Carey, H. M. (1992) *Courting Disaster: Astrology at the English Court and University in the Later Middle Ages* (New York: St Martin's). Important for its treatment of the increasing importance of astrology at the court of Richard II.

Conrad, L. I., Neve, M., Nutton, V., Porter, R. and Wear, A., eds (1995) *The Western Medical Tradition: 800 BC to AD 1800* (Cambridge: Cambridge University Press). A comprehensive and authoritative volume on medieval Western medicine, its origins and its longevity.

Curry, Walter Clyde (1960) *Chaucer and the Medieval Sciences*, 2nd rev. and enlarged edn (New York: Barnes & Noble; London: Allen). First published in 1926, but still a useful study.

Getz, Faye M. (1998) *Medicine in the English Middle Ages* (Princeton: Princeton University Press). Includes a number of fresh approaches to late medieval English medicine.

Hussey, M. (1967) *Chaucer's World: A Pictorial Companion* (Cambridge: Cambridge University Press). Reproduces astrological images, including Saturn, Mars, Venus and Mercury from illustrations based on *Planetenkinder* iconography.

In This Tretyse That is Cleped Governayle of Helthe (1489), facsimile repr., The English Experience 192 (Amsterdam: Theatrum Orbis Terrarum, 1969). An accessible edition of a popular Middle English regimen of health which was also the first printed medical book in English.

Kolve, V. A. (1984) *Chaucer and the Imagery of Narrative: The First Five Canterbury Tales* (Stanford: Stanford University Press). Especially important is chapter 3, 'The Knight's Tale and its settings', which includes numerous illustrations, including *Planetenkinder* images relevant to the Knight's Tale.

Lewis, C. S. (1964) *The Discarded Image: An Introduction to Medieval and Renaissance Literature* (Cambridge: Cambridge University Press). Valuable introductions for the modern reader are provided by sections 5, 'The heavens', and 7, 'Earth and her inhabitants'.

Lindberg, D. C. (1992) *The Beginnings of Western Science: The European Scientific Tradition in Philosophical, Religious, and Institutional Context, 600 BC to AD 1450* (Chicago: Chicago University Press). Standard history of pre-modern science.

Manzalaoui, Mahmoud A. (1974) 'Chaucer and science', in *Geoffrey Chaucer*, ed. Derek S. Brewer, 2nd edn Writers and Their Work (London: Bell), 224–61. Helpful for its taxonomy of medieval sciences, and for setting forth the place in medieval thought of what are now considered pseudo-sciences.

—— ed. (1977) *Secretum Secretorum: Nine English Versions*, Early English Text Society, original series 276. Several texts containing regimens of health and some discussion of humoral physiology.

North, J. D. (1988) *Chaucer's Universe* (Oxford: Clarendon). An immensely learned study by a historian of science; controversial, but ought not to be ignored.

Seymour, M. C., Liegey, G. M. et al., eds (1975–88) *On the Properties of Things: John Trevisa's Translation of Bartholomaeus Anglicus, De Proprietatibus Rerum*, 3 vols (Oxford: Clarendon). A primary source providing the scientific context of Chaucer's world. Particularly important sections in volume 1 are: 129ff, on bodies in relation to elements and qualities, with instructions on healthy habits; 147ff, on the origin of humours and their pathological manifestations; 321ff, on the non-naturals; and 473ff, on the planets and their influence.

Steele, R., ed. (1898) *Three Prose Versions of the Secreta Secretorum*. Early English Text Society, extra series 74, repr. 1975. Particularly useful for the James Yonge translation of 1422 (121–48, esp. 219–20, on bodies and personalities as determined by humours).

Tester, S. J. (1987) *A History of Western Astrology* (Woodbridge, Suffolk: Boydell). A concise treatment of the origins and history of astrology in Europe.

Voigts, Linda E. (1989) 'Scientific and medical books', in *Book Production and Publishing in Britain 1375–1475*, ed. Jeremy Griffiths and Derek Pearsall (Cambridge: Cambridge University Press), 345–402. Discusses scientific and medical writing circulating in England in the late Middle Ages.

——and Kurtz, P. D. (2000) *Scientific and Medical Writings in Old and Middle English: An Electronic Reference* (Ann Arbor: University of Michigan Press). A CD-ROM containing information on more than 8,000 scientific and medical texts in Middle English.

Wood, Chauncey (1970) *Chaucer and the Country of the Stars: Poetic Uses of Astrological Imagery* (Princeton: Princeton University Press). Another detailed discussion of Chaucer's use of astrology.

4

Chivalry

Derek Brewer

Medieval Europe was composed of many relatively small states and communities fiercely competing for scarce resources. The ability to fight was vital. Peace could be obtained only by war. At the centre of any community was the group of fighting men, in whom bravery and loyalty to leader and comrade were the crucial qualities. Since apart from the clergy, who aimed at a different way of life, the elite fighting men controlled most of the resources, it was they who could afford the prestige and power of horse and armour. They were in a small minority compared with the more numerous, less well-armed foot soldiers whom they led. The development of feudalism and larger groupings did not alter the essential structure. The body of 'knights', as they came to be called (in Latin *miles* originally meant 'a soldier'), developed into a 'professional class' in the eleventh and twelfth centuries, with varying wealth, but needing war for 'profit', i.e. loot. Within this class developed the system of ideals and norms we call chivalry, which became very complex. The need for a knight to have noble lineage developed early on, and this requirement remained essential; there were only rare exceptions.

The concept of the class of knights was encouraged by the old notion of the three-fold order of society, 'trifunctionality'. Three orders were envisaged: those who defended society (the knights); those who prayed, responsible for its spiritual health and welfare in the next world (the clergy); and those who tilled the ground to provide food for all (the ploughmen). Although Chaucer never refers directly to trifunctionality it is fundamental to his description of the pilgrims in the General Prologue to the *Canterbury Tales*, where the only persons not satirized are the Knight and Squire (with their follower the Yeoman), representing the knights and by Chaucer's time the chivalric ideal; the Parson and the Clerk, representing spiritual welfare and learning (clergy); and the Plowman, representing the peasants. William Langland expresses the same scheme more explicitly as concerns the knight (*Piers Plowman*, B-Text, passus VI, 22–58). A threefold classification of society is taken for granted in the Middle Ages in Europe and sometimes later.

Honour and Shame

The class of knights came to include even the king himself and of course their related ladies. An ethos of honour, again very ancient in origin and comparable with if not identical with that of many other ancient cultures, developed. For knights, bravery, loyalty, truth, fair play, disinterestedness; for their ladies, chastity, loyalty, bravery – indeed as far as called for – but not aggressiveness. Honour relies both on the claim to social reputation and on the corresponding sense of inner worth. As time passed, ideals of honour, expressed in many literary forms, social conventions and instances of exemplary behaviour, became more complex. Sometimes such ideals transcended social norms and achieved internalized independence, constituting a beauty in daily life, and illustrating physical and moral courage to the highest degree, duty, and self-sacrifice even to a solitary death.

The obverse of honour is shame, which men and women will do everything they can to avoid, and which cannot be effectively distinguished from the sense of guilt. Honour and shame are very much a part of hierarchical societies, and are intensely competitive, though they also unite certain groups – families, social associations – who 'share' each others' honour. What dishonours one member of the group dishonours them all. Hence complex responsibilities, as of fathers or lords, complex loyalties, feuds and the possibilities of painful self-contradictions. Honour is easily lost, and there is never (so to speak) enough to go round. One man's gain, as in winning a fight, is another man's loss. The honour of women is even more complex, with its origin in chastity, but comprising many other virtues, not least loyalty and obedience. Honour is at the centre of the chivalric ethos, the source of most of what we think of as admirable in it, and also of much of its arrogance, contentiousness and folly. A medieval Latin proverb translated by John Lydgate says that there are four things that make a fool of a man: wine, women, old age and honour. Yet the importance of honour and shame in medieval society and literature can hardly be over-rated.

The Role of the Church

Honour and shame were inextricably interwoven with religious life, though technically the clergy were excluded from the honour-group because they were forbidden to fight, and a strong vein in the New Testament rejects honour in favour of humility. But some of the New Testament and much of the Old is concerned with honour and 'a good name', while the chastity of women is a deep concern both of the Bible and of the honour system.

Just as the church could not but be involved in honour and shame, as the Parson's Tale illustrates in many ways, so it could not avoid the paradoxes of war for peace. The church took its origins from the Gospels, whose principal message is peace-making, but the Gospels do not offer a blueprint for society and the church both formed and was formed by the nature of the society in which it functioned. From the fourth century the church as an organization in the world had found it necessary to defend itself, and many of the clergy did take up arms despite the prohibition on so doing. In the sixth century Pope Gregory the Great had written that war was legitimate for converting the heathen. Hence the next thousand years of crusading which appealed simultaneously to the basest greed and the highest spiritual idealism available to fighting men.

As the church emerged as an order within society it rivalled the knighthood in its attempt to control society, in a mixture of co-operation and competition. Thousands of sermons condemned the sins of all classes, including the clergy. From the eleventh century the church attempted to christianize knighthood through doctrine and special ritual, and to harness military energy to the defence of religion. When a suitably qualified man was knighted he was formally 'dubbed', which was a secular ceremony consisting of a senior knight girding on the sword and in earlier days giving a blow on the cheek. In later times it became (and remains) a light touch on the shoulder with a sword. Sometimes men were knighted before a campaign, as was Edward Prince of Wales, aged fourteen, at Harcourt in the campaign that led to the battle of Crécy where he so distinguished himself. He in turn made a number of other knights, as had happened when his grandfather, later Edward II, was knighted in 1306 and then created many others. Chaucer could thus take it for granted that his young hero Troilus, at perhaps sixteen years old, could be a formidable warrior and a dubbed knight, and also that he led a group of young knights of about his own age in his company, where they behave as adolescent boys often do (*TC* I, 183–4). This primarily secular situation was early harnessed by the church and the creation of a knight in the fourteenth century could turn into an elaborate religious ceremony. Chaucer does not refer to this ceremony in detail, but makes clear the reason for it in the Parson's Tale: 'Certes the swerd that men yeven first to a knyght, whan he is newe dubbed, signifieth that he sholde deffenden hooly chirche' (766).

The crusades were by intention part of the attempt to christianize knighthood. The most notable crusading *coup* in the fourteenth century was the capture of Alexandria by Peter of Cyprus in 1365, applauded by everyone in Europe, including Chaucer. Peter of Cyprus, the leading crusader of the century, conducted other campaigns in what is now Asia Minor, in which Chaucer's Knight took part. Another branch of crusading that appealed to knights in northern Europe was the very different kind of fighting practised by the Order of Teutonic Knights in Lithuania and nearby areas, much easier to reach than the eastern Mediterranean. Many English nobles took part in these short campaigns, including the future Henry IV, and of course Chaucer's Knight, three times received as chief guest at the feasts. These crusades were a source of great honour and illustrated the disinterestedness of those who fought, for the loot to be won from the miserable heathen inhabitants was negligible.

Love of Women

The elements so far listed that contribute to the notion of chivalry – the ethos of fighting men, noble lineage, co-operation, competition, trifunctionality, honour, Christianity, a hierarchy – need at least two more major factors before we arrive at a full idea of chivalry: one is the attitude towards women, or at least ladies, and the other the all-embracing factor of literary representation.

Love of women cannot, indeed, be regarded as a new factor at any period of history; but it seems that towards the end of the eleventh century and in the twelfth, first of all in the small courts of Provence, a new sentiment of sexual love developed which distinguished ordinary male sexual desire by including within it the expression of deference to the lady, amounting sometimes to a parody of religious devotion, and which promised everlasting faithfulness in love independent of, though paralleling, the Christian doctrine of faithful married devotion. The lady is regarded as dominant, in contrast to women's normally inferior social position, the aspiring lover her servant. It is the reversal of the usual feudal relationship between lord and vassal, and of the medieval Christian view of the relationship between husband and wife.

In modern terms this *fine amour* is the progenitor of romantic love between the sexes. The expression of such love is found first in some of the lyrics by troubadours in the early twelfth century. Generalization conceals many individual differences of kind and attitude among troubadour poets, but the new note here and there is unmistakable. Many causes have been adduced, but whatever the nature of the mixture, the fact of a real change in attitude to ladies (not, at first, to women of lower class), of immense ultimate importance in cultural history, seems indisputable. It is equally important that we know about this new attitude from the *poetry* of the troubadours. Chroniclers and historians in the twelfth and thirteenth centuries do not remark the new sentiment of romantic love. We have to wait for Froissart for that. Nor do the earliest heroic narratives of knightly bravery and loyalty, of which the eleventh-century *Chanson de Roland* is the best known, have anything above love. Glory in battle, brave adventure, supreme loyalty, are not enough for chivalry, for they lack its ultimately defining characteristic: a high esteem for ladies, often shown as the hero's undying love for one beautiful lady. Combined with other influences the courtesy shown to the lady came to be extended to other women, even to other people in general. Chivalry, conceived in battle, was born of romantic faithful love.

The Literature of Chivalry

Contemporary with the troubadours in the less genial climate of England, and in Latin, appeared another literary work of great importance in helping to create the chivalric ideal. It was a fiction all the more important for pretending not to be: the *History of the Kings of Britain* (*Historia regum Britanniae*), by the archdeacon Geoffrey of Monmouth, written for the court of Henry I about 1135. This history purports to trace the sequence of 'British' (Celtic) kings from Brutus, the supposed grandson of Virgil's Aeneas who founded Rome, to the final advent of the Anglo-Saxons. In the long sequence of kings, many only briefly described, the account of Arthur, the greatest and almost the last, bulks large. There are brief references to Arthur in earlier writings in Latin and Welsh, including Welsh folktale, but it is Geoffrey who presents him as an heroic figure who makes great conquests but is at last betrayed and killed. Arthur provides the core of a potent myth of the great king who dies, which proved susceptible of many different treatments. His court with his great fighting men provided a nucleus for many heroes whose loves and adventures were eagerly followed throughout European countries until the sixteenth century. Chaucer, in brief references, is a rare example of scepticism.

For the Arthurian legend to come to that degree of fullness the theme of love, barely present in the *History of the Kings of Britain*, was needed. Its narrative form was provided by the romances of Chrétien de Troyes around 1180. Chrétien's romances drew on Celtic sources for magic adventure, and on the new courtliness for the emotion of love, reinforced by Ovid and the new interest in the movements of the feelings. His best known hero was Lancelot, not originally one of Arthur's warrior courtiers. Other leading heroes were Gawain and Tristan, whose roots were in Celtic stories. But the elegance, and especially the cultivation of the sentiment of love, are Chrétien's own, even if at times he presents the extremes of love with a touch of humour, and King Arthur himself recedes into the background. Chrétien's stories were retold and extended in French verse and prose, and in the thirteenth century a huge variety of romances of chivalric love and adventure were told throughout Europe. Although, as is characteristic of traditional literature, the same core narratives and characters were used again and again, they inevitably changed according to personal and social circumstance, and many new characters and new episodes were introduced. Not all chivalric romances necessarily had Arthurian themes. The rich stock of European folktale was drawn upon for new plots and characters. There were some sceptics and parodists of stories of chivalric love and adventure – not least, in part, Chaucer himself; but the remarkable thing about the whole body of chivalric romance in many European languages is how steadily, on the whole, it carries the chivalric ethos, to the extent that chivalric romance in the fourteenth and fifteenth centuries strongly influenced chivalric behaviour.

When the chivalric romances reached the English language in the thirteenth and fourteenth centuries they were largely translated from French and were in literary terms much less sophisticated than the French originals. There are around one hundred and fifty romances in English, mostly in verse, most of them in fifteenth-century manuscripts and many written in that century. They kept their vogue, though becoming more popular with the less educated through to the seventeenth century, and the list given at the end of the Tale of Sir Thopas shows that Chaucer expected his gentry-audience to know them. Thopas itself is a wonderful parody of their literary banality, though it is no criticism of chivalry as such.

Romances were not the only literary form that carried the chivalric ethos. Halfway between history and romance comes what has been called 'the chivalric biography', of which two conspicuous examples were written in England. The theme is the subject's pre-eminence in chivalric virtue. The earliest of all such works is the account, composed in Anglo-French about thirty years after his death, of William the Marshal (1147–1219), described by his eulogist–biographer as 'the best knight in the world'. The second example is the similar biographical eulogy of Prince Edward of Wales and Aquitaine (1330–76), known since the sixteenth century as 'the Black Prince', composed by the herald of the heroic Sir John Chandos (Pope and Lodge 1910). Chandos Herald sums up the prince as one who thought of nothing but *loiauté, franchise, valour* and *bounté*, was endowed with *proesce* and gave all his mind to maintaining *justice* and *droiture*. He practised *largesse* and his heart was full of *jolieté* and *noblesce* (65–80). He was 'Si prus, si hardi, si vaillant / Et si curtois et si sachant / Et si bien amot seinte Eglise' (84–6). Later he is praised for the way he overrode all the Cotentin and wholly burned and laid waste La Hogue, Barfleur, Carenton, Saint-Lô, Bayeux and up to Caen (161–80).

Chaucer as courtier must have known Edward and may well have served in his retinue in the prince's court in Aquitaine some time between 1360 and 1366, at which latter date Chaucer was travelling in Spain on an unknown mission. The description of Edward will be worth bearing in mind when considering Chaucer's description of the Knight in the General Prologue. Each of these 'biographies', it should be noted, concentrates on war, on a brave and devout character, and makes no mention of love. They are the reverse, historical, side of the medal of romance. The same is true with the portrait of Chaucer's Knight, except that Chaucer makes no mention of what may be called the 'administrative' side of a knight's duty, the maintenance of justice within the realm and defence against enemies.

Both William and Edward are praised for the fierce ravaging of enemy country-side, which though not mentioned by Chaucer also characterized the *chevauchée* of the Knight's son in Flanders, Artois and Picardy, where the Squire had acquitted himself well 'In hope to stonden in his lady grace' (GP 88). Jean Froissart, too, gives some instances in his chronicles of young knights, for example Sir Walter Manny, carrying out wild enterprises with the same motive.[1] These are examples of chivalry in the recent past or in Chaucer's own lifetime. There is no sign of tension in any of these accounts between chivalry and the practice of certain kinds of ruthless warfare. Nor is there any sign of loss of confidence in chivalry. This is partly because the chivalric class across Europe, despite local and national hatreds which certainly existed, also shared chivalric ideals independent of local non-chivalric classes. The classic case is when Prince Edward insisted on serving King John of France and treating him with great honour when John had been captured at the battle of Poitiers in 1356.

Besides romances and idealizing historical accounts of great knights, the theory, history and criticism of chivalry were written. The earliest and most influential such work was the Spaniard Raimón Llull's *Book of the Order of Chivalry*, written in Spain in 1265. The following century came Geoffroi de Charny's *Le Livre de chevalerie* and *The Tree of Battles* by the monk Honoré Bonet. These fully endorse the ideals of chivalry, including fierce ravaging of the countryside, though they include sharp criticism of current knightly practice: for them, true chivalry was always in the past. This is not the attitude of Chandos Herald, nor of Chaucer himself, whose Knight is fully contemporary, and is clearly drawn in part from the exploits of such contemporaries as Henry of Derby, later King Henry IV, son of John of Gaunt with whom Chaucer was closely associated.

Tournaments

For Chaucer himself, and for later ages, the tournament well represented the essence of chivalry. Tournaments began as dangerous war games with no rules, beyond the agreement to fight, between two large teams of knights. They were violent mêlées spreading over miles of countryside, doing much damage. The aim was practice for war, but also capturing and then ransoming opponents, thus winning honour and profit. The earliest of these fracas can hardly have had spectators; but something like a tournament, with ladies watching, is found in Geoffrey of Monmouth's *History*, and must have been the product of Geoffrey's imagination. Chrétien, too, portrays a very elaborate tournament in his *Lancelot (The Knight of the Cart)*.

These events became popular literary topics. Life and art influenced each other; Arthurian themes were frequent. Tournaments became more and more regulated and eventually reflected the growing individualism of the period when, instead of large numbers fighting each other, contests were limited to jousts between single knights. The actual frequency with which tournaments were held varied greatly. Edward III was very fond of them and staged many, often with elaborate dressing-up. Medieval culture was intensely visual and symbolic, and the tournament in both life and art became a kind of icon of chivalry. They had all the interest of sporting conflict, with colourful armour (rarely the burnished steel common in the sixteenth century, which remains the popular image), bright ladies to admire, inspire and be admired, and, after the sport, feasting and dancing (Barber and Barker 1989).

Rejecting Chivalry

'The tournament of the rich is the torment of the poor,' said the doughty Bishop Brinton of Rochester in Chaucer's day. This does not occur to Chaucer. There was, however, available to him a rejection of chivalry, of the whole chivalrous way of life, expressed not by other-worldly ascetics but by knights who seem to have been affected by the doctrines of Lollardy. These, in brief, rejected many of the institutions of the established culture, including marriage, the doctrine of the eucharist, crusades and pilgrimages, and along with them the whole panoply of the courtly life: a rejection more radical than anything in the Parson's Tale. Among the early adherents to this code were a group of knights known to Chaucer; some were perhaps his friends, and one, Sir John Clanvowe, was his poetic disciple. Clanvowe wrote a courtly Chaucerian poem, *The Boke of Cupide*. He also wrote one of the earliest religious treatises in English by a layman, *The Two Ways*, which rejects the whole chivalric and courtly ethos (Scattergood 1975). In witness to the divided mind of English culture, he died in 1391 on a journey to Constantinople when he must have been on a crusade or a pilgrimage; the previous year he had been on a crusade to Barbary.

Another kind of rejection, less dramatic but of some importance to Chaucer in his time, is suggested, though not expressed, by the great city merchants, who were active in the politics of the city of London. They were much richer than the average knight and mixed easily with the great lords of the court, even to the extent of occasional intermarriage. A few of them were knighted, for example, Sir William Walworth, the fiery Lord Mayor of London, who struck down Wat Tyler, leader of the Peasants' Revolt, in London in June 1381. But this was exceptional. By contrast with the latter part of the fifteenth century, when numerous lord mayors and London aldermen were knighted, very few were in Chaucer's day and earlier. It seems the honour was not desired; indeed, there was always a reluctance to be knighted among the English gentry. Chaucer, like many of his fellow esquires, must have shared this reluctance. Throughout the fourteenth century the government issued decrees called 'distraints of knighthood' to all parts of the country, requiring all those of good birth and a certain level of income to be knighted. It is plain that the unpaid administrative obligations of knightly status, for example to act as sheriff, attend Parliament, or sit on commissions, were not welcomed by most, even in the absence of military duties. There was always a shortage of knights in England.

The chivalric ideal, however, was not widely challenged, and its appeal – at least to city merchants, as well as enthusiastic nobles in England and the continent – increased in the fifteenth century.[2] By the end of the fourteenth century it was an intensely held personal ideal, reflecting a sense of inner worth and associated with firm ideals of honour, virtue and religion. Thus it could be recorded of Richard II in prison, deposed at the end of a disastrous reign, that he could claim to his gaolers that he was a loyal knight and had never forfeited his chivalry: 'Je ne forfis oncques shevalerie.'[3]

Chaucer's Knight and Squire (GP 43–100)

Chaucer took part as a youth or young man in Edward III's *chevauchée* ('In Flaundres in Artoys and Pycardie', 86), culminating in the unsuccessful siege of Reims in 1359–60, and including the usual brutal ravaging of the countryside. The Squire's *chivachie* (85) probably refers to the 'crusade' led by Henry Despencer, Bishop of

Norwich, in 1383, against the Flemish and French, deplored by some at the time for various reasons but evidently not by Chaucer.

Chaucer's earliest poems clearly state his own interest in the personal, civilizing, non-military aspect of knighthood, *fine amour*. In both the *Book of the Duchess* and the *Parliament of Fowls* chivalric valour is taken for granted and not discussed. Nobility of lineage, courtliness, faithful love, and the consequent problems, are the subject. In the *House of Fame* the poet, as Geoffrey Chaucer, repudiates the eager pursuit of fame, which is the extreme example of the social aspect of honour, because he sees fame as arbitrary and often undeserved. But, as in all honour systems, he has a very strong sense of his own inner worth (1870–92).

In Chaucer's writing the word 'chivalry' usually indicates the noble ideal, though it may mean 'company of knights'. The generic quality of being a knight is explicitly virtuous. The tone is set in the famous line describing the Knight in the General Prologue: 'He was a verray, parfit gentil knyght' (72). This is matched by the almost equally comprehensive description of Troilus as 'That trewe man, that noble gentil knyght' (*TC* II, 231). Simply to say a man is a knight is in Chaucer's poetry to imply all the chivalric virtues (KnT 959, 987).

When 'worthy' is applied to those knights whom modern historians think of as little better than scoundrels, the 'noble', 'worthy' Peter, 'glorie' of Spain (MkT 2375) and King Peter of Cyprus (2391), there is no reason to suspect irony. 'Worthy' means 'bold'. Though the Knight in the General Prologue was worthy, he was also 'wise' (68) meaning 'prudent'. 'Wisdom' goes with honour, 'fredom' (generosity) and worthiness, as well as all 'trouthe and gentillesse' in Pandarus' praise of Troilus (*TC* II, 160–1).

The portraits of Knight and Squire in the General Prologue together constitute a chivalric biography in miniature. The Knight's life is devoted to established ideals and his portrait may well be compared with Chandos Herald's praise of Prince Edward.

> A knyght ther was, and that a worthy man,
> That fro the tyme that he first bigan
> To riden out, he loved chivalrie,
> Trouthe and honour, fredom and curteisie.
>
> (43–6)

His life is defined by the record of his fighting on the frontiers of Christendom.

> And though that he were worthy, he was wys,
> And in his port as meeke as is a mayde.
> He nevere yet no vileynye ne sayde
> In al his lyf unto no maner wight.
> He was a verray, parfit gentil knyght.
>
> (68–72)

He is simply dressed, without ostentation but with excellent horses.

> With hym ther was his sone, a yong squier,
> A lovyere and a lusty bacheler,
> With lokkes crulle as they were leyd in presse.
>
> (79–81)

The Squire has seen some action, but he is notable for his flowery clothing, his singing, dancing, poetry, and being in love. To sum up:

> Curteis he was, lowely, and servysable,
> And carf biforn his fader at the table.
>
> (99–100)

These descriptions are brilliantly etched in declarative style, every word counting, every detail essential and adding to the concise, firm description. It is a sinewy muscular style of cogent nouns and verbs, in which the three powerful emotive chivalric adjectives of line 72 have all the more weight. They have entered the language with proverbial force to express a long-held ideal. There are no similes in the description of the Knight and only four brief light similes in the appropriately more decorative picture of the Squire. There is no intrusive authorial comment. The description is left to work for itself in an accepted form. As with all the other portraits in the General Prologue it is a bold creation, in extreme terms, of an ideal. A few modern critics have found this portrait ironical, but this is because they do not appreciate the nature of chivalry. They judge it in terms of modern pacifist, humanitarian, post-Christian ideals, which could not be shared by Chaucer.

Chaucer concentrates on the chivalric ideal to the exclusion of any reference to the ordinary day-to-day concerns of knights. He is not even concerned with justice. Nor does Chaucer's Knight fight in France, as did so many of Chaucer's own knightly acquaintances: he fights in crusades on the edge of Christendom, including Peter of Cyprus's crusade against Alexandria, the most resoundingly successful of the fourteenth century. Chaucer's own references, both here and in lamenting the murder of Peter (MkT 2391–8), whom he praises for his 'chivalrie', show that he took the usual fourteenth-century view. An oddity to modern eyes is the Knight's service with 'the lord of Palatye / Agayn another hethen in Turkye' (GP 65–6). It seems not to have been uncommon for Christian knights – at least in literature – to serve heathen emirs on occasion against other heathens. An example in literature contemporary with Chaucer is the fictional *Travels of Sir John Mandeville*. Such service does not make of him a mercenary like the English *condottiere* Sir John Hawkwood, one of those whose companies of soldiers ravaged France and Italy when not fighting for various lords or city states. (Hawkwood, however, was very highly valued by the city of Florence, which erected a memorial to him in the Duomo, still to be seen.)

The Knight has fought successfully in tournaments near the Muslim country of Morocco, and has been greatly honoured while fighting with the Teutonic Knights, like the future Henry IV and others. In a word, he has fought everywhere except against fellow Christians in France and Italy, which perhaps tells us something about Chaucer's political views '– though the Squire, like all of Chaucer's friends, and he himself, has fought in France.

The Squire represents an earlier stage in the life of a knight, before he has been knighted. Squires often took part in fighting, as Chaucer did, and many, from necessity or choice, remained squires. Though Chaucer was not a fighting man after 1360, the Squire exactly fits the ideal, as does Troilus.

The Knight's Tale

The fullest treatment of chivalry in Chaucer, where there is interest in fighting as well as in love, is the Knight's Tale. Pomp and splendid pageantry are found here, but also the harshness and stoical acceptance of suffering and death that are equally a part of chivalry. Those who wrote about chivalry were accustomed to justifying its glamour and rewards by pointing out the genuine hardships that knights suffered in war. Chaucer is not quite so explicit; but pain and grimness are the dark shadows which set off the brightness of the chivalric ideal. Not only fighting but love is pain, and love causes much of the pain of the virtuous knight.

The poem opens with Theseus, Duke of Athens, returning triumphant from his successful war against the Amazons, whose queen he has married. Before quite reaching home he sets off again on a war of revenge on Thebes, for pity (a chivalric virtue) of the widowed ladies of the town recently conquered by Creon, who has forbidden the burial of their dead husbands. He marches away in a passage where the very rhythm of the verse has a fine martial swagger:

> The rede statue of Mars, with spere and targe
> So shineth in his white baner large
> That alle the feeldes glyteren up and down;
> And by his baner born is his penoun
> Of gold ful riche, in which ther was ybete
> The Mynotaur which that he wan in Crete.
> Thus rit this duc, thus rit this conquerour
> And in his hoost of chivalrie the flour.
>
> (975–82)

Chaucer touches in references to pagan antiquity and mythology by references to Mars and the Mynotaur for the sake of local colour; medieval kings who led their armies into battle had their pennons (flags on a spear) as signs of knighthood, while the banners were vital both practically and symbolically, to mark the leader of the army and to act as a rallying point and inspiration to the fighting men, in the fourteenth century and for many centuries to come. After a successful battle the banners were (as they still are in England) hung in a church (2410). The great fourteenth-century

French theorist of chivalry, Geoffroi de Charny, author of the high-minded *Le Livre de chevalerie*, after a distinguished military career died defending the French royal banner, the *oriflamme*, at Poitiers in 1356.

In the Knight's Tale Theseus goes to Thebes in his just war, kills the usurper Creon ('manly as a knight') and destroys the town in typically ruthless chivalric fashion. He imprisons two Theban heroes for life. They fall in love from afar with the beautiful young Emelye, the sister of Theseus' wife. Arcite is released and Palamon escapes; then they unexpectedly meet on a May morning. Their confrontation is a model of chivalric (and human) competitiveness and honour. Arcite fetches armour and each arms the other (fourteenth-century armour needed assistance with straps and buckles), 'As freendly as he were his owene brother' (1653). Having thus illustrated the chivalric and honourable doctrine of 'fair play', they then fight each other on foot with sharp spears, like mad beasts (1656–8), though fighting on foot with spears rather than swords is highly unusual.

Theseus, out hunting with his wife and Emelye, discovers the combatants; at first enraged, he finally excuses them on the ladies' plea. The choleric but ultimately merciful prince, and the peace-making ladies, strike authentic chivalric notes. Eventually it is decided, in a way more characteristic of literature than of life, that the young heroes' quarrel will be decided by the outcome of a great tournament, to be held in a year's time; each hero will lead a hundred knights, and the winner will marry Emelye. Chaucer describes the lists with relish. They are a noble theatre, a mile in circuit, with grandstands of raked seating sixty feet high. Here is wild exaggeration, following Boccaccio, but characteristic of the hyperbolic imaginative splendours of romance, and grounded in reality of use, if not of scale. When Chaucer was clerk of the [king's] works he was himself responsible for the erection of the lists for the great tournament at Smithfield in 1390. The heroes return in due time, each with a champion and a noble company: every young man who loved chivalry, in England or elsewhere, says Chaucer, wanted to take part and fight for a lady (2113).

The extravagance of description is fully in the spirit of the chivalric court, and of the love of pageantry felt by all classes in the fourteenth century. The weaponry (2119–25) is entirely characteristic of late fourteenth-century armour, depicted with a half-apology on the poet's part for his ignorance of ancient weapons on the grounds that these things never change. The bustle of preparation for the lists and the speculations of the crowd are delightfully realistic, as are Theseus' rule that there should be only one course run by each knight with a sharp spear, though the safety measures to avoid loss of life were in reality less common. The conflict itself is the old-fashioned mêlée, unfamiliar in the fourteenth century but suitable to antiquity. Chaucer describes it vigorously in a bravura passage imitating alliterative verse which revelled in battle scenes. Arcite's fatal accident (2689–759) had its parallel in real-life tournaments, though Chaucer took the medical details of his wound from Bartholomaeus Anglicus' encyclopaedia. Such details mark the darker side of chivalry; but war would have no glory if it did not also have boredom and horror. Arcite's funeral pyre, though described in fanciful and perhaps slightly flippant pagan detail in a prolonged

occupatio, suits the chivalric love of funeral display. The Boethian speeches of
Theseus and Egeus at the end, often seen by modern critics as a collection of empty
clichés, are in fact the emotional, intellectual and chivalric climax of the whole poem,
honouring the dead Arcite, confirming the love of Palamon, reconciling joy and
sadness in a resolute acceptance of the good and bad of life. It is traditional, wise,
'sententious' poetry.

Troilus and Criseyde II, 624–31

The poem *Troilus* is implicitly a paean of praise for the 'true, noble, gentil', young,
hardy, fierce-at-need hero. In all these respects Troilus is the personification of the
chivalric ideal. By the late fourteenth century the young knight – and the ideal knight
is by definition young – is a lover devoted to a single lady, and it is this aspect of the
chivalrous ideal, along with all the moral imperatives of faithfulness, truth, honour
that come with love, that Chaucer chooses to emphasize in the poem. We can take
Troilus' fighting efficiency for granted. In a splendid passage he is shown on his return
from battle, in broken armour, on a wounded horse which he handles gently; a modest
but heroic, handsome considerate young man, cheered, to his embarrassment, by the
welcoming people.

> This Troilus sat on his baye steede
> Al armed, save his hed, ful richely;
> And wownded was his hors, and gan to blede,
> On which he rood a pas ful softely.
> But swich a knyghtly sighte trewely
> As was on hym, was nought, withouten faille,
> To loke on Mars, that god is of bataille.
>
> So lik a man of armes and a knyght . . .
>   (II, 624–31)

The repetition of the word 'knyght' as praise is typical of this style. This poetry
achieves its effects with powerful directness of diction where the words are themselves
loaded with accepted value – *man of armes*, *knyght*, *fressh*, *yong*, *weldy*. Concrete nouns
and active verbs predominate, coloured by the few adjectives. The selection of detail
is careful and highly significant – the damaged armour, the gentle treatment of the
wounded horse, the slight blush of boyish modesty. The touch of amusement at the
young man's embarrassment reinforces the earlier comment 'it was an heven upon
hym for to see', as an expression of the realistic, middle-aged but honestly admiring
observer. Chaucer does not show the battle. Troilus is, after Hector, the principal
defender of Troy (II, 644), but Chaucer is not interested, especially in this poem, in
battle. That has never been his purpose (V, 1765–71); he has, rather, set out to write
about Troilus' honourably chivalrous love.

It may seem paradoxical that Chaucer's greatest poem of love, with its insistence on the chivalric virtue of devotion to a lady, does not assume marriage to be the objective. Most (though not all) stories of chivalric love do tell of a love that aims at marriage. Troilus' own love is not adulterous. Neither he nor Criseyde is married. Chaucer's aim to show the intensity of love could best be shown by its steadfastness when betrayed, unsupported by any social or religious bond. Troilus' *trouthe* to a disloyal lover is the culminating chivalric virtue, standing on, validating and transcending valour, which comes to be taken for granted. *Trouthe* is a word and concept of great complexity in the fourteenth century,[4] including ideas of loyalty, faithfulness, and God himself, as in Chaucer's lyric, 'Truth' (cf. John 14: 6). The knight Arveragus in the Franklin's Tale says, and proves, that 'Trouthe is the hyeste thynge that man may kepe' (1479). Troilus' *trouthe* does not include loyalty to Troy, which he is ready to abandon if Criseyde will elope with him. Chivalry did not yet include patriotism. But Troilus would never be a traitor by fighting against Troy.

Ambiguities

Chaucer emphasizes the personal, not public, virtues of chivalry: bravery, and faithfulness to a person. He is not interested in the aggressive aspects which he takes for granted in a hero. On the other hand, he mocks lack of knightly manliness in his parody of the English romances and Flemish knighthood in the Tale of Sir Thopas. Sir Thopas qualifies in all the virtues of chivalry. His father is lord of 'Poperyng' (a real town in Flanders), he has as fine a pink and white complexion as any hero in romance and a splendid yellow beard – but down to his waist. He is a good archer and wrestler, both of them decidedly old-fashioned accomplishments in Edward III's or Richard II's court. Many a maiden loves him, 'But he was chaast and no lechour' (745). Chastity was a feminine virtue, and though the saving virtue of Sir Gawain in *Sir Gawain and the Green Knight* it was not very noticeable in Chaucer's circle and apparently deemed by Chaucer to be slightly risible in a man, even though Troilus is, it would seem, a virgin until he becomes the lover of Criseyde, and is always faithful to her. Sir Thopas falls in 'love-longing' as a young knight should (like, for example, the lover in the *Book of the Duchess*); but his devotion is absurd for its object is an unknown elf-queen. Then we come to the decking of Sir Thopas in his armour, where the traditional literary topos of the arming of the chivalric knight is used in order to mock both Sir Thopas and romance, especially English romance. The passage represents an interesting contrast with the comparable episode in *Sir Gawain and the Green Knight*, as in the insistence of Sir Thopas on sleeping out, his helmet for a pillow (909–14).[5] While Chaucer does not here mock the chivalric ideal, only its low-class imitation, a certain ambiguity remains. His repudiation of fame, though not of a consciousness of inner worth, independent of society, in the *House of Fame*, will be recalled.

The ending of *Troilus* is famously ambiguous. Perhaps Troilus is accepted into his pagan heaven; but there is a downright rejection of pagan religion and of all worldliness, not just chivalry, in the last few stanzas of the poem. In the pretended 'recantation' of *Troilus and Criseyde* that is the *Legend of Good Women* we revert to a fully chivalric standard of values, except that the heroes are the villains, the false knights who betray their *trouthe* to women, in each case having promised marriage. Knights are here condemned by their own standards. Here is no rebuttal of the accepted standards of chivalry, any more than is found in the preachers. In Chaucer's Parson's Tale the traditional pattern of acceptance and inconsistency appears. The newly dubbed knight is accepted as one who has been given a sword with which to defend holy church. The age-old and well-founded condemnations of the evil behaviour of knights and the luxurious self-indulgence of the rich are repeated (751). The fundamental equality of all mankind is asserted, along with the acceptance of the inequalities of society (764). The traditional solution to this problem is advanced: namely, that sin has brought in the need for inequality. The nature of thraldom is sin. There is no condemnation of the idea of lordship, still less of chivalry. Virtue is seen as 'gentillesse' (463), but the emphasis on sin, here as in most medieval preaching, leaves little room for emphasis on such positive virtues as are constantly recommended by the secular chivalric ideal, in this respect more attractive than the religious.

The vein of rejection comes to the surface again in Chaucer's Retraction at the end of the *Canterbury Tales*. This is not a rejection of chivalry as such; it is a rejection of all that is not in the narrowest sense ecclesiastical. Chaucer was not a Lollard, or he would have rejected the ecclesiastical establishment as well, but one is inescapably reminded here of Clanvowe's explicit rejection of the world's, and chivalry's, values. This radical rejection has nothing to do with any weakness of chivalry – rather, it opposes its worldly strength.

There is nowhere in Chaucer or other contemporary writers any sign of loss of confidence in chivalric values as such – unless we accept the view of some modern critics that the very pleasure in chivalric display and honour is a sign of an inner anxiety unrecognized by Chaucer himself or succeeding centuries up to the twentieth. But if we assume that triumphant martial display is a sign of inner anxiety, how would confidence be shown? By no display at all? By this argument chivalry cannot win. There was plenty of reason for anxiety and insecurity in every class in Chaucer's world: the assertions of chivalry represented a gallant and to some extent successful defence against and triumph over anxiety and insecurity. The code was still strong among the European nations in the First World War. It may well be that the idealism of chivalry itself was so easily perverted to serve men's natural aggressiveness and greed that it contributed to the problems of endemic war. Yet within the idealism was also a recognition of bravery and self-sacrifice in the service of the common good, of courtesy and of truth towards others, and a sense of high inner worth.

See also AUTHORITY; CHRISTIAN IDEOLOGIES; CONTEMPORARY ENGLISH WRITERS; CRISIS AND DISSENT; LANGUAGE; LOVE; SOCIAL STRUCTURES; VISUALIZING; WOMEN.

Notes

1 *The Chronicles of Froissart, translated by John Bourchier, Lord Berners,* ed. G. C. Macaulay (London: Macmillan, 1930), 78.

2 Sylvia L. Thrupp, *The Merchant Class of Medieval London, 1300–1500* (Chicago: University of Chicago Press, 1948; repr. Ann Arbor: University of Michigan Press, 1989); L. D. Benson, *Malory's* Morte Darthur (Cambridge, Mass.: Harvard University Press, 1976); Richard Barber, 'Malory's *Le Morte Darthur* and court culture under Edward IV', *Arthurian Literature* 12 (1993), 133–56.

3 'Chronique de la traison et mort de Richard II', ed. Benjamin White (London: English Historical Society, 1844), 67, trans. 218.

4 R. F. Green, 'Ricardian "trouthe": a legal perspective', in *Essays on Ricardian Literature in Honour of J. A. Burrow,* ed. Alastair J. Minnis, Charlotte C. Morse and Thorlac Turville-Petre (Oxford: Clarendon, 1997), 179–202.

5 Derek S. Brewer, 'The arming of the warrior in European literature and Chaucer', in *Tradition and Innovation in Chaucer* (London: Macmillan, 1982), 142–60.

References and Further Reading

Barber, R. (1995) *The Knight and Chivalry,* rev. edn (Woodbridge, Suffolk: Boydell). A standard history of European chivalry with emphasis on literary influences and tournaments; illustrated.

——, ed. (1979) *The Arthurian Legends: An Illustrated Anthology* (Woodbridge, Suffolk: Boydell). A wide selection, in translation, from the earliest Arthurian texts to those written in the twentieth century.

—— and Barker, Juliet (1989) *Tournaments* (Woodbridge, Suffolk: Boydell). An historical account of the history of European tournaments; illustrated.

Benson, Larry D. (1993) *A Glossarial Concordance to the Riverside Chaucer,* 2 vols (New York and London: Garland). Indispensable aid to the study of Chaucer's words and their poetic uses.

Boase, Roger (1977) *The Origin and Meaning of Courtly Love: A Critical Study of European Scholarship* (Manchester: Manchester University Press). Survey and critical analysis of the various theories.

Brewer, Derek S. (1963) *Chaucer in his Time* (London: Longman; repr. 1973). Courtly and chivalric life and references to Lollardy; illustrated.

——(1982) 'Class distinction in Chaucer', in *Tradition and Innovation in Chaucer* (London: Macmillan), 54–72. Class structures and 'trifunctionality'.

——(1984) 'The relationship of Chaucer to the English and European traditions', in *Chaucer: The Poet as Storyteller* (London: Macmillan), 8–36. Chaucer and especially the romances in English.

——(1992) *Chaucer and his World,* 2nd edn (Cambridge: Brewer). A wide-ranging survey.

——(1994) 'Chaucer's Knight as hero, and Machaut's *Prise d'Alexandrie*', in *Heroes and Heroines in Medieval English Literature: Essays Presented to André Crépin,* ed. L. Carruthers (Cambridge: Brewer), 81–96. Particular reference to the capture of Alexandria and the chivalry of Chaucer's Knight.

——(1998) *A New Introduction to Chaucer* (London: Longman). The latest general survey and references to honour and 'masculinity'. Further references to *fine amour.*

Brown, Peter and Butcher, Andrew F. (1991) *The Age of Saturn: Literature and History in the Canterbury Tales* (Oxford: Blackwell). An original account relating Chaucer to his intellectual and social background.

Chickering, Howell and Seiler, Thomas H., eds (1988) *The Study of Chivalry* (Kalamazoo, Mich.: Medieval Institute). Surveys by many scholars on all aspects of chivalry, designed to support the teaching of the subject in United States universities.

du Boulay, F. R. H. (1974) 'The historical Chaucer', in *Geoffrey Chaucer,* ed. Derek Brewer, rev. edn, Writers and Their Background (repr. Cambridge: Brewer, 1990), 33–57. A medieval historian's account of Chaucer's life.

Duby, G. (1980) *The Three Orders*, trans. A. Goldhammer (Chicago: Chicago University Press). Especially useful on 'trifunctionality'.

Gillingham, J. (1988) 'War and chivalry in the *History of William the Marshal*', in *Thirteenth Century England II*, ed. P. R. Coss and S. D. Lloyd (Woodbridge, Suffolk: Boydell), 1–13. Emphasizes the nature and importance of war in the chivalric ethos.

Keen, M. (1984) *Chivalry* (New Haven and London: Yale University Press). The standard history of chivalry, both sympathetic and critical.

Loomis, L. H. (1941) 'The tale of Sir Thopas', in *Sources and Analogues of Chaucer's Canterbury Tales*, ed. W. F. Bryan and G. Dempster (London: Routledge & Kegan Paul, repr. 1958), 486–559. Quotes sources and analogues and suggests Chaucer knew the fourteenth-century compilation, the Auchinleck manuscript.

McFarlane, K. B. (1972) *Lancastrian Kings and Lollard Knights* (Oxford: Clarendon). Biographies and comments on Chaucer's acquaintances, the Lollard knights, including Clanvowe.

Patterson, Lee (1991) *Chaucer and the Subject of History* (London: Routledge; Madison: University of Wisconsin Press). Another view of 'the crisis of chivalric identity' and learned essays on other aspects of Chaucer's poetry by a leading New Historical critic.

Pope, M. K. and Lodge, E. C., eds and trans (1910) *The Life of the Black Prince by the Herald of Sir John Chandos* (Oxford: Clarendon). Gives a contemporary view by an admirer.

Scattergood, V. J., ed. (1975) *The Works of Sir John Clanvowe* (Cambridge and Totowa, NJ: Brewer). An edition of his poem the *Boke of Cupide*, and his tract *The Two Ways*, with biographical introduction.

Vale, J. (1982) *Edward III and Chivalry: Chivalric Society and its Context 1270–1350* (Woodbridge, Suffolk: Boydell). Particular focus on Edward III's interest in chivalry.

Wright, N. (1998) *Knights and Peasants: The Hundred Years War in the French Countryside* (Woodbridge, Suffolk: Boydell). Historical account of the depredations of chivalry and the hostility between knights and peasants.

5

Christian Ideologies

Nicholas Watson

Now preye I to hem alle that herkne this litel tretys or rede, that if ther be any rhyng in it that liketh hem, that therof they thanken oure Lord Jhesu Crist . . . For oure book seith, 'Al that is writen is writen for oure doctrine', and that is myn entente. Wherfore I biseke yow mekely, for the mercy of God, that ye preye for me that Crist have mercy on me and foryeve me my giltes; and namely of my translacions and enditynges of worldly vanitees, the whiche I revoke in my retracciouns: as is the book of Troilus; the book also of Fame; the book of the XXV. Ladies . . . the tales of Cauntcrbury, thilke that sownen into synne . . . and many another book, if they were in my remembrance . . . that Crist for his grete mercy foryeve me the synne. But of the translacion of Boece de Consolacione, and other bookes of legendes of seintes, and omelies, and moralitee, and devocioun, that thanke I oure Lord Jhesu Crist and his blisful Mooder . . . (Ret 1081–8)

For generations of scholars and students, the last words of the *Canterbury Tales* and its author's career have been among the most annoying Chaucer wrote. In the fell swoop of a single biblical quotation – 'Al that is writen is writen for oure doctrine' (Romans 15: 4) – a seemingly monolithic didacticism descends on the variegated tapestry of the *Tales*. Whether we understand the phrase 'litel tretys' as referring to all the *Tales* or only to the Parson's Tale (which the Retraction follows), these words seem to demand that we rethink all Chaucer's oeuvre as serving a single religious project: that we winnow as chaff of 'worldly vanitees' the multiplicity for which he is famous, and soberly ingest the wheat of 'moralitee and devocioun' that remains. One recent critical movement (stemming from D. W. Robertson Jr's 1962 study, *A Preface to Chaucer*) has been eager to accept many of the terms of this demand, 'medievalizing' Chaucer as an unremitting poet of Christian ethics. But since so much writing on Chaucer in the past forty years has reacted against this movement, its unintended effect has been to make most scholars even more determined than they were earlier in the twentieth century to present him as a purely secular poet, sidelining both the Retraction and the more general topic of his religiosity. Only in the last few years has interest in the

Lollards and religious reform led to renewed attempts to align Chaucer with religious thought (Aers and Staley 1996).[1]

The key in dealing with Chaucer's religiosity lies in avoiding an all-or-nothing approach to the Retraction's assertion of a single *entente*, for neither approach seems to work on its own: either reading the passage as an extension of the Parson's rejection of verse and of 'fables and swich wrecchednesse' (ParsP 34–8), and thus as a belated attempt by a repentant poet to unwrite almost all the *Canterbury Tales*; or treating this revocation of most of his oeuvre as an *invocation* whose real *entente* – under the merciful eye of 'oure Lord Jhesu Crist and his blisful Mooder' – is to establish a canon of his writing (Scanlon 1994: 23–4). This chapter suggests that Chaucer's response to Christianity was no more consistent than late medieval Christianity itself. More specifically, it argues that many of Chaucer's encounters with religion reflect a division of expectation in fourteenth-century thought about the education, purity and zeal, not only of priests and other religious professionals, several of whom the poet imagines as pilgrims on his Canterbury journey, but also of the members of the laity who make up most of the party. The status of the laity in relation to the other orders was not the sole religious issue of the time; yet, partly because Chaucer's poetic persona is self-consciously lay, not clerical, partly because issues surrounding the laity touch on many others, these issues make a good starting-point for an analysis of Christian ideologies in his writing.

Christian Pedagogy and Laicization

One way of thinking about the laity – as objects of pastoral instruction by the clergy – can be traced back to the Fourth Lateran Council of 1215, where it was decided that all Christians had to make confession every year, and that a basic minimum of truths about the faith must be taught to all. Over the next century many lists of these truths were drawn up, including items like the Lord's Prayer, the *Ave Maria*, the Creed, the Ten Commandments, the sacraments, and the deadly sins and their remedies. Many more elaborate discussions of all these topics, in Latin and the vernacular, often organized around confession, were also written (Boyle 1985). The Parson's Tale is an example of this catechetical tradition, perhaps written as a penitential exercise (Patterson 1976), as in part is William Langland's *Piers Plowman*, which both embodies and explores the workings of this tradition.

Medieval pastoral theology is often imagined as a top–down affair, with the church dispensing pre-packaged religious information to a mass of illiterate lay people. The church represented by the Lateran Council was dominated by monks and hermits, who tended to think of separation from the world of the laity as a sign of holiness. Yet the development of pastoral instruction after 1215 coincided with a shift of energy away from these monastic orders towards informal religious groups such as beguines and anchoresses, as well as the laity and their ministers: secular priests, canons and friars (Vauchez 1993). Such shifts are always tricky to pinpoint. This one had roots in the century before the Council, which saw the establishment of the friars – for whom holiness involved conversion of the world, not separation from it – and in which apocalyptic thinkers like Joachim of Fiore prophesied a world about to be convulsed by godliness, when heaven would come to earth. Where earlier discussions of Christian living emphasize the superiority of the contemplative life of monks or nuns over the active one of the laity and priesthood, later medieval accounts often view preachers and the laity as of equal interest and status.[2]

This rethinking is clear in *Pearl*, where imagery that had long been used to praise vowed virginity is reworked as an argument for the spiritual worth of the lay aristocracy (Watson 1997a). The Wife of Bath also notes the 'greet perfeccion' of career virgins like nuns, while defending her right to 'persevere' in 'swich estaat as God hath cleped' her, as a member of the married laity (WBP 105–65). And the *Tales* are full of figures who imply the irrelevance of the religious orders and the ecclesiastical bureaucracy to the sober, practical Christianity represented by the Parson's Tale: the Monk, obsessed with hunting; the Canon, obsessed with alchemy; the friar in the Summoner's Tale, obsessed with money; and minor church officials like the Summoner and the Pardoner, who in many ways represent the church to the populace at large. Lay figures are often no better, but nor are they any worse than these religious ones. Most important, they and Chaucer, their lay creator, assume an equality with and freedom to criticize members of the religious orders and the church in general that would have been almost unthinkable to the participants in the Lateran Council.

Asceticism and Affectivity

As the *Tales'* portraits of swearing, hard-drinking, lecherous figures like the Reeve, the Cook and Harry Bailly suggest, late medieval discussions of the laity have a robust sense of the group's ignorance. Yet in Christian thought ignorance can also be idealized as simple faith, not troubled by theological knowledge that too easily substitutes for emotional understanding. The roots of this anti-intellectual tradition were a thousand years old by Chaucer's time, reaching back to the men and women of the fourth century known as the desert fathers, who followed the example of hermits like the remarkable St Anthony by choosing a life of harshly ascetic spiritual battle. Stories about these heroic Christians had a powerful impact on the twelfth-century reform movements which culminated in the Lateran Council, and were still a force in Chaucer's age. Langland is more aware of the desert fathers than Chaucer (*Piers Plowman*, B-Text, passus XV), but the Man of Law's Tale is redolent of the desert ideal, as must also have been the lost 'Orygenes upon the Maudeleyne' (listed in the *Legend of Good Women*, G 418). A patina of antiquity lies over these late fourteenth-century evocations of an ancient world of holy living, which seem to belong to an age of miracles whose lessons cannot be directly translated into the present. But even at that late date, aspects of the ideal were still powerful.

One result of the twelfth-century reform movement's encounter with heroic asceticism was that the ascetic ideal began to change under the influence of an affective
spirituality that was more inclusive. Asceticism was about disciplining the body –
not, as is often thought, rejecting it; but it was organized around a dichotomy between
flesh and spirit, in which the flesh (the sinning self) was seen as the main road-block
the soul faces on its journey towards God. Affective spirituality did not challenge this
dichotomy, but it did change it. First, it re-imagined the role of spiritual love, which
it saw as a desire as violent as sexual desire, with the power to burn away a lover's sin
in a way self-discipline alone could never achieve. This idea is not directly mentioned
by Chaucer, whose accounts of spiritual love invoke a Boethian vision of cosmic
harmony – especially in the third book of *Troilus and Criseyde*. Yet Troilus is purified,
and at the end of the poem perhaps even redeemed (V, 1807–27), by his experience
of erotic love, which the poem often evokes in religious terms.

Second, affective spirituality re-imagined Christ as an object of love. Late medieval
depictions of Christ focus not on the majesty of his divine nature but on the pathos
of his human one, revealed at his birth, when the 'hye God' sent 'His grace into a
litel oxes stalle', and at his death, when 'oure Lord Jhesu Crist aboghte upon his precious body ful deere' the 'disordinaunce and . . . rebellioun' of sin (ClT 206–7, ParsT
267). Christ's Passion was sometimes associated with women in particular. Julian of
Norwich – whose *Revelation of Love* was one of the most ambitious theological projects of Chaucer's day – arrives at her vision of cosmic redemption by focusing all her
attention on the meaning of Christ's bleeding head, while Chaucer gives Constance
evocatively imagistic prayers to the cross and the Virgin: 'Reed of the Lambes blood
ful of pitee'; 'Thow sawe thy child yslayn bifore thyne yen' (MLT 452, 848). Yet in
other texts it is Christian people as a whole – those 'symple soules', according to
Nicholas Love's *Mirror of the Blessed Life of Jesus Christ* (*c*.1409), 'that can not thenke
bot bodies or bodily thinges' (Wogan-Browne et al. 1999: 253) – who participate in
Christ's Passion through a compassion that affirms a human nature they share with
the incarnate God himself.

Christ's Body and Simple Faith

Affective spirituality in no sense replaced asceticism. But its focus on Christ's humanity, and on sensual love for his body as a way to heaven, were intimately bound up
with the rising spiritual status of the laity. Late medieval thought was rich in models
in which the ascent to truth was imagined as an ascent to contemplation, where the
body was progressively left behind. The last chapters of Walter Hilton's *Scale of Perfection* (*c*.1395) use terminology Augustine took from neoplatonism to describe how
the spiritual eye can unlock the mysteries of the Bible, the soul and heaven;[3] Chaucer's
Boece makes its own neoplatonic journey from collapse in the face of worldly turmoil
to acceptance that the 'Fadir, soowere and creatour of hevene and of erthes . . . gov-
ernest this world by perdurable resoun' (III, metrum 9, 1–3). Yet these ascent models

were increasingly in competition with other, incarnational models, in which the fact that Christ united his divinity with the flesh he created makes the sinful world by far the most important locus of truth. *Piers Plowman* and *A Revelation of Love* are two of many works that see body and world as transfigured by the incarnation: an event towards which the end of *Troilus and Criseyde* yearns in its address to 'yonge, fresshe folkes' (V, 1835–48) and which Langland and Julian imagine as a full manifestation of truth, both for humankind and for God himself (Watson 1997b). In a different sense, the *Canterbury Tales* also finds truth in this world, moving from the abstract philosophizing of the ending of the Knight's Tale – where Theseus signally fails to justify the order of the cosmos in the limited Boethian terms available to him – towards an incarnational aesthetic that governs even the Tale of Melibee and the Parson's Tale.

A public sign of the importance of the incarnation to the laity was the establishment in the late thirteenth century of the feast of Corpus Christi, which celebrates both the sacrament of the mass and the whole Christian community who represent Christ's body on earth (Rubin 1991). Corpus Christi became a symbol of municipal lay identity through the miracle plays performed on Corpus Christi day in English cities, in which actors and audience identified their lives with sacred history by playing it out, from Creation to Last Judgement, through the streets. The *Canterbury Tales'* evocations of Christ's body as a symbol of Christian community are more ambiguous, for they partly consist of a set of oaths spoken by the pilgrims that the Parson thinks sinful (MLE 1171): 'For Cristes passion'; 'For Goddes bones'; 'By Goddes sweete pyne'; 'by *corpus dominus*'; 'By corpus bones'; 'for cokkes bones' (CkP 4327; MLE 1166; Th 936; ShT 435; PardI 314; MkP 1906; ManP 9). It may be that these oaths tease out a punning link between the Host and the host (communion wafer) consecrated at the mass; Langland uses a related conceit in making his figure of lay sinfulness, Haukyn or *Activa Vita*, a minstrel and provider of communion wafers (*Piers Plowman*, B-Text, passus XIII). Yet this link need not be understood as satirical, for incarnational theology assumed that the world Christ redeemed was a world of sinners. Indeed, a radical way Langland and Julian understood the incarnation was as a sign that, despite threats of eternal torment, God was determined to save not only the whole Christian community but all humanity (Watson 1997c). Although there are many ways we can think about the Host – after all, taverns like the Tabard were referred to as 'the devil's churches' – Chaucer can be read here as offering his own optimistic vision of the fate of his community of pilgrims and their tales.

Affectivity also focused attention on the spiritual importance of the laity by elevating feeling over knowledge. Pastoral theology thought of lay ignorance as a problem. But affective spirituality – its roots sunk deep in ancient models of holy living as the imitation of Christ – could think of it as an advantage. The distinction between *scientia* and *sapientia* (head knowledge and heart knowledge) invoked in attacks on scholasticism was easily translated into an opposition between the hypocritical learning of clerics and the humble love for God felt by the unlearned. There is common ground between attacks on 'coriousté of moche clergie and letterly conning' in learned texts like the *Cloud of Unknowing* and the opposition in the Prioress's Tale between the devotion of the 'litel clergeon' from his 'litel scole' with his 'litel book' and the Jews' fidelity to their 'lawes' (495–564).[4] Despite their commitment to education, writers sympathetic with Lollard thought shared in this idealizing of lay ignorance, contrasting those who read with love, not wit, with 'veyn men' who 'jangelyn oonli of this blessid lawe to schewe here cunnynge abowe othere men' (*Holi Prophete David* [c.1400]; Wogan-Browne et al. 1999: 150). When the Shipman prevents the Parson from preaching in the Epilogue to the Man of Law's Tale, because he fears the Parson 'wolde sowen som difficulte, / Or springen cokkel in our clene corn', he may think he is defending religious orthodoxy, but his sentiment is as consistent with Lollard ideology as it is with standard teaching (1178–85).

Fourteenth-century Puritanism

To this point I have sketched an account of the laity in late medieval Christianity that treats this group as a single entity (the body of Christ on earth) and sees its supposed weaknesses of ignorance and carnality optimistically, as the very things that placed it at the centre of God's redemptive mission. Drawing especially on *Piers Plowman*, I have hinted at a reading of the *Canterbury Tales* in which the journey to Canterbury undertaken by the pilgrims is an authentic preparation for 'thilke parfit glorious pilgrymage / That highte Jerusalem celestial' proposed by the Parson (ParsP 50–1), which promises to end with the 'hooly blisful martir' Thomas healing them of sin (GP 17).

Yet Chaucer was also aware of a more severe strand of thinking about the Christian faith as applied to the laity, which made greater demands on those who accepted it and took a gloomy view of what would happen to those who did not. This puritanical version of lay religion accepted the Lateran Council's belief that all Christians must know about the faith, but interpreted it in idealistic terms taken from the twelfth-century reformers (partly via the Franciscans), showing frank hostility towards the lukewarm attitudes of everyone else. Instead of recognizing degrees of Christian living – active and contemplative, minimalist and perfectionist – puritanical religiosity claimed that only the few who pursue perfection can hope for salvation and be identified as the body of Christ on earth.[5]

There were no absolute boundaries between this strand of thought and the incarnational one I associated with the feast of Corpus Christi. Despite their rhetoric of spiritual elitism, there is a universalizing tendency in many puritan writings, which often address the whole Christian community as though everyone were capable of pursuing perfection. Indeed, incarnational and puritanical ways of thinking can be juxtaposed in the same text; Langland dramatizes the relationship between the two in the encounter between Haukyn, the minimalist lay Christian, and Patience (*Piers Plowman* B-Text, passus XIII–XIV). But lay puritanism had a firm enough profile to be lived and written about as a distinct set of attitudes – to be found among members of different social classes, from yeoman farmers all the way to the upper gentry – involving a dislike of showy wealth, a commitment to moderation, a contempt for hypocrisy, a fear of worldly entanglement (along with suspicion of monks, friars and nuns) and a deep sense of personal, as well as national, sinfulness. During Chaucer's lifetime, under the influence of John Wyclif, these traditional attitudes became aligned with a body of belief that was declared heretical: a process that led to the formation, under pressure of persecution, of what by the early fifteenth century was a separatist religious sect, the Lollards (Hudson 1988).

Chaucer may or may not have been interested in all the ideas associated with Lollardy. Fourteenth-century puritanism took different forms, and it was possible to have radical views on translation, or the church's duty to embrace poverty, or the virtuous layman's right to preach, or the purity required of a priest, or on pilgrimages and indulgences, while holding standard beliefs about confession, the mass, religious orders or obedience to bishops. Yet the vernacular religious culture that came into being around the Lollard controversy would have impressed anyone as well-placed as Chaucer – whose poetic universe may have been partly shaped by *Piers Plowman*; who could have met Wyclif through their common patron, John of Gaunt; who knew Wyclif's Oxford opponent, Ralph Strode; and whose friends included a group of Richard II's chamber knights who have been linked to Lollardy.

It is no surprise, then, that traces of lay puritanism and Wycliffite reformism are scattered throughout the *Canterbury Tales*. Not only does puritanism have representatives on the pilgrimage, the Parson and the Plowman – although neither of these could be described as a radical; as satire, it permeates the landscape crossed by four other characters – the Wife of Bath, the Pardoner, the Summoner and the Friar – and is enough of a presence elsewhere that it can be used as a lens through which to view the whole poem. There is nothing inherently false about sixteenth-century Protestant attempts to claim Chaucer as at least a moderate Wycliffite precursor. A puritan reading of the *Tales* might take as a motto a line from Chaucer's lyric 'Truth': 'Forth, pilgrim, forth! Forth, beste, out of thy stal!' (18). In such a reading, the Parson's spiritual 'parfit glorious pilgrymage' no longer stands in an easy relation to the Canterbury pilgrimage, but is at best suspicious of literal pilgrimage. The community of sinners on their way to buy indulgences at St Thomas's shrine is no longer performing a ritual with any intrinsic value. Indeed, the pilgrims begin to look uncomfortably like a group of false hypocrites, members of what a Lollard text like The *Lantern of Light* (*c*.1410) calls the church of Antichrist,[6] their vile language a particular sign of their reprobation; as *Piers Plowman* says of another group of blasphemers, they 'gnawen God with the gorge whanne hir guttes fullen' (*Piers Plowman*, B-Text, passus X, 57). Despite the Parson's disdain for 'fables and swich wrecchednesse' (ParsP 34), a puritanical reading of the *Tales* still has room for tale-telling as moral satire and is interested in the complexities of the relationship between tale and teller. Indeed, the ethics of satire – which preoccupies Langland and other reformist writers – often surfaces as a theme in the poem: in the quarrel between the Friar and the Summoner;

metaphorically, in Melibee's recurrently imprudent desire for vengeance on his enemies; and in the defence of satire in the Canon's Yeoman's Tale (992–1011). It is not clear how well the *Canterbury Tales* itself survives the corrosive effects of a puritan reading; Chaucer's interest in ironic or hypocritical juxtapositions between tales and tellers has the poem flirting all the time with the danger of being swept up into celebrating the sins it satirizes, as happens most chillingly with the Pardoner and his tale. But there is plenty of material to give such a reading power.

If the *Canterbury Tales* can be understood both as an optimistic account of a Christian community journeying towards salvation and as a pessimistic attack on a society whose members mostly merit damnation, how does this opposition affect our reading of individual tales? To address this question, I will look at two passages, from the Miller's Tale and the Clerk's Tale, both of which I read as commentaries on modern religion. Middle English religious writing is full of portents of the coming Doomsday, presenting the world as old and weak (as in Chaucer's lyric 'The Former Age'), where less can be expected of people than it was in the past. Some texts are harsh in their attitude to this deterioration, like *Dives and Pauper* (*c.*1410), which claims that these days 'the peple is unworthi and in despyt to alle Cristendam for her falshed . . . hatyd of God and of man'.[7] Others treat present weaknesses with indulgence; *The Contemplations of the Dread and Love of God* (*c.*1400) justifies the simplicity of the demands it makes by claiming that the desert fathers could live 'in wildernes bi gras and rotes . . . bi the streinthe of kinde that was in man tho daies' in a fashion that nowadays 'feblenes of man' makes impossible.[8] The Miller's Tale and the Clerk's Tale both echo this sense that humanity is not the same as it once was. Neither text, however, is clear on how tolerant it is proper to be towards the failings of the present.

The Miller's Tale, 3444–91

Nicholas's 'capyng upright' at the moon here is reminiscent of a satirical description of literalistic contemplatives who try to 'peerce the planetes, and make an hole in the firmament' in the *Cloud of Unknowing*, which views this exercise in self-deceit as profoundly dangerous.[9] This is how John also understands the rapture in which he finds Nicholas, and which he imagines has left the student in madness or despair, perhaps demonically possessed. John's assessment and relief at being a 'lewed man' not tempted to pry into 'Goddes pryvetee' is in tune with a good deal of religious writing that warns against visions and astrology: 'Aungelus office hit is hevenliche thyngus to knowe, and to wite the pryvytes that mow not be departed' says a contemporary text.[10] His response to the emergency is informed by a practical charity only slightly tarnished by its note of 'I told you so'. Full of compassion and arming himself with the holy name of Jesus, he uses physical force, prayer and exhortations to bestir Nicholas: 'thenk on Cristes passioun' is standard advice to a soul in despair, as Saint Frideswide is a proper saint to invoke in the presence of evil. Although his conjuring of 'elves' and 'wightes' would have met with mild theoretical disapproval from theologians, even his use of the 'nyght-spel' can be defended as a piece of practical charity suitable to a person of his station. In other words, John behaves as an exemplary member of the estate of 'men that swynke': a labourer like Piers Plowman, stepping briefly out of his sphere to help a fellow Christian of superior status by reminding him of the perils of *scientia* and the need to quit 'studyng' 'Goddes pryvetee' and 'thynk on God' in humility instead.

The problem with this reading, of course, is that John is being tricked in a way that cruelly exposes his stupidity and self-regard. Within a few lines of this passage, his 'ymaginacioun' (3611) has become as absorbed in 'Goddes pryvetee' – in the form of an image of himself as a second Noah saving Alisoun from drowning – as any false contemplative, falling into the 'marle-pit' (3460) of social humiliation with a completeness his knowledge of his 'bileve' can do nothing to prevent. Furnished though he is with proper slogans and attitudes, the very fact of his marriage to Alisoun shows that he lacks the self-knowledge that characterizes the simple spiritual wisdom he thinks he represents – his problems go a little deeper than the Miller's explanation that 'he knew not Catoun' suggests (3227). The Miller has promised us 'a legende and a lyf' (3141) of John and Alisoun – terms used for saints' lives like the Second Nun's Tale – and John does at first seem a worthy successor to his predecessor, Joseph the carpenter, an important lay saint who also married a younger woman. But in the event, the world is changed, and John is no more like Joseph than Alisoun is like the Virgin Mary or Nicholas the angel Gabriel (3216). The 'cherles tale' (3169) serves only to mock his spiritual pretensions.

Fabliaux are proof against moralization: that is their point. But fabliaux can satirize as well as burlesque, and so offer a broad moral commentary on what they depict: in the case of the Miller's Tale, an urban Christian community. The tale is rich in its evocation of a parish religion – replete with services, incense and local saints' cults (St Frideswide, St Neot) – in which devotion and sex, the everyday and the sacred, are inextricably mingled (cf. Duffy 1992). This is not entirely seen as a corruption of religious values. Unlike the tale's university student, whose energies are differently employed, the community of Oxford craftsmen has a strong work ethic – John is busy with the buildings in progress at 'Osenay' (3400), Gervays is up early to work his forge – and a sense of fellowship that only reveals its merciless side when John is 'holde wood in al the toun' at the end (3846). But religion here is at work in a world whose most obvious priorities are sex, social status and money. Absolon, the parish clerk, turns his ritual purification of the congregation into a fashion parade – 'Poules wyndow corven on his shoos' (3318) – unaware of the strictures on rich clothing in the Parson's Tale (415–35); eyes up the women; and woos Alisoun in the language of the Song of Songs (3698–707). Nicholas's rendition of '*Angelus ad virginem*' with psaltery accompaniment makes the angel Gabriel's visit to Mary sexy, rather than spiritual (3216). Alisoun's trip to church, 'Cristes owene werkes for to wirche' (3308), is described just after she has vowed her love to Nicholas, his hand between her legs, 'by Seint Thomas of Kent' (3291). And blind passion for his wife fools John, the tale's representative of 'men that swynke', into thinking that the Flood is coming again and that God has intervened directly to rescue his household.

As John's sense of history here suggests, this is above all a tale suffused by Corpus Christi plays, many of which mix religion and the secular in their own ways. Absolon, whose name and hair recall King David's son, 'pleyeth Herodes upon a scaffold hye' (3384), while the Miller introduces the tale 'in Pilates voys' (3124). Plays of the Annunciation and the Flood lie just below the narrative surface: Nicholas recalls Noah's troubles with his wife, often evoked in the plays, to persuade John to make three little arks, rather than one big one (3538–46). Gerveys's forge, where Absolon goes after committing his soul 'unto Sathanas' and where Gerveys himself swears 'Cristes foo!' (3750, 3782), precipitates a series of echoes of a stage hell – a place of heat, farts, arses and sodomy (3798–810). The feast of Corpus Christi – evoked in John's terrified 'Nay, Crist forbede it, for his hooly blood!' (3508) – celebrated the whole community's membership of the church of Christ, while the Corpus Christi plays swept this community up into a version of salvation history brought down to the local level. This was the incarnational vision that we saw was considered too inclusive by a puritan movement whose most powerful institutional base was Oxford: the very city in which the tale is set, and whose university participates in the harmonious jeering precipitated by John's downfall, which at last gives the academics something they can agree about: 'For every clerk anonright heeld with other. / They seyde, "The man is wood, my leeve brother"' (3847–8). The Miller's Tale stages a version of this inclusive vision that playfully unmasks its potential superficiality. Its characters are aware of the lessons of biblical history and can even inhabit biblical roles, but have learned none of the sober lessons the puritan movement found in the direct study of God's law. At the same time, the tale also leaves this vision intact, unchallenged by even a wisp of overt Wycliffite disapproval. Although it does imply that the inclusive axiom 'blessed be alwey a lewed man / That noght but oonly his bileve kan' is not enough, the fabliau eventually shoulders all such considerations aside, in favour of its algebraically perfect ending, and so leaves our judgement of parish religion, and consequently of its own community of pilgrim hearers, tantalizingly open.

The Clerk's Tale, 1142–69

What is startling about these stanzas and the ones that follow is not simply the shift of tone from lofty morality to cynicism but how the whole passage works two arguments at once. One argument steers us delicately through the pitfalls of the tale's allegorical meaning. The tale is about God and the soul, not about husbands and wives. But to say this is not to equate Walter with God: for God, knowing us perfectly already, tests us for our good, rather than playing with us out of curiosity. Still, we should submit to the suffering that God allows us, as Grisilde did to Walter, since, however bad it may be, all is 'for oure beste'. The other argument develops from the Clerk's presentation of his tale as distant in style, place, time and moral clarity from the world of his hearers, and is strictly literal. Grisilde's full submission would be 'inportable' for women to imitate because the present is an age of brass, not gold: 'This world is not so strong, it is no nay, / As it hath been in olde tymes yoore', as the Clerk also says earlier (1139–40). Indeed, potential Grisildes are now so rare that the tale's moral should be read backwards, in a spirit of fun – for 'Grisilde is deed, and eek her pacience' (1177). A man must not try what Walter tried, 'for in certein he shal faille' (1182), while women must not hope to be written about like Grisilde, but had best focus – like Grisilde's opposite, the Wife of Bath – on staying on top (1183–1212). This second argument would trail off into burlesque, were it not that the Clerk's picture of the bossy wife, 'of chiere as light as leef on lynde', letting her cowering mate 'care, and wepe, and wrynge, and waille' (1211–12) brings us sharply back to Walter's treatment of Grisilde, with the roles of the sexes reversed. Far from being comic, this second argument thus reinforces a general unease about the tale's implications.

One way of explaining this unease would be to suggest that the Clerk suspects his tale to be irrelevant to the present, when Grisildes do not exist, Wives of Bath run rampant with their demands for a life of pleasure sanctioned by religion, and God can no more test his people with due severity than husbands can test their wives. Patient Grisilde, on this reading, is like Custance in the Man of Law's Tale or Cecile in the Second Nun's Tale, who suffer with exemplary fortitude, but in a world so far in the past from the one in which the *Canterbury Tales* is set that the urgency of their heroic living and dying is dissipated. But I suggest that the opposite explanation – that the tale presses especially hard on the Clerk, his audience and Chaucer – is closer to being true. Despite the language of gold and brass, which imagines Grisilde and modern women in separate eras of world history, this is a modern saint's life, translated from a modern writer, Petrarch – hardly 'deed and nayled in his cheste' (29) – and set in a recognizable modern political system, north Italian absolutism. The Clerk may find ways to reiterate his insistence that 'Grisilde is deed' (1177) but, unlike Custance, she has not been dead for very long, even if her patience is now dead as well; she is still disturbingly relevant, as Custance is not. And she is especially relevant because, at least figuratively, Walter is not dead at all. Not only does he live in the absolutist pretensions of Chaucer's king, Richard II;[11] he lives as a version of God active in late medieval English religion, who demands his people conquer their lightest inclination to sin and loves only those who submit, as Grisilde did to Walter, to whatever trials he sends them.

Heroic Christianity as Constance or the desert fathers lived it can be admired but not imitated. Because it depends on God's constant intervention, it is reassuringly easy to dismiss as having little to say to people living under more normal conditions. Even though we are encouraged to compare her to Christ and Job (206–7, 440–1, 932–8), Grisilde's modernity is marked by the secular and unmiraculous nature of what she goes through. If she cannot be imitated either, this is because her suffering is too intense and her obedience to Walter too passionately embraced, not because she belongs in a different world. Any hearer of the Clerk's Tale could be called upon to endure as Grisilde did, assured that the 'sharpe scourges of adversitee' are good for them but also warned that, unlike her, they are unlikely 'now' to be capable of enduring. The warning is the more frightening because Grisilde is almost as close to occupying the space of 'now' as her opposite in the *Tales*, the Wife of Bath. Because the Clerk is clear that if people are to endure God's testing they still need the strength they apparently no longer have, all his rhetorical efforts to push Grisilde safely back into the past of the saints cannot exorcise the radicalism she represents from the world of his hearers.

Late medieval Christians knew that once in their lives, on their deathbeds, they would be subjected to God's scourge; a whole genre, the *ars moriendi* (art of dying), developed to prepare them for a moment when their endurance would be tested to the limit, as demons were permitted one last chance to drag them off to hell, held at bay only by faith and prayer. (One of Chaucer's most notable successors, Thomas Hoccleve, wrote one of these arts of dying.[12]) But puritan religiosity, which borrowed many of its attitudes from the ascetic tradition and advocated harsh repudiation of the smallest sins, saw the whole of life as adversity. True believers – all Christians serious about their salvation – were tested by the constant urge to sin generated by their fallen natures and the promptings of the devil; by life's many ups and downs; and by the jeers of the worldly, made uncomfortable by so much purity. Devout lay contemporaries of Chaucer eagerly read works with titles like the *Book of Tribulation* or *Remedies against Temptation*; during his lifetime *Ancrene Wisse*, the classic thirteenth-century account of the solitary life, more than half of which deals with tribulation, was adapted for lay readers needing even more of this material.[13] For these perfectionist readers, busy repudiating the laxity of contemporary faith, the heroic Christian past was not dead, and Grisilde's example not irrelevant. If the Miller's Tale's use of fabliau reflects an unease about the low expectations of knowledge and virtue that follow from defining religion around a sacramental community consisting of all the baptized, the Clerk's Tale – narrated by an Oxford clerk very different from the ones we meet in the Miller's Tale – reflects an equal anxiety about the high expectations of Christian endurance encouraged by the perfectionist religious outlook of late medieval puritanism.

'Thou sholdest knytte up wel a gret mateere'

The two readings I have offered here suggest that we can characterize the *Canterbury Tales'* general attitude to contemporary Christian ideologies as believing, fascinated, quizzical and uncertain. The poem is too ironically aware of the endemic corruption in the church, the earthly body of Christ, to endorse an incarnational religiosity without simultaneously stripping it of its pretensions; and the poem is at the same time too alert to the prejudices and hypocrisies that attend the use of satire to lay claim to that sense of righteousness with which puritan religiosity faces down the world. Yet Christianity is everywhere in the *Tales*, and not just as a backdrop for more interesting issues. Even where every possible religious outlook on life is made irrelevant by a given tale's genre, as with the fabliaux, this irrelevance can sometimes be part of the point; thus the Miller's Tale can be called religious in its depiction of a Christianity that pervades society but fails to achieve any deep purchase on human desire. However much there is going on in the *Tales* that has nothing to do with religion, it is a reflection of one of the poem's central preoccupations, not a sad lapse into religious dullness, when the Host asks the Parson to tell the last tale and 'knytte up wel a greet mateere' (ParsP 28).

None of this suggests that any moment in the *Canterbury Tales*, including the closing tale and epilogue, affirms any version of Christianity in a manner we are meant to take as an absolute directive as to how to read, or even how to live. The Retraction submits Chaucer's life-work to the mercy of Christ but only gestures vaguely towards the question of what poetry actually requires this mercy. Like Chaucer's two lost prose translations – of Innocent III's *De miseria condicionis humane* and the early 'Orygenes upon the Maudeleyne' (*LGWP*, G 414–18) – the Parson's Tale is presumably a sincere expression of religious belief. Yet in giving the tale to the Parson, an impressive but narrow-minded figure whose portrait in the General Prologue is of a man socially much inferior to the narrator or his audience (477–529), Chaucer refuses to accord even this careful expression of a moderate puritan outlook the privilege of standing for the truth. Penitence at once becomes a professional topic: something it is the Parson's job to preach and something that goes as well at the end of a long poem as it is a necessary attitude in facing the end of a long life.

It may perhaps be that there was something formalistic about the faith of a man who wrote poetry that can observe all the versions of Christianity it describes from the outside. Certainly Chaucer's whole mind was not swept up in the grand contradictions of faith in the manner of Langland, and he left no signs of ever having had an original or speculative theological thought. None the less, the demands of religion are not something Chaucer's explorations of the world ever ignore – any more than we should ignore them in our explorations of his poetry.

See also Authority; Chivalry; Comedy; Crisis and Dissent; Genre; Geography and Travel; Love; Other Thought-Worlds; Personal Identity; Science; Social Structures; Translation; Visualizing.

Acknowledgements

I thank Alison Conway, Richard Green, Fiona Somerset and Jocelyn Wogan-Browne for their help in writing this chapter.

Notes

1 See also Roger Ellis, *Patterns of Religious Narrative in the* Canterbury Tales (London: Croom Helm, 1986); *Chaucer's Religious Tales*, ed. C. David Benson and Elizabeth Robertson, Chaucer Studies 15 (Cambridge: Brewer, 1990).

2   Giles Constable, *Three Studies in Medieval Religious and Social Thought* (Cambridge: Cambridge University Press, 1995).

3   Walter Hilton, *Scale of Perfection*, trans. John P. H. Clark and Rosemary Dorward, Classics of Western Spirituality (New York: Paulist Press, 1991), 293–302.

4   *The Cloud of Unknowing*, ed. Patrick J. Gallacher, TEAMS Middle English Texts Series (Kalamazoo, Mich.: Medieval Institute Publications, 1997), 39.

5   Nicholas Watson, '*Ancrene Wisse*, religious reform, and the late Middle Ages', in *A Companion Guide to* Ancrene Wisse, ed. Yoko Wada (Cambridge: Brewer, forthcoming).

6   *Lantern of Light*, ed. L. M. Swinburn, Early English Text Society, original series 151 (1917).

7   *Dives and Pauper*, ed. Priscilla Heath Barnum,

2 vols, Early English Text Society, original series 275, 280 (1976, 1980), ii, 64.

8   *The Contemplations of the Dread and Love of God*, ed. Margaret Connolly, Early English Text Society, original series 303 (1994), 3.

9   *The Cloud of Unknowing*, ed. Gallacher, 84.

10 *Book for a Simple and Devout Woman*, ed. F. N. M. Diekstra, Mediaevalia Gröningana 24 (Gröningen: Egbert Forsten, 1998), 300.

11 David Wallace, *Chaucerian Polity: Absolutist Lineages and Associational Forms in England and Italy*, Figurae: Readings in Medieval Culture (Stanford: Stanford University Press, 1997), 261–98.

12 *Hoccleve's Works: The Minor Poems*, ed. F. J. Furnivall and I. Gollancz, rev. Jerome Mitchell and A. I. Doyle, Early English Text Society, extra series 61, 73 (1970).

13 Watson, '*Ancrene Wisse*'.

REFERENCES AND FURTHER READING

Aers, David and Staley, Lynn (1996) *The Powers of the Holy: Religion, Politics, and Gender in Late Medieval English Culture* (University Park, Pa.: Pennsylvania State University Press). Discusses Chaucer's poetry, with Langland and Julian of Norwich, in relation to religious and political crises of the late fourteenth century.

Boyle, Leonard E. (1985) 'The Fourth Lateran Council and manuals of popular religion', in *The Popular Religion of Medieval England*, ed. Thomas J. Heffernan (Knoxville, Tenn.: University of Tennessee Press), 30–60. Lucid account of the development of vernacular pastoral manuals in thirteenth- and fourteenth-century England and their significance.

Duffy, Eamon (1992) The *Stripping of the Altars: Traditional Religion in England, c.1400–c.1580* (New Haven: Yale University Press). Analysis and beautifully detailed evocation of parish religion in the period before and after the Reformation, with a controversial central thesis.

Hudson, Anne (1988) *The Premature Reformation: Wycliffite Texts and Lollard History* (Oxford: Clarendon). Classic textual study of the early decades of the Lollard movement, with especially useful final chapter on the intricacies of 'vernacular Wycliffism'.

Patterson, Lee (1976) 'The Parson's Tale and the quitting of the *Canterbury Tales*', *Traditio* 34, 331–80. Important and lucid general study of the Parson's Tale and its significance to the *Tales* as a whole.

Robertson, D. W., Jr (1962) *A Preface to Chaucer: Studies in Medieval Perspectives* (Princeton: Princeton University Press). Classic and controversial study of Chaucer as didactic poet: one of the most influential and controversial books on medieval literature ever written.

Rubin, Miri (1991) *Corpus Christi: The Eucharist in Late Medieval Culture* (Cambridge: Cambridge University Press). The theological, symbolic and social implications of Corpus Christi.

Scanlon, Larry (1994) *Narrative, Authority, and Power: The Medieval Exemplum and the Chaucerian Tradition*, Cambridge Studies in Medieval Literature 20 (Cambridge: Cambridge University Press). The relationship between clerical authority and lay power as it is negotiated in texts by Chaucer and others influenced by the exemplum tradition.

Vauchez, André (1993) The *Laity in the Middle Ages: Religious Beliefs and Devotional Practices*, trans. Margery J. Schneider (South Bend, Ind.: Notre Dame University Press). Multiperspective account of the process of laicization in later medieval Europe, its causes and effects.

Watson, Nicholas (1997a) 'The *Gawain*-poet as a vernacular theologian', in *A Companion Guide to the* Gawain-*Poet*, ed. Derek Brewer and Jonathan Gibson (Cambridge: Brewer), 293–313. *Pearl* and its companions as adaptations of ascetic religious thought for the aristocratic laity.

——(1997b) 'Conceptions of the word: the mother tongue and the incarnation of God', *New Medieval Literatures* 1, 85–124. Different ways of understanding the incarnation in relation to different understandings of the purpose of vernacular theological writing.

——(1997c) 'Visions of inclusion: universal salvation and vernacular theology in pre-Reformation England', *Journal of Medieval and Early Modern Studies* 27, 145–87. Argues that several Middle English writers accepted the notion of universal salvation and speculates about why.

Wogan-Browne, Jocelyn; Watson, Nicholas; Taylor, Andrew; and Evans, Ruth, eds (1999) *The Idea of the Vernacular: An Anthology of Middle English Literary Theory, 1280–1520* (University Park, Pa.: Pennsylvania State University Press; Exeter: Exeter University Press). Extensively annotated anthology of prologues to religious and secular texts.

6

Comedy

Laura Kendrick

In the light of surviving verse in Old English, the epithet 'father of English poetry', often accorded to Geoffrey Chaucer since it was coined by John Dryden, is a great exaggeration. We might more appropriately consider him to be the 'father of English comedy' for having elaborated the laughter-provoking fictions of the fabliaux among his *Canterbury Tales*, as well as for providing briefer moments of comic relief in his ostensibly serious works. Although not the inventor of comic writing per se (which emerged much earlier than the fourteenth century in Latin and continental vernaculars), Chaucer seems to have been the chief inventor of comic writing in the English language. In surviving Old English texts there is a remarkable dearth of comedy; in the twelfth and thirteenth centuries, after the Norman invasion, fewer texts of any sort were recorded in English. Only the brief, anonymous *fablel* or fabliau of *Dame Sirith* has survived in English from the thirteenth century, along with a fragment of a comic interlude featuring a dialogue between a cleric and a girl. However, in the fifteenth century, in the wake of Chaucer's example, comic writing of various sorts was done in English. Surviving from this period are fabliaux such as *The Lady Prioress*, burlesque lays such as *Sir Corneus* and humorous parodies of romance such as *The Tournament of Tottenham*.

What then, were the different strands of the comic tradition available in Chaucer's time, and what did he do with them? Let us begin with learned medieval notions of comedy and the comic, which were in some respects different from our own. Whereas we tend to think of a comedy as a dramatic genre and the comic as virtually anything provoking laughter, medieval definitions emphasize neither drama nor laughter.

Medieval Definitions of Comedy

The conventional medieval etymological definition of the Latin word *comedia* explained it as 'rustic song'; *comedia* was supposed to be a compound formed from *oda* ('song') and *comos* ('peasant' or 'rustic'). By this reasoning, comedy was rustic poetry dealing in an appropriately low vocabulary and style with peasant life ('low' matters such as cultivating the land, tending animals, and rural sexual activity). In some cases, to write in the vernacular, the 'vulgar' tongue, was enough to make a work into a comedy. Thus Dante's son Pietro explained his father's title, *The Divine Comedy*: 'Another reason was that the poet in comedy is meant to speak in a low rather than high manner, as Terence did in his comedies. . . . Dante used the vulgar tongue, just as rustics do' (Kelly 1989: 6, 27).

An alternate etymological definition emphasized a connection between comedy and festive banqueting or *commessacione* (Kelly 1989: 6). It is possible that this definition refers to one of the earliest surviving medieval comic texts, which features the pantheon of biblical characters behaving ludicrously 'in character' at a fictive banquet: Pilate brings the finger bowls, Herodiade dances, Judas kisses everyone. This Latin parody (or pastiche) of the Bible, known as *Cena Cypriani* (Cyprian's supper), was many times revised throughout the Middle Ages, most notably by Hrabanus Maurus in the ninth century, to entertain new audiences. One may well imagine the performance context of the *Cena Cypriani* to be a festive banquet at which it would be read aloud and possibly also mimed.

The derivation of the word 'comedy' from the word 'banquet' was probably also suggested by the more general observation that festive occasions (times for feasting) were in medieval life the traditional contexts for comedy, that is, for the performance and appreciation of comic texts. Annual seasonal festivities celebrated by both clergy and laity – such as the long holidays of New Year, with its Feast of the Boy Bishop in England and its Feast of Fools on the continent – were especially propitious for comedy, as were special occasions such as wedding feasts. By definition, these occasions were periods of transition, attempts to integrate novelty or to bridge difference, moments of expanded community. The copious ingestion of alcohol and food upon festive occasions encouraged the temporary relaxation – or even inversion – of the rules and distinctions that ordinarily governed social life. During the play time of the feast, crass materialism, physical pleasure and vulgarity in every sense of the term might take 'centre stage' in the performance of comic texts of a burlesque, debasingly parodic nature by professional entertainers or amateur ones: jongleurs, goliards, schoolboys, choirboys, courtiers and burghers.

Both etymological definitions of comedy – from 'rustic song' and from 'banquet' – fail to mention laughter, but they may assume it. A banqueting context would promote high spirits, and medieval clerical and aristocratic elites typically confirmed their own superiority by laughing at vulgarity – that is, rustic life and language. In an only slightly less estate-based sense than the medieval one, Aristotle had explained comedy in chapter 5 of his *Poetics* as 'a representation of inferior people, not indeed in the full sense of the word bad, but the laughable is a species of the base or ugly'.[1] Medieval etymological definitions of comedy suggest a festive banquet as the context for appreciating it and rusticity or vulgarity as its risible target.

To explain the title of Dante's masterpiece, Boccaccio had recourse to a more general definition of comedy: a narrative whose plot leads from sorrow to happiness. Thus a comedy could be almost any versified narrative that treated the lives of ordinary people and ended on a happier note than that on which it began (Kelly 1989: 47). This is much the same definition of comedy that John Lydgate gave in his fifteenth-century *Troy Book* (II, 847–51):

> A comedie hath in his gynnyng
> At prime face, a maner compleynyng,
> And afterward endeth in gladnes;
> And it the dedis only doth expres
> Of swiche as ben in pouert plounged lowe.[2]

This general notion of comedy seems to be what Chaucer contrasts to the 'tragedy' of *Troilus*, when at the end of that work he wishes that God would give him the power to compose a comedy before he dies (V, 787–8). Modern scholars have taken this as a foreshadowing of the *Canterbury Tales*, a work plotted as a storytelling contest among a group of pilgrims on their way to Canterbury, a contest that is supposed to end happily with a banquet in honour of the winner. However, its projected happy ending is by no means the only feature of the *Canterbury Tales* that has encouraged modern scholars, such as Lee Patterson, to define its genre as comedy:

> A tale-telling game that invokes a wide range of festive forms, an insistently 'voiced' text that foregrounds character at every turn, a collection organized according to intrinsic and self-generating formal principles, and a contest that gives full play to social antagonisms and grants unexpected authority to the voices of the socially ignoble: *The Canterbury Tales* is a comedy that declares its difference from courtly 'makyng' at every turn.[3]

Although Chaucer himself never explicitly used the term 'comedy' in referring to his *Canterbury Tales*, through the character of the Knight in the Prologue to the Nun's Priest's Tale he gave the conventional happy-ending definition of comedy as a description of the kind of story the Canterbury pilgrims would prefer to hear (instead of the Monk's 'tragedies' about the sudden decline of great men). Chaucer's Knight urges the telling of stories that are 'gladsom', that provoke 'joye and greet solas' through a happy ending: 'when a man hath been in povre estaat, / And clymbeth up and wexeth fortunat,/ And there abideth in prosperitee' (2774–7). Chaucer's Host heartily supports this view and nudges it in a more jocular direction. He emphasizes the lack of 'desport' and 'game' ('amusement' and 'play') in the Monk's 'tragedies' (2791).

John of Garland, an Englishman who taught in Paris during the first half of the thirteenth century, offered a definition of comedy in his *Parisiana poetria* that combined older notions with new specifics, such as that comedy should have five parts corresponding to its cast of five characters: 'a husband and wife, an adulterer and the adulterer's accomplice – or his critic – and the adulteress's nurse, or the husband's servant'.[4] This definition describes schoolish medieval Latin adaptations and imitations of classical comedy. These late twelfth- and thirteenth-century Latin texts were versified narratives including some dialogue whose characters, plots and subject matter (usually adultery and the outwitting of a jealous husband by his wife and a younger man) were virtually the same as those of the thirteenth-century French fabliaux (hence the theory that clerics were responsible for the invention as well as the preservation in writing of many vernacular fabliaux).

That Chaucer was familiar with the conventions of both Latin and fabliau comedy is certain. He knew, at the very least, those French fabliaux which he reworked in his *Canterbury Tales* (the Flemish tale of *Heile of Bersel* for the Miller's Tale, the French fabliau of *The Miller and the Two Clerks* for the Reeve's Tale, the French story of *The Priest's Bladder* for the Reeve's Tale). He must also have known Latin comedies such as *Lydia* (a source of the pear-tree episode in his Merchant's Tale, along with the Italian *Novellino*'s version) and *Pamphilus*, which he mentions by name in the Franklin's Tale (1110) and cites from three times in his Melibee (1556, 1558, 1561). His comic treatment of Pandarus as the lovers' go-between in *Troilus and Criseyde* likewise suggests his knowledge of the laughable go-betweens who serve the lovers and adulterers of medieval Latin comedies. Yet John of Garland readily admitted that not all medieval comedies had five such characters or parts and that 'sometimes any humorous treatment of a subject is called a comedy'. He continued by giving the conventional etymological definition: 'Comedy comes from *comos* "village" and *odos* "song" – a "peasant song" as it were, since it is composed of low and humorous matter.' A few lines later, contrasting the plots of tragedy and comedy, he remarked that 'a comedy is a humorous poem beginning in sadness and ending in joy'.[5] From John of Garland's discussion arise the notions that comedy deals with low and humorous matter and, more specifically, that this matter involves adultery, yet ends joyfully.

In none of these medieval definitions is comedy ever associated with drama or performance on stage, as it had been in classical times; instead, it is understood to be versified narrative. The Englishman Geoffrey of Vinsauf, in his twelfth-century Latin *Documentum de arte versificandi*, remarked that comedy such as Horace understood it (that played in the Roman theatres) no longer existed, but only 'humorous matter' ('jocosa materia'), that is, comic stories.[6]

Conventions of Medieval Comic Texts

Learned though they may be, these medieval definitions of comedy are not totally theoretical. They describe texts that really existed, whether solely in performance or also in writing: comic biblical parodies; tales of seduction, adultery and trickery; burlesque love lyrics or sermons; and even Dante's masterpiece. Chaucer's practice of comedy in English depended on his familiarity with comic texts in French, Flemish,

Latin and Italian – that is, versified narratives featuring vulgar speech and subject matter, especially adultery; rustic or lowly settings and characters; and risible or 'happy' outcomes.

The majority of surviving medieval comic texts, both in Latin and in the vernaculars, seem to have been invented by clerics or revised by them into the forms we know. This is not because the medieval clergy had more fun than other sectors of the population, but rather because literate men were the only ones capable of committing comic texts to writing, and thus preserving them in manuscript codices – and in the early Middle Ages, most literate men were clergymen. Many comic texts in Latin, especially parodies and burlesques of sacred texts or prayers – such as the Gospels, the Apocalypse, the Pater Noster – were attributed to 'vagrant', 'wandering' or 'ribald' clerics, or to 'goliards', that is educated men who played the role of Golias, or Bishop Golias, who was a laughably vulgar, low-minded narrative persona, a sort of comic mask through which to express what was ordinarily supposed to be repressed.

When Chaucer in the General Prologue to the *Canterbury Tales* called his Miller a 'janglere and a goliardeys' (560), he was associating him with both secular (jongleuresque) and clerical (goliardic) traditions of comic entertainment, the subjects of which were mainly 'synne and harlotries' (561), that is, lechery, adultery and other sins of the flesh. The very name Golias and the noun form 'goliard' were understood and etymologized in a number of ways, all of which Chaucer seems to allude to in his description of his Miller as a *goliardeys*. On the one hand, the Latin name for the Philistine giant whom David slew, and whom religious interpreters explained as a figure for sin and the devil, was Golias. This association emphasized the grotesque, monstrous, exaggeratedly sinful nature of the goliard. With his warty nose, huge black nostrils and furnace-sized mouth, Chaucer's *goliardeys* Miller has a grotesque physique worthy of Golias. Another Middle English spelling, *gulardous*, points to the Latin word *gula* ('throat' or 'gluttony'), and associates the goliard with festivity and excessive consumption of food and drink. Chaucer seems to suggest this sense of the term by emphasizing his Miller's enormous mouth (559) immediately before labelling him a *goliardeys*. Yet another Middle English spelling, *galiardeis*, suggests buffoonery or trickery, for *galier* meant 'to mock' or 'to make fun of' in medieval French. The word *goliard* may also evoke trickery through its relation to the Occitan *gualiar*, also spelled *galiar*, meaning 'trick' or 'seduce'.[7]

Nevertheless, in calling his Miller a *goliard*, Chaucer was stretching a term that conventionally applied to clerics who invented comic Latin texts for literate audiences capable of understanding them. Goliardic comedy was schoolish. The precondition for it was authoritarian instruction in Latin in cathedral or monastic schools under constant vigilance against various types of moral and linguistic misbehaviour. On festive occasions, such as the Feast of the Boy Bishop, the Feast of Fools, the Feast of the Innocents or the Feast of Asses, misbehaviour was tolerated for a while, and the lower orders of the religious hierarchy deliberately overthrew the rules of correct Latin grammar and correct textual interpretation. To comic effect, through their goliardic play, they deliberately pronounced or deformed classical or biblical words in rustic (vernacular, even dialectal) fashion, committing the linguistic sin of *barbarolexis*; they combined words, syllables or morphemes in irregular ways (*solecism*) to produce punning senses or innuendoes, especially erotic, scatological or otherwise vulgar and materialistic meanings (*cacemphaton*) that incongruously contrasted with and subverted a 'correct' or conventional understanding of the text. When he read medieval Latin parody, Mikhail Bakhtin heard two – or more – incongruous voices, the vernacular tongue vying with the learned one:

> The Latin 'parodia sacra' is projected against the background of the vulgar national language. The accentuating system of this vulgar language penetrates to the very heart of the Latin text. In essence, Latin parody is, therefore, a bilingual phenomenon: although there is only one language, this language is structured and perceived in the light of another language, and in some instances not only the accents but also the syntactical forms of the vulgar language are clearly sensed in the Latin parody. Latin parody is an intentional bilingual hybrid.[8]

Such goliardic play required an initiated audience, a 'school' of bilingual or multilingual interpreters. Because it used vulgarity to upset the conventional or ideal order of things, goliardic play has sometimes been called 'popular', following Bakhtin, but this view fails to take sufficient account of the role-playing involved in such temporary inversion of linguistic and social hierarchies. Golias or the goliard persona was a *mask* of vulgarity or rusticity.

In addition to deforming authoritative or sacred Latin texts through relatively small changes in their interpretation or performance (a kind of play that leaves no traces), goliards also invented 'new' texts that were loaded with puns and innuendoes emphasizing sensuality on all levels, comic texts – gospels, passions, masses, catechisms, confessions, prayers, sermons, hymns – that were debasing pastiches or parodies of their authoritative models. The goliardic cento was a patchwork of biblical or classical quotations and allusions rendered comic by their incongruously vulgar context. As Martha Bayless points out (1996: 135), these centos produced 'comedy of deflation, narrating salacious tales in biblical phrasing or wrongly applying scriptural quotations in unexpected and inappropriate contexts'. Instead of clerical or monastic chastity and discipline, goliard narrative verse celebrated sensual pleasures: illicit sex (which often involved a young cleric's outwitting of an older married man or a parish priest), drunkenness and gluttony, and linguistic licence or polysemy. For their comic effect, goliardic texts praising and revelling in various types of sinful behaviour relied heavily on incongruity and on the audience's capacity to detect irony. In his Clerk's Envoy, as we shall see, Chaucer exploits just this sort of goliardic irony.

In the vernaculars, jongleurs 'juggled' words to invent comic texts, which they memorized, improvised and performed on festive occasions. Yet unless someone literate went to the trouble of putting these texts into writing, and inscribed them on sturdy vellum pages to be bound into codices (rather than left as single sheets or rolls), they were eventually lost. This is one reason why comic texts in the vernacular have rarely survived prior to the thirteenth century. There are exceptions, such as a comic Occitan 'song', a short, narrative poem preserved in fourteenth-century manuscripts but attributed to the twelfth-century Count of Poitou and Duke of Aquitaine whom we know as William IX. In this lyric, a boastful and self-mockingly long-suffering first-person narrator tells how he tricked two married women into believing he was a deaf-mute pilgrim; how he silently suffered the claws of the cat that they dragged down his naked flesh to test him; and how the two wives, delighted with their discovery of a man unable to reveal their secret, used him for their sexual pleasure in their hideaway, so that he nearly broke his 'equipment' in fucking them 188 times ('tant las fotei com auziretz: / cent et quatre-vinz et veit vetz'); and how, at the time of the telling, he is still incapable of expressing the pain of his experience.[9] In its long version, the lyric begins with advice to wives to take knights as lovers, instead of monks or clerics, thus suggesting that the poem is a kind of comic response to goliardic verse praising clerical sexual prowess. Indeed, there was a long-running debate in medieval comic literature over the issue of who made the best 'stud', the clergyman or the layman. This debate or contest is the background against which Chaucer's Host (a layman), in the Prologue of the Monk's Tale, perhaps to prod the Monk into a bawdy fabliau of self-defence, taunts him by calling attention to his fine physique and apparent capacity for sexual prowess with laymen's wives (MkP 1932–64).

If William IX was indeed the inventor of the comic song attributed to him, we have an early example of a secular lord who undertook the entertainment of his entourage, perhaps delegating his song's performance to a professional jongleur. By the beginning of the fourteenth century, educated laymen were taking credit for the formal composition of comic texts in writing. One such was Gautier le Leu (Walter the Wolf or Walter the Light-Spirited). We do not know whether this composer of fabliaux was a jongleur who lived by performance, 'signing' his texts with his name, or whether he was a respectable burgher, that same 'Waltiers Li Leus, échevin de Valenciennes' mentioned, along with eleven other burghers of the same city, in a legal document dated 1296. In the latter case, the composer would probably confide his texts to a jongleur for performance. Waltiers and Gautier are different spellings of the same name, and both burgher and comic writer lived in the same place at the same time. Yet the modern editor of Gautier's fabliaux insisted that Gautier and Waltiers could not be the same man, because a magistrate of the city of Valenciennes could not possibly have the same mentality as the man who claimed to have composed in rhyme at least eleven fabliaux, among which are some of the most obscene and most sacrilegious surviving (Livingston 1951: 96–7). According to this logic, a respectable biblical exegete such as Hrabanus Maurus could not possibly have rewritten the *Cena Cypriani* either, and yet we know that he did.

At the end of the fabliau of *Les Deux Vilains* (The two rustics), which involves kissing a bottom in the night, trying to feed its 'mouth' and mistaking farts for bad breath – in short, imagining a face in the wrong place – Gautier le Leu explains his part in the story's transmission: he has merely set to rhyme a little fable or *fablel* told by 'Li Goulius' at Saint Amand and elsewhere and recounted by a young gentleman from Valenciennes who heard and retold it to Gautier (Livingston 1951: 206, lines 169–75). With this history of his part in its transmission, Gautier denies responsibility for the fabliau's obscene content. Like Geoffrey Chaucer later in his *Canterbury Tales*, Gautier presents himself as reporter and rhymer of other men's stories. In the case of the fabliau of *The Two Rustics*, the source he claims is a performer whose name sounds like a combination of Golias and gluttonous: 'Li Goulius'. Golias may have been, quite literally, a comic mask, and not merely a comic persona. If so, the mask was surely grotesque, featuring a huge mouth. One wonders if the mask might have been worn 'on the bottom' as well as on the top to heighten the comedy (giving the performer the look of certain creatures in the margins of Gothic manuscripts, who have grotesque faces in place of bottoms).[10] It is perhaps with reference to the Golias mask and to its downward displacement that Gautier le Leu in his fabliau (or, as he calls it, *roman*) of *The Widow*, used the term *Golias* to suggest the gluttony of the 'mouth down below': a young man complains that his wife's (the former Widow's) 'Golias' gapes too often and that he is incapable of satisfying its desires: 'Golias bee trop sovent. / Jo ne le puis asasiier' (Livingston 1951: 179, lines 436–7).

Eustache Deschamps

One of Chaucer's late fourteenth-century contemporaries and an admirer of his verse, the French royal officer Eustache Deschamps, also turned his hand to writing comic texts, but of more various types than Gautier le Leu. For example, Deschamps translated the medieval Latin comedy of *Geta and Amphitrion* (itself a revision of a play by Plautus) into octosyllabic couplets, interspersing third-person narrative with the characters' monologues and dialogues. As usual in medieval Latin comedy, the plot revolves around a successful attempt at adultery; in this case, the god Jupiter, to make love to the woman he desires, takes the form of her husband, and beats the real husband home from his long studies in Greece with his servant Geta, who has imbibed sophistry and logic there. Geta's monologue congratulating himself on his learning and projecting uses of it in his kitchen to turn fellow servants into beasts is one of the more humorous sections of the poem:

> Car sophismes sçay merveilleux
> Qui sont aussi tresperilleux,
> Car d'omme ou femme, vueille ou non,
> Puis je faire asnesse ou asnon,
> Changier les piez, muer la teste,
> Et prouver qu'il est une beste,
> Une heure beuf, l'autre heure chievre,
> Une brebis, connin ou lievre,

Un serpent ou une couleuvre;
Car logique sert de ceste œuvre,
Et fait par argumens sembler
Ce qui n'est pas et ressembler
Une chose a l'autre opposite;
Et fait de la copulative
Division estrangement
Qui forme bien son argument.
Quant je seray en ma cuisine,
J'ouverray de ceste dotrine.

(Œuvres, viii, 22,
lines 329–46)

For I know many wonderful sophisms that are also very dangerous, because I can make an ass, male or female, out of a man or a woman, in spite of them. I can change the feet, move the head, and prove that he is a beast, one moment a steer, another a goat, another a ewe, a rabbit or a hare, a viper or a gartersnake. Logic serves to accomplish this work so that, by means of argument, what isn't is made to seem to be, and a thing is made to resemble its opposite. And in order to make a good argument, the copula [linguistic link] is used to accomplish a strange division. When I'm in my kitchen, I'll put this teaching to work.

Geta substitutes sophistry and logic for common sense and eventually makes a fool of himself by arguing that he himself doesn't exist; he makes us laugh at sophistical learning, particularly ill-digested in the mouth of a rustic, grossly materialistic character. Chaucer's vulgar Host likewise associates learning with sophistry, and he intends to make fun of these when he chides the Clerk, in the Prologue to the Clerk's Tale, for not participating in the story-telling game due to his mental preoccupation with 'some sophism': 'I trowe ye studie aboute som sophyme' (5).

Deschamps also composed stanzaic poems – ballads, rondeaux and virelays – that were comic in their choice and treatment of subjects. For example, he wrote numerous self-mocking ballads on his physical person, his baldness, his ugliness, his bodily ills, even his unluckiness in love. In one three-strophe ballad of love complaint, the refrain presents a comical image of the lover's plight, one shoe on, one shoe off, incapable of getting anywhere:

J'ay en amours si grant desir eu
C'oncques mais homs n'y pot si grant avoir;
Mais ce desir m'a trop fort deceu.
Car il m'a fait un plaisir concevoir
Dont je ne puis guerredon recevoir.
Car quant je cuide estre bien avancié,
Je me treuve toudiz, au dire voir,
Que j'ay un pié deschaux, l'autre chaucié.

(iii, 314, lines 1–8)

I had such great desire for love that no man can ever have one as great, but this desire has disappointed me very severely, because it has made me imagine a pleasure for which there can be no satisfaction. Every time I think I am making progress, I discover that, in truth, I have one shoe off and one shoe on.

Curiously, this comic refrain evokes a near-pun on Deschamps' name in 'deschaux' and, in the rhyme word, an exact pun on 'Chaucier', the French pronunciation Deschamps used in his poem praising Chaucer (ii, 138–9) and proposing that they exchange works via Chaucer's friend Clifford, whose name appears again in Deschamps's verse as the rhyme word of a refrain (iii, 375–6).

In other ballads, the subject of Deschamps' amusement or mock indignation is his observation of table manners at the royal court or on his travels abroad in Bohemia. He describes the way people eat at dinner in grotesque detail, turning humans into animals in his mind's eye:

> Li uns sembloit truie enmi une voye,
> Tant mouvoit fort ses baulifres toudiz;
> L'autre faisoit de ses dens une soye,
> L'autre mouvoit le front et les sourcis;
> L'un requignoit, l'autre torcoit son vis,
> L'autre faisoit sa barbe baloier,
> L'un fait le veel, l'autre fait la brebis.
> Oncques ne vis gens ainsi requignier. . . .
> L'un machoit gros, l'autre comme souriz;
> Je n'oy oncques tant de joye ne ris
> Que de veoir leurs morceaulx ensacher . . .
> (v, 15–16, lines 9–22)

One of them looks like a sow in the middle of the road for the way he moves his chops so energetically; another uses his teeth like a saw; another moves his forehead and eyebrows; another bares his teeth; another contorts his facial features; another agitates his beard; another plays the calf; another the ewe; never have I seen people grimace that way . . . one chews by chomping; another nibbles like a mouse; nothing has ever lightened my spirits and made me laugh like watching them pack in their food . . .

In this poem, comedy arises, quite literally, from the feast, that is, from close observation of the feasters, from attention focused on their table manners, their bodies and faces, especially their mouths as they chew their food. In his detailed description of the Prioress's table manners in the General Prologue (127–36), Chaucer achieves a more subtle but analogous comic effect by praising her for the kind of table manners she avoids, focusing on the *faux pas* the eater does *not* commit (plunging her fingers into the sauce, dropping morsels on her breast before they reach her mouth, drinking with greasy lips from the common cup).

Among the vast collection of Deschamps' verse we also find stanzaic poems that are entirely dialogued and, according to a rubric, intended for performance ('a jouer par personnaiges'); one such is a comic altercation within a house between a ribald man and a ribald woman, presumably a couple. They hurl horrible accusations in the most vulgar terms at each other and cap them off, in the refrain of each stanza, by threatening each other with arrest. The man's tirade against the woman, after she starts the argument, goes as follows:

> Ribaude, cabas enfumez,
> Putain, sorciere, lorpidon,
> Qui mains enfans mourdri avez,
> Prestresse, que ne vous prant on!
> Larronnesse de cul et con
> Et des mains, qui avez destruit
> Maint homme et si avez seduit
> Mainte fillette a vostre temps:
> Mauvais renom contre vous bruit,
> Prevosts vous quierent et sergens.
>   (viii, 182, lines 11–20)

Ribald, crazy old bag, whore, witch, filthy hag, murderer of many infants, priest's mistress, may they arrest you! Robber with your bottom, cunt, and hands, you have destroyed many a man, seduced many a young girl in your time. Evil reputation clamours against you; provosts and police sergeants pursue you.

This comic battle between the sexes is interrupted by the arrival of the Provost of Laon and his police sergeant to arrest them; the authorities have the last words – 'Prevost vous *tiennent* et sergens' – and they threaten to torture the two until they tell the truth. The comic contest ends on an element of surprise when verbal threats, the conventional language of cursing, suddenly materialize and the provost appears at the door; their accusations have been their own undoing. Much the same sort of surprise ends the contest between the summoner and the old woman in Chaucer's Friar's Tale when a conventional curse ('The devil take him!') is suddenly realized, and the devil appears to haul the summoner off to hell, along with the widow's pan (1622–9). The Friar's Tale and many of Deschamps' comic poems make us laugh at the reprehensible; they make a mockery of sinful, vicious or merely uncourteous behaviour. Such comedy is normative and may be labelled today, because of its critical edge, 'satirical comedy'. In the Middle Ages, on the other hand, normative texts mocking vicious characters or criticizing sin with some wit were usually considered to be satire (or complaint) and not comedy.

Deschamps also wrote comic parodies for festive occasions, as for example the parodic charter of the 'Ordre des Fumeux' (Order of the quarrelsome) of which he himself was 'Emperor'. This mock charter, in the form of 259 lines of rhyming couplets, is dated 9 December 1368, a few days prior to the beginning of the Christmas and New Year season, with its festive burlesques and inversions. Deschamps, playing Emperor, describes the 'manner and condition' ('leur maniere / Et leur condicion') of the members of his order:

> Ilz parlent variablement;
> Ilz se demainent sotement; . . .
> Es tavernes vont voulentiers,
> Car c'est leur souverain mestiers;
> Aux eschés, aux dez et aux tables
> Jouent; en rien ne sont estables;
> Riotes mueuvent et contemps
> A leur pouoir en trestous temps;
> Estre ne vuellent a Raison
> Subgit, n'entrer en sa maison . . .
> S'uns prodoms dit aucune chose,
> Saiges sera, s'on ne li glose
> Sa parole diversement
> Au plus perilleux sentement.
> Ilz ne doubtent honeur ne honte,
> Prelat, empereur, duc ne conte,
> Pour ce que dame Oultrecuidance
> Maine chascun d'eulx a sa dance;
> Folie par la main les tient . . .
>   (vii, 313–15, lines 41–97)

They speak irregularly; they behave foolishly; . . . they play at chess, dice, and table games; in nothing are they stable; they incite brawls and disputes to the best of their ability all the time; they do not want to be subject to Reason nor to enter her service; . . . if a worthy man says anything, he will be clever indeed if they don't gloss his words for him differently, according to the most dangerous interpretation; they fear neither honour nor shame, prelate, emperor, duke, nor count, because Lady Arrogance leads each one of them to her dance; Folly holds them by the hand . . .

Such a foolish festive 'order', the reverse of a serious chivalric one, may actually have played at overturning hierarchy and proper courtly behaviour on the occasion of the New Year. We have accounts and images of analogous sorts of festive inversion being enacted at an even higher level, by the young King Charles VI and a group of young courtiers who disguised themselves as savages to perform a kind of court masque that unexpectedly turned into the 'Bal des Ardents' (Dance of burning men) when their wild-man costumes accidentally caught fire. It is also possible that Deschamps' 'Order of the Quarrelsome' is an entertaining fiction that was never realized. The comic vernacular writing of Deschamps is noteworthy for its variety of forms and subjects; in his effort to entertain himself and his entourage, this late fourteenth-century courtier and royal official tried his hand at virtually every sort of comic composition possible at the time.

Chaucer's *Ballade* 'To Rosemounde'

Geoffrey Chaucer also entertained himself and his entourage by experimenting with comic writing, and what is more, doing it in English, which was a novelty in itself. One of Chaucer's most innovative comic texts, seen against the background of serious love poetry, is his comic parody of a lover's complaint in his ballad 'To Rosemounde'. In order to appreciate the false notes in this complaint and laugh at the ineptitudes of its speaker, the audience had to be quite familiar with the conventions of love complaint. Modern readers who feel pity for this lover's frustration are missing Chaucer's mockery of his lover-persona.

His portrait of the beloved in the first stanza is nearly acceptable, except that he rather over-emphasizes the roundness of her red cheeks (for facial plumpness played no part in fourteenth-century ideals of noble beauty), and her merry, 'jocounde' dancing at revels:

> Madame, ye ben of al beaute shryne
> As fer as cercled is the mapamounde,
> For as the cristal glorious ye shyne,
> And lyke ruby ben your chekes rounde.
> Therwith ye ben so mery and so jocounde
> That at a revel whan that I see you daunce,
> It is an oynement unto my wounde,
> Thogh ye to me ne do no daliaunce.

This image of jollity in action seems more worthy of a peasant girl and clashes incongruously with that of the more abstract and formal opening, where the lover calls 'Madame' the shrine of beauty, shining like a crystal.

The first line of the second stanza begins with a real false note:

> For thogh I wepe of teres ful a tyne,
> Yet may that wo myn herte nat confounde;
> Your semy voys that ye so smal out twyne
> Maketh my thoght in joy and blis habounde.
> So curtaysly I go with love bounde
> That to myself I sey in my penaunce,
> 'Suffyseth me to love you, Rosemounde,
> Thogh ye to me ne do no daliaunce.'

A tub ('tyne') full of tears is simply too concrete. Lovers' complaints ordinarily do not measure the quantity of tears wept in this materialistic way. Frustrated poet-lovers may compare themselves to 'fountains' of tears (which are inexhaustible sources, hence poetic images), but never do they measure out their tears for their ladies in anything so crassly materialistic as a *tyne*, that is, a tub or vat used for brewing. Chaucer amuses us with this false note which results from a practical burgherly English voice (or mentality) sounding out loud and clear in a context where a more refined, noble one is expected. We laugh at the incongruity of the 'vulgar' note, much as we laugh at the vernacular pun that suddenly surfaces through the Latin in goliardic parody. A second image that surprises our expectations in this same second strophe is the lover's description of Rosemounde's voice, which he admires because she is able to 'twist it out' into such a fine thread of sound. Regardless of whether high, thin feminine voices were in style or not, this image is a false note because it is ignoble, being based on the mundane work of spinning, with which few noblewomen would want to be associated in the late fourteenth century, and which is never brought to the fore in conventional love poetry.

The fundamental vulgarity that renders this frustrated lover so inept shows through again in his crudely materialistic elaboration of conventional images of love's power to catch or hook, bind or ensnare the lover. For example, the prologue to the Latin comedy of *Milo* begins with such images: 'The hook of love (*hamus amoris*) is voracious and the net (*rete*) love casts is vaster than the world. Nothing escapes them; nothing satisfies them. This is my subject' (Cohen 1931: i, 168). Although the trope of love's hook implies that the lover caught by it is a fish, medieval poet-lovers do not develop the figure at length. Not so Chaucer's inept lover-persona who, in the third strophe, compares himself in ludicrous detail to a hooked and cooked fish: he is even more hopelessly wound up in love than a pike engulfed in galantine sauce:

> Nas never pyk walwed in galauntyne
> As I in love am walwed and ywounde,
> For which ful ofte I of myself devyne
> That I am trewe Tristam the secounde.
> My love may not refreyde nor affounde,
> I brenne ay in an amorous plesaunce
> Do what you lyst, I wyl your thral be founde,
> Thogh ye to me ne do no daliaunce.

Of all fish, why should the lover compare himself to a pike? Perhaps to suggest his frustrated desire, for the pike has a very large mouth that, when open, gives it a voracious look. We may imagine the lover's fishy analogue, the cooked pike, served up on the platter with a gaping mouth to make it look more lifelike and covered in imitation waves made of galantine sauce, for culinary realism was in style on festive occasions at court. After this grotesquely comic analogy, the inept lover incongruously bursts into an inflated comparison between himself and Tristam (or Tristan, one of the greatest lovers of medieval romance) only to return to a culinary and piscine register in the following line with the assurance that his love will never 'grow cold' or 'sink'. We cannot help but smile as he flounders through the conventions, claiming to be his lady's 'thrall' and to 'burn', not with the passion we would expect, but with a more comfortable flame: in this context, 'amorous plesaunce' is a bathetic let-down, yet another false note.

Even the sound patterns of this poem create false notes. Edmund Reiss remarked the awkward, mooing effect of the poem's predominant rhyme sound, which is also that of his lady's name: 'the sound *ounde* that appears twelve times as the *b* rhyme in the three stanzas of the poem brings in a touch of the ludicrous that could hardly have been accidental. The sound is far too heavy – too mooing even – for the praise of a lady and the assertions of love that follow.'[11] To pronounce *-ounde* requires pursing the lips, as does the repetition of the *w* sounds accompanying the image of the pike 'walwed' (twice) and 'ywounde'. Read aloud, this repeated pursing of the speaker's lips – as for a kiss – might well produce a comic visual impression. In such a context, the reproach of the poem's refrain, 'Thogh ye to me ne do no daliaunce' may evoke the most physical senses of 'daliaunce', that is, kissing, petting or sexual intercourse, rather than suggesting the lighter, more flirtatious or coquettish senses we would expect in refined speech.

The 'signature' provided for this poem in the sole surviving exemplar (Bodleian Library, MS Rawlinson Poetry 163, fo. 114) is the ultimate irony: under the last line, the word 'tregentil' is written on the left, and a line broken by two slashes leads to the name 'chaucer' on the right. Chaucer's name is both connected with and separated from the epithet 'very gentle' (refined, noble) beneath this comic parody of a love complaint in which a fundamentally vulgar voice and mentality keep breaking through, making us laugh at the lover-persona's ineptitude. We may wonder if Deschamps' ballad refrain punning on Chaucer's name, with its ludicrous image of the stymied lover, one shoe off, one shoe on ('Que j'ay un pié deschaux, l'autre chaucié') was written in appreciative response to Chaucer's comic, self-mocking image of himself in 'To Rosemounde'.

The Envoy of the Clerk's Tale (ClT 1177–1212)

Again in the Envoy following the Clerk's Tale from his collection of *Canterbury Tales*, Chaucer adapts goliardic comic devices to vernacular literature; he makes us laugh at the unexpected incongruity of his sudden inversion of an established or conventional hierarchy, and he plays bilingually with the sounds of words, especially rhyme words, to evoke connotations that clash ludicrously. Although these six strophes have a more virtuoso rhyme pattern than the tale and are labelled 'Lenvoy de Chaucer' in many manuscripts, including Hengwrt and Ellesmere, most Chaucer scholars understand them as spoken by the character of the Clerk in ironic, tongue-in-cheek conclusion to his tale. Indeed, the Clerk introduces these strophes by suddenly assuming the sort of youthful ('lusty . . . fressh and grene') festive voice characteristic of goliardic play. Out of love for the Wife of Bath and women like her, whom he facetiously beseeches God to maintain 'on top' ('in heigh maistrie'), he promises to recite a little poem ('seyn . . . a song') to entertain his audience and put an end to seriousness.

Whereas the Clerk's Tale offers an example of wifely perfection through the figure of the patient and obedient Grisilde, who suffers uncomplainingly through all of her husband's cruel tests, the Envoy bluntly inverts the message of the tale by urging wives to resist and overcome their husbands in the battle of the sexes. In its ironic inversion of the message of the preceding narrative, this Envoy recollects festive clerical games involving inversion of roles; as John Ganim has pointed out, it 'reveals a side of the Clerk that he has suppressed in his tale, a side traditional for his class and his profession . . . like the songs of the Goliard poets and the pranks of the Feast of Fools, [it] displays the carnival anarchy of university celebrations'.[12]

The Clerk's sudden reversal also evokes the blatantly ironic explicit morals of certain French fabliaux, which suddenly and incongruously invert the implicit message of the story (which we might summarize as a warning against women's wiles and their treachery) in order to urge greater trust in and compliance with women. For example, the fabliau of *Le Chevalier à la robe vermeille* (The knight with the scarlet mantle), a tale of a wife who outwits and cuckolds her husband, ends by urging husbands not to believe their eyes, but rather what their wives tell them:

> Cest dit as mariez pramet
> Que de folie s'entremet
> Qui croit ce que de ses ieus voie,
> Mes cil qui tient la droite voie
> Doit bien croirre sanz contredit
> Tout ce que sa fame li dit!
> (Noomen and van den Boogaard
> 1983–98: ii, 308, 312–17)

This story assures married men that it is folly to believe what one sees with one's eyes; whoever sticks to the right path must believe completely and without contradiction everything his wife tells him.

Likewise, we are surprised and amused by the incongruous moral Gautier le Leu draws for husbands at the end of his story of *The Widow*, which Chaucer probably used as a source for the character, the prologue and the tale of the Wife of Bath. Gautier recounts the newly widowed wife's excessive demonstrations of grief, rapidly followed by her insatiable search for a new husband, only to find herself united to a handsome younger man who grows tired of her sexual demands, insists on being paid and beats her up when she refuses the money; when she heals and they reconcile in bed, the former widow becomes a loving and solicitous wife. The implicit message of the story would seem to be the usual warning against the wiles of women, coupled with an example of how men can get the upper hand: by withholding sex and using physical violence. However, at the end of the story, Gautier inverts the implicit message to argue that the man who wants to live a pleasurable life must grant a great number of his lover's requests, however much it hurts him, and if she insults him, he had better ignore it and leave the scene rather than beating her with a log. In sum, sweet-tempered husbands have more pleasure than harsh-tempered ones who are always arguing and looking for a fight. Taking the side of wives with a knowing, ironic wink, Gautier caps his tale with advice that rivals the Wife of Bath's vision of wedded bliss:

> Gautiers Li Leus dist en la fin
> Que cil n'a mie le cuer fin
> Qui sa mollier destraint ne cosse,
> Ne qui li demande autre cosse
> Que ses bones voisines font.
> Je n'i vuel parler plus parfont:
> Feme fait bien que faire doit.
>   (Livingston 1951:
>   183, lines 585–91)

Gautier le Leu concludes by saying that the man who constrains or disputes with his wife is no true lover, nor should he expect anything more of her than what her good friends do. I don't want to go into it any further. Women do exactly what they ought to.

Gautier's audience – at least, the men in it – could probably be expected to take this moral with a guffaw. The sudden switch from ignoble language and sentiments to courteous ones is too incongruous to take seriously. During the course of the story, the widow's wiles and her sexual appetite are revealed and designated in demeaning terms – it is, for example, in this fabliau that 'Golias' refers to a gluttonous vagina – and the two spouses exchange vulgar insults and vulgar behaviour of all sorts. Their milieu and manners are anything but courtly. Gautier's concluding moral concerning the behaviour of the true lover, who always gives in to his lady's wishes, is ludicrously out of place in this fabliau context. His final sop to the women in his audience, if that is what it is, is an entirely ironic inversion, much like Chaucer's Clerk's Envoy addressed to wives. But whereas Gautier le Leu caps a fabliau battle of the sexes with a courteous moral, Chaucer's Clerk caps a courteous tale with a fabliau moral urging wives to dominate their husbands.

The Clerk's mock-epic exhortation of wives to battle, which begins with the second stanza, is laughable for its sudden juxtaposition of incompatible images. In only six lines we veer from overblown apostrophe addressing wives as noble and full of the highest wisdom to a grotesque, folkloric evocation of patient wives disappearing into the entrails of Chichevache ('Gaunt Cow', the Clerk's ruminant rendering of francophone oral tradition's starving monster with glowing eyes and 'gaunt face', the 'Chinceface', who devoured long-suffering wives):

> O noble wyves, ful of heigh prudence,
> Lat noon humylitee youre tonge naille,
> Ne lat no clerk have cause or diligence

> To write of yow a storie of swich mervaille
> As of Grisildis pacient and kynde,
> Lest Chichevache yow swelwe in hire entraille!
> (1183–8)

Again in the fourth stanza, the Clerk exhorts women through direct address, turning first to the strong ones, whom he calls 'archewyves' and urging them to defend themselves physically against any masculine offence. If we have conjured up an Amazonian image of these 'archewyves' in defensive posture, the Clerk quickly dissipates any dignity and renders the image grotesque by comparing their strength to that of a great camel: 'Ye archewyves, stondeth at defense, / Syn ye be strong as is a greet camaille; / Ne suffreth nat that men yow doon offense' (1195–7). For the francophones in his audience, there is a bilingual pun in the word 'camaille', which refers not only to the oriental beast of burden, but also to a piece of protective armor covering neck and breast (in English a *ventaille* and in French a *camail*).

The debasing bestial comparison is reinforced in the next lines addressed to 'slender' or frail wives, whom the Clerk exhorts to make up for their lack of physical stature by imitating the ferocity of an Indian tiger and the endless noise of a mill wheel: 'And sklendre wyves, fieble as in bataille, / Beth egre as is a tygre yond in Ynde: / Ay clappeth as a mille, I yow consaille' (1198–2000). A steady stream of verbal abuse is sure to get to any husband, no matter how well armoured, and even the frail wife can use jealousy to quell her spouse and make him behave like a frightened quail.

The final stanza elaborates on how a wife, be she pretty or ugly, may attract 'friends', either with her face and dress or with her generosity and lighthearted manner, and thereby provoke her husband's jealousy, leaving him to stew over his sorrows:

> If thou be fair, ther folk been in presence,
> Shewe thou thy visage and thyn apparaille;
> If thou be foul, be fre of thy dispence;
> To gete thee freendes ay do thy travaille;
> Be ay of chiere as light as leef on lynde,
> And lat hym care, and wepe, and wrynge, and waille!
> (1207–12)

One of the most clever comic devices in the Envoy is its bilingual wordplay, which adapts goliardic techniques to the vernacular. Instead of subverting a Latin sense with a crude, vernacular pun, Chaucer's Clerk subverts an English sense with a French one. Only the francophones in his audience or those familar with continental French would be likely to get the joke and appreciate the incongruity. On the one hand, the Clerk urges wives to greater belligerence against their husbands in the battle of the sexes; on the other hand, this exhortation is expressed through a veritable *tour de force* of eighteen rhyme sounds in *-aille* that suggest pain and distress by punning on familiar cries in French. *Ahi!* (or *ai!*) was – and still is – a cry expressing physical or mental pain; *aie!* (or *aye!*, *ahie!*, *ahaie!*) was a cry for help in its imperative verb form and it was also the noun meaning 'help'. In spite of the differences of orthography, these cries sound virtually the same as the rhyme *-aille* in its continental French pronunciation, with a palatalized *l*. There was even a loan word in English, borrowed from the French (*ahi!*) or the Latin (*ei!*), that sounded the same as *-aille*: this loan word was *ei!* (or *eighe!* or *eighie!* or *eighi!*), an exclamation of surprise mixed with fear or pain. Because of the punning sense of the many rhymes in *-aille*, it is as if the Clerk were at the same time urging wives on and mimicking their husbands' wailing. The plaintive undertone of the poem is emphasized by its last word and sound, descriptive of the suffering husbands: 'waille' (wail). It is as if the Clerk were exhorting the wives to battle with rhyme words ending in 'ouch!'. The contradiction between sound and sense serves to heighten the irony of this comic Envoy, in which the Clerk means just the opposite of what he says.

Chaucer was not the first to exploit the punning senses of *-aille* rhymes. Deschamps used them quite deliberately to reinforce the impression of misery in his *Double Lai de la fragilité humaine* (a free translation of Innocent III's treatise on the miseries of the human condition, which Chaucer also claimed to have translated); and he used them to suggest a cry of pain or a cry for help also in other poems, such as a 'begging' ballad wherein he prepared his request for a new coat by describing himself shivering in the cold to the repeated rhyme sound of *-aille* (*Œuvres*, ii, 270–1; iv, 314). It was Chaucer's genius to use the plaintive senses of this sound incongruously, to turn them to comic effect through the bilingual word play of the Clerk's Envoy.

The Miller's Tale (3687–739)

Chaucer's ballad 'To Rosemounde' is an innovative comic parody of love complaint, and the Envoy to the Clerk's Tale is a virtuoso use of sudden inversion and bilingual wordplay to comic effect; but most readers today would probably agree that Chaucer's consummate comic performance was given in the Miller's Tale through the 'vulgar' mask and voice of the Miller, which he described in detail in the General Prologue and in the prologue to the tale. The Miller's short, thick body and his facial features – broad red beard, wart garnished with red bristles on the tip of his nose, huge black nostrils, furnace-sized mouth – are incarnations of crudity and ugliness much like the Golias persona or the masks worn by the actors of antique farce. A few of these latter have been described by Margarete Bieber in terms that evoke the Miller's face (and draw upon the classical notion that ugliness and deformity are laughable):

> A terracotta statuette made in the factory of Vindex in Cologne, now in Bonn may be a Maccus, a stupid and gluttonous rustic . . . His enormous mask has a crooked face, a gigantic nose, a much too broad mouth with puckered corners, unsymmetrical

eyebrows and a wart on the forehead. The wart reappears on the fragment of a mask in Bonn . . . On a bronze head in the Metropolitan Museum of Art in New York warts are everywhere: on the crown of the pointed bare head, on the nose, and on both cheeks.[13]

In goliardic comedy, the narrative mask of foolishness or crudity – sometimes identified as Golias – does not preclude complex biblical parody or wordplay; likewise in Chaucer's Miller's Tale, which employs a range of comic devices beyond those we might expect of a real miller. In short, the comic mask (or persona) of rusticity or foolishness or drunken gluttony is a *licence* to take various sorts of liberties with authoritative texts, courteous discourse, and other social conventions and rules of conduct.

As Chaucer scholars have noted, the Miller's Tale contains much clever parody of biblical texts. The passage from the end of the tale, which I will discuss to exemplify Chaucer's comic techniques, begins with cento-like parody. Our laughter arises from recognition of well-known biblical language or speeches in incongruous contexts. Here Absolon, the pretty-boy parish clerk with pretensions to courtesy, after much private primping, goes out into the night to woo Alisoun, the old carpenter's luscious young wife. Rather than couching his love complaint solely in the imagery of secular love poetry, Absolon adapts a few well-known figures from the biblical Song of Songs – honeycomb, cinnamon, turtle-dove – which was understood allegorically in the Middle Ages as an expression of the love between Christ and his church (or Christ and the Christian soul).[14] The lover's imitation of an authoritative scriptural model is inept and inappropriate at the least, and it is rendered even more comically incongruous if we imagine not only that Absolon uses Christ's words to the church to woo Alisoun, but also that the big-mouthed, warty-nosed Miller repeats or mimics Absolon's wooing words. Goliardic comedy often involved multiple layers of impersonation: on festive occasions, a lowly cleric might assume a vulgar or foolish persona in order to play a hierarchical superior, and the role of bishop was superimposed on that of Golias.

Alisoun's crude response to Absolon's solicitation – 'Go fro the wyndow, Jakke fool . . . / Go forth thy wey, or I wol caste a ston' (3708–10) – is another comic misuse of biblical citation: in this case, Christ's defence of the woman taken in adultery by limiting stone-throwing (the conventional punishment for adulterous wives) to those who had never committed sin themselves (John 8: 7). That the adulterous Alisoun, still in bed with her lover Nicholas, would defend herself by 'casting the first stone' (at Absolon) is a ludicrous parody of Christ's message. The opportunity for a joke, not narrative realism, occasions this parodic threat. As scholars have remarked, it is highly unlikely that Alisoun would have a pile of stones to hand beside her bed, and to 'cast a stone' in her situation would be quite an exploit:

> The fact remains that it is dark. If Alisoun is used to walking toward her window, she is probably not used to throwing stones through it. If Alisoun knows where her window is, she still cannot see Absolon to aim at his head. Alisoun, then, threatens to cast an

unavailable missile at an invisible object. This itself renders the threat amusingly improbable, but it hardly competes with Alisoun's likely posture and activity as cause of the threat's ridiculousness. It is not so easy to cast a stone, let alone aim a stone accurately, when one is making love, presumably horizontally, underneath, and with even minimal zeal.[15]

The comic action immediately following this has to do with Alisoun's tricky substitution of her bottom for her face as an object for Absolon to kiss. The grotesque, bearded 'face down below' (her 'Golias', according to the euphemism in the fabliau of *The Widow*) is what Alisoun reveals to the unwitting Absolon, who very typically closes his eyes when he puckers:

> This Absolon gan wype his mouth ful drie.
> Derk was the nyght as pich, or as the cole,
> And at the wyndow out she putte hir hole,
> And Absolon, hym fil no bet ne wers,
> But with his mouth he kiste hir naked ers
> Ful savourly, er he were war of this.
> Abak he stirte, and thoughte it was amys,
> For wel he wiste a womman hath no berd.
> He felt a thyng al rough and long yherd,
> And seyde, 'Fy! allas! what have I do?'
> 'Tehee!' quod she, and clapte the wyndow to.
>   (3730–9)

Absolon's cry of regret, 'Allas . . . allas, I ne hadde ybleynt!' (3753) carries a double sense in the past participle of the verb *blenchen*: 'Alas, that I did not swerve aside!' and 'Alas, that I did not open my eyes!' The naïve Absolon is the object of Alisoun's, and the narrator's, derision here because of the way he has behaved up to this point: he has been excessively squeamish of bodily odours and functions (3337–8, 3690–3). The sudden juxtaposition of Alisoun's 'hole' (no cruder term could be used) to Absolon's perfumed breath and newly wiped lips is hilariously incongruous. The humour of the lines in which Absolon, in a frenzy of wiping, applies a whole series of available materials to his lips – 'Who rubbeth now, who froteth now his lippes / With dust, with sond, with straw, with clooth, with chippes' (3747–8) – is downright scatalogical, for these would seem to be the sorts of materials used for wiping excrement off bottoms in the Middle Ages. By kissing Alisoun's bottom 'ful savourly', Absolon is forced to treat his own face as a dirty bottom.

In the series of comic physical inversions of this fabliau, bottoms replace faces again when Nicholas replays Alisoun's trick in order to get his own bottom kissed. From here on the action accelerates, each gesture inevitably provoking the next in a causal chain leading up to the tale's riotous conclusion: when Nicholas farts in Absolon's face, Absolon takes aim with a red-hot coulter, which burns Nicholas's bottom, which makes him cry out for water, which awakens and prompts the Miller (awaiting the second Flood in his tub in the rafters) to cut the cord and come crashing down, which prompts Nicholas and Alisoun to cry out for help from the neighbours, who come running to the scene to take part in and laugh at the dispute over what really happened – on one side, the husband, on the other, the wife and her lover – and ultimately to join in the general mockery of the cuckolded husband's folly. The ending of the Miller's Tale is a riot in the comic sense of that term, which has a long history. But Chaucer does not dramatize this comic dispute; he narrates it very briefly through the voice of the Miller, leaving us to imagine the scene, which is dominated by what remains of the gigantic male genital configuration (two round tubs and an oblong one hanging in the rafters) at which the people all gape and crane their necks.[16] Although Alisoun's husband has taken a fall that broke his arm, endured his own cuckolding and the mockery of the whole neighbourhood, although Nicholas has a badly burned bottom, although Absolon has desecrated lips, deflated pride and destroyed illusions, the Miller's Tale ends exuberantly in laughter, which gives it the sort of 'happy' ending that medieval comedy required.

See also AUTHORITY; CHRISTIAN IDEOLOGIES; GAMES; FRANCE; GENRE; LANGUAGE; MODES OF REPRESENTATION; NARRATIVE; TEXTS; TRANSLATION.

NOTES

1 Aristotle, *Poetics*, trans. Hamilton Fyfe (London: Loeb, 1932), 9.

2 *Lydgate's Troy Book I*, ed. Henry Bergen, Early English Text Society, extra series 97 (1906), 168–9.

3 Lee Patterson, 'What man artow? Authorial self-definition in *The Tale of Sir Thopas* and *The Tale of Melibee*', *Studies in the Age of Chaucer* 11 (1989), 120–2.

4 *The 'Parisiana Poetria' of John of Garland*, ed. and trans. Traugott Lawlor (New Haven: Yale University Press, 1974), 81.

5 Ibid.

6 Geoffrey of Vinsauf, *Documentum de modo et arte dictandi et versificandi*, trans. Roger Parr (Milwaukee: Marquette University Press, 1968), 92–3.

7 For these spellings, see *The Middle English Dictionary*, ed. Hans Kurath and Sherman Kuhn (Ann Arbor: University of Michigan Press, 1952–); Frédéric Godefroy, *Dictionnaire de l'ancienne langue française du IXe au XVe siècles* (1885; repr. Geneva: Slatkine, 1961); and Emil Levy, *Provenzalisches Supplement-Wörterbuch* (Leipzig: Reisland, 1894–1924; repr. Hildesheim: Olms, 1973).

8 Mikhail Bakhtin, *The Dialogic Imagination*, trans. M. Holquist (Austin: University of Texas Press, 1981), 75–6.

9 'Farai un vers, pos mi sonelh' ('I will make a poem, because I'm dozing'), in *Guglielmo IX, Poesie*, ed. Nicolò Pasero (Modena: Mucchi, 1973), 125–32; a complete English translation may be found in Frederick Goldin, *Lyrics of the Troubadours and Trouveres* (New York: Anchor, 1973), 27–33.

10 For examples, see Lilian Randall, *Images in the Margins of Gothic Manuscripts* (Berkeley: University of California Press, 1966), figs 12, 82, 149; Michael Camille, *Image on the Edge: The Margins of Medieval Art* (Cambridge, Mass.: Harvard University Press, 1992), esp. fig. 18, from the early fourteenth-century Bardolf–Vaux Psalter (London, MS Lambeth Palace 233) showing in the lower margin a naked King David with a tamed lion at his feet and, on the left, mixed creatures with grotesque, bearded male heads (Golias masks?) in place of stomach and genitals.

11 Edmund Reiss, 'Dusting off the cobwebs: a look at Chaucer's lyrics', *Chaucer Review* 1 (1966–7), 63.

12 John Ganim, 'Carnival voices and the Envoy to the Clerk's Tale', *Chaucer Review* 22 (1987–8), 121.

13 Margarete Bieber, *The History of the Greek and Roman Theater* (Princeton: Princeton University Press, 1961), 248, figs 818–20.

14 R. E. Kaske, 'The *Canticum Canticorum* in the Miller's Tale', *Studies in Philology* 59 (1962), 479–500.

15 Macklin Smith, 'Or I wol caste a ston', *Studies in the Age of Chaucer* 8 (1986), 20–1.

16 Laura Kendrick, *Chaucerian Play: Comedy and Control in the* Canterbury Tales (Berkeley, Los Angeles and London: University of California Press, 1988), 6.

REFERENCES AND FURTHER READING

Bakhtin, Mikhail (1984) *Rabelais and His World*, trans. Hélène Iswolsky (Bloomington, Ind.: University of Indiana Press). On festive inversion and carnival in the late Middle Ages and the Renaissance.

Bate, Keith, trans. (1976) *Three Latin Comedies* (Toronto: University of Toronto Press). English versions of *Geta*, *Babio* and *Pamphilus*.

Bayless, Martha (1996) *Parody in the Middle Ages: The Latin Tradition* (Ann Arbor: University of Michigan Press). Good supplement to Lehmann (1963), offering critical analysis followed by Latin texts with English translations.

Bec, Pierre (1984) *Burlesque et obscénité chez les troubadours: le contre-texte au moyen âge* (Paris: Stock). Anthology of comic verse in medieval Occitan with modern French translations.

Chambers, E. K. (1903) *The Medieval Stage*, i (Oxford: Oxford University Press). Classic account in English of the Feast of Fools and of the Boy Bishop.

Cohen, Gustave, ed. and trans. (1931) *La 'Comédie' latine en France au XIIe siècle*, 2 vols (Paris: Les Belles-Lettres). Editions of Latin comedies, some by Englishmen, with facing French translations.

Deschamps, Eustache (1878–1903) *Œuvres complètes*, ed. A. H. E. Marquis de Queux de St-Hilaire and Gaston Raynaud, 11 vols (Paris: Firmin Didot). Critical edition of the complete works.

Dronke, Peter (1973) 'The rise of the medieval fabliau: Latin and vernacular evidence', *Romanische Forschungen* 85, 275–97. Contextualizes the fabliaux.

Faral, Edmond (1910) *Les Jongleurs en France au moyen âge* (Paris: Champion). Documentation on medieval entertainers.

Furrow, Melissa (1985) *Ten Fifteenth-century Comic Poems* (New York: Garland). Editions of comic writing in English after Chaucer.

Jost, Jean (1994) *Chaucer's Humor: Critical Essays* (New York: Garland). Essential collection of essays by contemporary scholars on Chaucer's comic writing, including a survey of its critical reception from the fifteenth century to the twentieth and an annotated bibliography of books and articles on the subject.

Kelly, Henry Ansgar (1989) *Tragedy and Comedy from Dante to Pseudo-Dante* (Berkeley: University of California Press). On medieval theories of comedy.

Kendrick, Laura (1983) 'Medieval satire', in *European Writers: The Middle Ages and the Renaissance*, ed. W. T. H. Jackson, 2 vols (New York: Scribners), i, 337–75. On medieval satire as a critical, polemical genre.

Lehmann, Paul (1963) *Die Parodie im Mittelalter*, 2nd edn (Stuttgart: Hiersemann). Includes editions of twenty-four medieval Latin parodies.

Livingston, Charles H. (1951) *Le Jongleur Gautier le Leu* (Cambridge, Mass.: Harvard University Press). Critical edition of Gautier le Leu's works including *The Widow*, excluded from Noomen and van den Boogaard (1983–98).

Noomen, Willem and van den Boogaard, Nico (1983–98) *Nouveau Recueil complet des fabliaux*, 10 vols (Assen: van Gorcum). New comprehensive anthology of the fabliaux, giving critical editions.

Rigg, A. G. (1977) 'Golias and other pseudonyms', *Studi medievali*, 3rd series 18, 65–109. Study of manuscript rubrications and ascriptions of verses to Golias.

Smithers, G. V. and Bennett, J. A. W., eds (1968) *Early Middle English Verse and Prose* (Oxford: Clarendon). Editions of comic writing in English before Chaucer, including *Dame Sirith* and the *Interludium de clerico et puella*.

7

Contemporary English Writers

James Simpson

The coronation of Richard II on 16 July 1377 experienced an odd glitch. At the end of the coronation mass, a heavily armed and mounted knight named Sir John Dymmok approached the doors of Westminster Abbey and claimed the right to defend the king's jurisdiction then and there, should anyone presume to challenge it.[1] As he approached the doors of the abbey, however, the king's marshal and constable moved towards the knight and told him that he had come at the wrong time: he was to postpone his arrival until the king's coronation feast, at which point Dymmok retired.[2] Is this an account of a carefully staged piece of royal theatre, or is it, on the contrary, an account of bungling the most carefully managed ritual of monarchy?

The monastic chronicler Thomas Walsingham, who recounts this event as an eyewitness, makes no comment on the moment of confusion, but his mini-narrative at least suggests that this is an account of bungled ritual; Dymmok was, Walsingham relates, himself challenged for the role of making the royal challenge by another knight, and so, it is implied, asserted his rights to the job in spectacular fashion. I am myself convinced that Dymmok's intervention was unscripted. It was an event of the kind that recurred throughout the reign of Richard II until his deposition in 1399: the perpetual youth of the king, that is, never managed successfully to rise above and control noble rivalries of which he was himself, finally, the victim. The fragility of Richard's power was exposed even in the very rituals designed to depict his claiming it. If, however, Dymmok did indeed act without authority, we should at least pause to recognize that his intervention is not entirely out of keeping with demonstrably scripted challenges to the king's authority, their apparently transgressive nature in fact an elaborate and knowing confirmation of the new status quo. For it was the case that a fully armed and mounted knight did ride into the coronation feast of late medieval kings;[3] and the mounted knight challenged anyone to a duel who refused to acknowledge the jurisdiction of the new monarch. Needless to say, no counter-challenge was made, since this is a theatrical exposure of vulnerability designed to neutralize it: the challenge concedes that opposition to the new king is at least possible, before the failure of anyone to take the challenge up anaesthetizes that very thought.

In this chapter I argue that Ricardian works of visual and literary art hover between the two models of theatrical experience so far considered, the theatrical bungle and the scripted theatrical challenge to royal authority. Many of the works of Chaucer's contemporaries raise the spectre of opposition before they seek to close it down. With varying emphases, however, the act of closing the danger down cannot help but expose the real possibilities that those dangers will escape royal management. The most consistent motif in the works to be considered is royal youthfulness, and the most frequent mode by which Richard's weakness is exposed is theatrical: no less than Chaucer himself, many of his contemporaries represent royally staged theatrical events within their poems that serve to admonish the royal child. Many of these texts, that is, are a form of children's theatre, constantly oscillating, as children's theatre does, between threat and comfort.

The Wilton Diptych

However much the Wilton Diptych tries not to illustrate this point, it cannot help but do so (figure 7.1). The very means at its disposal to assert the king's power also expose his vulnerability. The work was produced, by the latest scholarly account, in 1395–6, and formed part of the marriage arrangements between Richard II and Princess Isabelle of France.[4] This argument is principally reliant on the punning symbolism etched in, and overlaid on, Richard's gown. The splendid white hart badge worn by Richard both on and in his gown puns on his own name (*riche-hart*), while the broom cods etched in his gown by *sgraffito* and encircling his neck evoke the livery badge of Charles VI of France, as well as offering a punning reference to the lineage of both kings (*plant à gênet*).[5] The structure of the painting is divided between the secular and heavenly realms, and ostensibly has the secular deferring to the heavenly: Richard II has his patrons John the Baptist, King Edward the Confessor and King Edmund of East Anglia recommend him to the court of heaven; because Richard is on his knees in obeisance to a heavenly court, the eye must travel from left to right, rising from the earthly to the heavenly as it docs so. Even as the eye moves in this way, however, it is returned to Richard in a variety of ways. Most obviously the subtle play and pattern of hands across the whole image point not to the rulers of heaven but rather to the current ruler of England: while the hands of the patrons sustain Richard's own gesture of supplication, the answering manual gestures of both angels and Christ-child return the gaze back to its point of origin in Richard. Less overtly but much more ambitiously, the painter has subtly colonized the court of heaven, since the angels are wearing the king's own livery badge, the white hart. The subordination of heaven to England is implicit in the fact that the king's badge is elaborately decorated with pearls, while those of the angels are undecorated. This colonization of heaven is also probably implicit in the flag, which is most likely the

Figure 7.1   The Wilton Diptych (1395–6). London, National Gallery. [© National Gallery, London.]

flag of St George, the patron saint of England. That heaven is indeed carrying the flag for England is supported by the minuscule image, fully perceptible only under magnification, that is found on the very tip of the flagpole: a small island.

Under the cover of one earthly king offering supplicatory deference to a heavenly king, then, the diptych makes the most astonishing claims on heaven itself. More discreetly than the pantocratic gaze of the full-scale portrait of Richard now in Westminster Abbey,[6] the diptych nevertheless makes its own extraordinary claims for Richard's power to colonize even heaven. All that is other to Richard's jurisdiction, and to which he may appear subject, is brought within it, whether it be the Anglo-Saxon history represented by the patron kings, or the court of heaven. This hieratic royal theatre of sorts would seek to domesticate all that is different and other to Richard's control.

Even as it does so, however, it cannot help deploying the very signs of Richard's consistent weakness as king, in particular both his youth and the livery badges worn by the angels. Richard was in his eleventh year when he became king in 1377, possessing a youthfulness from whose vulnerability he never escaped. The *Record and Process* of his deposition in 1399, for example, consistently describes Richard as an impetuous and wilful child.[7] The sermon delivered at the deposition meeting concluded thus: 'When therefore a boy rules, will alone rules, and reason is in exile'.[8] Although the English rising of 1381 was not, in its explicit ideology at least, directed against the king, the Appellant challenge of 1387 certainly was. This challenge resulted in a very brief civil war in which Richard lost, and after which he was subjected to the rule of the Appellant lords until he assumed personal rule in 1389. The next eight years, until 1397 when Richard decided to take his revenge, were the most peaceful of his reign. It was during this period that the diptych was painted. So far from disguising his youth, however, Richard openly parades it: he is painted without a beard (he would have been thirty in 1396), and it has even been argued that the eleven angels are numbered so as to record Richard's age when he became king.[9]

Richard exaggerates his youthfulness, then, in such a way as to deny it as a source of vulnerability. The same is true of the deployment of badges, since these very signs were a hotly contested issue through parliaments from 1377 (Given-Wilson 1986: 236–45). Distributing livery badges was effectively a way of raising a private army, and the Commons of Parliament had complained bitterly against their use in both 1384, when the attack was directed to lords of the shires, and 1388, when the attack was directed to the King himself. In the second parliament of 1388, the Cambridge Parliament, the Commons requested that 'all liveries called badges [*signes*], as well of our lord the king as of other lords . . . shall be abolished' (Given-Wilson 1986: 238); only in 1390 was an ordinance issued that directed that no one below the rank of banneret be allowed to distribute badges, and confirmed the agreement of 1388 that no one below the rank of esquire should wear one. It was the king, however, who offended most flagrantly against these terms, in precisely the period of the Wilton Diptych: a petition of 1397 accused the king of distributing the badge of the white hart illicitly. One of the first statutes of Henry IV directed that the king alone shall distribute badges.[10] The power to distribute signs of client status, then, was very much in the interests both of the king and of his most powerful aristocratic rivals; in attempting to preserve his own capacity to raise private armies, Richard must equally allow the same capacity to those rivals. In the end it was the army of his cousin Henry Bolingbroke that toppled Richard in 1399. If the badges of the diptych enlist the distant court of heaven within Richard's livery, those same badges were incapable of resisting a much closer rival force in 1399.

The topic of this chapter is Chaucer's contemporaries, more specifically Chaucer's 'writerly' contemporaries. Even restricting the term further to those writing in the vernacular, contemporary with Chaucer's own literary career (*c.*1365–1400), those contemporaries comprise a very wide range of writers including, for example, John Trevisa, Julian of Norwich, Walter Hilton, the author of the *Cloud of Unknowing*, the translators of the Wycliffite Bible, Thomas Usk, John Clanvowe, possibly the writers of the alliterative works *The Destruction of Troy* and *St Erkenwald* (both of whose dating is uncertain), and many other anonymous authors, including those of the enigmatic texts persuasively attributed to activists of the English rising (Pearsall 1999). This is, clearly, an impossibly wide topic, and in the space remaining I choose to concentrate on a set of works that, like the Wilton Diptych, apparently espouse yet expose the ideological claims of Ricardian kingship. Each of these works sets royal youth into high relief, and each represents the public, often theatrical performance of royal control. These are, respectively, the set of texts attributed to William Langland and known as *Piers Plowman* (*c*.late 1360s to 1388); John Gower's *Confessio Amantis* (first published 1390, and twice modified by 1392–3); and *Sir Gawain and the Green Knight*, plausibly dated to the last decade of the fourteenth century. Each of these works is centrally concerned with management of the youthful will, sometimes explicitly a royal youthful will, and each stages the management of the will in public, often theatrical forms. I conclude by relating management of the boyish royal will back to some theatrical moments in Chaucer's poetry, and in particular to the Knight's Tale (first composed *c*.1386) and the *Legend of Good Women* (*c*.1386–8, revised *c*.1394).

William Langland, *Piers Plowman*

The prologue to the B-Text of *Piers Plowman* takes us directly back to the very coronation with which I began. After the narrator has witnessed various orders of society working or not working on the 'fair feeld ful of folk', the mode changes altogether as a king enters: 'Thanne kam there a Kyng: Knyghthod hym ladde' (112).[11] Whereas all the other orders of society have been susceptible to narratorial critique, presented as they are within an estates satire, the king is presented as an ideal, outside the scope of satire; he appears in procession, a form designed to invite an adoring gaze rather than critical detachment. The order of procession itself merges, indeed, with a scene of primal political constitution, as the scene unfolds:

> Thanne kam ther a Kyng: Knyghthod hym ladde;
> Might of the communes made hym to regne.
> And thanne cam Kynde Wit and clerkes he made,
> For to counseillen the Kyng and the Commune save.
> The Kyng and Knyghthod and Clergie bothe
> Casten that the Commune sholde hem communes fynde.
> The Commune contreved of Kynde Wit craftes,
> And for profit of al the peple plowmen ordeyned
> To tilie and to travaille as trewe lif asketh.
> The Kyng and the Commune and Kynde Wit the thridde
> Shopen lawe and leaute – ech lif to knowe his owene.
>   (113–22)

This founding moment of a political order pre-exists yet forestalls internal dissension. Justice (the very definition of which is encapsulated in the last half of line 122) is a matter of frictionless consent between sections of the governing class, whose decisions flow effortlessly downward in a model of harmonious acceptance. The contentious issues of labour relations in particular, which will quickly surface both within the poem and in the historical arena of Richard's England, are here presented as unproblematic matters of obedient consent.

Even in the regnal scene of the Prologue itself, however, discursive fractures become quickly apparent, and they do so in response to the youth of the represented king. Five separate sequences follow this enactment of foundational social order around the person of the king: a 'lunatik' prays for just rulership (123–7); an angel delivers a speech in Latin in which the king is exhorted to dispense justice with '*pietas*'; a 'goliard' critiques the angel by insisting on the king's single-minded pursuit of justice (139–42); the 'commune' blindly cries absolute obedience to the will of the king (143–5); and finally a crowd of rats and mice run on to debate the pros and cons of hanging a bell around the cat's neck so as to warn them of his dangerous approach. These scenes plausibly have connections with the coronation of Richard II and the issues raised by that coronation. The most explicit connection is the sceptical mouse's point that 'the court is ful elenge [miserable]' where the cat is a kitten, supported by citation from Scripture: 'Ve terre ubi puer est rex!' [Woe to the land whose king is a boy!] (194–6). If that anchors the scene, as it must, in the founding moments of the reign of the boy-king Richard II, the processional scene also evokes aspects of Richard's coronation, the first recorded royal triumphal entry in England. The king, for example, is here 'led' by knighthood: in the procession of Richard II through London to Westminster the day before his coronation he was led by the Duke of Lancaster (his uncle and guardian) along with other knights, in order to make a clear way for the young king;[12] as he made his way through Cheapside a theatrical and golden angel sat atop a fabricated castle, and offered a golden crown to the king as he passed. On the day of the coronation the Archbishop of Canterbury made a sermon 'concerning the matter of the realm and of rulership to the people, defining how the king should conduct himself to the people, and how the people should obey the king', after which the king promised to dispense justice and mercy in such a way as to elicit God's own mercy towards him. The people, invited to proclaim their acceptance of the king, cried with 'altissimo clamore' that they did indeed wish to submit to the rule of the new king.[13] Once Richard II had been invested with his regnal insignia, the coronation arrived at the point where Dymmok, as we have seen, interrupted with his ill-timed challenge.

Even if Langland clearly evokes Richard's coronation,[14] he renders that state event more theatrical and much less philosophically coherent. Whereas the voices that dominated the actual coronation of the king were those at the centre of power, and especially that of the archbishop, in Langland's scene these voices are more widely dispersed and marginal. Whereas a coronation pretends to 'speak' with one voice in an intensely solemn, quasi-divine manner, Langland's voices are drawn from the margins, and interact in the manner of clerical drama. The angel, no less than the 'lunatic' and the 'goliard' poet, are representationally drawn from the broadly theatrical modes associated with royalty: angels were regularly used in royal entries, and kings were accompanied by performing 'fool sages'. No authorized human voice expresses the ideology of kingship here, and the very language of that ideology is uncertain: the angel and the goliard both speak in learned Latin. The 'commune' themselves use Latin to express their absolute fidelity, not apparently understanding the real pressure of the preceding debate. Whereas a coronation seeks to efface division and speak with the single voice of the whole nation, Langland's scene rather suggests an ideological vacuum in which no one speaks but those whose authority derives from their very marginality: a lunatic, an angel and a clerical goliard. If the narrator unhesitatingly uses the first person plural possessive adjective earlier in the prologue – 'Oure Lord' (26), 'oure sight' (32) – here there can be no single or communal perspective from which the issues of kingship are expressed.

The sequence of the rats and mice that follows accounts for this anxiety, in both its mode and its content. The outspoken Bishop Brinton of Rochester had used the fable of the rats and mice in a sermon of 1376, in which he encouraged the 'belling of the cat' in the senescence of Edward III.[15] Langland's rats and mice are faced with a more complex problem, since the cat is not the king; here there is both cat and kitten, where the cat must refer to John of Gaunt, the king's guardian. With the apparent approval of Langland's narrator, the rodents here finally decide not to bell the cat: in the words of the finally persuasive mouse, 'shal nevere the cat ne the kiton by my counseil be greved' (203). This mouse apparently promotes a posture of complete submission to the capricious and now divided royal wills: he shall 'suffren as hymself wolde so doon as hym liketh – / Coupled and uncoupled to cacche what thei mowe' (206–7).

If this view favouring quiescence prevails, however, the narrative and its mode cannot help exposing a critique of royal wilfulness, and thereby offering a lesson to the young king. Fables are traditionally the form for instructing children; simultaneously, under cover of the puerile target audience, they are the transmitters of complex and otherwise unspeakable political truths. They express the realities of high political theory as experienced from the ground up, in the cat-eat-mouse world of lived political experience. Looked at from a distance, this fable does not so much express political quiescence, even if it covers its author by appearing so to do; its larger force is, rather, a sceptical recognition that kings (and their guardians) brutally consume their subjects. The very motive for the debate in the first place is that the rats and mice live in a state of constant fear:

> For a cat of a court cam whan hym liked
> And overleep hem lightliche and laughte hem at his wille,
> And pleide with hem perillousli and possed hem aboute.
>
> (149–51)

The sage mouse's argument against controlling the wilful cat is in no way couched in the terms of theoretical obedience to kings; it is, rather, born of a reflection on the inevitable brutalities of power. Were the rodents to rid themselves of the cat, they would have the even more capricious kitten in his place; the rodents themselves, the mouse ruefully points out, are not without their own rapacious will (185–201).

The argument that carries the day does so not as an expression of unthinking joy and fidelity at the coronation of a new king; on the contrary, while the very mode of fable serves to promise obedience of sorts, it does so by pointing out to the new king his inevitable rapacity. The first entrance of the king promises justice to all – 'ech lif to knowe his owene' (122); the last words of the resigned mouse replay that phrase with a sardonic twist: 'Forthi ech a wis wight I warne – wite [know/guard] wel his owene!' (208). Just as new kings were greeted by theatrical masques sketching the relations of royal power, so too does Langland insert a small and improvised parliamentary sketch into the coronation process, designed to instruct the new king. And, just as fables are most obviously designed for children, Langland's fabular theatre implicitly urges the young king not to exercise his inevitable rapacity against the innocent. Unlike the sealed, ideologically smooth surface of coronation ritual, this theatre of cruelty expresses much more than it can say. Langland's conclusion points to its dangerous interpretative enigmas, not the kind of thing one says at a coronation: 'What this metels [dreme] bymeneth, ye men that ben murye, / Devyne ye, for I ne dar, by deere God in hevene!' (209–10). The poet is in the same position as the rodents, who themselves protest the cat's ferocity by saying that 'if we grucche [complain] of his gamen he wol greven us alle' (153).

John Gower, *Confessio Amantis*

In the 1370s and 1380s both Chaucer and Langland lived in London. While they might have shared some readership (Kerby-Fulton and Justice 1998), and while Chaucer's General Prologue to the *Canterbury Tales* might be indebted to Langland's own Prologue,[16] Chaucer and Langland are on different sides of a contentious divide in London society. Chaucer's familial and professional affiliations are with the merchant oligarchy and the court (Strohm 1989: ch. 3), whereas Langland was in my view a supporter of the artisanal guilds in their battle against the merchant oligarchy's domination of London city politics in the late 1370s and early 1380s (Simpson 1993); he was also avidly read by the ideologues of the English rising of 1381, in whose writings Piers Plowman lives as a figure detached from Langland's poem.[17]

Chaucer's social affiliations lie with a bureaucratic class associated with the court, and this is broadly the society in which Gower represents himself as moving. Indeed, Chaucer and Gower refer explicitly and warmly to each other in their poetry.[18] John Gower (*c.*1330–1408) was a landowner in Kent, possibly a lawyer by training.[19] It might be that his financial resources allowed him a certain detachment from dependency on court and city patronage, unlike Chaucer and, at a lower level, also unlike the bureaucrat and writer Thomas Usk, executed in 1388 after having switched sides (Strohm 1990). From about 1377 Gower seems to have lived at St Mary Overeys in Southwark, which itself marks a slight geographical detachment from the city and court, since Southwark is outside the City of London proper. Certainly Gower represents himself in a detached relation with royal patronage: the first recension of the

Confessio Amantis begins, for example, with a casual meeting between himself and Richard II, both boating on the Thames, crossing each other's paths by chance; Richard commands Gower to write 'som newe thing', 'that he himself it mighte loke / After the forme of my [i.e. Gower's] writynge' (Prologue, *52–3). This detachment is also visible in the fact that the very dedication to Richard, such as it is, along with all declarations of fidelity to the king, were cut from the third recension of 1393.

Nevertheless, to whatever degree Gower appears to be less dependent on royal patronage than Chaucer for professional advancement, both poets approach politics and the problems of a young, impetuous king obliquely. Whereas at the very beginning of the reign in 1377 Langland represents the young king directly in the frame at least of an estates satire, by the later 1380s the dominant poetic mode is no longer satire but what may be called elegy. Satire in alliterative poetry reappears very soon after Richard's deposition in 1399, in *Richard the Redeless*, a poem ostensibly addressed to Richard, but clearly written after the deposition and capitalizing on the period of transition to instruct the new king Henry IV.[20] From the mid-1380s, however, when political relations with Richard II became dangerous both for dependants and enemies, politics is broached in poetry obliquely through Ovidian elegy, most sharply in the closely related *Confessio Amantis* and *Legend of Good Women*.[21] Once again, however, the key issues remain the rulership of impetuous, wilful youth, figured here as Cupid, the boy-prince who tyrannizes the heart. Both Gower's *Confessio* and Chaucer's *Legend* confront the problems of the royal Cupid's apparent monopoly on desire, to the punishing discipline of which subjects must submit.

This is too large a topic to pursue across the eight books and 33,446 lines of the *Confessio*; I restrict myself here to some examples of tyrannical young kings, notably Tarquin's son Aruns and Alexander. These are all framed, however, by the domination of almost the whole text by the young king Cupid, with whose iron rule I begin. The *Confessio* traces a narrative of psychic submission to and recovery from desire. In falling victim to Cupid's wounding and punishing arrow (I, 140–7), the narrator loses his proper identity and becomes Amans, an enactment of impersonal desire itself. Only through the long psychic rehabilitation produced by reflecting on the finally therapeutic narratives of Genius, Priest of Venus, can Amans reintegrate with the larger psyche of which he is a part and regain the proper identity of 'John Gower' (VIII, 2321). While Amans himself is a nugatory and often pathetic target for the encyclopaedic therapy of Genius, his symptoms are often dignified with real seriousness by being magnified: inescapable parallels are drawn between Amans and the wilful, impetuous, youthful rulers of world history, whose sexual and territorial rapacity exposes the menace of pathological submission to desire.

Most obviously, resonances are established between the pathetic Amans and the not remotely pathetic rapist Aruns. In Book VI Amans confesses to the 'sin' of what Genius calls 'love delicacy', an obsessive psychological gluttony that cannot help but 'feed' on the image of the object of desire (617–950). This might seem a purely personal psychopathology, but its consequences are magnified and politicized in the following book, when the young tyrant Aruns, son of Tarquin, psychologically 'feeds' in exactly the same way on the image of Lucrece before he rapes her. In his mind he 'pourtraieth hire ymage',

> And thus this tirannysshe knyght
> Was soupled, bot noght half aright,   [influenced]
> For he non other hiede tok,
> Bot that he myghte be som crok,
> Althogh it were ayein hire wille,
> The lustes of his fleissh fulfille.
> (VII, 4889–94)

Aruns's sexual rapacity has immediate political consequences, and is itself paralleled with territorial rapacity. Aruns comes to Lucrece after having violently deceived and defeated the Gabiens. And the consequence of his rape is, of course, the expulsion of the Roman kings. Publication of Lucrece's suicide provokes popular rebellion and memories of the long tyranny of the Tarquins: the 'commun clamour' initiates the Republic by expelling the sexually and territorially rapacious king: 'Awey, awey the tirannie / Of leccherie and covoitise' (VII, 5118–19). The republican impulses of the Lucrece narrative can be disguised only by truncating the story, as Chaucer does under orders from Cupid in the *Legend of Good Women*.[22] Gower, though, makes no effort to abbreviate or disguise the expulsion of kings. His placing of the narrative within Book VII, indeed, makes the very point of the narrative a political one, since the cursus of education in that book is a summary of 'Aristotle's' teaching of the young Alexander in his training for kingship. Just as the aged Aristotle teaches Alexander, and Genius teaches Amans, so too does the aged Gower implicitly admonish the young Richard II in this narrative of 'tyrannish' youth and its disastrous political consequences. The narrative is effectively prophetic, since once Richard II was deposed, charges of tyranny were readily made against him.[23]

The Lucrece narrative is designed in the first place, then, to teach the young king Alexander. The placing of Aristotle's teaching in Book VII itself expresses a scepticism, however, about the possibility of giving political instruction to the young and rapacious prince. For by the time the reader reaches Book VII, she has already heard other stories about how Alexander behaved (badly) *after* his education by Aristotle. In Book III, for example, we read the narrative of Diogenes and Alexander. If the Aristotelian tradition promises a successful marriage of philosophy and politics, Diogenes' mode of life would deny that altogether. He lives a solitary life in a barrel, the better to observe the heavens. Ordered by Alexander to appear before him, Diogenes refuses, and insults the king by calling him the servant of his servant. The conundrum is unravelled as Diogenes explains that his reason has always kept will 'soubgit':

> And thus be weie of covenant
> Will is my man and my servant,
> And evere hath ben and evere schal.

> And thi will is thi principal,
> And hath the lordschipe of thi witt,
> So that thou cowthest nevere yit
> Take o dai of reste of thi labour.
>   (III, 1279–85)

Because Diogenes does not identify his desire with that of the king, he is capable of a detached *otium*, or leisure, and also possessed of a 'proper' identity, naming himself as 'Diogenes' (III, 1299); all he really wants is Alexander to get out of the way of the sun, in order that he may continue his scientific observation. Later in the same book Alexander is confronted with much the same charge of being a servant to his will by a captured pirate. Whereas the narrative is premised on the stark differences between the world conqueror and the notorious pirate, it is resolved by the pirate's persuasive assertion of identity between the two men: the will of both is set on rapine, but because Alexander has been more successful he is called emperor. Alexander immediately sees the force of the argument, and takes the pirate into his service (III, 2363–437); in both cases 'will governeth the corage' (2429).

    These narratives are presented as occurring *after* the first-class education in practical philosophy that Alexander has received from Aristotle. Their depressing recognition of the uselessness of that education is also underscored by the immediate prelude to the *speculum principis* of Book VII, which relates Alexander's murder of his first tutor, Nectanabus. This first tutor had in fact deceived Olympias, wife of Philip of Macedon, so as to rape her. Later he becomes tutor to Alexander – officially Philip's son, but in reality his own – and they mount a tower to observe the heavens. As in the Diogenes story, Alexander blocks the philosopher's vision of the heavens, in this case by pushing him off the tower. Nectanabus had prophesied that he would be murdered by his own son, and Alexander, to prove the 'olde dotard' wrong, shoves him to his death (VI, 2280–366). While proving the philosopher right, and so the predictive strength of philosophy itself, the narrative equally proves the uselessness of philosophy before the brutality of the ignorant, wilful young king. If the most powerful reading of the *Confessio Amantis* sees it as an optimistic fable of the soul's power to reintegrate itself and so reintegrate the body politic, that reading must also register its haunting spectre: philosophy is helpless to redirect and educate the tyrant. If the posture of the *engagé* philosopher Aristotle fails, then the fallback position is that of the sceptic Diogenes.

Sir Gawain and the Green Knight

The date of *Sir Gawain and the Green Knight* is uncertain. The single manuscript in which it survives, along with *Cleanness*, *Pearl*, and *Patience*, dates from the end of the fourteenth century, and scholars also date the poem towards the end of that century, on the basis of architectural and sartorial evidence.[24] Like elegy, romance bears an oblique relation to history, and defies historicization precisely because the comic endings of romance defy history: romance protagonists are reintegrated within their society after the monstrous forces that threatened disintegration have been confronted and neutralized by the resources of human virtue. All that has been lost is found, and the ravages of time are set into reverse. In what follows I readily concede the speculative basis of dating the poem, but hypothetically proceed as if the poem were written in the reign of Richard II. Attempts to historicize this romance, and even to historicize its own apparent attempt to avoid the specificities of history, turn out to work well for the reign of Richard II. Such an attempt certainly chimes well with the themes of this chapter, since this poem too confronts the fragilities of royal youth. And, like *Piers Plowman*, it does so by both representing and critiquing royal theatre.

Although the dialect of the poem can be located in the north-west midlands, it has been plausibly argued that there is no necessary reason why it should not have London, or Westminster connections.[25] Certainly in the last three years of Richard's reign, the so-called 'tyranny' of Richard II, he was heavily reliant on a 300-strong body of Cheshire bowmen, and there was frequent commerce between both Richard's Cheshire principality and Lancashire on the one hand, and Westminster on the other.[26] The Stanley family in particular at that time both constituted the dominant power in Lancashire and had close contacts with court: John Stanley was controller of Richard's household for the last two years of his reign (Given-Wilson 1986: 168). Richard's cultivation of a north-western power base and the high-profile presence of many north-westerners in London may have had implications for metropolitan poets writing rhymed poetry: one scholar has suggestively remarked that Chaucer's Parson's assertion of his inability to 'rum, ram, ruf' 'by lettre' (ParsP 43) might be a slighting reference to the shift of poetic tastes towards alliteration in the final years of the 1390s.[27]

Certainly the poem itself is informed by an uneasy sense of the relations of locality and metropolis, as the ostensibly provincial court turns out to be every bit as sophisticated as the metropolitan centre, without definitively challenging that centre. And the festive events of the poem recall both royal Christmas entertainments and the legitimating theatre of coronations with which I began. Late medieval kings did spend the twelve days of Christmas in lavish style (Given-Wilson 1986: 41); and, just as the splendidly arrayed Green Knight enters the feast theatrically dressed in such a way as both to astonish and to frighten, as 'mon most' [the tallest man] (141), so too were frightening theatrical false heads common in late medieval England around Christmas: city ordinances prohibit the wearing of these socially disruptive costumes.[28] The very making of the poem might itself be a New Year's gift of the kind given in late medieval courts: Arthur refuses to sit down before he has received 'an uncouthe tale, / Of sum mayn meruayle', or else before a challenge has been made to one of his knights (91–9).[29] Although the giving of poems to patrons at New Year is not widely attested until early Tudor England,[30] it seems to me that the poem offers its own patron the (peaceful) textual alternative desired by Arthur. The most striking theatrical feature of the opening scene is, however, its connection with the coronation challenge discussed above. Like John Dymmok, the Green Knight rides into the hall and challenges the legitimacy of the king, whose youth, along with the youthfulness of his court, is stressed above all: the transgressive visitor wears no armour, since 'hit arn aboute on this bench bot berdlez chylder' (280). Hovering between the theatrical and the 'real', the Green Knight puts in question the court's power to generate only legitimating theatre. For whereas no one was expected to challenge the likes of John Dymmok, the Green Knight insists on playing a 'real' version of another theatrical tradition, an execution game involving a green man,[31] all the while calling it 'a Crystemas gomen' (283). The Green Knight offers brilliant children's theatre, expert as he is in the calibration of threat, astonishment and playfulness.

In *Sir Gawain and the Green Knight* the art of poetry claims to represent the art and artisanal forms of courtly life, such as armoury, architecture, embroidery and cloth work, just as painting in the Wilton Diptych represents many other art forms on a two-dimensional surface. This power to control the forms of representation is itself related to the performance of court life within the narrative of the poem itself, since Arthur's court absorbs anything that is apparently other to itself within the art form of courtly theatrics. When the Green Knight leaves, Arthur re-absorbs his transgressive irruption into the court by redescribing it as part of the 'laykyng of enterludez' that befits Christmas entertainment (472). Or when Gawain imports the green sash that is the sign of his failure at the end of the poem, the courtiers laughingly respond by adopting it as a communal sartorial sign of their fellowship. Part of the very luxury of court life is the semiotic luxury of being able to reinterpret signs of failure, labour and loss into tokens of plenitude and recovery. Courts have the power, that is, to construct the world in their own image, and they do so by rendering threat theatrical: theatrical threat acknowledges the existence of external danger but simultaneously neutralizes it by insisting that danger is a performance alone, and that it is 'not really happening'. In *Gawain*, indeed, the very threats would seem to collude with their theatricalization, since what is exterior and transgressive does acknowledge its ultimate dependence on the court: the wild green chapel turns out not to be the locus of danger, so much as the interior bedroom of Fit III, and those bedroom scenes themselves turn out to have been staged by Arthur's half-sister. Apparently real threats turn out to have been staged, and staged from within the dynamics of Arthur's own court; Hautdesert turns out to be 'pared out of papure' (802), of a kind with the decorative castles that adorned the tables of noble feasts.

If that were the whole story, then *Gawain* could be described as working very much in the way of the coronation challenge, in its standard form, with which I began: this is a poem that poses a threat to Arthur's court of 'berdles chylder', only to redescribe that threat as spectral, a theatrical shadow play designed to entertain the court from which its staging originated in the first place. Like most royal theatre, the poem by this reading would serve a purely legitimating function. Is it possible, however, to recognize that the work at least allows itself to be read as legitimating theatre that goes wrong? For all the court's power to produce images, might it be the case that the poem finally insists that there really is something 'out there' that is not merely theatrical? I end this discussion of *Gawain* by suggesting that this is indeed the way in which the poem marks the limitations of its own paraded power to neutralize history.

Deferred threat is a recurrent motif in *Gawain*. This is most obviously true of the extended and detailed moments of Gawain's waiting for the axe to fall across the entirety of his exposed neck in Fit IV. The prolonged and precisely narrated moment, however, evokes increasingly large time sequences of deferred menace: in Fit III Gawain is subject to an unspecified threat across three days as the finesse of the bedroom scenes is juxtaposed with the violence of the hunt and the ritual dismemberment of the animals; at the end of Fit I Arthur hangs the huge axe above and behind the royal seat on the dais, marking the threat overhanging Gawain for the coming year; and at the very beginning and end of the poem we are reminded of the world of history from which romance can hope to escape only provisionally: 'Sithen the sege and the assaut watz sesed at Troye' (1, 2525). Beyond this, outside the narrative time of the poem altogether, one might reflect that, like Troy, Camelot did indeed collapse, just as Richard II was indeed deposed and almost certainly murdered. *Sir Gawain and the Green Knight* operates *almost* wholly like legitimating royal theatre, with its sealed, ideologically smooth surface. The poem does indeed recognize the deep resources of the royal court, and of romance, to reconfigure all that threatens the court as part of the court's own performance. Gawain does, however, return with his own smooth surface having been ever so slightly disfigured. As with *Piers Plowman*, then, *Gawain* deploys the model of royal theatrics partly to critique the very power of that form to create the self-image of the court.

Royal Theatre: The Knight's Tale

Each of the Ricardian works so far considered, then, broaches questions of the youthful royal will, and each, while promising to legitimize the rule of a young king, exposes the fragilities and impetuosities of youthful rule. And in at least two of these works, the form chosen both to represent and to critique the court is that of royal theatre. In the mid-1380s Chaucer also deploys the model of royal theatre to contain youthful aristocratic rivalries. The Knight's Tale is referred to in the Prologue to the *Legend of Good Women* (F 420), and can therefore be assumed to have been composed prior to the *Canterbury Tales* period (1390–1400). In that poem Theseus contains and theatricalizes the rivalry of the Theban royal cousins Palamon and Arcite by constructing a theatre within which their violence can be played out. He

> . . . gooth so bisily
> To maken up the lystes roially,
> That swich a noble theatre as it was
> I dar wel seyen in this world ther nas.
> The circuit a myle was aboute,

> Walled of stoon, and dyched al withoute.
> Round was the shap, in manere of compas,
> Ful of degrees, the heighte of sixty pas,
> That whan a man was set on o degree,
> He letted nat his felawe for to see.
>
> (1883–92)

This is the very model of a royal theatre, since its perfectly symmetrical design ensures the control of the popular eye: spectators can be placed in such a way as to govern and concentrate their field of vision, its perfect circularity containing that vision at every point. It is also perfectly hierarchical, permitting as it does control of the distance from which the spectator watches. Its sacral design, too, mirrors and contains the cosmic energies that will be played out within royal control: temples to the younger generation of gods (Venus, Mars and Diana) are constructed at the eastern, western and northernmost points of the 'compas' respectively.

Theseus' architectural construction itself implies a position for Theseus himself. He is set 'ful riche and hye' in the coliseum, but his positioning is also designed to suggest analogies between his place in the theatre and the governance of the cosmos; in the speech of Theseus that closes the entire tale, he names Juppiter 'the kyng, / That is prince and cause of alle thyng' (3035–6), the very source of order in the universe itself. Just as Juppiter rules the universe, so too, the construction of Theseus' theatre implies, does Theseus return everything in the secular sphere to 'his propre welle', or source (cf. 3037). The theatre constructed by Theseus is designed in such a way as to imply that its structure mirrors the shape of the cosmos, and that its performance is not merely theatrical, grounded as it is in the deepest reality.

For all Theseus' attempt, however, to contain the rivalry of aristocratic young cousins within a theatrical space, darker, more entropic forces take over the performance. The theatre might be circular, but its power to contain violence is overtaken by another, much wider circle. Saturn, whose course runs widest in the cosmos, fixes the result of the violent encounter. Whereas Juppiter is powerless to quell the bickering between Venus and Mars (2442), the malignant grandfather figure Saturn arranges a spectacular and wholly untheatrical death for Arcite. Violent forces, beyond the power of Theseus to control, govern human rivalries with brutal despatch. The failure of the human, royal theatre to contain and temper human violence is evident in the very structure of Theseus' speech of congratulation at the end of the tournament: he comforts the losers by denying loss,

> For fallyng nys nat but an aventure,
> Ne to be lad by force unto the stake
> Unyolden, and with twenty knyghtes take,
> O persone allone, withouten mo,
> And haryed forth by arme, foot and too.
>
> (2722–6)

Theseus' attempt, that is, to disguise violence and embarrassment only serves to expose it. Against the ostensible thrust of his sentence, Theseus emphasizes chivalric humiliation and isolation: line 2725 prepares for the words of Arcite about to enter his 'colde grave / Allone, withouten any compaignye' (2779). Whereas the construction of this theatre has pretensions to ground performance within the cosmic order, things go wrong in such a way as to expose the theatre as a construction. Beyond the performance, and beyond human constructions, lies a reality whose forces cannot be managed by 'noble theatre'.

Theseus' theatrical attempt to govern and contain youthful royal wills points to the problem of royal desire and its management across Chaucer's *œuvre*: all the pre-*Canterbury Tales* amatory works (*Book of the Duchess, Parliament of Fowls, Troilus and Criseyde*, Knight's Tale, *Legend of Good Women*) circle around youthful aristocratic desire, but none so luridly or so theatrically as the *Legend*, which is perhaps the last of the court-centred poems before Chaucer sets off to Canterbury. In that poem the boy-prince enters wearing a sun-crown, just as Richard II himself bedecked himself with rising suns for processional display.[32] As a punishment for *Troilus and Criseyde*, Chaucer the narrator is condemned to write, as long as he lives, nothing but lives of virtuous women who are prepared to suffer for their rapacious royal lovers. As in each of the other Ricardian poems considered in this chapter, however, the attempt to execute the royal and cupidinous command cannot help but reveal other sources of desire beyond those of the childish king.

See also AUTHORITY; BODIES; CHIVALRY; CRISIS AND DISSENT; FRANCE; LONDON; MODES OF REPRESENTATION; PERSONAL IDENTITY; VISUALIZING.

NOTES

1   For Dymmok (father of the anti-Lollard polemicist), see Fiona Somerset, 'Answering the *Twelve Conclusions*: Dymmok's halfhearted gestures towards publication', in *Lollardy and the Gentry in the Late Middle Ages*, ed. Margaret Aston and Colin Richmond (Stroud: Sutton, 1997), 52–71 at 54.

2   Thomas Walsingham, *Historia Anglicana*, ed. Henry Thomas Riley, 2 vols, Rolls Series (1863–4), i, 337.

3   For the challenge at the coronation of Henry IV, for example, see Henry L. Harder, 'Feasting in the *Alliterative Morte Arthure*', in *Chivalric Literature*, ed. Larry D. Benson and John Leyerle, Studies in Medieval Culture 14 (Kalamazoo, Mich.: Medieval Institute Publications, 1980), 49–62.

4   Dillian Gordon, 'The Wilton Diptych: an introduction', in *The Regnal Image of Richard II and the Wilton Diptych*, ed. Dillian Gordon, Lisa Monnas and Caroline Elam (London: Harvey Miller, 1997), 19–26 at 20.

5   Ibid.

6   For which see Jonathan J. G. Alexander, 'The portrait of Richard II in Westminster Abbey', in *The Regnal Image of Richard II*, ed. Gordon, et al., 196–200 at 196.

7   *Record and Process*, in *Chronicles of the Revolution, 1397–1400: The Reign of Richard II*, ed. Chris Given-Wilson (Manchester: Manchester University Press, 1993), 168–9.

8   *Chronicles of the Revolution*, ed. Given-Wilson, 186.

9   Gordon, 'Wilton Diptych', 22.

10 *Statutes of the Realm*, ed. T. E. Tolmins et al., 11 vols (London: Dawsons, 1810–28; repr. 1963), 1 Henry IV (1399), statute 4, ch. 7; ii (1817), 113.

11   All references to the text of *Piers Plowman* are from *The Vision of Piers Plowman*, ed. A. V. C. Schmidt, 2nd edn (London: Dent, 1995).

12   Walsingham, *Historia Anglicana*, i, 331. For the importance of this entry in the history of royal processional, see Gordon Kipling, 'Richard II's sumptuous pageants and the idea of civic triumph', in *Pageantry in the Shakespearean Theater*, ed. David M. Bergeron (Athens, Ga.: University of Georgia Press, 1985), 83–103.

13   Walsingham, *Historia Anglicana*, ed. Riley, i, 332–3.

14   First suggested by J. A. W. Bennett, 'The date of the B Text of *Piers Plowman*', *Medium Ævum* 12 (1943), 55–64 at 57.

15   *The Sermons of Thomas Brinton, Bishop of Rochester (1373–1389)*, ed. Mary Aquinas Devlin, 2 vols, Camden 3rd series, 85 (1954), Sermon 69, ii, 315–21.

16   Helen Cooper, 'Langland's and Chaucer's pro-logues', *Yearbook of Langland Studies* 1 (1987), 71–81.

17   Steven Justice, *Writing and Rebellion: England in 1381*, The New Historicism 27 (Berkeley and Los Angeles: University of California Press, 1994).

18   Gower, *Confessio Amantis*, VIII, *2941; Chaucer, *Troilus and Criseyde*, V, 1856. All references to the *Confessio Amantis* are drawn from *The English Works of John Gower*, ed. G. C. Macaulay, 2 vols, Early English Text Society, extra series 81–2 (1900–1). An asterisk designates lines deleted in the second and/or third recensions.

19   John Hurt Fisher, *John Gower: Moral Philoso-pher and Friend of Chaucer* (New York: New York University Press, 1964), 37–69.

20   *The Piers Plowman Tradition*, ed. Helen Barr (London: Dent, 1993), 14–22.

21   For this tradition, see James Simpson, 'Break-ing the vacuum: Ricardian and Henrician Ovidianism', *Journal of Medieval and Early Modern Studies* 29 (1999), 325–55.

22   For the political emphases of this narrative in the *Confessio*, see James Simpson, *Sciences and the Self in Medieval Poetry: Alan of Lille's Anticlaudianus and John Gower's Confessio Amantis*, Cambridge Studies in Medieval Literature 25 (Cambridge: Cambridge University Press, 1995), 213–15. For the

Lucrece story more generally as a 'myth of revolution', see Ian Donaldson, *The Rapes of Lucretia: A Myth and its Transformations* (Oxford: Clarendon, 1982), ch. 6.

23   *Record and Process*, in *Chronicles of the Revolution*, ed. Given-Wilson. See also Nigel Saul, 'Richard II and the vocabulary of kingship', *English Historical Review* 110 (1995), 854–77. For the counter-case (that charges of tyranny against Richard were produced by Lancastrian propaganda), see C. M. Barron, 'The tyranny of Richard II', *Bulletin of the Institute of Historical Research* 41 (1968), 1–18.

24   *Sir Gawain and the Green Knight*, ed. J. R. R. Tolkien and E. V. Gordon, 2nd edn, rev. Norman Davis (Oxford: Clarendon, 1967), xxv–xxvii. All citations are drawn from this edition, with letter forms modernized.

25   Jill Mann, 'Price and value in *Sir Gawain and the Green Knight*', *Essays in Criticism* 36 (1986), 298–318; Ad Putter, *An Introduction to the* Gawain-*Poet* (London: Longman, 1996), 28–37.

26   John M. Bowers, '*Pearl* in its royal setting: Ricardian poetry revisited', *Studies in the Age of Chaucer* 17 (1995), 111–55 at 115–19; Michael J. Bennett, *Community, Class, and Careerism: Cheshire and Lancashire Society in the Age of* Sir Gawain and the Green Knight (Cambridge: Cambridge University Press, 1982).

27   Bowers, '*Pearl* in its royal setting', 154.

28   *Dramatic Texts and Records of Britain: A Chronological Topography*, ed. Ian Lancashire (Toronto: University of Toronto Press; Cambridge: Cambridge University Press, 1984), items 890, 921, 922, 935. Item 922 (London, Christmas 1418) prohibits anyone walking at night 'in eny manere mommyng, pleyes, enterludes, or eny . . . disgisynges', with pretended beards, painted visors, or 'disfourmyd or colourid visages'. The Green Knight offends in many respects.

29   For examples of lavish New Year gift-giving, see *John of Gaunt's Register, 1379–1383*, ed. Eleanor C. Lodge and Robert Somerville, 2 vols, Camden 3rd series 56, 57 (1937), i, 109–13.

30   D. R. Carlson, *English Humanist Books: Writers and Patrons, Manuscript and Print, 1475–1525*

(Toronto: Toronto University Press, 1993), 8–12.

31 Glynne Wickham, *The Medieval Theatre*, 3rd edn (Cambridge: Cambridge University Press, 1987), 136–43.

32 Lisa Monnas, 'Fit for a king: figured silks shown in the Wilton Diptych', in *The Regnal Image of Richard II*, ed. Gordon et al., 165–77 at 167–8.

REFERENCES AND FURTHER READING

Bennett, Michael J. (1992) 'The court of Richard II and the promotion of literature', in *Chaucer's England: Literature in Historical Context*, ed. Barbara Hanawalt, Medieval Studies at Minnesota 4 (Minneapolis: University of Minnesota Press), 3–20. Summary and judgement of debate regarding Richard II's promotion of literary and cultural activity.

Burrow, J. A. (1971) *Ricardian Poetry: Chaucer, Gower, Langland and the* Gawain-*poet* (London: Routledge & Kegan Paul; New Haven: Yale University Press). First book to delineate a distinctively 'Ricardian' aesthetic.

Given-Wilson, Chris (1986) *The Royal Household and the King's Affinity: Service, Politics and Finance in England 1360–1413* (New Haven: Yale University Press). Lucid account of the well-defined structure of the royal household and the more amorphous royal affinity.

Green, Richard Firth (1980) *Poets and Prince-pleasers: Literature and the English Court in the Later Middle Ages* (Toronto: University of Toronto Press). Survey of late medieval English court poetry in its institutional context.

Kerby-Fulton, Kathryn and Justice, Steven (1998) 'Langlandian reading circles', *New Medieval Literatures* 1, 59–83. Argues that London bureaucratic circles were the immediate target audiences for both Chaucer and Langland.

Kipling, Gordon (1998) *Enter the King: Theatre, Liturgy, and Ritual in the Medieval Civic Triumph* (Oxford: Clarendon). Survey of royal entries; stresses the importance of the reign of Richard II for royal pageantry.

Pearsall, Derek (1999) *Chaucer to Spenser: An Anthology* (Oxford: Blackwell). Includes a wide selection of writing from the later fourteenth century, with brief introductions.

Putter, Ad (1996) *An Introduction to the* Gawain-*poet* (London: Longman). Beyond excellent discussion of all works by the *Gawain-poet*, clear account of his possible London connections.

Saul, Nigel (1995) 'Richard II and the vocabulary of kingship', *English Historical Review* 110, 854–77. Focuses especially on the pantocratic pretensions of Richard II in his 'tyranny'.

Scattergood, V. J. and Sherborne, J. W., eds (1983) *English Court Culture in the Later Middle Ages* (London: Duckworth). Iconoclastic with regard to argument that Richard II's court promoted the production of cultural artefacts; see especially the essays by Sherborne and Scattergood.

Simpson, James (1990) *Piers Plowman: An Introduction to the B-Text* (London: Longman). Critical introduction to the whole poem.

——(1993) '"After craftes conseil clotheth yow and fede": Langland and London city politics', in *England in the Fourteenth Century: Proceedings of the Harlaxton Symposium*, ed. Nicholas Rogers (Stamford: Paul Watkins), 109–27. Argues that Langland aligned himself with the reform campaign of the artisanal crafts in London.

——(1995) *Sciences and the Self in Medieval Poetry: Alan of Lille's* Anticlaudianus *and John Gower's* Confessio Amantis, Cambridge Studies in Medieval Literature 25 (Cambridge: Cambridge University Press). For a fuller account of the presentation of Aristotelian politics in the *Confessio Amantis*.

——(1998) 'Ethics and interpretation: reading wills in Chaucer's *Legend of Good Women*', *Studies in the Age of Chaucer* 20, 73–100. Argues that Chaucer aligns himself with the abandoned women of the *Legend*; all are victims of Cupid's tyrannical desire.

Strohm, Paul (1989) *Social Chaucer* (Cambridge, Mass.: Harvard University Press). Includes a detailed historical account of Chaucer's reading publics.

——(1990) 'Politics and poetics: Usk and Chaucer in the 1380s', in *Literary Practice and Social Change in Britain, 1380–1530*, ed. Lee Patterson (Berkeley and Los Angeles: University of California Press), 83–112. Comparison of the way in which Usk and Chaucer responded to the crises of 1386–8.

Wallace, David (1992) 'Chaucer and the absent city', in *Chaucer's England: Literature in Historical Context*, ed. Barbara Hanawalt, Medieval Studies at Minnesota 4 (Minneapolis: University of Minneapolis Press), 59–91. Extended reflection on why Chaucer avoids engagement with London.

8

Crisis and Dissent

Alcuin Blamires

'Shew forth thy swerd of castigacioun.' This admonition from a concluding stanza to Chaucer's short moral poem 'Lak of Stedfastnesse' (26) is addressed to a 'prince' identified in one manuscript as Richard II. The admonition is about as close as Chaucer comes to engaging directly with the often dramatic politics of his time, when treachery, collusion, dissension, oppression, vindictiveness – the spectres raised in the preceding stanzas – persistently soured relations between king, magnates and people.

What particular crisis might have warranted the sword of castigation? One answer is that in its full context the line suggests the situation after an epoch-making parliament of 1386 stripped Richard II of power, impeached his favourite and appointed a council to run the country. Richard was left to summon a team of lawyers in 1387 to certify that such infringement of monarchal prerogative was illegal and punishable. The moment was ripe for Chaucer, a person formerly closely dependent on Richard's administration, to encourage the crown to restore royal *estat* with a show of strength (Scattergood 1987). Yet this hypothesis has to compete with attempts to link the poem with other crises, whether as early as 1381 in the aftermath of the Peasants' Revolt or as late as Richard's extension of his powers in 1397; and indeed it competes also with an equally strong conviction that the poem inscribes no crisis at all but merely appeals blandly for just rule (Pearsall 1992: 168).

We come straight up against factors which threaten the feasibility of assessing the articulation of 'crisis and dissent' in Chaucer's productions. Either he addresses contemporary issues (as here) through conventional generalities; or he addresses them obliquely, through narrative configurations. He subsumes political and social conflict within the private crises of fictional individuals, 'domesticates into literary narrative his response to the events of his day' (Pearsall 1992: 151; see also Brown and Butcher 1991: 18). Consequently there is a notorious dearth in his poetry of palpable reference to datable events. This parsimony, coupled with the large number of 'crises' during his lifetime, means that it requires firm nerve to elect a definitive crisis that a particular poem of no fixed date might be thought to address. So far as dissent is concerned some of the same factors apply, but an additional difficulty is that 'dissent' was an unstable phenomenon at this time, admitting of no very sharp definition except towards the very end of Chaucer's life.

The Nature of 'Crisis'

'Crisis' is a term easily bandied about, but a moment's reflection will suggest that one person's crisis may be another's triumph, and perhaps a matter of relative indifference to a third. The second half of the fourteenth century has been envisaged as so crisis-ridden that people may have felt they were moving 'from a series of crises to a general sense of crisis' (Brown and Butcher 1991: 205). If Chaucer does not communicate that general sense, or if he does not rise to the challenge of what with hindsight we see as momentous upheavals, it may sometimes be that we are ascribing the wrong sort of perceptions or alignments to him. In today's climate of insistence on the historical resonance of all writing, the old critical emphasis on Chaucer as a sublimely 'detached' poet is wearing thin. But this chapter will not assume that Chaucer indirectly addresses *as* crises all the crises we want him to. Some, we shall find, he does not recognize as such, or just brushes away.

The second half of the fourteenth century is characterized by horrifying epidemics of plague. At least 20 per cent of the population died across England in the first outbreak of the Black Death in 1348–9, and perhaps 40 per cent over the whole period.[1] The labouring population was immediately so reduced that survivors could put pressure on customary restrictions. Their increased mobility and wage bargaining alarmed landlords, who repeatedly tried to stem peasant aspirations through labour statutes. This was one major problem of governance which the ailing Edward III's administration misjudged in the 1370s. At the same time, the cost of sustaining the long-running war effort against France through repeated rounds of taxation was becoming a serious aggravation, especially since the campaigns no longer yielded victories and it was widely suspected that much of the subsidy was being creamed off. This was another acute problem of governance not well addressed. A third was the perception that justice was being undermined by gangs of liveried retainers hired to 'maintain' their lords' cause – usually by interfering in legal process.

Much of Chaucer's poetry was being written when the country was in the hands of one king in his dotage, then another at first too young, later temperamentally unqualified, to rule wisely. Not surprisingly, governance itself entered a period of crisis. Anger welled up over taxation and financial mismanagement; the 'commons' element (i.e. minor gentry and prosperous burgesses) in the English parliament asserted itself, achieving something close to a *coup* in 1376 (McKisack 1959: 387–93). Yet taxation was soon resumed in the new and harsh form of a poll tax, so inflammatory that it triggered the outbreak of open rebellion in 1381. By any standards the Peasants' Revolt was a national convulsion. Many thousands marched from various shires on London, took over the city, executed the archbishop-chancellor and the treasurer, and obliged the king to promise sweeping social change. The convulsion passed, the rebels disbanded – and the promises were revoked.

Chaucer's Response

How much of all this lives in Chaucer's writing? The terrifying suddenness and the awesome scale of plague do leave their mark. In the Pardoner's Tale, three revellers are interrupted by the funeral procession of a fellow reveller whisked away by Death the thief. Round figures have to be invoked in an attempt to grapple with the scale of Death's operation: 'He hath a thousand slayn this pestilence' (679). What the tale most registers is not clinical horror but rather, in a platitude not to be under-estimated, the random selectivity of Death. 'Beth redy for to meete hym everemoore' is the keynote (683). The plague foregrounds for Chaucer the question of spiritual preparedness or unpreparedness for death, or for what he and other medieval writers call *Goddes sonde*, God's dispensation. Death's suddenness resonates in other tales, too, whether striking in the twinkling of an eye, menacing uncertainly every age and rank, or consigning to the bier someone seen working 'on Monday last' (ClP 36–8, ClT 122–6; MilT 3427–30).

On the other hand, Chaucer appears perversely reticent so far as the notorious social and economic consequences of the plague are concerned. On the face of it he quite fails to embarrass modern readers, as does his contemporary John Gower, by whinge-ing on behalf of all landlords about the labour crisis of illegal peasant mobility and spiralling wages. Yet *implicitly* Chaucer reacts to the spectacle of a clamorous peas-antry. His version of a Plowman is an epitome of peasant docility and altruism, who lives in peace and will work for free ('withouten hire') to help others (GP 531–40). In the prevailing labour context, this representation constitutes an aggressive act of establishment propaganda (Stillwell 1939). Moreover, the Plowman's representation participates in an extended configuration in the General Prologue, whereby the crisis of rebellion is retrospectively contained, and the blame for it distributed away from the kinds of officials (embodied especially in the Franklin) whom the rebels them-selves held responsible. The Reeve, by precedent a peasant himself, is diagnosed as the real agent of oppression among the peasantry (Blamires 2000).

The classic critical hypothesis about Chaucer and rebellion, however, is that a Churls' Revolt is written into the *Canterbury Tales* when the Miller insists on being heard after the Knight and inaugurates a brief reign of 'low' narrative. Stephen Knight, for example, argues that this is part of a dynamic realization of historical forces. The 'murmure and the cherles rebellyng' mentioned in a catalogue of cata-strophes in the Knight's Tale (2459) grow into 'a poetic riot in the Miller's response'. Knight then acknowledges that Chaucer seems to arrange a self-destruct mechanism in 'this verbal peasant revolution against decency and linguistic order', leading to a re-imposition of authority in the person and tale of the Man of Law (Knight 1986: 92–5).

Knight partly accepts that 'Chaucer's own social position does not suggest he would sympathize with revolution' (69), and apart from the 'self-destruction' of his Churls' Revolt there is other evidence of disdain for popular activism. Sheila Delany has shown how Chaucer transforms the story of Appius and Virginia from a parable about popular uprising against oppressive oligarchy: in the Physician's Tale, class conflict disappears. Delany concludes that Chaucer 'will not show the people as collective hero, cleansing society with purgative revolt', because for him to do so would be 'utterly alien' to the views and circumstances of a 'socially conservative' courtier and crown servant, 'directly dependent for his living upon the good will of kings and dukes' (Delany 1981: 56–7).

The usual supposition about Chaucer's social positioning, by contrast, is that he straddles several social strata, and consequently 'rejects old certainties and probes for a new place to stand' (Knight 1986: 16–17: see also Patterson 1991: 39; Pearsall 1992: 245). Hence, while critics have very often sensed that the alignment of Chaucer's poetry in response to social crisis is no less hard-line than Gower's, they struggle with pre-conceptions about an alternative more radical alignment which they deduce from his 'anomalous' social background. But that has never been easy to reconcile with the tone of his one outright reference to the Revolt in a notorious passage in the Nun's Priest's Tale, which compares a farmyard fox-chase with the lynching cries of the 1381 rebels when they massacred Flemish workers in London (3393–7). Admittedly, responses to this as a 'trivialization' of the momentous implications of the Revolt sometimes overlook the mock-epic context: the point of the 1381 reference is to provide an outrageously disproportionate comparison with the fox-chase by widow, daughters, dogs, cows and calves. Nevertheless, the further details of the comparison juxtapose the rebels with squealing ducks or geese and with humans yelling like fiends in hell (3389–91): the rebels only keep company that is subhuman or horrendously devilish.

Just once, I believe, we can catch Chaucer pinpointing the prime cause of the Revolt. The Prologue to the *Legend of Good Women* (*c.*1386–8) includes a speech in which Queen Alceste urges that a king must not behave tyrannically like 'a fermour' (usually glossed 'tax collector') but should rather treat each subject as a liegeman, and as treasure in the royal coffers (F 376–80). Now, a *fermour* is actually 'one who under-takes the collection of taxes . . . *paying a fixed sum for the proceeds*' (*OED*, *farmer*, 1.a, my emphasis). Through Alceste, Chaucer is directly recalling the specific oppression blamed by the chroniclers for the rebellion; namely, the crown's contract with tax *fer-mours* to claw in revenues after what the authorities considered to be widespread evasion of the 1380 poll tax. The chronicler Henry Knighton explains how a royal official and his colleagues proposed commissions of inquiry to increase the inadequate returns. 'They contracted to give the lord king a large sum of money' for the right to pursue this (Martin 1995: 206–9; Dobson 1983: 135, and see 119, 124). It was the extortionate activities of the commissioners that provoked violent resistance in the south-east. While we have seen that Chaucer disdains the phenomenon of rebellion itself, Alceste's comment does acknowledge the malpractice most widely remembered as the cause of that rebellion.

Yet Chaucer generally draws much more attention to extortionate 'tax-farming' practices in the ecclesiastical sector. The kind of jibes frequently made in Chaucer's writings about religious operators – for instance, in the Friar's Tale that the summoner's 'maister hadde but half his duetee' (1352) – beg to be balanced, at this period, by more examples from the realms of secular taxation. The Speaker for the commons at the 1376 parliament was neither the first nor the last who 'reported that in their opinion the burden of taxation was the fault of certain councillors and royal servants who were enriching themselves at the king's expense' (McKisack 1959: 389).[2] Chaucer's emphasis (the single *fermour* allusion excepted) is instructive. Reading his poetry, you would think that there was a perceived national crisis of corrupt exaction only in the church, not in the state.

War and Tyranny

Although Chaucer's poetry seems conspicuous for dismissing the prospect of surging social discontent with indifference, belittlement or a deflective ideology of containment, we need at this point to distinguish carefully among different elements of 'crisis'. Important factors in the events leading to 1381 were the French war and the policies of a repressive nobility. When we move on to consider Chaucer's writing as a discourse about war and tyranny, and again when we ask about religious 'dissent', he will be seen to speak more positively of crises besetting late fourteenth-century England. He could do so because these were matters on which less solidarity bound the reactions of the authoritative social group to which he belonged.

The war with France had long been in progress by the time Chaucer began writing, and he had personal experience of it in 1359–60. The war tends to be most familiar to English literary students as a stirring story of battles, sieges, victories and reversals under individual command in France or at sea. That is only half the picture, however, for it under-represents among other factors the huge financial implications (Barnie 1974: 14–24). As the century wore on, the combination of expeditions that were expensive flops with a decreasing power to keep out Franco-Castilian coastal raids made the war policy less attractive. Of course, even amid the increasing national war-weariness and manifest military stalemate that gradually enabled Richard II to seek extended truces from the late 1380s, there were 'hawks' as well as 'doves'.[3] Thomas Duke of Gloucester was a notorious 'hawk'. Chaucer has been thought a 'dove'. He reserves for his 'own' contribution to the *Tales*, first, a parody which mocks the inanities of automatic chivalric aggression in popular romance, and second, a treatise which systematically critiques the lordly instinct for vengeful belligerence (Yeager 1987).

There remains for discussion the sensational saga of rumour-mongering, rivalry and vindictiveness centred on the person and rule of Richard II in the last decades of the century. The magnates grew openly restless with the behaviour of Richard as he emerged into his late teens 'capricious, headstrong, and irresponsible' (McKisack

1959: 436). There were alarming signs of violent temper, but above all, his choice and elevation of favourites angered the established nobility. As early as 1383 it was being claimed in parliament that evil counsellors were 'the cause of grave dissensions between the king and the lords' (McKisack 1959: 437). The absence of John of Gaunt in Castile facilitated a stand-off (at the very parliament which Chaucer attended as a Kentish representative) between Richard and a pressure group headed by his uncle the Duke of Gloucester and Bishop Arundel on the subject of the king's favourites. Richard's attempts to avoid humiliation and drum up support led only to the brink of deposition in 1388. The 'Lords Appellant' at the 'Merciless' parliament wrought the execution of various royal associates, including some with whom Chaucer had served on a commission for the peace in Kent.

Although Richard resumed full power in 1389, the legacy of these events remained to work itself out in the 1390s. Far from reining in his capricious autocratic tendencies, the king let them rip. Far from putting the episode with the Appellants behind him, he nurtured smouldering resentment. In a continuing atmosphere of plot and counter-plot, Richard created a huge armed bodyguard of archers, whom he eventually used to intimidate even parliament. In 1397 he set out to revenge himself on the Appellants and set in train the events which led to his actual deposition.

Do Chaucer's writings voice the acute tensions of this time? One answer can be seen in Lee Patterson's chapter, 'The *Knight's Tale* and the Crisis of Chivalric Identity' (Patterson 1991: 165–230). Patterson opts for a dating of the tale in the late 1380s, and argues that 'rivalry and governance', the 'two central topics of the tale', are 'also at the center of the problematic of the noble life in the England of the late fourteenth century' (179–80). Patterson describes England's military regression as reaching 'crisis proportions' in the 1380s, when Richard's own leadership of an expedition against Scotland neither achieved any strategic outcome nor succeeded in re-uniting the fractured governing class. The nobility's concern for honour was deteriorating into a hollow matter of public image-making, suggests Patterson. And Chaucer saw at the heart of this 'crisis of chivalric identity' the degradation of the concept of *trouthe* which he held dear as a behavioural ideal.

Is it possible to historicize the crisis politics of the tale more precisely? Brown and Butcher think so. They suggest that Chaucer highlights the chronic state of Richard's court and government in the late 1380s and 1390s in the cynicism of Arcite's opinion that 'at the kynges court' it is a case of 'Ech man for hymself, ther is noon oother' (1181–2; Brown and Butcher 1991: 211). They contemplate a historical shadowing whereby the tale's Duke Theseus might be a John of Gaunt figure, welcomed back from Spain in 1389 and thereafter attempting to solve the personal rivalry between Richard II and the Duke of Gloucester (Palamon and Arcite).

While such a thesis begs questions, not least about dating, it is a salient reminder of the contemporary frisson that Boccaccio's narrative could hold for Chaucer, who concludes the poem with obvious interest in the process of political reconstruction. Other scholars have focused more on the tale's questions about tyranny. Not only this text, but also others such as the Prologue to the *Legend of Good Women* and the

Manciple's Tale, have been considered parts of Chaucer's ongoing meditation on absolutist and collaborative political structures, spurred by his Italian experiences and by
his sense of personal precariousness as a royal servant (Wallace 1997: 104–24, 247–60,
337–78). Wallace interestingly advances the case that Chaucer may have thought
Richard's queen, Anne of Bohemia, a critical mediator (an Alceste figure) in relation
to an increasingly autocratic monarch.

Religious Dissent

The Manciple's Tale projects the extreme perils of utterance within a punitive household, yet it ends in a strange mocking patter about not-speaking, which puts one in
mind of Derek Pearsall's view that Chaucer will characteristically 'make a joke of what
might be very important to him or dangerous'. Pearsall actually makes that point
with reference to the dissenting movement known as Lollardy: 'we know that we are
unlikely to get any explicit comments on Lollardy from Chaucer: he will be his usual
cautious and evasive self' (Pearsall 1992: 182). In concluding this survey we shall
address the crisis of dissent witnessed in Lollardy which in turn introduced a crisis of
persecution as the fourteenth century concluded.

Disaffection with the hugely powerful institution of the church was already rife
in the period, and was aggravated by the spectacle of the papal Schism of 1378.
Christendom was suddenly and absurdly divided by the appearance of two popes, one
Italian and one French, whose rivalry infiltrated political alliances and led to outright
military 'crusade', one pope against another. Schism and papal warfare are obscenities
to Gower in the Prologue to his *Confessio Amantis*, which overlaps in date with
the *Canterbury Tales*. But the gap between willingness to censure those scandals and
willingness to countenance new directions in religious practice is demonstrated by
the fact that the same Prologue abhors 'this newe secte of Lollardie' as an evil manifestation of division, a heresy perversely linked to knowledge of 'al that the bible seith'
(346–55).

It was the Oxford theologian John Wyclif who had first courted trouble by advocating what his followers the 'Lollards' turned into the basis for a whole movement
– a return to pristine religion grounded in biblical text and necessitating institutional
and doctrinal change. Since Wyclif was initially under the protection of John of
Gaunt, and since Chaucer is widely thought to have been in Gaunt's patronage as
well, the idea of a meeting of minds between Wyclif and Chaucer is attractive. This
possibility is enhanced by the documented association of Chaucer with several of
Richard's 'chamber knights' who appear to have had Wycliffite sympathies. What
would Chaucer have thought of the gradual outlawing of Wyclif's beliefs and of
the Lollard movement which popularized them? The first crisis was a dramatic but
abortive 'trial' of Wyclif by bishops in London in 1377. The second was a formal repudiation of many of his tenets at a theological council in 1382, after which Wyclif
was retired to his rectory in Leicestershire. Further critical moments were a 1388

parliamentary commission to root out Lollard literature, then in 1395 the audacious publication on the doors of Westminster of the 'Twelve Conclusions' of the Lollards.

While Chaucer cannot be linked specifically to these developments, there are interesting signs that his writing breathes the wider 'crisis of dissent' in which they are landmarks. As David Lawton puts it in relation to the Parson's marked concern for the Gospels and 'Cristes loore' in the General Prologue; 'we run the risk of under-reading' if we overlook the Wycliffite context, though Lawton is inclined to see 'uncertainty' as much as 'sympathy' in Chaucer's attitude to Lollardy (Lawton 1987: 36). It is instructive that the Parson is complimented on biblical knowledge. Lollardy pursued a comprehensive policy of biblical translation from the inherited Latin so that the laity could access and discuss the whole sacred text for themselves. This was an enormous challenge to the church's control over doctrine, but Chaucer was a notably committed translator into English who may well have found some common cause with Lollardy in this respect.

Scholarship on Chaucer and dissent has tended to bog down in discussion of a specific reference occurring in a linking passage of tentative status in the *Tales* known as the 'Epilogue of the Man of Law's Tale' (1163–90). Here the Host makes satirical cracks about the Lollards' disliking of oaths and their high valuation of preaching. Another pilgrim, whose identity changes among the manuscripts, wants no preaching that might interpret the Gospels in such a way as to sow the weeds of difficulty into the company's faith. The lines prove that Lollardy and its controversial preaching were in the air at the time of writing – a matter for wrangling and simplification. But since the passage is sometimes omitted from authoritative manuscripts, Chaucer may eventually have cancelled it as being too risky for retention.

Chaucer's writings really require fresh concerted analysis from the point of view of Wycliffite polemic. The present consensus is that his engagement with that polemic is extensive and knowledgeable in contexts such as satire on friars or pardoners, or in contexts such as the question of the education of the simple laity; but that it is engagement by an interested and informed Christian, not by a partisan (Fletcher 1998: 278–9, 298–303). Despite Gower's hostile stance, people might think Wycliffite thoughts and read Lollard writings, for a while, without locating themselves in any *newe secte*. 'Only gradually did the full measure of Wyclif's heresy impinge, its tendency to encourage lay disobedience become clear, and the machinery of the ecclesiastical establishment activate itself to isolate those who had sympathy with any part of that heresy from the rest of society' (Hudson 1988: 393). Lollards did not suffer the horrific penalty of burning until after Chaucer's death.

In concluding this survey it needs to be reiterated, in the words of the first critic to write about 'poetry and crisis' in Chaucer's period, that in an absolutely literal sense 'the momentous crises and catastrophes of his time scarcely peep out' from his writing (Muscatine 1972: 27). Muscatine's own belief was that Chaucer mediates his articulation of a chronically unstable environment through Boethian philosophical reflection on instability itself, through irony, and through pathos (31–2, 113–14). Claims are made in this chapter, as they have been by recent critics, for ways in which crises map themselves into (rather than just 'peep from') Chaucer's writings. Uncertainties in the dating of the poems have long been acknowledged to endanger such claims. What is equally emphasized here is that pre-judgements about Chaucer's allegedly non-aligned social positioning may also skew our reckoning of how crisis is inscribed in the texts. Positioning him more centrally within the ruling ideology makes more sense of the strategies of containment that frequently figure in those texts. Since Wycliffite thought attracted the patronage both of John of Gaunt and of elements within Richard's court, Chaucer's espousal of Lollard thinking is no serious deviation from this positioning even if it would be a deviation from the strictest theological orthodoxy. In what follows, aspects of 'dissent' will be elicited from the Wife of Bath's Prologue; then, a politically correct response (by the standards of the day) to the crisis of governance will be explored at the very inception of the *Canterbury Tales*.

The Laity and Dissent: the Wife of Bath (WBP 14–29, FrP 1270–7)

Almost as soon as she begins to speak, Alisoun of Bath is arguing defensively about the doctrinal acceptability of having been married five times. Chaucer has borrowed the example she uses in lines 14–29 from the famous anti-matrimonial arguments of Jerome *Against Jovinian*, 1, 14. Jerome himself invokes the case of the Samaritan woman in a context where he admits that remarriages are more acceptable for widows than taking lovers, *if* Christ rebuked the Samaritan woman with whom he talked at a well because, having had five husbands, she was not in fact married to her current 'husband'.[4] Just what Christ did mean is open to interpretation, and Jerome leaves the door open. Alisoun pounces on the difficulty and dares ask *why* the fifth (Jerome would say, sixth) man was 'not a husband'. How many remarriages could the woman have? With a knowing scholastic tinge in her vocabulary of *diffinicioun* ('determination') upon the *nombre* she asks, what is the precise maximum? She adds sarcastically that 'men' (the construction can just mean 'people' at the time, but is perhaps gender specific here) speculate and stack up interpretations; but she herself knows that God expressly commanded 'us' (wives, or 'people'?) to increase and multiply.

Part of the fun of this is that Jerome himself had noted that the number of partners is not defined – that the Bible tacitly allows a woman to marry as often as her husband dies, a second, third, even eighth time (I, 15).[5] He had also attempted to neutralize the command to 'increase' – but Alisoun chooses to 'understand' the command to mean specifically a multiplication of marriages.

It makes all the difference in the world that a woman not a man, and worse still a laywoman not a nun, is posing questions about the Gospels and advancing personal readings. John, the carpenter in the Miller's Tale, who takes pride in knowing nothing but the Creed, typifies the 'official' line on simple lay piety, though this seems to leave him significantly vulnerable (Fletcher 1998: 239–48). The official line on lay*women* debarred them from theological study; and for them to preach was beyond the pale.

Yet this, precisely, was the spectre that Lollardy raised when it urged the dissemination of biblical knowledge in English among all lay people, in defiance of received doctrine which reserved study of the Bible to those in orders. Doubtless vernacularization was a trend of the time, but Lollards appropriated the trend. From about 1388, when a Parliament alarmed about heresy launched a crackdown on the dissemination of Lollard books in English (Martin 1995: 438–41), it began to be more unwise for non-professionals to promote controversy in the vernacular about matters of doctrine.[6] It was even more unwise to go around insisting on what Scripture 'expressly' said, as Alisoun does at lines 62 and 719 as well as here. This was a style of appeal to the naked biblical text which was fast becoming a trademark of Lollard polemic (Blamires 1989: 226–8). Eventually a Gospel paraphrase was issued specifically as an alternative to Lollard preoccupation with the word of the Bible (Hudson 1988: 437). The Wife of Bath treads dangerous ground.

It might be objected that the ground she treads is mostly ancient misogynous territory, not the new quicksand of Lollard error. Yet we should not consign the old debates on celibacy and marriage exclusively to 'tradition'. Two of the Lollards' published Conclusions in 1395 were antagonistic to chastity: in one case to the celibacy of the clergy and in the other to vows of sexual continence made by women, particularly widows. What an official opponent of the Lollards thought they meant by this was that female vows of chastity contravene the command to increase and multiply (Blamires 1989: 231–4). This strand in Lollard thinking must have injected contemporary urgency into the old arguments, since celibacy remained one of the movement's subsidiary targets (Hudson 1988: 114, 292, 357–8). If the paradoxical effect of Alisoun's reflections on marriage is to induce the Pardoner to blurt out that he will now think twice about his intention to marry (WBP 163–8), this serves to highlight further the issue of clerical celibacy, since Chaucer has asked us to think of pardoners as competitors with parish clergy and users of their pulpits.

However, the Wife's appropriation of clerical discourse is the most powerful symptom of dissent in her performance. The Pardoner's interruption refers to her as a *prechour* (WBP 165), and it is her trespass into the province of *prechyng* and *scoles of clergye* that is rebuked amid the Friar's flattery in the prologue to his tale (FrP 1270–7). This passage follows the Wife's tale and could be held to refer most specifically to arguments about Christ's poverty and other matters raised there, but that does not prevent us from taking it to encompass her prologue too. Condescendingly congratulating her for 'touching' rather well on complex theological issues, the Friar asserts that interpretation of texts (*auctoritees*) should be left to professionals – he probably means, to friars like himself. It is a defensive gesture from precisely the sector of the church most attacked by the Lollards, which retaliated when the Dominican Roger Dymmok systematically refuted their 'Twelve Conclusions' (Hudson 1988: 49).

One influential view of the Wife of Bath's Prologue and Tale is that it constitutes part of a strategy whereby Chaucer works to contain the boisterous peasant opposition to dominant ideology unleashed by the Miller's Tale. The Wife too is socially assertive, but Patterson argues that she is no agent of political or social change because she exists outside class moorings as a socially indeterminate 'private' subjectivity (Patterson 1991: 246). Differing from that view is the suggestion that Alisoun does identify herself as 'the voice of a maligned group, a group outside literate culture and thus disadvantaged at countering literate culture's authority' (Crane 1992: 215). The group in question are the rebels of 1381 (often styled illiterates by their opponents) who widely destroyed the legal records that authorized their servility.[7] The rebels burned books: Alisoun wants certain books of misogyny burned too. Crane hypothesizes that her prologue 'constitutes the most substantial response to the rising in Chaucer's works': it is a response in which elements of violence and illogic are felt to sabotage the claims of a suppressed group attempting to transcend its 'voicelessness' (216–17).

This argument is ingenious and usefully draws attention to literacy as an implicit instrument of repression. Yet it makes much more sense to situate the Wife's discourse within the incipient crisis of Lollardy than as an oblique response to the Peasants' Revolt. From at least as early as 1388 the identification and destruction of Lollard books was official policy (and ecclesiastical convention was to *burn* heretical writings). As the Friar's words to Alisoun prove, the real antagonists of the Wife of Bath are those who control theological interpretation and would curtail lay investigation of the Bible itself. Alisoun sometimes sounds amateurish in her interpretative raids – we are perhaps invited to 'spot the deliberate (authorial) mistake'. Lay people who presumed to enter the fray of dispute about *auctoritees* inevitably risked being labelled mere amateurs. Since Alisoun's prologue acknowledges that writing has hitherto been monopolized by her opponents, Chaucer may be said to account for the inevitability of amateurism in her articulation of alternative views, rather than gloat over it.

We may conclude that Chaucer manifests an informed and not unsympathetic attitude to at least some aspects of Lollardy, and that the Wife of Bath's Prologue encompasses this. Given that friars are the object of so much ridicule in Chaucer's poetry, the fact that it is a friar who is supplied to protect the monopoly of *scoles of clergye* from lay encroachment certainly suggests that Chaucer does not agree at all that interpretation of canonical texts is to be left to such *clergye*. If, however, this positioning implies a tincture of radicalism in Chaucer, the next example is offered as a sociopolitical statement that is fully supportive of dominant ideology.

The General Prologue and the Crisis of Governance (GP 777–87, 810–18)

The General Prologue is most often recollected as a sequence of discrete colourful descriptions, but its eloquent opening also emphasizes the formation of a *compaignye* (24) of diverse people thrown together into *felaweshipe* (26) by their common intention of pilgrimage. The passages at lines 777–87 and 810–18 come after they have begun to submerge their separateness, eating together and now responding to the

Host's proposal that they participate in a group pastime under his jurisdiction ('at his juggement'). The reading that will be pursued here identifies this interchange between Host and pilgrims as a political statement, comparable with statements about the much-needed unification of society made in the prologues of poems by Chaucer's two contemporaries, William Langland and John Gower.

The Host has been introduced as a figure of authority, fit to exercise the social protocol proper to a medieval gathering ('to been a marchal in an halle', 752). He is a large (perhaps also expansive), impressive person not lacking in *manhod* or 'courage' (756); the word includes an interesting chivalric nuance. Although he is described as entertaining and outspoken, any hint of indiscretion in that is cancelled out by insistence that he is wise and *wel ytaught* (755, 'informed, accomplished'). The Host, then, combines many valuable qualities: whatever shortcomings emerge later in the *Tales* are not to be read back into this able person, easily commanding respect, who welcomes the pilgrim company and offers a plan to enhance their journey.

Before spelling out the details, he tests the water in the first extract considered here, not presuming too much on their compliance. Will they unanimously (*by oon assent*) accept his jurisdiction and go along with his idea? Off with his head if the idea doesn't prove enjoyable! He asks for a show of hands. The *conseil* (advice) of the company is quickly forthcoming, for elaborate deliberation seems out of place; so they accept the Host's jurisdiction without further discussion and participate in the juridical spirit of his talk of *juggement* by requesting his 'verdict'.

Between these two passages, he explains the scheme of storytelling by the pilgrims en route. He further proposes to accompany them as guide, anyone defying his continuing jurisdiction being liable to pay the expenses of the rest. Again he asks whether they will accept (*vouche sauf*) the proposal.

In the second passage their agreement is enthusiastically and formally confirmed by oath. They further ask him to be, not just 'guide', but *oure governour* and 'judge' of their tales. They agree to be ruled in matters great or small *at his devys* ('as he wishes' in the Riverside gloss), so it is clear that they are now voluntarily yielding extensive power over their proceedings to their ruler. The interchange is pointedly rounded off by recalling the words with which it began. By *oon assent* they now fully agree to the Host's jurisdiction.

It will be apparent that this interchange invokes in the mind's eye several situations: we seem by turns to be in the realms of the judiciary, of the *ad hoc* public committee, and of parliament. Elastic though the options are, in my opinion the overriding implication concerns the politically resonant establishment of a harmonious social contract about government and leadership. Other commentators have offered analogous interpretations. One finds lines 810–18 'dense with the terminology and symbolic action of political life'; he reads in the General Prologue the adoption of an 'associational' political form characteristic of the medieval guild, whereby participants from different social niches form a corporate unity, though one that he conceives as being somewhat threatened by the Host's hierarchical instincts (Wallace 1997: 70 and 66–72). Another critic describes the Host's election to governance as an 'investiture', which binds the pilgrims into something more like 'a temporary *res publica* or polity' than a 'random fellowship'.[8]

What I think these critics miss is the coded urgency of what is envisaged, even though that urgency is implicit in the passage's anxious attention to *conseil*, assent and accord as components of workable government, and even though the urgency is clear as soon as one contemplates the relationship between this version of workable government and the crises of disunity damaging political relations at the time.

It is significant that both Langland and Gower respond to the late-century climate in comparable ways. The Prologue to Langland's B-Text of *Piers Plowman* imagines an originary monarchy harmoniously supported by lords and commons and counselled by clerks. However, the monarch's investiture is beset by anxieties about abuse of power, and leads to an acknowledgement that tyranny may have to be tolerated to avoid the potential anarchy that might follow curtailment of monarchal power (B Prologue, 112–208).[9] Gower's Prologue to *Confessio Amantis* is an apocalyptic discourse on *divisioun* as a root principle of disintegration in human morality and political stability. The world is so divided in warfare that vengefulness is everywhere, and division sets one house against another, threatening to overthrow all rule (896–9, 967–9). But this gloomy analysis is framed within icons of the opposite ideal. First, the poet represents himself as an obedient liegeman complying with his king's request for a book, and warns of the necessity of a reciprocal relation between a responsible ruler and compliant subjects whose *good conseil* the ruler gratefully accepts (39–75, 142–56). Then at the end he envisages an ideal ruler as a harpist able to soothe rampant social enmities so as to bring lords into *good acord* with commons, 'make pes where now is hate', and remove the fear that stands at everyone's door (1053–83).

Alongside Gower's distress over 'divisioun' we might place the Duke of Gloucester's reported rebuke to Richard II during the momentous parliament of 1386, declaring that the bright repute of the kingdom has now under his rule been 'shamefully abandoned through the division caused by bad government' ('per diuisionem male gubernacionis'; Barnie 1974: 23; Martin 1995: 360). What was clear to many, from the closing years of Edward's reign through the fraught years of Richard's, was that division stalked the land, both among the lords and between commons and lords. Chaucer's General Prologue begs to be seen in that context as a projection of the restoration of social and political amity or *felaweshipe*. The passages examined here require to be read as a projection, not of any 'threat' by the Host to a corporate commonalty, but of a proper working relationship between ruler and ruled. The problem of kingship is renegotiated through the fiction of a London hotelier and his guests. The Host, described as a natural and well-qualified leader (later he will speak to the Reeve 'as lordly as a kyng': RvP 3900) goes through a quasi-parliamentary process of 'consulting' his people. He looks for endorsement of his 'judgement', because monarchs were, in theory, elected – as well as formally responsible for the law. The pilgrim-subjects accept his proposal, not presuming to raise difficulties on this occasion. However, the very mention of the possibility that they might have deliberated sustains a kind of parliamentary right to offer alternative *conseil*: they implicitly assert, even as they register *acord* with his governance in this matter, that this is a power that they are giving him.

Where the monarchal analogy has been mooted before, the Host has been accused of 'willfulness and megalomania' for threatening with financial penalties any 'rebel' against his authority (Pichaske and Sweetland 1977: 183). This is surely to deny the medieval truism that a ruler should wield a 'sword of castigation'. While Chaucer's writings certainly disclose painful awareness of the effects of tyranny, the General Prologue nevertheless nostalgically affirms that the king *could* get things right. It affirms that a people's assent can be 'glad' and even almost unconditional (*in heigh and lough*) to a monarch with the right combination of consultative instincts, social wisdom and accomplishment. Anything less like the embittered relations between Richard, his Parliament and his people, especially after 1386, is hard to imagine. That is Chaucer's point.

See also AUTHORITY; CHIVALRY; CHRISTIAN IDEOLOGIES; CONTEMPORARY ENGLISH WRITERS; GAMES; LIFE HISTORIES; LONDON; LOVE; PERSONAL IDENTITY; SOCIAL STRUCTURES; TEXTS; TRANSLATION; VISUALIZING; WOMEN.

NOTES

1 The scale of mortality is disputed, as explained in Philip Ziegler, *The Black Death* (London: Collins, 1969), 227–30 and in M. H. Keen, *England in the Later Middle Ages* (London: Methuen, 1973), 169–73.

2 The details are investigated in George Holmes, *The Good Parliament* (Oxford: Clarendon, 1975), 100–58.

3 Anthony Tuck, 'Richard II and the Hundred Years War', in *Politics and Crisis in Fourteenth-century England*, ed. John Taylor and Wendy Childs (Gloucester: Sutton, 1990), 117–31.

4 *The Principal Works of St Jerome*, trans. W. H. Fremantle, Select Library of Nicene and Post-Nicene Fathers 6 (Oxford: James Parker; New York: Christian Literature Co., 1893), 346–416 at 358. The Latin text of *Adversus*

Iovinianum is in *Patrologia Latina*, ed. J.-P. Migne (Paris: 1844–64), xxiii, 221–352.

5 *Works of St Jerome*, trans. Fremantle, 359.

6 See Ralph Hanna III, 'The difficulty of Ricardian prose translation: the case of the Lollards', *Modern Language Quarterly* 51 (1990), 319–40; Susan S. Morrison, 'Don't ask, don't tell: the Wife of Bath and vernacular translations', *Exemplaria* 8 (1996), 97–123.

7 Steven Justice, *Writing and Rebellion: England in 1381*, The New Historicism 27 (Berkeley and Los Angeles: University of California Press, 1994), 1–66.

8 Paul Strohm, *Social Chaucer* (Cambridge, Mass.: Harvard University Press, 1989), 144.

9 *The Vision of Piers Plowman*, ed. A. V. C. Schmidt, 2nd edn (London: Dent, 1995).

REFERENCES AND FURTHER READING

Barnie, John (1974) *War in Medieval Society: Social Values and the Hundred Years War 1337–99* (London: Weidenfeld & Nicolson). An overview of the war and the politics of its funding, with a useful summary of contemporary opinion.

Blamires, Alcuin (1989) 'The Wife of Bath and Lollardy', *Medium Ævum* 58, 224–42. Argues that the Wife of Bath acquires Lollard traits as a laywoman engaging in biblical discussion of marriage and celibacy in the vernacular.

——(2000) 'Chaucer the reactionary: ideology and the General Prologue to the *Canterbury Tales*', *Review of English Studies*, November. Suggests that the General Prologue typifies Chaucer's political stance, dealing with the spectre of rebellion in a configuration which exculpates lordship and officialdom while displacing blame for oppression on to the peasantry – particularly the Reeve – and the church.

Brown, Peter and Butcher, Andrew F. (1991) *The Age of Saturn: Literature and History in the* Canterbury Tales (Oxford: Blackwell). Surveys methodologies for historicizing Chaucer and aims to demonstrate that he anchors society's crises in representation of individual experience. Case studies include: the dotage of Edward III as a constituent of the Merchant's Tale; and equivocal engagement with Wycliffite positions in the Pardoner's Tale.

Crane, Susan (1992) 'The writing lesson of 1381', in *Chaucer's England: Literature in Historical Context*, ed. Barbara Hanawalt (Minneapolis: University of Minnesota Press), 201–21. Investigates the role of literacy, illiteracy and attacks on documents in the 1381 rising. Speculates that, like the rebels, the Wife of Bath voices but cannot transcend the predicament of the inarticulate oppressed.

Delany, Sheila (1981) 'Politics and the paralysis of poetic imagination in the Physician's Tale', *Studies in the Age of Chaucer* 3, 47–60. Suggests that because of Chaucer's reluctance to articulate mass popular action he fudges the story's rationale of social protest.

Dobson, R. B., ed. (1983) *The Peasants' Revolt of 1381*, 2nd edn (London: Macmillan). Leads the reader through translated extracts from chronicles and other documents which report on the rising, its suppression and its aftermath.

Fletcher, Alan J. (1998) *Preaching and Politics in Late Medieval England* (Dublin: Four Courts). Informative essays on cross-currents of orthodoxy and Lollardy in some of the *Tales*.

Hudson, Anne (1988) *The Premature Reformation: Wycliffite Texts and Lollard History* (Oxford: Clarendon). The most comprehensive account of Lollardy, with helpful surveys of the movement's position on particular topics, e.g. 'War and Execution'.

Knight, Stephen (1986) *Geoffrey Chaucer*, Rereading Literature (Oxford: Blackwell). Marxist-

oriented investigation of ways in which the texts 'realize' socio-historical currents and become 'battlegrounds' for potent forces underlying the period's crises.

Lawton, David (1987) 'Chaucer's two ways: the pilgrimage frame of *The Canterbury Tales*', *Studies in the Age of Chaucer* 9, 3–40. Shows how opposed impulses of 'penance and play' in the ending and beginning of the *Tales* connect with Lollard thinking on true and feigned recreation.

McKisack, May (1959) *The Fourteenth Century, 1307–1399* (Oxford: Oxford University Press). Still an excellent starting-point for studying crises of governance in late fourteenth-century England.

Martin, G. H., ed. and trans. (1995) *Knighton's Chronicle 1337–1396* (Oxford: Clarendon). Text and translation of a description of crises in Chaucer's period from the point of view of a chronicler at a Leicestershire abbey, hostile to the Lollards and well disposed to John of Gaunt.

Muscatine, Charles (1972) *Poetry and Crisis in the Age of Chaucer* (Notre Dame, Ind.: University of Notre Dame Press). Summarizes the 'crises' and claims that Chaucer's response lies broadly in consolatory philosophy and in modes such as irony and pathos. A pre-New-Historicist view to be reckoned with.

Patterson, Lee (1991) *Chaucer and the Subject of History* (London: Routledge; Madison: University of Wisconsin Press). Includes an absorbing estimate of chivalric crisis in the Knight's Tale, and a classic exploration of the hypothesis that Chaucer's fabliaux release the energy of peasant aspiration into the *Canterbury Tales* only to retreat from political implications into representations of private subjectivity.

Pearsall, Derek (1992) *The Life of Geoffrey Chaucer: A Critical Biography* (Oxford and Cambridge, Mass.: Blackwell; repr. 1994). Fine modern biography of Chaucer, with insights into Chaucer's social and political situation and cogent speculation about his view of rebellion.

Pichaske, David R. and Sweetland, Laura (1977) 'Chaucer on the medieval monarchy: Harry Bailly in the *Canterbury Tales*', *Chaucer Review* 11, 179–200. Pioneering discussion of oblique political implication in the Host as 'ruler' in the *Tales*.

Scattergood, John (1987). 'Social and political issues in Chaucer: an approach to *Lak of*

Stedfastnesse', *Chaucer Review* 21, 469–75. Explains how Chaucer approaches contemporary issues through traditional genres and generalized statements. Speculates that 'Lak of Stedfastnesse' adapts the 'evils of the age' genre to Richard II's circumstances in the political crisis of 1386–7.

Stillwell, Gardiner (1939) 'Chaucer's Plowman and the contemporary English peasant', *Journal of English Literary History* 6, 285–90. Brief, cogent argument that the Plowman is so far removed from reality as to imply disapproval of rebellious peasantry.

Wallace, David (1997) *Chaucerian Polity: Absolutist Lineages and Associational Forms in England and Italy* (Stanford: Stanford University Press). Capacious discussion of alternative political structures within Chaucer's experience. Fresh insights into tyranny and into the Prologue to the *Legend of Good Women* and Manciple's Tale in relation to Richard II and Queen Anne.

Yeager, R. F. (1987) *'Pax poetica*: on the pacifism of Chaucer and Gower', *Studies in the Age of Chaucer* 9, 97–122. Makes the case that the Tale of Sir Thopas and Tale of Melibee establish Chaucer's distaste for war.

9

France

Michael Hanly

English courtiers at the time of Chaucer's birth were certainly fluent in French as well as their native tongue, and the court culture in which he came to age continued to look to France for its closest literary and intellectual models. The French language was heard everywhere at the court of London: in conversations between aristocrats, in pronouncements by justices, in speeches to parliament. And although poets living elsewhere in England were clearly drawing on indigenous modes, French poetic forms and fashions prevailed among the courtly crowd. This attraction continued despite the international tensions of the Hundred Years War, and despite a continuing stream of propaganda that vilified the French language and nation in an effort to elevate the status of English as the national language. Other writers have anatomized Chaucer's decision to write in English, and his indebtedness to the great French poets of the later Middle Ages has likewise been the topic of several long and magisterial studies; neither topic can be done full justice here. This chapter will briefly analyse his sustained engagement with French poets and poems, examine his personal experiences in France and with French diplomatic counterparts, and finally consider France as a centre of intellectual diffusion and the likely source for Chaucer's knowledge of the work of Italian poets, who with the French made up his most important poetic influences.

English society had been bilingual since the Norman Conquest, but despite the continued dominance of French culture at the court of London, it seems that by the mid-fourteenth century fewer aristocrats were routinely speaking French. In his seminal study of French influences, Charles Muscatine (1957: 251, n. 5) describes the change in the use of the French language in England during Chaucer's lifetime by citing two contemporary observations. In 1363, Ranulf Higden (*Polychronicon*) had objected to current practice:

Children in scole, ayenst the usage and manere of alle othere naciouns beeth compelled for to leve hire owne langage, and for to construe hir lessouns and here thynges in

Frensche, and so they haveth seth the Normans come first into Engelond. Also gentil men children beeth i-taught to speke Frensche from the tyme that they beeth i-rokked in here cradil . . .

But by 1385, John Trevisa, the translator and continuator of the *Polychronicon*, could say that 'now . . . in all the gramere scoles of Engelond, children leveth Frensche and construeth and lerneth an Englisch'.[1] English was permitted as the official language of the law courts in 1362, and of parliament in the following year; Muscatine adds that the earliest English proclamation of the city of London was issued in 1384, and the earliest known will in English in 1387. Even if, as Fisher (1981: 183) notes, French persisted as the language of polite society well into the fifteenth century – and, in the case of the legal community, until the end of the seventeenth – the dominance of the French language had begun to wane during Chaucer's youth. England, nevertheless, remained a bilingual society that spoke Anglo-Norman and English depending on class and occasion.

Equivocal Attitudes

What did Geoffrey Chaucer think of France and the French, and why did he make the historic decision to write his poems in English? Since we have no collection of letters from which to draw such conclusions, as in all other things scholars must depend on his writings, and Chaucer is notorious for his equivocal positioning of narrators and characters. The attempt to derive specific attitudes from individually contextualized allusions in his works, therefore, is no mean undertaking. The remarks in his poetry specifically regarding the French language and people are no exception: taken together, they indicate a markedly ambiguous attitude towards England's neighbour and rival. On the one hand, some of Chaucer's English characters manifest a sort of 'inferiority complex' in regard to the language and culture of France; but at the same time, since the French spoken by his characters sometimes serves ignorant and even debased purposes, France and its language can be seen in the text as a medium not of refinement but of vulgarity.

The French spoken by Chaucer's pilgrims – which is, of course, not the language spoken across the Channel but rather the insular Anglo-Norman, a breed apart ever since the Conquest – is felt to be a provincial dialect. The narrator observes that the Prioress spoke French 'After the scole of Stratford atte Bowe, / For Frenssh of Parys was to hire unknowe' (GP 125–6); in the context of his other observations about her dainty manners, she is presented as ridiculous for employing the local *koine* in an attempt to affect the high culture signified by Parisian French. Other Canterbury *poseurs* pretend to speak languages they cannot: the Summoner (GP 636–40) knows but a few terms in Latin he mutters while inebriated, and the chirking Friar (SumT 1832, 1838), in his quest to dupe the rustic couple, tries, like the Prioress, to make himself sound more learned and worldly by dropping French phrases into his discourse.

If the example of the Prioress's French works simply to exalt Paris and degrade Stratford (east London), the example of the Friar presents a mixed reading of the influence of France: French is lauded for its connotations of culture and refinement, but is also seen as an instrument of underhandedness. Indeed, Robert Holcot had just a few years earlier equated 'learning French' with 'learning to tell lies' (cited in Salter 1980: 240). The placement of the Shipman's Tale in mercantile St Denis signals moreover that anything and everything can be bought or sold, and that if France is a source of culture and refinement, it is also the locus of crass commercialism. Since France and England were almost continuously at war during this time, and the English were certainly behind their neighbours in poetry and other fine arts, it would be natural enough to find a certain degree of antipathy and envy in the expressions of English writers.

The Influence of French Literature at Court

However one finally interprets these texts, Chaucer's decision to make English the language of his poetic corpus cannot be seen as a simple reaction against a rival country and its language. For whatever the political environment, when Chaucer started out at the English court French enjoyed considerable prestige, and if conversations in French were declining in frequency, French love lyrics were still overwhelmingly popular in court circles. We do better to consider the young man delighting in the dominant artistic modes of his time, taking courage from the poetic accomplishments of another European vernacular and determining to attain the same status for his own. Chaucer had been part of the larger royal household since 1357, and was directly tied to the royal court from 1367 until he entered on a series of royal appointments in 1374. Even if we do not know for sure what Chaucer was doing between October 1360 and June 1367, we know that he lived in London from 1367 onwards and surmise that he was at court for most of that 'lost period' as well. And there is no doubt that Chaucer was writing poetry, in one language or the other, at the English court during this time. He takes responsibility, in the Retraction at the end of the *Canterbury Tales*, for the writing of 'many a song and many a leccherous lay'; his contemporary John Gower corroborates this claim, recounting how Chaucer 'in the floures of his youthe' filled the land with 'ditees and of songes glade' (*Confessio Amantis* VIII, 2943, 2945).[2] Given the cultural climate at court, moreover, there is every reason to believe that, like his friend Gower – who also recalls having composed 'folz ditz d'amours' ('foolish love poems': *Miroir de l'omme* 27340[3]) in his youth – Chaucer would have written these lyric verses in French (Robbins: 1978). Some of the French verses collected in a manuscript now at the University of Pennsylvania (French 15) may well have been composed by the young Chaucer himself (see final section, below).

The extant poems considered to be Chaucer's earliest efforts show a marked predilection for French models. *An ABC* (or *Prier à Nostre Dame*) is an English adaptation of the Marian poem intercalated in Guillaume de Deguileville's *Pèlerinage de la vie humaine* (*c*.1330). Chaucer also translated the first part of Guillaume de Lorris' 4,058-line opening section of the *Roman de la rose* (*c*.1237), a text known as Fragment A (1,705 lines) of the *Romaunt of the Rose*. Even though most scholars deny Chaucer's authorship of the other two long translated segments (Fragments B and C, 5,987 lines in all), there is no disputing the tremendous influence of the combined *Roman* – Lorris' first part and Jean de Meun's 17,722-line continuation (*c*.1270) – over his entire poetic career. The *Roman* informs everything Chaucer attempts in his works, from structures to characters to narrative strategies. For just a few examples of its influence, consider the dream architecture in the *Book of the Duchess*, *Parliament of Fowls* and the Prologue to the *Legend of Good Women*; the spring setting of the opening sentence of the General Prologue to the *Canterbury Tales*; the topic of Fame in *The House of Fame*; some of the Boethian matter in Troilus' speeches (drawn from Jean's Nature); and much of the material behind the character of the Friar (Faus Semblant) and the Wife of Bath (La Vieille). The French manuscripts for both the *Pèlerinage* and the *Roman* would have been easily available in the time of Chaucer's youth in the aristocratic courts of England, which was home not only to French intellectual modes but, for a time, to many French magnates and *literati* as well.

The cultural sophistication of the court of Edward III, who was closely related through his mother and wife to the French royal family, is often overlooked (Wimsatt 1991: ch. 2). Richard de Bury, after all, was Edward's chief minister, and Thomas Bradwardine a chaplain. But the 1360s certainly witnessed an increase in the court's level of cultivation, especially in the production of lyric poetry, then the preferred genre in France. An English courtier would not need to travel to France for a dose of French culture at this time, for the wars had brought French culture to London. King Jean II ('le Bon') was captured at Poitiers in 1356 and remained in England, a privileged prisoner, until 1360. He brought along with him his chaplain, the poet Gace de la Buigne, who began his *Roman de Deduis* there. Jean's brilliant court in Paris had supported Guillaume de Machaut and welcomed Petrarch, and the king is known to have continued his patronage of artistic interests in London (Salter 1980: 241). The fact that Jean was able to purchase French texts while in England, such as a *Roman de Renart*, a *Garin le Loherain*, and a *Tournoiement de l'Antechrist*, testifies to the currency of French modes even before his arrival. When the Treaty of Brétigny (1360) allowed the king's return to France to raise money for his ransom, among the royal hostages taking his place in London was his son Jean, Duc de Berry, arguably the greatest patron and collector of the age. The duke's leave-taking from his wife was commemorated by Machaut in the *Dit de la fonteinne amoureuse*, and it has even been argued (Wimsatt 1982: 49) that he imitated a line from Chaucer in a French ballade from 1389. In the 1360s, therefore, the English court must have been buzzing with talk of French poems and poets.

The supremacy of French verse was already well established in London, however. The poet Jehan de le Mote was known to Edward III and long honoured at the English court, probably from the late 1320s until the late 1350s. Le Mote's was the most significant poetry at the English court in the years before King Jean's entourage imported the reputation of Machaut. His developments in *formes fixes* lyrics and in narrative practice, as James Wimsatt observes, 'exerted a major influence on the poetic fashions to which Chaucer was exposed when he entered court life' (1991: 48). Le Mote may well have been 'the first prominent court poet Chaucer met' (50). His continental connections are impressive: le Mote was involved in a celebrated poetic 'quarrel' with the renowned poet–musician Philippe de Vitry, who was himself a friend of King Jean, of the scholar–translator Pierre Bersuire and of Petrarch, who esteemed him as 'poeta nunc unicus Galliarum' ('the only poet now among the French'), despite his customary denial of the existence of any poets outside Italy (Ouy 1978: 138). Jehan le Mote's familiarity with these major players on the European intellectual stage offers some tantalizing implications for the evolution of vernacular poetry. In any event, it seems inevitable that the presence in London of an illustrious French entourage would inspire an increase in the composition of lyric poetry in the style of Machaut's *dits amoreux* (see next section). It would also pave the way for the participation of English poets in later continental modes such as the poetic *débat* over the 'Flower and the Leaf' (see next section, and below).

Jean Froissart and Guillaume de Machaut

The royal party was not alone in exile: the French contingent in England also included the poet and chronicler Jean Froissart, who served as secretary to Edward III's queen Philippa from 1361 until 1369. Froissart was from the county of Hainault, an imperial territory just north of the French kingdom, the home both of Queen Philippa and of Chaucer's wife Philippa Roet. This Hainault connection could well have put the two poets in close contact during the years of their convergence at court. Froissart certainly had an influence on Chaucer's early poetry, his *Paradys d'Amours* inspiring much of the dream framework, not to mention the language of the introduction, in Chaucer's *Book of the Duchess* (see section below on *BD* 1–15); the *House of Fame*, too shows signs of influence by Froissart's *Le Temple d'Onnour*. There is also evidence of influence moving in the other direction: Froissart could well have taken the story for his *Dit dou bleu chevalier* from the *Book of the Duchess* (Wimsatt 1968: 129–33). In any case Froissart's *Joli Buisson de jonece* (1373), like Chaucer's *Book of the Duchess*, bewails the death of Blanche of Lancaster. The most important thing Chaucer drew from his association with Froissart, finally, is a familiarity with Machaut, who had the greatest influence on Chaucer of any contemporary French poet.

Guillaume de Machaut (*c.*1300–77) was the most important French artist of his century, a renowned musical composer as well as a poet. In music, he made substantial and long-lasting contributions in polyphony and rhythmic structure; in poetry, he pioneered lyric *formes fixes* such as the rondeau and ballade, as well as long love narratives called *dits amoreux*. Chaucer, who could possibly have met the much older French poet during one of his early trips to France (see next section), seems to have been aware of Machaut's works as early as the 1360s. His collected works display the influence of a good many of the Frenchman's lyrics, including all of Machaut's eight *dits* as well as two other long poems, the *Confort d'ami* and the *Prise d'Alexandrie*. But most significant to Chaucer's *œuvre* are five of these *dits*, and in particular a thematically linked pair that end in judgements made by royal patrons of Machaut, the *Jugement dou Roy de Behaingne* and *Jugement dou Roy de Navarre* (see Wimsatt 1968: 88–102).

Behaingne, a *dit* in debate form, is the most significant source for the *Book of the Duchess*, which shows numerous likenesses in characterization, action and language. *Navarre* does not supply the line-by-line likenesses to the *Book of the Duchess* that one finds in *Behaingne*, but is nevertheless a pervasive influence in Chaucer's work: the comic narrator Machaut presents in Navarre, consistent with the speaker in his *Voir Dit* and *Fonteinne amoureuse*, is the archetype for the obtuse, bumbling narrator of Chaucer's *Duchess*, *House of Fame* and *Parliament of Fowls*. The *Navarre*, furthermore, in that it serves as a retraction of the *Behaingne*, can be seen as Chaucer's model for providing the *Legend of Good Women* as a palinode to *Troilus and Criseyde*. *Troilus* not only draws overall themes and specific passages from *Behaingne*, but contains abundant tonal and formal evidence for considering Chaucer's poem as a participant in the tradition of the lyric *dits amoreux* pioneered by Machaut, and in the fourteenth-century phenomenon described by Wimsatt, borrowing Deschamps' phrase, as *musique naturele* (1991: 36–42).

Two other long *dits* by Machaut, this pair linked by their themes of lament and consolation, also appear to have served as inspirations for Chaucer. The *Remede de Fortune* offers thematic and verbal parallels to, as well as suggestions for character development in, the *Book of the Duchess* and *Troilus and Criseyde*. A large number of lines in the former (including the man in black's complaint against Fortune) are directly indebted to the *Remede de Fortune*; other notable resonances are the Boethian circumstances and the exhortations of Pandarus – ostensibly modelled after the words of Machaut's Esperance – in Book I of *Troilus*. His *Dit de la fonteinne amoureuse* was composed for the consolation of Jean, Duc de Berry, on the occasion of his departure as a hostage to England in 1361 (see section above on 'The Influence of French Literature at Court'); Chaucer's *Book of the Duchess* reflects the *dit*'s topos of overheard complaint and adopts both its version of Ovid's story of Ceyx and Alcyone and its application of this exemplum to the consolatory theme of the narrative. Machaut's *Dit de la fleur de lis et de la Marguerite* offers many parallels to the discussion of the daisy in the *Legend of Good Women* and numerous syntactical and verbal similarities to the opening of the *House of Fame*. It can be argued, finally, that Chaucer derived from Machaut's example the proclivity for inserting lyrics in his narrative poems, as well as his development of the comic narrator so important to his early poems and to individual *Canterbury Tales*. Chaucer's early emulation of Guillaume de Machaut left a tremendous and permanent impression. In the years following the *Book of the Duchess* he would write with a confidence and maturity born of this encounter with the works of the French master.

Chaucer in France

If Chaucer got his first exposure to French poets and their works at the English court, his knowledge of them cannot have been limited to his contacts with Froissart in London. The several recorded trips he made to France during his career would seem a likely point of convergence with other writers. However, no documentary evidence yet unearthed supports this hypothesis. It is at least possible that Chaucer met the venerable Machaut in 1359, when he was serving as a yeoman (*valettus*) in the army led by the Black Prince and had been captured by the French near Reims, Machaut's home. A meeting was also possible in 1360 at Calais, then full of nobles and their attendants from both sides fulfilling the terms of Brétigny. Among that company was Jean, Duc de Berry, bound for England; Machaut, who would commemorate this parting in verse; and the messenger, Chaucer. We have no evidence of a meeting, however, and, as in the case of his potential meeting with Boccaccio or Petrarch during his trip to Italy in 1372–3, it should be seen as possible but improbable, given the pressing official obligations on all occasions, not to mention Chaucer's relative obscurity as against the great renown of the older men. Their poems would influence Chaucer's verses whether or not he ever communed with them in person.

The records of his ensuing travels likewise yield nothing more than the potential for social contact with continental writers. Chaucer was abroad again, perhaps in France, for several weeks in 1368, and in September 1369 was with John of Gaunt's expeditionary force there. He was in France the following summer, again with the army, and in 1376–7 crossed the Channel on numerous occasions, all involving international diplomacy. Indeed, it is none other than Froissart, in Book I of his *Chroniques*, who establishes Chaucer's presence – a member of the English delegation alongside Sir Richard Stury and Sir Guischard d'Angle – at the 1377 peace negotiations at Montreuil-sur-Mer (see section below on Philippe de Mézières and the Order of the Passion). Disappointingly, none of these trips provides evidence of Chaucer's involvement in anything but official business. If he managed to make the acquaintance of poets, or acquire French or even Italian manuscripts while abroad, nothing remains to substantiate the fact, either in public records or in his writings.

But even if Chaucer never actually made the acquaintance of continental *literati* during his many journeys to France, those trips are emblematic of the incessant travels of a caste of cultivated diplomats like himself, whose breadth of experience and association in the courts of Italy, France and England strongly suggest their milieu as a network of literary exchange, with Paris at its centre (Hanly 1997). That envoys from all over Europe should constantly pass through the French capital is no surprise. The French court, however, under King Jean and his son, Charles V, who reigned 1364–80, became the site of a remarkable intellectual programme, whose centrepiece was the creation of France's first great library in a tower of the Louvre (Hanly 1990: 8–15). Pre-eminent among the works commissioned by Jean and Charles were the many translations of learned texts into French, including Bersuire's Livy, Jean de Sy's Bible, Denis de Foulechat's translation of John of Salisbury's *Policraticus*, Jean Daudin's rendering of Petrarch's *De remediis utriusque Fortunae* and Simon de Hesdin's Valerius Maximus. This absorption in ancient and 'serious' texts did not, however, preclude the appreciation of vernacular literature: the court of Paris provided patronage to French poets from Philippe de Vitry to Guillaume de Machaut to his protégé, Eustache Deschamps, a man of Chaucer's own age.

Eustache Deschamps, the 'Flower and the Leaf', and Oton de Grandson

Deschamps is known for his bold criticism of governmental policies and figures, a style very unlike the cautious navigation of political waters one finds both in Chaucer's poetry and in his official actions. And yet, like his English counterpart, he moved in circles close to the centre of power, and was himself present during at least one peace conference. The sole documentary evidence for their association is Deschamps' *ballade* 'O Socrates plains de philosophie' with its refrain 'Grant translateur, Geffroy Chaucier', which most scholars date in the mid-1380s (*Œuvres* ii, 138–40, no. 138;[4] see Wimsatt 1991: 248–62; and Crépin 1984: 61–7). Deschamps lauds Chaucer's poetic accomplishments and commends some of his own compositions to him, displaying conventional humility in calling them 'schoolboy poems' ('euvres d'escolier', 28). This poetic offering, he claims, was carried 'par Clifford', a surname referring almost certainly to the English knight Lewis Clifford, a member of Richard II's *camera regis* and of John of Gaunt's circle, a diplomat and a friend of Chaucer.

We do not know what other poems Deschamps entrusted to Clifford's care, but had his offering included four particular *ballades*, their presence could have caused Chaucer's first awareness of the fashionable 1380s trend called the 'Flower and the Leaf'. Its courtier adherents would take sides in a playful debate, in which principles of courtly love would be debated in terms of the superiority of either leaf or flower (Pearsall 1962: esp. 20–9). One of these four (*Œuvres* iii, 375–6, no. 536) presents a *demande d'amour* to be arbitrated by several authorities in love, most of them Frenchmen of the highest nobility but including 'l'amoureux Cliffort', whose inclusion here signals his familiarity with the French court and potential involvement in other episodes of literary exchange. Another (no. 764) describes Philippa of Lancaster, eldest daughter of Chaucer's benefactor John of Gaunt, as 'la fleur de valour', the patroness of the 'order' of the flower in England. If these lyrics had been among those dispatched to England along with the 'grant translateur' ballade, the conjunction could explain Chaucer's reference to the Flower and the Leaf in his *Legend of Good Women* (F 188–90). Nevertheless, whatever poems crossed the channel at this time, we should not make too much of the impact of Deschamps' poetry. Although it is clear that Chaucer knew his work, the evidence for its influence on his poetry is slight, involving the potential transmission of the poetic fashion described above, and some resonances between sections in the tales of the Wife of Bath and the Merchant and Deschamps' *Miroir de mariage*.

These scant traces of imitation notwithstanding, the simple fact of Chaucer's acquaintance with Deschamps implies a connection with the continental intellectual sphere that could prove more important to our knowledge of the broader influences on his work than any comparison of analogous lyrics. Deschamps not only knew and admired the poetry of Chaucer, but was acquainted with two of the English poet's close friends. The first, Lewis Clifford, has already been mentioned; the second, also featured in a Deschamps poem, is a figure much more significant both to Chaucer's poetry and to the diplomatic affairs of the era. This is Sir Oton de Grandson, a Savoyard who served the English crown for most of the period between 1369 and his death in a judicial duel in 1397, and was himself acquainted with a good many of the movers and shakers on the international political scene. Like Clifford, Grandson was an intimate of John of Gaunt, and both were acquainted with Chaucer. He knew Deschamps well enough to play a fairly harsh practical joke on him: in an episode recounted in one of Deschamps's ballades (*Œuvres* v, 79–80, no. 893), the poet crosses enemy lines to visit Grandson, who has his terrified friend seized by some brutish English soldiers before vouching for him. Like his friends, Grandson, as we will see in the next section, also had a certain reputation as a poet: correspondences between several of their poems point to an artistic partnership between himself and Chaucer, and he may have been responsible for assembling the French lyrics (including those of Deschamps) compiled in the 'Ch' manuscript at the University of Pennsylvania. But whatever effect he and his French concoctions had on Chaucer's poetry, the most significant role in Grandson's impressive career was his leadership in an international crusading order, the Order of the Passion.

Philippe de Mézières and the Order of the Passion

His co-operation with the Order of the Passion places Grandson in the sphere of Philippe de Mézières, the eminent author and propagandist of crusade who was the most vocal mediator between the French and English courts in the 1380s and 1390s (Hanly 1997). Mézières' familiarity with courts from Cyprus to London, combined with his extensive literary accomplishments, makes him a pivotal figure on the international scene. Some of the cultured diplomats who collaborated with him, furthermore, can profitably be considered as participants in the putative network of intellectual exchange mentioned above, and as potential 'carriers' of Italian culture. Mézières' lifelong fixation with leading a Christian crusade to stem Muslim expansion along Europe's eastern frontier made him one of the staunchest supporters of the long-drawn-out bilateral efforts to end the hostilities between England and France:

since no crusade could ever be mounted while the two greatest Christian nations were still at war, he and his circle, several of whom played crucial roles negotiating the frequent truces of the period, worked to achieve a permanent ceasefire.

The Order of the Passion, which Mézières had first conceived many years before but which finally materialized in the last two decades of the fourteenth century, would symbolize Anglo-French *détente* and supply the unified vanguard in the campaign against Islam. Some of the greatest French and English nobles joined its ranks, as did lesser figures like Clifford; Oton de Grandson was himself named one of the four 'evangelists' of the Order, with special responsibilities for disseminating its principles among the aristocracy on both sides of the Channel. Most significant is the fact that Geoffrey Chaucer was known not only to Clifford and Grandson, but to a number of Clifford's fellow Lollards and chamber knights as well, such as the poet John Clanvowe (see Scattergood 1983) and Richard Stury; all were active in the peace negotiations of the 1380s and 1390s, parleys in which Chaucer himself had taken part between 1377 and 1381. Stury, Chaucer's companion at Montreuil in 1377 and a long-time friend of Froissart, owned a copy of the *Roman de la rose* (now British Library MS Royal 19.B.XIII). And Clanvowe was himself a poet: his *Boke of Cupid* (also called *The Cuckoo and the Nightingale*) shows deep familiarity with Chaucer's *Parliament of Fowls*, and it has been argued that his *The Two Ways* displays a resistance to the warrior values of the aristocracy similar to that displayed in Chaucer's tales of Sir Thopas and Melibee (Scattergood 1981), an attitude that would seem to align Chaucer with the convictions of the broader 'peace movement'.

More noteworthy still is the fact that Philippe de Mézières was a long-standing friend of Petrarch. Petrarch's letter to Mézières of 1369 (*Epistolae rerum senilium* 13. 2), furthermore, suggests an awareness of Philippe's crusading principles (Hanly 1997: 309–10). Written shortly after the murder of Philippe's sovereign Pierre de Lusignan, the letter laments that loss while criticizing the lack of discipline displayed by Western knights in the Alexandria campaign of 1365, contrasting their disgrace with the lofty chivalric virtues of an unnamed mutual friend. Lusignan, interestingly enough, later became the hero of Machaut's *Prise d'Alexandrie* and the subject of a portrait in Chaucer's Monk's Tale. Mézières' interest in Petrarch, however, was not limited to their correspondence: in addition to his authorship of allegorical dream visions, Philippe also translated Petrarch's *Historia Griseldis*, the Latin rendition (*Epistolae rerum senilium* 17. 3) of Boccaccio's Griselda story (*Decameron* X. 10). Philippe's translation was in turn closely imitated by an anonymous French *Livre Griseldis* in the 1380s, which has itself been shown to be a source for Chaucer's own version of this story, the Clerk's Tale. This correlation between the work of Chaucer and that of Mézières is full of possibilities, especially given the Frenchman's association with Petrarch.

Could Philippe de Mézières and his circle have provided Chaucer with knowledge of the works of Petrarch and the other great Italian authors of the century, and even supplied manuscripts? We must keep in mind the importance of Paris as a centre both of learning and of international diplomacy, and consider as well the endless travels of courtiers at this time, in particular the members of the Order of the Passion and their circle, many of whom display the interest in literature most clearly manifested by their founder Mézières. Clifford travelled widely, Clanvowe more widely still, and there is some evidence that Oton de Grandson journeyed to Italy in Richard II's service before becoming one of Philippe's 'evangelists'. Envoys like these, furthermore, would have had frequent dealings with Avignon and its papal court, site of another fabled library and home to a thriving community of proto-humanists, many of them Italians, themselves involved in international diplomacy and in a veritable 'cult of Petrarch' as well (Simone 1961; Hanly 1997). And the earliest French translation of Boccaccio's *Il Filostrato* – a potential source for Chaucer's *Troilus and Criseyde* – could have been produced at the Angevin courts of Provence or Naples in this era (Hanly 1990).

The connections briefly sketched here point towards a late fourteenth-century Anglo-French cultural milieu in which literate diplomats would have been aware early on of the writings and the influence of the great Italian poets. If in his youth the presence of French courtiers and poets at the court of London gave Chaucer an essential grounding in poetic forms and motifs, his contact with other French figures later in life exposed him to additional continental themes and trends, perhaps even to the other most serious influence on his *œuvre*: the poetry of Petrarch, Boccaccio and Dante. Despite the endless, crippling war between the two neighbouring nations, France remained essential to England's cultural development. In what follows I will consider three passages from Chaucer's poetry emblematic of his transformation of the French language in his English style, his awareness of the debt he owed his French predecessors, and finally his appreciation for a French contemporary who, like him, had a career not only as a poet but also as a player in the turbulent political events of his day.

The *Book of the Duchess*, 1–15

We have observed that Chaucer's models as a youthful courtier in the 1360s would have been the fashionable French courtly lyric writers, such as Machaut or Froissart, and that he and all the other young poets at the English court would have been writing verses like those by 'Ch' in the Pennsylvania manuscript. We noticed, as well, that during Chaucer's lifetime the French language declined in prominence in England as that of English increased. But the native language, despite its new status in society, did not offer poets the flexible medium enjoyed by French practitioners. As Larry Benson puts it, 'before Chaucer could write English poetry he had to find an English poetic language and style' (1995: 247). Benson and Derek Brewer (1966) closely analyse the English tradition on which Chaucer drew as he fashioned his poetic medium, but since that tradition lies beyond the scope of this chapter, I will restrict the focus in the discussion of this first passage to Chaucer's appropriation and transformation of French language and conventions.

Benson (247–8) goes on to say that 'To write in English for an audience of fellow courtiers steeped in the French tradition Chaucer had to find a way to evoke the courtly style of French poetry in his own English verse.' The native poetic line available to him, the 'solid and workmanlike' four-beat English couplet augmented with the courtly language of the romances, was simple, direct and capable of some finesse. But to English poets who since their youth had lived and breathed the elaborate, ornamented courtly lyrics made famous by Machaut, this medium must have seemed crude and unwieldy. As an example of Chaucer's importation of the French tradition into English, let us briefly examine a single passage, the famous opening of the *Book of the Duchess*, alongside its source, the first twelve lines of Froissart's *Paradys d'Amours*:

Je sui de moi en grant merveille	I have gret wonder, be this lyght,
Comment je vifs quant tant je veille	How that I lyve, for day ne nyght
Et on ne poroit en veillant	I may nat slepe wel nygh noght;
Trouver de moi plus traveillant,	I have so many an ydel thoght
Car bien saciés que par veillier	Purely for defaute of slep
Me viennent souvent travillier	That, by my trouthe, I take no kep
Pensées et merancolies	Of nothing, how hyt cometh or gooth,
Qui me sont ens au coer liies	Ne me nys nothyng leef nor looth.
Et pas ne les puis deslyer,	Al is ylyche good to me –
Car ne voeil la belle oublyer	Joye or sorowe, wherso hyt be –
Pour quele amour en ce travail	For I have felynge in nothyng,
Je sui entrés et tant je veil.	But as yt were a mased thyng,
	Alway in poynt to falle a-doun;
	For sorwful ymagynacioun
	Ys alway hooly in my mynde.

My *literal translation of Froissart*: 'I am greatly amazed at myself, how I stay alive when I stay awake so much, and one could not find, among those who lie awake, one who is more tormented than I, for well you know that, as I lie awake, [troubled] thoughts and melancholies come often to torment me, which are bound within my heart and I cannot untie them, because I do not wish to forget the beautiful one for love of whom I am entered into this torment, lying so much awake.'

Chaucer's poem is remarkable both for its Frenchness and for its Englishness. Its sources are thoroughly French: the *Book of the Duchess* on the whole is greatly indebted to the work of Machaut, who (like Froissart) wrote in the tradition of the *Roman de la rose*. But its language is unrelentingly English. If in two previous renderings of French originals (the *ABC* and the 'Complaint unto Pity') Chaucer had gone out of his way to use French vocabulary, the opening lines to *The Book of the Duchess* display his commitment to another goal entirely. In his examination of this passage, Brewer observes that 'he seems even to avoid French words . . . Wherever Chaucer uses a French word, it is because there is no English equivalent available' (1966: 3). Benson notes that no Romance words are employed until the fifth line, and that these terms – 'purely' and 'defaut' – had already been in use in England since before 1300. Both

Benson and Brewer cite Joseph Mersand's affirmation of the 'overwhelmingly Anglo-Saxon proportion' of Chaucer's vocabulary: roughly seven per cent of the poem's words are Romance terms, the lowest ratio he found in all of Chaucer (Mersand 1939: 91). Chaucer elects, for example, to use the Old English 'wonder' in line 1 to render Froissart's *merveil*, though the Romance term 'marvel' had long been available in English. And even though Chaucer will employ conspicuously French stylistic tendencies at other points in this poem, such as abstract allegorizations or other courtly echoes of the *Roman de la rose*, he makes no effort here in the opening lines to provide the close translation of a French source witnessed in his *Romaunt*. The version of Froissart Chaucer uses to begin his poem shows no such inclination towards line-by-line reproduction. Chaucer's chatty paraphrase departs markedly from Froissart's comparatively listless passage, showcasing native asseverations and colloquial asides in the animated narrative style that would become one of his hallmarks, a style he seems to have acquired by way of an encounter with the English romance. This brief excerpt from the *Book of the Duchess*, therefore, can be considered the most competent Middle English verse yet attempted at that early date, but it nevertheless shows Chaucer at work in the shadow of the French courtly lyric, a tradition that both inspired and perplexed the English poets of his time.

The F Prologue to the *Legend of Good Women*, 66–83

However it was that Chaucer hammered out his own English style, his indebtedness to French authors and modes is indisputable, and even formed the subject for commentary in his poems. In the F Prologue to his *Legend of Good Women*, the narrator complains of the inadequacy of his language, acknowledging his dependence on poetic forerunners – and in the context here described, we can safely assume he means *French* poets, like Machaut or Froissart – in the effort to raise his own language to the poetic heights enjoyed by their vernacular:

> Allas, that I ne had Englyssh, ryme or prose,
> Suffisant this flour to preyse aryght!
> But helpeth, ye that han konnyng and myght,
> Ye lovers that kan make of sentement;
> In this cas oghte ye be diligent
> To forthren me somwhat in my labour,
> Whethir ye ben with the leef or with the flour.
> For wel I wot that ye han her-biforn
> Of makyng ropen, and lad awey the corn,
> And I come after, glenyng here and there,
> And am ful glad yf I may fynde an ere
> Of any goodly word that ye han left.
> And thogh it happen me rehercen eft
> That ye han in your fresshe songes sayd,

> Forbereth me, and beth nat evele apayd,
> Syn that ye see I do yt in the honour
> Of love, and eke in service of the flour
> Whom that I serve as I have wit or myght.

We recognize the context as that of the late fourteenth-century poetic fashion of the 'Flower and the Leaf'. In the first two lines of the passage, the narrator bewails his inability to praise the daisy's beauty. He claims to lack the 'Englyssh' for suitable adulation of the flower and, moving beyond the conventional topos of inexpressibility, suggests that his native tongue – and, by extension, the English poetic tradition – plays as much a role in this failure as his own ineffectual 'ryme or prose'. By announcing the deficiency of his own language, the narrator implies the potency of French, a sentiment underscored later in the passage (78–9) when he recalls the many times he has called upon the 'fresshe songes' of the poets of the Flower. And indeed, the ensuing five lines (68–72) represent a call for assistance from poetic predecessors who did in fact possess the tools necessary to praise this flower aright, those lovers 'that kan make of sentement' – who can write verses expressing (courtly) emotion. These poets, he declares, should strive to support him in his task, whatever side they have taken in this fashionable debate. The narrator displays customary humility before his ancestors, who have produced a rich crop of polished verses, the 'corn' of line 74. The field already harvested, he can only hope to find 'an ere / Of any goodly word' that they might have left behind, which he will then be obliged to rework, with deficient tools, in crafting a song of praise for this flower. As the passage concludes, the narrator asks his forebears not to misconstrue his imitations, since his borrowings are meant to serve, after all, the same poetic goal to which they dedicated their pioneering verses.

These lines, however, should not be read merely as self-deprecation. The *Legend of Good Women* may not be considered among his highest achievements, but since the poem most likely dates from the mid-1380s – when Chaucer was working at the peak of his abilities – neither can it be considered juvenilia. The narrator's protestations of inadequacy, therefore, should be taken more to manifest admiration and even reverence for the work of those French poets than to indicate frustration with his own.

The 'Complaint of Venus'

Chaucer's narrators often affect a humble stance, an attitude not only highly conventional but sometimes ironic, as in cases when the motif appears amid expert verses. Such a case occurs in our final passage, the last lines of Chaucer's envoy to his triple *ballade* 'The Complaint of Venus':

> And eke to me it ys a gret penaunce,
> Syth rym in Englissh hath such skarsete,

> To folowe word by word the curiosite
> Of Graunson, flour of hem that make in Fraunce.
> (79–82)

As in the passage from the *Legend* above, the narrator complains that his language impedes the poetic task at hand, here the rendering of rhymes found in the French original. There is no denying that the French language, then as now, is richer in rhymes than English. But given the fact that this *envoi* employs a much more complex rhyme scheme than is found in either the French poem Chaucer imitates or in the preceding seventy-two lines of English verse, one must question the seriousness of this stance (for a detailed reading of the poem and *envoi*, see Wimsatt 1991: 213–19). Furthermore, the narrator has just lamented that old age has taken a harsh toll on his poetic powers ('For elde, that in my spirit dulleth me / Hath of endyting al the subtilte / Wel nygh bereft out of my remembraunce', 76–8), a comment proclaiming the poem's 'maker' to be a seasoned, expert versifier. The poet adopts this humble stance conventionally, both before the 'Princes' (73) to whom the poem is dedicated, and before the poet whom Chaucer claims to have followed 'word by word', the illustrious Sir Oton de Grandson.

Grandson is celebrated as the 'flour of hem that make in Fraunce', which more likely signals prominence among warrior–poets than absolute superiority in a field that included Machaut and Froissart (Wimsatt 1991: 211); for, despite some fine verses and a decent reputation as a poet, Grandson was better known for his practice of arms than of versifying. The knight would have been acquainted with Chaucer at the English court, and their extant verses suggest a lively exchange of poems and ideas. Indeed, several of their works show they shared the notion that St Valentine's Day was the day when lovers would find mates, and some scholars even hold the two poets responsible for the origination of this myth. In addition to other more general themes and images in his poetry that show evidence of indebtedness to Chaucer's work, Grandson's *Complainte de l'an nouvel* imitates passages from the *Book of the Duchess*, and his *Songe Saint Valentin* from the *Parliament of Fowls*. One poem shows Chaucer directly imitating Grandson: the 'Complaint of Venus' (*c.*1385?) freely adapts three *ballades* from a five-*ballade* sequence, the 'Cinq ballades ensievans'.

The only manuscript presenting Grandson's *ballades* in the order imitated by Chaucer's 'Complaint' is MS French 15 at the University of Pennsylvania, a compilation dating from *c.*1400 which could well have been assembled by Grandson himself (see Wimsatt 1982). This codex contains 310 poems in all, most of them by Machaut, but including selections from Froissart, Deschamps and Grandson. Most fascinating, however, are the fifteen lyrics bearing the initials 'Ch', which seem to indicate authorship. Since we have no obvious candidate from among contemporary French poets, it has been argued that the 'Ch' could well stand for 'Chaucer'. Many of the poems in this anthology date from the 1350s and 1360s, when Chaucer was a young courtier and would quite likely have been composing French lyrics; the manuscript, therefore, not only is representative of the probable models for Chaucer's earliest efforts, but may even contain those efforts themselves. The Pennsylvania manuscript suggests a long complicity between the two poets, and an anthologist's perception of a poetic continuum reaching from Machaut through Chaucer.

This may well be what Grandson thought of Chaucer: the continuator of a rich lyric tradition, one who made his youthful contributions in French and now presented his mature creations in English. There could be no higher praise for a poet living in the bilingual England of his time. Whatever the impact of Grandson's poetry on Chaucer, finally, it is fairly clear that the two were friends who swapped books and ideas, and it is not difficult to imagine long conversations about poetry and poets, discussions of the works of their friend Froissart or their master Machaut, or even those of the Italian poets then coming into view. Perhaps Grandson profited more from their exchange than did Chaucer, and yet Chaucer is unquestionably the more important poet. As was the case with Deschamps, his connection with Grandson could very well have brought him benefits more difficult to trace than the imitation of individual lines. France was the source of Chaucer's earliest poetic inspiration and most likely of his first poetic language, the destination for many important professional travels, the home of some of his most significant literary influences and the point of contact between England and the cultural miracle of Italy. No matter what the two sides might have said about each other during their many years of war, England's intellectual debt to France cannot be over-estimated.

See also COMEDY; CONTEMPORARY ENGLISH WRITERS; GENRE; GEOGRAPHY AND TRAVEL; ITALY; LANGUAGE; LIFE HISTORIES; LONDON; MODES OF REPRESENTATION; NARRATIVE; TRANSLATION; VISUALIZING.

NOTES

1 *Polychronicon Ranulphi Higden Monachi Cestrensis . . .* , 9 vols, ed. C. Babington and J. R. Lumby, Rolls Series 41 (London: Longman, 1865–6), i, 159, 161.

2 *The Complete Works of John Gower*, ed. G. C. Macaulay, 4 vols (Oxford: Clarendon, 1899–1902), ii.

3 Ibid., i.

4 *Œuvres Complètes d'Eustache Deschamps*, ed. A. H. E. Marquis de Queux de St-Hilaire and Gaston Raynaud, 11 vols (Paris: Firmin Didot, 1878–1903), ii.

REFERENCES AND FURTHER READING

Benson, Larry D. (1995) 'The beginnings of Chaucer's English style', in *Contradictions: From Beowulf to Chaucer: Selected Studies of Larry D. Benson*, ed. Theodore M. Andersson and Stephen A. Barney (Aldershot: Scolar), 243–65. Examines Chaucer's development of a vernacular style out of two traditions – French and English – by the time he wrote the *Book of the Duchess*.

Braddy, Haldeen (1979) 'The French influence on Chaucer', in *Companion to Chaucer Studies*, ed.

Beryl Rowland, rev. edn (New York: Oxford University Press), 143–59. A concise review of the essential literary relations.

Brewer, Derek S. (1966) 'The relationship of Chaucer to the English and European traditions', in *Chaucer and Chaucerians: Critical Studies in Middle English Literature*, ed. Derek Brewer (University, Ala.: University of Alabama Press; London: Nelson), 1–38. Provides close historical contextualization and insightful readings in analysing the influence on Chaucer's poetry and prose of both the native English romance tradition and the French tradition (*Roman de la rose*, Machaut).

Calin, William (1974) *A Poet at the Fountain: Essays on the Narrative Verse of Guillaume de Machaut* (Lexington, Ky.: University of Kentucky Press). Comprehensive analysis of Machaut's poetic *oeuvre*, including discussions of historical context, manipulation of literary themes, imagery and narrative strategies; briefly discusses Machaut's influence on Chaucer.

Crépin, André (1984) 'Chaucer and the French', in *Medieval and Pseudo-medieval Literature*, ed. Piero Boitani and Anna Torti (Tübingen: Narr; Cambridge: Brewer), 55–77. Discusses influence of French language and poets, and of Chaucer's French experience; especially interesting for its treatment of Deschamps' 'Grant translateur' ballade, and its notion of Chaucer's role in the transmission of culture.

Fisher, John H. (1981) 'Chaucer and the French influence', in *New Perspectives in Chaucer Criticism*, ed. D. M. Rose (Norman, Okla.: Pilgrim Books), 177–91. Describes Chaucer's intimate familiarity with French language and poetry, and argues that this familiarity led to the development of an English style that allowed him to bring back a 'natural manner and conversational tone' that had been lost to English since the Conquest.

Green, Richard Firth (1980) *Poets and Prince-pleasers: Literature and the English Court in the Late Middle Ages* (Toronto: University of Toronto Press). The best available study of English court life in the late Middle Ages. Excellent archival documentation. Detailed discussions of (among other things) intellectual attitudes at late medieval English courts, the education of courtiers, patronage and the make-up of aristo-cratic libraries, composition of poetry by nobles and the role of translations in England.

Hanly, Michael (1990) *Boccaccio, Beauvau, and Chaucer*: Troilus and Criseyde – *Four Perspectives on Influence* (Norman, Okla.: Pilgrim Books). Examines putative relation between Chaucer's poem and a French translation of Boccaccio's *Il Filostrato*; first chapter provides brief overview of French intellectual climate and the library of Charles V.

——(1997) 'Courtiers and poets: an international network of literary exchange', *Viator* 28, 305–32. Scrutinizes careers of literate diplomats in placing the poetry of Chaucer in the context of contemporary continental artistic and political milieux.

Mersand, Joseph P. (1939) *Chaucer's Romance Vocabulary*, 2nd edn (New York: Comet). For a more recent work, see Christopher Cannon, *The Making of Chaucer's English: A Study of Words* (Cambridge: Cambridge University Press, 1998)

Muscatine, Charles (1957) *Chaucer and the French Tradition: A Study in Style and Meaning* (Berkeley, Los Angeles and London: University of California Press). Essential study of Chaucer's style as a response to French literature, to the 'courtly' tradition (represented by Guillaume de Lorris' section of the *Roman de la rose*) and the 'bourgeois' tradition (represented by Jean de Meun's).

Olson, Paul A. (1986) 'The Order of the Passion and internal order', in *The* Canterbury Tales *and the Good Society* (Princeton: Princeton University Press), ch. 2, 49–84. Most important for its speculations regarding the impact on the political elements of Chaucer's poetry of his participation in Anglo-French negotiations of the 1370s and 1380s, and connections with members of the supranational Order of the Passion.

Ouy, Gilbert (1978) 'La dialectique des rapports intellectuels franco-italiens et l'Humanisme en France aux XIVᵉ et XVᵉ siècles', *Rapporti culturali ed economici fra Italia e Francia nel secoli dal XIV al XVI*, proceedings of the 'Colloqui Italo-Francese', Rome, 18–20 February 1978 (Rome: Giunta Centrale per gli Studi Storici, 1979), 137–57. Meticulously documented appraisal of the French intellectual scene, and Petrarch's influence upon it, from *c.*1380 to 1417.

Pearsall, Derek, ed. (1962) The Floure and the Leaf *and* The Assembly of Ladies (Manchester: Manchester University Press). Text and authoritative explanatory notes for two poems representative of the late fourteenth-century courtly lyric tradition.

Robbins, Rossell Hope (1978) 'Geoffroi Chaucier, poète français, father of English poetry', *Chaucer Review* 13, 93–115. Argues persuasively that Chaucer would have written French lyrics early in his career; detailed, sophisticated contextualization.

Salter, Elizabeth (1980) 'Chaucer and internationalism', *Studies in the Age of Chaucer* 2, 71–9; repr. in Salter, *English and International: Studies in the Literature, Art and Patronage of Medieval England*, ed. Derek Pearsall and N. Zeeman (Cambridge: Cambridge University Press, 1988), 239–44. Excellent brief description of the intellectual culture at French and English courts in the mid- to late fourteenth century, with an especially fine account of the court of Edward III.

Scattergood, V. J. (1981) 'Chaucer and the French war: *Sir Thopas* and *Melibee*', in *Court and Poet*, ed. Glyn S. Burgess (Cambridge: Brewer), 287–96. Reads the two tales as arguing generally against chivalric excess, and particularly against the war with France; notes Chaucer's participation in negotiations.

——(1983) 'Literary culture at the court of Richard II', in *English Court Culture in the Later Middle Ages*, ed. V. J. Scattergood and J. W. Sherborne (London: Duckworth), 29–43. Corrective to Gervase Mathew's view of Richard's court; historical evidence shows prominence of French books and themes in England; fascinating account of Chaucer's contemporary audience, including career diplomats such as Clanvowe.

Simone, Franco (1961) *Il Renascimento francese: studi e ricerche* (Turin: Società editrice internazionale); abr. trans. by H. Gaston Hall as *The French Renaissance: Medieval Tradition and Italian Influence* (London: Macmillan, 1969). A pioneering study of the proto-humanist circles in fourteenth-century Avignon and Paris, the earliest examples of Petrarchan influence outside Italy.

Wallace, David (1986) 'Chaucer's continental inheritance: the early poems and *Troilus and Criseyde*', in *The Cambridge Chaucer Companion*, ed. Piero Boitani and Jill Mann (Cambridge: Cambridge University Press), 39–58. A perceptive encapsulation of the development of Chaucer's vernacular art through his engagement with the *Roman de la rose*, Machaut and Dante.

Wimsatt, James I. (1968) *Chaucer and the French Love Poets: The Literary Background of the Book of the Duchess* (Chapel Hill, NC: University of North Carolina Press; repr. New York and London: Johnson, 1972). Ground-breaking work on Machaut's career and contributions; analyses the development of the lyric *dit amoreux* from Guillaume de Lorris to Froissart, with a special focus on the indebtedness of Chaucer's *Book of the Duchess* to poems by Machaut.

——(1982) *Chaucer and the Poems of 'Ch' in University of Pennsylvania Manuscript French 15* (Cambridge: Brewer). Detailed study of the manuscript containing a collection of lyrics by Machaut, Grandson, Deschamps and others, perhaps including Chaucer ('Ch' signature).

——(1991) *Chaucer and his French Contemporaries: Natural Music in the Fourteenth Century* (Toronto: University of Toronto Press). Expands greatly upon his 1968 monograph, examining French lyric poetry from Jehan de le Mote to Deschamps with a view to establishing its influence on Chaucer, presenting all these poets as practitioners of 'natural music', the verbal euphony employed by fourteenth-century lyric poets involving the artful use of rhyme, alliteration and stanzaic patterning.

10
Games
Malcolm Andrew

The topic of 'games' as it applies to Chaucer's work has been taken to encompass literary representation of and allusion to a wide range of human activity, including recreations and pastimes of a broadly competitive nature, games of skill and chance, and all kinds of sport. It does not include social activities such as dancing and playing musical instruments, since these generally lack the element of competition which is fundamental to games.

Chaucerian scholars writing on these matters have been profoundly influenced by the seminal work of Johann Huizinga (1949) on play. Huizinga argues, in brief, that play is a fundamental and highly significant human activity, which has certain essential characteristics: it is voluntary, distinct from ordinary life, and not overtly productive; it occurs at specific times and in specific places, and is bound by rules; and, while ostensibly light-hearted, can be extremely serious. Just as V. A. Kolve (1966: 8–32) is relating these ideas to the English mystery plays, Richard A. Lanham (1967) applies them to Chaucer's poetry – in which he identifies three 'games', those of love, war and rhetoric. A complementary rhetorical tradition, that of 'jest and earnest in medieval literature', is traced to its classical origins in another seminal work, that of Ernst Robert Curtius (1953: 417–35). Glending Olson (1982) investigates a less well known but highly significant tradition, in which literature is justified for its therapeutic and recreational value, relating this concept to Chaucer's poetry, especially the *Canterbury Tales*. Several commentators, notably Carl Lindahl (1987), Laura Kendrick (1988) and John M. Ganim (1990) consider the *Canterbury Tales* in relation to ideas of carnival and the festive, associated with the work of Mikhail Bakhtin on Rabelais and C. L. Barber on Shakespeare.

All such discussions of game and play in Chaucer's work reflect an awareness of the importance of the words in which such ideas are expressed. Chief among these are, naturally enough, the Middle English *game* and *pleye* themselves. Each is conspicuously rich, both in its range of meaning and in its potential resonance. *Game* is used in a range of senses including pastime, amusement, sport, pleasure, fun, joke and trick, often in contrast to more serious matters, and potentially with a sexual connotation. *Pleye* occurs mainly as a verb, in a range of senses including 'to take part in a game, pastime, or contest, to take pleasure or enjoy leisure, to have fun, to jest' – again, sometimes with a sexual connotation. The cognate noun is used in an equivalent range of senses. Though Chaucer does, of course, use various other words and expressions in describing the (fictional) events and issues relevant to the topic of games, some of which are discussed below, these two words remain absolutely central. It is, therefore, no surprise to find that *game* and *pleye* occur repeatedly in connection with the most conspicuous game in Chaucer's work, the storytelling contest in the *Canterbury Tales*.

The *Canterbury Tales* as Game

The proposal that this contest should take place is initially described as a form of play on the part of the Host: the reader is informed that 'after soper pleyen he began' (GP 758). In elaborating his idea, the Host conceptualizes the process of storytelling as a form of play, explaining to the assembled pilgrims (who will become the tellers of the tales) that, according to his plan, 'as ye goon by the weye, / Ye shapen yow to talen and to pleye' (771–2). Once the Knight has been selected as the first teller by the drawing of lots (the 'cut'), his first words reflect the same concept: 'Syn I shal bigynne the game, / What, welcome be the cut, a Goddes name' (853–4). Thereafter, the storytelling contest is regularly described in terms of play and game. A few examples will suffice to illustrate this. At the end of the Knight's Tale, the Host observes that 'trewely the game is wel bigonne' (MilP 3117); subsequently, in encouraging the Monk to tell a tale, the Host requests that he should 'brek nat oure game' (MkP 1927). After his dreary succession of 'tragedies' has been interrupted, the Monk refuses the Host's invitation to tell another tale, asserting: 'I have no lust to pleye' (NPP 2806). Earlier, the Host has encouraged the Clerk to tell his tale by stating: 'For what man is entred in a pley, / He nedes moot unto the pley assente' (ClP 10–11).

This last quotation indicates that the tale-telling contest is governed by a set of rules – in which it conforms to one of the basic characteristics of play identified by Huizinga (as mentioned above). The Host does, in fact, stipulate the essential rules of the contest from the outset (GP 766–809): that each pilgrim should tell two tales on the way to Canterbury and two more on the way back; that he should himself travel with them and take charge of the contest; and that the winner should be treated to a dinner at the expense of the other pilgrims. At this juncture, the rules of the game are not specified in any more detail. While the Host seems to assume that he will have the right to make judgements on particular issues as the contest progresses, this notion does not meet with complete acceptance from the pilgrims. His authority is challenged most significantly on the question of the order in which the pilgrims should tell their tales. He has, apparently, assumed that this should conform to a descending order of social standing, but is challenged on the matter as soon as the first tale is over (MilP 3114–35). In this crucial passage, the Host, for all his apparent dominance and forcefulness, loses control over a significant aspect of the management of the game. Some commentators have linked this loss of control with the later revelation that he feels unable to control his wife (MkP 1891–1923). Whether or not such a notion may seem convincing, one of the recurring comic aspects of the *Canterbury Tales* is the portrayal of the Host's attempts to manage the tale-telling contest, to negotiate relationships with the various pilgrims and to maintain his authority as best he can.

These manoeuvres take place in the 'links' between the tales. They involve the Host in several related activities: manipulating relationships both among the pilgrims and between himself and various pilgrims; commenting regularly on the nature and quality of the tales immediately after they are told, and at times on the observations and statements of pilgrims in the links; and deciding what kind of tale would follow most appropriately at any given juncture. In making judgements of this last kind the Host would, presumably, be guided by some sense of what is desirable and appropriate in the tale-telling contest he has initiated. The most significant statement on this matter, made in his opening proposal, is that the winner would be the teller who provides 'tales of best sentence and moost solaas' (GP 798). Though the concept of 'sentence and solace' may raise some fundamental issues about the nature and purpose of literature (discussed further below), it also suggests the potential for a basic distinction between tales as edification and as entertainment.

According to Alan T. Gaylord (1967) in his article on Fragment VII of the *Canterbury Tales*, the Host's management of the tale-telling contest implies that he views tales as either edifying (*sentence*) or entertaining (*solace*), and that he favours an alternation between the two kinds of tale. The potential for the juxtaposition of edifying and entertaining tales to raise questions about literary taste and judgement is realized as early as the link between the first two tales (in the Miller's Prologue, part of which is discussed further below). At the end of this interesting passage, Chaucer offers a general appeal that 'men shal nat maken ernest of game'. Clearly, 'earnest and game' is a formula broadly equivalent to 'sentence and solace'. It becomes something of a motif in the *Canterbury Tales*, recurring, with minor variations, in the tales of the Clerk and the Merchant and in the prologue to the Manciple's Tale (ClT 609, 733; MerT 1594; ManP 100). It also appears, again with minor variations, in the *House of Fame*, *Troilus and Criseyde* and the *Legend of Good Women* (HF 822; TC III, 254, IV, 1465; *LGW* 2703). In each case, the formula tends to suggest something of the ambivalence and elusiveness of the concept of seriousness – most strikingly in the admission of Pandarus to Troilus that his role as a go-between has developed 'bitwixen game and ernest' (*TC* III, 254).

Tricks, Jests and Sexual Licence

By general consensus, these issues regarding 'earnest and game' are implicit in the opening sequence of the *Canterbury Tales*, where the elevated tone and matter of the

Knight's Tale gives way to comic bawdiness in the tales of the Miller and the Reeve, and in the fragmentary tale of the Cook. As it does so, some other aspects of play and game are introduced into the *Canterbury Tales*: those associated with trickery, jest and sexual licence. The treatment of such matters in the Miller's Tale may be particularly significant, since it is the first of the comic tales. Its essential characteristics include a neat and fast-moving plot based on trickery and deception, a small cast of stereo-typical but engaging characters, a setting in contemporary society, and a knowing and somewhat amoral view of conduct, especially with regard to sexual mores. While these features conform broadly to the generic norms of the fabliau (see chapter 11 on Genre), one distinctive quality is particularly striking. The tale is remarkable for its mingling of familiar details from everyday life with an utterly fantastic element: the warning that God is about to send a second Flood, and the bizarre measures taken in response to this threat. There is a striking disproportion between the effort required on the part of Nicholas to arrange this elaborate hoax and its ostensible purpose of allowing him to spend a night with Alisoun. Clearly, a significant aspect of the pleasure involved – for the protagonists as for the readers – lies in the playful ingenuity of the hoax.

The Reeve's Tale, which follows, is broadly similar in generic terms. While lacking the element of fantasy which is so conspicuous in the Miller's Tale, the bed-switch plot in the Reeve's Tale reflects a similar delight in plotting which is playful but vengeful. Serious issues and absurdity are, in fact, combined in both tales. The observations on the prospects of young women like Alisoun in the Miller's Tale (3268–70) and on the pretensions of the Symkyn and his wife in the Reeve's Tale (3926–86) constitute sharp social comment. It may also be noted that the pattern of retribution has a certain appropriateness – as, for instance, in the physical revenges suffered by Nicholas and Symkyn. Here, however, a word of qualification is important. While neat 'moral' conclusions can be derived from them, it is plain that the tales are, in essence, neither morally improving nor about the moral life: any such 'moral' would, in fact, advocate being careful rather than being good. The reader will surely be aware of this distinction as the Reeve asserts, with apparent relish, how his tale has demonstrated that 'a gylour shal hymself bigyled be' (RvT 4321).

This is, in fact, a fate shared by many of the 'gylours' in the *Canterbury Tales*. The plot element in which the person planning a trick or hoax is himself or herself deceived recurs in most of the fabliaux and other comic tales, including the tales of the Friar, the Summoner, the Pardoner, the Shipman, the Nun's Priest and the Canon's Yeoman. This basic feature does, however, occur in a variety of guises, as the following examples will suggest. In the pair of tales told against each other by the Friar and the Summoner, it is the obsessive pursuit of their own devious ends which renders each of the obnoxious protagonists vulnerable to the wiles of another trickster – respectively, Satan as hunter and the bedridden Thomas. In the Shipman's Tale, the wife is a willing accomplice of the monk, daun John, in duping her husband, but eventually becomes another victim of the monk's ingenious plotting. The pattern appears at its simplest in the Nun's Priest's Tale where, in a manner typical of the fable, daun Russell the fox first tricks Chauntecleer the cock and is then tricked by him.

It reaches a remarkable subtlety and elusiveness in the Pardoner's Prologue and Tale. Having frankly revealed in his prologue the methods by which he skilfully but cynically dupes his audiences into paying to touch his fraudulent relics, the Pardoner follows his tale with an apparent attempt to dupe the pilgrims in precisely the same way. Whether this is intended as a playful demonstration of technique or a serious attempt at a singularly audacious fraud is a matter of interpretation. It is, however, taken seriously by the Host, who responds viciously to the Pardoner's identification of him as the pilgrim 'moost envoluped in synne' (PardT 942), and therefore most in need of spiritual help. The Pardoner, whose power derives from an essentially verbal trickery, is rendered speechless by this cruel exposure (956–7). There may be some similarity between his response and that of Pandarus, who is reduced to silence when he has to acknowledge that Criseyde has forsaken Troilus (*TC* V, 1723–9). Though Pandarus hardly conforms to the pattern of the 'gylour' beguiled, he does act in a highly manipulative way – depending for his success on resourcefulness, ingenuity, persuasiveness and verbal dexterity – and appears utterly demoralized by the ultimate failure of his scheming.

It is notable that Pandarus repeatedly uses the words *play* and *game* with reference to his activities on behalf of Troilus (e.g. *TC* I, 868; III, 250–54, 961). Moreover, he shares with the Host an association with the word *jape*, one of the key words used by Chaucer, as both verb and noun, to describe both jesting and trickery (e.g. in *TC* II, 943, 1164; Th 693; ManP 4). The Cook memorably describes the Reeve's Tale as 'a jape of malice in the derk' (CkP 4338). The word often rhymes with 'ape' – the animal image representing the foolish victim of a hoax (e.g. in *TC* II, 1042, MilT 3389), just as 'fox' serves to suggest the guileful perpetrator (as in *TC* III, 1565, CYT 1080). Such activities also generate a wealth of lively expressions for the process of deceiving someone, including 'to set someone's cap', 'to blear someone's eye', or 'to make someone's beard' (e.g. MilP 3143, ManT 252, WBP 361). Among various other words used by Chaucer in this connection, it is worth mentioning the adjective 'sly' (as in CYP 655), and the cognate noun 'sleight' – which can signify either the abstract quality of cunning or trickery (*LGW* 931) or else a cunning trick (*TC* II, 1512). This may constitute the kind of behaviour suggested by the Parson's disapproving phrase 'knakkes of japeris' (ParsT 652). Chaucer's only other use of 'knakke' occurs in the *Book of the Duchess* (1033), where Blanche is praised for not using 'suche knakkes smale' as setting suitors hopeless or pointless tasks. One might contrast Dorigen's offer to Aurelius in the Franklin's Tale – which is, interestingly enough, said to have been made 'in pley' (988). The Franklin's Tale is a text in which Chaucer deals with one further aspect of trickery, that of illusion. The work of illusionists is also mentioned in the *House of Fame* (1259–81) and, briefly, in the Squire's Tale (217–19). The passage in the former includes an explicit reference to an entertainer named 'Colle tregetour' (i.e. magician). His trick, described as placing a windmill under a walnut shell (1277–81), has been taken to signify the ability of the human mind to encompass the world.

Games and Sports

Several other kinds of entertainment which may be included in the generic category of games (as defined briefly at the beginning of this chapter) are mentioned in Chaucer's work. The most prominent among these are wrestling, dicing, chess and hunting. Though he makes quite frequent reference to games and sports, it may be stated in general that he does not provide sustained accounts of such activities. Even his longest and most detailed passage of this kind – the description of the hunt in the *Book of the Duchess* (considered below) – clearly serves more to enrich the symbolic potential of that work than to provide an account of hunting for its own sake. A great majority of Chaucer's references to games and sports are either brief and allusive or else contribute to the presentation of a theme or character. The former may be exemplified by Chaucer's sole allusion to 'raket' (a kind of tennis), where the movement 'to and fro' in the game functions as an image of inconstancy (*TC* IV, 460), or by the reference to wrestling in the *Parliament of Fowls* (164–6), where the sporting allusion appears in a metaphor illustrating the distinction between theory and practice. The latter may be exemplified from Chaucer's remaining allusions to wrestling. Two of these appear in stories of remote and exotic events: the 'wake-pleyes' which follow the funeral of Arcite in the Knight's Tale (2961) include wrestling, as do the skills, more normally associated with young men, attributed to Cenobia in the Monk's Tale (2266–7). The others are more mundane. The success of Sir Thopas at winning the traditional prize of the ram in wrestling contests (Th 740–1) is generally taken to be comically inappropriate to one of his social rank. An equivalent prowess seems entirely appropriate to Chaucer's best-known wrestler, the Miller – who supplements conventional wrestling with the more dubious activity of door-butting (GP 547–51). The inclusion of wrestling among the accomplishments of Symkyn (RvT 3928) contributes to the impression that the Reeve has modelled him on the Miller.

If the image of wrestling in the local and contemporary world seems somewhat disreputable, that of dicing is emphatically so. Allusions to games of chance played with dice occur in three texts – the Pardoner's Tale, the Squire's Tale and the Cook's Tale – and all of them treat the activity as disreputable. In the Pardoner's Tale, dicing is first described as one of the typifying pursuits of a group of dissolute young people, and later censured in the most histrionic sermonizing style as a cause of much evil (463–71, 589–628). The Cook's Tale (4383–90) describes how Perkyn Revelour's fondness for dice leads him to waste money and steal from his master. This identification of dicing with low life, waste and dishonesty provides a context for the dismay expressed by the Franklin, at the end of the Squire's Tale (688–94), on the subject of his wayward son's fondness for dicing, inclination to profligacy and disregard for 'gentilesse'.

Chess, on the other hand, is associated with civilized and cultured life in the two texts which mention it, the *Book of the Duchess* and the Franklin's Tale. Both link chess with backgammon ('tables') – as an alternative to reading in the *Book of the Duchess*

(51), and among the pastimes enjoyed by Dorigen and her friends in the Franklin's Tale (900). The Parson's inclusion of 'tables' among activities conducive to sin (ParsT 793) reflects its potential association with gambling, and seems to constitute a somewhat strict view. No such dubious connotations are associated with chess. The only other allusion to it in Chaucer's work occurs at the heart of the *Book of the Duchess* (616–709), where the game of chess in which the man in black (signifying John of Gaunt) is defeated by Fortune serves to symbolize the death of his wife, the Duchess Blanche. The use of chess to represent a great personal loss suffered by a prince of the realm will indicate the esteem in which it was held.

Chaucer's work also reflects several aspects of hunting in the Middle Ages: the way in which it combined the recreational with the utilitarian, the variety of forms in which it was practised, and the range of symbolic associations which were attached to it. Though hunting is essentially recreational – as the application of the word 'game' to the hunt in the *Book of the Duchess* (539) may indicate – it served practical purposes relating both to the management of land and to the provision of food and other products. This mixed nature may be suggested by the existence of two kinds of deer hunt, the 'chase' and the 'drive' – both of which are described in Chaucer's work. While the chase is an essentially sporting pursuit of a single deer, the drive, in which a herd is driven past a shooting station, constitutes a means of culling the herd and securing a supply of food, hide and other valuable commodities. Evidence regarding the beasts hunted and the methods used is provided by the contemporary manuals of hunting, and surveyed by Mary Whitmore (1937: 193–208) and Teresa McLean (1983: 36–59). Chaucer's work includes accounts of or allusions to the hunting of deer, hare and more exotic quarries such as lion and bear, to various methods and techniques of hunting and, briefly, to hawking. It also reflects the main symbolic associations of hunting: that with love (typically using wordplay between 'heart' and 'hart'); that with a more explicitly sexual pursuit; that with chastity (through the tradition of Diana the chaste huntress); and that with death (partly derived from the biblical concept of Satan as a hunter). Two of these, the associations with love and with death, inform Chaucer's longest description of a hunt – that in the *Book of the Duchess*, which is considered below.

The other passages in which Chaucer describes or alludes to hunting range from the exotic to the mundane and from the symbolic to the literal. Three of these accounts of hunting may readily be designated as exotic: those of Dido in the *Legend of Good Women* (1188–1217), of Cenobia in the Monk's Tale (2255–70), and of Troilus, briefly mentioned in *Troilus and Criseyde* (III, 1779–81). The exotic quality is derived from the strangeness of the stories, the remoteness of the settings, the unusual quarries (including lions and bears) and, in the case of Dido's hunt, the sheer splendour of the horses and equipment. While the hunt in the *Legend of Good Women* suggests the passionate but disastrous love of Dido for Aeneas, that in the Monk's Tale presents Cenobia as a chaste huntress in the tradition of Diana. This tradition is depicted in the temple to Diana, described in the Knight's Tale (2051–88). The hunt of Theseus in this tale (1673–95) constitutes, despite the exotic setting, essentially a conventional chase for a 'hert', which derives some symbolic resonance from its juxtaposition with the conflict between Palamon and Arcite occasioned by their love for Emily. The deer hunt included in the visions created by the magician in the Franklin's Tale (1189–94), on the other hand, is clearly a drive – a form of hunting to which Pandarus makes an apt allusion in *Troilus and Criseyde* (II, 1534–5). The hunting sequence in the Franklin's Tale ends with a brief glimpse of hawking (1196–7), to which passing allusions are made in several other texts, including *Troilus and Criseyde*, the Wife of Bath's Prologue and the Friar's Tale (*TC* V, 65, WBP 415, FrT 1339–40). Hunting for deer and hawking are also included among the interests of Sir Thopas (Th 736–8) – though, according to the schemes which equated various birds of prey with the different orders of society (see Whitmore 1937: 206–7), his goshawk would have been appropriate to a mere yeoman rather than a knight.

Inappropriateness of a different kind may be suggested by the account of the Monk as an enthusiast for hunting the hare (GP 166–72, 189–92). Though the hare is a respected quarry, which was regularly hunted by 'pricking' (tracking the footprints), the pattern of innuendo in the description probably implies that the Monk has an interest in sexual love improper in one of his calling. Another pilgrim, the Yeoman, is portrayed in the traditional green garb of the hunter, as a forester – whose duties would have included the management of the game on his master's estate (GP 101–17). A hunter of a different kind, similarly dressed in green, appears in the Friar's Tale. Here Chaucer draws on a tradition derived from interpretation of a biblical text (Psalm 91 [Authorized Version 90]) in portraying Satan as a wily and resourceful hunter of human souls, with undeniably comic but utterly chilling effect.

This mingling of comic and serious elements is typical of Chaucer's treatment of games. It may readily be suggested by the two key formulae, 'sentence and solace' and 'earnest and game' (discussed further below) – which, in the context of Chaucer's work, draw the reader's attention to the complexity and elusiveness of such categories and of the judgements they are supposed to embody.

The Hunt in the *Book of the Duchess*, 344–86

The description of the hunt in the *Book of the Duchess* has regularly been identified as the most substantial and most specific account of hunting in Chaucer's work. While the accuracy of this view in terms of fact is not open to question, some helpful qualification of it may be achieved through consideration of other aspects of the passage. It can easily be forgotten that the description takes place within a dream sequence (which has begun at line 291), and reflects a conspicuous freedom from the need to represent the norms of the waking world. Thus, most notably, when the dreamer, who has been lying naked in bed listening to bird-song (292ff) hears the sound of the hunt (344ff), he simply takes his horse and leaves his chamber to join the hunters (356–9). When he does so, he asks one of them 'who shal hunte here?' – and is told, 'th' emperour Octovyen' (366–8). The setting – remote and unspecified in time and place, but vaguely romantic – provides further distancing from the literal and the everyday. Though the hunt itself is described sequentially from this point onward, Chaucer does not provide a full explanation of exactly what happens at each stage of the hunt. Commentators have, of course, quite justly noted the correct use of technical terms such as 'rechased' (379) and 'rused' (381), but have tended to ignore the lack of specificity in lines such as 'Every man dide ryght anoon / As to huntynge fil to doon' (373–4). The purpose of the technical terms is, perhaps, as much to give an impression of authenticity as to specify events and techniques precisely.

A similar lack of complete clarity pertains to the hunt's symbolic significance. It can plainly be stated that the hunt comes retrospectively to represent the death of Blanche, beloved wife of the man in black, and that the well-known traditions which associate hunting with love and death serve to facilitate this link. It is reinforced at the end of the poem, when the starkly brief revelation to the narrator of the exact nature of the loss suffered by the man in black is followed immediately by an equally brief allusion to the end of the hunt, evocatively termed 'the hert-huntyng' (1308–13). None the less, the precise significance of the hunt remains open to a variety of interpretations – the most prominent of which are surveyed in the note to lines 344–86 in the Riverside edition. It may well be concluded that the most thoughtful and sensitive readings will see the significance of the hunt as clear in general terms while remaining elusive in its particulars.

Sentence and *solace*: The General Prologue, 796–801

In a brief passage toward the end of the General Prologue, the Host specifies the rules of his proposed tale-telling contest, stating that the winner will be the pilgrim who tells 'Tales of best sentence and moost solaas' (798). This formula reflects the authority of classical literary theory, specifically the view expressed by Horace in his *Ars poetica* (333–4),[1] to the effect that the aim of poetry should be to provide benefit or delight, or a combination of the two. Though the formula 'sentence and solace' does not occur again in the *Canterbury Tales* or elsewhere in Chaucer's works, the individual words are used quite extensively. *Sentence* appears mainly in the senses of significance, essential meaning or wise saying, predominantly in the context of serious and ethical issues, as in the Tale of Melibee (975, etc.) and the Physician's Tale (157, etc.). *Solace* appears less frequently, in the senses of pleasure, comfort and relief – as in the Nun's Priest's Tale (3203) – and occurs several times in combination with 'joy', as in the Franklin's Tale (1019). Commentators have often seen these two words as having considerable potential to suggest alternative functions, according to the Horatian view, for the individual tales. The juxtaposition of these two functions has been perceived by some to indicate a conflict at the heart of the *Canterbury Tales*, with the Parson and the Host acting as champions for *sentence* and *solace* respectively. Whether or not this seems convincing, the contempt expressed by the Parson, in the prologue to his own tale, for what he terms 'fables and swich wrecchednesse' (34) is emphatic, and his subsequent tale constitutes an account of sin and penance rather than a work of fiction.

As observed above, the Host tends to divide tales firmly between the edifying (*sentence*) and the entertaining (*solace*), and his management of the contest has been taken to suggest a preference for an alternation between the two kinds of tale. Nowhere in the links does he show any sign of identifying a tale which meets his initial criterion of combining the two potential qualities of literature – though critics have regularly perceived such an achievement in various tales, especially that of the Nun's Priest. The links do, of course, provide plentiful evidence of the fallibility of the Host's judgement – revealing conventional literary taste, conservatism in social issues and pragmatism with regard to ethical matters and personal relationships. This last characteristic may be suggested here by the stipulation that the prize supper will be held at his own inn, the Tabard (GP 799–801) – an arrangement from which only he can profit. Be that as it may, his judgement is accorded no special authority in the *Canterbury Tales*. The formulation regarding 'sentence and solace', which he introduces in this passage, does, on the other hand, raise fundamental issues concerning the values of literature, which are of profound significance to any reading of the tales – and, indeed, of Chaucer's work as a whole.

Ernest and *game*: The Miller's Prologue, 3167–86

In an important passage at the end of the Miller's Prologue, Chaucer introduces another formula when he appeals to his readers that they 'shal nat maken ernest of game'. The broad similarity between this formula and 'sentence and solace' will be immediately apparent. It, too, has links with classical rhetoric: the derivation of the virtually identical formula 'jest and earnest' in medieval literature from its classical origins is traced by Curtius (1953: 417–35). This, likewise, postulates both the difference between edification and entertainment, and the possibility that the two might be mingled. As has already been observed above, the conjunction 'earnest and game' – unlike 'sentence and solace' – does recur, with variations, throughout the *Canterbury Tales* and the rest of Chaucer's work. The two formulae are, however, alike in that they are introduced into the *Canterbury Tales* at crucial junctures. While 'sentence and solace' occurs in the passage, discussed above, which establishes the rules of the tale-telling contest, 'earnest and game' appears at the end of the passage in which these rules are first put to the test. That passage is, of course, the Miller's Prologue. It may more helpfully be regarded as the link between the first two tales, those of the Knight and the Miller, since that fact explains its essential importance. Here, for the first time, certain fundamental aspects of the *Canterbury Tales* emerge: that the pilgrims will function as a fictional audience for the tales, and respond to them; that the order in which the tales are told will not follow any conventional or predictable sequence; that pilgrims will feel free to argue with each other and with the Host; that tales will be taken to express something of the (fictional) individual's social position, self-esteem and possibly even character; that one tale will be seen as responding to (*quitting*) another; and that tales may be discussed even before they are told. All these elements will have a profound influence on how the tales are told and the ways in which they create meaning.

At this intriguing but rather unstable juncture, the passage under discussion is presented as a personal statement by the poet. In its first nine lines, the repetition of the authorial 'I' is emphatic. Despite the implicit challenge to social stereotyping in the preceding encounter between the Miller and the Host, Chaucer here characterizes the forthcoming tales of the Miller and the Reeve as typical of 'cherles'. He apologizes, in advance, to 'every gentil wight' among his readers – the equivalent in his actual audience to the 'the gentils', who especially liked the Knight's Tale (MilP 3113), in his fictional audience – for any offence from the 'harlotrie' in such tales. In doing so, Chaucer reiterates the substance of an earlier, more general, apology (GP 725–46), which stressed in particular the author's duty to relate the tales just as they were told. Such a claim, made with reference to fiction by the creator of that fiction, is, of course, absurd; but it raises an entirely serious issue about the responsibilities of an author.

Here Chaucer adds a striking new argument, asserting that the reader also has responsibility, and can choose not to read something which might cause offence. He goes on to offer a kind of 'trailer' for the rest of the *Canterbury Tales* (3178–80): a summary of the varied material (apart from 'cherles tales') which can be found in the collection. The demand that readers should take responsibility for what they read is reinforced by Chaucer's emphatically reiterated refusal to accept blame: 'blameth nat me if that ye chese amys' (3181); 'avyseth yow, and put me out of blame' (3185). In both lines, the confrontation between poet and reader is clearly represented in the juxtaposition of first and second person pronouns. It is in this particular context that the formula 'earnest and game' emerges; indeed, 'blame' provides the rhyme for 'game'. While a rigorous moralist (such as the Parson) might well contend that some 'blame' attaches to all 'game', the pattern of the preceding passage, of the Miller's Prologue and of the developing work as a whole provides a far more open and questioning context for the formula.

The Miller's Prologue has shown the disparate group of pilgrims described in the General Prologue as they become involved in the business of the tale-telling contest on which they have embarked. In the process, they express views which are, essentially, varied and partial; none has any particular authority. Chaucer has strikingly reiterated and elaborated the attempt, made earlier near the end of the General Prologue, to qualify and limit his own special authority as author, and has demanded that his readers should accept their own responsibility for what they read. Like 'sentence and solace', 'earnest and game' might seem a formula designed to endorse stereotypical judgement. But the context, both general and particular, suggests the opposite: that these formulae will serve to raise fundamental questions about the purposes of literature and the nature of judgement. Such questions are typical of Chaucer's work, in which the element of play, as in the treatment of games and sports, does not preclude seriousness, but often challenges the reader to distinguish with any certainty between *ernest* and *game*.

See also AUTHORITY; COMEDY; CRISIS AND DISSENT; GENRE.

NOTES

1   *Horace: Epistles Book II and Epistle to the Pisones*
    ('Ars Poetica'), ed. Niall Rudd (Cambridge:
    Cambridge University Press, 1989).

REFERENCES AND FURTHER READING

Connolly, Margaret (1994) 'Chaucer and chess', *Chaucer Review* 29, 40–44. Argues that the chess metaphor in the *Book of the Duchess*, while apt in general, is problematic in some particulars.

Curtius, Ernst Robert (1953) *European Literature in the Latin Middle Ages*, trans. Willard R. Trask (London: Routledge & Kegan Paul). Includes a section tracing the tradition of 'jest and earnest' from its classical origins.

Ganim, John M. (1990) *Chaucerian Theatricality* (Princeton: Princeton University Press). Relates Chaucer's work to various aspects of performance in medieval society.

Gaylord, Alan T. (1967) '*Sentence* and *solaas* in Fragment VII of the *Canterbury Tales*: Harry Bailly as horseback editor', *Proceedings of the Modern Language Association* 82, 226–35. Discusses how these concepts are reflected in the Host's handling of the storytelling contest, particularly in Fragment VII.

Huizinga, Johann (1949) *Homo Ludens: A Study of the Play Element in Culture* (London: Routledge). Seminal account of the nature of play and its place in human society.

Josipovici, G. D. (1965) 'Fiction and game in *The Canterbury Tales*', *Critical Quarterly* 7, 185–97. Interprets the *Canterbury Tales* as a game played between Chaucer and his readers.

Kendrick, Laura (1988) *Chaucerian Play: Comedy and Control in the* Canterbury Tales (Berkeley, Los Angeles, and London: California University Press). A study of the nature and significance of the storytelling contest as a game.

Kolve, V. A. (1966) *The Play Called Corpus Christi* (Stanford: Stanford University Press). Includes consideration of the English mystery plays in relation to the ideas of Huizinga.

Lanham, Richard A. (1967) 'Game, play, and high seriousness in Chaucer's poetry', *English Studies* 48, 1–24; rev. repr. as 'Games and high seriousness: Chaucer', in Lanham, *The Motives of Eloquence: Literary Rhetoric in the Renaissance* (New Haven and London: Yale University Press, 1976), 65–81. Applies game theory to Chaucer's poetry, identifying three games: those of love, rhetoric and war.

Lindahl, Carl (1987) *Earnest Games: Folkloric Patterns in the* Canterbury Tales (Bloomington and Indianapolis: Indiana University Press). A study relating the *Canterbury Tales* to patterns of folk culture.

McLean, Teresa (1983) *The English at Play in the Middle Ages* (Windsor Forest: Kensal). A useful but little-known survey of play, games and sport in medieval England.

Manning, Stephen (1979) 'Rhetoric, game, morality, and Geoffrey Chaucer', *Studies in the Age of Chaucer* 1, 105–18. Applies game theory to Chaucer's work (cf. Lanham 1967), stressing ambivalence between seriousness and play.

Olson, Glending (1982) *Literature as Recreation in the Later Middle Ages* (Ithaca, NY and London: Cornell University Press). A study of medieval ideas concerning the therapeutic and recreational value of literature.

Thiébaux, Marcelle (1974) *The Stag of Love: The Chase in Medieval Literature* (Ithaca, NY and London: Cornell University Press). A study of the use of hunting to symbolize love in medieval literature.

Whitmore, Sister Mary Ernestine (1937) *Medieval English Domestic Life and Amusements in the Works of Chaucer: A Dissertation* (Washington, DC: Catholic University of America Press; repr. New York: Cooper Square, 1972). Includes a section on sports and pastimes.

Wimsatt, James I. (1968) *Chaucer and the French Love Poets: The Literary Background of the* Book of the Duchess (Chapel Hill, NC: University of North Carolina Press; repr. New York and London: Johnson, 1972). An authoritative study of the traditions informing this poem.

11

Genre

Caroline D. Eckhardt

A dozen or more literary genres are represented in Chaucer's work. Indeed, part of the pleasure of reading Chaucer lies in the play between generic recognition and surprise. Again and again the awareness of conventions of genre, a process which entails the arousal and fulfilment of expectations, is set into play against the element of surprise when generic traits are shifted, abandoned, juxtaposed or otherwise freely interpreted.

The concept of genre entails a double, and perhaps conflicting, agenda: the simultaneous perception of similarities (shared qualities that enable individual phenomena to associate together) and differences (qualities that differentiate one such group from another). Literary genres are commonly defined as clusters of traits pertaining to form, content or both. Aristotle's definition of tragedy, as 'an imitation of an action that is serious, complete, and of a certain magnitude . . . in the form of action, not of narrative; through pity and fear effecting the proper purgation of these emotions',[1] often serves as a touchstone, locating, as it does, the construction of genre in an interaction between qualities of the literary work and their effect on the audience, which in this case must feel pity and fear.

Medieval Classifications

Such an approach to genre – identifying traits in the formula of genus and species ('an imitation of an action' is differentiated from other imitations in specific ways) – rests on the assumption that genres possess a stable or even permanent identity. Medieval statements about genre tend to reflect the same assumption and thus to prescribe what a genre 'is'. The widely used encyclopedia of Isidore of Seville (d. 636), for instance, which draws upon classical sources in its genre theory, divides poetry into four kinds: not counting historical works, these are lyric, tragic, comic and theological (Kelly 1993: 112). Isidore also reports a tripartite division of narratives according to the kind of truth-claim they make: histories record true things that occurred, 'arguments' record things that did not occur but are possible, and fables record things that did not occur and are not possible because they are contrary to nature (Cooper 1991: 84). In the late eleventh century, Bernard of Utrecht divided the kinds of poetic song into epithalamium, lamentation, festive song (by which he meant hymns) and elegy (Minnis 1988: 135). In the twelfth century, Honorius of Autun, like Isidore, identified four kinds of poetry, here tragedies, comedies, satiric pieces and lyrics (Kelly 1993: 113); Matthew of Vendôme, also writing in the twelfth century, proposed the four genres of tragedy, satire, comedy and elegy, envisaging them as four women who attend Lady Philosophy within a dream. Early in the thirteenth century Geoffrey of Vinsauf's longer list of genres still included comedy ('any jocose poem', but especially 'a rustic song dealing with humble persons, beginning in sadness and ending in joy') and tragedy (a work 'showing the misfortunes of grave persons, beginning in joy and ending in grief', Kelly 1993: 113–14).

John of Garland, whose work dates shortly after that of Geoffrey of Vinsauf, mentioned forms such as legal and academic letters, elegies, comedies, tragedies and histories, and provided examples. His sample 'tragedy' is a rather odd piece about two washerwomen who supply various services to a garrison of soldiers under siege. John allowed for the blending of forms, offering an example of 'a poem that is simultaneously elegiac (dealing with the misery of love), amabeous (representing the characteristics of lovers), bucolic (with a pastoral setting and using humble style) and, finally, ethical (a hermeneutic category, meaning that it has an allegorical Christian dimension)' (Kelly 1993: 114–15). Such a conjunction between secular and religious approaches is also visible in, for example, the fourteenth-century work of Peter Auriol, who applies a secular scheme to Scripture when he classifies the forms of poetic song into songs of joy, as in Psalms; elegies or songs of sadness, as in the Book of Lamentations; and dramatic poems, as in the 'dramas of beauty and love' in the Song of Songs (Minnis 1988: 135).

Statements in encyclopedias, treatises or commentaries, being written in Latin, were intended for learned readers, but many implicit or explicit definitions of genres are embedded within vernacular literary works. Two Middle English poems, *Sir Orfeo* and *Lay le Freine*, explain that lays are stories, set to the music of the harp, which recount tales of wonder and adventure; since *Freine* involves no magical or supernatural elements, it seems somewhat at variance with its own generic description.[2] Boethius' *De consolatione Philosophiae*, which Chaucer and others translated and which thus became a vernacular text, implies a definition of tragedy in its rhetorical question: 'What other thyng bywaylen the cryinges of tragedyes but oonly the dedes of Fortune, that with unwar strook overturneth the realmes of greet nobleye?' (*Bo* II, prosa 2, 67–70). Dante refers to the story of Dido and Aeneas as an 'alta tragedia', a high tragedy (*Inferno* XX, 113), showing that the concept of tragedy could be applied to a narrative about unhappy lovers, in contrast to both Aristotle's definition, which was not generally available, and that of Boethius.[3]

Additionally, because the titles of texts were not standardized and a work might therefore be given different designations, scribal practice in the writing of manuscripts reveals variation in the understandings of genre. For instance, Latin or English rubrics in different manuscripts call Chaucer's Tale of Melibee variously *narratio* (narrative), *fabula* (tale/fable), 'tale', 'moral tale' or 'proverbis'; similarly, rubrics label the Manciple's Tale *narracio, fabula,* 'tale' or 'lytel tretis'.[4] Such variation can also be documented for earlier texts Chaucer may have known. The widely read legendary history by Geoffrey of Monmouth, now called the *Historia regum Britannie* (*History of the Kings of Britain*, twelfth century), is probably mentioned by Chaucer when he refers to 'Englyssh Gaufride' (*HF* 1470). All three of Isidore of Seville's narrative categories are included here – 'true' events such as Caesar's invasion of Britain, 'fictional' events such as the European conquests of King Arthur and 'fabulous' ingredients such as Merlin's being fathered by an incubus. The more than 200 manuscript copies of this work most commonly designate it as *historia* (history or story), but sometimes as *tractatus* (treatise), *cronica* (chronicles), *vita* (life), *editio* (edition), *gesta* (deeds) or simply *liber* (book).[5]

Evidence of an implied social hierarchy of genre, which determined the kinds of literature that medieval students (usually boys) would learn, can be found in schoolbooks such as the *Liber Catonianus*, a standard anthology of Latin readings. The genres it includes are the eclogue, fable, elegy, epic, and 'practical ethics' or philosophical maxims. Their presence in this textbook 'suggests that literary genres were used to embody and to teach young boys the process of moral decisions', with those five genres regarded as contributing to that edifying end.[6] Through other schoolbooks students read many more of the Latin classics, as well as finding models for writing in treatises such as the *artes dictaminis* (manuals of letter-writing) and *artes praedicandi* (manuals of preaching).

Medieval understandings of genre, then, were variable, just as later theories of genre have been. Theorists prescribed, but writers and scribes made their own choices. As Helen Cooper has aptly remarked, it is 'notoriously difficult to square medieval generic theory, with its classically-derived categories, with actual poetic practice' (1991: 86). One reason for the divergence derives from the theorists' reliance on classical models, while authors were also absorbing influences from non-classical sources and popular forms.

Generic Traits

Recent theory has shown a diversification in the features used to make generic distinctions and an awareness of the ideological functions of genre (Beebee 1994). Just as, in biological taxonomy, animals can be classified according to whether they lay eggs or not, or according to the shape of their toes or the food they eat, literary classifications too have used many traits – not only elements of form (such as metre), or subject (such as love or war), or style (such as high, middle or low), as in earlier theories, but other characteristics entirely. For instance, Northrop Frye sorted literary phenomena into genres in accordance with the four seasons of the year; Käthe

Hamburger according to the authenticity of the voice heard in the text; Emil Staiger and others according to the temporal situations of past, present and future; Thomas Beebee according to the use-values of literary forms (Beebee 1994: 269–70). Genre has also been correlated more closely to the reader's experience and to gender, as has been shown particularly for the romance ('just as the romance genre limits its characters' gendered possibilities, so do these defined gendered terms limit the genre itself', Weisl 1995: 3; cf. Crane 1994: 3). Tzvetan Todorov, to whom 'any description of a text, by the very fact that it is made by means of words, is a description of genre', notes that some genres (which he calls elementary) are defined by a single characteristic, while other genres (which he calls complex) are defined by several characteristics operating together.[7] As Beebee remarks, 'there is always an excess of generic markers to be sorted' and 'theorists of genre differ most radically precisely on this one point, on the 'things' in the text which will be compared in order to classify works' (1994: 269).

Similarly, one might ask, 'How large is a genre?' Some classifications assume that genres are very large indeed and there are only a few of them (Isidore's four; or just three – poetry, fiction and drama, or perhaps lyric, narrative and drama). In other contexts a plenitudinous array may be called genres, or sub-genres, or forms the aube, *ballade*, *chanson de geste*, chronicle, colloquy, complaint, dream vision, elegy, epic, epigram, fable, folktale, homily, lay, miracle, mystery play, novella, *prosimetrum*, riddle, romance, *roundelle*, saga, saint's life, sermon, sonnet, travel tale and *virelai*, to name a few medieval possibilities. Further, no genre really seems to be universal, permanent or self-sufficient. Genres change through time, each genre always exists in implicit differentiation from others, and literary genres meet, mate and hybridize, not only among themselves but also with the genres of other human modes of expression, such as film, painting, music, even architecture and urban design.

The Uses of Genre in Chaucer Studies

In this context of immense elasticity, not to say confusion, it might seem tempting simply to reject the utility of genre as a framework for Chaucer studies. However, two factors preclude such a dismissal. First is the recognition that variation in labelling does not mean that labels have no value, or that the differentiations they represent do not exist. To say that *Troilus and Criseyde* is an epic, a romance and a tragedy (as well as a 'litel bok') is to situate it within three (or four) literary contexts, each of which interacts with this text in crucial ways. In Chaucer's works there are simply too many generic signals and allusions to make it appropriate to ignore such interactions. The invocations to the Muses in *Troilus*, for instance, make little sense unless they are recognized as a conventional element of epic. For both writers and audiences of this period, literary meaning and value are bound up with genre.

Second, and equally important, is Chaucer's own use of terms suggesting literary forms or genres. He provides an unusually generous array of such words, including *avisioun*, *balade*, *carole*, *comedye*, *compleynt*, *cronicle*, *dreme*, *epistel*, *fable*, *geste*, *lay*, *legende*, *lyf, metres, miracle, omelies, parables, pleyes of myracles, preamble, prologe, prose, romaunce, rondel, ryme, sermoun, storie, sweven, tretis, tragedye, virelai, visioun, ympne* and *vers,* as well as the more general *book, song, tale* and *thyng* (this list is not exhaustive). The exact meanings of these terms are often debatable, and in some instances they may not necessarily designate genres. *Dreme,* for example, can refer to the experience itself, as well as to the text that records it. Nevertheless, such a lexicon simultaneously documents Chaucer's interest in genre and calls upon his audiences to bring it within their interpretative agenda as well.

Hundreds of critical studies have responded to that call. Space limitations preclude a summary, or even mention, of all the (imputed) Chaucerian genres and important analyses. What follows is only a small sampling, selected to demonstrate the pervasiveness and complexity of Chaucer's commitment to genre. As Robert Edwards remarks, 'Chaucer views established poetic doctrine as an unstable body of precepts open to change and new formations' (1989: 27), an assessment that I believe applies to his generic imagination as well as to his interpretation of other aspects of poetics. I will propose here that Chaucer's sense of genre begins with the desire to recapitulate many of the literary forms he knew, but that his extraordinary tendency to frame, modulate, combine, resist and otherwise reinterpret his models produces what may be called the creative derangement of genre. To be deranged does not mean, in this context, to depart from what makes sense, but instead to use conventional patterns as points of departure in order to make sense in ways not previously arranged. (I borrow the term 'derangement' from Charles Stanley Ross's analysis of what Boiardo did to the genre of heroic epic.[8])

The Dream Visions

Early in his literary career Chaucer had a special interest in dream poetry. His first three extant works, aside from the possibility that some undated lyrics might belong to this period, are the *Book of the Duchess,* the *House of Fame* and the *Parliament of Fowls,* all of which present a narrator who recounts a dream. Dreaming also occurs within *Troilus and Criseyde* and the *Canterbury Tales,* and Chaucer was working on a dream vision again in 1394 or afterwards, as he apparently revised the Prologue to the *Legend of Good Women* to reflect the death of Queen Anne. Thus in all major phases of his career, dreaming is a topic of poetic speculation.

The medieval dream tradition that is most important to Chaucer stems particularly from two texts. One is Macrobius' fourth-century Latin commentary on Cicero's *Dream of Scipio,* which sorts dreams (not necessarily clearly) into five categories. Three of these types, such as prophetic visions, are said to yield trustworthy insights, while the other two, such as the apparitions one might drowsily see between sleeping and waking, are not regarded as trustworthy (Russell 1988: 61–2). The second crucial text is the thirteenth-century French *Roman de la rose,* which Chaucer translated (*LGW* G 460) and in which several features of later dream visions are established: the poet (or the persona) falls asleep on an early summer day; he dreams that he encounters an enclosed garden, where he seeks something (in the *Roman*, an experience of love) within its inner world of natural abundance and allegorical representations; the poem provides opportunities to discuss aspects of love and desire.

Since A. C. Spearing's fundamental study,[9] many critics have explicated the ways in which the dream vision intersects with other modes or genres such as lyric, allegory, debate, philosophical discourse, complaint and confession. Two such possibilities will be mentioned here. J. Stephen Russell, who emphasizes the subjectivity of the narrator, argues that 'the dream vision is a species of the lyric mode' (1988: 115), moving from an initial lyric stage to a report that 'takes on the features of a narrative' and then returning to lyric at its close; thus 'a lyric experience masquerades for a time as a narrative one only to reveal at its conclusion that it is not and never was a narrative in any traditional sense' (1988: 129). Aside from the relation to lyric, in Chaucer's dream visions the philosophical and, to some readers, theological elements are also strong. (Kathryn L. Lynch would identify 'the philosophical vision' as a distinct sub-genre.[10]) Though the *Book of the Duchess*, given its commemoration of the dead lady White, is often described in terms of elegy, as well as dream vision, R. A. Shoaf has argued that in this work neither of those genres predominates. Instead, the element of confession is strong enough that 'Chaucer did not write an elegy' or 'a "conventional" dream poem' (1981: 181–2), but instead invented something new, 'a confessional or penitential form in which to display the gradual rectification' of the knight's behaviour (169), with the result that the 'form of *The Book of the Duchess* is autobiography by dream' (184). Whether 'autobiography by dream' can be considered a valid medieval literary form may be open to question, but Shoaf's and many other analyses demonstrate that even this early work displays a rich complexity of generic affiliations.

Epic, Romance, Tragedy and Other Models: *Troilus and Criseyde*

The generic associations of *Troilus and Criseyde* point towards diverse expectations that are not easily reconciled, building a formal tension that corresponds to the emotional, philosophical and religious tensions which accumulate as the poem elaborates its subject. In its first few pages the text suggests both epic (in its invocation of Tisiphone, for example) and romance (in its initiation of the love affair), establishing an initial generic interplay which continues. Chaucer subsequently refers to the poem as his 'litel bok' and as a tragedy (see below). In 1830 Thomas Campbell called *Troilus and Criseyde* a novel,[11] Kittredge subsequently discussed the poem as 'an elaborate psychological novel' (1915: 112) and countless readers since that time have felt that its process of character development, at least, is novelistic. Recent critics have found it fruitful to explicate the characteristics that link the poem to a plurality or hybridity of genres. As Derek Brewer points out, 'The complexity of this great poem is such that neither label, "tragedy" nor "comedy", nor even perhaps "romance", nor any combination of these terms, can do more than suggest one aspect of its Gothic multiplicity.'[12]

Monica McAlpine, for example, argues for the presence of both comedy and tragedy, but not as usually understood. McAlpine first differentiates Chaucer's generic intentions from medieval *de casibus* tragedy, which presents the fall from power of a ruler or other public figure, as in Boccaccio's collection of tales *De casibus virorum illustrium* (Concerning the falls of famous men), or in Chaucer's Monk's Tale. Because of the emphasis on Fortune in *de casibus* tragedy, she proposes that *Troilus and Criseyde* does not follow that genre, but instead draws upon Boethius to embody a double identity as both 'Troilus' Boethian comedy and Criseyde's Boethian tragedy' (McAlpine 1978: 219): Troilus emerges as 'a Boethian comic hero experiencing the agony and the triumph of being free' (1978: 151), while Criseyde illustrates Boethian tragedy, which depicts 'the inner degradation of a person caused by the free commission of an evil act' (73–4). Kelly points out, however, that Boccaccio does not label his *De casibus* tales as tragedies – he may have thought of them as moral exempla – and argues that there was no widely shared idea of tragedy in Chaucer's time: it was Chaucer himself who 'transformed Boccaccio's idiosyncratic exercise into a new genre, that of tragedy' (Kelly 1997: 91), which to him meant 'a well-told account of a lamentable fall from prosperity' (106). Accordingly, Chaucer created 'an elaborately wrought example of a tragedy of undeserved, or largely undeserved, misfortune in *Troilus and Crise*yde' (141).

Moving in other directions, and noting that *Troilus and Criseyde* is called a 'litel bok', Thomas C. Stillinger points out that two other crucial texts also describe themselves as 'little books': Dante's *Vita nuova* calls itself a *libello*, Boccaccio's *Filostrato* a *picciolo libro* (Stillinger 1992: 2). Stillinger does not propose that a 'little book', or what he calls the 'lyrical book' (179), constitutes a medieval genre, but his study provides a very useful reminder that whatever the predominant genre(s) of Chaucer's large and capacious poem may be, it also embeds smaller forms such as dream, song and letter – including, in two of Troilus' songs (*TC* I, 400–20 and V, 638–44), what are evidently the first English reflections or translations of Petrarchan sonnets (Stillinger 1992: 165–78). The most comprehensive web of generic affiliations proposed for *Troilus and Criseyde* is that of Barry Windeatt, who delineates its links to epic, romance, history, tragedy, drama (in the sense of 'scenic form in narrative', 1992: 161), philosophical dialogue, lyric, fabliau, allegory and commentary, concluding that Chaucer 'has produced a poem which through its very inclusiveness of genres becomes distinctively and essentially *sui generis*' (179).

An Anthology of Genres: The *Canterbury Tales*

The impression that in the *Canterbury Tales* Chaucer was intentionally displaying his generic virtuosity seems irresistible. After the General Prologue there comes a remarkable array of types of discourse, with variety both among genres and (as Benson 1986 shows) among different examples of the same genre. Some segments of the *Canterbury Tales* seem susceptible to association with a single genre, such as the fabliaux told by the Miller, the Reeve and the Shipman, or the prose discourses of the Parson and Melibee, or the saint's legend of the Second Nun, or the tragedies told by the Monk. But even these tales are situationally modulated by their placement within the pilgrimage framework. Thus in the Monk's Tale, the characters' apparent lack of responsibility for their downfall is ironized both by the ostensible religious calling of the Monk to whom the recounting of their fates is attributed, and by the pilgrimage setting as a whole. In other segments of the *Canterbury Tales* – such as the Knight's Tale, where epic and romance share the narrative space but do not exhaust the options, or the Wife of Bath's Prologue, where the transgression of the bounds of a prologue is signalled within the text by the Friar (WBP 831) – the identification of genre is complicated and perhaps finally elusive.

The Nun's Priest's Tale of Chauntecleer and Pertelote, one of Chaucer's most polished performances, partakes of mock-epic, beast fable, dream, debate and probably half a dozen other types. It also affords an opportunity to consider an aspect of Chaucer's writing that cross-cuts generic distinctions: his humour. In medieval theory, 'comedy' (as used with reference to Dante, for instance)[13] was often identified not with humour, but with a narrative trajectory that moved from sorrow to joy. Nevertheless, not only do genres such as the fabliau subsist upon situations that embody the grounds for laughter, but – in an almost Shakespearean manner – Chaucer can intersperse jokes into the most apparently solemn contexts. An extreme example occurs in the Retraction (is a retraction a genre?), where the teasing reticence of Chaucer's revocation of 'the tales of Caunterbury, thilke that sownen into synne' (1085) surely merits a smile at least. Which are the tales that tend towards sin? If the claim made only a moment before, 'Al that is writen is writen for oure doctrine' (1083), be true, there is nothing to revoke at all.

The Retraction brings us back to the whole 'book of the tales of Caunterbury', as the Ellesmere manuscript calls it, and to the question of the generic positioning of this remarkable book. Clearly it is a story-collection, and moreover one with a frame, which makes it a frame-tale; it is surely 'a Gothic miscellany', as Brewer calls it (1998: 395); and it is a *compilatio*, a compilation (Minnis 1988: 190–210) – not a mere coincidence of materials, but an organized array, though the organization of the *Canterbury Tales* varies in different manuscripts and may be partly attributable to Chaucer's editors.[14] In various ways it associates itself generically with many other composite works, including the *Ovide moralisé*, a retelling of tales from Ovid along with moralizing interpretations; the *Disciplina clericalis* of Petrus Alfonsus, to whom Chaucer refers several times in the Tale of Melibee (1053, 1189, etc.); Boccaccio's *Decameron*, which Chaucer may or may not have known; collections of saints' lives, a genre parodied in the *Legend of Good Women*; and the *Confessio Amantis*, on which Chaucer's good friend John Gower (*TC* V, 1856) may have been working at the same time as the *Canterbury Tales* were being written.

A final analogue to the *Canterbury Tales* may be the drama, the only major medieval literary genre that Chaucer seems not to have practised or parodied. The long cycles of plays on biblical subjects that were popular towards the end of the Middle Ages provide several structural parallels to the *Canterbury Tales*. They too present multiple episodes joined within one great framework; they too embody joy and sorrow, religious and secular preoccupations, humour and solemnity; they too re-arrange a great deal of traditional material for a new context. Chaucer must have seen performances of plays: the Miller's Tale and its prologue include references to players (MilP 3124; MilT 3384, 3534–43); and the Wife of Bath, while her husband was away, would put on her bright scarlet garments and go to 'pleyes of myracles' in order to see and to be seen (WBP 551–9). Chaucer's eighteenth-century editor Thomas Tyrwhitt commented on the affinities of the *Canterbury Tales* and the *Decameron* to 'comedies not intended for the stage',[15] and Kittredge argued that the *Canterbury Tales* is essentially a drama, with the pilgrims' stories functioning as 'long speeches expressing, directly or indirectly, the characters of the several persons . . . more or less comparable, in this regard, to the soliloquies of Hamlet or Iago or Macbeth' (1915: 155). If taken almost literally, as it was by some of Kittredge's followers, an interpretation of the *Canterbury Tales* as drama is way off the mark; but if taken instead as a recognition of Chaucer's unequalled generic receptivity, agility and (paradoxically) independence, there is value to such a claim.

The *Book of the Duchess*, 270–343

The *Book of the Duchess* participates in at least two main generic traditions, that of the dream vision and that of the elegy. This passage, in which the narrator falls asleep and dreams that he awakens in the springtime, illustrates primarily characteristics of the dream vision and of the similar type of poem known as the *dit amoreux* (lay of love; Phillips and Havely 1997: 38). Within a frame established by a dream or an alternative device, the *dit amoreux* presents an enclosed or secluded location such as a garden, island or castle, often with an idealized May landscape filled with flowers and birdsong. The centre of these poems frequently depicts a debate or love lament; classical tales with similar circumstances may be retold. The narrator, who is typically in a melancholy mood, may be the main character or else the observer of another's situation (Phillips and Havely 1997: 38–9). This form is not quite identical with the dream vision, since there can be dream visions on subjects other than love, while there can be *dits amoreux* without the framing device being a dream; but the two types are obviously closely related.

By a double process of allusion and imitation, the first passage associates itself with both dream vision and the lyric–narrative *dit amoreux*. The beginning of the passage, with its reiterative terminology (*me mette*, 'I dreamed', *sweven*, 'dream', *sweven*, *dremes* and *sweven* again), insists upon the narrator's experience as a dream and refers to the recognized authority on dreaming, Macrobius. Chaucer then makes it clear that he means not only the act of dreaming, but also a specific model for representing it in language, when he names the *Roman de la rose* (334). In addition to naming, he echoes the *Roman* verbally, as in the line 'Me thoght thus: that hyt was May' (291), which recalls the line 'That it was May me thoughte tho' (49 in the *Romaunt of the Rose*, the Middle English version of the *Roman*). Furthermore, he echoes the *Roman* and similar texts structurally when, within the frame established by dreaming, the narrator of the *Book of the Duchess* is awakened into a May dawn by the sound of birdsong that permeates his chamber.

The images depicted on the chamber's walls and within its window-glass, described in the second passage, are also paralleled in the *Roman*, where the dreamer sees a garden wall 'Portraied without and well entailled / With many riche portraitures' of personifications such as Hate, Felony, Vilany, Sorrow and others (*Rom* 140–1). Though the figures whom the dreamer sees in the *Book of the Duchess* are participants in the story of Troy, rather than personifications, a potential move towards allegory is signalled both by the naming of the 'Romaunce', whose allegorical qualities would have been known to many members of Chaucer's audience, and by the emphasis on the heavenly quality of the birdsong – including, as others have noted, a possible pun on the 'toune of Tewnis' (*BD* 310) as the tune of tunes or Song of Songs.

These densely intertextual passages can serve as an example, then, of Chaucer's tendency not only to write within the context of generic affiliations, but also insistently to call attention to them. In the two examples discussed below, this practice of generic referentiality is intensified and complicated, for the multiple genres to be invoked are partially conflicting, rather than being, as in this part of the *Book of the Duchess*, two very closely cooperating forms, dream vision and *dit amoreux*.

General Prologue to the *Canterbury Tales*, 1–42

In the opening passage of the General Prologue, Chaucer's tendency to modulate or disarrange generic expectations reaches a level that may produce a new kind of text altogether. The manuscript rubrics consistently call this first section of the Canterbury Tales a prologue: in different copies it is labelled *the prolog, prologus, the prolog of this boke, the prologe of the Kneytis tale, the prolog of the tales of Caunterbury, prologus fabularum Cantuar* or *the proheme of al the tal*.[16] Modern literary taste has reified the idea of this prologue into a free-standing entity (if not a genre), so that what we call the General Prologue has become the best-known segment of all of Chaucer's writings and the one most likely to appear in anthologies. Yet the practice of the medieval editors and scribes suggests, to the contrary, that the General Prologue was not understood as an independent text but, as its name implies, functioned as a verbal introduction inextricably linked to something else that was to follow. In no known medieval manuscript does the General Prologue appear as an excerpt standing alone, though other segments of the *Canterbury Tales*, especially the religious tales, are indeed separated out and anthologized with different materials. The exception to prove the rule is that part of the Parson's portrait was written into a blank column at the end of a manuscript of Boethius: clearly in that case it was not the Prologue as such, but instead this one portrait of a religious figure, that appealed.[17]

Middle English prologues to many works exist.[18] Not surprisingly, this prologue is extraordinarily complex. Starting with its opening phrases, it interprets its textual work, which is to introduce what will follow, as an opportunity to spin out lines of affiliation in multiple directions. The springtime topos with which the text begins summons up two main possibilities, the lyric (secular or religious) and the dream vision, both of which might conventionally call upon a landscape with flowers and birdsong. In the *Roman de la rose*, for example, as mentioned above, the inventory of the traits of springtime is similar, including the new moisture ('swote dewes', sweet dews, *Rom* 60) that relieves the earlier dryness; the growth of grass, flowers and foliage on the trees; the brightness of the sunshine; and the joyful singing of birds, such as the nightingale ('in her hertis is sich lykyng', *Rom* 76). After thirty-three lines in which these descriptive elements accumulate, the *Romaunt* offers its consequential 'Then—' clause to state the theme of secular love and desire: 'Than yonge folk enten-den ay / Forto ben gay and amorous' (*Rom* 82–3). To the extent that the opening lines of the General Prologue would have raised the expectation that a similar dream vision would follow, Chaucer's 'Then—' clause, which instead of amorous intent asserts 'Thanne longen folk to goon on pilgrimages' (12), would have functioned as a generic deviation, derangement or parody.

The pilgrimage narrative towards which the text seems to shift at this point was another widespread medieval type of writing. More than 500 accounts of the Jerusalem pilgrimage alone have survived (Howard 1980: 17). Aside from their subject of travel to a holy site, these accounts vary immensely and therefore may not have been associated with consistent generic expectations. Nevertheless, the General Prologue, in deflecting its trajectory from lyric or dream vision towards pilgrimage, is clearly moving in a different direction, if not precisely towards a different genre, for it starts to lay the groundwork for a travel tale. The narrator asserts his own preparedness for such a journey, saying that he was 'Redy to wenden on my pilgrymage' (21), and he offers a corroborating identification of the group of new arrivals at the Tabard: 'pilgrimes were they alle, / That toward Caunterbury wolden ryde' (26–7). But just as the theme of springtime fertility and sexuality was fore-grounded in the opening lines (1–11) and then seemed to recede from view when the pilgrimage motive was thrust forward (12–34), so now, in the portraits that follow, pilgrimage itself seems to recede, as attention is claimed by the new project of dis-playing 'al the condicioun / Of ech of hem, so as it semed me, / And whiche they weren, and of what degree, / and Eek in what array that they were inne' (38–41). Indeed, no full account of the pilgrimage is ever rendered, though later in the *Can-terbury Tales* a few locations along the route will be briefly glimpsed. In the General Prologue the portrait series predominates to the extent that Jill Mann proposed 'that the *Prologue* is an example of a neglected medieval genre – that both its form and its content proclaim it to be part of the literature dealing with the "estates" of society'

(Mann: 1973: 1); thus 'the form of the estates genre and the form of the Prologue are one and the same' (4).

In the opening passage of the *Canterbury Tales*, then, Chaucer has offered several generic signals, each overlain, though not obliterated, by the next. The springtime opening raises the possibility of lyric, though it soon becomes apparent that this is not a lyric. The springtime opening also establishes resemblances to the dream vision, though no dream, but instead a waking journey, is initiated. The turn to pilgrimage (at the 'Then—' juncture) begins to move the narrative into this new direction, though another deflection, this time into the extended series of portraits, occurs. The swift, fluid orchestration of generic options makes it clear both that genre is central to Chaucer's poetics, and that no single genre can long suffice to contain the energies of his text.

Troilus and Criseyde V, 1786–92, 1800–27

Towards the end of *Troilus and Criseyde*, positioned almost – but not quite – as an outer frame for the narrative, there occurs a passage in which Chaucer addresses his book as if it were a living creature and gives it an assignment: the book is to go forth and to kiss the steps where Virgil, Ovid, Homer, Lucan and Statius pass by (V, 1791–2). Then it will presumably travel onwards, for he prays that it will be understood wherever it is read or sung (1797–8). Such a 'go, little book' passage is a traditional ingredient that appears in Ovid's *Tristia*, Statius' *Thebaid* and other works Chaucer may have known. Chaucer's version recalls particularly the corresponding passage in Boccaccio's *Filocolo* where, as here, a sequence of five writers is named: Boccaccio's are Virgil, Lucan, Statius, Ovid and Dante. Chaucer's stanza refers, in rapid succession, to at least three generic contexts: (1) tragedy, which the 'litel book' is said to be; (2) comedy, with which the 'litel book' seems to be contrasted; and (3) via the five great poets, epic and history, from which, however, this story of Troilus is soon dissociated by its dismissive treatment of the hero's death in battle. Where scenes of combat and of death are often amplified in epic, here one line suffices to kill Troilus – 'Dispitously hym slough the fierse Achille' (1806). Even that single line is tilted towards Achilles; we are told that at this moment Achilles was fierce and cruel, but we can only assume that Troilus was brave and courageous to the last.

If this series of movements would seem to leave tragedy as the residual genre, that affiliation too is soon complicated. Within a few lines of his hastily announced death, Troilus, or his spirit, has ascended to the eighth sphere in the sky, where he hears heavenly harmonies and, looking down upon this 'litel spot of erthe' (1815), laughs at the sorrow of those who are grieving for his death. Just as the one-line description of the final battle has undercut the process of Troilus' dying, so now his laughter undercuts the lamentation that is characteristically associated with tragedy, a genre in which one would not expect to hear the (dead) protagonist's laughter at the end. Indeed, much has been written about this scene. John Steadman points out that the passage functions to invoke another literary tradition yet, that of the apotheosis, the journey to the heavens where the spectator gazes down at events on earth and realizes (sometimes with laughter) an important piece of wisdom, such as the relative insignificance of worldly concerns. Thus in Troilus' apotheosis, 'we may recognize a tradition that embraces Lucan and Cicero, Dante and Boccaccio, and that also displays marked affinities with Boethius's *De Consolatione*', which means that Chaucer 'may have expected his more judicious readers to interpret it against the background established by medieval and classical analogues' (Steadman 1972: 4). Though these analogues may not all belong to one genre, the point is that with Troilus' journey to the heavens the poem veers away from tragedy and opens itself to other options. (It will veer again before the close.)

Thus these five stanzas of *Troilus* display, as does the opening of the *Canterbury Tales* (see above), a highly compressed series of generic invocations and oscillations, and they seem designed to do exactly that. The text simultaneously is, and is not, each of several kinds. In *Troilus* and the *Canterbury Tales*, if not in all of Chaucer's works, a deft complexity in the presentation of genre – a resistance to categorical simplicities which, as a matter of principle, correlates with thematic and philosophical complexities as well – is a Chaucerian signature.

See also CHRISTIAN IDEOLOGIES; COMEDY; FRANCE; GAMES; GEOGRAPHY AND TRAVEL; ITALY; LANGUAGE; LIFE HISTORIES; MODES OF REPRESENTATION; NARRATIVE; OTHER THOUGHT-WORLDS; STYLE.

ACKNOWLEDGEMENTS

I would like to thank Robert R. Edwards and Thomas O. Beebee for comments on a previous draft of this chapter.

NOTES

1 Aristotle, *Poetics*, trans. S. H. Butcher, in *Critical Theory since Plato*, ed. Hazard Adams, rev. edn (Philadelphia: Harcourt Brace Jovanovich, 1992), 53.

2 *Sir Orfeo*, ed. A. J. Bliss (London: Oxford University Press, 1954), pp. xlvi–xlviii, 204.

3 For the definitions of tragedy and comedy in the *Epistle to Can Grande della Scala* attributed to Dante, see Alastair J. Minnis and A. B. Scott, with the assistance of David Wallace, *Medieval Literary Theory and Criticism c.1100–c.1375: The Commentary Tradition*, rev. edn (Oxford: Oxford University Press, 1991), 440–4, 460–1.

4 For rubrics and titles, see William McCormick with the assistance of Janet E. Heseltine, *The Manuscripts of Chaucer's* Canterbury Tales (Oxford: Clarendon, 1933).

5 Julia C. Crick, *The Historia Regum Britannie of Geoffrey of Monmouth*, iii: *A Summary Catalogue of the Manuscripts* (Cambridge: Brewer, 1989).

6 Paul M. Clogan, 'Literary genres in a medieval textbook', *Medievalia et Humanistica*, new series 11 (1982), 206.

7 Tzvetan Todorov, *The Fantastic: A Structural Approach to a Literary Genre*, trans. Richard Howard (Cleveland: The Press of Case

Western Reserve University, 1973; first pub. 1970), 7, 13–15.

8 Matteo Maria Boiardo, *Orlando Innamorato*, trans. Charles Stanley Ross (Berkeley: University of California Press, 1989), 19.

9 A. C. Spearing, *Medieval Dream-poetry* (Cambridge: Cambridge University Press, 1976).

10 Kathryn L. Lynch, *The High Medieval Dream Vision: Poetry, Philosophy, and Literary Form* (Stanford: Stanford University Press, 1988), 7.

11 Derek S. Brewer, 'Images of Chaucer 1386–1900', in *Chaucer and Chaucerians: Critical Studies in Middle English Literature*, ed. Derek S. Brewer (University, Ala.: University of Alabama Press; London: Nelson, 1966), 259.

12 Derek Brewer, 'Comedy and tragedy in *Troilus and Criseyde*', in *The European Tragedy of Troilus*, ed. Piero Boitani (Oxford: Clarendon, 1989), 109.

13 See note 3 above.

14 M. B. Parkes, 'The influence of the concepts of *ordinatio* and *compilatio* on the development of the book', in *Medieval Learning and Literature: Essays Presented to Richard William Hunt*, ed. J. J. G. Alexander and M. T. Gibson (Oxford: Clarendon, 1976), 115–41; A. I. Doyle and M. B. Parkes, 'The production of

copies of the *Canterbury Tales* and the *Confessio Amantis* in the early fifteenth century', in *Medieval Scribes, Manuscripts and Libraries: Essays Presented to N. R. Ker*, ed. M. B. Parkes and Andrew G. Watson (London: Scolar, 1978), 163–210.

15 Thomas Tyrwhitt, ed., *The Canterbury Tales of Chaucer, to which are added an Essay on his Language and Versification . . .*, 2nd edn, 2 vols (Oxford: Clarendon, 1798), i, 72.

16 McCormick and Heseltine, *Manuscripts of Chaucer's* Canterbury Tales.

17 The manuscript is London, British Library, MS Additional 10340; McCormick and Heseltine, *Manuscripts of Chaucer's* Canterbury Tales, 535. The single leaf from another manuscript with lines 298–368 of the General Prologue (Oxford, Bodleian Library, MS Douce, d. 4; McCormick and Heseltine, *Manuscripts of Chaucer's* Canterbury Tales, 537) is too fragmentary to determine its status.

18 Ruth Evans, 'An afterword on the prologue', in *The Idea of the Vernacular: An Anthology of Middle English Literary Theory 1280–1520*, ed. Jocelyn Wogan-Browne, Nicholas Watson, Andrew Taylor and Ruth Evans (University Park, Pa.: Pennsylvania State University Press, 1999), 371–8.

References and Further Reading

Beebee, Thomas O. (1994) *The Ideology of Genre: A Comparative Study of Generic Instability* (University Park, Pa.: Pennsylvania State University Press). Studies the nature of genre and its variations and use-values.

Benson, C. David (1986) *Chaucer's Drama of Style: Poetic Variety and Contrast in the* Canterbury Tales (Chapel Hill, NC: University of North Carolina Press). Proposes that the drama of this work is stylistic, consisting in part in the variety of genres.

Brewer, Derek S. (1998) *A New Introduction to Chaucer*, 2nd edn (London: Longman). Discusses each of Chaucer's works, with many comments on genre.

Cooper, Helen (1991) 'Generic variations on the theme of poetic and civil authority', in *Poetics: Theory and Practice in Medieval English Literature*, ed. Piero Boitani and Anna Torti (Cambridge: Brewer), 82–103. Correlates different uses of authority, including the citing of sources, with different genres.

Crane, Susan (1994) *Gender and Romance in Chaucer's* Canterbury Tales (Princeton: Princeton University Press). Argues that gender is central to Chaucer's interpretation of the genre of romance.

Edwards, Robert R. (1989) *The Dream of Chaucer: Representation and Reflection in the Early Narratives* (Durham, NC: Duke University Press). Demonstrates ways in which Chaucer presents dream vision as fiction and as speculation about the nature of poetry.

Hines, John (1993) *The Fabliau in English* (London: Longman). Places Chaucer's fabliaux within the context of French and other European versions.

Howard, Donald R. (1980) *Writers and Pilgrims: Medieval Pilgrimage Narratives and Their Posterity* (Berkeley: University of California Press). Describes pilgrimage narratives and draws comparisons to the *Canterbury Tales*.

Jauss, Hans Robert (1979) 'The alterity and modernity of medieval literature', *New Literary History* 10, 181–227. Presents an association of genres with 'attitudes' and discusses nine 'little genres'.

Kelly, H. Ansgar (1993) 'Interpretation of genres and by genres in the Middle Ages', in *Interpretation: Medieval and Modern*, ed. Piero Boitani and Anna Torti (Cambridge: Brewer), 107–22. Surveys medieval genre theory and Chaucer's contributions, emphasizing tragedy.

⎯⎯ (1997) *Chaucerian Tragedy* (Cambridge: Brewer). Studies in detail the concepts of tragedy pertaining to Boccaccio, Chaucer, Lydgate and Henryson.

Kittredge, George Lyman (1915) *Chaucer and His Poetry* (Cambridge, Mass.: Harvard University Press). Proposes that the *Canterbury Tales* is drama and *Troilus and Criseyde* a psychological novel.

McAlpine, Monica E. (1978) *The Genre of* Troilus and Criseyde (Ithaca, NY: Cornell University Press). Proposes that the genre of *Troilus* involves a combination of Boethian comedy and Boethian tragedy.

Mann, Jill (1973) *Chaucer and Medieval Estates Satire: The Literature of Social Classes and the General Prologue to the* Canterbury Tales (Cambridge: Cambridge University Press). Discusses estates satire as a genre and argues that Chaucer uses this literary form in the General Prologue.

Minnis, Alastair J. (1988) *Medieval Theory of Authorship: Scholastic Literary Attitudes in the Later Middle Ages*, 2nd rev. edn (London: Scolar; Philadelphia: University of Pennsylvania Press). Uses Latin prologues and commentaries as sources of medieval theory, including genre theory.

Phillips, Helen and Havely, Nicholas, eds (1997) *Chaucer's Dream Poetry* (Harlow: Longman). Provides overviews of the dream vision tradition and of each of Chaucer's dream poems.

Russell, J. Stephen (1988) *The English Dream Vision: Anatomy of a Form* (Columbus: Ohio State University Press). Analyses dream visions in relation to lyric, apocalypse, etc.

Shoaf, R. A. (1981) ' "Mutatio amoris": "penitentia" and the form of *The Book of the Duchess*', *Genre* 14, 163–89. Argues for the importance of the confessional tradition in this poem.

Steadman, John M. (1972) *Disembodied Laughter: Troilus and the Apotheosis Tradition* (Berkeley: University of California Press). Studies Troilus' ascent to the heavens in comparison to classical and medieval analogues of apotheosis.

Stillinger, Thomas C. (1992) *The Song of Troilus: Lyric Authority in the Medieval Book* (Philadelphia: University of Pennsylvania Press). Argues for the importance of lyric in *Troilus and Criseyde*.

Weisl, Angela Jane (1995) *Conquering the Reign of Femeny: Gender and Genre in Chaucer's Romance* (Cambridge: Brewer). Focuses on gender in *Troilus and Criseyde* and several of the *Canterbury Tales*.

Windeatt, Barry (1992) *Troilus and Criseyde*, Oxford Guides to Chaucer (Oxford: Clarendon). Provides in the chapter 'Genre' (129–79) a comprehensive analysis of ways in which *Troilus and Criseyde* draws upon many generic options.

12
Geography and Travel
Scott D. Westrem

The *Canterbury Tales* has become so familiar a work in the Western canon and its ornate first sentence has been memorized by so many generations of students that it is now impossible to recapture the surprise Geoffrey Chaucer's first readers or auditors probably experienced upon reaching the end of line 12 of the General Prologue. Nothing in the preceding dependent clause – with its balmy breezes, fecund earth and twittering birds – would have prepared them for the abrupt shift from latent eroticism to religious piety that occurs when 'corages' is made to rhyme with 'pilgrimages'. The road, which seemed to be leading in the general direction of 'mariages' (as, in fact, it does in WBP 557–8), heads unexpectedly toward a new destination. And yet, as Chaucer continues to narrow his focus from the universal to the particular in the ensuing six lines, he makes it seem that nothing could be more natural than this movement toward 'straunge strondes' or not-so-distant Canterbury in what Eliot called 'the juvescence of the year'.

While the first audiences of the *Canterbury Tales* may have been startled by an apparent volte-face in linguistic register and tone at its beginning, no one would have found the subject matter of its fictional frame to be unusual. Pilgrimage as an expression of personal devotion, a search for healing, a penance imposed by a confessor or a civil court, or an opportunity for social escape was a feature of late medieval European culture. It bolstered the economies of cathedrals and cities, it could be experienced vicariously through contractual arrangement with professionals ('palmeres', GP 13) who would visit shrines on another person's behalf, and it was the subject of numerous guidebooks and personal narratives of varying literary quality. Nor is it a surprise to find a pilgrimage at the heart of what is today the best-known work of a writer for whom geography and travel were matters of particular interest. This is evident throughout Chaucer's work, both early and late: Chaucer is the only medieval English writer for whom it has been thought necessary to compile a gazetteer for place-names (or toponyms) in his work (Magoun 1961). Although few critical studies of Chaucer include an entry for 'travel' or 'geography' in their indices, most scholars have assumed that he had a keen understanding of both, as arguments regarding the 'proper' ordering of the *Tales* have shown since F. J. Furnivall first addressed the question, prompted by Henry Bradshaw, in 1868. Chaucer's indebtedness to Dante, Petrarch, Boccaccio, Deschamps and many others may be traced definitively in his work; he borrowed less obviously from pilgrimage accounts, travel narratives or geographical treatises. Still, discussing such lesser-known texts in relation to Chaucer may enrich our appreciation of him, since among medieval European writers only Dante is his rival in demonstrating knowledge about the surrounding world 'bitwixen Orkades and Inde' (*TC* V, 971).[1]

Chaucer's Own Travels

Born into a vintner's family in a ward of London populated by merchants from Italy and elsewhere on the continent, Chaucer no doubt learned in his youth of distant lands and different customs (and perhaps also some foreign languages, including Italian). Among the 493 pieces of direct evidence that together are known as the *Chaucer Life-records* (Pearsall 1992), not one refers unambiguously to his career as a poet, but several document his travels for a variety of reasons in Europe: he was a soldier in France, an ambassador to Italy and possibly a pilgrim in Spain. No other early English writer is known to have journeyed so widely as Chaucer. The effect this experience had on his work is uncertain – we do not know if he was abroad or at home when he encountered the French and Italian writings that so influenced him – but we may assume that it gave him an increased appreciation for different settings, ethnicities and members of the human 'compaignye'.

Chronologically the second record notes the payment, on 1 March 1360, of a ransom for 'Galfrido Chaucer', who had been captured by the French while in the company of Lionel, Earl of Ulster, on a campaign that began in September 1359 and ended with a truce on 10 March the following year. The date and location of his capture are not given, but Lionel was part of Prince Edward's army, which landed at Calais and proceeded to Reims, which the English besieged until January, when they advanced into Burgundy. The notice offers no indication of the degree to which Chaucer became acquainted with things French; Derek Pearsall points out that Guillaume de Machaut and Eustache Deschamps were both in Reims during the siege, but that conditions were inopportune for conversations about poetry. Nevertheless, like the Squire in the *Tales* (GP 82), Chaucer had crossed the Channel under the banner of war by the time he was about twenty, even if the cause for which he fought did not consider this territory 'foreign' (Pearsall 1992: 40–1).

Chaucer's whereabouts are uncertain between late 1360 and 20 June 1367, when he is recorded as being a *valettus* (esquire) to the king: he may have accompanied Lionel to Ireland in September 1361, joined part of the royal household in Aquitaine or remained in England. In all likelihood he spent time in Prince Edward's entourage in Aquitaine, for in the spring of 1366 he was in Spain on unstated business; the letter of safe conduct from Charles II of Navarre that Chaucer and three 'compaignons' received for the period from 22 February to Pentecost (24 May) was routinely given to pilgrims, and Pearsall surmises that he may have been under way to Compostela or on a secret mission connected with Pedro I of Castile (MkT 2375–90).[2] Chaucer was granted permission to cross the sea again in July 1368, with a letter of exchange (for £10) sufficient to have covered expenses for travel as far as Rome. Scholars continue to debate whether he was present at the celebrations of Lionel's wedding to Violante Visconti in Milan that summer and autumn. He was advanced the same amount of money a year later, probably in connection with John of Gaunt's expedition in northern France (Pearsall 1992: 47, 51, 53–4). There is no documentary evidence for the claim, however tantalizing it may be, that Chaucer was among the pilgrims who thronged to Canterbury in response to the Jubilee indulgence of 1370 (Sumption 1975: 150).

Chaucer must have acquired diplomatic experience on these early journeys abroad because on 1 December 1372 he received a handsome travel advance of 100 marks to cover his expenses as a member of a delegation sent to negotiate a trade agreement with Genoese merchants. He was abroad until 23 May 1373. The journey from England to Genoa would have taken approximately six weeks, and thus he probably spent at least three months in Italy.[3] His statement of expenses indicates that he also visited Florence, which like Genoa had a population of over 100,000 (at least double that of London). The city was making every effort to redeem itself for exiling its most famous son; the established lecture series on Dante for 1374 was delivered by Boccaccio, another citizen of great reputation. There is no record that Chaucer mixed business with literary pursuits in Italy, but he cannot have returned from Florence without a keen sense (and perhaps evidence in the form of books) of the stunning contributions made by Italians to knowledge and culture during the 1300s. Their impact on him, Pearsall writes, would have been 'staggering, but also liberating' (Pearsall 1992: 102–3).[4]

Chaucer made several shorter journeys during the next five years. In November 1373 he travelled to Dartmouth to arrange for the release of a Genoese merchant-ship to its master (his experience there may be recalled in the portrait of the Shipman, GP 389, 410). Just before Christmas that year, he and Sir John de Burley (brother of Richard II's future tutor) went somewhere on the king's 'secret business'. On 17 February 1377 he obtained an advance to go to Flanders, although when he returned (on 25 March) he submitted receipts proving that he had been in Paris and Montreuil; additional, sizeable advances were paid out to him on 11 and 28 April. He accounted for fourteen more days abroad on 26 June. These journeys were probably all connected to peace-treaty negotiations with France. On another visit to Italy, between 28 May and 19 September 1378, Chaucer accompanied Sir Edward Berkeley in talks with Bernabò Visconti, the lord of Milan (MkT 2399–406) and Sir John Hawkwood, a notorious English mercenary soldier. The substance of their discussion is uncertain, but the English throne had an obvious interest in maintaining good relations with the powerful banking establishments of Lombardy and influential political powers who might be useful in dealings with the French (Pearsall 1992: 105–7).

Chaucer is not known to have made any other trips overseas again, except perhaps to Calais, which was considered English territory, during the politically turbulent summer of 1387. As clerk of the king's works (from 12 July 1389 to 17 June 1391) he was responsible for several royal properties, mostly in or near London, including 'Eltham' and 'Sheene' (*LGWP* F 497). While serving in this capacity, probably travelling between manors, he was robbed (perhaps as many as three times) and thus learned at first hand one of the primary hazards of the road. Chaucer accepted the post of deputy forester at North Petherton in Somerset some time during the 1390s, but no evidence shows that he ever lived in western England. One of the last records of his life, from 4 May 1398, is a royal warrant granting him protection while 'going about the various areas of England on the arduous and urgent business' of the king [my translation], but its function and context are uncertain (Pearsall 1992: 206–7, 210–11, 213, 223–4).

The Aims and Practice of Pilgrimage

Chaucer's purposes as a diplomat and, perhaps, a pilgrim can only be inferred, but this is true of many medieval travellers, whose motives cannot always be established. Medieval men and women undertook pilgrimages for a variety of reasons. Their *entente* – one of Chaucer's favourite words and crucial to the proper prosecution of any spiritual exercise – varied in kind over time, and the texts that record the activity are dissimilar. Some seized at an opportunity for escape from the confinements of home; in the 1220s Jacques de Vitry, who had been resident Archbishop of Acre in the Holy Land, chastized those who went 'on pilgrimages not out of devotion, but out of mere curiosity and love of novelty'. These 'light-minded' people left little written record of their vagabondage (Sumption 1975: 13, 257). Certainly many travelled to Palestine and adjacent territory out of pious desire to walk in the footsteps of Jesus Christ and other notable figures of the Old and New Testaments; others visited sites connected to the deeds of the apostles and early Christians in Rome. Most of the 150 Holy Land pilgrimage accounts, guidebooks and descriptions written between 1200 and 1400 seem to have been composed to impart spiritual or practical understanding in readers.[5]

As individual saints became associated with a variety of salutary powers, especially between the eleventh and early fourteenth centuries, pilgrims visited shrines in search of healing from physical and mental illness or, like the members of Chaucer's entourage, out of gratitude for cures already experienced. According to one scholar, 'the desire to witness or experience a miracle was the principal motive for many pilgrimages' (Sumption 1975: 76, 140). We know of such motivations chiefly from hagiographical records, which at times reveal a spirit of competition in recording supplicants' claims to have visited other shrines fruitlessly before finding success with the saint, or candidate for sainthood, in question (Sumption 1975: 150–2, 239; Loxton 1978: 100; Webb 1999: 22).

As early as the 1100s people convicted of crimes from disorderly conduct to rape and murder might be required by secular courts to undertake pilgrimages as acts of penance, enabling some to escape the death penalty. By 1250 inquisitors were forcing penitent heretics to visit shrines on journeys whose distance and difficulty reflected the gravity of their offences. Around 1320 the Dominican Bernard Gui compiled a list of suitable pilgrimage sites, four major (Rome, St James of Compostela, St Thomas in Canterbury and the Three Kings of Cologne) and nineteen minor. By the 1300s the Dutch had become particularly inventive in ridding their towns of malefactors and public nuisances by sending them on holy journeys elsewhere (Sumption 1975: 98–113; Webb 1999: 51–63, esp. 59). As Chaucer's Parson makes clear, such penance might be meted out to groups of people: 'Commune penaunce is that preestes enjoynen men communly in certeyn caas, as for to goon peraventure naked in pilgrimages, or barefoot' (ParsT 105). Penitential pilgrimages are known chiefly through legal documents.

As the church clarified its teaching on issues such as purgatory, especially after the eleventh century, it developed the concept of indulgences, by which means a specific quantity of penance might be remitted. The church never posited the idea that indulgences themselves were a replacement for an individual's expression of guilt – this required a formal act of contrition and confession before a priest, who then pronounced absolution – but stated only that they might reduce the amount of penance (as a period of time or a proportion of the total amount 'due') required of the sinner to make restitution. Indeed, official doctrine held that a pilgrimage was effectual only if embarked on by individuals who had made full confession within their own parish. This fine point of theology escaped most people (see *Piers Plowman*, B-Text, Prol. 46–9 [Repentaunce offers 'correct' teaching at V, 224–8, 270–2]), and as indulgences came increasingly to be regarded as tickets out of posthumous agony, they increased in both popularity and potency. Before 1292 churches in Rome offered pilgrims an indulgence for only around seven years (or less) of purgatorial suffering. The indulgence that Boniface VIII declared for the Jubilee year of 1300 was plenary – and, according to Sumption, a response to popular demand – thus covering an individual's entire penitential obligation. An estimated two million pilgrims flocked to the Holy City (Dante recalls the traffic jams in *Inferno* XVIII, 28–33). A second Roman Jubilee year occurred in 1350, after which papal dispensations occasionally extended the benefit of plenary indulgence to pilgrims to other shrines; Martin V complained in 1420 that prelates at Canterbury had failed to secure his approval before granting it to visitors celebrating the 200th anniversary of Thomas's translation to his sumptuous tomb (Sumption 1975: 70, 143–4, 231–2; Webb 1999: 64–82). By Chaucer's day many pilgrims were visiting holy places as part of well-organized experiences of working off their ultimate debt. Some in fact did so as proxies for individuals who were dead, infirm or simply unwilling to go on a long journey, after the Synod of Arras (1205) declared that 'penance could be as effective for the dead as for the living'

(Loxton 1978: 96). This motivation is most evident in wills, chronicles, papal bulls and other ecclesiastical records.

For pilgrims and other travellers covering long distances almost any route – by land, river or sea – meant a combination of discomfort, novelty, confusion, awe, danger and boredom. Chaucer knew this from his own journeys within Europe and England. Pilgrims were expected to fast – at any rate to abstain from fancy food or copious amounts of it – but they sometimes had little choice. A poor transportation infrastructure made nearly all supplies local. The chronicler Ralph de Diceto (d. *c*.1202) reports that John, Bishop of Norwich, on a single day in 1176, passed through one region in central France where food was abundant, then entered another where people were starving by the side of the road and even fodder was unobtainable. Voyagers on sea lanes to Compostela or the Holy Land were served stale food and water amid chaotic conditions (Sumption 1975: 73, 185–6). Inns were notorious for poor cuisine. Harry Bailly presumably has more than just the Cook's bad sanitary habits in mind when he tells him, 'Of many a pilgrym hastow Cristes curs' (CkP 4349).

Roads were linear obstacle courses and travellers, usually carrying ample sums of money, were prey to robbers. The property of pilgrims who died en route often remained at the hospice or inn at which they received care. Innkeepers and their employees had a reputation for ruthlessness and overpricing, or at least for offering poor value to travellers (Sumption 1975: 89, 91, 93, 203; Webb 1999: 83, 87–8). The Host is thus acting to type when he volunteers to accompany the Canterbury pilgrims and do them 'som confort' by supervising a tale-telling contest that will reward the victor with 'a soper at oure aller cost' (GP 776, 799), a game at which he is sure to win some profit even if it is not quite the feast that the Parson has in mind (ParsP 46–7). The risks travellers faced are summed up in Chaunticleer's first exemplum testifying to the veracity of dreams. Two men who set out 'On pilgrimage, in a ful good entente' arrive 'in a toun' where the 'congregacioun' of people exceeds its 'herbergage'. One can be comfortably accommodated, but the other is forced to spend the night in a ox stall, where he is killed by an innkeeper after his gold, who nearly gets away with the murder of someone he perhaps assumed would not be missed (NPT 2984–3062). (Chaunticleer's second story hinges on the hazards of a sea voyage [3064–104].)

Despite its perils, a pilgrimage held out venal appeal to some. The logistics of travel and the anonymity people enjoyed away from home brought opportunitites for sex and fraud. As early as 813 the Council of Châlons addressed the issue of individuals who committed crimes *because* they were going on a pilgrimage or levied taxes 'on the pretext of a journey to Rome or Tours'. Pilgrims were generally immune from lawsuits for a period of one year (Sumption 1975: 168; Webb 1999: 32). This may explain a difficult passage in the Shipman's Tale, in which a merchant describes the anxieties that businessmen endure, observing 'We may wel make chiere and good visage, / And dryve forth the world as it may be, / And kepen oure estaat in pryvetee, / Til we be deed, or elles that we pleye / A pilgrymage, or goon out of the weye' (230–4). He seems to mean that 'chapmen' must choose either to put on a good face to stave off creditors or to do so by claiming to be going on a pilgrimage (or simply disappearing). The Merchant himself has mastered the first approach (GP 279–82), and his presence on the road to Canterbury may suggest he is engaged in the second.

Like all members of medieval society, pilgrims were easily recognized by their clothing and accoutrements. They wore a sclavein (a long tunic made of coarse cloth, sometimes with a hood), carried a staff (a solid wooden stick, usually with a metal toe) and had strapped to their waists a scrip (a bag, generally made of leather, for food-stuffs, money and other necessaries). Some protected themselves from sun and wind with a distinctive wide-brimmed hat. The garb was homogeneous enough to allow prominent, wealthy people to travel incognito, presumably to escape notice and hazard (Sumption 1975: 83, 171–4, 264–5; Webb 1999: 124–9). It did not wipe out all traces of identity, however. Troilus abandons the rather whimsical notion to disguise 'Hymselven lik a pilgrym' and gain access to Criseyde in the Greek camp when he realizes that 'he may nat contrefete / To ben unknowen of folk that weren wise, / Ne fynde excuse aright that may suffise / If he among the Grekis knowen were' (TC V, 1576–81). The pilgrim's experience and guise both served as cultural icons of sorts. In a handbook of model sermons in Latin compiled around 1300, probably by a Franciscan, a homily devoted to explaining how 'Christ's life here on earth was like a pilgrimage' portrays him as afflicted with miseries and pains, known to few people, treated unjustly, considered a vagabond and exposed to dangers and death. It con-cludes with this exhortation: 'if we wish to be true pilgrims and followers of Christ, we must have, as he did, a robe of charity against envy, a hood of humility against pride, a bag of generosity against avarice, a staff of mildness against wrath, sandals of liveliness against sloth, a girdle of chastity against lechery, and a gourd of soberness against gluttony'.[6]

Since pilgrims were expected to be in uniform, as it were, the narrator's promise in the *Canterbury Tales* to describe each member of the company by vocation (or, at least, profession), specifying 'what array that they were inne' (GP 41), should have been an early signal to audiences that the 'viage' to Canterbury would not be, strictly speaking, realistic. On the other hand, the Parson, who walks with a staff in attend-ing to his parishioners' needs (GP 495) and who answers to the Host's request to 'shewe us what is in thy male' (ParsP 26) is arrayed like a pilgrim in his day-to-day life.[7] Returning pilgrims often wore badges, by the 1300s made of lead or pewter, with an emblem of their destination: a cockleshell for Compostela, crossed keys for Rome, palm branches for Jerusalem and a head with mitre between crossed swords for Canterbury; the last of these likely carried with them ampullae filled with 'water of St Thomas', a dilution of the martyr's own blood that was obtained from a great cistern and was consumed as one of the great medicines of the later Middle Ages. Gerald of Wales recalls that when he was returning to Southwark from a visit to Canterbury, the Bishop of Winchester knew where he had been from the *signacula* hanging from the necks of his companions (Webb 1999: 125).

The Canterbury Pilgrimage in Practice and in the *Tales*

Chaucer's Canterbury pilgrims travel on horseback without incident, except that the drunken Cook cannot stay in the saddle (ManP 46–9). The easy pace at which they and others like them proceeded is the source of the verb 'to canter'. A royal proclamation in 1396 attempted to regulate the hiring of horses, which were prominently branded to keep them from being stolen, fixing the cost at 24d from Southwark to Canterbury, one way. At the time, a bed in England cost around a penny and a dinner with beer a bit more; candles and fodder were extra, but specially provisioned monasteries were gratis (Sumption 1975: 203–4; Webb 1999: 199; Loxton 1978: 89, 104, 109). Chaucer's pilgrims begin their storytelling contest at the 'Wateryng of Seint Thomas' (GP 826), a stream near the second mile-post on the Canterbury road where a gallows was established by the county of Surrey, offering a grim reminder to passers-by of the consequences of misdeeds and suggesting that pilgrims did not need to wait for the Parson to provide a suitable image of mortality.

Members of the company make only casual reference to the fifty-mile journey: they pass Deptford and Greenwich (RvP 3906–7), but we hear nothing about the ferry service over the Darent at Dartford, or the bridge over the Medway at Rochester (in 1387 a stone structure replaced a wooden one), and we do not know they have stopped at a 'hostelrie' (presumably at Ospringe, around five miles from Boughton [Street], where the Maison Dieu could accommodate the king) until after they leave it the following morning (CYP 554–7, 588–9). No other overnight stops are mentioned – the one-way journey from London under normal conditions took around three days – and the 'joly compaignye' is last seen at the entrance to an unidentified village, although none exists between Canterbury and Harbledown, if that is the 'Bobbe-up-and-doun, / Under the Blee, in Caunterbury Weye' that the narrator seems to believe is so well known (ParsP 12, 14; ManP 2–3). In the Ellesmere manuscript sequence of tales, the Host calls attention to the proximity of Rochester (MkP 1926) after the company has reached Sittingbourne, which is in fact ten miles *closer* to Canterbury (the 'error' assumes a connection between the Summoner's threat in WBP 847 and the 'towne' of SumT 2294). Whatever the validity of various scholars' claims that the grouping of tales in other manuscripts preserves accurate geography and must therefore reflect authorial intention, arguments on all sides attribute to Chaucer a keen sense of geographical precision, even though he leaves his 'compaignye' and his audience in a kind of limbo.[8]

Actual Canterbury pilgrims visited five particular places within the cathedral precinct: the site of Thomas's martyrdom (in the north-west transept), the high altar (where the archbishop's body was laid out), the crypt (where he was entombed between 1170 and 1220), the altar of the crown of St Thomas in the Corona (a place in the easternmost apse specially built to house the part of the saint's head that was sliced through at his murder) and the tomb of the saint that was erected in Trinity Chapel (east of the high altar) in 1220 (Loxton 1978: 150–4, 176–8). The tomb, with its exquisite designs in opulent jewels and gold, would have bedazzled anybody: when Henry VIII destroyed it in 1538, bringing the Canterbury pilgrimage to an end, he took away twenty-six cartloads of precious material (Sumption 1975: 154–5).

As the endlinks in the *Canterbury Tales* make clear, the work acquires some of its coherence from an underlying understanding that human life itself is a kind of pilgrimage. The metaphor has scriptural authority (Psalm 118 [AV 119]: 54, Ecclesiasticus 7: 1, Hebrews 11: 13) and it is central in such seminal works as Augustine's *City of God* and his *Confessions*. In 'Truth', which exists in more manuscript copies than any other of his shorter lyrics, Chaucer sounds a distinctly Augustinian note in a series of imperatives that direct the reader to flee ambitious crowds eager for worldly gain – 'Her is non hoom, her nis but wildernesse' – and lead to this exhortation: 'Forth, pilgrim, forth! Forth, beste, out of thy stal! / Know thy contree, look up, thank God of al; / Hold the heye wey and lat thy gost thee lede' (17–20). Chaucer found the metaphor congenial, or at least useful. Egeus consoles Theseus on Arcite's death by explaining, perhaps somewhat reductively, that 'This world nys but a thurghfare ful of wo, / And we been pilgrymes, passynge to and fro' (KnT 2847–8); Theseus later asks why anyone would complain about Arcite's escape from 'this foule prisoun of this lyf' (3061). Chaucer's recurrent interest in his characters' *entente* – their true, deliberate ends – makes it seem almost inevitable that he would be attracted to a practice which, as noted above, was to be undertaken only after full confession to one's parish priest and could be effectual only if conducted with the proper spirit.

Travel Literature

The Canterbury pilgrimage was not the subject of personal accounts or guidebooks; we know about it from hagiographies, wills, church documents and royal statutes (Webb 1999: 284, s.v. 'Canterbury'). Visitors to Rome and Compostela left little record of journeys there, although some descriptive works exist (Figg et al. 2000: s.v. Rome, Santiago de Compostela). Pilgrimages to the Holy Land, on the other hand, are the subject of a rich literature from as early as the fourth century, some of it produced in England (even if in some cases the travellers are not known to have been English).[9] Scholars debate the degree to which 'travel literature' existed as a genre with identifiable characteristics during the Middle Ages, but their discussions have shown that it is futile to attempt to treat travel narratives and pilgrimage accounts as distinct categories (Campbell 1988; Guéret-Laferté 1994; Richard 1981; Tellenbach 1977).

During the century before Chaucer, several Europeans made (or claimed to have made) the arduous journey to east Asia and their reports, even if fictional, constitute the most significant and most satisfying travel books of the Middle Ages. The *Book of John Mandeville* (*c.*1360) was unquestionably the most successful. Drawing heavily on the travel accounts of William of Boldensele and Odoric of Pordenone, but amplifying each to more than double its original length, the *Book*'s anonymous writer combines accounts of an alleged pilgrimage to the Holy Land (while serving the sultan of Egypt as a mercenary) and a journey across Asia to the courts of the Great Khan and the legendary emperor Prester John (the manuscript tradition is divided about whether he served in the army of one or both). Claiming to be a knight from St Albans who was abroad from 1322 until 1356 (or 1357), the author composed the *Book* in French. It was quickly translated into nine medieval languages (including Czech, Danish and Irish) and survives in at least 300 manuscripts, some forty-four of them in one of six translations into Middle English (four of these appear to date from the late fourteenth century).

The writer strikingly depersonalizes both of his main sources by casting them in the third person and punctuating them with occasional truth-claims, such as his assertion that he made a respectful visit to the mosque built on the site of Solomon's temple in Jerusalem, which William had clearly stated was off limits to Christians and Jews. The *Book* sets itself up to be a guide for both actual and vicarious pilgrims. It also emblematizes the experience of travel in narrative units that alternate geographical information and stories one might hear along the road. None of these – the dragon-woman of Lango, the frightening journey through the Perilous Valley, the report of one man's circumnavigation of the earth, the depiction of turbulent seas near the Earthly Paradise – surfaces in Chaucer's work, but the association between travelling and tale-telling has an obvious resonance. The *Book*'s singular tolerance of the non-Christian world – except for Jews, who are treated throughout as enemies of nearly everyone – seems to present its readers and listeners with a world united by semi-Christian principles, indeed a world that will one day be universally Christian and is well on its way towards becoming so.

The immediate and general popularity of the *Book* makes it extremely likely that Chaucer at least knew of the work, with its affable, sometimes self-critical narrator. Distant echoes suggest that he had read it. The Mandeville-writer explains that the word Nazareth means 'Flour of the Gardyn', adding 'and be good skylle may it ben clept flour, for there was norisscht the flour of lyf that was Crist Ihesu' (ch. 13), an etymology also advanced by the Parson ('*Nazarenus* is as muche for to seye as "floris-shynge"', ParsT 288).[10] According to the *Book*, among the 'dyuerse contrees' east of Palestine are the kingdoms of 'Schithie' and, adjoining it, 'Amazoyne, that is the lond of Femynye', located in the area between the river Don and the Caspian (ch. 16, repeated in ch. 17). Chaucer's own Knight might have found some confirmation there of details in Statius and Boccaccio relating to Theseus' battles in 'many a riche contree', culminating in his conquest of 'the regne of Femenye, / That whilom was ycleped Scithia' (KnT 866–7), however much Magoun contends that this 'geography makes utter nonsense' (Magoun 1961: 140).

The Squire's Tale, which is set 'At Sarray, in the land of Tartarye', a realm at war with 'Russye' (SqT 9–10, 46), transfers several thousand miles to the west (to the region between the Black and Caspian seas) the Mongol world of Mandeville, accurately reflecting the dramatic decline of that empire brought about by the rise of the Ming Dynasty in 1367. Nevertheless, as Josephine Waters Bennett has pointed out, the Squire, in claiming to have learned of the peculiar culinary preferences of the 'Tartres' from the tales of 'knyghtes olde' – and in pointing out that there is 'no man that may reporten al' the wonders of Cambyuskan's court (SqT 69, 72) – apparently refers to the *Book*, which is the only medieval text concerning the Mongols attributed to a knight (the passages in question are in chapters 26 and 34).[11] In chapter 23 the Mandeville-author dilates on the wonders of the Great Khan's court, including his 'grete palays' which is 'merueylleousely atyred' and in which is located 'the emperoures throne fulle high where he sytteth at the mete' and other 'solempne festes' at tables of gold. The Squire recalls these phrases in describing how Cambyuskan 'In roial vestiment sit on his deys, / With diademe, ful heighe in his paleys, / And halt his feeste so solempne and so ryche' (59–61). Later in the chapter Mandeville is said to have served in the khan's army for fifteen months and the reader is reassured that his claims, however 'merueylouse' they may be, are completely true.

Geography and Maps

Medieval Europe lacked a scientific vocabulary with which to discuss and develop geography: the very word *geographia* was hardly ever used before the fifteenth century. Key words had multiple meanings: a *mappamundi* was both a pictorial representation of the earth (usually schematic but occasionally a highly accurate navigational chart) and an entirely verbal description of it. In Latin, *mundus* is as multivalent as is the English 'world', a word Chaucer employed at least 365 times. To a large degree, medieval Europeans inherited their geographical assumptions from antiquity, which reached them via four principal sources: the *Collectanea rerum memorabilium* (Collection of memorable things) of Caius Julius Solinus (*c.*230–40), which digested Pliny's sprawling *Natural History* (before AD 79); Macrobius' lucid *Commentary on the Dream of Scipio* (*c.*400), approximately half of which treats cosmographical material (see the discussion of *PF* 64–70, below); Martianus Capella's equally sophisticated epitome of classical learning, *De nuptiis Philologiae et Mercurii* (The marriage of Philology and Mercury), produced between *c.*410 and 439; and the *Historiarum adversus paganos libri VII* (Seven books of history against the pagans), which Paulus Orosius completed in 418. These four books were key sources for many encyclopedic compendia written during the Middle Ages, almost all of which include sections specifically dedicated to geographical knowledge.

Given the circulation of these books and the place of some of them in the schools, we may assume that moderately educated medieval Europeans – and anyone with a modicum of curiosity – would have understood the earth to be spherical; Aurelius is stating a general fact, not a debatable assertion, when he refers to the 'wyde world, which that men seye is round' (FranT 1228). As Chaucer indicates in *HF* 1339, the earth's land area was thought to be comprised of the three adjacent 'parts' of Asia, Europe and Africa (almost all geographical texts refer to *partes*, for which 'continents' is an anachronistic translation), Asia taking up approximately half the space, with the rest occupied by Europe and Africa (early works divide the remaining half equally, but by the fourteenth century Europe was thought to exceed Africa's size considerably, as Ranulph Higden's *Polychronicon* attests [I, 7]). This land area spanned a great distance from Britain and Scandinavia at the western extreme to the Far East, or 'Ynde', as the Wife of Bath (and everyone else) called it (WBP 823–4). Vast as this expanse may have been, the surrounding Sea-Ocean was even larger, occupying the hemisphere between Spain and China, as well as much (or even all) of the globe south of the equator.

The Bible, the incontrovertible word of God, contributed several other concepts to medieval geography. The Terrestrial Paradise, or the Garden of Eden, was an actual site, usually thought to be inaccessible and beyond the eastern coast of Asia. According to Genesis 2: 10–14, four great rivers flow out of this Paradise, each with specific properties; these were usually understood to be the Nile, Tigris, Euphrates and Ganges. The Greco-Roman tripartite division of the earth's land mass received Judeo-Christian endorsement in the claim that after the Flood Noah distributed territory among his sons (Genesis 9: 18–19), the eldest, Shem, deserving the largest inheritance (Asia), while Japhet received Europe and Africa went to Ham (usually spelled Cham or Chan). Jerusalem was figured to be at the centre of the earth's land mass (the city was known *not* to lie on the equator), based on Psalm 73 [AV 74]: 12 and Ezekiel 5: 5. References to the earth's 'four corners' in Isaiah 11: 12 and Revelation 7: 7 were understood in terms of cardinal directions.

Medieval Europe's complicated understanding of geography – as a theoretical and a practical science – is reflected in its cartography. Maps were generally of two kinds. Those depicting the entire earth, today called *mappaemundi* or 'world maps', were in almost all cases idealized or schematic in the sense that they did not attempt to represent space on the surface of a sheet of vellum (or paper) in proportion to what it occupies in reality. Most of the 1,100 exemplars known today are oriented to the east; around 900 are in manuscript books. Meanwhile (and probably by the late 1100s), marine charts, in English often called 'portolans', depicted more localized land areas (usually the Mediterranean littoral, sometimes including the Black Sea) in such a way that seamen could use the maps to chart a course from one port to another. These maps, oriented to the north, almost always include a marker for scale, a series of 'rhumb lines' emanating from central points that were useful for sailing by compass and single-word (or -phrase) legends identifying coastal cities or topographical features that may be colour coded to represent size or dominant religion. Approximately 180 such charts and atlases are known today (Woodward and Campbell in Harley and Woodward 1987: 286, 291–2, 336–7, 376–80).

A small, delicately drawn design in Lambeth Palace Library MS 371 (fo. 9ᵛ), which dates from *c.*1300, displays some of the characteristic features of a *mappamundi* (see figure 12.1). The Lambeth Map, as I will refer to it here (it has never before been examined or published), is oriented to the east (the semicircle at the top is labelled 'paradysus'), has Jerusalem nearly at its centre and allocates territory schematically (almost all cities, regions and nations are represented by circles with identical diameters). The world is rendered in terms both theological and geographical. Set

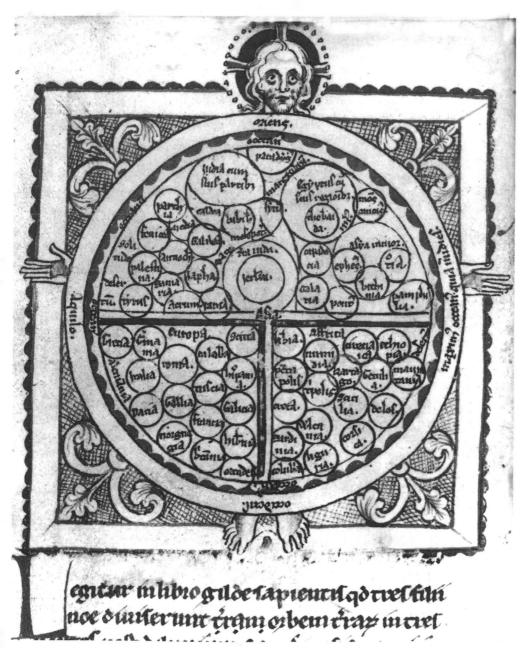

Figure 12.1 The Lambeth Map (or *mappamundi*). From Nennius, *Historia Britonum* (a free-standing excerpt from chapter 17). London, Lambeth Palace Library, MS 371, fo. 9ᵛ (*c.* 1300). [By permission of the Lambeth Palace Library.]

against the figure of Christ, who is shown both in the position of a crucified man and with the nimbus of the resurrected Lord, the earth takes the place of Jesus' body, with Jerusalem approximately in the position of his navel, like a cartographic representation of the eucharistic host. The square frame of the map measures $3 \times 2^{15}/_{16}$ inches (77 × 75 mm); with the head of Christ included, the design measures $3^{7}/_{16} \times 2^{15}/_{16}$ inches (87 × 75 mm) on a vellum page $9^{9}/_{16} \times c.6^{3}/_{4}$ inches (243 × 170 mm).

The design of the Lambeth Map is traditional. The world's three land areas – or *partes* – are clearly demarcated within an O-shaped frame that is bisected by a diameter bar showing the courses of the Don and Nile rivers, at left and right of centre, respectively, although neither is named. The lower (western) semicircle is further halved by a radius line representing the Mediterranean Sea (also unidentified); these waterways are all coloured blue on the original. This tripartite division of the terrestrial land mass has its origins in Greek and Roman geography, and it appealed to Christian theologians by accommodating the biblical record of human history after the Flood, when Noah's three sons 'overspread' the whole earth (Gen. 9: 19). The cartographical image, described in the 1420s as a 'T within an O' – today referred to in English as a T–O map – is the basis for hundreds of surviving medieval world maps (Woodward in Harley and Woodward 1987: 301–2). Most of them show the earth's land area within at least one set of concentric circles, which, at a time when artists had not yet invented a means for depicting three-dimensional perspective, was shorthand for the figure of a sphere. Thus, the medieval eye saw a ball and not a disc in this rendering of the earth. The names of the four cardinal directions appear in the outermost ring; a second ring has three legends that read 'occeanus', all references to the great Sea-Ocean thought to occupy one-half to three-quarters of the earth's surface (see *Bo* IV, metrum 6, 13–14), a 'fact' no map needed to depict. The earth's three parts are labelled just above or below the diametrical waterway. Within each of the three resulting sections, cities and regions are depicted as circles: sixteen in 'Europa', twenty-nine in 'Asia' and seventeen in 'Affrica'.

The cartographer viewed his map as an idealization: 'roma' and 'Italia' are separate circles of equal size in Europe, as are 'kartago' (Carthage) and 'ethiopia' in Africa; four circles in Asia are drawn large enough to accommodate smaller ones, but the rationale seems hierarchical rather than spatial, since 'India' (which contains 'caldea' and 'babilon') is no bigger than the Land of Judah ('terra iuda'), at the core of which is Jerusalem. The distribution of land areas on the map has no connection to spatial reality (few individuals who seriously thought about the world imagined Sicily ['Scicilia'] to be in central Africa, and even a casual reader of the New Testament knew that 'asya minor' does not lie due south of the Holy Land and south-west of Egypt). On the other hand, the extremes of this earth do conform to imagined reality: the 'orcades' (Orkneys), just above Christ's right foot in the far west, are as distant from India, just to the left of Paradise, as Chaucer thought (*TC* V, 971). Other features of the Chaucerian landscape are here as well: in addition to Babylon, Carthage, Chaldea, India, Italy, Jerusalem, Rome and Paradise, named above, they include 'Galicia' (GP 466), 'Galilee' (WBP 11), 'Grecie' (KnT 962 and *passim*), 'hispania' (*HF* 1117;

Figure 12.2 The Gough Map of Britain. Detail of south-eastern England, with London near the centre and Canterbury near the uppermost extent of land. The map is oriented to the east. Oxford, Bodleian Library, MS Gough Gen. Top. 16 (1350–70). [By permission of the Bodleian Library, University of Oxford.]

GP 409; PardT 565, 570; MkT 2375 – all spelled 'Spaigne', or a variant, except in the heading before MkT 2375), 'libia' (*HF* 488; *LGW* 959, 1123; *Bo* IV, metrum 7, 50–2), the Red Sea or 'mare rubrum' (*Bo* III, metrum 3, 5; see also MLT 490), 'Scitia' (KnT 867, 882; *Anel* 23, 37), 'syria' (MLT 134 and *passim*), Egyptian 'thebaida' (KnT 1472) and 'tyrus' (*Bo* II, metrum 5, 11, 14; III, metrum 4, 3). Located just to the left of Christ's left hand is 'troia'. 'Dacia', placed between 'alemania' (not given a circle) and Norway in the far north-east of Europe, probably refers to Denmark (WBP 824) rather than a region roughly coterminous with modern-day Romania.

A very different representation of space is found on the Gough Map of Britain (of which a detail is shown in figure 12.2), which measures 22 × 46½ inches

(56 × 118 cm) on two unequally sized vellum sheets sewn together. (It takes its name from Richard Gough [1735–1809], an antiquarian who owned it.) Unlike the schematized T–O image in the Lambeth Palace Library manuscript, the map in full offers the modern eye appreciable cartography: one can identify it immediately and the fact that it is free-standing, rather than part of a codex, makes it *seem* like a map. Most scholars date it between 1350 and 1370, and while its original function is not known one can imagine that it would have been extremely useful to a man in Chaucer's positions as controller in the custom house or clerk of the king's works. Although it is reminiscent of portolan charts (except that, like the Lambeth Map, it is oriented to the east rather than the north), the Gough Map is geared for the traveller by land, not sea: it quite accurately defines the island's coastline, but the cartographer focused on what might be called British infrastructure. Rivers and roads link nearly 600 named towns, the distances between many of them measured in miles.

The map's practicality is limited to Britain, however. While it shows the shore-lines of Ireland, Norway, Denmark (named 'Dacia') and France – as well as the Orkney Islands – these lands are included to place Britain in a context; the only place-name outside Britain and the Orkneys accompanied by any ornamentation is Calais ('Caleys'), which was an 'English' town after 1347. Only thirteen other national or city names appear (four legends identify parts of the sea). By contrast, England is depicted with at least 405 cities, twenty-two offshore islands and thirty-two other topographical features (including regionalisms and names of mountains and forests); another twenty-four legends are indecipherable. Wales has sixty-two cities, six islands and six other topographical features; six more names cannot be read. In Scotland are sixty-nine cities, two islands and thirty-six other topographical features; an additional seventeen names are obscure. At least seventy-three British rivers are legibly named; many others cannot be deciphered (Parsons and Stenton 1996: 21–35). Along a network of some twenty-four main and secondary roads, which are marked in red ink, are at least 176 Roman numerals that give distance measurements between cities (Parsons and Stenton 1996: 36–7). Colour is instrumental in conveying information: the surrounding sea, like the many rivers, is green, and this creates the island's coastline. City names are usually in red, but some are brown. Larger cities are both named and displayed in architectural renderings of various sizes, variously combining crenellated walls, towers and spires, most of which are outlined in brown with red highlights.

Although the Gough Map lacks typical features of the portolan chart – it is not oriented to the north, has no loxodromic lines or scale and does not identify port cities in legends written at a ninety-degree angle to the coastline – it shares one principle of marine maps in its attempt to depict space on a flat surface in direct, consistent proportion to its distribution in reality. Thus, unlike the Lambeth Map, it might have been usefully consulted by a traveller planning a journey. Indeed, P. D. A. Harvey, in observing that scale is inconsistent on the Gough Map, observes that it must have been 'constructed around a route or routes with distances entered', and that it is a small step from this point to 'due proportion' (Harley and Woodward 1987: 496). At the same time, the historical concerns of *mappaemundi* are present here too: off the Devonshire coast is the legend 'Here Brutus landed with the Trojans' ('hic Brutus applicuit cum Troianis'), affirming the island's settlement by an eponymous first ruler, as celebrated by Geoffrey of Monmouth, Layamon and the *Gawain*-poet.

Chaucer's early readers could have consulted the Gough Map (or its likeness) to find the relative locations of several towns along the route of the pilgrimage company – including 'lo*n*don' (GP 382; WBP 550; CYT 1012 and *passim*), 'Rowchestr' (MkP 1926), 'sithingborn' (WBP 847), 'ospring' (Ospringe, five miles from Boughton, CYP 589) and, of course, the goal of 'Cantuar*is*' itself. They could have measured the distance between 'Berwike' in Northumberland and 'ware' in Hertfordshire, an expanse within which the Pardoner had no rival (GP 692–3; the Cook is from Ware, CkP 4336). They would have found 'oxonia' (GP 285; MilT 3187, 3329; WBP 527; ClP 1; *Astr* Prol. 106); 'dertemouth' (GP 389), 'hull' (GP 404), 'Boleyne' (GP 465), 'Norfolk' (GP 619), 'Kant' (MilT 3291), 'Cantebrege' (RvT 3921, 3990), 'sheffeld' of steel-making fame (RvT 3933), 'Brumholm' (RvT 4286), 'Wallia' (MLT 544), 'donemowe' in 'Essex' (WBP 218), 'Dacia' (WBP 824 ['Denmark']), 'Holder-nesse' in 'Yorkshire' (SumT 1709–10), 'h . . . les' [Hales or Hayles] (PardT 652), 'lincoln' (PrT 684), 'Insula de Orkeney' (*TC* V, 971) and 'wynsor' (*Rom* 1250). The Gough Map does not show locations for the other British place-names in Chaucer's works. The presence of so many toponyms from the Gough Map in Chaucer's poetry demonstrates the extent to which he – like John Gower, in the *Confessio Amantis*, but more literally so – in each of his works was writing 'A bok for Engelondes sake' (Prol. 24).

The *Book of the Duchess*

Chaucer's knowledge of the literature of travel and geography is already evident in the *Book of the Duchess,* his earliest major poem (most scholars date it between 1369 and 1372), a work of consolation commemorating the life of Blanche, wife of John of Gaunt, Duke of Lancaster and Earl of Richmond. This dream vision recalls her death (1368) and underscores its poignancy in two artful ways: the narrator's 'sweven' (176, 179, 290) occurs *after* he has fallen asleep reading about the grief Alcyone experiences on learning that her husband Ceyx has drowned at sea (62–217), and the sleeping narrator encounters a regal man in black whose answers to somewhat naïve questions demonstrate the virtues of the wife whose loss he mourns (but does not articulate until the very end) and whose love shaped an ideal marriage in which 'Al was us oon' (1295). The dream setting allows the story to unfold in spatial obscurity – locations are inde-terminate and the knight suffers in a splendid 'woode' (414, 430, 444) that evokes a sense of social rather than geographical place – yet the poem makes several specific geographical references and thus incorporates the physical world into the dreamer's landscape. Among the magnificent gifts the narrator promises Morpheus in exchange for sleep are pillowcases from Rennes (255) and satin sheets from the Middle East. The word 'doutremer' at line 253 may mean 'foreign', but it literally means 'from across the Mediterranean', the 'Grete Se' in which Ceyx has perished on his voyage (140). The narrator falls asleep and hears birdsong so melodious that he would not trade it 'for the toun of Tewnes [Tunis]' (310), a peculiar exchange only a dreamer could envision, and he distinguishes his 'sweven' from those of Joseph of 'Egipte' and Scipio, 'the Affrikan' (281, 287), whose survey of world geography in Macrobius' well-known *Commentary* is described below.

Curiously, however, the poem's most concentrated references to the real world come from the distracted and sorrowful knight in the dream, whom Chaucer craftily allows to be Blanche's eulogist. In praising her singularity he compares her to 'The soleyn fenix of Arabye' (982), using language employed by Isidore of Seville in his *Etymologiae* (XII, ch. 7, 22) and echoed in many later texts, including bestiaries (the Virgin Mary is likened to the 'Fenyx of Arraby' in the *Gawain-poet's Pearl* 430). He would have loved her best even had he possessed the riches of the most opulent places within the earth's three *partes*: Babyloyne (Chaucer may mean the city or the region), Cartage, Macedoyne, Rome or Nynyve (1060–3), a list that lacks spatial or chronological order (except that all flourished in antiquity). In his most unusual observation, however, the knight distinguishes Blanche from a 'typical' noblewoman by claiming that she never sent 'men into Walakye, / To Pruyse, and into Tartarye, / To Alysaundre, ne into Turkye', nor did she ever command anyone to 'Goo hoodles into the Drye Se / And come hom by the Carrenar' (1024–6, 1028–9). With this list of toponyms, the knight refers to a convention of the courtly love tradition in which a woman explicitly or implicitly makes her favour contingent on a knight's valiant chivalric service. Blanche's reserve and judiciousness are established by the knight's hyperbole: the little whimsies – or 'knakkes smale' (1033) – she does *not* display would send suitors to the Transylvanian Alps, the south-east coast of the Baltic Sea, east Asia, Egypt, Turkey and the Gobi (in that frenetic order).

Yet Chaucer's toponyms do not come from the geography of romance: young men in Blanche's service are not spared exploits in never-never-land, the world of King Arthur or even the contemporary arena, but from the political and mercantile affairs of his own day. Wallachia, in modern Romania, is still Roman 'Dacia' in John of Plano Carpini (the more up-to-date William of Rubruck refers twice to 'Blakia'), Prussia was at this time controlled by the evangelical Teutonic Knights from 'alle nacions' (GP 53) and the outpost Carrenar (Qara Na'ur, 'Black Lake') lies east of the Gobi in Outer Mongolia.[12] The image of a knight obeying a command to ride 'hoodles' – without a chain-mail head covering – recalls contemporary descriptions of protective measures needed for desert crossings. The contemporaneity of the place-names in the passage both underscores the occasionally wild absurdity of dreams and links the idealized landscape of the vision to the real world from whose space Blanche has bodily disappeared.

The *Parliament of Fowls*

Chaucer's novel list of fourteenth-century place-names in the *Book of the Duchess* depends on a very different kind of geographical knowledge from that displayed in the *Parliament of Fowls*, in which a narrator once again approaches the kernel of his story via an act of reading. In this case it is not insomnia but intellectual eagerness that spurs him to spend an entire 'longe day' reading what he calls 'Tullyus of the Drem of Scipioun' (21, 31), by which this narrator means the 'Dream of Scipio' – or *Somnium Scipionis* – the only part of Marcus Tullius Cicero's *De re publica* known during the Middle Ages.[13] It circulated together with a detailed commentary by the late fourth-century polymath Macrobius, whose expansion of the original text to some sixteen times its original length justifies the assertion that he cared not just a little about it (*PF* 111). The *Commentary*'s discussion of astronomy, geography, physics and philosophy in the context of Roman imperial history made it an attractive pedagogical text and it was read in many medieval schools.

Chaucer refers to the work with notable frequency (*BD* 284–9; *HF* 514, 916–18; *NPT* 3123–6; *Rom* 6–10) and some inaccuracy (Scipio was not a king, as three of these passages style him, nor did his vision of immortal souls include a view of 'helle', as asserted in *HF* 918 and *PF* 32–3). His summary of Tullius' 'sentence' in *PF* 36–84 could have been taken entirely from Cicero's original (it nowhere contains a detail unique to the Macrobian commentary). In it the narrator recounts how the Roman general Scipio, near the height of his fame in exploits against Carthage, dreams that his adoptive grandfather Africanus comes to him in a dream and, from a lofty height, offers a lesson in geography, good citizenship, secular transitoriness and the immortality of souls. Africanus directs Scipio's attention to the 'nyne speres' within which 'the lytel erthe' is both at the centre and of relative insignificance: these are, in order, earth, the moon, Mercury, Venus, the sun, Mars, Jupiter, Saturn and the fixed stars (*PF* 57–63), whose composition constitutes, and literally effects, stunning cosmic harmony. Africanus poses a lesson in the form of a request:

> Than bad he hym, syn erthe was so lyte,
> And dissevable and ful of harde grace,
> That he ne shulde hym in the world delyte.
> Thanne tolde he hym, in certeyn yeres space
> That every sterre shulde come into his place
> Ther it was first, and al shulde out of mynde
> That in this world is don of al mankynde.
>
> (64–70)

The transition from the physical 'erthe' to the moral 'world' in the first three lines of this stanza corresponds to a section of the *Commentary* in which the move occurs much more slowly and from which Chaucer would have received a succinct lesson in world geography (II, 5–9).

Macrobius draws primarily on Greek sources to sketch out a spherical earth, with a circumference corresponding to its modern measurement, that is divided into five zones (or 'climata'). Three of these are uninhabitable, owing to frigidity at the poles and heat at the equator, and two are temperate bands that are populated but separated by impassable seas. Variations in temperature occur even within these two equable zones: thus Egypt and Ethiopia experience heat and drought, while the sufferings of the northern Scythians can only be surmised (II, 7 [19]). In expanding on this concept, medieval writers associated different climatic regions with a range of human behaviours, making the setting of a story particularly important since it could determine, or at least explain, a character's actions. A *mappamundi* found today in many manuscript copies of the *Commentary* graphically displays these concepts – the text calls for an 'accompanying diagram [that] will lay everything before our eyes' (II, 9 [7]) – so Chaucer's narrator may have been reading a text *and* an image: over 150 'Macrobian' maps are known (Woodward in Harley and Woodward 1987: 300, 353–4).

As is often the case in pre-modern geographical works, space gives way to time in Africanus' explanation of the 'great year' (II, 11): the time it takes for all the planets and the stars to make one complete orbit in this geocentric universe, a period of some 15,000 years, long enough to eradicate the fame of any one man and to recommend that humans dedicate themselves to virtue rather than exploits. The physical details and the moral lesson are thoroughly traditional, as was the status of the *Commentary* in Chaucer's day, an authoritative, 1,000-year-old source for geographical knowledge. The birds fail in their attempt to 'argue' the issue of love to a logical conclusion – Chaucer sounds like Langland in suggesting that the competing tercelets prove themselves through their intent 'For to do wel' (663) – but unite in singing a French roundel, which, with its repeated refrain, seems an appropriate, if distant, echo of the music of the spheres Scipio was privileged to overhear.

See also AFTERLIFE; BODIES; CHRISTIAN IDEOLOGIES; FRANCE; GENRE; ITALY; LIFE HISTORIES; LONDON; SOCIAL STRUCTURES; VISUALIZING.

NOTES

1   Peter S. Hawkins, '"Out upon circumference": discovery in Dante', in *Discovering New Worlds: Essays on Medieval Exploration and Imagination*, ed. Scott D. Westrem (New York and London: Garland, 1991), 193–220. Repr. in *Dante's Testaments: Essays in Scriptural Imagination* (Stanford: Stanford University Press, 1999), 265–83, 336–41.

2   Few people journeyed to Santiago de Compostela during Lent. In 1366 Easter fell on 5 April, which would have enabled Chaucer

to be both a diplomat and a pilgrim. See further Martha S. Waller, 'The Physician's Tale: Geoffrey Chaucer and Frau Juan García de Castrojeriz', *Speculum* 51 (1976), 292–306.

3   Travel to and from Italy had probably not become much more rapid since the days of Archbishop Sigeric of Canterbury, whose itinerary of his pilgrimage to Rome in 993 lists all his overnight stops, of which there are approximately forty-five between the vicinity

of Genoa and the English Channel: see Diana Webb, *Pilgrims and Pilgrimage in the Medieval West*, International Library of Historical Studies 12 (London and New York: I. B. Tauris, 1999), 18–19, 33–4. Given the fractious relations between France and England, Chaucer may have travelled up the Rhine, which was somewhat more time-consuming; he would thus have passed Cologne, another major pilgrimage site.

4   Robert A. Pratt speculates that Chaucer may have visited the new church of St Cecilia, rebuilt near the Piazza della Signoria, with its altarpiece showing the saint and eight scenes from her life that are recounted in the Second Nun's Tale. See his *The Tales of Canterbury* (Boston: Houghton Mifflin, 1974), 442–3. This church may still have been under construction in 1373: it replaced one that was razed in 1367 and was itself demolished in the late 1700s. The altarpiece is in the Uffizi. Pratt also observes (295–6) that en route from Genoa to Florence Chaucer would have passed through Pisa, perhaps seeing the great cloister of the Camposanto, a burial ground made up of earth shipped from the Holy Land, with Francesco Traini's fresco of *The Last Judgement*, in which a defecating Satan recalls the Summoner's scandalous 'visioun' in SumP 1675–99.

5   For a census of such works and a dated but still quite reliable listing of known manuscript copies, see Reinhold Röhricht, *Bibliotheca Geographica Palaestinae. Chronologisches Verzeichniss der auf die Geographie des Heiligen Landes bezüglichen Literatur von 333 bis 1878 und Versuch einer Cartographie*, rev. David H. K. Amiran (Berlin, 1890; rev. edn Jerusalem: Universitas Booksellers of Jerusalem, 1963), 45–101. For information about all travellers and geographical writers mentioned below, see Kristen Figg, John Block Friedman, Gregory Guzman and Scott D. Westrem, *Travel, Trade and Exploration in the Middle Ages: An Encyclopedia* (New York and London: Garland, 2000).

6   *Fasciculus Morum: A Fourteenth-century Preacher's Handbook*, ed. and trans. Siegfried Wenzel (University Park, Pa. and London: Pennsylvania State University Press, 1989),

261, 263 (Latin on facing pp. 260, 262). Cf. 475/7, 474/6.

7   The Parson's moral opposite is the friar who, 'With scrippe and tipped staf, ytukked hye', snoops around the town; when he arrives at Thomas's house, he lays 'adoun his potente [walking stick] and his hat, / And eek his scrippe', then sits, but only after driving off the lounging cat (SumT 1737, 1776–7).

8   Chaucer's early readers evidently sensed a locational indeterminacy in the *Tales'* 'ending': by the early 1400s additions to the corpus were appearing. In the prologue to the *Tale of Beryn* the pilgrims enter the cathedral, where the Pardoner and the Miller, at first transfixed by the stained-glass windows, steal pilgrim badges. See *The Canterbury Tales: Fifteenth-Century Continuations and Additions*, ed. John M. Bowers, TEAMS Middle English Texts (Kalamazoo: Medieval Institute, 1992).

9   See Scott D. Westrem, 'Travelers in an antique land: inhabitants of the holy lands in reports by three European pilgrims of the 1330s', forthcoming in a volume of essays connected with the conference 'Way and Wayfarer: Travels in the Medieval World', held at Pennsylvania State University on 3–4 April 1998.

10   Citations here are from the Cotton Version of the *Book*, an English translation from *c*.1390/1400 (*Mandeville's Travels*, ed. M. C. Seymour [Oxford: Clarendon, 1967]), but Chaucer may have read the work in French. The remark makes more explicit William of Boldensele's observation (in the Mandeville copy-text) that 'In hoc loco florido initium nostrae salutis effloruit'; see C. L. Grotefend, ed. 'Die Edelherren von Boldensele oder Boldensen', *Zeitschrift des Historischen Vereins für Niedersachsen* 1 (1855), 209–86 at 279.

11   *The Rediscovery of Sir John Mandeville*, Modern Language Association of America Monograph Series 19 (New York: Modern Language Association of America, 1954), 224–7. Bennett believed that Chaucer knew the *Book* in the French original. See also Kathryn L. Lynch, 'East meets West in Chaucer's Squire's and Franklin's Tales', *Speculum* 70 (1995), 530–51.

12 See John Livingston Lowes, 'The Drye
Sea and the Carrenare', *Modern Philology* 3
(1905), 1–46, esp. 20–6, and his discussion of 'Chaucer's world' in *Geoffrey Chaucer
and the Development of His Genius* (Boston

and New York: Houghton Mifflin, 1934),
39–48.
13 Macrobius, *Commentary on the Dream of Scipio*,
trans. W. H. Stahl (New York: Columbia
University Press, 1952).

REFERENCES AND FURTHER READING

Campbell, Mary B. (1988) *The Witness and the
Other World: Exotic European Travel Writing,
400–1600* (Ithaca, NY and London: Cornell
University Press). Offers a detailed examination
of eight texts, from Egeria's fragmentary letter
recounting her pilgrimage to the Holy Land
(late fourth century) to Sir Walter Ralegh's
Discoverie of . . . Guiana (1595), with insightful references to many others, particularly
their rhetorical strategies for coming to terms
with the alienating experience of being
abroad.

Figg, Kristen; Friedman, John Block; Guzman,
Gregory; and Westrem, Scott D. (2000) *Travel,
Trade and Exploration in the Middle Ages: An Encyclopedia* (New York and London: Garland). Contains 435 entries by 177 scholars from around
the world, including specific descriptions and
evaluations of all real and putative pilgrims,
other travellers and geographers mentioned in
this chapter.

Guéret-Laferté, Michèle (1994) *Sur les Routes de
l'empire mongol: ordre et rhétorique des relations de
voyage aux XIIIe et XIVe siècles*, Nouvelle Bibliothèque du Moyen Age 28 (Paris: Champion).
Surveys the work of twenty-three individuals
who claim to have travelled the 'roads of the
Mongol Empire' between 1238 and 1360 and
develops a vocabulary and taxonomy that
facilitate sophisticated, theoretically informed
discussions of travel literature.

Harley, J. B. and Woodward, David, eds (1987)
The History of Cartography, i: *Cartography in
Prehistoric, Ancient and Medieval Europe and
the Mediterranean* (Chicago: University of
Chicago Press). Particularly relevant for the
student of medieval English literature are the
contributions by J. B. Harley on the development of cartography as a discipline (1–42),
David Woodward on medieval *mappaemundi*
(286–370), Tony Campbell on portolan (marine)

charts (371–463) and P. D. A. Harvey on local
and regional maps (464–501).

Higgins, Iain Macleod (1997) *Writing East: The
Travels of Sir John Mandeville* (Philadelphia: University of Pennsylvania Press). Elegantly traces
the ways in which the Mandeville-author made
his *Book* a 'multi-text' by assembling it from the
literate pilgrimage narratives of William of
Boldensele (1336) and Odoric of Pordenone
(1330) and several other works on travel and
geography, but also by manipulating, or 'over-
writing', these sources for his own ends; and
points out several suggestive parallels between
the Mandeville-author and Chaucer.

Howard, Donald R. (1980) *Writers and Pilgrims:
Medieval Pilgrimage Narratives and Their Posterity*
(Berkeley: University of California Press). Makes
a strong case for accepting at least some
medieval 'writings' about travel as having literary qualities, which in turn emerge in imaginative works such as the *Canterbury Tales*.

Loxton, Howard (1978) *Pilgrimage to Canterbury*
(London: David and Charles; Totowa, NJ:
Rowman & Littlefield). A biography of Thomas
of Canterbury, an overview of saints' relics and
pilgrims, and a careful procession to Canterbury
following the medieval roads from both
Winchester and London.

Magoun, Francis P., Jr (1961) *A Chaucer Gazetteer*
(Chicago: University of Chicago Press). A 'dictionary' of place-names in Chaucer's works that
is invaluable both for its identification of
toponyms and for the very fact that it needed to
be written – and in the form of a book – as a
testimony to the poet's acute awareness of
geography.

North, J. D. (1988) *Chaucer's Universe* (Oxford:
Clarendon). Contends that Chaucer was deeply
learned in astronomical and astrological lore and
that his poetry contains many allusions to
planets and stars.

Parsons, E. J. S. and Stenton, Sir Frank (1958) *The Map of Great Britain circa AD 1360 Known as the Gough Map*, Royal Geographical Society Reproductions of Early Manuscript Maps 4 (Oxford: Bodleian Library; repr. 1996). This efficient 38-page account of what little may be ascertained about the Gough Map's origin and purpose includes a transcription and identification of its legends and designs, arranged by topographical names, rivers and roads, with distance markers.

Pearsall, Derek (1992) *The Life of Geoffrey Chaucer: A Critical Biography* (Oxford and Cambridge, Mass.: Blackwell, repr. 1994). Relying on the 493 documentary items published by Martin M. Crow and Clair C. Olson in the *Chaucer Life-records* (Oxford: Clarendon, 1966), and providing incisive readings of Chaucer's works, Pearsall constructs – and makes every effort nowhere to invent – the poet's biography.

Richard, Jean (1981) *Les Récits de voyages et de pèlerinages*, Typologie des sources du Moyen Age Occidental 38 (Turnholt: Brepols). Argues that medieval travel writing constitutes 'un genre multiforme' (8), consisting of guidebooks, pilgrimage accounts, works about the Crusades, reports by ambassadors and missionaries, merchants' records, descriptions by adventurers and imaginary voyage narratives.

Sumption, Jonathan (1975) *Pilgrimage: An Image of Medieval Religion* (Totowa, NJ: Rowman & Littlefield). Provides a panoramic view of European Christian pilgrimage, from its origin in the context of the veneration of relics to its near-demise in the 1500s.

Tellenbach, Gerd (1977) 'Zur Frühgeschichte abendländischer Reisebeschreibungen', in *Historia Integra*, ed. Hans Fenske, Wolfgang Reinhard and Ernst Schulin (Berlin: Duncker and Humblot), 51–80. Analyses themes in travel narratives – measurements of distance, delight in monstrosity, descriptions of storms at sea – in an early attempt to establish travel writing as a genre, although the effort is somewhat weakened by an over-reliance on texts from the fifteenth century.

Webb, Diana (1999) *Pilgrims and Pilgrimage in the Medieval West*, International Library of Historical Studies 12 (London and New York: I. B. Tauris). Features English translations of primary source material (seldom longer than a paragraph and an impressively eclectic assortment) on various aspects of pilgrimage; the section on 'Pilgrimage in one country' covers English pilgrims abroad, pilgrimage within England and Scotland, and visitors from abroad (163–232).

Westrem, Scott D. (2000) *Broader Horizons: Johannes Witte de Hese's* Itinerarius *and Medieval Travel Narratives* (Cambridge, Mass.: Medieval Academy of America). An edition and translation of the first imaginary travel narrative (*c.*1391) not overtly based on other written sources, with a long introductory chapter on aspects of pilgrimage and other journeys 1240–1400.

Wright, John Kirtland (1925) *The Geographical Lore of the Time of the Crusades: A Study in the History of Medieval Science and Tradition in Western Europe*, American Geographical Society Research Series 15 (New York: American Geographical Society; expanded repr. 1965). Remains the most comprehensive and exact survey of its kind in English.

Zacher, Christian K. (1976) *Curiosity and Pilgrimage: The Literature of Discovery in Fourteenth-century England* (Baltimore: Johns Hopkins University Press). Examines different meanings and implications of *curiositas* during the Middle Ages and applies them to three fourteenth-century English works: Richard de Bury's *Philobiblon*, *The Book of John Mandeville* and Chaucer's *Canterbury Tales*.

13

Italy

David Wallace

Italy, since the fall of the Roman Empire, has been more poetic fantasy than political entity. Despite clearer geographical definition than, say, France, Italy has always struggled to constitute itself as a national space. Petrarch, in his great canzone 'Italia mia', notes with satisfaction that 'Nature provided well for our country [*nostro stato*] when she deployed the Alps to screen us from the German rabble [*la tedesca rabbia*],' 128. 33–5): but even as he writes – at Parma, in the winter of 1344–5 – he is surrounded by Italian lords fighting, each with his band of German mercenaries.[1] Dante, two generations earlier, had dreamed of Italy as the heartland of a newly unified Empire: but Henry VII, his chosen Emperor, died before descending on Italy from Germany to fulfil such hopes; Dante's *Commedia* stands as a ruined monument to such aspirations. Loyalties in Italy were and have always been local: to Siena, before Italy; to a particular district in Siena, before Tuscany. Cities continually warred with one another, and many different forms of polity – republic, merchant oligarchy, monarchy, despotism – prevailed. Northern Italy perpetuates traditions of family, work and devotion associated with Germanic Lombardi; the Duomo at Milan turns its back on Tuscan style to embrace northern Gothic. Naples has deeply infused Arabic and Byzantine influences; Sicily lies less than two hundred miles from the African coast. 'Italy', for both Chaucer and ourselves, then, remains a concept both self-evident and endlessly complex.

Chaucer's Italy

Chaucer's family held property on Thames Street, one block north of the river in Vintry Ward; his father, John, was a successful wine merchant. From his earliest days, then, Chaucer was accustomed to seeing and hearing Italian merchants at work on the quays. In 1374 – like his father and grandfather before him – Chaucer was appointed to work among such merchants as a customs officer; he remained in charge of the export tax on wool until 1385. For much of this period he had daily dealings with merchants transporting wool from London to Flanders and Florence (where it would be worked into high-grade fabric); many of these merchants – and the men who bankrolled them – were Italian. Before returning to the London quays in 1374, however, Chaucer had been spirited away to serve in first aristocratic and then royal households. His first master, Prince Lionel (whom he served from 1357 to 1360) travelled to Italy in 1368 to marry Violante Visconti, daughter of the infamous Milanese despot Bernabò. Chaucer 'passed at Dover' on 17 July 1368. It is possible that he travelled down to Milan as letter-carrier to Lionel; he is sure to have heard much about the sumptuous Visconti wedding – attended by Petrarch – and about the rapid and mysterious death of Lionel, his old master. By the time he set off on his first securely documented journey to Italy late in 1372, then, Chaucer had acquired some complex impressions of the Italian peninsula. In no sense, however, was he aware of journeying from 'medieval' to 'Renaissance' cultures: Italy, for Chaucer, formed part of a greater European nexus of diplomacy, marriages, capital, warfare and wool in which (as servant of the crown) he habitually moved.

On the quaysides of Genoa, his first Italian port of call in 1373, Chaucer negotiated with shipping interests (and encountered slaves imported from the Levant). Travelling on to Florence, he encountered more slaves – almost all young women – forming the almost invisible substratum of a most complex polity: a republic that had banished magnates (the most powerful aristocrats) from office. This regime was, by any pre-modern standard, remarkably inclusive and notoriously talkative: the Florentine Republic remains the best-documented state of medieval Europe. All levels of this society shared in the perils and profits of mercantile trade. The chief office-holders were capitalist entrepreneurs; upper and lower guildsmen also served in the Signoria. Beneath this level surged the *popolo minuto*, a mass of unorganized, unenfranchized and propertyless labourers (many of them wool-workers).

At the time of Chaucer's 1373 visit the Florentine economy was in recession and political conditions were volatile; in the summer of 1378, when he next returned to Italy, the Florentine regime was overthrown by Ciompi (rebellious, unemployed wool-workers). Fortunately for Chaucer, his 1378 visit had brought him not to Florence, but to Milan; here he sought to enlist the aid of Bernabò Visconti in England's interminable war with France. For the Visconti, pioneers of a despotic or absolutist polity that would prove prototypical for much of Europe – one thinks of England under Henry VIII – the fall of the Florentine regime was inevitable: such a republic lacked the strong and single-minded leadership necessary to keep down the rabble. Chaucer no doubt reflected on all this in 1381 as rebellious peasants and artisans occupied the capital (and Richard II locked himself in the Tower of London). But there is no suggestion that he hankered for Visconti-style despotism: indeed, he has his good queen Alceste urge her irascible spouse, in the *Legend of Good Women*, *not* to be 'lyk tirauntz of Lumbardye' (F 374). Marquis Walter, the pathological Lombard of the Clerk's Tale, is hardly exemplary; Bernabò Visconti, 'God of delit and scourge of Lumbardye', rates one Monk's Tale stanza – following his murder in 1385 – as just one more toppled tyrant (2399–406).

Literary and Political Models: Petrarch, Albertano and Boccaccio

Direct experience of ideological, military and cultural rivalries between Milan and Florence in the 1370s offered Chaucer an intensified vision of alternatives back home. In Visconti territories, 'Lumbardye', he found a courtly, Francophile society organizing itself around the person of a single male ruler (as forceful and volatile as a 'God of delit', or God of Love). He also encountered the legend of Petrarch, the great 'lauriat poete' (ClP 31) who had accepted the physical security afforded by despotism in order to excogitate dreams of Laura (an ethereal beloved: *l'aura*, the air) and the dead of classical antiquity. Petrarch, from whom Chaucer's Clerk reportedly 'learns' (ClP 27) the story of Lombard tyranny that begins Fragment IV of the *Canterbury Tales*, had hoped for an easy time with the Visconti; in fact, they employed him to great effect during his sojourn at Milan from 1353 to 1361 as ambassador, political negotiator and general cultural celebrity.

Chaucer, throughout his career, devoted much energy to imagining how a poet might flourish (or survive) within the ambit of powerful lordship. His early *Book of the Duchess* sees the poet himself, or his first-person surrogate, attempting dialogue with an unhappy magnate; the later prologue to the *Legend of Good Women* sees 'Chaucer' again attempting to converse with a powerful (and unhappy) lord. In the later text, Chaucer has himself rescued from his own (supposedly maladroit) rhetoric by the decisive intervention of Alceste, an eloquent wife. Chaucer invests great faith in wifely rhetoric: the Tale of Melibee, which he assigns to himself as a Canterbury pilgrim, functions as a handbook for any eloquent wife wishing to dissuade an irate and powerful spouse from acting out violence in the public sphere. The historical surrogate interpellated here is clearly Anne of Bohemia, the much-loved, companionate wife of Richard II. Such scripting of female eloquence was hardly an option for any poet under the Visconti: Bernabò, at one stage in his career, was credited with having thirty-six living children and eighteen women in various stages of pregnancy. When Anne of Bohemia died in 1394, much of the immediate historical relevance of Chaucer's writing – particularly his devotion to female eloquence – died with her. Richard without Anne has customarily been characterized as a tyrant; the Lombard scenario – the nightmare of Fragment IV – loomed more threateningly than ever during Chaucer's final years. Alone in a milieu of despotic violence, a poet might come to greater understanding of Petrarchan sensibility: a sense of loneliness and vulnerability; an impulse to hide in airy abstractions. This might explain, of course, the timely and intense rediscovery of Petrarch by poets under Henry VIII (the first English monarch to behead his queen).

Chaucer's Tale of Melibee also derives from an Italian source: the *Liber consolationis et consilii* of Albertano da Brescia. Albertano (professionally active 1226–51) wrote three works in which, in effect, he attempted to equip his fledgling home-town republic with the rhetorical and ethical tools necessary for the conduct of civic life. The chief threats to such a project were the Emperor Frederick II (Albertano wrote his first text, the *De amore et dilectione Dei et proximi*, while held prisoner by imperial forces) and the magnates: leading aristocratic families, unwilling to recognize any broader-based polity, who preferred to settle affairs themselves (often by way of *vendetta*). Dante, throughout his writings, is acutely aware of the destructive tendency of magnates to tear the fragile fabric of the city states (an awareness made the more urgent by recognition of impulses within himself to glory in his ancestors and carry forward their quarrels).

The Italian city-state republics, hailed by Marx as one of the greatest political achievements of the Middle Ages, would indeed ultimately succumb to magnate violence: for dynasties such as the Medici – like the Visconti before them – were no more than magnates who had outlasted other magnates and infiltrated (before ultimately collapsing) republican structures. During Chaucer's lifetime, however, the end was not yet in sight. A number of Italian republics had succumbed to despotism, but other communes – most notably Florence – proved more resilient. Boccaccio was a lifelong servant of the Florentine Republic; Petrarch never persuaded him to move north to Milan. His *Decameron* was clearly conceived as an attempt to rejuvenate Florentine cultural life – sustained, as ever, through endless debate – after the devastating Black Death of 1348, which killed half the population (including Boccaccio's father, a merchant and city official). The *Decameron* clearly inspired Chaucer's swerve away from the court-centred poetics that had dominated the first half of his career. Courtly poetics form a vital part of the *Canterbury Tales*, of course, but only a *part*: we hear from a knight and squire, but also from and in concert with figures such as a miller, a reeve, a cook of London, a wife of Bath, a manciple, a merchant, a shipman and an alchemical yeoman from the suburbs. The example of the *Decameron*, then, encourages Chaucer to reach beyond court circles centred on Westminster to the greater imaginative world of London; to explore the rivalries of specialist guilds and to reveal their trade secrets.

The Influence of the *Decameron*; the Miller and Licisca

While there is little doubt that Chaucer was profoundly inspired by the *Decameron*, there is (as yet) no hard evidence that he owned a manuscript, complete or incomplete, of Boccaccio's great work. It is irrefutably clear that he owned, or had frequent access to, copies of both the *Filostrato* (source of *Troilus and Criseyde*) and the *Teseida* (source of the Knight's Tale; of the ending of the *Troilus*; and of poetic elaborations in many other works, most notably the temple of Venus in the *Parliament of Fowls*). It is clear, further, that Chaucer was a brilliantly gifted Italianist who understood complex clauses of Boccaccio's poetry that still cause modern translators to stumble. So he was perfectly capable of learning a great deal from the *Decameron* in a short space of time. Petrarch, in a letter written to Boccaccio in 1373, tells of his own rather rapid reading of the *Decameron*: 'I leafed through it,' he declares, 'like a hurried traveller who looks around from side to side without halting' (*Seniles* 18. 3; ii, 655).[2] Chaucer, who might first have learned of the *Decameron* from courtly, diplomatic or mercantile acquaintances, may have adopted a similar mode of reading. And, having grasped what the *Decameron* had to teach as a great framed collection, he may not have felt an urgent need to obtain his own copy of the work. Boccaccio, a great admirer of Dante who copied out the entire *Commedia* in his own hand more than once, was shocked to learn that Petrarch possessed no copy of Dante's great poem. Petrarch defended himself by insisting that he acknowledged Dante's merits, but that he wished to achieve something on his own account. Poets and novelists do sometimes shield themselves from illustrious predecessors: twentieth-century British writers, for example, often turned back to Hardy while skirting Joyce or Yeats. Chaucer's *Canterbury Tales*, I am suggesting, owes a great deal to the *Decameron* in just this semi-acknowledged way. It is, I think, of limited use to compare the two works within conventional source-study frameworks. But in reading the two works against one another, we do find moments of both likeness and dissimilarity that sharpen understanding of the distinctive qualities of each (and of their formative milieux). Let us consider, for example, moments of rebellion as enacted by Chaucer's Miller and Boccaccio's Licisca, a kitchen maid.

It is evident that Harry Bailly intends the order of storytelling in the *Tales* to follow a conventional order of social precedence: first the Knight, then 'sir Monk' (MilP 3118) and so on down. This plan is challenged by the drunken and vociferous Miller, who proposes to 'quite' the 'noble storie' of the Knight with a 'noble tale' of his own:

> Oure Hooste saugh that he was dronke of ale,
> And seyde, 'Abdyd, Robin, my leeve brother;
> Som bettre man shal telle us first another.
> Abyd and lat us werken thriftily.
> 'By goddes soule,' quod he, 'that wol nat I;
> For I wol speke or elles go my wey.'
>
> (3128–33)

By 'bettre man', the Host clearly means 'a man of greater degree, of superior social standing'. But this principle is soon defeated by a higher one: for once the Miller threatens to 'go my wey', that is, break the newly formed, newly sworn integrity of the pilgrim *compagnye*, the Host immediately invites him (in the very next line) to 'tel on'. From the beginning of the Canterbury journey to the end, group integrity is of paramount importance: pilgrims unite to identify and expel the late-arriving alchemical Canon in Fragment VIII; in Fragment IX the whole pilgrimage comes to a halt to put the drunken Cook back in the saddle. The ethos of a pilgrim *compagnye* is that suggested by its etymology (from late Latin and Old French): companions are those who share in the same bread. Such eucharisitic overtones make it difficult to discern, within the context of a pilgrimage to Canterbury (finally figured as 'Jerusalem celestial', ParsP 51), who is indeed the 'bettre man'. Discernment is therefore deferred to the 'day of doom' glimpsed at the very end of the *Tales*, when each pilgrim hopes to 'been oon of hem . . . that shulle be saved' (Ret 1091).

All this is very different from the *Decameron*, where, it seems, the day of doom has already arrived; the plague (as the text opens) is carrying off fully one-half of the population. Part of the intense suffering of this time, Boccaccio recalls, follows from the breakdown of gendered proprieties and social order: sick women expose themselves to anybody with a glimmering of medical knowledge; a new guild of *becchini* or gravediggers pops up to traffic in corpses. The group or *brigata* of ten storytellers formed at Santa Maria Novella that takes to the countryside clearly aims to uphold standards of gendered and social decorum that have fallen away in the city. This group is homogeneous: the ten men and women are young, aristocratic and related by ties of kinship or amorous intrigue. They are accompanied by what might be termed a shadow *brigata*: a group of seven servants (four women, three men) who service the needs of the storytellers while remaining, for the most part, silent and invisible. It is only at the beginning of the *Decameron*'s sixth Day – which is to say, at the midpoint of the work – that this lower stratum erupts into the storytelling to hold, momentarily, centre stage. For just as the queen-for-the-day is about to call for the first story, 'something happened' (Boccaccio tells us) 'which had never happened before, namely, that she and her companions heard a great commotion issuing from the kitchen' (p. 445; 6. Intr., 4).[3] Two servants, it transpires, are in vehement disagreement over the sexual *mores* of young women. Licisca, the maidservant, is heatedly contemptuous ('in sul gridar riscaldata', 7) of the naïvely complacent views of Tindaro (manservant and bagpiper): 'I swear to Christ,' she says, '. . . that not a single one of the girls from my district went to her husband a virgin; and as for the married ones, I could tell you a thing or two about the clever tricks they play upon their husbands' (445). ('Alla fé, di Cristo . . . io non ho vicina che pulcella ne sia andata a marito, e anche delle maritate so io bene quante e quali beffe elle fanno a' mariti', 6. Intr., 10).

Licisca's extended rant is as sudden and forceful as the explosive introjection – 'by blood and bones' – of the Miller after the Knight's Tale (MilP 3125). And the things she promises to tell of local wifely trickeries suggest tales to come that might rival – in sexual energy and social register – those of Chaucer's Miller, Reeve and Cook. But she never does get to tell her 'thing or two', her 'quante e quali'. Her torrent of language, which renders the aristocratic ladies helpless with laughter ('you could have pulled all their teeth out', p. 445; 11), is perceived by the queen as a threat to social order. Threatened with whipping, Licisca is ordered back to the kitchen: for otherwise, Boccaccio says, there would have been nothing else to do for the rest of the day *but* listen to her ('attendere a lei', p. 446; 15). In the *Canterbury Tales*, of course, Fragment I does nothing else for its duration but attend to the Licisca-like narrations of the Miller, Reeve and Cook. Licisca and Tindaro are remembered at the end of the

Decameron's sixth Day: Tindaro is commanded to play his bagpipe so that the aristocrats might dance; Licisca's theme (the trickeries wives play upon husbands) is recalled and adopted as the topic for the seventh Day. But there is never any question of Licisca being recalled to speak *in propria persona*; the voice of the lower orders recedes even as it becomes the invisible source of supply for upper-class entertainment. All this makes the hijacking of tale-telling by Chaucer's Miller seem, by comparison, remarkably bold. It also helps explain why the homogenized *novelle* of Boccaccio proved more acceptable to sixteenth-century English taste than the heterogeneities, social and generic, of Chaucer.

It might seem odd that Boccaccio, who worked tirelessly for the Florentine Republic and against the despots of Lombardy, should favour a rotating, one-day monarchy as his *Decameron*'s model of governance. Such a model represents a strange, personally peculiar, amalgam of influences. The brevity of office recalls the exceptionally short terms enjoyed by office-holders in Florence: priors, for example, served for just two months. Boccaccio's imagining of monarchy itself perhaps recalls the highly idealized view of courtly culture he had developed as a young man in Naples (serving as an apprentice merchant to the Florentine Bardi, his father's company, under the general protection of King Robert the Wise). It is ironic that Boccaccio's evocations of feudal court cultures – often incestuous and set in the south: the paradigmatic example is in *Decameron* 4. 1 – proved so influential in later centuries; for his courts are fantasy spaces that show little of the practical understanding of courtly discourse, its perils and pitfalls, so brilliantly exemplified by Chaucer in his Prologue to the *Legend of Good Women* and elsewhere. Boccaccio's evocation of England in Decameron 2. 3 forms part of such fantasies: the astute young Florentine on the make, the *novella* suggests, can get rich by mortgaging barons' castles; he might then be seduced by an abbot (who turns out to be a princess in disguise), reconcile the King of England with his errant son and be created Earl of Cornwall before, finally, conquering Scotland. All this serves to remind us that, to Trecento Italians, Britain was (geographically and culturally) an eccentric place. Tales of 'Barbary' (the north African coast) abound in medieval Italian narrative, and the Mediterranean is clearly home territory: the Bardi had offices and warehouses in Cyprus, Constantinople, Majorca, Rhodes, Tunis, Marseilles, Jerusalem and Barcelona as well as in Seville, Paris, Bruges, Avignon and London.

Boccaccio's Latin Encyclopedism and the Monk's Tale

After 1350, the year in which he first met Petrarch, Boccaccio turned increasingly away from composition in his Italian vernacular, or mother tongue, towards the Latin encyclopedism that formed an early phase of humanist endeavours. He remained, however, a great champion of Dante: in 1350 he travelled to Ravenna to present Sister Beatrice, Dante's daughter, with fifty gold florins on behalf of the Florentine public; in 1373 (the year of Chaucer's visit to Florence) he was chosen to deliver a series of *lecturae Dantis* to the Florentine citzenry; and he also wrote and twice revised a

Trattatello in laude di Dante. But the kind of grand-scale vernacular project essayed by Dante's *Commedia* was by now out of fashion in Italy: Petrarch chose to write his *magnum opus*, the *Africa*, in Latin. The earliest commentaries on Dante were written in Italian, but later commentators – including Pietro, Dante's son – favoured Latin. Boccaccio, for his part, attempted (on behalf of the Florentine authorities) to lure Petrarch, the greatest of Latinists, to Florence with the offer of a chair at the Studio (which Petrarch refused; he preferred Avignon). Boccaccio also promoted the teaching of Greek at the Studio and attempted to procure translations from Homer. Such enthusiasms are developed through the lengthy encyclopedic works with which Boccaccio busied himself until his death in 1375. His *Geneaologia deorum gentilium*, begun in 1350, was to circulate widely throughout Europe during the next three centuries; its defence of poetry in Books XIV and XV proved particularly influential. But two works in particular seem to have impressed Chaucer: *De mulieribus claris*, which influenced the design (if not, to any great extent, the verbal texture) of the *Legend of Good Women*; and *De casibus virorum illustrium*, a compilation of great men's lives imitated by the Monk of the Canterbury pilgrimage.

Chaucer is evidently keen to accentuate the Latin encyclopedist lineage of his Monk's Tale: '*Heere bigynneth*,' he declares, '*the Monkes Tale De Casibus Virorum Illustrium*' (MkT, p. 241). What follows is by no means a systematic imitation of Boccaccio's treatise. Adam, Hercules, Nero and Sampson suggest the influence of the *De casibus* (and Zenobia, huntress and warrior-queen of Palmyra, somehow migrates in from Boccaccio's *De mulieribus*). The terrible, brain-biting narrative of Dante's Ugolino is loosely translated from *Inferno* 33, and three other 'modern instances' of the fall of great men are added to the ancient exempla. Once again, it seems, Chaucer works chiefly from his memory of Italian texts rather than from exemplars at his elbow. And yet he is evidently keen to convey, indeed to imitate at some length, the encyclopedic *modus agendi* of these fashionable Italian works. He also decides to submit it (the *modus agendi*, or way of proceeding as an author) to the judgement of his own itinerant English public, the Canterbury pilgrims. Reviews are not good: indeed, the Knight is moved to intervene ('Hoo!') and relieve or *stynte* the Monk of his tale-telling. His grounds for objecting are the unrelieved misery and monotony of the Monk's tragic tales: one great man falls, then another, and no man 'clymbeth up and wexeth fortunat' (NPP 2776). The Host soon chimes in to second these objections: 'Youre tale', he tells the Monk, 'anoyeth al this compaignye' (2789). The term *anoyeth* carries suggestions of physical discomfort not fully carried forward by our term 'annoy': to be subjected to tedious or incompetent narrativizing, for medievals, was to suffer acute physiological symptoms. In *Decameron* 6. 1, for example, Madonna Oretta, forced to endure the botched storytelling of a knightly companion, sweats, has palpitations and fears she will die (p. 447; 10). In the *Canterbury Tales*, the Physician's dismal tale of decapitated Virginia provokes fears of cardiac arrest in the Host (and delivers him to the curative narrativizing powers of the Pardoner); the Squire's rhetorical ineptitude inspires the cunning intervention of the Franklin. So it is, then, that the Monk's monotonous *de casibus* narratives are decisively rejected by the Host:

> Wherefore, sire Monk, daun Piers by youre name,
> I prey yow hertely telle us somwhat elles;
> For sikerly, nere clynkyng of youre belles
> That on youre bridel hange on every syde,
> By hevene kyng that for us alle dyde,
> I sholde er this han fallen doun for sleep,
> Althogh the slough had never been so deep;
> Thanne hadde youre tale al be toold in veyne.
>
> (2792–9)

Although couched in broad language, this actually offers a rather complex aesthetic and moral critique of the Monk's performance. Monotonous narrative, the Host suggests, defeats good authorial intentions by lulling its auditors to sleep; and *de casibus* narrative can be nothing but monotonous, since its protagonists must fall from fortunate beginnings, just as the Host – very nearly – slips from the saddle. Latin-derived encyclopedism, then, seems unlikely to please the kind of heterogeneous social body suggested by the pilgrim *compagnye*: a body that seems disinclined to hear anything savouring of 'Heigh style' (ClP 18) Latinity. Even the Clerk, who is proud to announce a tale 'lerned' from 'Fraunceys Petrak, the lauriat poete' (ClP 27, 29), feels obliged to cut the extensive geographical description with which Petrarch opens his Grisilde story: all this, he admits, 'a long thyng were to devyse' (52). The humanist encyclopedic impulse exemplified by Petrarch's topographical survey is thus considered surplus to current requirements; the Clerk duly cuts it from his Englishing as 'a thyng impertinent' (52, 54). The guiding principle of matching narrative strategy to immediate audience need would, however, have been readily grasped by followers of Petrarch and his 'rethorike sweete' (32). In the *Decameron*, for example, the overwhelming immediate need is to distract attention from the horrors of enfolding plague. The fourth Day, under the rule of the unhappily love-struck Filostrato, is dedicated to 'those whose love ended unhappily' (opening rubric, p. 284). Following the epic, incestuous and suicidal tale of Tancredi and Ghismonda that opens this Day, Filostrato requests 'some gruesome tale that has a bearing on my own sorry state' (p. 302; 4. 2. 3). Pampinea, more sensitively attuned to 'the mood of her companions' (p. 302; 'l'animo delle compagne', 4. 2. 4), defies this command to tell the comic story of Frate Alberto, alias the Archangel Gabriel and Monna Lisetta; and Fiammetta, at the end of the Day, chooses for the next Day the theme of loves that end in happiness. Balance is thus restored: the same kind of balance achieved by Chaucer's pilgrim body when, following the Knight's demand for counterbalancing tales of 'joye and greet solas' (NPP 2774), the Monk is supplanted by the Nun's Priest. Rejection of the Monk need not be read as a defeat for Latinity, but rather the substitution of one kind of Latinity for another: Aesopian fable for Latin neo-humanist encyclopedism.

It is immediately evident why Chaucer entrusts his tale of Chauntecleer, a cock who services hens, to a priest serving nuns. But why, then, should he have entrusted the newly fashionable, Italianate *de casibus* stories to a monk? The clinking of the Monk's bridle bells – which serve to keep the Host from sleeping in the saddle – neatly accentuates the anomaly of a travelling Monk: for a monk was bound to his monastery by a vow of stability; the only bells we should associate with a monk are those calling him to office five times a day. Monasteries, with their ancient traditions of chronicling and record-keeping, had long been pre-eminent institutions for the making of history and the conservation of literary texts. Most humanist 'discoveries' of ancient authors were, in fact, made in monastic libraries: Petrarch's celebrated reconstruction of the text of Livy owed much to monastic librarians; Boccaccio energetically copied manuscripts at Montecassino in 1355 (just as he was beginning his *De casibus*). Throughout the fourteenth century, however, monks – traditionally anchored to their monastic estates – had been increasingly eclipsed (and, in England, displaced as royal confessors) by the highly mobile new orders of friars. The career of John Lydgate (*c.*1370–1449) may be seen as a vigorous response to such changes: for Lydgate preferred to travel (to Paris, for example, with Warwick in 1426) rather than to stay home with his fellow Benedictines at Bury St Edmunds; and he preferred writing of Thebes, Troy and the fall of great men to the compiling of *pastoralia* in time-honoured, monkish fashion. Chaucer's portrait of a travelling monk who is keen to English Italian-derived Latin *de casibus* seems, then, extraordinarily prescient of Lydgate's whole career. Or perhaps it was precisely his attentive reading of Chaucer that inspired Lydgate to attempt (via the mediating French translation of Laurent de Premierfait) his own Englishing of Boccaccio's *De casibus virorum illustrium* as *The Fall of Princes* (1430).

Translating Boccaccio, Petrarch and Dante: *Troilus and Criseyde*

It is, perhaps, in Chaucer's great narrative of Troy that his particular debts to Boccaccio, Petrarch and Dante may be most readily evaluated. Chaucer's reading of his chief source for *Troilus and Criseyde*, Boccaccio's *Filostrato*, was evidently both close and long-meditated. The earlier theory that Chaucer made use of an intermediary French translation in approaching Boccaccio's text has been comprehensively disproved: close comparisons of Italian and English stanzas show Chaucer directly engaged with Boccaccio's text in minute local detail. Chaucer evidently recognized both the classicizing ambitions of Boccaccio (who was anxious to suggest familiarity with the *auctores*, especially Statius) and his more basic indebtedness to popular, oral-derived forms. Boccaccio's *ottave rime* owe much to the *cantare*, a tradition of popular narrative passing from oral performance to written form in the course of the fourteenth century. Sure signs of popular provenance are supplied by the tag phrases that provide rhymes or moments of redundancy when the auditor's attention might, momentarily, relax. Such tags are a familiar feature of English as well as Italian popular narrative; the stanzaic *cantare* has much in common with English tail-rhyme (the verse form of one-half of all surviving Middle English romances). Many of these phrases, often designed to evoke an idyllic courtly world, are common to both traditions: 'a grande onore', 'with muche honour'; 'di possanza oltre misura', 'ful of might'; 'con chaira fronte', 'brighte of ble'; 'con canti e festa', 'with gamen and pley'. In such a world we might discover a hero 'queynte of gynne' ('cortese e saputo'), 'proude in pride' ('di coraggio fino'), or 'fair and gent' ('valloroso e isnello'). This last example ('fair and gente') occurs in Chaucer's affectionate parody of tail-rhyme, the Tale of Sir Thopas (715). In mimicking this popular English tradition (it has long been recognized), Chaucer bites the hand that feeds him: for he was never, even in his most elevated poetic performances, shy of attributing 'armes two' (a phrase he uses ten times) to a heroine or of speaking (as do canterini and romancers) of what 'bokes us declare' (when no immediate written source comes to mind). In Boccaccio, then, Chaucer recognized a kindred attachment to both illustriously Latinate and vernacular, popularly derived traditions of poetry. He also recognized a deep devotion to Dante: phrases from the *Commedia* (sometimes employed as, or as if, poetic tags; sometimes deployed with more deliberate, allusive intent) pervade Boccaccio's poem.

Petrarch, unlike Boccaccio, took the utmost care to protect his poetry from anything that might smack of minstrelsy; if he lighted on a phrase suggestive of such origins that had somehow passed into his verse he would root it out and rewrite the poem. Petrarch also took the utmost care to ensure that his writings would not be contaminated by premature circulation; his texts were therefore very difficult to obtain. When Chaucer somehow got hold of the Petrarchan sonnet 'S'amor non è' (sonnet 132 in the *Canzoniere*) he knew that he had captured quite a prize; his translation 'If no love is', slotted neatly into Book I of *Troilus* (400–20), is in fact the only extant English translation of a Petrarchan sonnet made before the sixteenth century. This 'song', sung by Troilus (I, 397), is thus introduced with considerable fanfare: Chaucer as author promises to give us not only the 'sentence' of this song, but also, 'save oure tonges difference', 'every word' of the original (attributed to 'Lollius', the fictive author of his text). And this promise, albeit impossible to fulfil, is approached through quite brilliant feats of translation. Chaucer devotes one of his seven-line stanzas to Petrarch's first four lines, then a further stanza to the next four; the remaining sestet is then accommodated by a third and final stanza. Some Petrarchan paradoxes are thus unpacked over several lines; others, such as 'O viva morte, o dilectoso male' (132. 7), are captured in a single line ('O quike deth, O swete harm so queynte', 411). Chaucer seems not quite to have grasped the self-negating force of Petrarch's penultimate line, 'ch'i medesemo non so quel ch'io mi voglio' ('that I myself do not know what I wish for': Chaucer's hero is blown by contrary winds, in more orthodox dialectical fashion). But he does grasp the imaginative potential of a hero afloat 'senza governo' ('Al sterelees', i.e. rudderless, 416), a motif that returns later (to disastrous effect, as it turns out) when Troilus acclaims Criseyde as 'my steere' (III, 1291).

The fact that Chaucer takes twenty-one lines to translate Petrarch's fourteen need not be taken to indicate prolixity. For, by adding seven lines, Chaucer neatly aligns his translating of Petrarch with the traditional three-stanza format of French *ballade*. This alignment neatly symbolizes Chaucer's dual indebtedness to these two mature vernacular traditions: there is no need to suppose, as critics once insisted, that Chaucer passed from the tutelage, or preponderant influence, of French to Italian. Indeed, the next pivotal 'Troian song' to be sung, that of 'Antigone the shene', owes more to Guillaume de Machaut than it does to any Italian author (II, 824–5, 827–75). Boccaccio, who wrote the *Filostrato* on the fringes of a French-derived court culture at Angevin Naples, was happy to countenance French influence: indeed, he even concocts a legend of French birth for himself (which sees him born at Paris, fruit of a Florentine merchant father and a French princess). Petrarch, by way of promoting visions of 'Italia mia', polemicized against French writing (although he spent the first half of his career in or near Avignon and was burdened with the name Francesco). Dante, similarly grudging, is similarly suspicious of French dynastic ambitions. And yet, without Brunetto Latini's sojourn in French domains (1260–6) and the precedent of the *Roman de la rose*, which Brunetto helped transplant in Italy, his *Commedia* – that long pilgrimage to a celestial rose – would read quite differently. In matters of poetics, then, Chaucer borrowed freely across various European borders. Both French and Italian verse had distinctive things to teach. One of the basic features of Italian, however, was of especial importance (in suggesting continuities with English that French does not): the use of *caesura* in a hendecasyllabic line, with two major stresses in each half-line (and a fifth stress, often lighter, always available). The accentual cadences of the *Commedia*, in particular, suggest certain possibilities of dramatic emphasis that accord well with the fundamental structures of Middle English verse.

The *House of Fame* suggests that Chaucer's first encounters with Dantean *terza rima* made him acutely conscious of the limits of the octosyllabics he had adopted from the French *Rose*. Book III of his poem, which begins by imitating the opening of Dante's third *cantica*, the *Paradiso*, soon retreats into self-parody: where Dante promises to crown himself with laurel as all-conquering poet, Chaucer proposes to seek out a laurel tree 'And kysse it' (1108). By the time of *Troilus*, however, Chaucer had achieved a more settled and subtle relationship to Dantean precedent, one that we might briefly evaluate by considering the ending of his first, third and fifth Books.

Chaucer's desire to suggest comparison or alignment with the *Commedia* is most forcefully registered at the ending of Book V. By instructing his 'litel book' to 'kisse the steppes' (1791; more kissing) trodden by Virgil, Ovid, Homer, Lucan and Statius, Chaucer implicitly awards himself sixth place in an illustrious tradition linking antique authorship to the Christian present: the very same configuration Dante imagines for himself in meeting five ancient *auctores* in Inferno 4 and assuming his place as 'sesto tra cotanto senno' ('sixth among such intellects', 102).[4] Chaucer strengthens suggestive alignment with the *Commedia* by opening his last stanza of all with very close imitation of one last song: that of the spirits in *Paradiso* 14. 28–30 who count out the mystery of the Trinity ('Quell' uno e due e tre'; 'Thow oon and two and thre', V, 1863). Such an ending is both like and unlike Dante: for whereas Dante achieves his final vision in the company of, or in mysterious proximity to, Beatrice, Chaucer has perforce parted company with both Criseyde and Troilus. And yet such difficult estrangement in Chaucer reminds us that Dante has a second beloved, namely Virgil; and Virgil was lost at the *paradiso terrestre*. The painfulness of this loss for Dante (as Kenelm Foster so eloquently writes) can hardly be over-estimated; Dante loses some part of himself. In reading *Troilus* against the *Commedia*, then, we may achieve a fuller sense of the loss implied in that final, very late lurch to mathematical Trinitarian certainty. Such a reading, which Chaucer seems to invite, can dispense with the rash of exclamation marks ('Swich fyn hath, lo, this Troilus for love!', V, 1828) with which modern editors turn the contemplation of loss into strident melodramatics.

The ending of Chaucer's third Book achieves a moment of peaceful equilibrium, as Troilus, 'in luste and in quiete / Is with Criseyde' (III, 1819–20). Such a moment, which might be sustained by a pause in reading or recitation, is dispelled at once by the opening stanza – indeed, the opening word: 'But' – of Book IV. But the latter part of Chaucer's middle Book – like the latter part of Dante's middle *cantica* – achieves a *paradiso* of sorts: an earthly paradise, a terrain that inspires the most complex cross-hatching of pagan and Christian terms of reference. In Chaucer as in Dante, this is a densely allusive space: a place of amazement, enigma and difficulty that will not stabilize. Chaucer's use of Dante in this part of his poem augments such complexities. In Troilus' three-stanza song or hymn to love, for example ('O Love, O Charite!', III, 1254–74), Chaucer closely imitates a Dantean tercet that speaks of the need to seek grace; he who will not do so, Dante argues (and Chaucer after him) would fly without wings ('sua disïanza vuol volar sanz' ali', 33. 15; 'his desir wol fle withouten wynges', III, 1263). Dante's argument occurs in the very last canto of the *Commedia* as part of St Bernard's prayer to the Virgin; Troilus here prays to a more abstract concept of 'benigne love' (III, 1261). It is remarkable, then, that Chaucer should here evoke (terms of reference are difficult to establish: should we say 'echo'? 'allude to'?) the highest reaches of the Dantean *paradiso*, yet end his poem's last Book with *paradiso*-in-process, canto 19. However, the human being to whom St Bernard appeals does indeed appear in Chaucer's last stanza. She is, in fact, the very last person named in the poem, as Chaucer appeals to 'Jesus . . . / For love of mayde and moder thyn benigne' (V, 1868–9). Perhaps that last adjective does betoken some hope for the pagan Troilus, looking down on 'this litel spot of erthe' (V, 1815), as the 'benigne love' to which he prayed assumes, finally, a human face.

Troilus and the *Vita nuova*

At this point it is worth noting that the five-book structure of Chaucer's poem, a design that facilitates such suggestive alignment with Dante, radically reworks its chief source: the *Filostrato* is written in nine 'parts' of unequal length (or in eight-plus-one parts, since part nine consists of an eight-stanza coda or envoy in which

Boccaccio sends his book forth to his lady). Chaucer's design is the more remarkable in that it seems to embrace the full duration of the Dante–Beatrice relationship: that is to say, the *Commedia* prefaced by the *Vita nuova*. I am not remotely suggesting that Chaucer knew or had even heard of Dante's youthful *prosimetrum*; I am suggesting that a reading of the *Vita nuova* against *Troilus* yields remarkable congruences (that might prompt us to think further about the two informing cultures, Italian and English). For young Dante was never so Troilus-like (he was never Troiolo-like) as he is in the *Vita nuova*; and the structure and development of *Troilus and Criseyde*, Book I, parallels that of the *Vita nuova* from beginning to end.

Each text – the *Vita nuova* and *Troilus*, Book I – begins with *innamoramento*: young male protagonists are rapidly subjected to Love (imagined as a feudal lord of absolute authority), a process that wears away at the body, encourages progressive withdrawal from society and inspires the copious writing of *planctus*, or poetic complaint. Each ends with re-entry into society, new hope and a determination (above all) to please the lady. Passage between these distinctive phases depends upon a crucial moment of reappraisal or (in Rilke's terms) *Wendung*, a fundamental re-orientation of attitude that escapes solipsism, obsessive self-regard. Neither protagonist can achieve this for himself; both depend upon the radical intervention of well-disposed friends. In Dante's case this is supplied by crucial interrogation within a female circle; the chief inquisitor is a woman of exceptional, light-tongued eloquence ('di molto leggiadro parlare', 18. 2): if, she argues, the aim of his verse-making has been (as he insists) to praise his lady, he has failed, since he is more concerned with analysing his own condition ('la tua condizione', 18. 7) than with praising her.[5] This simple truth, albeit painful to acknowledge, soon releases Dante into a new life of outward-focused creativity; its first fruit is the great *canzone* addressed to these women, 'Donne ch'avete intelletto d'amore'. In the case of Troilus, the crucial interrogation is undertaken by Pandarus: a more problematic figure, to be sure, but one just as effective in redirecting his friend from grimly inward-focused complaints at his own condition, alone in his room, to an outwardly directed, joyful mode. Pandarus' winning argument concludes thus:

> What sholde he therfore fallen in dispayr,
> Or be recreant for his owne tene,
> Or slen hymself, al be his lady fair?
> Nay, nay, but evere in oon be fressh and grene
> To serve and love his deere hertes queene,
> And thynk it is a guerdon hire to serve,
> A thousand fold moore than he kan deserve.
>   (I, 813–19)

There is no doubt that this *is* a winning argument: 'of that word', we are told in the very next line, 'took hede Troilus' (I, 820). And in the very next stanza he asks the crucial, moral (*quod agas, moralia*) question: 'What is me best to do?' (I, 828). Of course, it is Pandarus who performs much of the needful doing for Troilus before

Criseyde is won; the parallel with the *Vita nuova* is not perfect. But it extends far enough to suggest how closely such refined psychic dynamics, expressive of despair and hope, are realized in Chaucer and Dante. And it is in this crucial moment of transition – at a place in *Troilus* where the *Filostrato* is not active as a source – that they come closest of all.

There is, I am suggesting, a particular kinship between Dante and Chaucer as poets of a vernacular lyricism that, European in scope, extends back at least as far as the court of Frederick II (1194–1250). But the kinship runs closer than that: for each is engaged, at a critical juncture in the history of his particular language, at decisively enlarging the capacities of his *lingua materna*, or mother tongue. In works such as *De vulgari eloquentia* and the *Convivio*, Dante advanced detailed arguments for the wisdom and utility of this process. Chaucer made no such extensive theoretical statements, but his translating of works from Latin (especially *Boece*, so crucial to *Troilus*) implicitly acknowledges Dante's programme for an illustrious vernacular, or *vulgaris illustris*: a mother tongue that infuses learned capacities from *Latinitas* without compromising its capacity for spontaneity and expressive vigour. Such emphases passed out of fashion in Italy shortly after Dante's death; for later Trecento writers, Latin seemed the only legitimate medium for a culture aspiring to escape erosions of time and vagaries of place. Dante does not finally dispute such arguments concerning the fragility of vernacular eloquence: indeed, through Adam in *Paradiso* 26, he rejoices in them. For human reasoning, Adam argues, is itself fragile, subject to erosion and change; the vernacular tongue thus most fittingly expresses, participates in, the human condition (124–38). Chaucer's poetic – most gloriously embodied, perhaps, in that highly rhetorical creature of Adam's rib, the Wife of Bath – is attuned to all this; study of Latinity strengthens vernacular eloquence from within. In fifteenth-century England, Latinity was to be applied from without: that is, aureate terms would be applied or slapped on to the surface of an English poetry. By then, of course, qualities of spontaneity and expressive vigour in English writing – especially religious writing – were out of political favour.

It may not be altogether gratuitous, then, to consider Chaucer to be Dante's most authentic continuator as Trecento vernacular poet; their dates are different, but (in certain vital but delimited respects) their times are the same. Literary culture in Italy had moved on from aspects of Dante's achievement with which English writing had yet to engage; and although we now more fully recognize that Chaucer had company and forebears as *makere* in and of English, we can still acknowledge the singularity of his engagement with Italy. For in the wing of the House of Fame dedicated to English writers, or writers in English, who have grappled decisively with Italian language, literature and culture, we find just four busts (on columns of diverse metals): Chaucer, Milton, Shelley and Giacomo Joyce.

See also FRANCE; GENRE; GEOGRAPHY AND TRAVEL; LANGUAGE; LIFE HISTORIES; LONDON; LOVE; MODES OF REPRESENTATION; PAGAN SURVIVALS; SOCIAL STRUCTURES; TRANSLATION.

NOTES

1 Citations from the *Canzoniere* follow the edition of Ugo Doti, 2 vols (Rome: Donzelli, 1996).
2 *Letters of Old Age: Rerum senilium libri I–XVIII*, trans. Aldo S. Bernardo, Saul Levin and Reta A. Bernardo (Baltimore: Johns Hopkins University Press, 1992), 18. 3; ii, 655.
3 References to works of Boccaccio follow *Tutte le opere*, ed. Vittore Branca, 12 vols (Milan: Mondadori, 1964–). Translations follow *The*

Decameron, ed. G. H. McWilliam, 2nd edn (Harmondsworth: Penguin, 1995).
4 Citations follow *La Commedia secondo l'antica vulgata*, ed. Giorgio Petrocchi, 4 vols (Milan: Mondadori, 1966).
5 Citations follow *Vita nuova: Italian Text with Facing English Translation*, trans. Dino S. Cervigni and Edward Vasta (Notre Dame, Ind.: University of Notre Dame Press, 1995).

REFERENCES AND FURTHER READING

Boitani, Piero, ed. (1983) *Chaucer and the Italian Trecento* (Cambridge: Cambridge University Press, 1983). A collaborative volume featuring historians, Latinists and literary critics.
——(1984) *Chaucer and the Imaginary World of Fame* (Woodbridge, Suffolk: Brewer). Ranges from Homer to the scholastics, the Trecento Italians and Chaucer (especially the *House of Fame*).
Balduino, Armando, ed. (1970) *Cantari del Trecento* (Milan: Marzorati). A selection of *cantari*, poems of the genre (comparable with English tail-rhyme romance) that influenced Boccaccio's *Filostrato* and *Teseida*.
Constable, Giles (1980) 'Petrarch and monasticism', in *Francesco Petrarca: Citizen of the World*, ed. Aldo Bernardo (Padua: Antenore). Petrarch's vital relationship to defining aspects of medieval tradition, spiritual and textual.
Foster, Kenelm (1977) *The Two Dantes and Other Studies* (London: Darton, Longman & Todd). On Dante's simultaneous attachment to Christian and classical traditions.
——(1984) *Petrarch: Poet and Humanist* (Edinburgh: Edinburgh University Press). An engaging account of the full range of Petrarch's writing.
Havely, Nicholas R., ed. and trans. (1980) *Chaucer's Boccaccio* (Cambridge: Brewer). Reliable translations of the Boccaccian texts deployed in Chaucer's Knight's Tale, Franklin's Tale and *Troilus*, plus a succinct but invaluable introduction.
Jacoff, Rachel, ed. (1993) *The Cambridge Dante Companion* (Cambridge: Cambridge University

Press) Essays on basic topics, including Dante's fortunes in English translation.
Kirkpatrick, Robin (1995) *English and Italian Literature from Dante to Shakespeare: A Study of Source, Analogue and Divergence* (London: Longman). An invigorating survey with a fine ear for poetry.
Koff, Leonard M. and Schildgen, Brenda D., eds (2000) *The Decameron and the Canterbury Tales: New Essays on an Old Question* (Cranbury, NJ and London: Associated University Presses). Explores diverse aspects of Chaucer's borrowing.
Larner, John (1980) *Italy in the Age of Dante and Petrarch, 1216–1380* (London: Longman). A readable and reliable basic history.
Minnis, Alastair J. and Scott, A. B., eds, with the assistance of David Wallace (1991) *Medieval Literary Theory and Criticism: The Commentary Tradition, c.1100–1375*, rev. edn (Oxford: Clarendon). How medieval literary theory (English and especially Italian) emerges from scriptural exegesis.
Neuse, Richard (1991) *Chaucer's Dante: Allegory and Epic Theater in the Canterbury Tales* (Berkeley: University of California Press). Argues that Chaucer read Dante the way Dante read Virgil.
Schless, Howard H. (1984) *Chaucer and Dante: A Reevaluation* (Norman, Okla.: Pilgrim Books). Lists parallel passages from Chaucer and Dante and weighs evidence for each putative instance of borrowing.
Stillinger, Thomas C. (1992) *The Song of Troilus: Lyric Authority in the Medieval Book* (Philadelphia: University of Pennsylvania

Press). On the interplay of lyrical and exegetical elements in Dante, Boccacio and Chaucer.

Taylor, Karla (1989) *Chaucer Reads the* Divine Comedy (Stanford: Stanford University Press). Studies poetic influence, temporality, autobiography.

Thompson, Nigel S. (1996) *Chaucer, Boccaccio and the Debate of Love: A Comparative Study of the* Decameron *and the* Canterbury Tales (Oxford: Clarendon). Comparative study of fictional themes and techniques.

Wallace, David (1991) *Giovanni Boccaccio:* Decameron (Cambridge: Cambridge University Press). Emphasizes issues of gender, politics and history.

——(1997) *Chaucerian Polity: Absolutist Lineages and Associational Forms in England and Italy* (Stanford: Stanford University Press). On literary texts, political forms and changes over time; concentrates on the *Canterbury Tales*.

Wimsatt, James I. (1991) *Chaucer and his French Contemporaries: Natural Music in the Fourteenth Century* (Toronto: University of Toronto Press). On the French sources that complement Chaucer's borrowings from Italian poets.

Windeatt, Barry, ed. (1984) *Troilus and Criseyde* (London: Longman). The definitive edition of Chaucer's poem, with the *Filostrato* in parallel text (and textual variants plus detailed annotation in two extra columns).

14
Language
David Burnley

Chaucer's language is a variety of Middle English. The word 'middle' implies a historical perspective, which sees it as transitional between the highly inflected Germanic language, Old English, and the relatively uninflected, syntactically ordered, standard literary language of today. But from the point of view of the modern reader, who does not see it in the context of major linguistic changes from Old English, the overwhelming impression of Middle English is of a language in chaos, with disordered spelling, unfamiliar words, syntactic licence and unexpected inflexions. These impressions cannot be entirely denied, although they can be explained historically; but it is impossible to enter into detailed discussion here. Instead, we should be aware that Middle English was not a standard language, but a collection of dialects and, to a considerable extent, the product of contact with other languages.

From French to English

Scandinavian settlement from 865 and the Norman Conquest two centuries later both contributed to English in different ways. Scandinavian languages had dialectal impact in a broad belt extending across the country from Cumbria and Lancashire in the west to Yorkshire and Lincolnshire in the east; but this influence was more or less restricted to a speech-based culture, so that its effects filtered only slowly into the written language. French borrowing, however, took place in a literate environment throughout Britain, and the borrowings often consisted of words and phrases denoting abstract ideas with socially elevated associations, since the aristocracy were predominantly of French descent. The pace at which words entered the vocabulary from French increased during Chaucer's lifetime, reaching a peak about 1375.

These bare facts help to set the linguistic stage, but give little impression of the extreme importance of French to Chaucer, an Englishman writing English in the second half of the fourteenth century. In fact, French language and culture dominated his world. His father was successful in the French wine trade, which enabled him to place his son in an aristocratic household, where he could learn the French cultural norms of *curtesie* and a more esteemed idiom than the business French used by merchants. Anyone who wished to read secular literature of any sophistication had to turn to French or Latin sources, and in the household of John of Gaunt, for whom Chaucer wrote the *Book of the Duchess*, there was a tradition of French literacy. Some of his associates at the court of Richard II composed verse in French and maintained contacts with French authors, and French poets were welcome at court. Chaucer may even have composed French poetry in his youth. As a royal official, Chaucer would have had to conduct much of his business in French. For diplomatic business, this was an absolute rule and, as clerk of the works, although verbal negotiations with tradesmen were probably conducted in English, he would have had to deal with documents in French as well as in Latin. Similarly, during his short spell as knight of the shire for Kent, debates in parliament were likely to have been in French and the records kept in French or in Latin. At his court appearance in 1386, the proceedings were recorded (and probably conducted) in French. Letters received from elevated members of the court circle would have been composed in French. And yet, although his contemporary, John Gower, remarked that 'fewe men' did so, Chaucer chose to compose his major poetry in English.

It seems at first an inexplicable choice: the language of the ruled rather than the rulers; a language lacking credible literary models, lacking an influential and wealthy clientele, lacking any stable standard and possessing a relatively restricted vocabulary. However, Chaucer could have answered all these objections. French still enjoyed enormous prestige, but learning it had become an obstacle for Englishmen, one which they had to overcome if they were to progress in any profession, or be taken for a gentleman. Many found it insurmountable. But English composition could assume the prestige of French by judicious borrowing from domains where French still held sway. Indeed, the great increase in borrowed French words during Chaucer's lifetime was a sign both of broader English literacy exploiting this technique and of declining ability in French. Also, as a royal employee with administrative duties, Chaucer was free of dependence on literary patronage and was therefore not compelled to serve conservative linguistic tastes. As a poet, he saw that French in England was becoming largely a technical language, or the language of old books tucked away in libraries and aristocratic bequests, and as such lacked the nuances and associations for its readers which language gains from everyday use. By choosing English as a medium, he would gain a nuanced colloquial language which could be enriched at will with literary associations by recourse to French and Latin.

Modern authors are inclined to summarize Chaucer's debt to French in terms of simple statistics: 51 per cent of his vocabulary is of Romance origin; 1,102 of his Romance words are new in the English language. The question of what constitutes a French word is often begged by this kind of study. In any case, such statistics are of limited value in understanding the true nature of Chaucer's language. It is rather as if we were to assert that all the inhabitants of Glasgow are Scottish by definition. This may seem an adequate truth, but it ignores the variety actually present in that city and does not properly represent the perceptions of its inhabitants, for whom more subtle discrimination is necessary. Chaucer, like popular romances before him, reflects what seems to be a colloquial use of French phrases: *bele chose, graunt mercy, ma foy, maugree, paramours, pardieux, paraventure, parchance, par compaignye, par consequence, par cas, par may foy, par charitee*. These can be paralleled by French address forms such as *sire* and *ma dame*. Phrases like *have pitee on, do me a grace, do vileynye, catch a routhe*, were partly or wholly translated from French models and, like the borrowings *avauntour, congeyen, conveyen, facound, vouchesauf, nurture, parage* and *vileyn*, were associated with social sophistication whose origins lay in French literature. Both Chaucer and Gower group *balades, roundels* and *virelais* as French verse forms. But, besides this explicit acknowledgement of aristocratic French culture, the language also provided the channel through which technical vocabulary entered English, much of it rather obviously adopted from Latin and even Arabic: from alchemy *distill* and *lambic*; from astronomy *ascend, aspect, elevation, elongation*; from medicine *cardinacle, humour, sarsanure*; from law *adversarie, amercement, perpetuel prison, strong prison*; from philosophy *accident, appetite, conclusioun, contrary, convertible, felicitee*; from geometry *centre, cercle, ligne, equal, perpendicular*; and from literary practice *glose, prohemye, rubrik, texte*. Ordinary users of English, however, were not concerned with the etymological history of these technical terms; but they were very much concerned with their associations and the status conferred by their use.

Often, strange or learned words were used mainly for show. Chaucerian examples are the adjectives *ardaunt, celebrable, convertible, perdurable, columbyn, artificial, celestial, cerial, furial, palestral* and *unparegal*, or the verbs *stellifie* and *condescend*. In the case of *urne* (*TC* V, 311) and *amphibologie* (*TC* IV, 1406) Chaucer emphasized the unfamiliarity of his word choice by explaining the meaning in context. Such words have Franco-Latin form and are the consciously literary precursors to the aureate vocabulary of the fifteenth century; but it is worth adopting a modern perspective. Consider the modern word pairs *tricky–deceptive, happy–felicitous, lucky–fortunate, end–conclusion*. It is likely that we should regard the second item of each pair as more literary and elevated than the first. This impression is only indirectly connected with their etymologies, since the former are a disparate collection: French, Scandinavian, Dutch and Old English respectively. The latter form a more coherent group and are all Franco-Latin. But this coherence has more to do with the contexts in which we find such words, and with their word structure, than with etymology. They are multi-syllables which use formative affixes such as *-ive, -ous, -ate, -ion*. We are used to finding them in contexts with other words with elevated associations.

Until the sixteenth century, affixes like these (and *-al, per-, in-, -able, -ible, -aunt, -yn*) were very rarely or never used to form derivatives from English or Scandinavian base forms. These affixes at once defined and helped to maintain a substantial body of English vocabulary which, although it was Franco-Latin in origin – and educated users might have recognized that and been able to specify technical associations – would for most people give an impression chiefly and simply of stylistic elevation.

Indeed, much borrowing was not recognized as either foreign or elevated: Chaucer himself translates the Latin *fructus* and Greek *leos* into what he calls the 'Englissh' *fruyt* and *peple* (ParsT 869; SNT 106) and Edward, Duke of York, writing about 1406, tells us that the French *quest* translates into 'Englissh' as *serchyng*. Neither author was conscious of the fact that these were historically French borrowings. French borrowing was important to the development of Chaucer's English, but simple etymological classification tells us little about how he conceptualized his language.

Linguistic Variety

The city of London in the time of Chaucer was by far the largest in Britain. It had been a mercantile centre for centuries, situated at the junction of the old kingdoms of Kent, Wessex and Mercia. Royal government had been established at nearby Westminster since the time of Henry I. This combination naturally attracted not only foreign merchants and diplomats but immigration from the English. Indeed, Chaucer's own family had been part of an early fourteenth-century immigration from Suffolk, which left linguistic traces in the popular romances of his childhood. His poem 'Envoy to Scogan' is addressed to a court colleague from northern Norfolk, and the parliamentary record of Justice Thirnyng's words to Richard II at his deposition is full of forms reflecting his early career in the north. The variety of dialects which could be heard in London was thus built on a combination of geographical location and extended immigration. During the fourteenth century, the nature of the London language changed from a southern-based dialect to a language with a predominantly east Midland grammar and phonology.

Variety is not only the spice of life; it may be the stuff of poetry. The ability to rephrase permits nuances of meaning, but new patterns of words also confer flexibility on versification and expand the range of possible rhymes.

> 'By god, right by the hopur wil I stande,'
> Quod John, 'and se how that the corn gas in.
> Yet saugh I nevere, by my fader kyn,
> How that the hopur wagges til and fra.'
> Aleyn answerde, 'John, wiltow swa?
> Thanne wil I be bynethe, by my croun,
> And se how that the mele falles doun
> Into the trough; that sal be my disport.
> For John, y-faith, I may been of youre sort;
> I is as ille a millere as ar ye.'
> (RvT 4036–45)

In the above passage from the Reeve's Tale, Chaucer imitates the speech of two northern students. Their dialect is evident in the forms *gas, wagges, falles, sal, fra, swa* (usual

Chaucer forms: *goth, waggeth, falleth, shal, fro, so*). *Ille* is a Scandinavian-derived word not usually used by Chaucer. *I is* is a combination restricted to this tale and *ar ye* occurs only once outside it. These northernisms play a role in the characterization of the tale, but linguistic variety can also be useful in other ways, by contributing to versification. Chaucer's later verse is based on a five-stress line with ten or (when the last is unstressed) eleven syllables. Variation between the infinitives *be* and *been* permits a proper syllable count in line 4044. See below for more details of how Chaucer can exploit formal variety for metrical purposes.

Metre

The preceding paragraph begs an important question about Chaucer's intentions as a poet. We have simply assumed that he was concerned to write metrically correct and exactly rhyming verse, but to some readers Middle English may seem disordered and Chaucer's versification rough. We cannot know Chaucer's intention for any individual line, but pointers from both inside and outside his works suggest his scrupulousness. His theory of language was based on the Franco-Latin metrical one of 'word', 'syllable' and 'letter', and he was well aware that the lack of a syllable might be considered a defect in metre (*HF* 1098). The French poet Eustache Deschamps, who wrote a theoretical work on rhyme and versification, accepted Chaucer as an author of equal literary merit. In an envoy almost entirely dependent on borrowed French rhyme words, Chaucer complains of the difficulty of matching in English the rhyming skills of the French poet Oton de Granson (*Ven* 82). This perception of versification as a demanding craft does not suggest a slipshod attitude, and it is reasonable to assume a literary environment which presupposes correctness in composition.

It is a picture substantially reflected by his practice. Chaucer and his imitator, Thomas Hoccleve, are among a very few authors in the London area at the close of the fourteenth century who carefully maintain the syllabic value of final *-e* in their verse. This is most striking in the case of monosyllabic adjectives. But before considering examples, it is necessary to emphasize that what follows does not apply to disyllabic adjectives, such as *clene* and *grene*, whose stem ended in *-e* in Old English. Consider instead the adjective *good*. This is the 'strong form' which is found after the indefinite article (*a good man*) or with no article (*by good ensaumple*). However, the 'weak' form of the adjective (*goode*) is found after the definite article (*the goode man*), demonstratives (*this goode man*), a possessive pronoun (*oure goode man*) and in address forms (*goode sire*). The plural form has final *-e* (*goode men*) whatever the context. Final *-e* is usually elided before another vowel and silent *h* + vowel, but elsewhere it is pronounced and forms part of the metrical pattern. This usage extends also to rhyme, where forms with *-e* do not normally rhyme with forms without. Final *-e* is a grammatical constraint around which Chaucer constructs his versification.

Although maintaining this south-eastern adjectival grammar, Chaucer was willing to look further afield for metrical flexibility. In the northern dialect of the Reeve's Tale we find the line 'Now are we dryve til hethyng and til scorn' (4110). This is the only place in the *Canterbury Tales* where the locative preposition *til* ('to') is used before a consonant or a sounded *h*. Elsewhere, it occurs only before vowels and silent *h*. The distribution of *fro*, however, is the mirror image of this, since it occurs almost always before consonants. The phrase *til and fra* (RvT 4039) is a Scandinavian-derived northernism which Chaucer had adopted with certain restrictions. He used the usual London English *to* and *from* and *til* with time reference (i.e. 'until') quite freely, but his use of the northern *til* and *fra/fro* is conditioned by phonological context: creating euphony and controlling elision. The adoption of these dialect variants was motivated by a poetic purpose.

Rhyme

In rhymes too, Chaucer shows careful craftsmanship. The stanza of *Troilus and Criseyde* rhymes ababbcc, which makes the following somewhat disconcerting:

> This Troilus, withouten reed or loore,
> As man that hath hise joies ek forlore,
> Was waytyng on his lady evere more
> As she that was the sothfast crop and more
> Of al his lust or joies heretofore.
> But Troilus, now far-wel al thi joie,
> For shaltow nevere sen hire eft in Troie!
> (*TC* V, 22–8)

The rhyme scheme seems to have been obscured in the first five lines. But appearances are deceptive, since Chaucer made a distinction in the pronunciation of two long *o* sounds. The words *loore* and *evere more/evermore* have rhyme vowels derived from the raising of Old English long *a* (pronounced like modern *sore*), while in the words *forlore*, *more* and *heretofore* the long *o* derives from the lengthening of Old English short *o* (like *so*). Chaucer's language makes a similar distinction between two variants of long *e*, which largely corresponds to the modern spellings in words like *meet* and *meat*. *Mete* 'meet' was pronounced *mate*, whilst *mete* 'meat' was pronounced with a vowel more like that in *fare*. Chaucer carefully observes this Midland distinction in his rhyme schemes. The rhyme scheme of the following passage is aabaabbab, where the a-rhymes are like *mate* and the b-rhymes like *fare*:

> And shal I preye and weyve womanhede? –
> Nay! Rather deth then do so foul a dede! –
> And axe merci, gilteles – what nede?
> And yf I pleyne what lyf that I lede,
> Yow rekketh not; that knowe I, out of drede;

And if that I to yow myne othes bede
For myn excuse, a skorn shal be my mede.
Your chere floureth, but it wol not sede;
Ful longe agoon I oghte have taken hede.
(*Anel* 299–307)

Chaucer normally avoids the sets of half-rhymes which were a feature of popular romance, but there are exceptions – the rhyme *sike* with *white* (*TC* II, 886) – and he may seem to break his own rules more generally by rhyming together words which, by the standards of an east Midland-based London English, ought not to rhyme exactly (for example, rhyming *do* with *so* and *dede* 'deed' with *dede* 'dead'). Once again, appearances are deceptive. Chaucer's English contained variant pronunciations from earlier London and the south-east, and he was prepared to use them in rhyme. He used the south-eastern pronunciations *feere* and *leste* alongside the east Midland *fire* and *liste* (cf. Old Kentish *fer*, *lestan* with Anglian *fyr*, *lystan*) and Kentish long *e*, which was always pronounced with the closer (*mate*) sound. However, Kent did not supply the variants which permitted the unexpected rhymes *do* with *so* and *bifore* with *moore*, or, for that matter, of *strete* with *grete*. Such rhymes already existed in the Auchinleck manuscript, indicating the earlier development of closer pronunciation variants of Midland long, open *o* and *e*. These rhymes do not demonstrate Chaucer's carelessness. His pronunciation was not a free-for-all, but a considered selection from the range of permissible spoken variants; and it is reasonable to assume that what prompted his selection was concern with his role as versifier. Internal procedures and external evidence therefore agree in declaring Chaucer, despite the occasional lapse, a careful metrical craftsman working within the constraints of his language.

Decorum

However, Chaucer's selection of pronunciation variants was determined by considerations other than their grammatical correctness or their usefulness in versification: in particular, by their acceptability to his audience. Northernisms might function in characterization and might be useful in metre, but some seem to have been unacceptable to a London audience. The convenience of being able to rhyme noun plurals with third person present tense verbal endings in *-es* is obvious, but Chaucer generally avoided this, just as he avoided *til* + consonant. Chaucer's audience apparently also expected a certain decorum in his choice of words. This is apparent from his arch apologies for vulgarity (GP 725–42; MilT 3167–86; ManT 210). In the Merchant's Tale (2363) he considers the word *swyve* to be *uncurteis* – a view apparently shared by the scribe of the Hengwrt manuscript, who substituted *etcetera* for this word (ManT 256). Medieval ideals of politeness and refinement were enshrined in the ideal of *curteisie*, and certain language might be approved, while other linguistic choices indicated *vileynie*. The latter included swearing and vulgarity, but also insulting or disparaging address. *Curteis* speech, by contrast, avoided vulgarity and served to reinforce the self-esteem of the addressee. It was marked by indirect questions and commands, by the use of address forms like *sire* and *madame*, and by the use of tentative conditional constructions when making statements. These ideals of courtliness were part of the cultural inheritance which English owed to French, and their linguistic manifestation had the same source. This is most strikingly apparent in the pronouns used for address in Chaucer's English.

The second person pronoun in modern English is *you* (with *thou* persisting in some dialects and the religious register). In early Middle English, there were two second person pronouns, the T-form (*thou*) and the V-form (*ye*). The T-form was used in address to a single individual, the V-form in addressing more than one: a distinction based simply on number. By the middle of the thirteenth century this had begun to change under the influence of French, and by Chaucer's time the V-form could be used in address to a single individual as an indication of respect. It is important to realize that the new distinction between T-form and V-form according to social relationship was not a substitute for the old distinction based on number, but was additional to it and existed alongside it. In the new courtly system the V-form was expected when addressing individuals of equivalent or higher social status, one's elders, or persons with whom the speaker was unfamiliar. The T-form was used to persons of inferior status, to express familiarity and solidarity between men, and in prayers to God. These basic guidelines demanded tact and subtlety in their use, and were subject to interpretation and to rhetorical exploitation. The deliberate breach of the expectations of address is common, and the use of the T-form when a V-form is predicted may be a calculated insult; alternatively, the V-form may be used to cajole and flatter. A fairly subtle modulation of interpersonal relations can be charted by shifts in these forms of address in the course of a dialogue. However, not everyone in Chaucer's England observed this courtly usage. It was the property of polite society, and those who did not belong to polite society did not use it.

These outsiders were of two types: the ignorant and the learned. People who had no status in society, and therefore little exposure to French cultural values, did not know or care about this courtly device. Learned men rejected it from a mixture of principle and self-interest. The use of the V-form to individuals was seen both as grammatically incorrect and as evidence of worldly self-aggrandizement; so they insisted on the use of the T-form. The T-form was used by preachers and by those licensed to instruct, and so scholars could wrap themselves in its moral authority, claiming unworldly disinterest, even when admonishing the monarch. Chaucer's poetry reflects these contradictions and complexities. In a courtly work such as *Troilus and Criseyde* the norms of courtly address are carefully observed, but in his fabliau tales they are not. His clerics use the expression *leve brother*, which naturally leads on to the T-form. Burgesses' wives, who felt that 'It is ful fair to ben ycleped madame' (GP 376, RvT 3956), no doubt felt the same about the V-form of address, which is usually associated with the address forms *madame*, *dame*, *my lord*, *my lady*, *sir*, *maister* and *sire*.

Idiom

As an associate of the court, Chaucer participated in the court's administrative business as well as its social values, and so he learned the idiom of its official documents. In the Squire's Tale (110–67), when seeking to catch the eloquence of an enchanted knight, he turns to the devices of formal letters such as those written by the city corporation to the king. These letters, written in what modern scholars call 'curial style', were marked by an accumulation of qualifying clauses leading to very long sentences, very intrusive devices for internal coherence (*the which*, *the said*, etc.), indirect forms of address by titles, use of the V-form, and latinate and technical vocabulary. The knight's speech does not reproduce these strategies in full, but it adopts some features and some specific verbal echoes. For example, the line 'Salueth yow as he best kan and may' (112) employs a favourite device of such letters in its use of the auxiliaries *kan* and *may*.

It has been noted by critics from Quintilian to Mikhail Bakhtin, in Latin and in Russian, that where a language is used for a wide range of purposes, it becomes full of such echoes. The exploitation of them is as much the skill of the wit and raconteur as of the serious author. However, with a few exceptions, this associational 'architecture' is unrecognizable in earlier Middle English, when English literacy was very restricted. By Chaucer's time the literate use of the English language was various enough for it to be possible to allude, not so much to other texts (except for allusions to the wording of the English portions of the marriage service in Usk's *Testament of Love* [9] and Chaucer's Merchant's Tale [1287–90]), but to a whole range of recognizable styles. The address *goode men and wommen* (PardP 377) and phrase *Heere may ye se and heer by may ye preve* (MerT 1330) both echo the language of the preacher; the use of the words *hende, love-longing, oore* and *swete bridde* in the Miller's Tale recall the language of popular lyric; and the parodic Tale of Sir Thopas is a storehouse of the diction and devices of popular romance. The phrasing of French romance is encountered in words like *fetys, tretys, wel ytaught, debonaire, eyen gray*.

This newly developed associational resonance of English enabled Chaucer to achieve literary effects which had not been attempted by previous authors. In the *Parliament of Fowls*, the *House of Fame* and especially in the Nun's Priest's Tale, Chaucer imagines speaking birds. But birds do not speak, so Chaucer has to find them voices from people he heard around him. The result is that the birds emerge as recognizable social types from the *ways* in which they speak. The style of the eagles in the *Parliament* is modelled on courtly eloquence (415–41); that of the duck ('Wel bourded,' quod the doke, 'by myn hat!' [589]) upon churlish abruptness. The eagle in the *House of Fame* uses the directness of address and the T-form, with the technicalities of the instructor. His tone is echoed to some degree in the words of Chauntecleer to Pertelote (NPT 4160–73), but here the cockerel also addresses the hen as *madame*, with the use of the V-form in the manner of husband and wife in a cultivated household. The dramatic creation of character through 'voice' adds subtlety also to the portraits in the General

Prologue where, for example, the Friar's voice is heard inappropriately using phrasing appropriate to a city merchant (246–9) while the merchant in the Shipman's Tale reflects on *chapmanhede* in a language more appropriate to a philosopher (1414–28). The multiplicity of late fourteenth-century London life and the widening use of the English language in all its departments gave Chaucer a poetic medium which had not previously existed in England; but he had the individual gifts and experience which enabled him to exploit it and fully to justify his choice of English.

Sound

But how did Chaucer's poetry actually sound? It is clearly impossible to give a detailed account, and the best impression may be gained from listening to good recordings being read by competent scholar–actors; but some hints can be given.

Short vowels are pronounced as in modern English, except that *o* before *n*, *m*, *v* (in words like *come, love, sonne, tonge*) is pronounced as *u*. Modern English pronunciation is a guide here. Long vowels have the same quality as in modern European languages: *a* is pronounced as in *bar*, *e* may be as in *mate* or in *fare*, *i* as in *meet*, *o* either as in *home* or as in *store*, *u* as in *spoon*. Modern English uses diphthongs in some of these examples, but Middle English had pure vowels. Middle English scribes did not consistently mark vowel length, but spellings with doubled vowels (*graas, maad, heere, deeth, loore, good*) or with a final *-e* after a single intervening consonant (*grace, made, grete, here, lore*) are helpful, and modern pronunciation may also be a guide. Two diphthongs require special notice: *ei* and *ai* are both pronounced somewhere between modern *eye* and (*h*)*ay*. The spelling *au* (more often *aw*) represents the diphthong in modern *town*, but the spelling *ou* represents the pure long *u*, as in modern *spoon*. However, *au* before *n* or *m*, especially in French loan-words (*chaumbre*, but also *Caunterbury*), may be pronounced as a nasalized *a*. Initially, before another vowel, *y* is a consonant like that in modern English (*yive, yong, youthe*), but initially before a consonant, and finally, it is a vowel pronounced as in modern *funny* (*ycleped, ybrent*). Medially, it is simply an alternative spelling for *i*.

The consonants in Chaucer's English are mostly like those in modern English, but there are no silent consonants. This means that the initial consonants are pronounced in words like *knight, gnof, writen*. It means also that postvocalic *r* was pronounced in words like *harde, lerne* and *wordes*, and postvocalic *l* in words like *half* and *folke*. Some digraphs, such as *gg, gh, th* require special consideration. The first of these can be simply demonstrated by the word *brygge*, whose meaning and pronunciation are the same as modern 'bridge'. The second, when it occurs in words with back vowels like *thoght, soughte* and *trogh*, represents a fricative like that in modern Scottish *loch*, but in words with front vowels like *lighte* and *nyght* it represents a fricative like that in German *nicht*. Finally, *th* represents the same sounds as in modern English, but they are differently distributed. Between vowels *th* is pronounced as in modern *brother*, but initially and finally as in modern *thin*. This means that words such as *the*, *this*, *that* and *there* were pronounced without voicing, as in *thin*. A similar distribution is found in the case of *s*, so that final *s* in words like *is* and *was*, as well as the plural inflexion *es*, was pronounced without voicing, as in modern *miss*.

The stressing of words in Middle English was the same as that in modern English, except that some French borrowings might still retain their original stress patterns. This is particularly true of words in rhyme, where the rhyme often occurs on stressed French suffixes. *Daliaunce* rhymes with *purveiaunce* and *stable* rhymes with *unresonable*. However, some words seem to be usable with either English or French stress patterns: so *poverte* can rhyme with *herte* and *sherte* when stressed on the root syllable, but also with *be*, when stressed on the final syllable. French pronunciations also affect the correct syllable count of the line, so that *condicioun* has four syllables and the *c* is pronounced as *s*, and *visioun* has three syllables and the *s* is pronounced as *z*, as in French.

The Franklin's Tale, 1571–1619

We may now consider two extended passages of Chaucer's verse in the light of the above. The first is a passage at the end of a tale in which a young squire returns to repay a debt owed to a scholar.

Nouns

Modern English also uses an uninflected plural after a numeral with nouns of measurement: *two yeer* (1582), *thousand pound* (1613).

Personal Pronouns

The subject forms of the second person are *thou* and *ye*; the object and prepositional forms *thee* and *yow*. The corresponding possessives are *thy* and *youre*. However, before a vowel or silent *h*, the form *thyn* would be used. Compare *myn heritage* (1584) and *my dette* (1578) – and modern English *a tax* but *an axe*.

Verbs

The third person singular, present tense ends in -*(e)th*. Plural is in -*(e)n*: *han* (1594). Past participles are more variable: *quyt* (1578), *herd* (1593), *lost* (1600), *holden* (1587), *cropen* (1614). The latter two are strong past participles with the ending -*en*. The form *ypayed* (1618) retains the *y*- prefix which is dialectally more southern than the others. The choice of form has metrical implications. Infinitives also vary widely, from the plain form after an auxiliary – *be* (1578) and *reherce* (1594) – to prepositional forms *to been* (1599) and *for to respiten* (1582). Final -*n* in both past participles and infinitives is optional. Its absence in lines 1575, 1594 permits elision, and its presence in 1580 and 1616 contributes a syllable to the metre. Chaucer makes more frequent use of the subjunctive (*were I*, 1583 and 1614) than is usual in modern English, and its use in wishes and after words such as *if* and *though* explains apparently endingless third person singular present tense forms such as *god forbede* (1610) and *if thow kan* (1591).

Syntax

The object usually follows the verb, as in modern English, but personal pronouns acting as object frequently precede it: *he . . . hym bisecheth* (1574). In addition to impersonal constructions with the subject *it* (*it nedeth nat*, 1594), Middle English uses an impersonal construction in which the subject is not expressed: *as thee liketh* (1589), *how looth hire was* (1599). In these expressions the personal pronoun is the indirect object: 'as it pleases (to) thee', 'how hateful it was to her'. Double negation is fairly frequent in Chaucer's verse, where it is often intended emphatically (1615). There are a number of idioms, for examples *to goon abegged* 'to go begging' (1580) and *hadde levere* 'would rather' (1596).

French Influence

French influence is apparent in such phrases as *make avaunt* (1576), *wolde ye vouchesauf* (1581) and *han . . . greet pitee* (1603) as well as in lexical borrowing, but is most interesting in the use of T-/V-forms. The *squier* uses courtly address with the V-form throughout; the *philosophre* uses the T-form proper to his role as learned instructor, beginning with the address *leeve brother*. Because he uses this singular mode, his use of the imperative (*tel me*, 1591) is also singular. The plural (and more elaborated) form would have been *telleth*.

The Franklin's tale of gentillesse appropriately uses a system of address forms which belongs to courtly society. This was not inevitable in Chaucer's use of language, but was a conscious stylistic choice which he does not make, for example, in the Miller's or Reeve's tales. But it goes beyond the polite use of *ye* address, since it reflects the finer detail that the Clerk of Orleans prefers to use *my leeve brother* with *thou*. Here Chaucer is faithfully echoing a preference of clerks, who used this as a mark of their status and their rejection of worldly pretensions. The Clerk, then, intends no insult to Aurelius, but is simply maintaining his role as disinterested adviser. His choice of usage gives a special palpability to the closing question in the tale, which asks who was the more *gentil*, the self-conscious practitioners of *curtesie* or the clerk who explicitly rejects its practices.

Troilus and Criseyde II, 1–42

The second passage is the stylistically elevated prologue to a courtly poem. (Features noted in the first passage are not repeated here.)

Nouns

The phrase *lady grace* (32) is an idiom in which *lady* is an endingless possessive from an Old English weak noun.

Personal Pronouns

The third person pronouns are the same as modern English in the singular. In the plural the subject form is *thei/they* (25, 40) and the object and prepositional form *hem* (25). The plural possessive was *hire* (41). The modern singular *its* did not exist and *hise* was used (42). Simple pronoun forms may function as reflexives: *me* (12), 'myself'.

Verbs

The third person singular -*eth* possessed a variant in which the *e* was not pronounced and the *th* was assimilated to a preceding *t* or *d* in the stem, so that instead of *wendeth* and *haldeth*, we find *wente* (36) and *halt* (37). The final -*e* in *wente* (present in the manuscript) has no metrical implication and has been removed by the modern editor, since it is a scribal error. These are southern variants used by Chaucer for metrical purposes.

Syntax

The complex syntax of the first stanza is better understood by recognizing that *gynneth* (2) is a polite imperative addressed to the wind; the object is *weder*, 'storm'. The discontinuous phrase 'boot . . . of my connyng' is a literal translation of Italian *la navicella del mio ingegno*, 'little boat of my wit', taken from the source. Generally, Italian influence on Chaucer's language is negligible. The negating particle *ne* sometimes combines with monosyllabic verbs and auxiliaries to produce contracted forms: *nyl* (15) from *ne + wyl*, 'do not wish'; *nold* (33) from *ne + wold*; *noot* (35) from *ne + woot*, 'do not know'.

Style

The rhyme *newe is—hewis* (20–1) suggests a variant pronunciation of the plural inflexion -*es*, which would be found in the north Midlands.

In addition to their demonstration of some of the variety in linguistic forms in Chaucer's composition, these stanzas exhibit two common features of his practice as a poet. They begin with the relatively close translation of a foreign source, then drift away from it into free composition; and with that departure, the stylistic level diminishes from elevated diction and complex syntax to something more approaching colloquial address to his audience. He starts out to impress and finishes by seeking to communicate. The rhetoric gives way to familiar phrases and proverbs, which he clearly expects to share as part of the linguistic competence of his audience. Interestingly, part of his early strategy to impress involves claiming a prestigious Latin source.

Italian, which he and Lollard writers thought of as 'Latyn corrupt' did not have the required status (although providing a useful secret source of inspiration). Besides foreseeing this linguistic prejudice in his audience, he expected them in Book V, 1793–4 to have noticed the dialectal diversity in English, and it is sometimes claimed that in this passage (22) he thought they might be aware of the diachronic development of linguistic forms. This is wildly improbable. Medieval people were primarily interested in language in a highly pragmatic way: in the power which its mastery could give them. Language in society required competence in a range of appropriate formulations and styles. The point which Chaucer is making is not that linguistic forms change, but that the uses of language in social interaction are subject to change. As with the appropriate use of *ye* and *thou*, the skills that preoccupied Chaucer's generation were a knowledge of the proper time to speak and the best way to phrase an utterance (or a letter), not the philological history of the English language.

See also AFTERLIFE; CHIVALRY; COMEDY; FRANCE; GENRE; ITALY; LIFE HISTORIES; LONDON; SCIENCE; STYLE; TEXTS; TRANSLATION.

REFERENCES AND FURTHER READING

1   The Cultural and Linguistic Background

Burnley, J. D. (1992) 'Lexis and semantics', in *The Cambridge History of the English Language*, ii: *Middle English*, ed. N. F. Blake (Cambridge: Cambridge University Press), 409–99. General account of the vocabulary in Middle English.

Burrow, J. A. and Turville-Petre, T. (1996) *A Book of Middle English*, 2nd edn (Oxford: Blackwell). Widely used textbook of Middle English, which contains grammatical information as well as illustrative texts.

Cannon, Christopher (1998) *The Making of Chaucer's English: A Study of Words*, Cambridge Studies in Medieval Literature 39 (Cambridge and New York: Cambridge University Press). Study of Chaucer's vocabulary as it is reflected in dictionary materials. Emphasizes neologisms and borrowings from the Romance languages.

Dekeyser, X. (1986) 'Romance loans in Middle English', in *Linguistics across Historical and Geographical Boundaries: In Honour of Jacek Fisiak on the Occasion of his Fiftieth Birthday*, ed. A. Szwedek and D. Kastovsky, 2 vols (Berlin:

Mouton de Gruyter), i, 253–65. Latest in a tradition of studies charting the impact of French borrowing on Middle English vocabulary. Repeats earlier findings of Jespersen and Baugh (which were based on less complete data) that the pace of borrowing peaked around 1375.

Prins, A. A. (1952) *French Influence in English Phrasing* (Leiden: Leiden University Press). Study of the influence of French, not simply on single word borrowings but on phrases which may be wholly or partially translated from French originals. Addenda published in *English Studies* (1959, 1960).

Rothwell, W. (1994) 'The trilingual England of Geoffrey Chaucer', *Studies in the Age of Chaucer* 16, 45–67. Emphasizes the importance of a naturalized form of French in medieval England and the way in which French, Latin and English are interwoven in use.

Samuels, M. L. (1972) *Linguistic Evolution: With Special Reference to English*. (London: Cambridge University Press). The book deals with wider issues of historical linguistics, but pages 165–70 update information first given in an *English*

Studies (1963) article concerning the linguistic situation in Chaucer's London.

——(1985) 'The great Scandinavian belt', in *Papers from the Fourth International Conference on English Historical Linguistics, 10–13th April 1985*, ed. R. Eaton, O. Fischer, W. Koopman and F. van der Leek (Amsterdam: Benjamins), 269–81. Demonstrates that Scandinavian linguistic influence was most penetrating in those parts of northern England where the settlement was most dense: a belt including Cumbria, north Lancashire, north and east Yorkshire and north Lincolnshire. Examines in details some of the effects on Middle English dialects.

2   General Studies of Chaucer's Language

Burnley, D. (1989) *The Language of Chaucer* (Basingstoke: Macmillan). Re-issue of *A Guide to Chaucer's Language* (1983). Chapters cover grammar, textual coherence, vocabulary, pragmatics and stylistic variety of Chaucer's language, but omit details of pronunciation and metre.

Davis, N. (1974) 'Chaucer and fourteenth-century English', in *Geoffrey Chaucer*, Writers and Their Background, ed. Derek S. Brewer (London: Bell), 58–84. Good basic account of Chaucer's language in its fourteenth-century context. Deals with some details of phonology, rhyme and metre.

Elliott, Ralph W. V. (1974) *Chaucer's English* (London: Deutsch). Compendious account of Chaucer's language and style, based largely on vocabulary choices.

Sandved, A. O. (1985) *Introduction to Chaucerian English* (Cambridge: Brewer). Account in structural linguistic terms of Chaucer's morphology and phonology; also contains useful data on pronunciation and rhyme.

3   Chaucer's Pronunciation and Versification

Burnley, D. (1982) 'Inflexion in Chaucer's adjectives', *Neuphilologische Mitteilungen* 83, 169–77.

A study in detail of final *-e* in Chaucer's adjectives in the Hengwrt manuscript of the *Canterbury Tales*. Developed from a note by M. L. Samuels in *Notes and Queries* (1972).

Cowen, J. M. (1987) 'Metrical problems in editing *The Legend of Good Women*', in *Manuscripts and Texts: Editorial Problems in Later Middle English Literature*, ed. D. A. Pearsall (Cambridge: Brewer), 26–33. Contains details of the use of final *-e* in the versification of the *Legend of Good Women*, noting the grammatical contexts where *-e* appears obligatory and those in which endingless variants may occur. The same collection contains an essay on Hoccleve's versification by Judith Jefferson, which is valuable as a comparison.

Ikegami, M. T. (1984) *Rhyme and Pronunciation: Some Studies of English Rhymes from King Alisaunder to Skelton* (Tokyo: Hogaku-Kenkyu Kai, Keio University). An extensive study of rhyme technique among Middle English poets, which contains accounts of the practice of Chaucer and Gower.

Kökeritz, H. (1961) *A Guide to Chaucer's Pronunciation* (Stockholm: Almqvist & Wiksell). A brief account of Chaucer's pronunciation, which includes extended passages transcribed into phonetic notation.

4   Stylistic Studies

Benson, L. (1988) 'Chaucer and courtly speech', in *Genres, Themes and Images in English Literature*, ed. P. Boitani and A. Torti (Tübingen: Narr), 11–30. Looks at some ideals of courtliness as reflected in speech, including the *thou/you* distinction and euphemistic expressions as well as vulgarity. For a different approach, see J. D. Burnley, 'Courtly speech in Chaucer', *Poetica* 24 (1986), 16–38.

Burnley, J. D. (1991) 'On the architecture of Chaucer's language', in *This Noble Craft: Proceedings of the Xth Research Symposium of the Dutch and Belgian Teachers of Old and Middle English and Historical Linguistics, Utrecht, 19–20th January 1989*, ed. E. Kooper (Amsterdam: Rodopi), 43–57. An account of the concept of the stylistic and associational architecture of a language, with examples of Chaucer's poetic exploitation of this linguistic feature.

Donaldson, E. Talbot (1970) *Speaking of Chaucer* (London: Athlone). Contains an essay, first published in *English Institute Essays* (1950), which demonstrates Chaucer's use in the Miller's Tale of words and phrases characteristic of popular lyric poetry.

15
Life Histories
Janette Dillon

Readers of both fictional and non-fictional writing about people expect the written text to enable them to 'place' these people, to arrive at an understanding of them by situating them imaginatively within their cultural context. But one of the biggest problems for readers and writers, especially when the subject at the centre of the piece of writing is distanced from them in time and place, is the temptation unconsciously to apply false frameworks of categorization in describing or apprehending the life history in question. The categories within which we operate and by which we define ourselves are so strongly rooted as to seem given, even inevitable. It is scarcely surprising, therefore, that biographies routinely have certain areas of enquiry in common: for example, birth and parentage; nationality; education; occupation; love; marriage; religious beliefs; political affiliations. Yet there are problems with these categories, one being that the very terminology is so familiar that we may forget how differently the terms signify in different times and places. When we think of Englishness we almost automatically respond from within a context of present-day geographical and political awareness that situates England within the United Kingdom, Europe, the affluent West and the dominance of English as a world language; when we think of education we envisage schoolrooms or lecture halls usually mixed by gender and segregated according to age and stage. But both of these responses are inestimably wide of the mark for arriving at an understanding of the concepts of nationality and education in late fourteenth-century England.

Chaucer's Biography

We may begin by looking at Chaucer's own biography to establish some of the differences between his world and ours (and, it follows, between the meaning of certain very familiar words then and now). With Chaucer we must begin by acknowledging what cannot be known at this distance in time because of the incompleteness of extant records. So we do not know exactly when or where he was born, though we can date his birth to some time in the 1340s and hazard a reasonable guess that he was born in London. ('London' itself represents another of those entities we may totally mis-conceive at this distance in time: its population in Chaucer's day was a mere 40,000, largely confined within the square mile or so of the walled city.) Then there is the further problem of what records, where they exist, can and cannot tell us. The deed releasing Chaucer from the '*raptus*' of Cecilia Chaumpaigne, for example,[1] reveals that Chaucer was involved in either the rape or the abduction of this woman; it cannot tell us which of these two ways of translating the Latin applies in this case, or whether Chaucer was a principal or an accessory. Such uncertainties, however, may offer a salutary way of reminding ourselves at the outset that knowledge of another person can never be complete, no matter how full the records. Paradoxically, perhaps, access to fictional persons may be in some ways more complete, or at least less contestable, since if a writer tells us that a character was, for example, born in Edinburgh, or hated her father, we have no grounds for disputing the truth of these statements. With real people, however, while evidence regarding place of birth may or may not be verifi-able, deductions about attitudes, feelings and motivations are unreliable. Biographers produce them and readers enjoy reading them, but in both cases the engagement with such explanations is invested with needs and desires which are independent of the subject of the biography.

We know that Chaucer grew up in London; that his father, John, was both a wealthy vintner and employed in various positions in the king's service; and that the family owned several properties in the Vintry ward in London. Yet this accumulation of infor-mation precisely prevents us from making any easy categorization of Chaucer's social status in modern terms. While John Chaucer's success in trade might initially make us think of the term 'middle-class', we soon find that his other occupations expose such labelling as misguided pigeon-holing. John Chaucer, like both his own father and his son, Geoffrey, held posts in the customs service; but we must remind our-selves that posts at the level to which Chaucer was appointed were not anonymous, pen-pushing jobs, but trusted and potentially lucrative positions to which people were appointed by the king; positions, moreover, likely to yield occasional large profits, such as Chaucer made on goods forfeited by a certain John Kent in 1376. And in the same year as Chaucer made that profit through the customs he was also paid for trans-acting 'secret business of the king'.[2] The range of work he might be asked to do was evidently very different from the careful separation now made between routine civil service administration and espionage. As T. F. Tout has argued, 'the men of the middle ages did not clearly distinguish between the king in his private and public capaci-ties'.[3] Paul Strohm's careful analysis of Chaucer's rank of *esquier* (an appellation used of him from at least 1368, if not 1366), via a range of fourteenth-century documents, demonstrates how the term was undergoing constant redefinition and challenging the traditional distinction between gentle and non-gentle status. Chaucer himself was ambiguously situated, Strohm shows, within an already ambiguous ranking (Strohm 1989: 5–13).

Questions of nationality similarly need to be approached by very different routes from present-day conceptions of Englishness. We may collude with Dryden in celebrating Chaucer as the 'father' of English poetry, yet one incontestable element of his life history is the French derivation of his name. This points us towards the massive impact of the Norman Conquest on English social life and the extent to which the French language colonized the upper echelons of English society. French was still widely known and spoken at court and in other elite environments in Chaucer's lifetime, and Chaucer would almost certainly have begun his writing career by writing in French. Certainly his English verse is moulded by his familiarity with French forms, and the sources to which he is indebted are most commonly French or Italian (and are sometimes written in Latin, which was still the language of international European communication). England owned territories in France and was at war with France throughout Chaucer's lifetime, contesting sovereignty over French lands; yet during the four years that the French king and some of his nobles were held hostage in England following the battle of Poitiers, the hostages were treated as honoured guests at the English court, mixing freely with Englishmen whose marriages and ancestry linked them in innumerable different ways with their French prisoners. One of the hostages even married the king's daughter. And Chaucer followed a similar model in making his own marriage to one Philippa de Roet, daughter of Gilles de Roet, King of Arms for Aquitaine, who had come to England from the Low Countries in the service of Edward III's queen, Philippa of Hainault.

It is likely that Geoffrey and Philippa Chaucer both spoke English and French. Their bilingualism, however, would have been more the result of their milieu than of any formal education, and evidence of Chaucer's social education is much more forthcoming than any evidence of institutional schooling. The earliest known document to name him is a record in the household of the Countess of Ulster, wife of King Edward's third son, Lionel. It records the purchase of clothes for Chaucer, indicating that he belonged to the countess's household, probably as a page.[4] Growing up in the service of a noble household brought with it an education in various social skills, from courtly manners to singing, dancing, riding and other sports, including the kind of exercise that provided a rehearsal for war; and Chaucer certainly took part in the French war, probably in the service of Prince Lionel. It is clear from Chaucer's writing that he was widely read in several languages; but this more academic schooling could as easily have been acquired through private household instruction as through elementary and grammar schooling, though Chaucer might have experienced some combination of the two. There are no records of Chaucer's attendance at any educational institution; and precisely because his social position was so fluid in allowing him access to so many different areas of London courtly and mercantile society, it is impossible to be sure where he is most likely to have acquired his education.

One area on which we do need to focus is a category much less obvious and immediate in our own contemporary world: the question of patronage. At every stage of Chaucer's life, both as a writer and as a paid employee of the court, the importance of a powerful and prestigious patron cannot be overrated. Prince Lionel offered a strong starting point, but a year before the prince's death in 1368 Chaucer had become a member of the king's own household. From this point on, both Chaucer and his wife were to remain in service with Edward III, or with his fourth son, John of Gaunt, or with Edward's grandson, who succeeded him as Richard II. A poem Chaucer addressed to Richard's successor, Henry IV (eldest son of John of Gaunt), who came to the throne the year before Chaucer's death, demonstrates both the importance and the potential fragility, from the point of view of the client, of the client–patron relationship. Chaucer, as a relatively old man, faced a risky and awkward situation in 1399. Having remained loyal to Richard through various political upheavals, including the quarrel between Richard and Henry, who now acceded to the throne by virtue of his forceful deposition of Richard, Chaucer needed to find a position acceptable to the new king, henceforth of necessity his intended patron. 'Complaint . . . to His Purse' voices that need, and the poem's envoy, not surprisingly, welcomes the 'conquerour' as 'verray king' by both descent and 'free eleccion'. The terms of address remind us how crucial the issues of time and place are in determining what it is possible or necessary to write.

Realism and Subjectivity: The *Parliament of Fowls*, 1–21 and 693–9

As we bring twentieth-century assumptions into our attempts to imagine fourteenth-century life, so we bring twentieth-century assumptions to our interpretations of how fourteenth-century literature functions in representing life histories. Probably the most widespread and potentially blinding of these is the realist assumption: that is, the notion that literature usually aims to produce realistic or 'rounded' impressions of real people, and therefore that many, if not most, of its features are devoted to producing this mimetic picture. But if we work on the premise that realism is the only, or even the primary, function of medieval poetry, we will miss a great deal that the poet expects his audience to find in the poem; and it is especially important that in considering the presence and functioning of life histories in literature we should be aware of the limitations of such an approach.

On the other hand, while we need to recognize that realism is not a naturalized premise in the writing of medieval literature, we should not assume that personhood and subjectivity are absent from its concerns. As David Aers and Lee Patterson have argued, critics who date the appearance of interiority to an originary moment at the close of the sixteenth century, when Hamlet confesses that he has 'that within which passeth show' (a view most recently espoused by Harold Bloom, with his insistence on Shakespeare's 'invention of the human'[5]), have paid insufficient attention to medieval literature and to the Christian tradition of confession and self-examination. Subjectivity most certainly is evident in Chaucer and other medieval texts; but the demonstration and elaboration of subjectivity is never the sole object of a medieval writer. It always co-exists with other agendas represented by specific rhetorical strategies. In seeking to demonstrate how Chaucerian life histories serve different agendas we may start with an example of the life history at its most misleading: where the presence of the first person 'I' suggests to the modern reader a subjectivity, perhaps even to be equated with the poet's own, but where the construction of a subject is in fact almost wholly subservient to other literary purposes.

In Chaucer's work, as in most medieval poetry, the use of the first person is most characteristically associated with beginnings and endings. For a medieval poet, prologues and epilogues were recognizable rhetorical structures. The very fact that they were identifiable by these names indicates a formal way of thinking about them. For a modern audience, however, conditioned by twentieth-century confessional poetry to read for an equation between the 'I' of the poem and the person of the poet (Ted Hughes's *Birthday Letters* representing the popular face of poetry at the time of writing this chapter), the very different use of the first person in a medieval prologue or epilogue may take some getting used to. The opening three stanzas and the closing stanza of the *Parliament of Fowls* may serve as exemplary.

The first puzzle for a reader working on the assumption that the poem's first person is to be understood as a window into the poet's inner life would be the first half of the first sentence, which is as formal and distanced as a passage of verse can be, despite its first-person subject. The sentence in fact occupies the whole seven-line stanza, but the first three and a half lines are discernibly different in style from those that follow. The reader has to wait for the grammatical subject, the 'I', to emerge:

> The lyf so short, the craft so long to lerne,
> Th'assay so hard, so sharp the conquerynge,
> The dredful joye alwey that slit so yerne:
> Al this mene I by Love . . .
>
> (1–4)

The initial impression is of a highly rhetorical address, made up of balancing phrases built up in grammatical parallel in a way that deliberately postpones the subject represented by each of these carefully wrought units: love. The 'I' is scarcely prominent at all here, either rhythmically or syntactically; it is merely the designated agent of meaning, the supposed source of the verse that struggles so elegantly with literary artifice to express the inexpressible. The central topic of the poem, the single monosyllable positioned so carefully in the middle of the fourth line, is love. Yet the 'I', merely slipped into the line that highlights love, becomes gradually more insistent over the remaining lines of the stanza, which turn to examine the bewildering effect on the writer of this concept of

> . . . Love, that my felynge
> Astonyeth with his wonderful werkynge
> So sore, iwis, that whan I on hym thynke
> Nat wot I wel wher that I flete or synke.
>
> (4–7)

These lines seem to begin to open up the poet as more than a mere vehicle, as a source of meaning in himself, an individual with a particularly strong response to love. This 'I' thinks and feels: when he thinks about love he is astonished, bedazzled, unsure of self or surroundings. He feels small in the face of a force as immense as love; yet the very fact that he gives expression to a subjectivity that feels may seem to enlarge him with an inner life. The detail of an individual life is then apparently fleshed out by the revelation in the next stanza that this speaker is not himself a lover, but knows love only through books. He becomes a distinct, even eccentric, personality.

A reader determined to equate this poetic 'I' with Chaucer's own life history encounters a problem at this point. While a conception of poetry as a consistent, continuing revelation of the writer's self might find useful confirmation of the speaker dazed by love in another dream prologue, the prologue to the *Book of the Duchess*, that same prologue also provides a straightforward contradiction of the second element: the lack of experience in love. The narrator of the *Book of the Duchess*, though he describes himself as 'a mased thyng' (12), is dazed not by the thought of what love is or might be, but by the condition of being in love himself (there is, he says, only one physician who may cure him). What we have here, then, is not a poet lying about himself, but a poet making different use of the conventions of dream poetry and *dits amoreux* (see further Spearing 1997, esp. 42–7).

The speaker's tone in the prologue to the *Parliament of Fowls* becomes increasingly colloquial and intimate: 'But "God save swich a lord!" – I can na moore' (14); 'On bokes rede I ofte, as I yow tolde' (16). The apparent self-revelation of line 16 is again a detail both intimate and elsewhere attested (as in *HF* 652–8 and *LGWP* F 29–39); but it is scarcely a revelation for a writer of books, and is more important in any case as a vehicle for introducing reading matter into the poem as a deliberate and relevant signpost to the poem's meaning. The third stanza, in the same conversational tone, has the narrator ask rhetorically why he is telling the reader all about his reading, precisely in order to highlight its functionality. On one occasion, he tells us, he was reading a book for a particular reason: in order to learn 'a certeyn thing' (20); and because he wanted to learn that 'certeyn thing', he says, he read quickly and eagerly all day long. The poet does not directly tell us at that point what the certain thing was, but we may assume, since he introduces it, that the book he is reading, which he summarizes in the poem, does in fact shed some light on the subject (an argument I pursue at more length in Dillon 1993: 80–90).

The final stanza of the poem shows the narrator returning to his reading none the wiser and taking up his search for learning again:

> I wok and othere bokes tok me to,
> To reede upon and yit I rede alwey.
> I hope, ywis, to rede so som day
> That I shal mete some thyng for to fare
> The bet and thus to rede I nyl nat spare.
>   (695–9)

Here, if anywhere, the priority of functionality in the use of the first person seems self-evident. The return to the question of learning from books via the apparent failure to learn on the part of the narrator is not a way of giving prominence to the narrator's personality for its own sake; it is a way of reminding the reader that the narrator embarked upon his reading to learn a certain thing, and of thereby prompting the reader to think back over his own reading to establish what that thing is. It goes without saying, I think, that what the narrator seeks to learn must be one and the same thing as what the poem seeks to teach. The framing of the uninformed and slow-witted persona who reads, but not sharply enough, functions to push readers towards a more actively thoughtful and interpretative role, explicitly putting the burden on them to make sense of what they have read. It must be obvious that Chaucer, as writer of the poem, cannot 'be' the narrator who fails to understand the material at the heart of that same poem. It follows, then, that the first-person 'I' serves another and, in this case, more didactic function.

The Functions of Character: The Reeve's Tale, 3941–86

Criticism of the *Canterbury Tales*, and especially of the General Prologue, has been less tempted to make an equation between the first-person narrator and the poet than between the represented characters and people Chaucer may have known or heard of. J. M. Manly and Muriel Bowden are particularly associated with the search for real-life counterparts to literary portraits; but Jill Mann's work on estates satire has clearly demonstrated that Chaucer, in writing the General Prologue, was working within an established, pre-existent literary genre stretching back to at least the twelfth century. As Mann has pointed out, however, her approach, while differing from Manly's, is not necessarily opposed to it. The importance of Manly's contribution, she argues, lay in showing 'the relevance of the *Prologue* to its contemporary social life rather than to a world of eternal human types' (Mann 1973: 2); and Mann's own concern is to examine Chaucer's literary portraits within the context of social stereotyping, not to demarcate a simplistic boundary between literature and life. In looking at character, then, we need to dispense with reductive critical binaries such as that between literature and life, and inspect the variety of ways in which particular kinds of detail can function.

The Reeve's Tale follows the Miller's Tale, in which the Miller puts a foolish carpenter at the centre of his narrative. The prologue to the Reeve's Tale begins by showing the Reeve, who is a carpenter by trade, take offence at this story and hence deliberately set out to tell a story that will 'quite' the Miller through its focus on the 'bleryng of a proud milleres ye' (3864–5). It is thus made clear that the characters of the Reeve's Tale are to be understood within a context of personal bias; and indeed there are marked similarities between the Reeve's fictional miller and the (also fictional) Miller who has offended him (aggressiveness, skill in wrestling, bagpipe-playing and, stereotypically, a tendency to steal grain). The miller's daughter has the

longest and fullest life history visible in the tale, in that she can be understood within
the context of her parents', and even one grandparent's, social positioning, the nuances
of which are supplied with some care. Though the daughter of a miller, she is also
the daughter of a woman with higher social pretensions, 'ykomen of noble kyn', 'yfos-
tred in a nonnerye', 'well ynorissed and a mayde' (3942–8). But this mother's 'nobility' is heavily compromised, since it comes via her descent from 'the person of the
toun' (3943), which makes her not only a bastard ('somdel smoterlich', 3963), but
the child of a priest sworn to celibacy. The aims and thought processes of both the
parson and the miller are seen in the eagerness of both for the marriage: the parson
gives Symkyn plenty of money to marry his daughter, and Symkyn himself prizes the
woman's education and her virginity as necessary to his proud sense of his own yeoman
status. The miller's daughter is thus precisely placed as the offspring of absurd pride
and pseudo-elegance on the part of all three forebears: mother, father and grandfather.
While mother and father seek to over-compensate for their social shortcomings by
parading themselves in slightly absurd matching finery –

> On halydayes biforn hire wolde he go
> With his typet wounde aboute his heed,
> And she cam after in a gyte of reed;
> And Symkyn hadde hosen of the same
>   (3952–5)

– grandfather makes difficulties about her marriage in his determination 'to bistowe
hire hye / Into som worthy blood of auncetrye' (3981–2).

   The degree to which she reflects both the pretension and the absurdity of her
background is conveyed through the literary cross-reference of her physical description, which juxtaposes elements of romance (such as Chaucer draws on in his portrait
of the Prioress in the General Prologue) with a contradictory coarseness that in turn
directly echoes the physical description of the miller. She is both 'thikke and wel
ygrowen' (3973; the pilgrim Miller is 'a thikke knarre', whereas the Prioress is 'nat
undergrowe', GP 549, 156); she has a 'kamus nose' and 'eyen greye as glas' (3974;
the pug nose constitutes an unfortunate genetic inheritance from the miller, whereas
the Prioress has eyes grey as glass, GP 3934, 152); and while her breasts are round
and high, her broad buttocks somewhat spoil the picture of elegance.

   Yet the detail of this life history is not there for its own sake, simply so that we
should appreciate the miller's daughter in all her fullness. It functions within the tale
to make literary and satiric points which gesture outwards towards both the wider
frame of the *Canterbury Tales* and social practice in the fourteenth century. If, instead
of cutting off the quotation about the parson's aspirations for her marriage where it
ends above, we carry it on to the next two lines, we see a change of direction in the
rhetoric, signalling a new poetic objective:

> For hooly chirches good moot been despended
> On hooly chirches blood, that is descended.

Therfore he wolde his hooly blood honoure,
Though that he hooly chirche sholde devoure.
(3983–6)

The mode of writing here is at odds with anything that has gone before. The repetition of 'hooly chirche' and 'hooly blood' underlines the moral outrage against the parson's double sin: not only has he sired an illegitimate daughter, but he has laid out money that belongs to the church by right on having her educated in a convent and buying her a good marriage, and now seeks to ensure that the rest of his immoral hoard is passed on through his immorally descended offspring. The life history of the miller's daughter makes space for a different and more vitriolic brand of satire. The primary direction of the tale is not anticlerical satire, nor does the tale return to the figure of the parson again; but for a brief moment here Chaucer invites his audience to take, as it were, time off from the main concerns of the tale to participate in what is nevertheless a very central concern of the *Tales* as a whole: disgust with corruption in the church.

The portrait of Symkyn's daughter thus operates in at least four ways. First, it functions to create an impression of an individual living in a particular place and time; second, it operates within the literary framework of the larger work, the *Canterbury Tales*, which demands that it be read against other portraits, other tales and the opening gambits of the General Prologue; third, its place within the *Canterbury Tales* implicitly situates the miller's daughter within the larger framework of literary tradition, which demands that any given work is understood by comparison with those other literary works that either resemble or differ from it, thus creating the defining parameters of genre which shape the experience of reading; and fourth, it functions as a vehicle for the expression of an authorial view on matters of common concern outside literature, as here in the sudden attack on an instance of clerical corruption.

Criseyde as Subject: *Troilus and Criseyde* II, 50–147

Both the Reeve's Tale and the *Parliament of Fowls* construct life histories intermittently and with varying degrees of fullness; but a rather different test case is offered by *Troilus and Criseyde*, in which the figure of Criseyde is much more fully developed as a subject, not just in the sense that she is presented as having an inner life, but also in the sense the poem encourages that she is constructed as she is by powerful social forces literally 'subjecting' her. The opening of Book II finds her sitting in a 'paved parlour' with two other ladies while a maiden reads to them from a romance. This clarity of detail has the effect of rooting Criseyde in a continuing daily life at an elite social level. Like any well-born widow in fourteenth-century England, she is mistress of her own household, where she has leisure to sit with female companions and to command the services of others. Yet the other side of this comfortable indoor

life is the fact that it is narrow and restricted. As a widow, without a male protector
to take control of and responsibility for her and the household, Criseyde must be
careful that the life she leads does not incur charges of immodesty; and, as the daughter of a traitor, she must take care not to give offence to those upon whose good opinion
she is dependent.

Her cloistered leisure is interrupted by an invasion of the outside world in the
shape of Pandarus, who comes to soften her up on Troilus' behalf. Since Pandarus is
her uncle and his plans are less for her good than for his friend's, we are reminded
perhaps of Criseyde's expressed sense of vulnerability at the beginning of Book I, when
her father turns traitor, leaving her 'allone / Of any frend to whom she dorste hir
mone' (97–8) and pleading with Hector to take pity on her despite her father's treachery. Here again, the focus is on her vulnerability as a woman without a male protector, dependent on the good will of other males for her safety. As Pandarus arrives,
Chaucer gives Criseyde both social and inner richness by showing her warm welcome
of her uncle immediately move into confiding mode, thereby furnishing a glimpse
into her private life:

> 'Ey, uncle myn, welcome iwys,' quod she;
> And up she roos and by the hond in hye
> She took hym faste and seyde, 'This nyght thrie,
> To goode mot it turne, of yow I mette.'
> And with that word she doun on bench hym sette.
>
> (87–91)

The apparent openness of both the welcome and the self-revelation, together with the
visible physicality of 'sitting' her uncle down, work to give her a rounded presence
which is made simultaneously physical, socially interactive and inwardly alive. We are
given the impression of having open access to both a conscious and an unconscious life.

This is extended and enhanced as the dialogue with Pandarus continues to present
easy intimacy, fullness of interaction, colloquial freedom of speech and a capacity
to tease and laugh. Criseyde's playful remark, ' "Uncle," quod she, "youre maistresse
is nat here" ' (98), demonstrates a surprising knowingness and unguarded immodesty
which extend her status as subject by taking her beyond the stereotyped realm of
the romantic heroine, who would not normally be shown as playful or knowing about
love. The fact that Criseyde knows either that Pandarus has a lover, or that he might
be expected to have one, intensifies our sense of her range and awareness and also puts
her momentarily in a position of power over him which sets her free of the gendered
stereotype installed by passages like the kneeling to Hector in the previous book (I,
105–12). She also gains fuller subjectivity by virtue of being shown to have social
awareness and self-consciousness. When Pandarus invites her to 'Do wey youre barbe
and shew youre face bare; / Do wey youre book, ryse up and lat us daunce, / And lat
us don to May some observaunce' (110–12), we are alerted not only to the social code
embodied in Criseyde's dress (she is covered from chin to breast by a 'barbe', worn by

nuns and widows), but to the fact that both she and Pandarus adopt a position in relation to it, Pandarus boldly challenging Criseyde to take it off, while she responds with seeming outrage: ' "I! God forbede!" quod she. "Be ye mad? / Is that a widewes lif, so God you save?" ' (113–14).

Yet the fullness of social detail in this potential life history of a noble widow outraged by the suggestion that she compromise her position is made to look thin by comparison with the more complex self-awareness that is given to Criseyde when she situates that conventional response against her own practice by pointing out the unconventionality and unsuitability of her own chosen reading material. Even as she refuses Pandarus' invitation to throw off the trappings of respectable status, she acknowledges the extent to which she falls short of ideal widowhood by reading romances in her parlour rather than saints' lives in a cell: 'It satte me wel bet ay in a cave / To bidde and rede on holy seyntes lyves; / Lat maydens gon to daunce and yonge wyves' (117–19).

This accumulation of detail seems to suggest an almost impossible fullness of access until we remember that that fullness is always compromised by gaps in what has gone before; so that while we know Criseyde to be a widow, for example, a woman alone without father or husband, we know nothing whatsoever of that first husband, nor even whether she has any children. And this absence of knowledge is quite deliberately foregrounded: 'But whether that she children hadde or noon, / I rede it naught, therfore I late it goon' (1, 132–3). The gaps may be read, paradoxically, as both countering and enhancing our access to Criseyde's subjectivity: while they restrict what we may know of her life history, they simultaneously hint at unknowability as a sign of richness and fullness beyond the documented facts.

The passage in Book II is itself written in such a way as to continue the construction of Criseyde as a creature of gaps, one who has an inner self that deliberately keeps apart from the visible public persona, one who may seem outgoing and spontaneous, but who is in fact always planning her next move. Strategic intent is clearly signalled by Chaucer's description of her behaviour in trying to extract Pandarus' secret from him:

> Tho gan she wondren moore than biforn
> A thousand fold and down hire eyghen caste;
> For nevere, sith the tyme that she was born,
> To knowe thyng desired she so faste;
> And with a syk she seyde hym atte laste,
> 'Now, uncle myn, I nyl yow nought displese,
> Nor axen more that may do yow disese.'
>
> (141–7)

The discrepancy between the urgency of her wish to know, stated in the text, and the gesture and speech of submissive resignation to remaining ignorant, build up an interiority that is made known to the reader by its very refusal to make itself known socially.

Harder to read are the signs of a self-consciousness that is not merely social but literary. When Criseyde voices the awareness that she should be reading saints' lives rather than romances, her subjectivity seems almost to expand beyond the confines of the romance within which she finds herself – except that such a formulation cannot really make sense. The expansion is in fact one that must contain Criseyde. Though 'Criseyde' is given the momentary awareness that lives can be constructed, such awareness of the way in which literary genre constructs within particular limits in fact rebounds on the apparently widening subjectivity of the character who utters it by reminding the audience of her constructedness. This is a moment that pushes against the limits of what a literary subjectivity can encompass: as it mimics the capacity of a non-literary subjectivity to articulate a sense of the literary, it encounters breaking-point and is reduced by what it seeks to encompass.

This produces an irony that rhymes with the irony more regularly produced by setting the characters in unconscious juxtaposition with their literary sources. This kind of literary play surrounds and limits the characters by calling on readers' wider knowledge of ancient history and mythology. Twice in this passage Chaucer calls on those surrounding frameworks to put Criseyde into an ironic perspective that goes beyond the time-frame within which she operates and thus reminds us of the arbitrary constructedness of the subjectivity attributed to her by this particular literary work, as opposed to everything else that has been written on Criseyde, the Trojan war, or romantic heroines generally. (And immediately prior to the passage, of course, is the prologue to Book II, in which a wider view of love in different times and places, and an insistence on the poem's translated status and cultural difference, are articulated.) The first of these moments is the stanza describing how Pandarus is wakened out of his half-sleep by the swallow, Procne, chattering of 'How Tereus gan forth hire suster take' (69). The reference is to the rape of Philomela by her sister's husband, Tereus. Its violence and tragic outcome (Procne is metamorphosed into a swallow and Philomela into a nightingale after avenging the rape) insert a sense of foreboding alongside the optimism of the May setting, undercutting the way birdsong usually functions as part of the gladness of spring. Besides hinting at betrayal in love, furthermore (and the prologue to Book I has already warned us that this is a story of sorrow in love), the mythic reference also serves to remind the reader of that other rape, explicitly recalled at the beginning of Book I, the 'ravysshyng . . . of Eleyne' by Paris (62), the event that set in train the entire Trojan war.

The second point at which the reader's awareness is made to swing out beyond the story of Troilus and Criseyde in order to compare it with a different myth and thus call to mind its own writtenness and intertextuality is Criseyde's account of the romance she is reading. Just as the rape of Procne pointed to the rape of Helen, so the siege of Thebes points to the siege of Troy. The distant myths comment on the myth currently under (re)construction. And the story of Thebes, as even Criseyde's brief summary shows, is another story of death and destruction, interrupted, rather pointedly here, at the moment where a character has just died and gone to hell. Though Book II is poised at the moment where the reciprocation of love is about to take root and at a point where Criseyde is light-hearted and unsuspecting, Procne and

Thebes do not bode well for the outcome of love, and the light-hearted banter of this encounter is deliberately framed by negative parallels that keep the harsher perspective in view.

The framing, however, is not just a matter of setting one tone against another that undermines it, but of setting one way of writing a life history against another with which it is barely compatible. From one angle, the fullness of Criseyde's subjectivity is privileged, giving us a sense both of access to her and sympathy with her, and prioritizing her inner life as a focus of the action. From the other, the worlds that subject her, both historical and literary, are prioritized, creating a sense that Criseyde's life history is both predetermined and arbitrary, defined by the authorial force that brings her into being as a character, as well as the forces of the fictional world she occupies, and that Criseyde 'herself' is therefore entirely without agency. By deliberately oscillating between the long view of Criseyde's life history (the full span of her life and history, to separate out the terms) and the synchronic fullness of the moment, Chaucer cultivates our sense of the paradox of subjectivity. To be a subject is to be both impossibly full and impossibly dwarfed. And in writing the poem as he does, with blatant emphasis on the literary devices through which these two kinds of fullness may be constructed, Chaucer calls attention to the artifice that goes into the making of literary life histories and the wider agendas they serve. The act of telling, moment by moment, we are made fully aware, subjects the lives of characters to rhetorical strategies that make use of them to speak to audiences in particular and premeditated ways.

See also AFTERLIFE; BODIES; CRISIS AND DISSENT; FRANCE; GENRE; GEOGRAPHY AND TRAVEL; ITALY; LANGUAGE; LONDON; LOVE; MODES OF REPRESENTATION; NARRATIVE; OTHER THOUGHT-WORLDS; PERSONAL IDENTITY; SOCIAL STRUCTURES; VISUALIZING.

NOTES

1 *Chaucer Life-records*, ed. Martin M. Crow and Clair C. Olson (Oxford: Clarendon, 1966), ch. 15.
2 Ibid., 42–4.
3 *Chapters in the Administrative History of Medieval England: The Wardrobe, the Chamber and the Small Seals*, 6 vols (Manchester: Manchester University Press, 1920–33), i, 19.
4 *Life-records*, ed. Crow and Olson, 13–18.
5 Harold Bloom, *Shakespeare: The Invention of the Human* (London: Fourth Estate, 1998).

REFERENCES AND FURTHER READING

Aers, David (1986) *Chaucer* (Atlantic Highlands, NJ: Brighton: Harvester). The work of David Aers and Lee Patterson has done most to move historicist literary criticism away from earlier approaches that treated history as mere background, to a more self-conscious and dynamic model of practice.

——(1992) 'A whisper in the ear of early modernists; or, reflections on literary critics writing the "History of the Subject"', in *Culture and History 1350–1600: Essays on English Communities, Identities and Writing*, ed. David Aers (London: Harvester Wheatsheaf; Detroit: Wayne State University Press), 177–202. Specifically challenges the view commonly expressed by critics of the early modern period, that the subject does not emerge as a concern in literature written before that time.

Bowden, Muriel (1948) *A Commentary on the General Prologue to the* Canterbury Tales (New York: Macmillan). Builds on Manly's approach (below), through contextual and topical contemporary detail.

Brown, Peter and Butcher, Andrew, F. (1991) *The Age of Saturn: Literature and History in the* Canterbury Tales (Oxford: Blackwell). Examines the possible interactions between literature and history with particular emphasis on the *topos* of Saturn.

Coleman, Janet (1981) *English Literature in History 1350–1400: Medieval Readers and Writers* (London: Hutchinson). An historian's discussion of some of the more important areas of history that need to be taken into account in the study of medieval literature.

Dillon, Janette (1993) *Geoffrey Chaucer* (Basingstoke and London: Macmillan). A historicist approach to a selection of Chaucer's poetry.

Ellis, David, ed. (1993) *Imitating Art: Essays in Biography* (London and Boulder, Col.: Pluto). An exploration, through selected essays, of some of the problems and issues around biography.

Green, Richard Firth (1980) *Poets and Prince-pleasers: Literature and the English Court in the Late Middle Ages* (Toronto: University of Toronto Press). A clear account of the relationship between Chaucer's writing and his courtly environment. Chapter 3 outlines the kind of social and intellectual education that attachment to one of the royal households would have involved.

Knapp, Peggy Ann (1990) *Chaucer and the Social Contest* (New York and London: Routledge). Examines selections from the *Canterbury Tales* with emphasis on the ruptures and discontinuities in traditional social thinking coming to the fore in the late fourteenth century.

Leicester, H. Marshall, Jr (1990) *The Disenchanted Self: Representing the Subject in the* Canterbury Tales (Berkeley, Los Angeles and London: University of California Press). A deconstructionist

reading of a few of the tales urging that the pilgrim tellers be read as the products rather than the producers of their tales.

Manly, John M. (1926) *Some New Light on Chaucer* (New York: Holt; London: Bell; repr. Gloucester, Mass.: Peter Smith, 1951). An investigation of the *Canterbury Tales* through contemporary social contexts, including proposed real-life counterparts for some of Chaucer's poetic characters.

Mann, Jill (1973) *Chaucer and Medieval Estates Satire: The Literature of Social Classes and the General Prologue to the* Canterbury Tales (Cambridge: Cambridge University Press). An important contextualization of the General Prologue within the traditional expectations produced by estates satire.

Patterson, Lee (1987) *Negotiating the Past: The Historical Understanding of Medieval Literature* (Madison: University of Wisconsin Press). Questions earlier historicist and non-historicist critical approaches and includes analysis of a fifteenth-century reader's response to *Troilus and Criseyde* (ch. 4).

——(1991) *Chaucer and the Subject of History* (London: Routledge; Madison: University of Wisconsin Press). Looks in detail at Chaucer's own approaches to history and subjectivity.

Pearsall, Derek (1992) *The Life of Geoffrey Chaucer: A Critical Biography* (Oxford and Cambridge, Mass.: Blackwell; repr. 1994). A clear assessment of what is known and what kinds of speculation may be most valuably hazarded about Chaucer's life.

Rigby, S. H. (1996) *Chaucer in Context: Society, Allegory and Gender* (Manchester and New York: Manchester University Press). An historian's approach to some potential social meanings of the *Canterbury Tales*.

Salter, Elizabeth (1988) *English and International: Studies in the Literature, Art and Patronage of Medieval England*, ed. Derek Pearsall and Nicolette Zeeman (Cambridge: Cambridge University Press). An indispensable account of what Salter calls 'the obsession with the continent'.

Spearing, A. C. (1976) *Medieval Dream-poetry* (Cambridge: Cambridge University Press). An important assessment of the conventions of the genre and the way Chaucer and other English poets developed it.

——(1997) 'A Ricardian "I": the narrator of *Troilus and Criseyde*', in *Essays on Ricardian Literature in Honour of J. A. Burrow*, ed. Alastair J. Minnis, Charlotte C. Morse and Thorlac Turville-Petre (Oxford: Clarendon), 1–22. A brief analysis of criticism to date on Chaucer's use of narrative persona, followed by an analysis of its characteristically variable and non-unified functioning in *Troilus and Criseyde*.

Strohm, Paul (1989) *Social Chaucer* (Cambridge, Mass.: Harvard University Press). A detailed investigation of Chaucer's social positioning within his different environments.

16

London

Michael Hanrahan

When Chaucer writes about London, he tends to avoid it, to refer to it obliquely, or to explore it haltingly. *Troilus and Criseyde*, set in ancient Troy, undoubtedly conjured London for fourteenth-century readers, for whom the city was commonly and sometimes notoriously known as New Troy. The General Prologue to the *Canterbury Tales* opens with the pilgrims assembling at the Tabard Inn in Southwark, the suburb and borough south of London across the River Thames, infamous for its unsavoury industries, ranging from brothels to tanneries. The Canon's Yeoman's Tale treats the chicanery of a London priest but falls short of realizing the city beyond naming it in passing. And the Cook's Tale, Chaucer's most developed London narrative, ends abruptly. The fleeting and fragmentary appearance of the city in Chaucer's poetry is not an instance of the poet's avoidance of history, but is rather more appropriately seen as a condition of history. To Chaucer and his contemporaries, as David Wallace has argued, London existed as a 'discourse of fragments, discontinuities, and contradictions'. The very cultural conditions of London – a place repeatedly beset by cataclysmic crises and irresolvable internal tensions – precluded the possibility of representing it as a 'single, unified site' (Wallace 1992: 59, 82).

Chaucer's London

Late fourteenth-century London had its share of problems. The city's craft guilds and merchant oligarchs were engaged in a prolonged feud that spanned the reigns of Edward III and Richard II; it was invaded during the rising of 1381, and the ensuing chaos enabled disgruntled insiders and outsiders alike to exact revenge on their enemies in the streets of the capital; Richard II strove to enlist the support of the city in his political struggle against the Lords Appellant throughout the 1380s; and he plunged the city into crisis when he took the government into his own hands in 1392. The various attempts to seize or defend control of the city produced competing representations of events. A wide variety of texts, from poems to chronicles to parliamentary petitions, record motivated interpretations of London history that assert a given group's interested version of who should govern the city and how.

Medieval London, like Chaucer's poetry, did not exist in isolation. The rebels' invasion of the city in 1381 establishes its accessibility and significance to agrarian workers and rural townspeople; their invasion also enacts in a dramatic fashion the daily threat presented by the masses of urban poor who immigrated to London from the countryside in search of work. Besides its rural bonds, London was also dependent on and interconnected with its suburbs. Southwark to the south served as London's 'dumping ground' (Wallace 1992: 60): the foul industries of urban life that were banned within the city limits sprung up there. There, too, outside the city's jurisdiction, the criminals who preyed on London sought refuge. To the west of London lay Westminster, where Parliament sat when it met in London and where, by Richard II's reign, the royal administration and bureaucracy were firmly established. The walled city of London may have been a symbolically delineated space, but its boundaries were 'permeable': the city space existed in relation to the countryside and its suburbs (Lindenbaum 1999: 284).

Chaucer's place in London – his social, financial and professional position – depended largely on his association with the royal court. Chaucer's education and career as a courtier began as a retainer, perhaps a page, in the household of Elizabeth de Burgh, Countess of Ulster and wife of Prince Lionel, the second oldest surviving son of Edward III.[1] Elizabeth's and Lionel's households were merged when Lionel came of age in 1359, and Chaucer subsequently entered the service of the prince. At some point during the 1360s Chaucer became a member of the royal household: the details of how this came about have not survived, but a record of 20 June 1367 lists him as receiving from Edward III a life annuity of twenty marks. Life annuities were the normal means of rewarding royal retainers for services rendered. From this point on, Chaucer appears to have supported himself by means of his court affiliation. By conducting the king's business as a royal emissary, or by occupying royally appointed posts, such as controller of customs (1374), controller of the petty customs (1382), clerk of the works (1389) and deputy forester (1391), Chaucer made his living. The royal appointment to the controllership of the customs coincided with his obtaining the rent-free lease to the living quarters above Aldgate, one of the six gates in the city wall. Chaucer's connection to the court of King Edward III secured his return to London in the 1360s; his withdrawal from the city in the 1380s was, in turn, hastened by his association with the court of Edward's grandson and heir, Richard II.

During the 1380s Richard II suffered several humiliating political defeats at the hands of the Lords Appellant, a group of dissident magnates so named because they ultimately appealed several of Richard's favourites on charges of treason. In an attempt to reform and control the royal court, the Appellants impeached the king's chancellor and appointed a commission to help Richard govern during the 'Wonderful Parliament' of 1386. In the aftermath of this parliament, which Chaucer is known to have attended as an MP for Kent, he resigned from his customs posts and, having already surrendered his living quarters in Aldgate, withdrew from London to Kent. Among the petitions presented by this reform-minded parliament was one particularly relevant to Chaucer: the commons sought to have those controllers of customs appointed for life removed from office on account of financial malpractice.[2] Although Chaucer's was not a life appointment, and although he may have been in the process of removing himself to Kent, the atmosphere of the parliament, which sought to weaken Richard's administrative hold on the realm, no doubt quickened Chaucer's withdrawal from the city and the king's affinity. The Wonderful Parliament ended on 28 November 1386 and, within a matter of weeks, Chaucer resigned from his controllerships. Whether these actions are interpreted as witnessing Chaucer the astute political player (the great reader as well as writer) or Chaucer the victim of the commons' reform, the basic scenario remains the same: Chaucer withdrew from London during a period when Richard's servants and favourites were increasingly under attack and in danger.

The 'Merciless Parliament' of 1388 established the political ascendancy of the Appellants, who used this parliament to execute or exile Richard's favourites. Among the petitions presented to it was one aimed at Richard's practice of recruiting members to his affinity by granting life annuities. Singled out were those persons who had been granted life annuities by Edward III and who had received further grants from Richard.[3] The 1367 annuity that Edward granted to Chaucer may have technically fallen into the category targeted by the 1388 petition.[4] Perhaps in response to the petition, Chaucer resigned his annuities on 1 May 1388, while the Merciless Parliament was still in session. Such an action suggests that the bloody purge of Richard's court by his enemies warranted additional self-protective steps by royal servants, like Chaucer, who had already distanced themselves from the city and court. If at the very least an indirect victim of the Appellants' reform of the Ricardian court, Chaucer was very much the direct beneficiary of Richard's return to power. Two months after assuming his majority in May 1389, Richard appointed Chaucer clerk of the works.

The overlapping and mutually informing contexts of Ricardian court and London civic politics provide a discursive space in which to locate Chaucer's London. The factional strife of the period not only affected the real lives of individuals and writers, like Chaucer or Thomas Usk, but also produced a wide range of texts that variously represented and reproduced the struggles. The Cook's Tale, which Wallace has called 'Chaucer's solitary attempt at pure London fiction' (Wallace 1992: 59), provides an initial, useful entrance to the tumultuous world of late fourteenth-century London.

'Oure citee', Public Order and Riot: The Cook's Tale

In his prologue and tale, the Cook refers to 'oure citee' (4343, 4365), an inclusive verbal gesture that enlists not only the pilgrims but also the audience of the text, all of whom are embraced as part of an imaginary plurality that is unnamed but understood – London. His reference to the city simultaneously asserts a proprietary claim to it that insinuates the Cook into the exclusive group of citizens or freemen. The basic social distinction in medieval London was between the enfranchised and the unenfranchised: according to Sylvia Thrupp, 'only the former, who had sworn loyalty to the city government and undertaken to bear their share of taxation and public duty, could style themselves citizens or freemen and claim the various privileges that were guaranteed to the community by royal charter' (Thrupp 1948: 2–3). One was not a citizen by virtue of living in London. Citizenship was instead achieved through inheritance, apprenticeship or purchase. The majority of London inhabitants were non-citizens, known either as 'foreigners', whether born in London or elsewhere in the realm, or 'aliens', if born overseas (Thrupp 1948: 2–3). Roughly three-quarters of the male population of medieval London were non-citizens,[5] and all women were excluded from *full* citizenship. Women married to citizens, and the widows of citizens, were afforded the economic privileges bestowed by their husbands' status (to keep shop, trade retail in the city, pay taxes and train apprentices), but they were excluded from exercising the political privileges of that status, namely holding any ward or civic office (Barron 1989).

By invoking 'oure citee' the Cook asserts a claim to London and by extension to the exclusive ranks of citizenship. The Cook is by no means disqualified from citizenship because of his social class or occupation. Nor is he a citizen simply because he is 'of London'. Rather than a citizen, the Cook, originally from Ware, seems to be a representative example of the mobile poor, who moved to London from throughout England and who, in seeking apprenticeship, more often than not ended up providing the capital with cheap labour. He is, after all, not making the pilgrimage on his own but is attending to the guildsmen.

The Cook's Tale itself has provided rich material for reconstructing the social and political world of Chaucer's London (Wallace 1992; Strohm 1994). Through its narrative cues and description of Perkyn's revelry, the tale establishes its narrator's concern with the dominating political and social idea of medieval London – public order (Thrupp 1948: 16, 75; Wallace 1992: 70–5). Its opening couplet, 'A prentys whilom dwelled in oure citee, / And of a craft of vitailliers was hee' (4365–6), as Wallace has noted, conjures the factional strife that plagued the city: 'it would hardly be possible, for a contemporary audience, to think of the London victualers without thinking of their binary pairing, the nonvictualers and of the affrays, riots and disputes between these rival parties' (Wallace 1992: 71). With the exception of a brief period in the late 1370s and early 1380s, political power in London was concentrated in the hands of a merchant oligarchy (Thrupp 1948: 65–80; Bird 1949: 30–43).[6] Chaucer's adult London years coincided with this aberrant period in civic politics, when the craft guilds, comprised mainly of artisans and led by John Northampton, threatened the merchants' oligarchic hold on city government. The struggles between the competing factions came to a head in the London mayoral election in 1383, when Nicholas Brembre, the powerful merchant and favourite of the king, defeated the incumbent mayor, John Northampton.

Besides the opening couplet, with its freighted associations with London factional strife, the Cook's narrative invokes additional concerns about civic peace when it condemns Perkyn's riotous behaviour as illustrating the mutual incompatibility of truth (or faithfulness) and a revelous servant: 'Revel and trouthe, as in a lowe degree, / They been ful wrothe al day, as men may see' (4397–8). Paul Strohm has noted that the comment illustrates one instance of the Cook's ventriloquizing the voice of a pulpit moralist (Strohm 1994: 164). The comment also further situates the poem in the broader context of late fourteenth-century factional politics. The concept of truth as faith or loyalty to the city and king figured prominently in textual accounts of London civic struggles – struggles that show how these loyalties were in theory consonant but in practice often divisive.

Trouthe and the Case of Thomas Usk

After losing the London mayoralty to Brembre in 1383, Northampton conspired to take it back by force and was subsequently arrested for inciting a riot. During his trial before the king at Reading in 1384, Northampton's personal secretary and co-conspirator, Thomas Usk, stepped forward and provided testimony against his former lord and employer. Usk revisits his role in the trial of Northampton in Book I of his prose allegory, *The Testament of Love* (c.1386). In this fictional account of the events of 1383–4, Usk's persona defends his betrayal of his co-conspirators as an instance of his loyalty to the king:

> For my trouthe and my conscience ben witnesse to me bothe, that this (knowinge sothe) have I sayd, for no harme ne malice of tho persones, but only for the trouthe of my sacrament in my ligeaunce, by whiche I was charged on my kinges behalfe. (I, ch. 6, 162–6)[7]

Besides justifying his actions as an instance of allegiance, Usk's version of events also provides a self-defence against the possible charge that he defamed his former colleagues by publicly declaring their crimes. Usk's choice of language, that he intended 'no harme or malice', engages the legal definition of defamation, which English canon law defined as the malicious imputation of a crime. He also deftly assumes the common defence of persons accused of slandering another by asserting that he simply spoke the truth ('sothe').[8]

Usk inspired a special loathing among his contemporaries. He was executed during the Merciless Parliament because of his alleged role in certain royal plots against the Appellants, but contemporary accounts of his execution and death dwell on his treachery towards Northampton. The source of his contemporaries' hatred seems to have been the particular nature of his treason, namely the betrayal by a servant of the trust of his lord. In his condemnation of Perkyn's disobedience and disloyalty, Chaucer's Cook exhibits a similarly class-informed attitude towards the apprentice, whose disloyalty, especially his stealing from his master, exemplifies the Cook's assertion that loyalty and revelry in a social inferior are incompatible.

Usk's fictional justification and defence of his betrayal of Northampton resort to certain charged terms and concepts ('truth', 'allegiance' and 'defamation') that were readily deployed in other motivated accounts of London civic history. In 1386, for example, the London guild of Mercers submitted a petition to parliament complaining against former mayor Nicholas Brembre.[9] Among other grievances, the petition claims that Brembre had slandered the Mercers by challenging their truth or loyalty to Richard II:

> And we ben openlich disclaundred, holden vntrewe & traitours to owre Kyng, for the same Nichol sayd bifor Mair, Aldermen, & owre craft that xx or xxx. of vs were worthy to be drawen & hanged, the which thyng lyke to yowre worthy lordship by an euen Juge to be proued or disproued, the whether that trowthe may shewe, for trouthe amonges vs of fewe or elles no man many day dorst be shewed.[10]

The obsessive concern with truth in this passage serves to assert the Mercers' loyalty in the face of Brembre's slander, as well as in the face of their fellow citizens' general disregard for truth. Through their petition, the Mercers identify themselves as genuinely faithful to the king and city. Usk relies on a similar strategy of self-identification with truth. However, unlike the Mercers who challenge Brembre's authority, Usk's narrative ultimately endorses Brembre's version of civic events (namely, that Northampton is a traitor and the source of civic unrest). Given this charged environment, the Cook's Tale's concern with truth and a servant's rebelliousness acquires a referentiality that further realizes its engagement of London factional politics. The tale's abrupt ending cuts short its version of these matters, but Chaucer is not altogether through with them. His other London narrative, the Canon's Yeoman's Tale, revisits the city and returns to the same matters of loyalty, treason and slander which figured so prominently in the political discourse of the day.

Loyalty and Treason: The Canon's Yeoman's Prologue and Tale

The Canon's and Yeoman's dramatic entrance in the *Canterbury Tales* re-enacts a conflict explored in the Cook's Tale – a servant's rebellion against his master. After catching up with the pilgrims, the Canon's Yeoman explains to the Host that he and his master have overtaken the group because his 'lord' and 'soverayn' (590) loves company. The Yeoman's respect for and loyalty towards his master are, however, extremely short-lived. His conversation with the Host raises the suspicion and ire of the Canon, who accuses his servant of no less than slander:

> Hoold thou thy pees and spek no wordes mo,
> For if thou do, thou shalt it deere abye.

Thou sclaundrest me heere in this compaignye.
(693–5)

After launching this accusation, the Canon beats a hasty retreat. The Yeoman, meanwhile, encouraged by the Host, proceeds to realize his lord's accusation by betraying the Canon's trust in him to the pilgrims: 'Syn that my lord is goon, I wol nat spare; / Swich thing as that I knowe, I wol declare' (718–19). The Yeoman effectively switches allegiance and joins the party ruled by the Host, who in the General Prologue had been elected the pilgrims' 'governour' (813). The Yeoman's change of allegiance also encapsulates the main features of Usk's notorious betrayal of Northampton – a servant of one lord allies himself with another whose protection allows that servant to declare all that he knows about the secret practices of his former master.

The points of congruence that exist between Usk's and the Canon's Yeoman's treasons are neither best explained nor fully exhausted by allegory. Narrative accounts that are suggestive or even representative of actual historical events or persons do not, as Strohm has forcefully described, exist in a relation of reference or one-to-one correspondence; instead, literary texts exist in 'a relation of participation within a larger system' or symbolic field (Strohm 1994: 168–9). The Canon's Yeoman's Tale, Usk's allegory and the Mercer's petition constitute and are constituted by the symbolic field of allegiance that figured prominently in London civic politics. The pilgrims themselves acquire a distinct political association within this cultural milieu. While it might be overstating the case to say that the Yeoman switches political parties, he does join a group with an express purpose. Such organizations were always suspect in Chaucer's London. Wallace, discussing the anti-associational rhetoric of the period (Wallace 1992: 75), singles out a mayoral proclamation of 1383 that forbids assembly: 'Noman make none congregaciouns, conuenticles, ne assembles of poeple, in priue nen apert . . . ne ouer more in none manere ne make alliances, confederacies, conspiracies, ne obligaciouns, forto bynde men to gidre.'[11] The opening setting of the *Canterbury Tales* not only makes sense but acquires a contemporary currency within this context: in Southwark, outside the jurisdiction of the city, the pilgrims are free to organize themselves into a company.[12]

The Yeoman's ability to join the pilgrims implies the group's potential inclusiveness, which contrasts sharply with the regulated and exclusive membership of the London citizenry. The Yeoman's betrayal of his master, however, surfaces again and again during his initiation into the group, which takes the form of telling a tale. The tale begins with a complaining disquisition against the misguided practices of alchemy and concludes with a story of a certain canon who deceives a London priest. The subject matter of the first part of the tale, alchemy, metaphorically reinforces his own recent transformation from servant to the Canon to member of the pilgrimage. The second part of the tale explores from a variety of perspectives his betrayal of the Canon – a betrayal that both enables his change of allegiance and also undermines his capacity for allegiance.

According to Wallace, betrayal is the ' "key motif" of the tale': the priest betrays a London canon; the London canon, according to the Yeoman, betrays his brethren; and finally the Yeoman betrays his lord and master (Wallace 1992: 82). This last act of bad faith is recognized by the Yeoman at two points in his narrative: he interjects that he is neither talking about his master in particular (1088–91) nor slandering canons in general:

> But worshipful chanons religious,
> Ne demeth nat that I sclaundre youre hous,
> Although that my tale of a chanoun bee.
> . . .
> To sclaundre yow is no thyng myn entente,
> But to correcten that is mys I mente.
> This tale was nat oonly toold for yow,
> But eek for othere mo . . .
>
> (992–1001)

The Yeoman emphasizes that it is not his intention to slander those of whom he speaks (canons explicitly and his master implicitly), but instead to correct what is amiss. Like Usk's fictional persona in the *Testament*, the Canon's Yeoman insists that he is not speaking maliciously but only telling the truth. Besides further enmeshing its narrative within the political discourse of the period, the tale's invocation of the fine distinction between slander and speaking the truth brings us full circle to the Cook's Prologue.

Slander, Truth and Sexual Practice: The Cook's Prologue and Tale

In the prologue to his tale, the Cook's announcement that he will tell 'A litel jape that fil in oure citee' (4343) prompts the Host to joke at the Cook's expense. Harry Bailly accuses Roger of selling inferior and spoiled pies, a common practice that warranted civic attention (Wallace 1992: 70). After casting aspersions on the Cook's business and culinary practices, Harry assures Roger that he is telling the truth in sport: 'A man may seye ful sooth in game and pley' (4354). The Cook accepts the terms of the Host's argument with the understanding that true jokes are nevertheless bad jokes (4356–7). He takes comfort, however, in the knowledge that he can return the Host's jesting, truthful attacks in kind: 'But er we parte, ywis, thou shalt be quit' (4362). Roger's threat captures the inevitable escalation of charges and counter-charges that result from slander, whether intended as jest or character assassination.

Chaucer's playful engagement of slander contrasts sharply with its enlistment by Usk and the Mercers. Usk's fictional account of his role in the Brembre–Northampton feud is at once a strategy to re-establish his good fame and an attempt to win the patronage of Nicholas Brembre, whose interests and agenda are promoted in Usk's version of events. The Mercers' petition strives to preserve their reputation while challenging Brembre's power and influence in the city. The Canon's Yeoman's Tale provides a potentially critical examination of provisional allegiance but, like the Cook's Tale, avoids any overt political alignment. Other writers more desperate and therefore less circumspect than Chaucer readily align themselves factionally by laying claim to truth and strategically enlisting the allegation of slander. In doing so they not only represent but also reproduce the political struggles of Ricardian London.

Chaucer's London tales and the Mercers' petition share one last feature: in each the assertion of truth is accompanied by the assumption of a moral perspective. Richard Firth Green, commenting on the petition, detects the 'unmistakable echoes of the aphoristic rhymes on the evils of the times with which contemporary pulpit moralists peppered their sermons'.[13] Chaucer's Yeoman offers a thinly veiled attack on his master as a corrective for others. And the Cook condemns the lax morals of the apprentice, as well as those of the master who fails to reel in his wayward servant. The Cook's rebuke of his tale's subjects, especially his disapproval of the apprentice's disruptive sexuality, illustrates another aspect of the tale's multi-faceted engagement of London civic matters. Civic authorities actively sought to regulate sexual practice, especially prostitution, and John Northampton's notorious campaign of moral rectitude provides a final London context for the Cook's Tale.

During the early part of the 1380s, Northampton sought to have prostitutes and their clientele, including priests, tried at civic courts. The chronicler Thomas Walsingham describes Northampton's programme of reform: 'Londoners at this time began to grow haughty beyond measure. Relying on the arrogant authority of the mayor of that year, John Northampton, they usurped episcopal rights, occasioning many disgraces by apprehending fornicators and adulterers.'[14] According to the chronicler, the women arrested were first imprisoned, then shorn of their hair and 'paraded before the assembled inhabitants of the city, accompanied by trumpeters and pipers'.[15] The *Liber albus*, a fifteenth-century compilation of London's customary law, lists certain ordinances that prescribe a similar punishment for adulterers: 'If any person shall be impeached of adultery and thereof lawfully attainted, let him be taken unto Newgate and from thence, with minstrelsy, through Chepe, to Tun on Cornhulle.'[16] In the Cook's Tale, one of Perkyn's pastimes consists of accompanying processions of accused criminals being led with minstrelsy to Newgate. Strohm has observed that 'Perkyn, led with revel to Newgate', anticipates his future starring role in a similar parade (Strohm 1994: 170–1). I would add that given the tale's abrupt ending – Perkyn moving in with a compeer and his wife, who supports herself, her husband and perhaps Perkyn as well by prostitution – anticipates the specific kind of crime for which he will be paraded: fornication.

The Cook's disapproving commentary on Perkyn's behaviour exemplifies the indignant attack on lax morals that figured in Northampton's programme of good governance. James Simpson, discussing Northampton's reforms, notes: 'To please the prudish-minded elements among the Londoners (strong it would seem among the lesser guildsmen), he conducted a campaign against sexual immorality in London and did not hesitate to trespass on the rights of the Church courts to do so' (Simpson 1993: 123). The need to regulate sexuality is a conventional reformist idea that applied equally to civic and court practices. Writers of the period commonly drew on an analogy linking sexual propriety and right rule. Book VII of *Confessio Amantis*, John Gower's manual of advice to princes in general and Richard II in particular, cautions rulers against lechery, lest it lead to misgovernance and deposition:

> The Philosophre upon this thing
> Writ and conseileth to a king,
> That he the surfet of luxure
> Schal tempre and reule of such mesure,
>
> . . .
>
> So that the lustes ignorance
> Be cause of no misgovernance
> Thurgh which that he be overthrowe.
> (4559–67)[17]

Walsingham, criticizing the lecherous habits of the royal counsellors and favourites, likewise suggests that the political reform of Richard's court requires sexual reform.[18] Regulated sexuality on the streets of London or in the court of the king is the key to peace and good governance.

Chaucer's Cook, like the 'prudish-minded elements among the Londoners', condemns unruly persons, like Perkyn, whose sexual practices threaten to disrupt civic peace and order. Given this cultural milieu, the king's relation to the city, commonly described in amorous terms, generates problematical associations. Richard Maidstone's account of the king's reconciliation with the city in 1392 draws on erotically laden images and language that underscore the ambivalent relation between king and city.

In June of 1392, Richard took London into his own hands: he revoked the customary liberties of the city, removed the courts to York and arrested the mayor, sheriffs and aldermen. The traditional explanation for Richard's actions is that he was avenging himself on certain London merchants who had refused him a loan. In August 1392, a symbolic reconciliation between the king and city was enacted in a royal procession through the streets of London. Maidstone, who commemorates the event in his *Concordia: facta inter regem Riccardum II et civitatem Londonie* (Concord between Richard II and the city of London, *c.*1393), depicts the reconciliation as a wedding in which 'The people hasten forth from the city to meet their king and spouse' (171).[19] Maidstone further develops the wedding metaphor as he explains how envious slanderers had momentarily turned the king/groom against his city/bride: 'An

invidious throng had turned the king in anger against you and caused your bridegroom to forsake his bridal chamber . . . The biting, detracting tongues could not
prevent your bridegroom from desiring to come to his bridal chamber, for he that
took all customary liberties from you now returns ready to give them back in greater
number' (167, 169). Maidstone's representation of the slandered city as both bride
and bridal chamber ('*thalamus*') not only conceives of Richard's entrance into London
in terms of sexual penetration,[20] but also imagines that penetration as fruitful: 'he
that took all customary liberties from you now returns to give them back in greater
number'. Given that Richard's then marriage to Anne of Bohemia was childless, the
king's symbolically reproductive second marriage to London illustrates one instance
of the anxiety about succession that attended the last decade of Richard's rule. To
ensure lawful succession and peace in the realm, and to guarantee the property rights
of his subjects, a king was obligated to produce an heir. Richard, notoriously, failed
to fulfil this basic obligation.

The Clerk's Tale as a London Narrative

The concerns of succession that surface in Maidstone's account of Richard's relations
with the city of London provide a context for considering the Clerk's Tale as a London
narrative. Just as the Cook's and Canon's Yeoman's Tales invoke certain key terms and
contested concepts that were regularly deployed in the factional struggles of the
period, the Clerk's Tale engages the crisis of an heirless realm that haunts Maidstone's
poem. Scholars have long recognized that the Clerk's Tale offers a study in governance,
or misgovernance, since Walter exhibits the tell-tale signs of a tyrant. Just as significant, however, and more specific, is the way the tale entertains Richard's failure as
a ruler because he has not produced an heir.

Like Queen Anne, who is relegated to the role of mediator during the crises of
Richard's reign, Grisilde plays an intercessory role in the crises of Walter's realm:

> Ther nas discord, rancour, ne hevynesse
> In al that land that she ne koude apese,
> And wisely brynge hem alle in reste and ese.
> (431–4)

In Maidstone's narrative, Anne assumes the role of intercessor in Richard's so-
called 'quarrel' with London when she prostrates herself at the feet of the king and
begs that he restore the city's liberties. Like Grisilde, who prepares the house and
bedchamber for Walter and his new bride, Anne effectively prepares for the wedding
of Richard to London. In each case, the ruler's first wife functions as a bawd for her
husband.[21]

Maidstone's symbolic wedding between Richard and the city conceives of an alternative available to the heirless king – a second wife. Chaucer's Clerk Tale imagines

the same alternative. During the course of his trial of Grisilde, Walter fabricates rumours of his subjects' disapproval of his marriage to a peasant. According to Walter, the people complain that when he is dead and gone they will have Janicle's grandson for a ruler: 'Thanne shal the blood of Janicle succede / And been oure lord, for oother have we noon' (632–3). Grisilde's social inferiority and unworthiness ultimately justify Walter's subsequent scheme to remarry. According to his subjects, Walter's new bride, who happens to be his daughter, is fairer and nobler than Grisilde:

> For she is fairer, as they deemen alle,
> Than is Grisilde and moore tendre of age,
> And fairer fruyt bitwene hem sholde falle,
> And moore plesant, for hire heigh lynage.
>   (988–91)

In a departure from his source materials, Chaucer highlights the lineage and breeding potential of Walter's second wife, who will produce the heir ('fairer fruit') that compelled his people to urge him to marry in the first place.[22]

By translating a story deeply concerned with succession in the last decade of Richard's reign Chaucer, intentionally or not, turns to a past text to imagine the events of his day. Henry Bolingbroke's eventual usurpation was successful in no small measure because of Richard's failure to produce an heir. In 1399 Chaucer and London find themselves in similar positions. London, as Ruth Bird notes, always temporized in times of crisis and invariably sided with the ascendant power (Bird 1949: 118). After Henry returned to England from exile in France, London withheld its support of the usurper until he threatened the city with violence (Barron 1990: 141–2). Only then did it commit itself. London's change of allegiance is played out on a much smaller scale by Chaucer. Faced with a new king and the old problem of securing his annuities, Chaucer out of necessity forswears decades of allegiance to Richard and presents Henry with the begging poem, 'Complaint to his Purse'. The poem recognizes the 'conqueror' whose grace alone will guarantee the poet's continued receipt of his annuities. London's and Chaucer's inevitable capitulation to Henry reinforces what has already been illustrated in the Canon's Yeoman's Tale – allegiances are oftentimes provisional.

To locate London in Chaucer's poetry, finally, is inseparable from the concomitant and reciprocal process of locating that poetry in medieval London. Chaucer's London and London's Chaucer are by necessity inextricable textual constructions. Chaucer relied on a common set of culturally specific symbols and politically charged terms with which to construct his version of London; and any attempt to situate Chaucer and his writings in the cultural context of London constructs its own version of London's Chaucer, one that owes as much to Chaucer as to Chaucer's contemporaries.

See also AFTERLIFE; AUTHORITY; CONTEMPORARY ENGLISH WRITERS; CRISIS AND DISSENT; FRANCE; GEOGRAPHY AND TRAVEL; ITALY; LANGUAGE; LIFE HISTORIES; PERSONAL IDENTITY.

NOTES

1 *Chaucer Life-records*, ed. Martin M. Crow and Clair C. Olson (Oxford: Clarendon, 1966), 13–18. These earliest surviving records to mention Chaucer date from the late 1350s and also list him as a Londoner, 'Galfrido Chaucer Londonie'.

2 *Rotuli Parliamentorum* (London: 1783), iii, 223. For discussions of this petition, see Derek Pearsall, *The Life of Geoffrey Chaucer: A Critical Biography* (Oxford and Cambridge, Mass.: Blackwell, 1992; repr. 1994), 203–4; Paul Strohm, *Social Chaucer* (Cambridge, Mass.: Harvard University Press, 1989), 37.

3 *Rotuli Parliamentorum*, iii, 246. See Pearsall, *Life of Geoffrey Chaucer*, 208 and Strohm, *Social Chaucer*, 38.

4 *Chaucer Life-records*, ed. Crow and Olson, 338.

5 A. R. Myers, *London in the Age of Chaucer* (Norman, Okla.: University of Oklahoma Press, 1972), 144–5.

6 Pamela Nightingale challenges this view of London civic history. See her 'Capitalists, crafts and constitutional change in late fourteenth-century London', *Past and Present* 124 (1989), 3–35.

7 Citations of Usk's *Testament* are from *The Complete Works of Geoffrey Chaucer*, ed. W. W. Skeat, 7 vols (Oxford: Clarendon), 1897), vii, 1–145.

8 According to Richard H. Helmholz, editor of *Select Cases on Defamation to 1600* (London: Selden Society, 1985), the provincial Constitution of the Council of Oxford (1222) is the effective origin of the English law of defamation (14). See ibid., pp. xxx–xxxii, for a discussion of truth as a defence against the charge of defamation.

9 My discussion is indebted to Richard Firth Green, *A Crisis of Truth: Literature and Law in Ricardian England* (Philadelphia: University of Pennsylvania Press, 1999), esp. 1–10, which describes the dense and shifting meanings of 'truth' in late fourteenth-century England.

10 *A Book of London English, 1384–1425*, ed. R. W. Chambers and Marjorie Daunt (Oxford: Clarendon, 1931), 35.

11 *The Memorials of London and London Life*, ed. Henry Thomas Riley (London: Longmans, Green and Co., 1868), 480–1. Wallace also discusses the issuing of writs at the Cambridge parliament of 1388 that required 'all guilds, fraternities, mysteries and crafts to give an account of themselves to the Royal Chancery': see David Wallace, 'Chaucer and the absent city', in *Chaucer's England: Literature in Historical Context*, ed. Barbara A. Hanawalt, Medieval Studies at Minnesota 4 (Minneapolis: University of Minnesota Press, 1992), 75. According to Simpson, the Cambridge writs recognize fraternities and guilds as 'potentially subversive in the late 1380s': see James Simpson, '"After craftes conseil clotheth yow and fede": Langland and London city politics', in *England in the Fourteenth Century: Proceedings of the 1991 Harlaxton Symposium*, ed. Nicholas Rogers (Stamford: Paul Watkins, 1993), 121.

12 David Wallace, *Chaucerian Polity: Absolutist Lineages and Associational Forms in England and Italy*, Figurae: Readings in Medieval Culture (Stanford: University of Stanford Press, 1997), pursues this aspect of the pilgrim assembly: 'The most powerful instantiation of associational ideology in Chaucer comes through the formation of the pilgrim *compagnye* at the opening of the *Canterbury Tales*' (2).

13 Green, *Crisis of Truth*, 2.

14 Thomas Walsingham, *Historia Anglicana*, ed. Henry Thomas Riley (London: Stationery Office, 1864), ii, 65: 'Londonienses isto tempore coeperunt ultra modum insolescere. . . . Revera freti Majoris illius anni, Johannis de Northamtone, auctoritate superciliosa, praesumpserant episcopalia jura, multas dehonestationes inferentes, in fornicationibus vel adulteriis deprehensis.' (Unless otherwise indicated, translations are mine.)

15 Ibid.: 'Circumduci fecerunt in conspectu cunctorum inhabitantium civitatem, praecedentibus tubicinis et fistulatoribus.'

16 *Liber albus*, ed. Henry Thomas Riley (London: Richard Griffin and Co., 1861), 394–6 at 396. *The Calendar of Letter-Book H*, ed.

Reginald Sharpe (London: John Edward Francis, 1907), 189, mentions certain 'ordinances made by the Mayor, Aldermen and Common Council for the punishment of bawds, harlots, unchaste priests and the like'. For discussions of these ordinances, see Ruth Bird, *The Turbulent London of Richard II* (London: Longmans, Green & Co., 1949), 64–5; Ruth Mazo Karras, *Common Women: Prostitution and Sexuality in Medieval England* (New York and Oxford: Oxford University Press, 1996), 15.

17 *The Complete Works of John Gower*, ed. G. C. Macaulay, 4 vols (Oxford: Clarendon), 1899–1902), ii, 1–519, iii, 1–386.

18 In his well-known 'knights of Venus' passage from the *Historia Anglicana*, ed. Riley, ii, 156, Walsingham describes how the court's lecherous pastimes have led Richard to neglect cultivating the pursuits befitting a king.

19 Citations of Maidstone are from *Concordia: Facta inter Regem Riccardum II et Civitatem Londonie*, ed. and trans. Charles Roger Smith, unpublished PhD thesis, Princeton University (Ann Arbor: University Microfilms, 1972), with page numbers following the English translations. Paul Strohm, 'Queens as intercessors', in his *Hochon's Arrow: The Social Imagination of Fourteenth-century Texts* (Princeton: Princeton University Press, 1992), 107 and Sylvia Federico, 'A fourteenth-century erotics of politics: London as a feminine New Troy', *Studies in the Age of Chaucer* 19 (1997), 121–55 at 145–52, discuss this erotically laden metaphor.

20 See Strohm, 'Queens as intercessors', 107–8; Federico, 'A fourteenth-century erotics of politics', 145–6. Walsingham's criticism of Richard's court, mentioned above in note 18, describes Richard's favourites as more valiant in the bedchamber (*thalamus*) than on the battlefield.

21 Commenting on the 'complicated dynamic of the king's real wife giving him a second one', Federico notes that Anne functions as a bawd in this scene: 'A fourteenth-century erotics of politics', 152.

22 See Warren S. Ginsburg's commentary on the poem in the *Riverside Chaucer*, 883, 990–1n.

REFERENCES AND FURTHER READING

Barron, Caroline (1989) 'The "golden age" of women in medieval London', *Reading Medieval Studies* 25, 35–58. London customary law guaranteed wives and widows of citizens most of the economic but none of the political privileges of citizenship.

——(1990) 'The deposition of Richard II', in *Politics and Crisis in Fourteenth-century England*, ed. John Taylor and Wendy Childs (Gloucester: Sutton), 132–49. Revisits the chronicle evidence of Richard's deposition and qualifies the traditional view that Richard turned into a tyrant in the later years of his reign.

Bird, Ruth (1949) *The Turbulent London of Richard II* (London: Longmans, Green & Co.) Understands London civic politics as having been organized into two opposing parties – the crafts, led by Northampton and the merchant capitalists, led by Brembre. Argues that Northampton sought to challenge the merchants' monopolistic control of city government.

Carlin, Martha (1996) *Medieval Southwark* (London: Hambledon). Traces the development of Southwark from AD 50 to 1550. Focuses on the period from 1200 to 1550 before this suburb of and 'jurisdictional affront' to London became incorporated into the city.

Federico, Sylvia (1997) 'A fourteenth-century erotics of politics: London as a feminine New Troy', *Studies in the Age of Chaucer* 19, 121–55. Discusses the symbolic and political referentiality of 'New Troy' in late fourteenth-century texts.

Lindenbaum, Sheila (1999) 'London texts and literate practices', in *The Cambridge History of Medieval English Literature*, ed. David Wallace (Cambridge: Cambridge University Press), 284–309. Surveys London textual production and reception from 1375 to 1485 and identifies three broad phases: 'discursive experimentation' during the reign of Richard II; 'the imposition of normative discourse' during the Lancastrian rule; and the 'intensive ritualization of culture' toward the end of the fifteenth century.

Nightingale, Pamela (1989) 'Capitalists, crafts and constitutional change in late fourteenth-century London', *Past and Present* 124, 3–35. Proposes that London factionalism was more fluid and provisional than the two-party model delineated by Bird.

Pearsall, Derek (1992) *The Life of Geoffrey Chaucer: A Critical Biography* (Oxford and Cambridge, Mass.: Blackwell; repr. 1994). This authoritative biography situates Chaucer's art in the context of the period. Considers the ways in which 'the *Canterbury Tales* will be the fullest record of London life, in its specific historical circumstances and conditions, in the 1380s and 1390s'.

Simpson, James (1993) '"After craftes conseil clotheth yow and fede": Langland and London city politics', in *England in the Fourteenth Century: Proceedings of the 1991 Harlaxton Symposium*, ed. Nicholas Rogers (Stamford: Paul Watkins), 109–27. Situates Langland's *Piers Plowman* in the cultural milieu of London civic politics from the mid-1370s to the mid-1380s. Focusing on the pentecostal scene in passus XIX of the B-Text, explores how Langland imagines a resolution to the factional strife of internal London politics.

Strohm, Paul (1989) *Social Chaucer* (Cambridge, Mass.: Harvard University Press). Situates the poet and his writings in the shifting and transitional contexts of his social milieu, factional affiliation and professional circle.

——(1990) 'Politics and poetics: Usk and Chaucer in the 1380s', in *Literary Practice and Social Change in Britain, 1380–1530*, ed. Lee Patterson (Berkeley and Los Angeles: University of California Press), 83–112. Considers the contrasting lives and writing practices of these two London writers. Whereas Usk recklessly pursued royal favour during this treacherous period, Chaucer cautiously withdrew from the king's affinity.

——(1994) '"Lad with revel to Newegate": Chaucerian narrative and historical metanarrative', in *Art and Context in Late Medieval English Narrative: Essays in Honor of Robert Worth Frank, Jr*, ed. Robert R. Edwards (Cambridge: Brewer), 163–76. The Cook's Tale participates in the 'symbolic field' of riotous behaviour to which writers of the period turned and, in turning to, helped construct in their accounts of the rising of 1381.

Thrupp, Sylvia, L. (1948) *The Merchant Class of Medieval London, 1300–1500* (Chicago: University of Chicago Press; repr. Ann Arbor: University of Michigan Press, 1989). This social history, which tends to view social class as a static entity, treats the merchants as a distinct group.

Wallace, David (1992) 'Chaucer and the absent city', in *Chaucer's England: Literature in Historical Context*, ed. Barbara A. Hanawalt, Medieval Studies at Minnesota 4 (Minneapolis: University of Minnesota Press), 59–90. Discusses the Cook's and Canon's Yeoman's Tales in the context of the civic conflicts and tensions that beset Ricardian London. Argues 'there is no idea of a city for all the inhabitants of a space called London to pay allegiance to; there are only conflicts of associational, hierarchical and antiassociational discourses'.

17

Love

Helen Phillips

Love is Chaucer's most important subject. Not only does his writing encompass most elements of human love – desire, delight, obsession, selflessness and sensuality – as well as some aspects of religious love, but his exploration of other subjects, particularly literature, political power relations and philosophical issues, is frequently conducted through consideration of the subjects of love and sexual relations.[1] Love is rarely treated as a subject in isolation: it is the site of the interplay of often contradictory forces and concepts. Thus, when Chaucer treats of the tragic power of love in the Knight's Tale, he muses also on the order and purpose of the universe, on harmony and desire, discord and pain; writing of the god of love's cruelty and of betrayed women in the *Legend of Good Women* he thinks also in terms of a political discourse of 'tyrannye' and 'oppressyoun', and of the literary, hermeneutic (even Wycliffite) issues of interpretation and intentionality (e.g. *LGWP* G 355, *LGW* 1868). The Clerk's Tale, which, in its Italian sources, was an exemplification of wifely obedience or the soul's relation with God, becomes also, in Chaucer's hands, a study in tyranny and *gentillesse* – fitness to rule. The marital power struggle between man and woman in the Wife of Bath's Tale similarly evolves into a treatise on *gentillesse*, social rank and poverty. The Nun's Priest's Tale, arguably the only tale in which a trace of the 1381 rising and conservative reaction against it can be discerned, is another study of marital 'maistrie' and extends the sexual battle for power to the areas of learning and textual exegesis. The Tale of Melibee combines a reversal of the usual relationship between husband's and wife's authority with a similarly challenging view of the exercise of political lordship, and a plea for the domination of the rule of reason over the rule of might. The Merchant's and Shipman's tales treat sexual negotiations as financial negotiations. In *Troilus* the 'double sorrow' of desire and loss in love becomes indissoluble from questions about fate, free will and mutability, and – ultimately – about the ontological status of individual subjective consciousness. The *Legend of Good Women* and Wife of Bath's Tale, dealing with 'wo that is in mariage' (WBP 3) and in sexual relationships, contemplate also gendered literary tradition and its misrepresentation of women, as well as the issues of textual intention and interpretation.

The Effects of Love

The dominant impression of love in Chaucer's writing is of its force, of the pain that seems its inevitable concomitant, and of its apparently paradoxical implications:

> The lyf so short, the craft so long to lerne, . . .
> The dredful joye alwey that flit so yerne;
> Al this mene I by Love, that my felynge
> Astonyeth with his wonderful werkynge
> So sore, iwis, that whan I on hym thinke
> Nat wot I wel wher that I flete or synke.
> (*PF* 1–7)

In the Knight's Tale, Arcite the soldier cries 'A!' as if stabbed to the heart, at his first sight of Emelye. For faithful Anelida, as for the falcon in the Squire's Tale, love cannot be abandoned, and brings unending grief. The *Legend of Good Women*'s good women are good because they have suffered in love: faithful martyrs to Cupid. Similarly, the temple of Venus in the *Parliament of Fowls* is filled with pictures of famous lovers and their deaths, and the flames on its altars are fanned by sighs of pain. The *Complaint of Mars* asks why God created love, whose power humans seem unable to resist yet which brings only either sorrow or a joy that lasts but a twinkling of an eye: an example of the readiness with which Chaucer turns from the sorrows of love to questions about the purpose and order of the universe. Love in the *Book of the Duchess* is as absolute as death, silencing (it seems) any arguments for moderation. In *Troilus* love's power and its capacity for all-absorbing pain become an overtly philosophical issue, embodied in a provocatively dialogic design: not only is the love narrative constantly interleaved with borrowings from its most important intertext, Boethius' *De consolatione Philosophiae*, but the structure of the text itself presents the reader with an unresolved dilemma about the relative claims of individual emotional consciousness and transcendental philosophy; for, through five long books, the subjective experiences of love, its ecstasies and sorrows, dominate the text, until it ends in a sudden volte-face, with the assertion that such experiences are not important, almost nonexistent, their apparent substantiality an illusion (*TC* V, 1821–55). The same kind of question is created by the shift from the *Canterbury Tales* to the Retraction, though that explicitly has a wider reference, not just to love but all 'worldly vanitees', and 'enditynges' about them. Though the final stanzas of *Troilus* proclaim that the phenomenon of human love can be dismissed and subsumed into a reality which has truth and substance in another world, beyond this one, the uncomfortable disproportion and inconsistency between the conclusion and what went before (paralleled in the contradictions in the narratorial stance which have puzzled critics) are likely to leave readers with the sense that love is a subject that raises ontological and ethical issues which the available philosophy cannot encompass.

Love at the end of *Troilus*, like secular and sexual fictions in the Retraction, seems to become an experience which represents temporal life and consciousness in general: human individual particularity, desire for physical, emotional and secular forms of happiness, and acceptance that events in the realm of time and contingency may have high significance and dignity for humans, alongside universal truths of reason and the soul. These temporal values are, of course, the stock-in-trade of the narrative writer, and in modern times, especially, of the novelist; Chaucer's questions about love are also questions about the scope and dignity of his own art.

The conclusion to *Troilus*, like the Retraction to the *Canterbury Tales*, appears disruptive but sincere: the only answer medieval culture, imbued with its dualist and universalist heritage, could offer to these existentialist and aesthetic issues. None the less, meaning in literature inheres more in how we travel than in where we arrive, and the sheer irreducible substantiality of those preceding five books of *Troilus* poses a philosophical question about the place and status of subjective, emotional phenomena in the official medieval universe. *Troilus* is a philosophical text, ultimately, less because it incorporates intertextual elements from Boethius than because it poses this question, even if no answer can be offered. The *Parliament of Fowls*, having set up the issue of the order of the universe early on, through its allusion to *Somnium Scipionis*, as the context for all that follows, proceeds to locate love, interrogatively, between the deities of Venus and Nature: the one beautiful but tragically destructive, the other elevated by God as his 'vicaire' on earth, yet representing a phenomenon, the mechanism of reproduction, which is far too limited to account for the aspirations and ideals that accompany human love, including its courtly and chivalric cultural manifestations. Are the humble, biological purposes of sexual desire its truest, most rationally justifiable and important aspect, since God the Creator blesses these, through Nature? Or is the extravagant, emotional absolutism that the aristocratic eagles express the highest form of this emotion, since theirs seems an experience full of idealism, self-sacrifice and a constancy enduring through vicissitude? We might note, too, that the birds' parliament contains the built-in assumption that the ways of love for the upper classes, the 'gentil' birds of prey, will differ from those of the lower orders, being more refined, more absolute, more faithful – and more literary in their expression.

In some texts, love's sorrows prompt explicit questioning of God's design. Just as the *Complaint of Mars*, contemplating a fugitive and jealous love, asked why God would create an experience as uncontrollable, unstable and unhappy as love (218–71), the Franklin's Tale asks how a loving Creator could fashion a world full of cruel and irrational dangers for the humanity whom he is supposed to love (V, 865–93). This challenge to orthodox constructions occurs in the fictional context of a love conundrum, a story in which good people, because of experience of love that seems in each case presented as innocent, find themselves in danger and at risk of harming others, and their own reputations and honour. The question so boldly asked in *Mars* should make us pause before accepting the critical view that, because *Troilus* contains echoes of Boethius and finally asserts a transcendental world view, it necessarily endorses the Boethian position, which accords human love and earthly passions no importance or dignity.[2] It may not reject it, but it certainly problematizes it.

Two recurrent Chaucerian topics are jealousy and rivalry in love. The illogicality of an emotion such as human love, where partners do not pair off neatly and permanently two by two, is a problem obviously relevant to a mind like Chaucer's, that so insistently ponders the relationship of sexual desire to the concept of an ordered and stable creation. Betrayal, too, preoccupies him. In *Troilus* it is allied to questions about mutability; in *Anelida* and the *Legend of Good Women* it provides opportunities for exploration of other favourite Chaucerian themes, including pathos and pity, and the love-experiences of women.

In Chaucer's religious writings, divine love is not an important theme, but divine mercy is. His pre-eminent religious themes are penitence and mercy (which dominate his two most exclusively religious texts, the *ABC* and the Parson's Tale); the harmony of the Creator's universal design (a theme often placed interrogatively in relation to the disruptive forces in human experience); and the paradoxical strength of those – usually women – who are spiritually strong amid worldly oppression and vicissitudes. Though these women, such as Custance, Grisilde and St Cecile, may show loyal benevolence towards their allotted partners, their fixed and passionate devotion, the love that keeps them strong, is for God, and for spiritual certainties beyond the world of change. Chaucer's most substantial representation of divine love is, startlingly, Troilus' song of happiness at the zenith of his love affair with Criseyde at the end of Book III of *Troilus and Criseyde* (1744–71):

> 'Love, that of erthe and se hath governaunce,
> Love, that his hestes hath in hevene hye . . .'
>   (1744–5)

This song ends with a very secular prayer for the softening of unresponsive lovers' hearts. Yet the bulk of it is an adaptation of a Boethian metrum (II, viii) in praise of that celestial order that, precisely, represents the opposite of the sorrow-stained pursuit of earthly joys and desires. Here, as so often, Chaucer is most controversial when being most intertextual, especially in the context of the subject of love.

Chaucer seems unable to leave the topic of cosmic order, yet also unable to contemplate it without troubled awareness of the conflict, instability and pain of human experience, especially when these are wrought by sexual desire, itself allegedly a source of harmony, love and union. This dichotomy, at the heart of his writing, constitutes the central theme of his two philosophical romances, the Knight's Tale and *Troilus*.

Troilus and Criseyde, III, 1184–1274

Chaucer brings together many of the irreconcilable elements of the text at the consummation of Troilus' passion. He prays here not straightforwardly to the god of Love, the Amors of the *Roman de la rose*, but to a diverse miscellany of love deities that draws into juxtaposition disconcertingly incompatible forces: first 'Love', perhaps the *Roman de la rose* Amors, but apostrophized here immediately and unexpectedly also as 'Charite'; then Venus, first as the goddess 'Citheria', but next in the form of the planet, in favourable aspect (directing attention to cosmic order, not sexual experience). Then comes Hymen, god of marriage: but this is an extra-marital love affair, and one of the literalist reader's puzzles about *Troilus* is why Troilus did not marry Criseyde – so the reference seems provocatively obtrusive. Finally comes a Boethian celestial power, 'Benigne Love, thow holy bond of thynges' (1261–74), a philosophical element in this miscellany of deities, that becomes doubly confusing for any observant reader who recognizes echoes of Dante's praise of the Virgin Mary bound up in this passage (*Paradiso* 33, 14–18). 'Charite', disconcerting enough in this context, even if it means either charitable benevolence or the Creator's *caritas*, may be used in a specialized Boethian sense, for the concept of a naturally imbued life force that animates living creatures (*De consolatione Philosophiae* III, prosa XI, 96; see Windeatt, 1992: 102–3): a far from erotic, romantic or courtly concept. Chaucer here runs through almost all the species of love deity available to his culture – except any of the potentially negative personifications of passion and physical sex, such as the goddess Venus as patroness of pain (as in the *Parliament*), Priapus, Cupid/Amour, Nature or Luxuria ('lechery'). Yet the immediate occasion is not one of philosophical insight into the cosmic design, nor a union that proves to have been blessed by the planets with longevity and stability, nor a marriage, nor an obvious instance of *caritas*, and certainly not virginal; it is Troilus' rapturous stroking of Criseyde's body. The diversity of love deities invoked poses precisely the question, 'What is Love?', foregrounded powerfully by the first *Canticus Troili* in Book I: 'if love is, what thing and which is he?' (I, 401). It encourages the reader to ask whether Chaucer presents sexual passion as akin to these grander, more authoritatively moral, celestial powers, or wholly at odds with them (as exegetic critics would have us believe).[3]

The evidence from artistry, within the writing, however, shows Chaucer lavishing all his art on the documentation of physical foreplay and its attendant emotions: this is not a dephysicalized description but one full of the movements of approaching union: 'felte hire . . . ytake', 'quake', 'felte . . . in armes folde', 'in arms gan hire streyne', 'with many a twiste', 'Bytrent and writh', and so on, evolving from individual to shared movement: 'Gan ech of hem in armes other wynde.' After the sparrowhawk image, discussed below, Chaucer does not allow negative elements to enter the writing. The reader's own approval and sympathy are engaged by insertions of both narrator and narratees, adulating Troilus' experience, at lines 1193–7, 1217,

1225 and 1246, and by the invitation to the reader to form his/her own judgement in lines 1310–37.

This passage illustrates something of Chaucer's use of framing devices in Book III: this moment of (temporary) joy and harmony is located in a highly unstable, threatened place: a secret meeting, in a bed with servants sleeping outside, in a house during a storm in a besieged city (which the reader knows must fall), with the enemy encamped around. Its intense, elevated and lyrical presentation is framed by the comic presence of Pandarus, whom Chaucer removes, with his benevolent but mocking valedictory *double entendre*, in lines 1188–90, to bring him back with ribald and officious cheerfulness, deflating the dignity of the sexual union that has intervened, in the morning, at lines 1555–82. His fabliau presence both frames the consummation, provocatively, and yet is prevented from spoiling its mood (see Muscatine 1957, on the interplay of fabliau and romance generic expectations in Chaucer).

This description of sexual arousal is created predominantly through the male experience: no female-oriented celebration of Troilus' hairy chest or delicately chiselled hips balances the itemization of Criseyde's naked charms. Though joy, trust and embracings become mutual, the event is still conceived primarily as Troilus' achievement, the moment when he 'hath his lady swete', line 1245. The sparrowhawk image (1191–2) conveys aggression, predatory possession and annihilation. Love in this image is not woman-friendly but a matter of male triumph, at odds with the mutuality conveyed in the woodbine image (1230–2), and the discourse that presented Troilus earlier in the narrative as Criseyde's humble slave. Its abrupt assertion of a concept of sex as an assault on a woman matches the Man of Law's Tale's equally abrupt comment (708–14), that brides, however holy, must put up with whatever sexual 'necessaries' are pleasing to the men who have wedded them. We cannot ask whether Chaucer merely follows contemporary assumptions, unexamined, or whether these statements and their world view, sharply discordant to the modern reader, are introduced with some consciousness of their provocative moral and emotional status. What we can say, however, is that Chaucer turns the predatory hawk image into a question for the reader to consider, both by using question form here and by withdrawing authorial responsibility for interpretation ('I kan namore', 1193).

Predatory language has a brief reprise at line 1207, ' "Now be ye kaught" ', but at this point accompanied by the text's manipulative insistence that Criseyde has consented, freely, to the sexual behaviour the sparrowhawk image has presented as rape-like, in the charming response Chaucer gives to her at this point: ' "Ne hadde I er now . . . Ben yolde, ywis, I were now nought heere." '[4] The disconcerting image of Criseyde as the victim lark, juxtaposed with the text's fleeting concession that the experience could have been presented from her point of view ('What can the sely larke'), is of a piece with Chaucer's exploration in Books II and IV of the complexities and miseries, from her point of view, of the changing situations that fate and men throw at her: a study not simply of a woman falling in love (like Chrétien's Laudine or the *Roman d'Eneas* Lavine), but of what it is to be the disempowered object of masculine desire. Chaucer is often, and justifiably, seen as a conservative author; but this compulsion to acknowledge within his writing the conflicts that challenge dominant ideology, even while he ostensibly endorses that ideology, is one of his most profound, and anti-conservative, characteristics as a writer. As one of the key passages in *Troilus* for presenting the poem's problematization of love, and its troubled awareness of the co-existence of impulses towards sacred and sensual, tragic and comic, within human perceptions of love, lines 1184–1274 exemplify also that sense of unresolved multiplicity and contradiction that is the mainspring for much of Chaucer's most powerful writing and his most provocative narrative structures.

The Franklin's Tale, 761–802

This bravura exploration of love and marriage, and of authority and obedience between spouses, challenges some medieval expectations. First, by its very act of questioning and discussing the unequal power relations between husband and wife; second, by its presentation of this as an attitude which men and women share: both sexes, it asserts, naturally desire liberty (268–9), and it is a man here who proposes that the husband's right to require obedience should not be enforced (745–50); and third, by reformulating the marital relationship as one best regarded as one of love and friendship. The last point is perhaps the most original: spouses are tellingly introduced as 'freendes'(762), and in this move Chaucer draws the discussion of sexual relations cleverly into the discourse of *amicitia*, an elevated scholarly and moral topic from the twelfth century on, with an idealization of true friendship as a pure, consensual and unselfish affection between equals (see Burnley 1979: 134–50). *Amicitia*, 'friendship', in this tradition, was a unisex or masculine bond, free of the tainted (for a medieval audience) associations of marriage, and elevated by association both with the classical treatises on friendship, especially Cicero's *De amicitia*, and with celibate monastic ideals. Moreover, the emphasis on 'pacience', on learning 'to suffre' (= 'to endure without complaint'), 'temperance', 'governaunce' and 'suffrance' ('tolerance'), in Chaucer's advice on how to preserve love (771–86), transforms sexual love into a moral education (see Burnley 1979: 64–98, on this complex of moral ideas).

While these elements and strategies construct a plea for a new view of marriage, reconceived as a relationship centred on love, friendship, consent and respect for the other partner, rather than the traditional assumptions that marriage was essentially a contract that gave power to the husband and required obedience from the wife, there are, especially noticeable for modern readers, counter-elements that convey much less liberal ideas (for a negative reading see also Aers 1980: 160–9). In making the man propose that he will ask only for obedience that is freely given, Chaucer falls back on a model for social and marital structures he offers elsewhere, one that is essentially conservative. The person to whom medieval society usually gave domination will still be in control, but his partner will have accepted the subordinate role voluntarily. The same 'solution' to unequal power and inherent conflict is given in the Wife of Bath's Tale (1177–1206, 1241–57), applied there as a recipe for a happy state, politically, and a happy marriage (see Phillips 2000: 101–2); the Wife claims that inequalities between rich and poor can produce a harmonious society if the rich use their power morally and the poor are contented. The bride in that tale, having gained self-determination from her husband, then gives it up, choosing, like Dorigen, to be a completely obedient wife – a decision resulting, we are told, in a perfect marriage (we might recall that conflicts between characters in the Franklin's Tale are solved, finally, by acts of selfless generosity, a solution implying an analogous vision).

This is a model for reforming human power struggles not by radical restructuring of society, the economy or marriage, but through individuals behaving unselfishly in whatever sphere God has placed them. That Chaucer cannot leave the point without some sense that it is problematic is shown by the disturbances to smooth textual coherence evident immediately after the theory is proposed, both in the Wife of Bath's Tale, which moves into disconcerting and disruptive, crudely aggressive pro-feminist attitudes (1259–64), and in the Franklin's Tale. There, the presence of unanswered questions in the 'voluntary obedience' model produces some distinctly confusing writing, for example in lines 751–2, where the formula about saving 'the name of soveraynetee . . . for shame of his degree' is verbally and intellectually baffling; and, in lines 781–805, which accelerate to an equally baffling torrent of paradoxical word-play and end with an insistence, in the problematizing form of an interrogative, that marriage (*always?*) produces 'joye . . . ese, and . . . prosperitee' between husband and wife. In lines 791–8, the syntax insists that paradoxes are being reconciled – servant *and* lord; servant in love *and* lord in marriage; lady *and* wife *also*; *both* lordship *and* servage; *both* lady *and* love – with assertions like *thus*, *nay*, *sith*, *certes*; but the incompatible terms chop and change in an increasingly dizzy manner. In practice, Arveragus will demand obedience from Dorigen, over her promise, rather than simply maintaining an outward show of authority ('name of soveraynetee') – not because Arveragus is conceived as dishonest, but because the text, having bravely suggested a modification of patriarchal control, falls back on containment of the woman when it envisages action or decision-making taking place.

This is, then, a passage where liberal and illiberal principles, conservative and radical impulses, are in conflict: a conflict signalled by some very strange verbal formulas. It explores heterosexual relationships in characteristically Chaucerian terms of power and paradox. Other favourite Chaucerian preoccupations make brief appearances: the nature of true *gentillesse*; the philosophical virtues of *pacience* and *governaunce*; the inadvisability of revenge or tyranny ('rigour'); the vision of perfect love as a state of being 'in quiete and in reste' (cf. *TC* III, 1819–20; MLT 1131). Anyone will find here some perennially wise advice on marriage, especially on tolerance, yet the totality of these individual parts is not reassuring. The passage begins with a statement of 'accord' and ends with 'acordeth to' (798), but it is not the conclusion, the happy ending of a story; it is the start, a calm before the storm, before the unresolved conflicts of medieval marriage, and of this passage, break out. It is a conclusion in which nothing is concluded, and everything is still open to be proved or disproved by experience. Of course, experience serves only to reinforce the incompatibility of these opposites, yoked in a theoretical 'accord' of love and marriage: the wife, through loving her husband so much, puts herself in the hands of a would-be adulterer; the husband, offering her freedom to keep her word, enforces on her the duty of adultery.

This story, which in Boccaccio's two versions is a tale of magic and of a wife's extrication from a fatal promise, becomes a problem piece for Chaucer's audience, explicitly enquiring of them 'Which was moost fre?', but also raising questions about order. It questions the divine order of the Creation in Dorigen's speech (865–93); it implicitly questions social rank and order, showing a non-*gentil* professional and *clerk* more honourable and unselfish than two *gentils*; and it holds up to the puzzled scrutiny of its audience the whole structure of married order: the husband's power to command, the wife's duty to obey, and the issue of the two forms of honour, female honour as chastity and male honour centred on oath-keeping.

Courtly Love

This passage takes for granted a particular discourse that modern culture has labelled 'courtly love': it contrasts marriage with the relationship of a 'lover' and his 'lady', in which the man is the humble servant of the woman and woos her by demonstrating the force of his love through his 'peyne', 'meke obeysaunce' and deeds of prowess. Her love is conceptualized as an act of 'pitee'. This form of relationship is here shown to have its natural outcome in happy marriage, yet to be a radically different type of relationship from that normally ordained for medieval marriage, where the husband has 'lordshipe' and 'maistrye' over a wife sworn to obedience. Later, both Dorigen (815–64) and Aurelius (939–59) manifest similar symptoms of the sincere and intense lover: insomnia, life-threatening sickness, fasting, obsession, weeping, melancholy and poetic outpourings (on lovesickness, see Wack 1986). Whether or not we label that discourse 'courtly love', a label that can imply acceptance of the now-mistrusted theory of a reified 'code' of rules for lovers' behaviour, rigidly followed by writers from the eleventh century on, it seems clear that by the late fourteenth century Chaucer had a sense of such a discourse, of which he could use a few key elements as shorthand to indicate that Arveragus' love is sexual love in its most elevated form: pure, total, devoted and part of his character as a *gentil* warrior. Even if 'courtly love' did not spring into being fully formed in eleventh-century Provence, as C. S. Lewis claimed, something like it was certainly familiar to Chaucer and contemporary writers as a literary style that they could use and readers would recognize. Parody is always a good indicator of the cultural acceptability of a literary language, and a parody of the romantic vocabulary of popular romance is used in the Miller's Tale, to mock the provincial pretensions of the artisan-class lovers.

Derek Brewer discusses courtly love in relation to chivalry in chapter 4 of this volume. It is a truism that courtly love was an invention of the nineteenth century, an exaggeration but a salutary one: the terms 'courtly love' or *amour courtois* are almost never found in the medieval period, and indeed the whole concept proves in practice problematic to relate to medieval literature. It was Gaston Paris in an 1883 article about Chrétien de Troyes' *Conte de la charrette* who claimed that the romance created an 'amour *courtois*', in which a man involved in a clandestine and obsessive love affair idealizes his mistress, is completely in thrall to love and her will, seeks to win her approval through prowess, and becomes, through the educative powers of such total devotion, a more perfect knight and human being. Subsequent criticism took Paris' relatively cautious observations and built an all too solid-seeming phenomenon on them: courtly love, sometimes described as a 'code', 'convention' or 'doctrine'. For English-speaking readers the most influential of these critics was C. S. Lewis, in his irresistibly forceful and learned *Allegory of Love* (1936).

Certain of the claims attracted almost immediate controversy: was it true, as Lewis beguilingly announced, that courtly love arose quite suddenly in eleventh-century Provence? It was clear that such themes could be found in many societies both before and after that period. The appearance of the troubadours, Marie de France and Chrétien de Troyes in the late eleventh and twelfth centuries may seem sudden, but that probably reflects the failure of earlier erotic vernacular texts to survive. Did perfect love in medieval literature always have to be adulterous? Chaucer's Franklin's Tale was only one of many texts to disprove that. How did the courtly love these critics described operate in medieval Christian society? D. W. Robertson, Jr (1962, 1968) questioned the sincerity of many texts that seemed to celebrate courtly passion, demonstrating how often such texts could be read ironically. These challenges chipped away at weak points in the edifice of courtly love, but it was the very impression of an edifice that was the real weakness. The reification and unification involved in the concept, the talk of rules, conventions and system, puzzled the thoughtful reader, giving the impression of a coercive social code: were the critics describing the behaviour of real people in society, or of authors composing fictions? One answer, explored with particular success by David Burnley (1998), stressed the extent to which 'courtly love' is a phenomenon of language, a style of writing. Fifteenth-century 'Chaucerian' poets and Elizabethan sonneteers demonstrate that by the end of the Middle Ages there was a recognizable register for love poetry. If we substitute for the old talk of 'codes' and 'conventions' the more modern critical concept of 'discourse' – a language which encapsulates a society's way of regarding and prioritizing particular experiences – we gain a recognition of the powerful ways in which literature affects social behaviour and the correspondingly powerful ways in which real people construct their own experiences as consistent with dominant literary patterns.

The passage from the Franklin's Tale examined above explores heterosexual relationships in characteristically Chaucerian terms: those of power and paradox. The unequal power relations of the lover and his mistress are reversed once marriage brings about the different power relationship of the husband's 'lordship' and the wife's obedience. The text asserts that power conflicts, and the contradictory attitudes to women in real-life marriage and in love literature, can be reconciled; yet we have seen that the rhetoric, with its increasingly disquieting rapid interchange of incompatibilities ('humble', 'servant . . . and lord', 'servant in love and lord in marriage', 'Servage? Nay

. . . lordshipe', etc.) fails to support this assertion. As so often, Chaucer's writing holds together contradictory impulses, radical and conservative. The passage is full of statements which, individually, contain excellent advice for harmoniously managing relationships, based on a primacy of love to defeat conflict: friends must obey each other; partners should tolerantly make allowances for difficulties arising from time to time as a result of such influences as anger, sickness, wine or woe, and so on. Yet the totality of these individual parts is not reassuring.

The clichés of love poetry become in Chaucer's poetry vehicles for new and polyphonic effects. The images of love as a sickness and a wound, already present in Boccaccio's *Il Filostrato*, are expanded in *Troilus*, especially in Book II, turning his Troilus into a hero characterized by passivity and receptivity, one who spends far more of his time in bed than his Italian counterpart. This helps to make *Troilus* into a study of interiority and subjective consciousness; it also facilitates comedy, with Pandarus as the active and cynical foil to Troilus, and it gives extensive space in the text for musings and discussions on the nature of love and philosophical dimensions related to it. Insomnia, attributed to the narrator of the *Book of the Duchess*, never explicitly said to be caused by love, becomes a multivalent state, akin both to death and to dreams with their enlightenments. The courtly literary discourse that uses the terms 'lady', 'mercy' and 'servant' in depicting the passion a lover feels during the pre-marriage courtship period is used in the Franklin's Tale to introduce a study in power and class, as well as a study of marriage.

One medieval association that seems to evoke Chaucer's humour and tenderness (characteristically linked faculties) is that between lovers and birds. He disarmingly thinks of birds themselves as suffering from love: the nightingale sings 'in his briddes wise a lay' of love to Criseyde as she lies musing (*TC* III, 921); the tercels in the Squire's Tale and *Parliament of Fowls* suffer agonies of unrequited devotion; in the General Prologue, 'smale fowles', unable to sleep for love, and the Squire, sleeping 'namoore than dooth a nythtyngale', are counter-images of each other. It is hard not to feel that Chaucer loved birds, and his style of equating birds and lovers suggests a combination of vulnerability, comicality and ethereality as the characteristics of love. Chauntecleer and Pertelote, acting out the marital battle for 'maistrye' all too recognizably, convey also, through the associations of the beast fable, political, theological and parodic double meanings. The urge for liberty in love (another theme that expresses love's unrestrainable power) is figured as the bird's natural desire to fly free, not only in the Franklin's Tale, but in the Manciple's and Squire's. The crow in the Manciple's Tale symbolizes the court poet, and the poet adopts the voice of a bird himself to present the *Complaint of Mars*.

The Miller's Tale, 3255–311

One of the problems the *Canterbury Tales* poses for its readers is how sexual desire — anarchic, unhappy and frequently immoral in its workings — fits into any serious or moral world view, and especially into a world view like that of medieval Christianity, with its strongly dualistic inheritance. Fabliau and romance jostle together in the *Tales*. The Miller's Tale, following on from the Knight's Tale, presents as great a challenge to the elevated, philosophical and tragic treatment of love in the preceding story as the Miller himself does to the gentlefolk in his aggressive prologue to this fabliau tale. The tale presents lust in a style which seems simultaneously innocent and immoral, callous and joyful, and the passage illustrates one method of suggesting innocence: Alisoun and Nicholas are associated with images of young animals, natural life and music. It also shows, in lines 3298–300, the arrogant masculine rivalry and aggression which will run through the text and be almost as central a motive for the plot as the male–female dynamics.

Chaucer was traditionally often seen as a pioneer realist; this passage illustrates why, but also shows how intermittent is his realist technique, and how much it is concentrated in details of speech and gesture (for example, colloquial register at line 3285: 'Lat be!'; gesture accompanying speech at line 3276: 'prively he caughte hire by the queynte'); or the sociolinguistic dimensions of speech, as when Alisoun distances Nicholas linguistically as well as physically with her switch to the formal second person plural form 'youre' (3287).

Chaucer's popular reputation is as a poet of lust and bawdy, not love. This passage contains the famous 'queynte' couplet, an example of the scattering of taboo discourse typical of this text (despite the demonstration by Larry Benson [1984] that the coarseness in the couplet here is a more refined coarseness than first appears, since the second 'queynte', while indicating the genitals, was in the fourteenth century probably still a euphemistic term). We see here the employment of clerkly cunning in the pursuit of self-gratification, characteristic of the fabliau, and the linguistic *vraisemblance* in references to the body, to work and to a lower-class physical environment which are also expectations of the genre: 'lendes', 'fartynge', 'was at Oseneye', 'whan she leet hir werk', 'laten blood, and clippe and shave', ' brewhous ne taverne'.

The Miller's Tale specializes in unexpectedly harsh revelations: the analogies between Alisoun and a coin, weasel and weapons (3235, 3256, 3264–6) prefigure reluctant awareness that, though sexy, she is not very nice; the unexpectedly blunt reference to farting (3337–8) prefigures Absolon's unwelcome encounters with the unfragrant elements of sexual physicality, and parallels his instinct (3341) to cover women in clouds of incense. Taken together, the imbalances in his demeanour, as shown later in the tale – courtly and infantile, eager and timid, sexually obsessed and over-idealistic – create an element of psychological comedy, with probably an underlying current of homophobia.

Bawdy is not the only foregrounded register; the Miller's Tale is an extravaganza of many registers and multiple forms of comedy. Juxtapositions of disparate registers and modes characterize its presentation of sexual attractions and sexual behaviour. Courtly language ('derne love', 'lemman'; see Donaldson 1970) clashes with uncourtly behaviour and language in lines 3275–87, as will be the case later with the courtly register associated with Absolon ('love-longynge', 'curteisie', 'paramours').

Parodic religious references intriguingly enter into the depiction of fabliau sexuality: Alisoun's radiant face (3255, 3310), for example, a religious motif to which critics have not in the past paid any attention, recalls the gleaming face of Mary, Jesus and God in mystery plays. It belongs with a stream of religious allusions, especially to Mary, the Annunciation and the Nativity, and to their popular representation in plays and narratives, which runs through this most irreverent text. Alisoun and Absolon's own interpenetration of sexual preoccupations into religious observance (3307–11, 3339–47), matches this verbal interweaving of religion and sex. The language of love, in this social satire on lower-class pretensions in the successful tradesman class of the period, has a tinsel air, rather like Alisoun's 'latoun'-pearled purse and her over-emphatic, and therefore unladylike, taste in fashion. The cheapness of these provincial young people's charms is, however, perceived through the eyes of a snobbish observer, at home with the highest London modes (certainly not the fictional Miller): Absolon's curly hair and fancy fashions, like his provincial vigour in dancing, are mocked from a narratorial viewpoint that seems, earlier, in the General Prologue, to feel nothing but respectful admiration for the love-lorn Squire's rather similar style. Chaucer here shows himself the conservative member of the princely, courtly, circles in which he was a civil servant and retainer. E. T. Donaldson (1970) pointed to a register of *déclassé* popular love poetry running through the text: words like 'lemman', 'hende', 'derne', 'ore', 'blosme upon the ris'. Some, including 'lemman', overlap with a group of terms which were in process of acquiring negative sexual assocations (examples here include 'wenche' and probably 'pyggesnye', which by the nineteenth century, according to the OED, meant something like a 'floosy'). Words with simultaneous innocent and smutty senses contribute to a recurrent undertow of *double entendre*, seen in the passage in 'spille' and Nicholas's busy figures on his 'sawtrie'. The language of the tale often endorses the celebration of youthful lust that motivates the protagonists: in the description of Alisoun, for example, the image of her mouth, sweet as 'bragot or the meeth', encourages the reader to assent to intoxication, and the comparison with a 'hoord of apples' suggests that her sweetness has been stored up, unappreciated, far too long (recalling Song of Songs 2: 5). Yet much of the comedy of the Miller's Tale is launched from a position of social superiority to the protagonists; the cruelly snobbish calculation of Alisoun's sexual rating as good enough for a lord to bed or a 'good yeman' to marry makes this plain. It is the socially superior and intellectually arrogant clerk, Nicholas, to whom the tale awards the pleasure of Alisoun; in some ways, the tale itself is an amusing and titillating slice of lower-middle-class sitcom served up for the entertainment of upper-class readers.

Despite that, the tale's uncritical enjoyment of sexual pleasure and selfish cunning challenge powerfully the orthodox high-mindedness of the Knight's Tale. Such anomalies as the insistence on reminding the reader of religious values, while disregarding religious sanctions against such activities as it describes, with no attempt to resolve conflicts between the tale's sympathies and orthodox morality, leave the reader to make sense of the phenomenon of sexual lust. And this, in its own way, is analogous to the question raised by *Troilus*, about the significance of passion in a world of mutability and in a philosophy of dualist contempt for the body and emotionality.

See also AUTHORITY; BODIES; CHIVALRY; CHRISTIAN IDEOLOGIES; CRISIS AND DISSENT; ITALY; LIFE HISTORIES; MODES OF REPRESENTATION; OTHER THOUGHT-WORLDS; PERSONAL IDENTITY; VISUALIZING; WOMEN.

NOTES

1   On cultural, economic and political themes in Chaucer's depiction of marriage, see David Aers, *Chaucer, Langland and the Creative Imagination* (London: Routledge & Kegan Paul, 1980), 143–73.

2   Boethius reduces sexual passion to a briefly mentioned, contemptible pleasure of the 'most vile and fragile body' (III, prosa 7, 8), in a world that is only the size of a pinpoint in comparison with the size of the heavens (II, prosa 7).

3   By representing Cupid/Amour/Love as 'Charite', and Venus under the defamiliarizing name Citheria and as a benign planetary conjunction, Chaucer dignifies and desexualizes these two references.

4   The text's precautionary insistence that women actually enjoy being sexually forced is found also in the Reeve's Tale, 4230, 4240–8.

REFERENCES AND FURTHER READING

Aers, David (1980), *Chaucer, Langland and the Creative Imagination* (London: Routledge & Kegan Paul). Undermines many previous assumptions, demonstrating the underlying topicality of both Langland and Chaucer; an exploration of the ideological implications of style.

Benson, Larry D. (1984), 'The *"queynte"* puns of Chaucer's critics', *Studies in the Age of Chaucer: Proceedings* 1, 23–50. Like Donaldson (1970; see below), explores the use of refined language in a bawdy context in the Miller's Tale, arguing that *queynte* still had a courtly and euphemistic sense when applied to the female genital area.

Burnley, David (1979), *Chaucer's Language and the Philosophers' Tradition*, Chaucer Studies 2 (Cambridge: Rowman & Littlefield). Demonstrates the network of philosophical and moral ideas running through much of Chaucer's writing, especially on the themes of kingship, power, moderation and patience.

——(1998) *Courtliness and Medieval Literature* (Harlow: Addison-Wesley-Longman). Probably the best, most wide-ranging and balanced account of the controversial themes associated with the *courtois*.

Donaldson, E. Talbot (1970), 'The idiom of popular poetry in the Miller's Tale', in *Speaking of Chaucer* (London: Athlone), 13–29. Important study of Chaucer's use of a register of romance and courtly love-poetry which, Donaldson suggests, would have sounded hackneyed and stale to sophisticated Londoners by the end of the fourteenth century.

Falconer, William A., ed. and trans. (1928), Cicero, *De officiis, De amicitia, De senectute*, Loeb Classics (London: Methuen). Edition with facing-page translation.

Knight, Stephen (1986) *Geoffrey Chaucer* (Brighton: Harvester). Presents Chaucer as a far from apolitical author and as one who, though he characteristically retreats into conservatism, presents fictionally in the *Canterbury Tales* the English society, and its social, economic and political tensions, that created and followed on from the 1381 rising.

Lewis, C. S. (1936) *The Allegory of Love: A Study*

in Medieval Tradition (London: Oxford University Press; repr. 1958). All later studies of the topic are indebted to this seminal work, however strongly some have questioned its arguments.

Muscatine, Charles (1957), *Chaucer and the French Tradition: A Study in Style and Meaning* (Berkeley, Los Angeles and London: University of California Press). Shows the interplay and conflict of registers and generic expectations, in particular those of fabliau and romance, that characterize much of Chaucer's writing.

Phillips, Helen (2000) *An Introduction to the Canterbury Tales: Reading, Fiction, Context* (Basingstoke: Macmillan). Focuses on Chaucer as a conservative who none the less enacts topical conflict within his style; explores the *Tales* as a series of studies of aspects of the medieval book: authorship, reading and textuality.

Phillips, Helen and Havely, Nicholas, eds (1997) *Chaucer's Dream Poetry* (Harlow: Longman). Editions of the dream narratives with critical studies of each.

Robertson, D. W., Jr (1962) *Preface to Chaucer: Studies in Medieval Perspectives* (Princeton: Princeton University Press, 1960). The single most important book in the 'exegetical' school of criticism, interpreting Chaucer from the perspective of an Augustinian belief that all literature can and should be read as Christian didacticism, either directly or through allegorical exegesis.

——(1968) 'Courtly love as an impediment to the understanding of medieval texts', in *The Meaning of Courtly Love*, ed. F. X. Newman (Princeton: Princeton University Press). Dismantles simplistic assumptions about 'courtly love' from an erudite and trenchantly 'exegetical' position.

Wack, Mary (1986), 'Pandarus, poetry and healing', *Studies in the Age of Chaucer: Proceedings* 2, 127–33. One of several studies of lovesickness by this author.

Windeatt, Barry (1992) *Troilus and Criseyde*, Oxford Guides to Chaucer (Oxford: Clarendon). An edition which provides excellent notes and parallels from Boccaccio.

——ed. (1984) *Troilus and Criseyde* (London: Longman). A full, learned and illuminating study of all aspects of the text.

18

Modes of Representation

Edward Wheatley

Modes of representation are the rhetorical tones and patterns of meaning that inform texts. This chapter surveys five modes of representation in Geoffrey Chaucer's work: allegory, exemplum, satire, parody and realism. To the modern reader these terms may seem too disparate to allow for consideration together; indeed, while the three latter modes above remain popular today, the first two are relatively unimportant in modern discourse. However, in the Middle Ages, not only were all of these modes popular (with the modern favourite, realism, being the least common), but also they often inhabited the same text.

Modes of discourse are not to be confused with genres, because almost any textual example of a genre can be recast in different modes: for example, tragedy can have an allegorical or satirical dimension, comedy can be exemplary or parodic, and romance, though a fantastic, imaginative genre, can draw on realism.

The intersection of modes of representation and genre was important for Chaucer, who generally translated or adapted texts, some of which were widely known and valued as cultural currency in his era. Even if the genres of these texts were well known – for example, Virgil's *Aeneid* as an epic, or the *Roman de la rose* as a vernacular allegory – Chaucer could refashion them into different modes. Indeed, some of Chaucer's most creative work exploits the ironic tension or cognitive dissonance between a source text and the modal manipulations that he exercises upon it. I will discuss his work in relation to its background texts in several parts of this chapter.

Allegory and the Burden of Literary Tradition

Both personification allegory and narrative allegory were held in high esteem in medieval Europe. The former is based on a character who symbolizes and embodies a certain human characteristic and who moves through a dialogue or plot in which that characteristic is demonstrated. In Chaucer's work, the most frequently cited allegorical figure is Fortune, who was based on classical models representing the uncertainty of human destiny; she is iconographically associated with a turning wheel upon which humans rise and fall. Fortune dominates Chaucer's short poem of that title in which a plaintiff legalistically rebukes her cruelty, and she responds that misfortune teaches its victims the difference between truth and falsehood, mutability and stability. She is also central to the seventeen *de casibus* tragedies of the Monk's Tale, some of which border on parody in their drastically abbreviated redactions of the falls of famous people from power.

Fortune is the shadow adversary in the most popular Latin personification allegory of Chaucer's era, the *Consolation of Philosophy* by Boethius (*c.*480–524). A philosophical treatise in allegorical mode, it presents a dialogue between the imprisoned narrator and the personified Lady Philosophy, who teaches him the value of adversity. Chaucer himself translated Boethius' treatise quite closely, and it is the only classical Latin work in the Chaucerian corpus to receive such treatment; clearly Chaucer felt the weight of authority here.

A direct philosophical descendent of Boethius' *Consolation* was Albertanus of Brescia's twelfth-century *Liber consolationi et consilii*, in which a woman named Prudentia counsels her husband Melibeus about proper moral behaviour towards men who have broken into their house and assaulted their daughter. As in the *Consolation*, the allegory remains a vehicle for philosophical teaching rather than a literary end in itself. This work was translated into at least six vernacular languages, and the French translation by Renaud de Louens served as the source for the Tale of Melibee, the prose tale that Chaucer the pilgrim tells after the Host has interrupted the Tale of Sir Thopas. Chaucer added to the source text only an allegorical name for the daughter, Sophie, and a few phrases that contribute little new meaning. Again he seemed to feel constrained by the weight of the didacticism for which allegory was primarily read.

Dominating the French tradition of allegory was the *Roman de la rose*, a long poem begun by Guillaume de Lorris around 1237 and completed by Jean de Meun about forty years later. It comprises both narrative allegory in a dream vision of a young man questing for his beloved, the rose, and personification allegory in the numerous characters with such names as Idleness (Oiseuse), Nature and False-Seeming (Faus Semblant). In the prologue to the *Legend of Good Women*, the God of Love castigates Chaucer the narrator for having translated the ostensibly antifeminist *Rose*, but the surviving Middle English translation attributed to him may be his only partially or not at all.

Although the Middle English *Boece*, Melibee and *Romaunt of the Rose* attest to Chaucer's appreciation of allegory, in his own poetry he favoured the reduction of allegory to the human level. For example, the Old Woman in the *Rose* is adapted as the Wife of Bath, and False-Seeming becomes the Pardoner. In relation to plot, Chaucer often accomplishes this modal modification through the use of a dream-vision framework. For example, the dreamer in the *Parliament of Fowls* is literally pushed into a 'garden of love' populated by personification allegories resembling those in the *Rose*. However, unlike the Boethian narrator of the *Consolation*, Chaucer's narrator remains a detached observer, unable to engage with these characters or the fowls in Dame Nature's court. The *Book of the Duchess*, which allegorizes John of Gaunt's mourning after the death of his wife Blanche, opens with the narrator reading the story of Ceyx and Alcyone from Ovid's *Metamorphoses*; while tacitly encouraging the reader to map this story of the death of a spouse on to the tale of the black knight, whose lover has died, Chaucer thwarts direct allegorical correspondence not only in the grotesque revivification of Ceyx's drowned body but also in the satirical tone of the redaction of the episode from Ovid. The *House of Fame* apparently allegorizes the challenges facing a poet who must negotiate between classical and vernacular subject matter. A golden eagle takes the dreamer Geffrey from the court of the personified Fame (a parodic reincarnation of Boethius' Lady Philosophy), which is decorated with statues of classical and religious authors, to the whirling wicker house of Rumour, where lowly vernacular speech acts take wing and fly out to test themselves at Fame's court. The poem might have become Chaucer's most consistent allegory if he had finished it – but the unfinished state of this relatively early piece may indicate his frustration with the sustained employment of this mode.

With the exception of Melibee, univalent narrative allegory is absent from the *Canterbury Tales*. Even the Nun's Priest's Tale, a beast fable of a cock and a fox, defies conventional fabular simplicity by focusing on a barnyard debate about the predictive power of dreams. Chaucer similarly tempts his readers to find allegorical significance in the two tales with superhuman heroines, the Man of Law's Tale and the Clerk's Tale. Although Custance and Grisilde are mortal, their remarkable spiritual strength, patience and innate wisdom defy logical human limits. Chaucer pushes the tale of Grisilde towards allegory first by having the Clerk compare her patience to Job's (a comparison absent from the source texts; 932–8), and later addding Petrarch's quasi-allegorical moralization of the tale:

> For sith a womman was so pacient
> Unto a mortal man, wel moore us oghte
> Receyven al in gree that God us sent;
> For greet skile is he preeve that he wroghte.
> (1149–52)

This statement, more comparison than interpretation, does not fit the text retrospectively, because Walter is anything but godly. Chaucer further complicates interpretation by adding the Clerk's praise of the Wife of Bath and her 'secte' (1170–2) in an envoy explicitly discouraging wives from remaining as pliable and silent as Grisilde (1177–1212).

Richard Neuse (1991: 103) has described this interpretative impasse as one of the occasions in the *Canterbury Tales* 'when the reader is confronted with a kind of "allegorical crisis", the dilemma or necessity of deciding between a literal and a metaphoric reading . . . [due to] the absence of a formal metaphysical or theological framework that would direct the flow of allegorical meaning and establish a hierarchy of relationships between literal and metaphoric, physical and spiritual, and so forth'. Chaucer fully exploits the ambiguity of his quasi-allegorical texts, implicitly challenging both his original audience and his modern readers to re-examine the sometimes simplistic formulae of interpretation associated with allegory in the Middle Ages.

In the twentieth-century history of Chaucer criticism, one of the most vitriolic debates has centred on whether all of Chaucer's work might have an allegorical dimension. D. W. Robertson Jr's *A Preface to Chaucer*, one of the best-known and most disputed critical monographs of the later twentieth century, claims that serious medieval poetry was based on the Augustinian assumption that all good writing necessarily leads to an interpretation teaching Christian charity. Augustine and other medieval patristic philosophers believed that allegory and figurative language presented pleasurable puzzles to readers who learned more effectively from interpretation requiring intellectual effort. Thus poetry, like Scripture, had a superficial 'husk' or 'shell' concealing the allegorical fruit that benefits perceptive readers. Robertson and the patristic school of critics believed that Chaucer's frequent recourse to biblical allusion and symbolism was the poet's invitation to the reader to engage in pseudo-exegetical allegorical interpretation leading to moral instruction. Opponents of patristic criticism see its precepts as necessarily resulting in reductive readings that rely on 'imposed' allegory that grows out of a reader's response to the text rather than 'intentional' allegory constructed by the author. Patristic criticism has declined in popularity during recent decades, not least because of the less determinist interpretative possibilities that post-structuralism has introduced to academic discourse.

The Exemplum and its Modal Inadequacies

An exemplum is a narrative leading to moral instruction; such tales ornamented medieval sermons, providing narrative instantiations of relevant scriptural lessons. Unlike allegories, in which readers find correspondences between the narrative and an over-arching interpretation, exempla conclude with general, often proverbial interpretations.

Chaucer problematized the telling and reception of exempla in the *Canterbury Tales* by inviting his readers to examine supposedly moral tales in relation to the morality of their narrators. Although St Augustine asserted that any moral message drawn from Christianity would reveal its truth to believers, even if it were voiced by an immoral person, Chaucer seemed less sure. One of the least moral of the Canterbury pilgrims, the Pardoner, tells an exemplum of three rioters who ultimately murder each other for money that they have found; this exemplum elucidates the scriptural text 'Radix malorum est cupiditas' (Greed is the root of evils). However, the morality of the Pardoner's performance is occluded by his honesty about his dishonesty: he preaches about this text as a way of convincing gullible Christians to buy his false relics and inauthentic pardons for their sins. Even if the message of the Pardoner's sermon is incontrovertibly moral from a Christian standpoint, his character causes both readers and other pilgrims – notably the Host – to question or reject its validity in the context that Chaucer has created. Thus the straightforward morality of an exemplum becomes complicated.

The Pardoner's closest cohort in ecclesiastical crime is the Summoner, whose exempla show him to be less self-aware than the Pardoner. In order to avenge himself upon the pilgrim Friar who has told a scurrilous tale about a summoner, the Summoner tells of a friar trying to wheedle contributions out of a sick man, Thomas, in exchange for the mendicant brothers' prayers that the man be restored to health. Thomas responds angrily that the friars' prayers have not proven efficacious, prompting the friar to deliver a series of exempla condemning anger. Nevertheless, Thomas's anger increases to explosive proportions. Thus the Summoner believes himself to have demonstrated the uselessness of exempla in friars' sermons, though in another sense, his satire backfires because the Summoner, telling his tale for wrathful revenge upon the pilgrim Friar, has failed to internalize the message of the exempla that he recounts.

Chaucer brings the power of exemplary literature to bear on his own narratorial persona in the *Legend of Good Women*. In the prologue, Chaucer sees Cupid and Alceste, who chastize the poet for writing more stories of wicked women than good ones. Alceste demands that Chaucer undertake penance by collecting tales of virgins and women who were true in love but betrayed by false men – in effect, exempla of good female behaviour. The poet complies by writing stories of Cleopatra, Dido and others, but perhaps most indicative of the modal imperatives of exemplary literature is the story of Medea (see below). He implies that when moral reading becomes the sole aim of literature, it must necessarily oversimplify complexities of plot and character.

Satire as a Medieval and Modern Mode

At its most basic level, Chaucer's satire is as accessible to modern readers as it was to medieval ones. The *locus classicus* of Chaucerian satire remains the General Prologue of the *Canterbury Tales*; any reader who knows two or three conventional characteristics of a doctor, a nun, a sailor or an oft-remarried woman can see through Chaucer's gimlet eye the ribbing that these pilgrims receive. However, the portraits of the pilgrims also draw upon a particularly medieval type of satire that Jill Mann has discussed in *Chaucer and Medieval Estates Satire*. Mann contextualizes the portrait of each pilgrim within the body of medieval literature that addresses the interests, concerns and foibles conventionally attributed to the pilgrim's class or occupation. The largest body of estates satire relates to corrupt clergy, especially friars, but in comparison to much antifraternal literature, Chaucer's portrait of the pilgrim Friar is relatively gentle in its satire. The poet expanded the anticlerical tradition by satirizing a summoner, whose occupation had not received such malicious attention earlier.

Although the poet–narrator of the *Canterbury Tales* is at least partially a Chaucerian self-portrait, he too becomes the object of the poet's satire, especially when sketching the portraits of the pilgrims. Thus each portrait presents an amalgam of estates satire and Chaucer's satire of his narrator's skewed, myopic perceptions – a satire of the estate of poetic 'maker'. This combination appears most clearly in the portraits of pilgrims whom the narrator admires and whose foibles he willingly excuses. Among these is the Monk, whose portrait is examined below.

Chaucer translates the gentle satire of his own narrator in the General Prologue into his treatment of pilgrim narrators as they tell their tales; both Chaucer the narrator and his pilgrim companions show a lack of self-awareness that results in dramatic irony. For example, the Knight remains consistently befuddled by the opacity of his characters' pagan beliefs; when Arcite dies, the Knight says, 'His spirit chaunged hous and wente ther, / As I cam nevere, I kan nat tellen wher' (KnT 2809–10); he goes on to add bluntly, 'Arcite is coold, ther Mars his soule gye!' (2815). The narrator's matter-of-fact acknowledgement of his own ignorance is humorously incongruous with the conventional emotions associated with the death of a young hero. Similarly, the Knight's son, the Squire, becomes the butt of Chaucer's satire for his concomitant emphasis on the craft of storytelling and apparent inability to construct a cohesive tale of reasonable length.

Within their tales, pilgrim narrators often satirize characters resembling other pilgrims towards whom the narrators have developed rivalry or antipathy. For example, we have seen the Summoner's biting depiction of the friar, a direct response to the pilgrim Friar's satire of a summoner in his tale. The Reeve aims his satirical barbs at the central character of his tale, a dishonest miller, as a direct response to the Miller's tale about a carpenter, which happens to be the trade of the Reeve. Unique among the narrators who satirize their characters is the Merchant, whose aged, self-deluding January, blindly intent on marrying a young woman, reflects the Merchant himself, who bemoans his unhappiness as a newlywed in his prologue (1213–39). In this instance the narrator's satirical self-awareness largely displaces any satire by Chaucer the poet: an author does not need to deflate a character who deflates himself.

Among Chaucer's numerous satires of courtly love, 'To Rosemounde' features the Chaucerian persona describing his love with a comically inept comparison: 'Nas never pyk walwed in galauntyne / As I in love am walwed and ywounde'. The image of a fish profoundly immersed in galantine sauce seems best suited for whetting appetites other than amatory. The satire of courtly love appears in fuller form in such Canterbury tales as those told by the Knight, the Miller and the Franklin, and in several other major poems (e.g. the *Book of the Duchess* and the *Parliament of Fowls*). However, Chaucer exploits this satire most completely in *Troilus and Criseyde*. Troilus himself derides love and its 'folye' as he witnesses its excesses among the revellers at the very festival where he sees and falls madly in love with Criseyde. His feeling for Criseyde ultimately becomes so debilitating that as the carefully arranged moment of consummation approaches, he faints (III, 1086–92).

It is hardly an over-statement to assert that elements of satire appear in nearly every major poem written by Chaucer; the only works that avoid it focus on religion and didacticism, such as the Second Nun's Tale, the Tale of Melibee and the Parson's Tale.

Parody and Medieval Genres

Parody represents the least sincere form of literary flattery, though it flatters never-theless: it requires that readers know and understand the work or genre that an author chooses to parody, so even as it inverts or debases its source text, it tacitly acknowl-edges that text's cultural significance.

Chaucer's best-known parody is recounted by his own pilgrim persona: the Tale of Sir Thopas effectively lampoons popular chivalric romance for both its form and its content. The hero exhausts himself by merely riding his horse, he runs aways from the giant Oliphant rather than bravely engaging in battle, and he wears dandified armour more suitable for pageantry than combat. Significantly, however, the Host silences Chaucer not for the mishandled subject matter but for the 'drasty rymyng' (Th 930). The stylistic blunders that the Host reviles relate to the tale-teller's mis-handling of conventional English romance verse forms such as the six-line tail-rhyme stanza that begins Thopas and the single-stress 'bob' line that punctures later stanzas. Equally parodic of the oral craft of minstrels are the numerous metrical tags and fillers ('it is no nay', 'par ma fay', 'par charitee') with which the tale mockingly echoes a style for which Chaucer had little appreciation.

Another romance, the Knight's Tale, briefly parodies yet another verse form associated with Middle English romance, the alliterative line. This stylistic survival from Old English employs alliterating stressed syllables instead of rhyme as the organizing principle for each line. Chaucer uses alliterative verse in the highly chivalric setting of the tournament between the groups led by Palamoun and Arcite:

> There shyveren shaftes upon sheeldes thikke;
> He feeleth thurgh the herte-spoon the prikke.
> Up spryngen speres twenty foot on highte;
> Out goon the swerdes as the silver brighte;
> The helmes they tohewen and toshrede;
> Out brest the blood with stierne stremes rede;
> With mighty maces the bones they tobreste.
> He thurgh the thikkeste of the throng gan threste;
> Ther stomblen steedes strong, and doun gooth al . . .
> (2605–13)

In a sense Chaucer belittles the alliterative line by managing a convincing (though not entirely consistent) mimicry of it while retaining the decasyllabic couplets.

Chaucer's parodies of genres and associated styles inform other works as well. The Nun's Priest's Tale, for example, presents an amalgam of beast fable and mock-epic, humorously aggrandizing barnyard animals by means of comparisons to such epics as the *Aeneid* and the *Song of Roland*. Although the seventeen tragedies comprising the Monk's Tale belong to the *de casibus* sub-genre popular in the Middle Ages, their extreme abbreviation may represent a Chaucerian parody, a *reductio ad absurdum* that in some cases prevents readers from engaging with one story before the next displaces it.

Although Chaucer apparently favoured the generic types of parody described above, he turned to parody of a specific text for his early dream vision, the *House of Fame*. Here the poet Geffrey, in search of suitable subject matter, is borne aloft by a talking eagle that resembles the eagle that performs a similar service for the pilgrim Dante in Purgatorio IX of the *Divine Comedy*. Suggesting a further parodic revision of Dante's spiritual voyage, the *House of Fame* centres on a poet–pilgrim in need of education. However, given the fact that Dante was practically unknown in the England of Chaucer's day, this parody may not have been recognized by Chaucer's contemporaries.

Realism and its Discontents

Modern readers with a set notion of what constitutes 'realism' are unaccustomed to applying that literary mode to poetry in general, and to medieval poetry in particular. The medieval aesthetic prized artifice over realism, and medieval writers favoured romance ideals of heroism, adventure and fantasy over attempts to depict the world 'as it was'. Indeed, since medieval Christianity stressed the mutability and transience of the world, why did that world deserve a realistic rendering in literature?

I would argue that all four of the popular medieval modes of representation discussed above are essentially unrealistic. Allegory may reflect aspects of 'real' human experience, but the understanding of that reality comes from generalized interpretation by the reader, not 'realistic' characterization or description by the author. While an exemplum may have overtones of realism, its modal requirement of a moral conclusion necessitates narrative closure that is antithetical to realism. In order for readers to recognize satire, the author must present an unrealistic world in which she amplifies and implicitly criticizes the unfavourable character traits and corrupt institutions that are her satirical targets. And parody, as defined above, is art satirizing art, two steps away from reality.

What Chaucer offers instead of sustained realist treatments of society and psychology are intermittent moments of realism that he often adds to his source texts. These moments tend to be those in which he confronts ugliness, unpleasantness or anguish, since more positive emotions and experiences tend to resemble the idealized moments of high romance.

Readers new to Chaucer's work often appreciate what they identify as the 'realistic' descriptions of the pilgrims in the General Prologue of the *Canterbury Tales*. Certainly Chaucer's attention to the Clerk's emaciation, the Wife of Bath's hearing impairment, the Miller's warty nose and the Summoner's skin diseases reminds us of how imperfect humans are in reality. But while these character traits and others clearly have a realistic dimension, some of them – for example, the Clerk's slenderness – were conventions of estates satire, and others – such as the Summoner's bad complexion – bespoke a very different 'reality' to medieval people (who believed that certain leprous skin diseases were related to syphilis). These issues indicate a paradox: in spite of its name, 'realism' is not the same for all people in all times and places. Rather, it is constructed by the experience and knowledge that is most taken for granted in a given time, place and culture.

The Wife of Bath's deafness relates to another instance of realism for which Chaucer's work is prized in the late twentieth century: his description of power struggles within marriage. The Wife's fifth husband, Jankyn, has deafened her by striking her on the ear after she has torn three leaves from his 'book of wicked wives' (WBP 634–6, 788–99). But as the Wife describes the constant negotiation and frequent discord that typify her marriages, she is also citing a plethora of authorities on the institution drawn from a remarkable variety of sources – pagan and Christian, ancient and contemporary. These *auctoritates* recast the Wife's experiences within marriage as exempla in a scholastic examination of the virtues of marriage: 'realistic' moments punctuate her prologue instead of providing a foundation for it.

The Canon's Yeoman's Prologue and Tale offer Chaucer's most sustained effort in realism of physical detail. Chaucer's modal choice here fits his subject matter well, since the tale-teller's goal is to debunk the false ideals of alchemy, the attempt to transform base metals into gold. The Canon's Yeoman and his master gallop from behind to join the pilgrims who have departed days earlier from the Tabard Inn: the Canon's horse, over-exerted to the degree that foam stands around his collar (564), 'So swatte that it wonder was to see' (560) and 'So swatte that unnethe myghte it gon' (563). The narrator compares the dripping of the Canon's sweaty forehead to the process of distillation (580), a simile that anticipates the tale of scientific processes of transformation. The realistic emphasis on the physicality of sweat here contrasts with its idealized absence from the previous tale, the Second Nun's life of Saint Cecilia, whose martyrdom includes twenty-four hours in a boiling bath that 'made hire nat a drope for to sweete' (522).

As if to prepare his reader for the generic shift from a saint's life to a tale of deceit, Chaucer structures the Canon's Yeoman's Prologue around a radical shift in mode. At first, the Yeoman hyperbolically praises the cleverness and wealth of his alchemist master; however, when the suspicious Host asks the Yeoman why the rich man is dressed so poorly, the Yeoman begins to reveal the Canon's quackery. In spite of the Canon's scolding, the Yeoman vows to continue to tell the truth, and the Canon flees 'for verray sorwe and shame' (702). His departure having opened the field for truth-telling, the Canon's Yeoman recounts a tale of a cozening canon who uses sleight of hand with alchemical equipment to dupe a priest out of forty pounds. Interestingly, the Canon's Yeoman emphasizes that the canon in his tale is not his recently departed master. Thus, within the fiction of the pilgrimage framework, the audience must understand the tale as a realist fiction of the narrator's own making, instead of detailed reportage of events in his master's laboratory. Chaucer's evocation of the gritty, smoky, sweaty atmosphere of a medieval alchemist's work is so realistic that in the fifteenth century it earned him the reputation of having been an alchemist himself (*Riverside Chaucer*, 948).

Satire in the Monk's Portrait: General Prologue, 165–207

In one of the longest portraits in the General Prologue, that of the Monk, Chaucer the poet satirizes both the pilgrim and the narrator who describes him. The narrator indicates the Monk's lack of interest in religion almost immediately.

> A Monk there was, a fair for the maistrie,
> An outridere, that lovede venerie,
> A manly man, to been an abbot able.
> (165–7)

The Monk's primary interest, hunting, shows that he is not as concerned with religion as he should be; however, the attention to the Monk's fine, masculine appearance betrays the narrator's equal lack of interest in the Monk's spirituality. Chaucer structures this sentence so that the Monk's ability to serve as an abbot appears only as an afterthought on the narrator's part.

After praising the quality of the Monk's horses and the merry sound of the bells on his bridle, the narrator returns to the subject of monasticism.

> The reule of Seint Maure or of Seint Beneit –
> By cause that it was old and somdel streit
> This ilke Monk leet olde thynges pace,
> And heeld after the newe world the space.
> He yaf nat of that text a pulled hen,
> That seith that hunters ben nat hooly men,
> Ne that a monk, whan he is recchelees,
> Is likned til a fissh that is waterlees –
> This is to seyn, a monk out of his cloystre.
> But thilke text heeld he nat worth an oystre;
> And I seyde his opinion was good.
> What sholde he studie and make hymselven wood,
> Upon a book in cloystre alwey to poure,
> Or swynken with his handes, and laboure,
> As Austyn bit? How shal the world be served?
> Lat Austyn have his swynk to hym reserved!
> (173–88)

The Monk eschews the Benedictine rule because of its age and strictness. The narrator explains the Monk's preference in terms of an interest in 'the newe world', although temporal fashions should not attract clerics. The monastic rule forbidding monks to leave the monastery would naturally forbid hunting, but this Monk would give neither a plucked hen nor an oyster for the venerable edict. Thus the narrator alludes to the Monk's interest in food, again at odds with the austere life that he should lead. Chaucer satirizes the narrator for praising the Monk's refusal to be rule-bound, since the narrator is not qualified to offer an opinion in such matters. The reader also senses that the narrator is working harder than he should to ingratiate himself with the Monk. Chaucer the poet then has the narrator raise – and miss – the important point that the study and labour of monks are not meant to serve the world, but rather to serve God.

Having rendered unto Augustine what was Augustine's, the Monk is free to engage fully in hunting in a stylish manner suited to the bourgeoisie or aristocracy:

> Therfore he was a prikasour aright:
> Grehoundes he hadde as swift as fowel in flight;
> Of prikyng and of hunting for the hare
> Was al his lust, for no cost wolde he spare.
> I seigh his sleves purfiled at the hond
> With grys, and that the fyneste of a lond;
> And for to festne his hood under hys chyn,
> He hadde of gold ywroght a ful curious pyn;
> A love-knotte in the gretter ende ther was.
> His heed was balled, that shoon as any glas,
> And eek his face, as he hadde been enoynt.
> He was a lord ful fat and in good poynt;
> His eyen steepe, and rollynge in his heed,
> That stemed as a forneys of a leed;
> His bootes souple, his hors in greet estaat.
>   (189–203)

The Monk's expenditures on the accoutrements of hunting add a satirical dimension to the portrait, again betraying his love of luxury. His expensive tastes are reiterated in the description of his fur-lined sleeves, gold cloak pin and supple boots. The love-knot in the Monk's pin deepens the satire: a man so apathetic toward monastic rules might also be lax in observing rules relating to chastity.

The narrator keeps himself before the reader with the phrase 'I seigh' (193), and his somewhat voyeuristic tone continues through the portrait's final lines.

> Now certeinly he was a fair prelaat;
> He was nat pale as a forpyned goost.
> A fat swan loved he best of any roost.
> His palfrey was as broun as is a berye.
>   (204–7)

Again the narrator emphasizes the Monk's physical appearance, praising him for being fair while undermining the observation by reminding the reader that rule-bound monks are conventionally pale and ghostly. The Monk's favourite roast, a 'fat swan', reminds us of the scornful remark about the plucked hen earlier: mere chicken is beneath contempt when one aspires to swan on the table. The reader might also ask how the narrator has learned about the Monk's preferred poultry: has the Monk told the narrator about it, or have the pilgrims seen the Monk merrily tucking in to a fat swan breast? Either reading contributes to the satire.

This overview of satire in the Monk's portrait is based on a handful of verbal cues and rudimentary knowledge of how monks should behave; readers who would like to understand the full breadth of Chaucer's satire in its historical context should consult Mann's *Chaucer and Medieval Estates Satire* (1973), which devotes twenty pages to an historically informed interpretation of the portrait.

The Exemplary Tale of Medea: The *Legend of Good Women*, 1662–79

The *Legend of Good Women* presents a particularly fruitful field for exploring the exemplary mode as Chaucer understood it, for the narrator Chaucer here has been instructed by Alceste to atone for his works about faithless women by writing about faithful ones betrayed by fickle men. These stories thus become the exemplary literature that the Chaucerian narrator should internalize in order to understand proper, moral behaviour.

After recounting Jason's desertion of Hypsipyle, Chaucer describes the hero's arrival at the court of Medea's father, King Aeetes. Having fallen in love with Jason, Medea predicts danger for him in procuring the Golden Fleece, danger that her magic can prevent; he agrees to accept her magical aid and to marry her. Jason wins the fleece but betrays his helper by taking a third wife, leaving Medea behind with 'his yonge children two' (1657). The narrative closes as follows:

> This is the mede of lovynge and guerdoun
> That Medea receyved of Jasoun
> Ryght for hire trouthe and for hire kyndenesse,
> That lovede hym beter than hireself, I gesse,
> And lafte hire fader and hire herytage.
> And of Jason this is the vassellage,
> That in his dayes nas ther non yfounde
> So fals a lovere goinge on the grounde.
> And therfore in hire letter thus she seyde
> Fyrst, whan she of his falsnesse hym upbreyde:
> 'Whi lykede me thy yelwe her to se
> More than the boundes of myn honeste?

> Why lykede me thy youthe and thy fayrnesse,
> And of thy tonge, the infynyt graciousnesse?
> O, haddest thow in thy conquest ded ybe,
> Ful mikel untrouthe hadde ther deyd with the!'
> Wel can Ovyde hire letter in vers endyte,
> Which were as now to long for me to wryte.
>
> (1662–79)

The summative moralization in the first lines of this verse paragraph is typical of exemplum: it emphasizes Medea's misfortune and Jason's betrayal as moral lessons to be gleaned from the story. The heroine also sums up her mistake as she perceives it, adding another dimension to the moral message.

The final couplet of this passage names one of Chaucer's source texts for this and other legends: Ovid's *Heroides*, letters from classical heroines to their lovers. Since Ovid's Medea writes the letter between the time of Jason's departure and the infanticides, the poem does not directly mention the murders, but any reader familiar with Medea's story will understand the foreshadowing in such lines as 'Whither my ire leads, I will follow', and 'Something portentous, surely, is working in my soul!' The other Ovidian text from which Chaucer drew material here, the *Metamorphoses*, mentions the murders outright (VII, 30), and Chaucer could have relied on many readers using their knowledge of this popular text to flesh out his version of Medea's story.

In order to make an exemplum of proper female behaviour from the story of Medea, Chaucer edited the story radically by emphasizing her helpful magic arts and ignoring her crime, thus erasing much of the literary history of the story. But where does this modal refashioning leave Chaucer the poet? If, as seems likely, he knew that his readers would be able to complete the story of Medea, then he is using dramatic irony to undermine his narrator's project: in this instance, the goal of praising female virtue is destined to fail, because Medea is not remembered primarily for her virtue. If the request of Cupid and Alceste represents an allegorization of a similar demand from Chaucer's readers for him to focus on positive examples of womanhood, then Chaucer is effectively problematizing the issue here by indicating that even relatively villainous literary figures can be recast as virtuous.

Realism in the Franklin's Tale, 1474–84

If the Wife of Bath's Prologue analyses marriage in scholastic terms, the Franklin's Tale examines it against the ideals of courtly love. Before Arveragus and Dorigen marry, they come to an agreement about the dynamics of power in their relationship: he will neither take 'maistrie' upon himself nor show jealousy, but for the sake of their social status he will maintain the appearance of sovereignty outside the domestic sphere. In return for his generosity, she swears never to cause conflicts between them

(729–60). It is no surprise that such an idealistic agreement should fail, and Chaucer shatters it in a moment of considerable psychological realism that does not appear in his primary source and analogue, respectively Giovanni Boccaccio's *Il Filocolo* and *Decameron* 10. 5. When Dorigen reports to her husband that the terms of her rash promise to Aurelius have been fulfilled and that she must have sex with him in order to keep her part of the agreement, Arveragus introduces his response in the idealistic fashion that informs his relationship with his spouse, but then he breaks down in genuine anguish:

> This housbonde, with glad chiere, in freendly wyse
> Answerde and seyde as I shal yow devyse:
> 'Is ther oght elles, Dorigen, but this?'
> 'Nay, nay,' quod she, 'God help me so as wys!
> This is to muche, and it were Goddes wille.'
> 'Ye, wyf,' quod he, 'lat slepen that is stille.
> It may be wel, paraventure, yet to day.
> Ye shul youre trouthe holden, by my fay!
> For God so wisly have mercy upon me,
> I hadde wel levere ystiked for to be
> For verray love which that I to you have,
> But if ye sholde youre trouthe kepe and save.
> Trouthe is the hyeste thyng that man may kepe' –
> But with that word he brast anon to wepe,
> And seyde, 'I you forbede, up peyne of deeth,
> That nevere, whil thee lasteth lyf ne breeth,
> To no wight telle thou of this aventure –
> As I may best, I wol my wo endure . . .'
> (1474–84)

In neither of Boccaccio's versions of the tale does the husband show anguish or rage: those characters remain uncomfortably idealized models of propriety as they urge their wives to fulfil their promises, in a manner similar to Arveragus' in the first lines of his response. Chaucer, however, has created a realistic moment at which Arveragus realizes the unreasonable price that must be paid if he and his wife are to live according to an absolutist conception of 'trouthe'. And Arveragus shows further realism by responding to his powerlessness by appropriating power over his wife in two ways. First, his imperious tone ('I yow forbede') represents an assumption of the 'maistrie' over his wife that he forswore in their marriage agreement, and second, he threatens her with the most dire appropriation of power over her: he will kill her if she divulges her secret liaison to anyone.

Furthermore, Arveragus' distraught response works retroactively to make his initially sanguine demeanour seem more realistic than it does in the Italian source texts. In Boccaccio's versions the Arveragus figure's consistent idealism makes him a one-dimensional character and causes the reader to focus on the Dorigen character's moral dilemma. This contrast helps us to see that Chaucer's Arveragus feigns contented non-chalance because he is clinging for as long as possible to the unattainable ideals upon which he and Dorigen have based their marriage. His bluff question of whether com-mitting adultery is all that Dorigen has on her mind takes on a tone of desperation as he sees the nature of his marriage change utterly. The attention to Arveragus' stake in the rash promise is consistent with Chaucer's addition of the couple's marriage agreement to his version of the tale; that agreement is completely absent from Boccaccio's texts.

See also AUTHORITY; COMEDY; CONTEMPORARY ENGLISH WRITERS; FRANCE; GENRE; ITALY; LIFE HISTORIES; LOVE; NARRATIVE; SOCIAL STRUCTURES; STYLE; TRANSLATION.

REFERENCES AND FURTHER READING

Fichte, Jörg O. (1993) 'Images of Arthurian litera-ture reflected in Chaucer's poetry', *Archiv für das Studium der neueren Sprachen und Literaturen* 230, 52–61. Fichte establishes the larger social and literary contexts of Chaucer's parodic use of Arthurian literature by distinguishing among pretext, intertext and the text itself. He con-cludes that Chaucer's main parodic target in Sir Thopas was the tail-rhyme romance, which was no longer appreciated in the late fourteenth century.

Kooper, E. S. (1984) 'Inverted images in Chaucer's Tale of Sir Thopas', *Studia Neophilologica* 56, 147–54. Kooper bases this discussion of Chaucer's parody on the assertion in medieval lapidaries that the topaz (for which 'thopas' is a variant spelling) has the property of reflecting images upside-down like a concave mirror. The article examines a number of inversions, includ-ing the tale's parodic connection to the preced-ing tale told by the Prioress, and the following one, Melibee.

Leicester, H. Marshall, Jr (1990) 'Structure as deconstruction: Chaucer and estates satire in the General Prologue, or reading Chaucer as a prologue to the history of disenchantment', *Exemplaria* 2, 241–61. Leicester uses post-structuralist theory and its foundation upon what he calls 'disenchantment' to reread Mann's book (see below). He asserts that the General Prologue 'challenges the traditional assumptions of estates satire . . . , in the mode

of deconstruction: by enacting or miming traditional classifications themselves in such a way as gradually to bring out the tensions and contradictions that underlie and constitute them' (255).

Mann, Jill (1973) *Chaucer and Medieval Estates Satire: The Literature of Social Class and the General Prologue to the* Canterbury Tales (Cam-bridge: Cambridge University Press). Mann dis-cusses each Canterbury pilgrim's portrait in relation to the medieval satirical literature that addressed various estates. This book remains the most comprehensive study of Chaucer's satire in its historical context.

Neuse, Richard (1991) *Chaucer's Dante: Allegory and Epic Theater in the* Canterbury Tales (Berke-ley: University of California Press). Neuse exam-ines the affinities between the *Divine Comedy* and Chaucer's tales, arguing that as spiritual autobi-ography, the works move beyond the medieval allegory to early humanist concerns.

Rigby, S. H. (1996) *Chaucer in Context: Society, Alle-gory, and Gender* (Manchester and New York: Manchester University Press). Rigby, an histo-rian, discusses contemporary critical approaches to the works of Chaucer in order to 'provide an assessment of competing perspectives'. Readers interested in allegory will appreciate his rehearsal of the conflict between allegorical and 'humanist' interpretation.

Robertson, D. W., Jr (1962) *A Preface to Chaucer: Studies in Medieval Perspectives* (Princeton: Princeton University Press). Although Robertson's ideas about the pervasiveness of allegory in Chaucer's work are considered extreme by most modern scholars, he provides helpful historical information about medieval allegoresis.

Russell, J. Stephen, ed. (1988) *Allegoresis: The Craft of Allegory in Medieval Literature* (New York: Garland). This collection of essays includes recent theoretically informed approaches that take allegorical reading beyond patristic criticism. Particularly helpful are Julia Bolton Holloway's 'The Pilgrim in the Poem: Dante, Langland, and Chaucer' and the editor's 'A Seme in the Integument: Allegory in the *Hous of Fame*'.

Scanlon, Larry (1994) *Narrative, Authority, and Power: The Medieval Exemplum and the Chaucerian Tradition*, Cambridge Studies in Medieval Literature 20 (Cambridge: Cambridge University Press). Defining exemplum as 'narrative enactment of cultural authority', this excellent study contextualizes the *Canterbury Tales* and works by other authors in relation to both sermon exempla and exempla relating to government. Scanlon examines the ways that this mode of representation achieved authority in the emerging vernacular literature of the late fourteenth and early fifteenth centuries.

Walker, Denis (1985) 'The psychological realism of fictional characters', *Neuphilologische Mitteilungen* 86, 337–42. Walker cautions against treating characters in the *Canterbury Tales* as if they were fully realized historical figures with psychological histories beyond the verbal construction of Chaucer's poem.

Wimsatt, James I. (1979) 'Realism in *Troilus and Criseyde* and the *Roman de la Rose*', in *Essays on Troilus and Criseyde*, ed. Mary Salu (Cambridge: Brewer), 43–56. Wimsatt asserts that *Troilus and Criseyde* exemplifies realism in 'circumstantial detail, unidealized incident, psychological interaction, and a love story that unfolds according to a common and natural pattern' (43). He traces these elements to the so-called 'cosmic allegories' of various Latin writers and to the *Pamphilus* and the *Roman de la rose*.

19
Narrative
Robert R. Edwards

Narrative technique refers to the strategies and aesthetic devices used by writers to convey their stories. Technique occasionally serves as an authorial signature (as for example in James Joyce's stream-of-consciousness), but it is usually regarded as a formal aspect of literary discourse. Consequently, it tends to be analysed apart from historical and cultural contexts. Its chief elements – structure, characterization, viewpoint, setting and verbal complexity – are treated as features of storytelling directly available to all writers and accepted by all readers. Chaucer's narrative technique is broadly formal in this sense, yet it remains deeply embedded in a historical context and literary tradition. His strategies and particular devices have their roots in medieval poetic and rhetorical theory, in the techniques of classical and vernacular authors, and in the sources from which he draws his stories. Chaucer's achievement is to employ these resources within a distinctive and fully realized artistic vision that sketches richly imagined fictional worlds while complicating what they mean and how we might understand them. In other words, his narrative art draws from the conventions and practices of his age but is not reducible to them. Moreover, Chaucer, like his best English contemporaries and European counterparts, uses technique thematically to express symbolic meaning and reflect on the nature of his art.

Past Approaches

Like Chaucer's narrative technique, discussion of his craft has a history and context. Renaissance readers, building on the sense of Chaucer established by John Lydgate (c.1370–1449/50), Thomas Hoccleve (c.1368/69–1426), and other fifteenth-century self-appointed literary disciples, valued Chaucer as a rhetorician who embellished the language and established English as a worthy counterpart to classical languages and Dante's 'illustrious vernacular'. They saw him chiefly as a master of linguistic ornament and style, features of technique they regarded as largely extrinsic to the imaginative centre of narrative. As Derek Brewer points out in his judicious surveys of Chaucer's reception, it is John Dryden, arguably the first professional writer in a modern sense, who establishes Chaucer's reputation as a literary craftsman working to create fictional realms that writers and readers in other ages could immediately recognize. Dryden identifies Chaucer, with Boccaccio, as a writer of 'Novels' (short stories), and his emphasis falls particularly on Chaucer's skill in characterization ('Manners'), hence on a dramatic principle in the *Canterbury Tales*: the pilgrims stand imaginatively before Dryden just as if he had joined their company at the Tabard. Dryden's further observation that 'Chaucer follow'd Nature every where, but was never so bold to go beyond her' (Brewer 1978: i, 164) stands at the head of two centuries of commentary on Chaucer's capacity to represent his age and its social world realistically (Brewer 1966: 259).

In modern criticism, interest in Chaucer's skill with narrative and storytelling divides into several phases, each with its own assumptions about literature. Nineteenth- and early twentieth-century critics share a tradition of genteel appreciation which emphasizes Chaucer's realism in depicting character, landscape and social conditions. With the professionalization of literary studies and the interpretative technology of the New Criticism, Chaucer's narratives are studied for their formal patterns and verbal nuance; to analyse Chaucer's technique means simultaneously to describe formal effects and to advance the claim, tacitly or overtly, that medieval poems satisfy the evaluative standards applied to texts from other periods. In recent decades, narrative technique has been a useful approach for scholars and critics interested in historical, feminist and ideological concerns; for the study of technique offers a way of answering the essential questions of contemporary revisionist reading: who is speaking for whom and to what purpose? Narrative technique is now as much an issue of the politics of representation as of Chaucer's verbal artistry.

Voicing Events

Narrative requires, at a minimum, a sequence of events and a speaker or voice to describe them. Implicitly, it requires as well a structural transformation in events (reversal, repetition, crisis and resolution, parallels, contrasts) and an internal hermeneutic, whether moralizing, ironic or consciously ambiguous. Medieval poetics, based on the precepts of classical rhetoric, distinguished between natural and artificial order in the sequence of narrative events. Poets could recount their stories in chronological sequence from beginning to end, or in a structure of their own devising that might begin in the middle or at the end; in addition, they could open at any of these three positions with a *sententia* (maxim) or *exemplum* (historical case with the authority named). In a form like the dream vision, the prevailing fiction is that the narrator recounts his adventures in the sequence in which they occurred or, more precisely, in which he supposedly remembers them. The *Parliament of Fowls* follows the natural order of recollection but begins with a *sententia* ('The lyf so short, the craft so long to lerne') that seems to evoke a commonplace about art but refers instead to love, the theme of the poem. Romance and fabliau, by contrast, frequently depend on artificial structures of balance and repetition, with independent but finally converging lines of action. The narrative proper of *Troilus and Criseyde*, for instance, begins in the middle of the larger Troy story, with Calkas' defection to the Greeks. Whatever the genre, topic or mode (realistic, symbolic, allegorical or psychological), Chaucer's narrative presents action as a carefully articulated series of discrete units or episodes linked by emphatically marked transitional devices, such as the following transition in the Knight's Tale: 'And in this blisse lete I now Arcite, / And speke I wole of Palamon a lite' (1449–50).

The complement to devising a narrative sequence and giving it a significant form is the voice of a speaker conveying the story. Medieval rhetoricians, following classical tradition, distinguished the so-called 'narrative' voice of a poet addressing his audience and telling his story both from the 'dramatic' voices of characters speaking directly for themselves and from a 'mixed' form in which the voices of the author and characters alternate. The sources for Chaucer's narrative voice lie closer, however, to his own age in the practice of his contemporaries and vernacular predecessors. The *Roman de la Rose*, which Chaucer translated early in his career and echoed throughout his writing, establishes its narrator as a centre of action and meaning, a locus of consciousness through which we simultaneously learn the story and form judgements about it and the figure recounting it. The lyric–narrative *dits amoreux* of Guillaume de Machaut, which served Chaucer as early poetic sources, accentuate the focus on the narrator as a device and subject of storytelling. Boethius' *Consolation of Philosophy*, a work Chaucer translated in mid-career but encountered earlier in the *Rose*, maps an internal trajectory of understanding and self-awareness in its colloquy between master and disciple. In Dante, Chaucer discovered the conception of a narrator who is grounded in his own historical moment yet able to negotiate the confrontation of classical and Christian culture. In his *Confessio Amantis*, Chaucer's friend John Gower fashions himself as a fictive Lover (61 gloss) led through penitential dialogue and exempla to a decisive self-recognition.

Narrators, Invention and Disposition

The defining feature of Chaucer's narrative technique is the literary dialectic between mimetic representation and the narrator's self-presentation and performance. A sense of action – of characters doing things or experiencing them through language – informs stories that range from dreams recalled to tales of love and war in the ancient world, moral exempla, allegories, fables, saints' legends and sexual comedy. Even in his fragmentary narratives (the *House of Fame*, *Anelida and Arcite*, and the tales of the Cook, Squire and Sir Thopas in the *Canterbury Tales*), Chaucer conveys a sense of action developed through a succession of episodes, though the direction is more evident in some than others (Edmund Spenser 'completed' the last two, which are the most problematic from a technical standpoint). Yet in all the stories, Chaucer's narrator is the shaping force of storytelling. Twentieth-century critics have debated how one might differentiate the historical Chaucer of London and Westminster (Chaucer the man) from the artist who creates the narrative fictions (Chaucer the poet) and the character who recounts the story (Chaucer the narrator); most would allow some overlap or uncertainty among the roles, especially in their potential for comedy and irony. What remains clear is that the 'I' of the poem is an essential part of Chaucer's technique of storytelling, above all in the complex modulation of tone. Only in an experimental work like *Anelida* and an exemplary 'legend' like Cleopatra's (*LGW* 580–705) does the narrator recede in significant measure behind action, though his descriptive and interpretative presence is still evident.

The narratives that Chaucer recounts through this dialectic of imitation and performance are, in almost every instance, stories that he discovered ('invented') in other writers. Medieval poetics furnished a conceptual framework for rewriting these antecedent texts and thereby made technique an issue from the very outset of literary composition. The most important step in the process is the initial phase of invention, in which the poet imagines an abstract plan or idea (*archetypus*) for his work. The thirteenth-century rhetorician Geoffrey of Vinsauf, in a passage Chaucer incorporates and parodies in *Troilus and Criseyde* (I, 1065–71), likens invention to an architectural design for a house and urges that the interior compass of the mind first circumscribe its subject matter. For material already put into verse, poetic theory offered specific protocols of invention. Geoffrey advises elsewhere that the new work not follow its predecessor slavishly, retracing its footsteps or reproducing its speech, but look instead for areas of expression that remained unexploited in its source. The poetic *matere* discovered through invention thus depends on a critical understanding and aesthetic reconception of the poet's sources.

The work that emerges from this textual engagement takes actual form through disposition, the arrangement of parts in a coherent literary structure. Geoffrey of Vinsauf envisions this arrangement as a pathway with a natural or artificial beginning and subsequent development modulated by amplification or abbreviation, the techniques of elaborating or condensing material. The highly articulated quality of Chaucer's narratives – their clear division into discrete units with prominent transitional devices joining them – reflect this concern with the concrete embodiment of an abstract plan of composition. Here, in the mysterious transit from invention to disposition, narrative moves from idea to story. To some extent, such modulation is inherent in a well-shaped narrative plot. The narrator of *Troilus and Criseyde* remarks that it would be 'a long thyng' (III, 495) and a strange poetic practice if he reported everything Troilus said to Criseyde, and John Burrow (1982: 74–5) rightly notes that Chaucer, like other courtly poets of the age, invests the small details of social life and personal exchanges with special meaning by enlarging their scale within the narrative. At a stylistic level, rhetorical colours, particularly figures of diction and thought, support this redistribution of the source narrative into a new structure. Metaphor, simile, images, rhetorical questions and digressions, dialogue and interpretation help give texture to action. On occasion, Chaucer uses these figures to thematize narrative technique. *Occupatio*, which allows a speaker to describe scenes and events while claiming that he does not have time for an adequate description, becomes as much a signature of Chaucerian narrative as the first-person narrator. In the Squire's Tale, the frantic accumulation of self-reflective narrative devices dramatizes the failure of authorial invention and disposition in contrast to the Knight's rhetorical control.

Structure

Invention and disposition provide, then, historical and analytical categories for understanding the narrative patterns that underlie Chaucer's work. Among modern critics, Robert Payne (1963: 115) finds three major structural models in Chaucer's poetry: 'combinative structures', as in the dream visions, which connect the elements of old books, experience and dreams; 'single narratives', which directly retell an old story; and framed collections such as the *Legend of Good Women* and the *Canterbury Tales*. Piero Boitani (1982: 137) argues that Chaucer works in three basic forms – dream poems, collections and romances – and that he is the only medieval European writer besides Boccaccio to combine all three in his narrative works. Other critics refer to the 'Gothic' quality of Chaucer's narratives. Robert M. Jordan's earlier work (1967), qualified to some degree by his later turn to post-modern theory (1987), draws on Erwin Panofsky's equation between high medieval church architecture and the complex divisions and subdivisions of scholastic thought to explain Chaucer's intricate structural patterns. In a similar way, V. A. Kolve (1984) proposes that the 'narrative images' of medieval visual culture are structural and thematic elements of the *Canterbury Tales*. Whether read for their novelistic plot or for the ground-plan of their 'Gothic' arrangement, all of Chaucer's narratives reflect the poetic task of reconceiving source material within a complex structure of narration.

Chaucer's early narratives show many of the characteristic features of his craft. All three early dream visions have a carefully developed introductory section focusing on the narrator (see section below on *BD* 1–60). Their structural disposition literally follows Geoffrey of Vinsauf's metaphor of a pathway, as the narrator proceeds from one locale and episode to another. All three poems use the device of *ekphrasis*, the verbal portrait of an artwork, for amplification and thematic effect. The dreamer of the *Book of the Duchess*, for instance, falls asleep on a book of romance and awakens in a room blazoned with images from the *Romance of the Rose* and the Troy story, two foundational texts for medieval aristocratic culture. Book I of the *House of Fame* retells Virgil's *Aeneid* as a sequence of visual images focusing mostly on Aeneas and Dido and incorporating Dido's viewpoint from Ovid's *Heroides* as a counter-epic. The *Parliament of Fowls* redacts the description of Venus' temple from Boccaccio's *Teseida* before introducing Dame Nature and the assembly of birds who gather to find mates on Valentine's Day. A section like the Ceyx and Alcyone story in the *Book of the Duchess* may have been written earlier and incorporated into the poem, but it forecasts what

Chaucer will do elsewhere with Ovidian material (notably in the *Legend of Good Women*) by shifting the emphases and suppressing the frame and original ending. The three dream visions also show Chaucer's recurrent difficulty in bringing narrative action to full closure. The *Book of the Duchess* ends with the narrator's awakening and pledging himself to a new project of writing out his dream fully. The *House of Fame* breaks off as a 'man of gret auctorite' (2158) is introduced; William Caxton added a perfunctory ending that continued to appear in printed editions until the nineteenth century. The *Parliament* ends with the narrative crisis unresolved, a roundel, and the narrator determined to continue his reading.

Writing Antiquity

In the F Prologue to the *Legend of Good Women* (c.1386), where he mentions 'al the love of Palamon and Arcite / Of Thebes' (420–1) and 'the lyf also of Seynt Cecile' (426), Chaucer discloses that he has been working with another kind of narrative. It is uncertain when exactly this work began or even whether the poems as we have them reflect their original state or a later adaptation to the *Canterbury Tales*. But evidently, by the second decade of his career, Chaucer moved from the dream frame to a form that shifted the balance back from narratorial performance toward narrated action. *Anelida and Arcite* may be a transitional piece in this shift; its formal lyric complaint is set in a narrative invented from Boccaccio's *Teseida*. Chaucer's focus on antiquity (including Christian antiquity), which is his dominant project in the 1380s, requires a form of narrative less anchored rhetorically in performance for an intimate audience and more concerned with the internal structure of action. Chaucer's contemporaries viewed antiquity as the origin of their political states and cultural values and as a mirror for princes and noblemen. Its story had to be intelligible as a record of human action aided by reason alone, before the prospect of redemption. Its expressive forms are romance–epic and tragedy.

In the Knight's Tale, the twelve books of Boccaccio's *Teseida* (originally structured in imitation of Statius and Virgil) are rewritten with a tighter narrative and thematic focus. The two introductory books that explained the appearance of Arcita, Palemone and Emilia in Boccaccio's poem are cut, as is Arcite's apotheosis at the end of the poem. The text of Chaucer's poem, especially in the formal divisions recorded in the Ellesmere manuscript, shows a careful pattern of structural symmetry. Indeed, this formal pattern, as analysed by Charles Muscatine (1957: 181), has become the focus for revisionist efforts to deconstruct the poem's theme and ideology of order. In *Troilus and Criseyde*, Boccaccio's *Filostrato* is shorn of its frame-tale, reconfigured from nine cantos of varying length into a five-part symmetrical structure and given a new ending, based on Arcite's apotheosis in the *Teseida*. So powerful is Chaucer's conception of structure that Lydgate uses it as a model to retell the background story of Troy, rearranging the thirty-nine chapters of Guido delle Colonne's *Historia destructionis Troiae* into the five books of the *Troy Book* he composed on commission from Henry V.

But, as John Norton-Smith remarks, no other English writer possessed the skill to control the simultaneous conclusion and continuation that Chaucer shows at the end of each book of *Troilus* (1974: 90–4).

If the project of writing antiquity requires a free-standing narrative, the craft needed for such a form can be applied to still other topics and to genres beyond romance–epic and tragedy. One view of the *Legend of Good Women* is that its stories of classical heroines, modelled generally on the elegiac complaints of Ovid's *Heroides*, provide the occasion for honing narrative techniques subsequently employed with consummate skill in the *Canterbury Tales*. Robert W. Frank, Jr argues that the stories taught Chaucer the importance of selection, proportion, summary and telling detail for a brief verse narrative (1972: 169–87). Cupid sets the poet–narrator to work with the admonition, 'Sey shortly' (F 577). The poet absorbs the lesson confidently enough to address Virgil in the legend of Dido, 'In thyn Eneyde and Naso wol I take / The tenor, and the grete effectes make' (928–9).

Framed Tales

The most tightly crafted stories in the *Canterbury Tales* – the tales of the Miller, Reeve and Pardoner – combine the economy of exemplary narratives such as the legends with the interior logic of their own fictions. Not only does the Miller's Tale ironically reprise elements of the Knight's Tale, but Nicholas's fiction of a second Flood connects the subplots at the climactic moment when he cries out, 'Help! Water! Water! Help, for Goddes herte!' (3815). Equilibrium controls the Reeve's Tale, not just in the Reeve's intention to 'quite' (3916) the Miller or in Aleyn's vengeful, self-serving notion of 'esement' (4179) but even in the details of exchanging and converting material goods and sexual services. The Pardoner's Tale, for all its resonance with the narrator's self-performance, turns on the stark literalism of rioters seeking Death. In other respects, the carefully plotted structures Chaucer devises for his *matere* not only convey a story but provide a source of symbolic meaning themselves. Within the confines of the fabliau, the Miller's Tale embodies the romance technique of interlacing plot lines. The Franklin's Tale, labelled by its narrator a Breton lay, suppresses the extended mythographic journey that dominates its source, in order to tell a story of married love in which the desire of an aristocratic rival threatens to create a fabliau.

The *Legend* and the *Canterbury Tales* introduce a further dimension to Chaucer's narrative technique by framing their stories within a larger fiction. Precedents for this strategy can be found in the embedded classical stories of Alcyone, Dido and Scipio Africanus, which appear early in the dream visions and set up parallels and contrasts with the main action. The Prologue to the *Legend* returns to the dream frame, and in it Queen Alceste seems to furnish an interpretative key to the subsequent narratives by instructing the narrator to write 'a glorious legende / Of goode wymmen . . . / That weren trewe in lovyng al hire lyves; / And telle of false men that hem bytraien' (F 483–6). The two versions of the Prologue complicate these issues by framing the stories in different ways: in the F Prologue, the stories are part of the continuing dream, while in the G Prologue (presumably a later version), the dreamer awakens and gets immediately to work. That Chaucer follows Alceste's instructions equivocally at best is a commonplace of criticism on the poem. Feminist interpreters have questioned further whether the legends escape the misogyny they are ostensibly written to remedy and whether men escape patriarchy (Hansen 1992: 1–25).

The *Canterbury Tales* employ a markedly more dynamic frame than the *Legend*. The narrator stands between the poet and the pilgrims whose stories he narrates. Telling 'a tale after a man' (GP 731), he combines his fictional voice with the impersonated voice of other narrators. George Lyman Kittredge (1915: 152–6) famously described the General Prologue to the *Tales* as a portrait gallery and formulated the 'dramatic principle' whereby the narratives are read predominantly as illustrations of their pilgrim–narrators. In recent years, critics have challenged the primacy of the roadside drama set in motion by the Host's storytelling contest and sustained (fitfully) by links between tales (Benson 1986). Some observe that the assignment of tales varies, others that Chaucer's artistic emphasis is on narrative rather than dramatization, still others that the dramatic principle confers an illusory unity on an unfinished work. Many scholars find the structuring principle of the *Tales*, as with John Gower's *Confessio Amantis*, in the medieval scholastic *compilatio* – a gathering of source materials in a purposeful order (Parkes 1976).

Chaucer never fully executed his overall plan of composition, and textual evidence shows that he modified it as he worked. As it survives, the frame structure, seen most clearly in the Ellesmere order, connects only two of the ten fragments into which the tales are gathered (the Manciple's Tale and Parson's Prologue of Fragments IX and X). Yet within individual fragments it allows for accident, chance and misunderstanding to intervene in the meta-narrative of the pilgrimage and for patterns of similarity and contrast to emerge between tales. The stories of Fragment I are connected by a sequence of paired narrators (Knight–Miller, Miller–Reeve, Reeve–Cook), but they also trace a decaying arc from romance–epic to fabliau, thence to the Cook's unfinished story of low-life and prostitution in contemporary London. The placement of the Man of Law's Tale in Fragment II of Ellesmere may represent an effort to rehabilitate the frame-tale and begin on a new moral high ground. Kittredge, following Eleanor Hammond's slightly earlier suggestion, proposed that a debate on marriage begins with the Wife of Bath's Prologue and finds its resolution in the ending of the Franklin's Tale (Fragments IV–VI). The Monk's collection of tragedies from the fall of Lucifer to the deaths of Chaucer's contemporaries presents a miniature *compilatio* within Fragment VII, which in turn collects a variety of literary genres. Fragment VIII uses *chiasmus* (a formal pattern that reverses sequence at its middle: abccba) to counterpose the structural units of the life of Saint Cecilia, now assigned to the Second Nun, with corresponding divisions in the stories of alchemy told by the Canon's Yeoman as he joins the pilgrimage.

Character

The structural patterns that Chaucer invents and arranges for individual narratives and collections of narratives depend on character for poetic enactment. In medieval rhetoric, a description of character (*notatio*) can be written by using the 'attributes' and commonplaces (e.g. way of life, behaviour, goals, appetites, eloquence, age, status, homeland) enumerated by Cicero and Horace for character types. Subsequent medieval theorists adapted these traits to represent the *interioris hominis proprietates* – the 'inner man' and the properties of his soul. When the Merchant describes the ageing Lombard knight January at the beginning of his tale, he does so by listing the Ciceronian attributes of homeland, birthplace, fortune, way of life and status. Within the dramatic frame of the *Tales*, this list is a parodic inversion of the attributes that the Clerk employs to describe Walter, the Marquis of Saluzzo, at the beginning of his tale. Jill Mann (1973) has shown that the portraits of the pilgrims in the General Prologue to the *Canterbury Tales* draw significantly on the stereotypes associated with medieval social estates and occupations. This strategy of characterization, recognized by medieval poetic theorists, aims not so much to create character directly from stereotypes as to establish our initial expectations of a fictional character (see section below on *TC* I, 281–322). In this respect, character as an aesthetic element of narrative is what lies beyond or apart from our initial expectations; it is the unanticipated supplement, complexity or contradiction that individuates a figure within our readerly expectations.

To some degree, Chaucer's characters reflect E. M. Forster's celebrated distinction between flat (stereotypical) and rounded (realistic, lifelike) characters. Much of Chaucer's writing is indeed populated with characters whom we could easily describe as flat and functional – the narrator's foils in the dream poems, everyone except the three principal characters and the narrator in *Troilus and Criseyde*, the minor characters in most of the *Canterbury Tales*. Recent criticism, incorporating the precepts of post-structuralism and post-modernism, has challenged the rounded, lifelike characterization on which much of Chaucer's literary reputation has depended for three centuries. On this view, Chaucer's characters do not portray autonomous individuals or selves but subjects shaped by discourse. Discourse in this case means the relation of language to power and institutions as well as the distinctive linguistic registers of occupations, social classes and cultural types. Consequently, Chaucer's characters do not tell us who they are by how they act, look and speak; there is no 'interior man' awaiting disclosure through the content and style of verbal portrayal. Instead, characters fashion themselves through pre-existing cultural forms, borrowed terms and political arrangements. One criticism of this approach to character is that it seems to restrict Chaucer's characters to a hegemonic world that absorbs any possibility of artistic individuality or ideological resistance. Another is that it does not offer a fully coherent explanation of the role of language in defining character. For if the subject is constituted in a borrowed vocabulary, it is none the less the individuating power of language that creates the most distinctive literary effects.

Chaucer's two greatest characters are his own narrative persona and the Wife of Bath. Both of them appear in his narratives without framing or other authenticating devices. The opening move of all Chaucerian narratives is for the narrator to position himself or herself with respect to story and audience. The longest delay for the narrator's entrance in the Chaucer canon occurs in the General Prologue to the *Canterbury Tales*, where the 'I' of the poem does not appear until after the opening periodic sentence celebrating the harmony of nature and man in springtime renewal. While earlier criticism stressed the narrator's authorial disguise, the recent tendency is to see the first-person narrative as part of the narrative code. The narrator's identity, as David Lawton remarks (1986), shifts from one poem to another, and within individual stories there are notable inconsistencies and breaks in self-characterization. In the *Book of the Duchess*, for example, the narrator overhears the man in black's lament for his dead lady White but seems oblivious to the fact until he is told at the end, 'She ys ded' (1309). In the F and G Prologues to the *Legend of Good Women*, written a decade apart from one another, the narrator praises Alceste, seemingly unaware of her presence before him until the God of Love remarks it (F 508–16 and G 496–504). The most complex interaction of story and narrator occurs in *Troilus and Criseyde*, where the 'I' of the poem introduces himself as a historian and servant of love's servants, experiences an intense identification with his characters, but ends by rejecting their fallen, mutable pagan world and the literary tradition that preserves it in favour of Christian redemption. In the Miller's Prologue, the narrator seems to step out of character altogether and speak directly: 'The Millere is a cherl; ye knowe wel this' (3182).

The Wife of Bath appropriates what Chaucer's first-person narrator does everywhere else – she speaks herself into existence from the very outset of her tale in a bravura performance of self-assertion. The manuscript evidence of the *Canterbury Tales* suggests that her prologue is a comparatively late development in Chaucer's overall plan and that Chaucer originally intended to assign the Shipman's Tale to her. None the less, all the textual witnesses introduce her as a powerful speaking voice. Although four manuscripts have spurious links to the Merchant's Tale or the Squire's Tale, there is no authentic link to connect her prologue to any frame except that established by her own performance. The immediate effect is dramatized self-definition, the constitution of an imaginative subject out of a misogynistic discourse on women (see section below on WBP 469–80). But as H. Marshall Leicester, Jr observes, there are dimensions to her performance beyond a self-authorizing speaking voice: 'because of the unfolding or dramatized character of the Wife's performance, it is particularly evident from the beginning that she *encounters herself* in her telling and that this encounter is more than a *compte rendu* of a preexistent self' (1990: 133). This technique of constituting a character who recognizes himself or herself appears throughout Chaucer's narrative canon. The therapy that the dreamer applies to the man in black in the *Book of the Duchess* leads him through the stages of erotic adept and devoted servant in love to a realization of his present condition. In the *House of Fame*, the narrator refuses to reveal his name in the wicker house that merges truth and falsehood. One of the clearest articulations of this double consciousness is given by the Pardoner as he summarizes his textual practice of gulling the credulous for profit: 'For though myself be a ful vicious man, / A moral tale yet I yow telle kan, / Which I am wont to preche for to wynne' (PardP 459–61). Perhaps the most fascinating case is that of Criseyde. Chaucer shows her mind at work in Book II, as she weighs the alternatives of accepting or rejecting Troilus' love, and in Book IV, as she argues against simply fleeing Troy; he injects the verbal parallels between Troilus' desire and hers; he reports her awareness of what will become of her reputation once she betrays Troilus. Still, Criseyde remains a figure of mystery, hidden on the one hand from the narrator who cannot tell when precisely she embraces or betrays Troilus, and hidden on the other from herself. For all his reliance on cultural types and pre-existing discourse, a defining element in Chaucer's greatest characters is irreducible contradiction.

Inbuilt Interpretations

No narrative operates without some form of interpretative framework, even if it is the mere sequence of action and episodes. Throughout his career as a narrative writer, Chaucer repeatedly stages the act of interpretation within his stories and opens them up to interpretation by other characters, imagined audiences and his readers. He uses a wide variety of devices and techniques borrowed from rhetoric, generic conventions and the discourses associated with his topics. Allusion is a pervasive device, from the list of classical and biblical suicides mentioned by the narrator in the *Book of the Duchess* (721–39) through to the Manciple's references to Solomon, David and Seneca and the Parson's citation of sapiential and ecclesiastical authorities at the end of the *Canterbury Tales*. Closely allied to allusion are the proverbs that figure so prominently in the discourses of the Wife, Pardoner, Melibee, Dame Prudence and the Parson, which dramatize argument and persuasion. Local, at times seemingly improvisational, these devices invite comparison between narrative events and received wisdom, while revealing the character of the speaker. But if allusions and proverbs convey the promise of meaning, the comparisons they make more often convey point of view and tone than authorial intent or final significance. The Wife, to take the most obvious example, makes her point precisely by inverting the *sentence* of authorities. And in Chaucer's conscious gestures toward Dante and Boccaccio, the meaning of Chaucer's references must lie beyond persuasion in the realm of poetic tradition, for he is the writer who introduces their works to English literature and the only contemporary English reader to whom they would be fully significant.

Besides rhetorical figures, Chaucer uses his own devices to connect narrative and interpretation. Setting establishes initial expectations of genre and theme, but it is frequently a landscape to be reclaimed or reformed, as in the paradisal garden of the *Book of the Duchess* and the *Parliament of Fowls*, or the poetic emblems of the *House of*

Fame. Chaucer's poems on classical antiquity present the pagan past as a temporally discrete realm of different ritual observances but immediately accessible philosophical problems (free will, determinism, divine beneficence). These poems frequently begin their action with mentions of time, place and textual authority: 'Whilom, as olde stories tellen us' (KnT 859), 'Yt is wel wist how that the Grekes stronge / In armes with a thousand shippes wente / To Troiewardes' (*TC* I, 57–9), 'In Tessalie, as Guido tellith us' (*LGW* 1396). What follows usually belies the simplicity of style and assurance of authority. Theseus' governance symbolizes the problem at the heart of the Knight's Tale; Trojan history eventually intervenes in Troilus' love story; Guido delle Colonne opens his version of that history with the internecine conflict and erotic treachery of Jason. The details of setting lend much to the realistic effects of the *Canterbury Tales*, both in the familiar, local territories of the fabliaux and in remote places – Syria, Tartary, Asia and Armorik. By contrast, the Tale of Melibee derives its moralizing and allegorical power precisely by being located nowhere in particular, hence in every court and household. Other settings establish symbolic and topical meanings. The Flanders of the Pardoner's Tale is a landscape of riot. Lombardy is a realm of tyranny portrayed in quite different ways in the Clerk's and Merchant's Tales.

At both a rhetorical and a structural level, Chaucer connects narrative and interpretation through techniques of repetition. In the dream visions, terms like *thyng* and *sweven* refer to the narrator's dream and to poetic fictions. His vocabulary, phrasing and imagery create a form of autocitation. In *Troilus and Crisyede*, the rhyming pairs *Troye / joie* and *Criseyde / deyde* forecast the shape of tragic action. Ian Bishop points out that repetitions establish adjacent and remote comparisons throughout the *Canterbury Tales* (1987: 14). The oft-repeated phrase 'pitee renneth soone in gentil herte' echoes throughout the *Tales* and links them to the *Legend* (KnT 1761, MLT 660, MerT 1986, SqT 479, *LGW* F 503). 'Pryvetee' is a concern throughout Fragment I of the *Canterbury Tales* and elsewhere, ranging from unknown forces in the universe to human secrets and secret places. Surely, one of Chaucer's most satiric repetitions occurs with the phrase 'atte leeste weye'. As Palamon uses the phrase (KnT 1121) he expresses his idealistic, courtly desire at least to see Emily, if he cannot obtain her mercy and grace. As Absolon uses it, the phrase designates the anatomical destination of his misguided kiss for Alisoun: 'at the leeste wey I shal hire kisse' (MilT 3680).

All these figures and techniques have a communicative function. They furnish cues that point towards meaning and lead the reader to the connections and provisional conclusions that comprise critical engagement with a poetic text. A similar process unfolds within Chaucer's stories for both his narrators and characters. The dreamer in the *Book of the Duchess* awakens determined at some point 'to put this sweven in ryme / As I kan best' (1332–3), while his counterpart in the *Parliament of Fowls* renews his reading in the hope to dream 'som thyng for to fare / The bet' (698–9). The narrators of *Troilus and Crisyede* and the *Legend* ostensibly adopt a reception aesthetic, placing the meaning of their stories in a courtly audience of amateur poets and lovers. The Host in the *Canterbury Tales* sets a Horatian criterion for the tale-telling contest

– 'Tales of best sentence and moost solaas' (GP 798). Yet the hermeneutic guides within Chaucer's mature narratives intensify rather than resolve the problems of narrative. The narrator of the *Legend* quickly outdistances 'Ye lovers that kan make of sentement' (*LGWP* F 69) as well as Virgil and Ovid; he finds himself appalled and 'agroted' (2454) by his *matere*, and finally captured by the very ambiguity he has injected into both the frame tale and the legends: 'Be war, ye wemen, of youre subtyl fo, / Syn yit this day men may ensaumple se; / And trusteth, as in love, no man but me' (2559–61). The narrator of *Troilus* adjures 'the forme of olde clerkis speche / In poetrie' (V, 1854–5). The Host, like all the Canterbury pilgrims, finds his reading of tales open to continual challenge and debate.

Chaucer's characters play out the same dilemmas. Criseyde and Pandarus quibble over the book she is reading with other women when he begins his mission, and the meaning of words, gestures and letters is continually weighed. At the end of the poem, though Troilus rejects Cassandra's interpretation of his dream, the pressure of history progressively cancels out all his misreadings. Diomede knows how to read Criseyde as soon as he sees her, and Troilus at length learns to construe her letters rightly and to realize that the brooch captured from Diomede is the unequivocal sign of her betrayal. In the *Legend*, Piramus and Thisbe, Hypsipyle and Medea are the victims of signs misread. Philomela, able to read and compose but not write, is stranded between semiotic codes until she weaves the letters that tell of her violation and finds the gestures to send her text to Procne. Lucrece, like Virginia in the Physician's Tale, becomes a cultural symbol of tyranny over female bodies and traditional patriarchal rights. In the Manciple's Tale, the last narrative told on the Canterbury pilgrimage, Ovid's tale of Phoebus and the crow is over-determined in meaning and made to illustrate the virtue of silence. Its ambivalent lesson is anticipated by the Nun's Priest's Tale, Chaucer's most subtle reflection on the complex relation of narrative to interpretation. The Nun's Priest's final exhortations to the pilgrims urge two kinds of traditional reading: 'Taketh the moralite, goode men' (3440) and 'Taketh the fruyt, and lat the chaf be stille' (3443). His beast fable challenges moralization and allegorical interpretation while asserting that narrative and interpretation are inseparable. In the same way, the traditional techniques that Chaucer uses to tell his stories are inseparable from the new possibilities of meaning that he uncovers in them.

The *Book of the Duchess*, 1–60

In the *Book of the Duchess*, Chaucer inaugurates his career as a narrative poet by imitating and transforming the opening of Jean Froissart's *Paradys d'Amours*, a courtly dream vision indebted to Machaut's *Remede de Fortune* and emblematic of the social and literary milieu for which Chaucer wrote before beginning the *Canterbury Tales* in the late 1380s. Like Froissart's speaker, Chaucer's narrator suffers insomnia and melancholy:

> I have gret wonder, be this lyght,
> How that I lyve, for day ne nyght
> I may nat slepe wel nygh noght;
> I have so many an ydel thoght
> Purely for defaute of slep
> That, by my trouthe, I take no kep
> Of nothing, how hyt cometh or gooth,
> Ne me nys nothyng leef nor looth.
> Al is ylyche good to me –
> Joye or sorowe, wherso hyt be –
> For I have felynge in nothyng,
> But as yt were a mased thyng,
> Alway in poynt to falle a-doun;
> For sorwful ymagynacioun
> Ys alway hooly in my mynde.

The cause of distress in Froissart is 'la belle . . . / Pour quele amour en ce traveil / Je sui entrés et tant je veil' ('the fair one, for love of whom I entered into this torment and suffer such sleeplessness'). His poem goes on to evoke a garden with various allegorical personnel and the lady who occasions his torment. Chaucer makes oblique reference to a courtly lady, the 'phisicien' (39) who alone might heal his mysterious eight-year sickness, but never mentions her again, for his focus is entirely displaced from Froissart.

Chaucer rewrites Froissart's opening into an exploration of authorial subjectivity and poetic imagination in their most radical form. The 'pensées et merancolies' that occasion Froissart's vision produce in Chaucer's narrator the 'ydel thoght' that levels all perception. The sequence of his phrasing makes it clear that the hierarchy of cognition has collapsed. He loses, in order, the power of attention ('I take no kep / Of nothing'), the ability to discern patterns ('how hyt cometh or gooth'), and the capacity to make judgements ('Ne me nys nothyng leef nor looth'). The result is a paradox – 'felynge in nothyng'. His mind is occupied, literally and figuratively, by 'sorwful ymagynacioun' and the 'fantasies' that 'ben in myn hede / So I not what is best to doo' (28–9). The remedy he seeks is 'a book, / A romaunce' (47–8), which displaces melancholy, by driving away the night that symbolizes his distraction. The 'written fables' (52) of clerks and other poets, brought within the formal order of verbal art and therefore able to be read and 'to be in minde' (55), introduce a corresponding moral order. These tales were written 'While men loved the lawe of kinde' (56), and they portray a world of aristocratic lives and 'many other thinges smale' (59).

Chaucer introduces into Froissart's scene a psychological language that takes the metaphor of melancholy in a literal, even spatial sense. By this technique, he opens up the possibility of a radical subjectivity beyond courtly discourse and conventional authorial poses. The style he employs is at once simple and complex. Derek Brewer (1966: 2–7) emphasizes the debt in colloquial tone and phrasing to Middle English rhyming romances (the kind Chaucer will parody in Sir Thopas), while Payne (1963:

121–4) shows the concentration of rhetorical topoi and figures. The effect it achieves is the conversational tone of courtly address, the 'noble talkyng' and 'communing' of an aristocratic social world seen from the inside. Even more important here is Chaucer's skill in compacting multiple meanings into seemingly transparent words and phrases. The melancholic narrator suffers 'ydel thoght' because it is both inconsequential and deprived of moral significance. He has 'felynge in nothyng' – a state of no feeling and a sensation that emanates from distraction. His 'sorwful ymagynacioun' is at once the means and symptom of distraction. Dante ('Letter to Can Grande della Scala') makes this kind of polysemy a characteristic of poetic language. What Chaucer does at the inaugural moment of his career is to attach it to terms that seem univocal and purely functional. His capacity to infuse language with texture and nuance has no Middle English counterpart, except perhaps for the *Gawain*-poet.

Troilus and Criseyde I, 281–322

The scene in the temple where Troilus first sees Criseyde is built on the rhetorical figure of *effictio* (a verbal description of someone's appearance). In medieval rhetoric and poetics, *effictio* is an ornament of style that presents the external counterpart to the description of character (*notatio*). Chaucer uses it throughout his poetry to introduce and locate his characters in a narrative setting, but in this passage his technique has a thematic dimension, too. Troilus moves through the crowd of young people at 'Palladiones feste' (I, 161), reproving lovers and looking from one woman to another, unaware that, as in the *Romance of the Rose*, Love will soon claim him in vengeance. And, like the lover in the *Rose*, by chance ('upon cas') he allows his gaze to penetrate to one object where it rests and he, in turn, is transfixed by his gaze. Troilus quickly recovers himself and resumes his mocking posture, but the scene develops on two simultaneous levels, for Troilus maintains a public face radically at odds with his turbulent interior experience.

Modern critics read this scene not as a first moment of romantic love but as an instance illustrating the dynamics by which the male gaze constitutes its object of desire. Troilus looks at Criseyde, but Chaucer's technique emphasizes what and how he sees. His piercing eye reaches to a figure whom he already recognizes as something to be described – someone 'so feyr and goodly to devise' (277). In Chaucer's source, Boccaccio's *Filostrato*, this thematic framing of the lover's vision does not exist. Thus what Troilus sees is an object within his own economy of desire first created by language ('devising') and then preserved by memory and will within the lover. When Chaucer shows Criseyde in the next stanza, she is transformed from Boccaccio's social creature into a rhetorical figure:

> She nas nat with the leste of hire stature,
> But alle hire lymes so wel answerynge
> Weren to wommanhod, that creature

> Was nevere lasse mannyssh in semynge;
> And ek the pure wise of hire mevynge
> Shewed wel that men myght in hire gesse
> Honour, estat, and wommanly noblesse.
>
> (I, 281–7)

Boccaccio's Criseida is simply 'grande', but Chaucer describes her with understatement ('nat with the leste of hire stature') and in conformity with the portrait he will later sketch of her in Book V (806–26), using Joseph of Exeter's *Ilias*. Both Boccaccio and Chaucer observe the rhetorical protocol that ornament must be proportionate, but they differ in their purposes. In Boccaccio, Criseida's limbs answer fittingly to her size, and her face and appearance reflect the *donna angelicata* of Italian lyric, whose loftiest expression is the Beatrice of Dante's *Vita nuova*. Criseyde's limbs denote 'wommanhod' instead, and Chaucer again uses understatement to enforce the point: 'creature / Was nevere lasse mannyssh in semynge'. In a detail that has no counterpart in Boccaccio, Chaucer goes on to connect physical description to the description of character. Criseyde's appearance and movement signify her interior qualities: 'men myght in hire gesse / Honour, estat, and wommanly noblesse'.

What Chaucer does in this passage through the conventional techniques of literary description is not just to introduce Criseyde into the story but to reveal how she is seen. We view her through Troilus' eyes, through the perceptions of any culturally literate observer of bodies and virtues, ultimately through the power of language to constitute subjectivity and desire. This effect depends generally on the discursive properties of language, but Chaucer imbues his language with specific resonance and added meaning. Criseyde is not mannish 'in semynge', and this minor phrase refers doubly to the way she appears and the way we perceive her. The 'men' who infer honour, social position and nobility from her appearance are (according to standard Middle English usage) men and women alike, but 'men' echoes directly off of 'mannyssh', and this scene is above all one staged through the male gaze. Chaucer confirms the last point by the narrator's report that Troilus, watching her movement, thought he had never seen 'so good a syghte' (294). Whoever Criseyde may be as a character, she enters the poem as an object of Troilus' specular pleasure.

Chaucer's adaptation of the rhetorical *effictio* thus goes beyond the practical means of storytelling to establish and complicate his love theme. The rhetorical portrait is a device of amplification, and it allows Chaucer to foreground a small, interior moment within the larger scene of pagan ritual observance. Indeed, the intimate and the interior utterly displace the social and public action. In portraying the inception of Troilus' desire, Chaucer shows that it is circular and solipsistic. He immediately adds a stanza to Boccaccio's text that conveys the continuing effects of seeing Criseyde. Criseyde's 'look' (295) generates 'So gret desir and such affeccioun, / That in his herte botme gan to stiken / Of hir his fixe and depe impressioun' (296–8). The 'look' repeats the 'syghte' of the preceding stanza, and this subjective experience of seeing produces desire and affection – synonymous terms that designate feeling as against reason. In this way, Chaucer tracks the movement of the soul towards its love object and then back towards itself. Just as Troilus' gaze penetrates the crowd and rests on Criseyde, so her look returns to impress itself on him. Chaucer's language employs the commonplaces of faculty psychology by evoking the power of visual images (both external and self-generated) to press themselves on consciousness, much as wax is imprinted or letters are incised on a writing tablet. It also shows – again through the nuance of phrasing – the transformative power of sight and desire. The impression of Criseyde both reaches to the core of his being ('his herte botme') and lodges there permanently ('fixe'). Troilus has become fixed by his own desire. In this way, Cupid secures his oblique vengeance, and the scene closes with Troilus' striving to maintain a public face now totally at odds with his emotions. When Chaucer comes to write the companion scene in Book II, in which Criseyde sees Troilus enter the city after battle, he uses the conventions of the *effictio* with the same language and effect.

The Wife of Bath's Prologue, 469–80

The Wife of Bath's Prologue is divided into structural units that grow progressively specific and localized as her discourse on the 'wo that is in mariage' (3) unfolds. The opening section, punctuated by the Pardoner's ill-advised intervention, sounds her themes of experience and authority, textual interpretation, power, economic exchange and sexuality. The middle section rehearses Alisoun's tactics for governing her husbands and ends with the example of the fourth husband, whose excesses come closest to the Wife's own. The final section is devoted to her fifth husband, the clerk Jankyn, and it serves in many ways as a thematic and structural mirror for her subsequent tale of the knight–rapist who eventually surrenders 'maistrie' (1236) to the hag whom he is compelled to marry for saving his life. The Prologue follows a strategy by which the Wife appropriates, enlarges and inverts the commonplaces of medieval antifeminism. Historicist critics have remarked that she appropriates misogynistic discourse without merely reproducing it, and feminist critics have emphasized that both her body and her speech are the sites of resistance and identity. The energy of her performance establishes her rhetorical ethos: she is a credible, sympathetic character because she seems to disown no part of her appetite, even though she insists 'myn entente nys but for to pleye' (192).

At the same time, she has a capacity for moments of introspection that break the illusion of outwardly directed performance. Such a moment occurs at the end of the middle section of her prologue, as she suspends the description of her fourth husband and shifts to an elegiac mode:

> But – Lord Crist! – whan that it remembreth me
> Upon my yowthe, and on my jolitee,
> It tikleth me aboute myn herte roote.
> Unto this day it dooth myn herte boote

> That I have had my world as in my tyme.
> But age, allas, that al wole envenyme,
> Hath me biraft my beautee and my pith.
> Lat go. Farewel! The devel go therwith!
> The flour is goon; ther is namoore to telle;
> The bren, as I best kan, now moste I selle;
> But yet to be right myrie wol I fonde.
> Now wol I tellen of my fourthe housbonde.
>
> (469–80)

This passage is in one sense an amalgam of sources. Most of it derives from Jean de Meun's portion of the *Roman de la Rose*, while the final image sounds proverbial (it appears only in this text). But, as in her borrowings from St Jerome and other authorities, the Wife relocates and recontextualizes meanings to disclose a new significance in the act of speaking. In the *Rose*, the Old Woman (La Vieille) instructs the allegorical figure Fair Welcome (Bel Accueil) in the art of love as a way of wreaking vengeance on men, who have misused her in youth and now despise her in old age. She mourns the loss of her beauty, yet thinks back on her youth with pleasure. Jean's verb for memory – *pourpenser* – is an intensified form that echoes rhetorically in the next line with *pensee* ('thought') and conceptually with the theme of pleasure. The Old Woman finds delight in recollection, and her pleasure is sensory and immediate as well as retrospective: 'me resbaudissent li membre' ('all my body is enlivened', 12939).[1] Thinking back is a form of interior, erotic experience and a means of transformation, for the body is made young ('Tout me rajouvenist le cors', 12943) by such memory and the Old Woman finds worldly bliss ('Touz les biens dou monde'), despite the deception of men.

The Wife of Bath translates this passage into an entirely different attitude. The Old Woman's asseveration 'Par Dieu' becomes her forceful and surprising interjection 'Lord Crist!' The impersonal construction 'it remembreth me' replaces the active verbs of memory. If memory affects all the Old Woman's body ('li membre' and 'le cors'), it concentrates on the Wife's heart, the primary site of sense perception, and amuses as well as pleases her. Memory stimulates desire for the Old Woman, much as it does for Troilus, but it furnishes an occasion for reflection to the Wife. Youth and pleasure are experiences to understand. In this way, the Wife reaches an accommodation that finds lyric expression: 'I have had my world as in my tyme.' Worldly goods are not external, as they are for the Old Woman, but stand within the Wife's power. And the agent of loss is not a man who misuses or scorns the Wife but time, which governs all creatures. Perhaps the Wife's most powerful statement is her colloquial dismissal of time's limits: 'Lat go. Farewel! The devel go therwith!' Evoking the hermeneutic imagery of wheat and chaff and troping her earlier image of wives as 'barly-breed' (144), she places herself within a naturalized economy of time and faded beauty: 'The flour is goon; ther is namoore to telle; / The bren, as I best kan, now moste I selle.' Her defining act of will is her resolve 'to be right myrie' in the face of contingency.

See also AFTERLIFE; COMEDY; FRANCE; GENRE; LIFE HISTORIES; PAGAN SURVIVALS; PERSONAL IDENTITY; MODES OF REPRESENTATION; VISUALIZING; WOMEN.

NOTES

1   The references in this section are taken from Guillaume de Lorris and Jean de Meun, *Le Roman de la rose*, ed. Armand Strubel (Paris: Livre de Poche, 1992).

REFERENCES AND FURTHER READING

Benson, C. David (1986) *Chaucer's Drama of Style: Poetic Variety and Contrast in the* Canterbury Tales (Chapel Hill, NC: University of North Carolina Press). Argues against the 'dramatic principle' as an organizing structure and in favour of Chaucer's experimenting with different genres.

Bishop, Ian (1987) *The Narrative Art of the* Canterbury Tales*: A Critical Study of the Major Poems* (London: Dent). Offers close critical readings of most of the *Canterbury Tales*.

Boitani, Piero (1982) *English Medieval Narrative in the Thirteenth and Fourteenth Centuries*, trans. Joan Krakover Hall (Cambridge: Cambridge University Press). Identifies the dream poem, story collection and romance as the major literary structures in Chaucer and examines narrative strategies in each form.

Boitani, Piero and Mann, Jill, eds (1986) *The Cambridge Chaucer Companion* (Cambridge: Cambridge University Press). Contains useful essays on Chaucer's realism, literary structure, narrator and style as well as thematic topics.

Brewer, Derek S., ed. (1978) *Chaucer: The Critical Heritage, 1385–1933*, 2 vols (London: Routledge & Kegan Paul). Prints texts that document the history of Chaucer's reception *c.*1385–1933 and supplements Caroline Spurgeon's *Five Hundred Years of Chaucer Criticism and Allusion, 1357–1900* (1925).

——ed. (1966) *Chaucer and Chaucerians: Critical Studies in Middle English Literature* (University, Ala.: University of Alabama Press; London: Nelson). Gathers essays emphasizing verbal artistry and structure in major narratives and on Chaucer's legacy.

Burrow, John A. (1982) *Medieval Writers and Their Work: Middle English Literature and its Background 1100–1500* (Oxford: Oxford University Press). Discusses Chaucer's narratives in relation to context, genre and reception.

Cooper, Helen (1983) *The Structure of the* Canterbury Tales (London: Duckworth). Reviews traditions of story collections and examines the groupings of stories and themes.

Edwards, Robert R. (1989) *The Dream of Chaucer: Representation and Reflection in the Early Narratives* (Durham, NC: Duke University Press). Argues that Chaucer's early narratives are both poetic fictions and speculations on the nature of poetry.

Frank, Robert Worth, Jr (1972) *Chaucer and* The Legend of Good Women (Cambridge, Mass.: Harvard University Press). Reads the *Legend* not as a project abandoned out of boredom but an experiment in the techniques of writing narrative.

Hansen, Elaine Tuttle (1992) *Chaucer and the Fictions of Gender* (Berkeley and Los Angeles: University of California Press). Interprets major narrative poems in terms of representation of women and contradictions of patriarchy.

Howard, Donald (1976) *The Idea of the* Canterbury Tales (Berkeley and Los Angeles: University of California Press). Stresses both the medieval analogues (visual arts, memory systems) and the dynamic quality of structure in the *Tales*.

Jordan, Robert M. (1967) *Chaucer and the Shape of Creation: The Aesthetic Possibilities of Inorganic Structure* (Cambridge, Mass.: Harvard University Press). Analyses Chaucer's narratives in context of structuring principles within medieval art and philosophy.

——(1987) *Chaucer's Poetics and the Modern Reader* (Berkeley, Los Angeles and London: University of California Press). Emphasizes the interruptions, digressions and transformations within Chaucer's narrative patterns.

Kelly, Douglas (1991) *The Arts of Poetry and Prose*, Typologie des sources du moyen âge occidental, fasc. 59 (Turnhout: Brepols). Provides overview and guide to Latin and vernacular treatises on poetics.

Kittredge, George Lyman (1915) *Chaucer and his Poetry* (Cambridge, Mass.: Harvard University Press). Establishes many of the major categories for interpreting Chaucer's narrative – *Troilus and Criseyde* as a psychological novel, the 'dramatic principle', and the marriage group of the *Canterbury Tales*.

Koff, Leonard Michael (1988) *Chaucer and the Art of Storytelling* (Berkeley and Los Angeles: University of California Press). Argues that Chaucer's storytelling does not contain obscure meanings but is directed, rather, to a community of readers with a public aim of testing morals and truth through fiction.

Kolve, V. A. (1984) *Chaucer and the Imagery of Narrative: The First Five* Canterbury Tales (Stanford: Stanford University Press). Interprets tales from Fragments I and II against the conventions and techniques of late medieval visual culture.

Lawton, David (1986) *Chaucer's Narrators* (Woodbridge, Suffolk: Brewer). Challenges traditional views of narrators and argues that the poet's 'I' is an 'open persona' who serves as a device for controlling narrative and tone.

Leicester, H. Marshall, Jr (1990) *The Disenchanted Self: Representing the Subject in the* Canterbury Tales (Berkeley, Los Angeles and London: University of California Press). Applies post-Freudian psychoanalytic theory to Chaucer's portrayal of character and social arrangements.

Mann, Jill (1973) *Chaucer and Medieval Estates Satire: The Literature of Social Classes and the General Prologue to the* Canterbury Tales (Cambridge: Cambridge University Press). Places Chaucer's characterization of the Canterbury pilgrims in the context of late medieval literary and social conventions about social classes and occupations.

Meech, Sanford B. (1959) *Design in Chaucer's Troilus* (Syracuse, NY: Syracuse University Press). Examines in detail Chaucer's transformation of Boccaccio's *Filostrato*.

Mehl, Dieter (1986) *Geoffrey Chaucer: An Introduction to his Narrative Poetry* (Cambridge: Cambridge University Press). Emphasizes relation of poet to audience and reader as source for strategies of narration and aesthetic indeterminacy.

Muscatine, Charles (1957) *Chaucer and the French Tradition* (Berkeley, Los Angeles and London: University of California Press). Connects analyses of style and form in Chaucer's major poems to theme and ideology.

Norton-Smith, John (1974) *Geoffrey Chaucer* (London: Routledge & Kegan Paul). Focuses on poetic form in close readings of Chaucer's major works.

Parkes, M. B. (1976) 'The influence of the concepts of *ordinatio* and *compilatio* on the development of the book', in *Medieval Learning and Literature: Essays Presented to Richard William Hunt*, ed. J. J. G. Alexander and M. T. Gibson (Oxford: Clarendon), 115–41. Describes two important medieval literary concepts and applies them to Middle English works.

Payne, Robert O. (1963) *The Key of Remembrance: A Study of Chaucer's Poetics* (New Haven and London: Yale University Press). Argues for the importance of medieval poetic theory within Chaucer's practice and disputes earlier attempts to dismiss rhetoric as an element of his artistry.

Schaar, Claes (1955) *The Golden Mirror: Studies in Chaucer's Descriptive Technique and its Literary Background* (Lund: Gleerup). Analyses Chaucer's sources and practice in describing emotions, character and landscape.

20
Other Thought-worlds
Susanna Fein

'He semeth elvyssh by his contenaunce'
(ThP 703)

Summaries of Chaucer's literary canon typically note that it begins in visionary dream-worlds and ends in the realistic here and now of the Canterbury pilgrims. But 'elvyssh' Chaucer never quite abandons a method of counterpoising the world of everyday life, its routine interactions and responses, duties and pleasures, with alternate worlds of fantasy and unpredictability. Chaucer's realms of the bizarre – of faery, dream or folk-lore – play against the real and exist within it, opening up the emotional, psychological and subliminal realms that dwell in the inner self. In this chapter I examine how Chaucer's other worlds are rooted in primal instincts, which are manifested in ways perceived as strange but which turn out to emanate from the perceiver's own self. When lost in other thought-worlds, Chaucer's protagonists encounter things alien to themselves that force self-recognitions. New knowledge arrives through jarring shifts in perspective involving gender, class, even species, accompanied by surreal encounter and irrational occurrence.

In vigorously exploiting what is strange, Chaucer highlights deficiencies in the perspective of a protagonist figured as 'normal' and projecting ordinary foibles and complacencies. In Chaucer this norm tends to be male, socially advantaged and embedded in the experiential world of humans. In early dream visions the protagonist is closely bound in identity to the poet, though many have observed how these self-portraits are distorted with parody. In Chaucer's repeated use of the dream genre, putting someone like himself at the centre, we may detect the poet's desire for knowledge outside immediate sense perceptions and for empathies that enlarge personal response. The poet's later use of other-worldly setting is coloured by similar desires. The texts examined here – the *House of Fame*, Wife of Bath's Tale and Pardoner's Tale – are chosen to illustrate three types of fantastic medium invoked by Chaucer as he pushes the limits of individual experience. Each kind of event is marked by genre: amid the free associations of dreams the subject becomes creative thought; in the realm of fairies what is magical and strange is woman's experience; and in ancient lore voices of the dead haunt the land.

Dreams: The *House of Fame*

The *House of Fame* is the Chaucerian poem that most directly confronts the issue of what a dream might be in psychological terms. The fertile literary dream traditions lent to Chaucer from biblical, classical and medieval sources congregate thickly in this poem about the poet's debt to precedent authorities and his own aspirations to join them. The poem seems inherently to concern Chaucer's inner life, a serious subject delved with humour and irreverence through his persona Geffrey. Dreaming, Geffrey first finds himself in a temple of glass, which he senses belongs to Venus; then, in a house-of-mirrors effect in which he mimics Aeneas in Carthage (*Aeneid* I, 642–97), he views images that tell the Virgilian story, beginning with the famous opening lines and proceeding through Troy's fall, Dido's tragedy and Aeneas' dream-like descent into hell to the final triumph in Italy. The dreamer is both passive and active witness to the epic, absorbing details given him by an artist–author and participating deeply in characters' emotions. Dreamily augmented with visual and aural effects, the mental after-experience of reading is made external.

By associational thinking Geffrey becomes like the wandering Trojan hero when he suddenly wonders where his own journey has taken him: 'But not wot I . . . / where I am' (474–5). Although the theory-filled Proem I had obsessively defined dreaming as an experience of indeterminate origin (1–51), no option given there proposes that actual travel will occur. The narrator has none the less dreamt himself *somewhere*: a temple where he was both stationary and transported through fictional travel. Chaucer clearly has proposed another origin of dreams: the imaginative prompt of a book. When the *Aeneid* ends, however, the dreaming man loses his bookish grounding – itself ephemeral – and cannot fathom his spatial location. The dream setting then reveals the mind's inner blankness: 'Then sawgh I but a large feld, / As fer as that I myghte see' (482–3). This moment brings stark terror: what if, behind and beyond the book and the dream, there is nothing? That dreams require originary explanations suggests that they come from external stimuli, not spontaneously from inner invention. As derivative responses, they would hold no meaning in themselves. The blank plain denotes the blank mind, the blank page, and the human or authorial fear that if experience is inadequate, reliance on authority is no better because it masks inner emptiness.

Feeling lost, the dreamer calls outside of himself to a source of ultimate meaning: '"O Crist," thoughte I, "that art in blysse, / Fro fantome and illusion / Me save!"' (492–4). The request is for a meaning in images and words – not illusion and fantasy – and for inspired knowledge that will rescue him from a frightening wasteland that is apparently his own mind or soul. The answer to his prayer materializes immediately, swooping down from the sunny heaven into which he has cast his eye: a gigantic, fantastical eagle, Dantesque in source, but also evocative of mythological, astrological and biblical imagery.

Thus the dreamer who seemed overly dependent upon an outside author loses the secure grounding of a book, flounders momentarily in desperate solitude and finally seizes on his own imaginative powers divinely granted. What follows – in Proem II – is the first invocation to the muses in English literature: 'Now faire blisfull, O Cipris, / So be my favour at this tyme! / And ye, me to endite and ryme / Helpeth, that on Parnaso duelle, / Be Elicon, the clere well' (518–22). The narrator next invokes his own mental powers:

> O Thought, that wrot al that I mette,
> And in the tresorye hyt shette
> Of my brayn, now shal men se
> Yf any vertu in the be
> To tellen al my drem aryght.
> Now kythe thyn engyn and myghte!
>
> (523–8)

This second invocation glosses classical convention with updated meaning: the Muses denote invention from the rich treasury of one's own thinking brain. Apparently the wasteland was illusory, or merely a transition point, for in the mind lies a repository of true words and images. 'Thought', God-given and God-inspired, has the power to bring the dream to *written* form (it 'wrot al that [he] mette'). At this point the dream becomes consciously doubled as experience and text. The authorial task is to write dreams down so that others ('men') shall 'see' whether one's thought has the skill ('vertu') to 'tellen al [his] drem aryght', that is, to write so that whatever meaning it has may be deciphered. Telling the dream 'aryght' means more than knowing its origin. As individualized filters of a person's past reading, dream visions give fuel to Thought, which brings them to written form. The cycle from reading to dream to authorial thought and action is continuous and fertile as long as Thought can make known ('kythe') its skill and power to a new readership.

Loss and despair are therefore answered by sublime aspirations and a renewal of hope. After this grand apostrophe Chaucer returns confidently to the dream, suspended just as the eagle made its descent towards the hero. Bound in a dream-world, Geffrey has up to now met what may be accounted for in worldly causes: he read the *Aeneid* and then dreamt it; the dream-book ended, and the mind made vicariously dependent upon it went blank. Now enters the truly strange and fantastic: a larger-than-life eagle, endowed with speech. The perspective shifts to that of the swooping bird, and the narrator Geffrey, envisioned as a clear target upon an open field (537–40), becomes easy prey. Is he being 'saved' in answer to his prayer, or is he to be eaten? The eagle, after all, is behaving as a hunting bird does by nature. Where is the confidence the poet has just shown in the apostrophe to Thought? Now, instead, he is puny, weak, and elevated in a most unusual manner – not by lofty Philosophy, as were his distinguished predecessors, but by means of natural flight in the talons of an enormous bird.

Obviously, Chaucer is using the traditions to have some fun, and the *House of Fame* is certainly one of the most playful if mentally restless and anxious poems he ever wrote. The eagle soon orders the swooning narrator to 'Awak!' in a 'mannes vois' that Geffrey finds oddly familiar and probably familial (555–62). The swoon creates inside the dream-poem a sleep within a sleep, and a reader may justifiably grow confused as the 'astonyed' narrator is ordered to be 'awak' but not really awake. An embodied parody of Boethius' definition of Thought – 'A thought may flee so hye / Wyth fetheres of Philosophye, / To passen everych element' (973–5) – the feathered, philosophical eagle raises Geffrey high above the clouds and takes him upon a didactic tour of the airy sphere above the firmament. The dream encounter in Book II is with a creature unlike the narrator in many ways: authoritative, strong, avian rather than human, and capable of flight. The mundane Geffrey, mocked by the eagle as perpetually 'daswed' from reading heavily (655–60), has been made to explore the world 'experientially' (though actually in a dream) and to see it literally in overview. The bookish and house-bound Geffrey's encounter with a soaring eagle forces him to confront something utterly unlike his own habitual self; yet what he meets in comic, exaggerated and massively externalized form is actually originating from somewhere within himself his own creative thought processes. Digging deeper, past the blank space, and relying on traces of God's image in him, the dreamer becomes the visionary poet.

It is impossible to reduce the *House of Fame*, a challenging and complex poem about knowledge, art and indeterminate meaning, to any simple formula, and such is not my intent. But the central figure of an eagle is well, if rather elliptically, glossed by the poet. When the Chaucer addresses Thought in Proem II, he is writing down the dream, not experiencing it (each proem interrupts the dream account). Within the dream the lost Geffrey had prayed for succour, eliciting a gigantic bird, so in the dream per se the prayer is the only apparent prompt for the eagle. The interruptive proem conjoins, however, with the prayer, adding the Muses and Thought to the meanings we might attach to the eagle. Finally, the dreamer himself, in the clutches of the eagle, utters the saying of Boethius that connects Thought to 'fetheres of Philosophye' (974). Thus Chaucer is not being obscure about what the eagle symbolizes. Poor Geffrey has released powers from within that he can barely handle; indeed, he is entirely at the eagle's mercy, and the bird feels obliged frequently to reassure this quivering lump of humanity captive in his claws that his motives are protective, benevolent and wisely pedagogical.

And so begins the vision of Fame's house, prefaced by Virgil's *Aeneid* and the flight of an eagle. I have dwelt upon these entry points to Geffrey's vision because they illustrate well Chaucer's early experiments in alternate worlds of thought. Both offer the psychological feel of a dream: an obsessive rehearsing of vivid details and images as the mind replays an exciting book; the sensations of flight and fear that can overtake one in sleep. Moreover, they originate in the narrator's own waking preoccupations, though coloured by a heightened subjectivity. Most importantly, they are themselves about the very nature of thought. Chaucer turns the dream process upon itself, so that the free flight of associational thinking – images and ideas and feelings – that occurs in a dream is literalized into a dream of flying on a thoughtful bird and listening to its scientific theories upon the subject of where the sounds of words that feed one's thoughts eventually end up. And the written dream vision is itself, ultimately, the product of conscious Thought.

Faery: The Wife of Bath's Tale

While the *House of Fame* may be the most self-conscious of Chaucer's poems upon the subject of thought, a poem in which he makes it a soaring conceit, elsewhere and later in the canon Chaucer continues to toy with altered realities that reshape ordinary perception. Like dreams, the realm of fairies offers a rich stage for other-worldly encounters. That there could be a kingdom of creatures transparent to the human eye is another trick reality might play on ordinary human beings. Since human perception is limited to what we can know by our five senses within a specific spot in space and time, perhaps – so the thinking goes – there are stimuli and signals we are not equipped to receive. If such a world exists, it is clearly subject to different laws and free of mortal constraints. While belief in fairies was hardly compatible with Christianity in the Middle Ages, religion's upholding of unseen efficacious powers did little to dissipate folk stories of faery sightings. The medieval form most drawn to faery lore is the romance, and even more so the short romances known as *lais*, said to be from old Celtic stories told by the Bretons.

Chaucer composes two Breton *lais* for the *Canterbury Tales*: the tales of the Wife of Bath and the Franklin. I will focus on the Wife's tale which, as Chaucer's only Arthurian story, has a setting fully licensed to invoke the curious world of faery. As with the *House of Fame*, what I explore is the hero's point of entry into an alien world and how contact with that world comes to be educative and transforming. The encounter comes about, though, by means of a paradoxical combination of extreme wilfulness and extreme compulsion, as if it denotes a process unconsciously self-willed and inevitable, a process of learning initiated by one's own ignorant impulses.

An anonymous knight – a 'lusty bacheler' – has no known history before we witness him commit a savage act:

> And so bifel that this kyng Arthour
> Hadde in his hous a lusty bacheler,
> That on a day cam ridynge fro ryver,
> And happed that, allone as he was born,
> He saugh a mayde walkynge hym biforn,
> Of which mayde anon, maugree hir heed,
> By verray force, he rafte hire maydenhed.
>
> (882–8)

Riding from a river, 'allone as he was born', he forces himself upon an innocent maiden. The primal quality of this plot — a solitary, unknown 'generic' man originates as if from a river and violates a female as if he were born to do so — vividly underscores the subject of sexual difference that haunts the tale. The man is stronger, the maid defenceless, except for legal recourse after the fact. Her virginity gone, she is changed and diminished in body. He gains, and she loses.

The tale thus opens with a powerful paradigm by which to read a story of sovereignty designated by gender. Another opening, however, has prefaced this one by naming a presence that suffuses and surrounds the realm of men: the land 'fulfild of fayerye' (859) is ruled by a feminine 'elf-queene', and the place retains such magic that men in those days could actually see fairies on occasion dancing 'in many a grene mede' (861). The time is set before the existence of 'lymytours' (866) — the term refers to licensed friars, but also, figuratively, to territorializing masculinity, that is, those who would set up artificial boundaries. Given this superarching rule of faery, the government of King Arthur is a human delusion, satisfactory for those in it, but a delusion none the less. A maternal presence supersedes laws fixed by the king, and it bypasses such boundaries as men may set.

In fact, Chaucer's Wife's story is conceived upon notions of boundaries changing and shapes shifting. The Wife of Bath's Tale seems to be Chaucer's attempt to create a tale in terms of a woman's embodied aesthetic but, of course, Chaucer's understanding of what this is remains bound within his own maleness. None the less, his experiment in feminine tale-telling is fascinating for its insistence that men's subjugation of women is a form of self-subjugation. When the young knight rapes the maid, he has literally shifted her shape by means of forced entry. Women's closed bodies are made permeable by men. What happens afterwards to the knight is a strange entry into 'woman's world' (identified with the faery realm), something he did not bargain on in his impulsive act of apparent superiority and possession. In the Wife's Breton *lai* Chaucer has blended together old notions of faery shape-shifting with intriguing ideas about female sexuality and the polarization that exists between the genders.

The action that ensues from the rape is both inevitable and elegant in terms of the Wife's aesthetic. The maid disappears from the tale, having been erased by the man's theft of her virginal essence. The knight remains in the story, but he must pay for his crime. The rest of the tale is about his reparation of something that cannot be restored. Bound to die by Arthur's law, the knight is reprieved by petition of the queen, whose own juridical method is different though no less rigorous. By a communal court of ladies he is set upon a quest to learn 'What thyng is it that wommen moost desiren' (905). Thus feminine intervention shifts the ground away from what was a case of clear-cut crime and punishment. Now the knight's condition is fraught with ambiguity, and one might argue that he suffers a 'living' death in which his execution has merely been stayed one year. The question — itself a riddle — appears to be impossible to answer in a way that would satisfy all women. Facing a world filled with individual females, the knight senses there is a myriad of responses, which the Wife herself confirms is the case (922–49). Thus the quest is defined by a real sense of futility. Dejected, the knight finally turns 'homward' (988).

At this point of utter despair and relinquished control, and in the midst of a forest setting (where human–faery encounters often occur in romance), the knight stumbles across a wondrous sight:

> And in his wey it happed hym to ryde,
> In al this care, under a forest syde,
> Wher as he saugh upon a daunce go
> Of ladyes foure and twenty, and yet mo.
>
> (989–92)

Despite the scene's charm, many phrases in it echo a prior, less charming event: the year before the knight 'cam *ridynge*', and it '*happed* that . . . / He *saugh* a mayde' (884–6). The change is from one maiden to many, in just the way his adventure has changed from ill-advised pursuit of one to enforced petition of many. He is attracted to the circle of dancing ladies: 'Toward the whiche daunce he drow ful yerne, / In hope that som wysdom sholde he lerne' (993–4). While the knight sensibly hopes now to learn some wisdom from women, one readily perceives that their beauty and grace hold an erotic appeal as well, to which he responds 'ful yerne'. The women's lithe bodies presumably dance in a ring (as fairies were reputed to do), a shape symbolic of feminine gender, and the knight instinctively seeks to enter their circle. In so doing, his action may be read as figuratively sexual, repeating on a symbolic level the behaviour that got him into trouble before. The blend of desire with wisdom-seeking does, however, indicate some degree of maturation.

Although the ladies have not explicitly been identified as fairies, the teller has allowed this expectation to arise in the reader, particularly after her preface about the 'elf-queene'. Even so, their sudden disappearance is a surprise, and what remains on the spot – an ugly, old crone – is said to elicit revulsion among men:

> But certeinly, er he cam fully there,
> Vanysshed was this daunce, he nyste where.
> No creature saugh he that bar lyf,
> Save on the grene he saugh sittynge a wyf –
> A fouler wight ther may no man devyse.
>
> (995–9)

As the many ladies revert to just one, the loathly woman's foulness negates the *déjà vu* sense of seduction and now, instead, ideas of death are invoked: 'he saw no creature that bore life, except for . . .' The phrasing underlines how old and decrepit the woman looks to the young knight. It also implies how naïvely this 'lusty bacheler' still sees his questing in terms of life-charged pursuits: the active desires of women and, of course, his own. But since he is virtually on death row, in his failure to achieve the quest, an image of *memento mori* is appropriate.

The knight's second encounter with a solitary woman is thus shrouded in faery mystery and intrigue. Unlike the young maiden, whom he mistakenly took to be instantly accessible, the woman he meets now is fully marked as distant and 'other': old, ragged, foul, ugly, magically bizarre. She has control of the hapless man, instead of the other way around. His own motive has changed from pleasure-seeking to primal survival. She offers him a reassuring greeting: 'Tel me what that ye seken, by youre fey! / Paraventure it may the bettre be' (1002–3). The knight's response acknowledges her maternal authority: in addressing her as 'leeve mooder' (1005), he seems indeed to have travelled figuratively 'homward'. His solitary trek 'fro ryver' having gone sorely astray, the knight returns to an originary point, denoted as 'mooder', the source of life and knowledge. And he understands well the dire nature of his dilemma: 'I nam but deed but if that I kan seyn / What thing it is that wommen moost desire' (1006–7).

The old woman – a creature of faery, of course, and perhaps even the Faery Queen herself – holds the answer to the impossible question. She possesses knowledge that every woman has but no single woman could articulate. Benevolently she gives it to the knight, but in return she wins his pledged 'trouthe' (1009–13) to grant her demand after his life is saved. Indeed, his life is safe, for not a single woman in the queen's court can contradict his new-found answer: that women desire sovereignty over husbands or lovers (1038–45). The knight is set free of his sentence of death – but now, suddenly, he finds himself newly constrained, for the old woman claims his troth more literally than he had ever imagined: she requires that he marry her. His response is immediate, visceral and evocative of a rape victim: 'Allas and weylawey! / . . . Taak al my good and lat my body go' (1058, 1061). If experience is the truest form of knowledge, the rapist–knight is about to learn the ultimate truth of what he did. The queen's sentencing of the knight has been overtaken, it would appear, by the faery realm, which would carry it even further.

One may pause here to examine the notions of justice in the Wife of Bath's Tale, because it is crucial to see how the faery realm interacts with the world of Arthur and his queen. Arthur's law would have dealt final punishment for rape – decapitation – a literalism of the crime of 'rafte maydenhede' that would seem to render the victim as 'dead' as the perpetrator will become. Paternal law cannot restore maidenhood, the loss of which seems a form of death. However, softened by the queen's law, the punishment meted out to a rapist allots him a chance (albeit a slim one) to live by redeeming himself. The queen's sentence – death or wisdom – allows for reform, as if the maiden's loss might be read as male sexual initiation, and with it his freedom from women. A sexualized young man is apparently womanhood's potential gain, so long as he can be made subject to woman's rule. The queen's logic would not consider the maiden irreparably damaged, although in acting so impetuously the knight did sin against women and deserves stern attention. The queen seems to be enacting a maternal justice that takes a more flexible view of women's bodies, while the king's law is absolutist on the question of female virginity.

Although the old woman's faery justice is, like the queen's, recuperative, it is similar to Arthur's law in demanding, in altered form, 'an eye for an eye': a rape for a rape. Yet in the exchange from worldly king to other-worldly queen, the authoritative definition of impetuous sex shifts radically: in the realm of men, when man overpowers woman, sex (rape) means death for both parties; but in the realm of fairies (or women, the Other of men), such action invites womanhood to overpower the man, reconstituting forced sex as marriage (and life). The strange world of faery in the Wife of Bath's Tale is therefore much allied to the feminine, which is understood as utterly foreign to men, whose polarized viewpoint is taken to be the social norm. The rapist–knight, by unthinking choice and penetrative act, has entered, quite literally, 'femenye', and he may now never return to a state of separated maleness. The change is absolute, whether he knows it or not. The 'faery' view of sexual experience – even rape – appears to connect it primally to birth, an attitude situated in decidedly maternal terms. It is almost as if, figuratively, the realm of feminine faery surrounds, womb-like, the masculine world of Arthur and his virile knights. Women are figured as willing, in benevolent fashion, to let men pass through their bodies so long as they grow, learn and mature in time. Rape is therefore interpretable as a budding man's premature readiness to complete the circle from infant birth to mature heterosexuality. This 'faery' way of thinking conflates the mother's birth canal with the mistress's erotic recesses. The mother who bore the boy would want him to grow and 'return' to her in the form of another woman, and if he errs along the way, she will guide and teach him.

Hence, in Chaucer's 'faery' thought, devised for the Wife's tale, woman with her permeable body is the archetypal shape-shifter, and, by some eerie truth, mother and mistress are one. Like fairies, women experience transformation as they physically subsume the male (husband or son). Men deny that they themselves change as they change women's bodies, but such denials are ignorant. Maternally viewed, the rapist is a poor, misguided boy, confused in his maturation and need for women. He lacks 'faery' wisdom, and the women of the tale seem desirous to impart it (if only instinctively and ineffably) because it makes men revere women – especially their wives – when they recognize their own origin in the mother who bore them. Although the knight's stepping into the circle resonates with his old crime, it also foreshadows his new understanding as he addresses the old woman as 'mooder'.

None the less, faery thought is so bizarre in the real world that the ensuing plot becomes a tragi-comedy centred on the young man's humiliation and revulsion in having to marry a loathsomely ugly old woman. His life is saved, but the knight undergoes a new sort of death: the demise of his aristocratic 'heritage'. In agony, the newly affianced man exclaims, 'Allas, that any of my nacioun / Sholde evere so foule disparaged be!' (1068–9). From an old wife there will be no progeny, and with this peasant marriage his noble line will die. Just as loss of virginity erased the maid, so too will a low marriage erase the aristocrat. The knight's consciousness of this loss is everywhere implicit in the woman's long speech on *gentillesse*, as she asks him to focus upon nobility within the individual (1153–8). It is maternal wisdom, not paternal blood, that advises the young man here, and he recognizes the truth of what she tells him, his understanding actually coming from within himself, God-given: 'Thy gentillesse cometh fro God allone' (1162).

The Wife of Bath's Tale ends magically with the final faery transformation: having gained sovereignty over her acquiescent husband, the old woman changes into a young, beautiful and faithful wife. In so doing, she restores the promise of aristocratic heirs and thus brings the knight, whose existence has been perpetually under threat, fully to life. But, of course, a correspondent transformation occurs in the male 'hous' of Arthur: the young knight learns who he is in the context of women – mothers and wives – and he accepts his condition with reverence and humility. This scene of recognition and change brings with it glorious union, a wondrous faery-tale ending: 'For joye he hente hire in his armes two. / His herte bathed in a bath of blisse' (1252–3). The last image in the tale is a blissful 'bath', ideal union becoming (in fulfilment of the teller's name) physical and spiritual complementarity, with men understanding that possession is also to be possessed. This scene completes the tale's threefold consummation of the feminine faery ring, as each step marks the man's educative journey: first brutal rape, an act of male indifference; then seductive maidens who vanish and dissolve into an old maternal crone, a figure of intense difference; and last a 'bath' of merged sexual happiness.

In Chaucer's Arthurian faery tale, then, other-worldly encounter develops from violent, polarized confrontation. The normed pleasure-seeking male naïvely but aggressively hunts the feminine Other. He is the first to breach the divide between genders, but by this deed he brings the full force of mystical 'femenye' down upon his own body and mind. His stupid, instinctive act of rape eventually brings him to a meeting with the faery 'mooder', whose stringent pedagogy forces him to a self-recognition. In entering a woman, the foolhardy protagonist literally enters faeryland, a magical abode of shape-shifting and fuzzy limits, where he comes to understand his contiguous existence in a communal world of mothers and fathers, daughters and sons. Chaucer uses the other thought-world of fairies to elucidate for men a different perspective – one fashioned as the physically permeable perspective of all women who are sexualized by men – a perspective that seems likely to elude men in their self-enclosed, complacent worlds, where they live within masculine bodies that seem stably fixed.

Folktale: The Pardoner's Tale

In the narratives explored so far Chaucer used other-worldly mediums – dreams, fairies – to explore invisible psychological terrains beyond the ken of rationality. A third medium for bizarre, truth-telling occurrence is the folk tale, which uses narrative rather than analysis to convey an internally recognized truth. Chaucer's tale of three wastrels who precipitously meet death is such a tale. The Pardoner explains how and why he uses folk tales in his sermons:

> Than telle I hem ensamples many oon
> Of olde stories longe tyme agoon.
> For lewed peple loven tales olde;
> Swiche thynges kan they wel reporte and holde.
>   (PardP 435–8)

The rhyming phrases emphasize that the stories are multiple in number, venerable in age and oral by long custom. These are the stories people love to recall and retell, forming a collective memory of lore.

In naming his audience 'lewed', that is, illiterate, simple and gullible, the Pardoner betrays contempt for common folk. Exceedingly proud of his rhetorical skills, he holds himself above the 'lewed' and is pleased that he can manipulate their stories for his own strategic gain, namely to win gold. The irony, of course, is that the old story warns against love of money. The Pardoner gloats at how he can hoodwink the congregation by covert reversal of the message, though as he gains materially, his alienation from his fellows increases. Thus the teller illustrates in himself the negative side of his own exemplum, as if he is most in need of the folk wisdom he is unable to receive.

Much of the complexity in the Pardoner's character derives, therefore, from his self-proclaimed and enacted distance from the folk who preserve the stories. And yet, as he retells the old tale he is, in spite of himself, a folk-teller. The Pardoner's oral performance spirals inwards: first the public confession, where he tells how he is set apart from his church audiences, ending, 'Now hoold youre pees! My tale I wol bigynne' (462); then the skilful sermon on vices, ending, 'But, sires, now wol I telle forth my tale' (660); and at last the powerful story of three revellers, which concludes when the Pardoner reverts to his sales pitch: 'But, sires, o word forgat I in my tale' (919). The Pardoner's use of 'tale' denotes the exemplum only, exclusive of his double prologue and epilogue (which he 'forgot' because it has no place in the tale). The paradox of a non-folksy folk-teller lends tension to the performance. Chaucer, of course, provokes this tension. Within a written text that portrays a fictional series of spoken performances, the genre adopted by the Pardoner is intrinsically without intervening medium. Orality underscores its immediacy. An old tale well told haunts the recesses of the unconscious with half-disclosed truths. Such a narrative possesses genuine story-telling magic, and its efficacious moral may even foil the speaker's ill motives. In packaging it as an enactment of a preaching performance, Chaucer reinscribes its orality, even as the Pardoner's character would seem to divide it from folk performance.

Hence, aside from the complications of speaker and motive, there is the tale itself. The surreal world it creates challenges the rational one we inhabit. The plot is in fact ancient: a group of companions (usually numbered three but sometimes two) discover a treasure, and the common bonds of friendship break as individual greed leads to betrayal and homicide. The analogues, which stretch in recorded time from the fourth or third century BC (a Buddhist story) to the present (the latest reported one comes from Zaire), testify to an enduring sense of the story's claim to truth: it seems to witness wryly to a wayward human propensity to seek gain even to the point of harm to others. The catch to the story is that such heedless pursuit of personal 'good' entraps each plotter, who does not see his own destruction coming.

The plot also testifies to a human disinclination to learn from collective experience. Often it includes an outside figure who offers counsel or who presages the deaths to come, becoming a figure of unheeded *memento mori*. In the Pardoner's Tale, however, there are, all told, three admonitory figures who serve as truth-tellers: a boy, a taverner and an old man. The riotous threesome ignore counsels from three others and quickly meet their fate. In Chaucer's hands the old tale becomes a story of tales told and retold through generations; that is, it is a folk tale about folk tales, as if its story is the most primordial of all, and to brush it off is so foolish as to be inconceivable. Yet the plot follows men who do bypass the truth-tellers; and it intimates, further, that the oft-told story is tragically repudiated on a daily basis.

The first of the internal tellers is the boy, who gives an odd answer when he is asked to name the corpse being borne off to its grave:

> 'Sire,' quod this boy, 'it nedeth never-a-deel;
> It was me toold er ye cam heer two houres.
> He was, pardee, an old felawe of youres,
> And sodeynly he was yslayn to-nyght,
> Fordronke, as he sat on his bench upright.'
> (670–4)

The boy says that his knowledge precedes the rioters' presence by a mere two hours, and, devoid of personal experience, he just repeats what he has heard. He identifies the passing corpse as a man who drank heavily, an 'old felawe' of the three rioters. The man's name is unimportant ('it nedeth never-a-deel'), but, eager to tattle-tell, he does volunteer the name of the murderer, a 'privee theef' who slays with a spear:

> Ther cam a privee theef men clepeth Deeth,
> That in this contree al the peple sleeth,
> And with his spere he smoot his herte atwo,
> And wente his wey withouten wordes mo.
> He hath a thousand slayn this pestilence.
> And, maister, er ye come in his presence,
> Me thynketh that it were necessarie
> For to be war of swich an adversarie.
> Beth redy for to meete hym everemoore;
> Thus taughte me my dame; I sey namoore.
> (675–84)

The boy's words were taught him by his mother, and they conclude with a warning both ominous and innocently parroted: 'be war of swich an adversarie'. What is most strange about this speech is its introduction of Death as a character, someone unmet but already set up as a challenger of the three rioters' prowess. Death does not appear bodily in the story, and his ways are silent, but the boy betrays him through a tale.

The taverner's voice enters next by invoking the blessed mother and avowing that the boy speaks truth (685–91). As second truth-teller, the taverner also warns of the homicide Death, specifying his locale (about a mile away) and length of stay (a year), thereby further particularizing the idea that Death may be sought and found. Compared to the boy, the taverner has a wider reach of experience. The rioters respond to the cues of both as they vow to join as 'brothers' and hunt down and slay the enemy Death (698–700). The tale's third truth-teller is the old man, who delivers a lament and warning that exactly counterpoise the boy's simplicity. The rigours of going through the world a 'longe tyme' (726) have wasted the old man's 'flessh, and blood, and skyn' (732). Bearing the wisdom and pain of long experience, the old man invokes his 'mooder' not as origin of knowledge but as desired end of time, a view reversing the boy's lens.

Each of the three admonitory figures in the Pardoner's Tale has a speech that expresses his life-phase, his maternal relationship and his range of experience. Each demonstrates intimate knowledge of death, whom they all name as if it were a person – one rather distant from themselves, but corporealized and threatening for the rioters. The three emblematic figures all have 'mothers' who oppose death: the instinctive, inborn desire to avoid death (boy); Mary's saintly intercession and, implicitly, her bearing of Christ/Life into the world (taverner); a restorative rest after an existence of wasting away (old man). Death as defined by these maternal concepts is black oblivion.

The tale's haunted aura develops from the three interactions between the warners and the warned. Each threesome seems to inhabit its own existential space and to communicate with the other three as if across a divide. In the third meeting the old man fixes a steady gaze upon the 'proudest' of the rioters, a look emanating from a pair of penetrating eyes, his body swathed in clothing save for the 'ful pale and welked' face (716–38). The gaze is mutual, a young man perusing the face of age, the old man staring back (720). The image is a mirror of time. The boy, taverner and old man derive from a familiar scheme for depicting man's times of life as three ages – Youth, Middle Age, Age – a pattern imitative of lived experience (past, present, future) and best known elsewhere in Middle English in the *Parlement of the Thre Ages*. The specific three-age variation used here is closely allied to *memento mori* imagery: the legend of the Three Living and the Three Dead. This popular motif was a widespread theme painted upon church walls in Chaucer's England – exactly the sorts of churches in which the fictional Pardoner would have preached. Such illustrations depict a scary set-scene of surreal encounter in which three worldly characters find themselves all at once dominated by three walking dead, figures who resemble corpses and brandish ominous weapons. The dead warn of impending death, the ravages of which are made forcefully apparent. The motif is one of encounter with

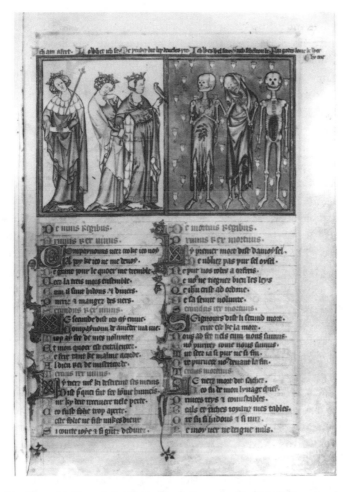

Figure 20.1 The Three Living and the Three Dead. From the De Lisle Psalter. London, British Library, MS Arundel 83 II, fo. 127 (after 1308). [By permission of The British Library.]

the strange and yet real: the undeniable fact of one's own death and the bodily change that must occur with it.

In many pictorial representations, such as that in the De Lisle Psalter (*c.*1310), the three dead appear to be in successive stages of decay, and the three living seem differentiated, too, by prop and gesture: a falcon held by Youth; a fearful gesture made by Middle Age; and a sceptre grasped by Age in his royal prime (see figure 20.1). Similar elements appear in the sole Middle English poem on the theme, the alliterative *De tribus regibus mortuis*. This work opens with a riotous hunt led by three kings, but the action quickly freezes into the conventional artistic tableau of encounter when the enlivened apparitions of the dead materialize. At that point the poem becomes a chillingly formal set-piece: living and dead speak one stanza each in a kind of stylized dialogue between two worlds. The De Lisle Psalter page displays the same rigour:

living and dead are each held within their own frames, cognizant of the other side but also entirely separate. Speeches, too, appear in separate columns, as if to set present life before a mirror of its inverted future. In medieval art the dead are often rendered in stiff poses while the living react in a panic of movement. Likewise, the three 'riotours' are, in name and activity, caught up in frenzied behaviours, and epithets differentiate them: 'proudest', 'worst', 'youngest'. The second threesome are narratively static and occupy a fictional space that interacts with the rioters but exists in a different dimension, where like eerie folk-tellers they utter age-old wisdom.

In the primal folkloric thought of the Pardoner's Tale life is a blind journey towards death. Recklessly seeking to quell Death, the three rioters are propelled through time, passing markers of ageing. Their journey covers the space of a symbolic day; the demise of their 'old felawe' occurred the previous night (672–3), a sign, apparently, of how humanity plays out the story in endless cycle. They plan to traverse a full mile in quest of Death, but in their precipitous haste they encounter the Old Man at less than 'half a mile' (711). Meanwhile, the three truth-tellers continue dream-like and perpetually 'alive' in a place where men pass by every day. Earlier ages bequeath lore, but the living disregard it, because, presumably, the one simple existential truth common to ancestors – namely, death – is the one fact that all living will inherently deny. The collective voice of generations tells this fatal tale; but, if heard closely, it also tells better news of a maternal, sheltering salvation.

In ways that seem both pre-ordained and individually willed, the three wastrels of the Pardoner's Tale suicidally cross the boundary of life. After they hurry past the old man, signpost for their imminent deaths, they find little pardon. His not-so-cryptic words explained that hope lay in a willingness to exchange youth for age. If the rioters were to trade places with him, Death would die. The answer is Christian: imitate Christ, who died in his mortal prime so that humanity, in its collective agedness, could live. As the old man says, he 'lafte' Death 'under a tree' (762–3). In rushing to the oak and finding gold (that is, material death), the rioters lose the treasure of their immortal existence, which abides unseen at the sacramental tree.

The Pardoner mirrors the heedlessness of folk to folklore when he uses a folk tale perversely to trick people. Though the tale exists for the benefit of later living generations, he would knowingly break the chain of efficacious telling. No matter how potent, the lore of folk – and even of Christ – seems futile because it tries to reach those in the midst of life, those who by nature attend only to their own immediate, death-pursuing impulses. But, as the Pardoner concedes, the story's inherent virtue may break through in spite of his own determined cynicism (403–10, 429–32).

The three protagonists' meeting with something other in the Pardoner's Tale thus fits with the rest of Chaucer's works examined in this chapter. What they find ultimately is death, the exact opposite of what they are as living creatures. They do not, however, meet a character, Death. Instead they meet figures of themselves as they age in time, figures who speak for earlier generations to whom they are related by common human thread. Chaucer fashions from an old folk tale a story about folklorishness, with its final chilling conclusion that the living dead speak both to us and ever out of range of our unhearing, deadened ears. And among the dead, most intriguingly and perhaps most scarily, is Christ the living.

While Chaucer uses dreams to explore the inner world of thought, and faery realms to explore the bodily experiences of women, he uses folklore to explore the cumulative meaning of the dead who lived before. In each type, the confrontation is primal and strangely unrecognizable: one does not know where one is upon initial contact, and one feels strangely lost, disoriented and threatened. The comforts of one's normed sense of self are disrupted by a challenge from outside. But in each case it is the protagonist who initiates the encounter, which emanates from within himself and through his own actions. Thus the Other, delivered by process of surreal thought-worlds ('swevenes', 'faery', 'oold tales'), is only a strangely refracted mirror of oneself.

See also BODIES; CHRISTIAN IDEOLOGIES; GENRE; LIFE HISTORIES; LOVE; PAGAN SURVIVALS; PERSONAL IDENTITY; WOMEN.

REFERENCES AND FURTHER READING

Allen, Sr Prudence (1997) *The Concept of Woman: The Aristotelian Revolution, 750 BC–AD 1250*, 2nd edn (Grand Rapids, Mich.: Eerdmans). A history of sex polarity and sex complementarity in Western thought.

Binski, Paul (1996) *Medieval Death: Ritual and Representation* (London: British Museum Press). The macabre, the Three Living and the Three Dead, and the De Lisle Psalter page reproduced.

Boitani, Piero (1989) *The Tragic and the Sublime in Medieval Literature* (Cambridge: Cambridge University Press). The Old Man's alterity and death's uncanniness in the Pardoner's Tale.

Burrow, John A. (1995) 'Elvish Chaucer', in *The Endless Knot: Essays in Honor of Marie Borroff*, ed. M. Teresa Tavormina and R. F. Yeager (Cambridge: Brewer), 105–11. Discusses what 'elvish' means and how the word fits Chaucer.

Crane, Susan (1994) *Gender and Romance in Chaucer's* Canterbury Tales (Princeton: Princeton University Press). Magic, shape-shifting, and the uncanny in the Wife of Bath's Tale.

Delany, Sheila (1972) *Chaucer's* The House of Fame: *The Poetics of Skeptical Fideism* (Chicago: Chicago University Press). Essential reading on the *House of Fame*.

Dinshaw, Carolyn (1998) 'Rivalry, rape, and manhood: Gower and Chaucer', in *Violence against Women in Medieval Texts*, ed. Anna Roberts (Gainesville, Fla.: University Press of Florida), 137–60. Rape theorized as crime of 'indifference' (man blind to feminine Other).

Hamel, Mary and Merrill, Charles (1992) 'The analogues of the Pardoner's Tale and a new African version', *Chaucer Review* 26, 175–83. Folklore types that correspond to the Pardoner's Tale.

Kruger, Stephen F. (1993) 'Imagination and the complex movement of Chaucer's *The House of Fame*', *Chaucer Review* 28, 117–34. In the context of dream the *House of Fame* operates in the realm of the imagination.

Laskaya, Anne (1995) *Chaucer's Approach to Gender in the* Canterbury Tales (Cambridge: Brewer). The faery world and flux in the Wife of Bath's Tale.

Lebbe, Christophe (1998) 'The shadow realm between life and death', in *The Pagan Middle Ages*, ed. Ludo J. R. Milis, trans. Tanis Guest (Woodbridge, Suffolk: Boydell), 65–82. [Original work published 1991.] Cultural anthropology used to contextualize stories of the walking dead.

Lindahl, Carl (1987) *Earnest Games: Folkloric Patterns in the* Canterbury Tales (Bloomington and Indianapolis: Indiana University Press). Chaucer's folk rhetoric.

Lindley, Arthur (1992) ' "Vanysshed was this daunce, he nyste where": Alisoun's absence in the *Wife of Bath's Prologue and Tale*', *ELH: English Literary History* 59, 1–21. The women of the tale blend together; magic, not education, reconciles the sexes.

Phillips, Helen and Havely, Nicholas, eds (1997) *Chaucer's Dream Poetry* (Harlow: Longman). Most recent treatment of the dream genre in Chaucer.

Purdon, L. O. (1992) 'The Pardoner's Old Man and the second death', *Studies in Philology* 89, 334–49. Theology of second death provides a way to understand the Old Man's deathless state.

Russell, J. Stephen (1988) *The English Dream Vision: Anatomy of a Form* (Columbus: Ohio State University Press). A study of the dream genre; the *House of Fame* discussed as 'the end of lore'.

Spearing, A. C. (1976) *Medieval Dream-poetry* (Cambridge: Cambridge University Press).

Medieval dream theory, with a fine discussion of the *House of Fame* and the affinity between dreams and poetry.

Tristram, Philippa (1976) *Figures of Life and Death in Medieval English Literature* (New York: New York University Press; London: Elek). Background on *memento mori* imagery, including the Three Ages, and the Three Living and Three Dead.

Wenzel, Siegfried (1996) 'Another analogue to The Pardoner's Tale', *Notes and Queries* 241, 134–6. A version of the tale used as exemplum in a medieval English sermon.

Williams, E. Carlton (1942) 'Mural paintings of the Three Living and the Three Dead in England', *Journal of the British Archaeological Association*, 3rd ser. 7, 31–40. Documents the prevalence of such paintings in English parish churches.

21
Pagan Survivals
John M. Fyler

In *An Elegant and Learned Discourse of the Light of Nature* (1652), the Cambridge Platonist Nathanael Culverwel condemns all pagans to eternal reprobation, conceding only that the virtuous will be punished less severely than the vicious:

> *Socrates* shall taste a milder cup of wrath, when as *Aristophanes* shall drink up the dregs of fury; if divine justice whip *Cicero* with rods, 'twill whip *Catiline* with Scorpions. An easier and more gentle worm shall feed upon *Augustus*, a more fierce and cruel one shall prey upon *Tiberius*; if justice put *Cato* into a prison, 'twill put *Cethegus* into a dungeon. (p. 204)

To most late medieval contemplators of classical antiquity this gradation within utter degradation would be shocking, as much as would be finding the Roman Stoics among the heaped carcasses in Spenser's House of Pride. But Culverwel's is a particularly vivid, if late, answer to a paradox that many medieval writers felt: that the great minds of classical antiquity, who had lived virtuously and had pushed speculative thought and literary genius as far as human reason, unaided by revelation, could push, must none the less spend eternity in torment, denied a heavenly reward merely, it would seem, by the historical accident of their birth-dates.

Medieval Affinities with the Pagan Past

The sharp awareness of this paradox, its demand for a mixture of sympathy and cold dismissal, constitutes an important part of a larger issue: the ambiguous relationship of the Christian Middle Ages to pagan antiquity. This relationship was at once more tentative and more assured than our own. For if the date of the Incarnation marked an eternal barrier between Christians and those who lived before Christ – a barrier that Culverwel must have been one of the last to insist on so rigidly – the simultaneous lack of historical sense that we so often find in medieval literature marks a much closer, unreflective feeling of kinship with ancient times. Even in so sophisticated and historically aware a writer as Chaucer, Pandarus evidently lives in a fourteenth-century house; and Theseus in the Knight's Tale is an exemplar of chivalry, though he rules in ancient Athens (with its conspicuous examples of pagan alterity, the colosseum Theseus constructs and the 'wake-pleyes', the funeral games for Arcite). As we have often been reminded, the discovery of a sense of history marks the Renaissance; in art it manifests itself, as Jean Seznec (1953) and Erwin Panofsky (1960) have shown, in the reunion of classical figures with classical forms: Romans start wearing togas once again and Roman gods adopt once more the poses they adopt in classical sculpture, as they inhabit anew their ancient iconography. But this sense of history offsets its gains in accuracy with the loss of proximity and intimacy: the relics of the antique past, whether Ciceronian periods or statues of Venus, now lie on the other side of a gulf marked by the Middle Ages; and the attempt to recreate them always threatens to degenerate into a merely nostalgic effort to copy an unrecoverable past. In Panofsky's words, 'the classical past was looked upon, for the first time, as a totality cut off from the present; and, therefore, as an ideal to be longed for instead of a reality to be both utilized and feared' (1960: 113).

By contrast, the relation of the Middle Ages to classical antiquity is often one of unreflecting affinity; and the result of this medieval affinity with the ancients is the predictable attempt to mitigate the severity of reprobation – as it were, to sneak a few pagans into heaven. The thirteenth-century pseudo-Ovidian poem *De Vetula* tells us that Ovid, as an old man, worshipped the Blessed Virgin. The issue is centrally important for Dante, who regretfully condemns Virgil and his peers to Limbo, but manages to place Cato and a Christian Statius in Purgatory, and Trajan and the just Ripheus (a minor character from *Aeneid* II) in Paradise. For other medieval writers the works of the ancients, if not the ancients themselves, can be saved, overcoming an uneasiness about the awkward fit between classical style and Christian verity that goes back to SS Jerome and Augustine. Virgil's *Fourth Eclogue* predicts the coming of the Messiah; the star that Ovid identifies as the apotheosized Julius Caesar, in *Metamorphoses* XV, is in fact – the *Ovide moralisé* ingeniously argues – the Nativity star, which Ovid misidentifies so that he may curry favour with Augustus, in the hope of ending his exile.

Chaucer's Paganism

Chaucer's treatment of the virtuous pagan, and of classical literature, develops the concerns of his predecessors, but does so within a peculiarly fourteenth-century, and peculiarly English context – one that has been well explored by Beryl Smalley's book on the fourteenth-century classicizing English friars (Smalley 1960). The primary intention of these friars – notably Robert Holcot and John Ridewall – is to provide a repertory of sermon exempla; but in the process they make the body of classical myth and legend available as stories, to poets and their audiences; and their own antiquarian response to the pagan past is surprisingly generous. Although their purposes are different, they share many interests with Chaucer's fourteenth-century Italian sources, Dante, Petrarch and above all Boccaccio, whose fascination with arcane detail surpasses them all (as in his glosses to the *Teseida* and in his treatise on the *Genealogy of the Gods*). Chaucer rarely exhibits the same level of antiquarian knowledge, or for that matter interest; but in other respects he is at one with the English friars and Italian poets in his knowledge of and sophisticated use of the Latin classics. Indeed, in episodes he adds to Boccaccio's *Il Filostrato* when he revises the Italian poem for *Troilus and Criseyde*, he relies directly on Statius' *Thebaid* and Virgil's *Aeneid*: at the end of Book II, when he mentions Polyphete (an obscure character mentioned once in *Aeneid* VI), he is clearly composing with the *Aeneid* open on the table in front of him. Although when possible Chaucer makes use of medieval translations and adaptations of classical material – probably the *Ovide moralisé*, certainly the French *romans antiques* of the twelfth century – he also goes back to the original Latin texts of Ovid, Virgil and Statius. And in the Prologue to the *Legend of Good Women* he indulges in some Ovidian myth-making of his own, by inventing the metamorphosis of Alceste into a daisy; in this effort to go beyond Ovid, he copies the more self-conscious and self-advertising myth-making of Dante and Froissart.

Astrology, the goddess Fortune and magic can all be seen as pagan survivals as well, though they are also very much at home in a medieval setting. In the realm of magic, the pagan assumes a wider meaning, that of faery, the world summoned up in the Tale of Sir Thopas and the tales of the Wife of Bath, Squire and Franklin. Indeed, in the Merchant's Tale, as in the anonymous *Sir Orfeo*, classical myth and fairyland are conflated, when Pluto and Proserpina are the 'kyng of Fairye' and his queen. Chaucer's scientific interests make themselves evident in his use of astrology; and though astrology appears in a number of tales set in the Christian world (those of the Miller and Man of Law, for example), it does serve, in pagan settings, as a metaphor for pagan fatalism, and the manifested power of the pagan pantheon. Astrology and Fortune suggest a continuity in human experience. 'The deeth of every man' is written in the stars, according to the Man of Law, 'but mennes wittes ben so dulle / That no wight kan wel rede it atte fulle' (196, 202–3). Just as the god of love can still pluck a proud peacock, as much as he could in pagan times (*Troilus* I, 210, 232–8), so the stars and Fortune exercise a continuing power over human affairs. But they also define a difference between past and present. For the medieval Christian is exhorted to resist the predispositions that the stars mould in human character, not give in to them as the Wife of Bath exuberantly does in her prologue: 'I am al Venerien / In feelynge, and myn herte is Marcien' (609–10); 'I folwed ay myn inclinacioun / By vertu of my constellacioun' (615–16). As Dorothy Bethurum Loomis notes (1968: 152), Bishop Bradwardine's *De causa Dei* – to which the Nun's Priest alludes (3241) – 'is a great defence of Augustinian predestination but opposes vigorously stellar determinism'. So, in a Boethian context, we know that Troilus is in trouble when he complains of Fortune's unfairness: 'Have I the nought honoured al my lyve, / As thow wel woost, above the goddes alle?' (IV, 267–8).

The choice in both these instances, for the medieval writer or reader looking back on the pagan past, is to discriminate between what is to be accepted and what rejected (or escaped), what incorporated and what refused as alien to the healthy and specifically Christian mind and soul. In this respect, the issue of pagan survivals – the 'despoliation of the Egyptians', in Augustine's phrasing (Minnis and Scott 1988: 38) – becomes part of a larger question, that of purity and contamination (Douglas 1966) in its medieval form. These concerns can appear in a distrust of the 'foreign', which for fourteenth-century Londoners can mean anyone not from London or, for that matter, people of low estate within London itself; xenophobia; or fears of contamination by an unclean Other (see Moore 1987).

In the *Canterbury Tales*, Chaucer often reveals the ethical quality of his characters by their degree of magnanimity, their toleration for otherness, in the ways they people their tales. This characteristic is particularly noticeable in the three tales about non-Christian Asia: those of the Man of Law, the Prioress and the Squire. Two of the three recoil from the otherness of Islam and of medieval Jewry; only the Squire treats his subject, the Mongols, with toleration and an engaged sympathy, bestowing praise upon Cambyuskan as a virtuous heathen – 'He kepte his lay, to which that he was sworn' (18) – and after dinner, we are told, his court goes 'Unto the temple, as reson was' (296). All three tales are concerned with issues of contamination, the risks of confronting the alien, the broad cultural issues of contact, resistance and assimilation. They are tales, moreover, where xenophobia and resistance to the other mark a parochial and confining self-enclosure.

The Otherness of Jews: The Prioress's Tale

The Man of Law's Tale, itself confined, implicitly comments on the Prioress's even more extreme narrowness of vision. The two tales are alike in their xenophobic alarm at the world outside Christian Europe, but they differ strikingly in the place at which they draw that boundary. The Man of Law, in his effort to mark off the world of Mahound in Syria and pagan belief in Northumbria, quite comfortably includes the Judaic and classical past within the Christian present. In this he is exactly in accord with the famous catalogue of the Nine Worthies: three Jews, three classical pagans and three Christians. He notes God's power in saving Daniel and Jonah; in keeping the 'peple Ebrayk' from drowning in the Red Sea (473–90); in saving Susannah (639); in giving courage to David and Judith (935–40). In the Prioress's Tale, by contrast, the naming of the little clergeon's mother as 'This newe Rachel' (627) is conspicuous by its singularity and by its failure to recognize that Rachel, like the mothers of the Holy Innocents whose Mass the Prioress quotes (457–9), has some connection to this 'cursed folk of Herodes al newe' (574) that she so vehemently castigates.

The Prioress's Tale visualizes its setting, despite the abstraction of its being in an unnamed city in Asia, in a notably vivid way. The Jews are confined to a ghetto, sustained there by the city's ruler 'For foul usure' (491): usury as the exchange of money contaminated by the taking of interest. But despite the mix of practical necessity and political corruption implicit here, the pretence remains that uncontaminated separation remains possible. Through the street of the ghetto 'men myghte ride or wende, / For it was free and open at eyther ende' (493–4). Language, the quintessential medium of exchange, is what provokes the murder of the 'litel clergeon' – but indeed, sacral and not necessarily comprehensible language. He memorizes the *Alma redemptoris* without understanding its meaning, and learns it from a friend who himself does not understand it; nor is it clear that the Jews understand its words, though they know its significance. As the Prioress implies, a more worldly silence would have kept him alive. Instead, his innocent, uncomprehending speech provokes the retaliatory attempt at unclean corruption. The disposal of the boy's body in a common privy is purposely shocking, but as ineffective as the attempt to silence his voice. When he begins to sing again, lying upright in the privy with his throat cut, he is called 'This gemme of chastite, this emeraude', and the 'ruby bright' of martyrdom (609–10). The Prioress's Tale ends with a progression of images to restore the visible purity or integrity of what cannot be corrupted in any case: the gem in the privy, the grain that when at last removed can restore the boy's tongue to silence, the final enclosure of his 'litel body sweete' 'in a tombe of marbul stones cleere' (681–2).

In the context of thinking about pagan survivals, and the Jews as a special instance of such survivals from antiquity, this tale is given an interesting counterpoint by the anonymous alliterative poem *St Erkenwald*, in which the saint's tears baptize the entombed body of a man who was 'never kyng ne cayser ne yet no knyght nothyre, / Bot a lede of the lagh that then this londe usit' (199–200).[1] The body and clothing of this righteous pagan judge have remained 'unwemmyd' (266), uncorrupted, all through the pagan age of Britain, all through its Roman Christianization, all through the time when the pagan Saxons had defeated the Britons 'And pervertyd all the pepul that in that place dwellid' (10) – as if lying in wait for the Saxons' own conversion in turn by St Augustine. Erkenwald the Bishop of London, a town tied to its origins by its name New Troy, wishes to rededicate and sanctify the devils' temples, to throw out their idols, change their names, and use them to house saints and Christian worship. In the excavations at St Paul's the judge's body is unearthed, so richly clothed and so well preserved that he appears to be merely sleeping. Once his soul is miraculously saved and ascends to heaven, his body and burial clothes immediately blacken and disintegrate.

The central image in these two narratives calls to mind, however coincidentally, Panofsky's vivid summary of the difference between Middle Ages and Renaissance: 'The Middle Ages had left antiquity unburied and alternately galvanised and exorcised its corpse. The Renaissance stood weeping at its grave and tried to resurrect its soul' (1960: 113). The author of *St Erkenwald* and the Prioress are both engaged in galvanizing corpses, but with a notable difference. *St Erkenwald*, by keeping the judge's body immune to the vagaries of historical change – Britain's long history of settlement, conversion, perversion and final redemption – both exorcizes and saves the pagan past. The Prioress's obsession with purity and danger, cleanness and contamination, comes to seem, by contrast, merely a monstrous version of her fastidiousness in table manners.

The *Book of the Duchess*, 1048–87

This passage, from Chaucer's first extant major poem, shows his interest in and detailed – even bookish – knowledge of classical legend and history from the start of his poetic career. The dreamer–narrator somewhat grudgingly allows the man in black, whom he meets in his dream, the claim that White was, in his eyes at least, the best and fairest of all; and his scepticism provokes the mourning lover's reply, which insistently measures himself and his dead beloved by the absolute standards of ancient example. Chaucer takes this practice of an overloaded catalogue of antiquity from his French contemporaries – notably Guillaume de Machaut, in the *Remede de Fortune* – and he is indebted to French poetry for many of the details as well: Alcibiades, for example, is praised for his beauty in the *Roman de la rose*, and the Lucrece allusion – despite Chaucer's naming of the Roman historian Livy – is indebted to the *Rose* and its source, Walter Map's letter from 'Valerius' to 'Rufinus' on the dangers of marriage.

In his later poems, Chaucer occasionally expands on the details of myth and legend, presumably for the instruction of his audience: Pandarus, for example, mentions 'Ticius in helle, / Whos stomak foughles tiren evere moo / That hightyn volturis, as bokes telle' (*TC* I, 786–8); if this seems like unnecessary detail in its immediate context, the detail is skilfully and unobtrusively enough conveyed. In the *Book of the Duchess*, by contrast, the youthful poet seems to be parading his knowledge somewhat awkwardly when he indulges in such elaborations of detail, whether the brief digression on Algus and arabic numerals (435–40) or, in the passage considered here, the account of Achilles' death for love of Polyxena (1066–71) – although one might argue that the excursus on love and death is appropriate to the mourning man in black and the larger elegiac concerns of the poem.

The reference to Dares Phrygius (1071) also reminds us that medieval knowledge of the Trojan war does not come from Homer, but from Latin versions of the Troy story, including this famous forged eye-witness account, which hands down to the Middle Ages such details as Achilles' stabbing Hector in the back (see *TC* V, 1559). Even more interesting, perhaps, is the easy cohabitation of biblical and pagan references in these allusions to antiquity: Babylon and Nineveh fit easily into a catalogue of ancient cities. Such cohabitation is even more conspicuous in the Man of Law's Tale, where Jewish and pagan traditions comfortably belong to Us, set against the alien, hateful Them of Islam.

The final comparison of the lady White to Penelope and Lucrece is of particular interest. The two ancient names come not from Livy, to whom the poet attributes the story of Lucrece, but from the *Roman de la rose* and the letter of 'Valerius' against marriage, where these heroines are named as the pre-eminent examples of a virtuous womanhood that no longer exists (Fyler 1979: 78–9, 183–4). Praising White as their equal implicitly answers a facile misogyny, in which the example of ancient pagan women is used to browbeat modern Christian ones, but also asserts the possibility that ancient virtue survives in the modern world.

The Knight's Tale, 2438–78

This passage, from the end of Part Three of the Knight's contribution, comes from a tale whose narrator, a lifelong defender of Christian Europe, paradoxically tells a story about a pagan exemplar of chivalry and a pagan world in which divine influence seems arbitrary and indifferent to human desires, if not malign. In this passage, as in other places in Chaucer's poetry, the gods are ambiguously members of the pagan pantheon and planets, and their influence is both as pagan gods (hence, potentially at least, demonic figures) and astrological beings. (The astrology is almost entirely Chaucer's addition to his source, Boccaccio's *Teseida*.) Describing the gods as planets solves some potential difficulties for a medieval poet, by emptying them of their specifically pagan and hence problematic meanings, while suggesting that the human emotions they guide or perhaps merely reflect are universals, not dependent on a pagan religious dispensation. The 'strife in heaven' could of course refer either to gods or planets, but when Saturn proclaims his 'cours, that hath so wyde for to turne', he is speaking as a planet.

In this tale as elsewhere, Chaucer uses the astrological properties of planets, exploiting his interest in scientific knowledge, as an elaborate, and often intellectually demanding, form of wit. The *Complaint of Mars* is notable for its effortless blurring of astronomy and myth; and in the Knight's Tale itself, Venus' tears of vexation 'for wantynge of hir wille' (2665) are evidently raindrops. Saturn appears again in Book III of *Troilus and Criseyde*, in conjunction with Jupiter and the moon in the sign of Cancer (624–5) – an astronomical configuration that occurred in May 1385 for the first time since 769, and that Chaucer means us to read as an omen of the fall of Troy, though Pandarus uses it merely to predict an opportunely heavy rainstorm. This is an interesting moment in a poem full of such moments. It suggests at once that the stars influence Fate for pagans and Christians both, that the carefully distinguished pagan observances – the festival of the Palladium in Book I, a pagan equivalent to Easter (a detail Chaucer takes from Boccaccio), or Pandarus' jarring invocation of the 'Immortal god . . . that mayst nought deyen, / Cupide I mene' (III, 185–6) – obscure a universality in human experience: Cupid even now can take revenge on those who mock him, just as he did in ancient Troy.

In the Knight's Tale the conception of the gods as stars creates a striking eclecticism of reference: Saturn takes credit for the undoing of Samson and 'the cherles rebellynge', including the recent instance in 1381; the paintings in the temple of Mars picture the killing of Julius Caesar, Nero and Antony: 'Al be that thilke tyme they were unborn, / Yet was hir deth depeynted ther-biforn / By manasynge of Mars, right by figure' (2033–5). And Saturn's promise to reconcile Mars and Venus, though they are not of one 'compleccioun', mingles the psychology of the humours with astronomy, as Mars and Venus sum up not only the two parts of the chivalric ideal, but the basic human impulses in the arena of experience that is the world, and specifically as well the arena that Theseus constructs.

Even so, the pagan gods in the Knight's Tale are still gods; and the bleakness of the tale's view of human life has much to do with the fatalism that Alastair Minnis has identified as Chaucer's defining characteristic of pagan antiquity. Like the Merchant's Tale, in which the gods are hypostases of the tale's human characters (Pluto and Proserpina are January and May writ large), the Knight's Tale proposes such analogies: Egeus, like Saturn the old wise man whom one can outrun but not 'atrede' (2449), is superseded by his son, like the more benign Jupiter in his effort to create order from violence and chaos. But the tale's conclusion, in which Theseus' political expediency and pessimism qualify his impulse to impose a fairy-tale happy ending, leaves us with little in the way of optimism about justice in the universe; and since Theseus is himself also a surrogate for the Knight–narrator, who responds to Arcite's death with his own curt agnosticism (2809–15), the power of the pagan survives its historical terminus as a deeply meditated pessimism about human experience.

The Franklin's Tale, 1243–96

This passage differs greatly in tone and meaning from the account of Saturn's influence in the Knight's Tale; and the differences have centrally to do with the voice and attitudes of the tale's narrator, who talks about the details of astrology as

> . . . swich folye,
> As in oure dayes is nat worth a flye –
> For hooly chirches feith in oure bileve
> Ne suffreth noon illusioun us to greve.
>   (1131–4)

The Franklin prefaces his tale by confessing that he is a plain speaker, unversed in the subtleties of rhetoric, and, like the innocent Dorigen within his tale, he resists the threats of illusion, deceptive appearance and the potential sophistry of poetic language – all summed up here in the 'supersticious cursednesse' of astrology, which makes the rocks disappear, or merely seem to disappear, by magic. In the world of the tale, astrology and magic are aligned with other versions of delusion and self-delusion, notably Aurelius' devotion to an impossible fantasy of adulterous love, which is set against Dorigen's clear-headed rejoinder to his protestations, when she asks why a man should 'love another mannes wyf, / That hath hir body whan so that hym liketh?' (1004–5). This fantasy is anatomized in his 'general compleyning' (945), as he works through the gamut of medieval lyric genres in poems of complaint that Dorigen has never understood to be about her; and in the vision of chivalric wish-fulfilment offered him in the magician's book-lined study, a vision of hunting, jousting and 'his lady on a daunce, / On which hymself he daunced, as hym thoughte' (1200–1).

Chaucer gives this story a pagan setting, in such details as Aurelius' prayer to Apollo for aid (1031–79), and he does so in large part to facilitate the Franklin's debunking view of astrology as a form of black magic. Unlike his creator, the Franklin knows 'no termes of astrologye', though he then offers us a catalogue of precisely such terms, starting with the Tolletan tables. But this list sounds very much like the Canon's Yeoman's confused list of alchemical terms: specific meaning is less important than, and indeed gets lost in, its primary purpose – to mark itself as specialized jargon, meant to impress non-practitioners with the arcane, and suggest the numinous magical power in the terms themselves. In both cases, though, specialized terminology may also serve to suggest the self-delusion of the practitioner: the magician's astrological list seems oddly parallel, in fact, with the list of Aurelius' lyric genres.

The opening lines of this passage vividly set the season for the tale's climactic moment; and this winter setting is Chaucer's addition to the story, though it picks up the wife's request in Boccaccio's original for a May garden in January. Its details about Janus, the boar's head and even 'Nowel' are consistent enough with the tale's pagan setting; but Chaucer's addition of these details also suggests a deeper symbolic meaning to these celebrations of the winter solstice and New Year. The Franklin's Tale argues, in the person of Arveragus, that 'Trouthe is the hyeste thyng that man may kepe' (1479). Against all our expectations and the expectations of the tale's characters, keeping one's word repeatedly leads to an answering gift of mercy and *gentillesse*, as Aurelius releases Dorigen from her rash vow and the magician releases Aurelius from his threatened bankruptcy. Particularly in the context of the Franklin's pointed comments on heathen folly and illusion, we may well read in this passage a symbolic re-enactment of a favourite medieval paradigm, the progress from Old Law to New Law, from the Old Testament to the new dispensation of mercy and grace. (In its idealizing argument for equality in love, the tale also hearkens back to a still older law, the natural law of the Golden Age.) It may be more than a coincidence that in Shakespeare's late romance *Cymbeline*, which has a character named Arveragus, a similar dispelling of pagan illusion takes place – its story set in the age of Augustus, a time suffused by a heavenly power that seems to affect these pagan characters without their knowing it, as forgiveness and a newly achieved clarity of focus bring about the happy ending.

See also BODIES; ITALY; NARRATIVE; OTHER THOUGHT-WORLDS; SCIENCE; VISUALIZING.

NOTES

1   In *A Book of Middle English*, ed. J. A. Burrow
    and Thorlac Turville-Petre (Oxford: Blackwell,
    1992), 199–212.

References and Further Reading

Anderson, David (1988) *Before the Knight's Tale: Imitation of Classical Epic in Boccaccio's* Teseida (Philadelphia: University of Pennsylvania Press). A scholarly, detailed and very interesting discussion of Boccaccio's response to classical epic, which illuminates Chaucer's somewhat different purposes in the Knight's Tale.

Baswell, Christopher (1995) *Virgil in Medieval England: Figuring the* Aeneid *from the Twelfth Century to Chaucer* (Cambridge: Cambridge University Press). An expert account of Virgil's reception and influence, with very helpful chapters on medieval manuscripts of the *Aeneid* and their annotations, and on Chaucer's use of Virgil.

Brown, Peter and Butcher, Andrew (1991) *The Age of Saturn: Literature and History in the* Canterbury Tales (Oxford: Blackwell). A stimulating reading of several of the *Canterbury Tales* in their historical and social contexts, as Chaucer's presentation of an age of Saturn.

Douglas, Mary (1966) *Purity and Danger: An Analysis of Concepts of Pollution and Taboo* (New York: Praeger). A thought-provoking anthropological discussion, using dietary codes in particular to illuminate broad issues of pollution and taboo.

Fleming, John V. (1990) *Classical Imitation and Interpretation in Chaucer's* Troilus (Lincoln: University of Nebraska Press). Argues that Chaucer imitates the classics in order to fashion 'a classical, Christian tragedy'.

Fyler, John M. (1979) *Chaucer and Ovid* (New Haven: Yale University Press). A reading of Chaucer, particularly the dream visions, as most influenced by, and having a special affinity with, Ovid.

——(1984) '*Auctoritee* and allusion in *Troilus and Criseyde*', *Res Publica Litterarum* 7, 73–92. Using Petrarch's annotations to the *Aeneid* as an analogy, argues that Chaucer alludes directly to the Latin classics in *Troilus and Criseyde*.

Loomis, Dorothy Bethurum (1968) 'Saturn in Chaucer's Knight's Tale', in *Chaucer und seine Zeit: Symposion für Walter F. Schirmer*, ed. Arno Esch (Tübingen: Niemeyer), 149–61. A succinct exposition of Chaucer's debt to twelfth-century Chartrian learning, and his place in the context of fourteenth-century views of astrology.

Minnis, Alastair J. (1982) *Chaucer and Pagan Antiquity*, Chaucer Studies 8 (Cambridge: Brewer). Shows authoritatively that Chaucer's sympathetic interest in the ancient world fits within a context of similarly sympathetic fourteenth-century English writers; the second half of the book offers readings of pagan fatalism in *Troilus and Criseyde* and the Knight's Tale.

Minnis, Alastair J. and Scott, A. B., eds, with the assistance of David Wallace (1988) *Medieval Literary Theory and Criticism c.1100–c.1375: The Commentary Tradition* (Oxford: Clarendon; rev. edn 1991). An essential compendium of medieval theory and criticism, much of it concerned with classical literature.

Moore, R. I. (1987) *The Formation of a Persecuting Society: Power and Deviance in Western Europe, 950–1250* (Oxford: Blackwell). A thought-provoking study, with interesting implications for Chaucer's poetry.

Nolan, Barbara (1992) *Chaucer and the Tradition of the Roman Antique*, Cambridge Studies in Medieval Literature 15 (Cambridge: Cambridge University Press). Very helpful on the transmutations of classical epic in twelfth-century French romance, and the influences of the *roman antique* on Boccaccio and Chaucer.

North, J. D. (1988) *Chaucer's Universe* (Oxford: Clarendon). A scholarly, detailed and informative description of medieval astronomy and astrology, as Chaucer knew them; less persuasive in its readings of particular works.

Panofsky, Erwin (1960) *Renaissance and Renascences in Western Art* (Stockholm: Almqvist & Wiksell). A masterly and profoundly interesting discussion of what differentiates the Renaissance from earlier renascences, particularly in their responses to classical mythology and art.

Patterson, Lee (1991) *Chaucer and the Subject of History* (London: Routledge; Madison: University of Wisconsin Press). Particularly useful in the context of 'pagan survivals' for its readings of *Troilus and Criseyde* and the Knight's Tale, as they show Chaucer's understanding of history and, in particular, Theban history.

Richardson, H. G. (1960) *The English Jewry under the Angevin Kings* (London: Methuen). An illuminating account of the Jews in medieval England, leading up to their expulsion in 1290.

Seznec, Jean (1953) *The Survival of the Pagan Gods: The Mythological Tradition and Its Place in Renaissance Humanism and Art*, trans. Barbara F. Sessions (New York: Pantheon Books; first publ. 1940). A detailed and highly interesting account of the transmission of classical mythology and astronomy to the Middle Ages and beyond.

Smalley, Beryl (1960) *English Friars and Antiquity in the Early Fourteenth Century* (Oxford: Blackwell). A ground-breaking study, with wide implications for Chaucer and other late fourteenth-century English poets.

Wetherbee, Winthrop (1984) *Chaucer and the Poets: An Essay on* Troilus and Criseyde (Ithaca, NY: Cornell University Press). A powerful reading of *Troilus and Criseyde* in the context of Chaucer's debt to the classical poets; the chapter on Statius is especially useful.

Wood, Chauncey (1970) *Chaucer and the Country of the Stars: Poetic Uses of Astrological Imagery* (Princeton: Princeton University Press). Argues that Chaucer's attitude towards astrology was sceptical. Detailed readings of several works, including the *Complaint of Mars*, the Man of Law's Tale and the Franklin's Tale.

22

Personal Identity

Lynn Staley

Chaucer's attention to voicing in the *Canterbury Tales*, as well as his deployment of a persona in all of his major poems, provides evidence for his own interest in identity, its composition and its scope. The vividness of his characters constantly tempts us to take them as real and to use our own tools of psychological analysis to read them that way. However, not only are Chaucer's characters not real, but Chaucer thought about personal identity in ways that are radically different from our own. I would like to provide a historical context for questions of identity that makes it possible to see both why and how the subject might have been of interest to Chaucer. Stephen Greenblatt's *Renaissance Self-Fashioning*[1] argued for a specific set of cultural and political situations that obtained during the sixteenth century in England and that prompted a process of self-creation and re-creation that always, but not exclusively, happened through language. Greenblatt's argument that that particular period in English history gave rise to a new cultural phenomenon has been challenged by medievalists, particularly David Aers and Lee Patterson, who outline historical reasons for looking further back than the sixteenth century for expressions of a discursively formed selfhood. As these scholars, following the lead of philosophers like Charles Taylor, indicate, selfhood cannot be treated without reference to the community which surrounds it, giving it the very systems of meaning that allow it to begin to distinguish between the inner and the outer realms.

For reasons relating to social, political, economic and theological shifts and conflicts, the England of the late fourteenth century was a time when many groups sought to articulate an identity that distinguished them by giving them an authority at once traditional and unique. Group identity is not, of course, the same as personal identity. However, Chaucer's handling of personal identity suggests that what we conceive of as personal (such as emotion, subjectivity, memory, character or piety) is always enmeshed in webs of contingency. Whether those webs are understood as woven by society, history or literary convention, any effort at self-knowledge is doomed without reference to a greater, and usually public, contextuality. In linking identity to what

Taylor has referred to as 'frameworks' designating the horizons within which we live our lives (Taylor 1989: 27), Chaucer does not imply that the self is merely socially constituted, but that the self can only be understood by reference to some greater context. Chaucer's handling of the self underlines its inherent agency, but his hand-ling of the frameworks for the self also suggests how difficult an endeavour it is to articulate a fully realized personal identity apart from the webs within which we con-ceive ourselves.

Definitions

First, let me offer a caveat, since the very term 'personal identity' did not exist in Chaucer's time. The adjective 'personal' was used as a word of clarification (as in 'per-sonal quarrel'), in order to indicate that an act was performed by or against a specific person. 'Identity', drawn from the Latin 'idem', meaning the same, thus identical, was not used in our sense of self or selfhood at all. It is not until the late seventeenth century that the phrase was used to designate the continuity of the personality throughout the phases of existence (*OED*). A related definition that seems to point the way to a world we might find more congenial is the single entry in the *Middle English Dictionary* for the word 'personality': 'Al þe personalite of man stondiþ in þe spirit of him'. The author of such an astonishingly modern statement was a Lollard, a follower of John Wyclif and one of the authors of the heterodox Wycliffite sermons that were written in the late fourteenth century and circulated throughout the fif-teenth. Rather than linking personality to external attributes or to behaviour, he locates the personality in the human spirit, thus in belief.

Perhaps we can come closest to a sense of what Chaucer might have understood by the term 'personal identity' by seeking to understand the Middle English applications of the noun 'persoun', especially those that cite Chaucer. The *Middle English Dictionary* lists Chaucerian usages for 'persoun' that suggest an understand-ing of personhood as firmly linked to physical as well as to spiritual identity. Thus Chaucer describes Criseyde's response to Troilus, 'Hire liked al in-fere, / His person, his aray, his look, his chere' (*TC* II, 1266–7). 'Person' here seems to indicate Troilus' public self, the impression made by his clothing, his manner of carrying himself, and his countenance or demeanour. In the *Canterbury Tales* Prudence tells Melibee, 'Ye shal do youre diligence to kepe youre persone and to warnestore your hous' (2487), suggesting that Melibee's 'person' is not distinguishable from his public holdings, that keeping his person is somehow like fortifying his house. On the Canterbury pilgrimage Harry Bailly digs at the pilgrim Geoffrey by asking, 'What man artow?', going on to comment upon his looks and mannerisms before asking him for his tale. In the Second Nun's Tale, Almachius' first judicial question to Cecile seems a sly echo of Harry Bailly's previous one to Chaucer, 'What maner womman artow?' Their courtroom interchange captures two interconnected ways of under-standing selfhood:

> 'I am a gentil womman born,' quod she.
> 'I axe thee,' quod he, 'though it thee greeve,
> Of thy religioun and of thy bileeve.'
>
> 'Ye han begonne youre questioun folily,'
> Quod she, 'that wolden two answeres conclude
> In o demande; ye axed lewedly.'
>   (SNT 425–30)

Almachius' question about identity and Cecile's aggressive response suggest, like Harry Bailly's quizzing of Chaucer, that any enquiry into the nature of personhood is, inevitably, an enquiry into the relationship between the private self and its public manifestation (see Aers 1988).

Authority

The confrontation between Cecilia, the Christian martyr-to-be, and Almachius, her Roman judge, also suggests that the idea of personal identity is, in addition, bound up with a concern for the nature of authority. Both Almachius and Cecilia present themselves in terms of authority: his civil authority is more than matched by her spiritual authority, and their conversation plays out the distinction between the two that was fundamental to the Lollard challenge to ecclesiastical authority during the late fourteenth and fifteenth centuries. Reverence for authority was embedded in both the Latin and vernacular cultures of medieval Europe, but Chaucer's interest in personal identity as related to the subject of authority has a particular relevance for the historical and cultural conditions of Ricardian England. The search for identity, or for the basis of identity in a pre-existing authority, was not only the common concern of many types of groups during the late fourteenth century but gave Chaucer one of his major themes throughout his writing life. What began in a fairly conventional way as a search for authorial identity ends in the edgy variety of the Canterbury tales and their detailing of the processes by which identities are constructed, consciously or not. For all the richness of Chaucer's handling of his persona in early works like the *Book of the Duchess*, the *House of Fame* and the *Parliament of Fowls*, none of these poems offers the incisive enquiry into identity that we can find in *Troilus and Criseyde* and the *Canterbury Tales*. To some extent, by deflecting attention from himself, or by effacing the author, Chaucer thrust forward the more riveting (and potentially dangerous) subject of identity as it is related to broader social and political categories.

Those processes through which or by which identities are made can be categorized in ways that underline Chaucer's keen appraisal of the frequently contradictory impulses that he saw as driving the world in which he lived and wrote. The interchange between Cecile and Almachius captures some of those contradictions – Is identity performative? Upon what basis does self-understanding rest? Is self-understanding bound to be at issue with authority? If Cecile plays for time (and her life) by taking the question as referring only to lineage, Almachius asserts the more modern (or Lollard) view and links identity to belief. Like an ecclesiastical inquisitor, Almachius searches out what might threaten a status quo rooted in lineage and power. Chaucer here stages in miniature a drama of semantic confrontation that is played out many times among the Canterbury pilgrims who, in creating themselves for their fellow pilgrims, allow Chaucer to demonstrate ways in which identities are pasted together, textually, socially, culturally, spiritually and materially. These 'personal' enterprises staged throughout Chaucer's works cannot be separated from a broader contemporary search for ecclesiastical and regal images whose authority lay in their carefully fashioned identities. It would be inaccurate to use a term like *national search*, since the very concept of a 'national' identity lay some years in the future, but the self-consciousness and the porosity that allow for identity-making is certainly apparent in the political world of the late fourteenth century.

Identity in Crisis

These are years during which England's actual power (in the sense of military power and economic might) fluctuated, primarily in relation to those of France and the continuing impact of the Hundred Years War; but they are also years when the prestige of English institutions came under a good deal of internal stress. In 1376 the Black Prince, Edward III's oldest son and heir to the throne, died. In 1377 Edward himself, who had been an absent and senile monarch for the last years of his reign, died, and in 1378 a child, Richard, acceded to the throne. In that same year Pope Gregory XI died, and Christendom was for thirty years ruled, depending upon its political allegiances, by one of two popes. Moreover, from about 1377 or 1378 until he died in 1384, John Wyclif began to question the very basis of papal and clerical authority and to hammer further at the foundations of ecclesiastical identity by questioning the doctrine of transubstantiation by which the elements of the Mass were physically changed from bread and wine into the body and blood of Christ. The English rising of 1381 and the developing crisis of regal authority which was focused upon Richard's apparent inability to satisfy parliamentary commons with his fiscal solvency, or the nobility with his zeal for war, contributed to a situation of profound social change, one that must have seemed in need of a defining rhetoric. However, as William Langland's *Piers Plowman* demonstrates through its three successive versions, written between approximately 1368 and 1388–9, the need for such a rhetoric and the identity crisis such a need can prompt did not suddenly emerge with the accession of Richard or with the controversies that swirled around Wyclif.[2]

The origins for the social aspect of the crisis can be traced further back to the catastrophic effects of the Black Death, which first appeared in 1348 and reappeared in waves thereafter, killing possibly one-third or one-half of the population. The Statute of Labourers, which attempted to ignore the economic changes consequent on demographic disaster by fixing wages (but not prices) at earlier levels, along with the steadily rising taxation that the war with France demanded, created a volatile situation in the English countryside. At the same time, during the last quarter of the century, the parliamentary commons began to forge a rhetorical identity for itself as the conscience of the realm, describing itself as a body that was representative, that acted for the good of the 'commonwealth'. Though the members of the commons more often tended to act for the good of the landed class that they, in fact, represented, their attempt to define themselves in terms of a broader, communal identity found its own shrewd echo in the voices of those who rejected the tax of 1380 and the attempts in 1381 to collect it. Thus the rebels of 1381 called themselves the 'true commons', defining themselves *against* a body whose authority was being so radically questioned. As studies by David Aers (1988), Steven Justice (1994), Derek Pearsall (1989) and Paul Strohm (1992), as well as the collections of contemporary documents written about the rising edited by R. B. Dobson (1970), indicate, social identity was one of the deeply contested issues in the rising and in the attempts by contemporary chroniclers to record it for posterity.

An even more studied effort to forge an identity is described by the efforts of Richard II in his maturity. Criticized by parliament for his heedlessness, then directly threatened by the Appellant Lords in the Merciless Parliament of 1388, Richard found himself potentially without a throne, then certainly without his closest friends and advisers, who were either dead or in exile. From 1389, when he declared his majority to parliament, to his forced abdication in 1399, Richard sought to create a regal identity that would serve to define not simply himself but the scope of his power. Works like the Wilton Diptych (Gordon 1993) can be seen as royal icons, created for Richard's own private devotions. However, though private, the Wilton Diptych is also a representation of Richard's own carefully put together public or regal myth: he kneels, flanked by the saints Edmund, Edward the Confessor and John the Baptist, to hail the Christ child who, held in Mary's arms and flanked by angels wearing Richard's badge of the white hart, hails the boyish king (see figure 7.1, p. 116 above). The private Richard who would have knelt before this picture of his kneeling youthful self was always and also a public figure, whose increasingly formal and ritualistic manner blurred the distinction between the two realms (see Saul 1997: 435–67). Richard's determined presentation of the sacral nature of English kingship, his devotion to the deposed Edward II, his ancestor, his emphasis upon the iconic nature of his rule, may tell us something about Richard himself, but they also reflect a contemporary awareness of the processes by which identities are made.

Self-definition: Arms, Badges, Wealth

Chaucer would certainly have been alert to such processes. Called as a witness at the Scrope–Grosvenor trial before the Court of Chivalry in 1387, Chaucer was directly involved in one of the major disputes of the time which centred on the right to bear certain arms. His status as a king's esquire, as a diplomat, and as a representative to the commons in 1386 would have made him keenly aware of the ways in which coats of arms served as definitions of identity, and thus of privilege (Patterson 1991: 180–5). Chivalric disputes about the right to bear arms, as well as the pernicious and disputed habit of distributing badges to bands of retainers, which Richard himself emulated with the badges of the white hart that identified those closest to him, were all means of establishing a symbolic identity. Chaucer's tradesmen in the General Prologue, who bear the liveries of their fraternities, likewise define themselves in terms of an urban world of trade and piety.

These are all instances by which individuals seek to make communally sanctioned identities for themselves, linking an articulation of personal identity to a recognition of its social contingencies, the lineage or wealth or striving by which we are known. Alan Macfarlane (1978), in particular, has argued that the impulse to self-definition that can be found in late fourteenth-century England can be traced to the profound impact of the Black Death and the loosening of ties between families and specific plots of land. The more active land market, the increased mobility of labourers and the greater availability of goods in an already vigorous market economy that were some of the results of the plague would inevitably have influenced ways of thinking about personal identity as not necessarily tied to status and birth, thus as potentially flexible. Not only does that possibility include the possibility of failure and so of insecurity, but these conditions would also produce a corresponding anxiety in the already privileged, since what is at issue is the foundation upon which privilege rests. In the chronicle accounts of the rising of 1381, written by monks as histories, the dread and sense of impending chaos, of boundaries transgressed, of the social fabric rent, signal how terrible a thing such strivings were for those who controlled land and culture.

As Sylvia Thrupp demonstrated in her study of merchant wealth and corresponding influence, the England of Chaucer's time was not simply the fiefdom of the nobility or of a few wealthy monasteries, nor was it the property of angry rebels. It contained means by which a man of relatively modest background might well go far. After all, when Richard II wanted a loan in 1391, he turned not to the ancient nobility but to the city of London, or to the merchants who commanded that city. When they turned him down, he moved the government to York, returning only when the city oligarchy was willing to apologize, grant him the sums he needed and produce a pageant of reconciliation. Not even those gestures were enough for Richard: he commissioned the Carmelite monk, Richard Maidstone, to write a poem in Latin supposedly recounting this pageant, a poem that would capture Richard's image and that of the city for posterity (Staley 1996: 248–50; Strohm 1992: 107–11). As fifteenth-century texts like the Paston letters, the *Book of Margery Kempe*, vernacular drama and Lollard trials demonstrate, the worlds of the gentry community, of the city or of small artisan groups were increasingly sites for the tensions associated with individuality. Linking the process of realizing a personal identity to goods, or to increased economic opportunity, inevitably draws a line between material wealth or flexibility and inner possibility. Chaucer's own focus upon the acquisition of wealth, particularly in the *Canterbury Tales* and pilgrims and characters who either have it or want it, suggests his own profound scepticism about the benefits of capital gain to the inner person.

Spiritual Categories

If Ricardian England provided a likely social and political context for the business of 'self-fashioning', the traditions of Christian spirituality had an even more powerful sanction for the belief in and development of an inner life. Though a focus upon inner truth, upon one's personal involvement in salvation, is fundamental to the New Testament, the medieval language for self-scrutiny can more surely be traced to St Augustine's *Confessions*. Here, as Taylor has argued, is the text that 'shifts the focus from the field of objects known to the activity of knowing' (Taylor 1989: 130). In his careful use of the language of inwardness, in his reflexive stance upon the self, as well as his emphasis upon memory as key to self-definition and understanding, Augustine provided the West not simply with a way of mapping the self, but with a rationale for doing so. In the devotional literature of the Middle Ages, both Latin and, increasingly vernacular, we can find strong evidence for a focus upon the inner self. Frequently, and particularly in vernacular devotional treatises, we can also find expressions of a painful but necessary tension between the articulation of an inner reality and the necessity of maintaining a public self. It is here, in the late medieval literature of spirituality, from the writings of the mid-fourteenth-century Richard Rolle, through Langland's effort to define a private and a public self and Julian of Norwich's anguish over the meaning of her revelations, to the Lollard confessions and treatises that are extant, that we can find a large and polished body of writing that proclaims the agonies, the dangers and the freedoms that accompany statements of personal identity.

Chaucer seems to espouse neither the dreams of the cultural materialists nor the visions of the devotees. He appears rather, as I hope to show in my following discussions of selected passages, to insist always upon the contingencies, the frameworks, within which each of his voices, including his own, is set. That identities were made and remade he demonstrates, but how personal those identities are, or how truly they can be realized, seem questions that render his work as ambiguous as it is searching. Or, put more bluntly, Chaucer's quizzing of identity very often questions the likely outcome, or the worth, of the process. A realization of personal identity inevitably involves a break with an old, unrealized, self, a process that St Augustine's *Confessions* analyses in great and sophisticated detail. Whether the conflict is fought on spiritual or social grounds, selfhood comes by and through conflict. And it is at conflict that Chaucer often baulks, asking instead if the game is worth the candle. Or he asks what can come of the sort of violent wrench that signals the birth of a new order of being, a being whose continuity over time is self-consciously distinct. The anguish that can be found in a Rolle or a Langland or a Julian is, in Chaucer, submerged in a variety of scepticism that questions the motives that lie behind the impulse to articulate a self. Contingencies, or frameworks, what Julian finds a way through, Chaucer utilizes as the means by which selfhood is always enmeshed in communal reckoning. His techniques for questioning the processes involved in identity-making are many, all of them masterful.

The irony that is Chaucer's trademark complicates any rhetorical performance. But more insinuative are the literary frameworks within which he enmeshes many characters who can seem to speak with such shocking immediacy or individuality. Many of his contemporaries would have recognized that Chaucer himself had pasted the identities of his characters together: from estates satire (Mann 1973), from exegetical materials (Robertson 1962, Fleming 1990), from Latin, French and Italian poetry (Fleming 1990, Patterson 1991, Robertson 1962, Wetherbee 1984); and the very traditions many of them deny provide them with the language through which they constitute themselves. By such means, Chaucer at once speaks through traditional forms, creating what appears new, and also leaves little room for the sort of manoeuvring found in writers like Langland or Julian, who seek spiritual authority for their acts of identity. Is the irony of secular limitation Chaucer's irony, or is he, too, caught in its web? The Parson's Tale traces a way out of one community into another, but, there too, the identity espoused is credal: the 'I believe' is always 'we believe'. The selfhood towards which the Parson points is the *imitatio Christi*, where the penitential re-creation he outlines ends in the old self made new, through Christ, like Christ. If radical change enables declarations of personal identity, Chaucer constantly qualifies our optimism about the effects of either secular or spiritual striving.

The General Prologue, 731–46

> Whoso shal telle a tale after a man,
> He moot reherce as ny as evere he kan
> Everich a word, if it be in his charge,
> Al speke he never so rudeliche and large,
> Or ellis he moot telle his tale untrewe,
> Or feyne thyng, or fynde wordes newe.
> He may nat spare, althogh he were his brother;
> He moot as wel seye o word as another.
> Crist spak hymself ful brode in hooly writ,
> And wel ye woot no vileynye is it.
> Eek Plato seith, whoso kan hym rede,
> The wordes moote be cosyn to the dede.
> Also I prey yow to foryeve it me,
> Al have I nat set folk in hir degree
> Heere in this tale, as that they sholde stonde.
> My wit is short, ye may wel understonde.

This is one of many authorial statements scattered strategically throughout Chaucer's works, all of which seem to declare an identity by effacing it or by merging it into a formalized persona that would have been familiar to him from contemporary French poetry. In the *Book of the Duchess*, *House of Fame* and *Parliament of Fowls*, Chaucer presents himself within the framework of the dream vision, as lovesick, unsuccessful and uncomprehending, as someone whose wisdom comes less from personal experience than from those primarily classical and authorizing texts that serve him as guides or models. In *Troilus and Criseyde*, Chaucer further problematizes his presentation of identity, using the narrator, who speaks in the first person, as an intermediary between the poem's audience and the texts (some of them spurious) that are transmitted into English vernacular by the narrator. The narrator's role is extensive and demonstrates Chaucer's mastery of narrative distancing and of narrative irony, as well as his increasingly ambiguous relationship with the materials he purports to be translating (see e.g. Fleming 1990; Patterson 1991; Robertson 1962; Wetherbee 1984). The above passage seems at once vintage Chaucer and a subtle departure from his earlier 'personal' statements.

Though the narrator here certainly names authorizing texts for his own practice, the words of Christ and the works of Plato, he presents himself as an intermediary not between his audience and a pre-existing text, but between his audience and the voices of the pilgrims. That the pilgrims themselves are his creations goes without saying, but he presents them as though they speak and he reports upon them. There is more than a move here into vernacular textuality, or into the authority of the vernacular; Chaucer establishes a complicit relationship between himself and his audience that is rooted in our experiential understanding of the world in which all of us live. Thus, he insists, we know as well as he that telling stories others have told demands that we repeat the exact words of others, even at the risk of offending. But Chaucer does even more here than seek to validate possibly rude tales; he takes as given our common worldliness, our awareness of social degree and consequently of rhetorical degree. Moreover, he takes for granted that our vision of society is rooted in an orderly attention to degree since he apologizes for his violation of that order in the final four lines of the passage. His slyness masks a knowing rearrangement of the social body, whose members will attempt to create themselves in language that often signals that rupture with the past that seems to accompany all declarations of new identity. The Miller will push ahead of the Monk; the Reeve will seek to best the Miller; the Wife will discount authority in favour of experience; the Friar and Summoner will squabble; and Chaucer will have presented a world that may have described itself in terms of orderly hierarchies but that seems held together only in the most tenuous sense.

Chaucer's authorial statement also contains a degree of unease about his relationship to the community, an unease that can be found in more anguished form in Langland or Julian. Langland uses his persona–narrator, Will, to question the likelihood that any of the world's communities or institutions (including those of the church) can offer the searching spirit any true guide. Not only does Langland place the self in the foreground of the poem by externalizing inner faculties of that self, he links the self's recognition of its own distinction, or separateness, from the community to its search for authorial identity. Similarly, Julian struggles in her *Revelations* to mediate between what she has seen and what she has been taught, and the *Revelations*, particularly the long text, can be read as just such a struggle to articulate an identity that is personal and therefore distinct from the communal identity she has hitherto accepted. Both of these writers are contemporaries with Chaucer. Langland's works were certainly known by him, since both men lived and worked in London. Although Chaucer is not directly concerned with the issue of spiritual authority that gives Julian's work much of its tension and Langland's such power, throughout the *Canterbury Tales* he confronts the idea of authority, whether it be political, historical, social or ecclesiastical, as serving to check statements of selfhood.

This particular statement, in all its cagey allusiveness, suggests that Chaucer thought that much was at stake when a man chose to tell a tale, his own or someone else's. In the penultimate tale in the Canterbury book, his creature, the Manciple, can only advise his listeners that the first virtue is to 'keep tongue'. That is dangerous advice for courtiers, merchants or writers; but it underlines Chaucer's evaluation of the self as potentially at odds with the communities that provide it with its language, its livelihood and its public identity. If the Parson in his tale asks us to shed those public selves in confession in favour of a private, he none the less describes that private self in remarkably communal terms. Chaucer's own small confession in this passage that begins with an apology and ends with a statement of his 'short' wit at once acknowledges that to write is to risk offence to some, that an authorial identity is potentially disruptive, and reinserts the writer into a community of tellers (Christ and Plato) and a community of highly socialized listeners who may be more scandalized by violations of social degree than of rhetorical. By this time, Chaucer's original audience would have known that his signature statement of identity was the naïf, the man of scant wit who could not be held truly accountable. And while stoutly denying it, he surely suggests that selfhood is agency, an agency he must muffle in communal wrappings in order to write what he wants to write. What Chaucer may not say overtly when speaking of himself, he can say through the mouth (beak) of a rooster.

The Nun's Priest's Tale, 3424–32

In a passage from near the end of the Nun's Priest's Tale, Chaucer gives Chauntecleer, his splendidly feathered rooster, a speech whose comic assertion of agency suggests means by which self-understanding might not involve rupture with the past:

> 'Com doun, and I shal telle yow what I mente;
> I shal seye sooth to yow, God help me so!'
> 'Nay thanne,' quod he, 'I shrewe us bothe two.
> And first I shrewe myself, bothe blood and bones,

If thou bigyle me ofter than ones.
Thou shalt namoore thurgh thy flaterye
Do me to synge and wynke with myn ye;
For he that wynketh, whan he sholde see,
Al wilfully, God lat him nevere thee!'

The Nun's Priest's Tale is a prime example of Chaucer's ability to speak through traditional forms. He draws upon French fables and beast epics, upon homiletic materials, and upon anecdotes and proverbs, creating a tale whose outlines would have
been thoroughly familiar to his audience, but also a tale of such perfectly balanced
tone that its fundamental absurdity and humour serve to underline a seriousness of
purpose available to anyone who wishes it. The plot is a simple one of a vain and
foolish rooster and a clever, flattering fox. Foxes in French fables were typically named
either Reynard or Russell; this one is Russell. Chauntecleer postures and lectures his
hens, especially Pertelote, his 'sister' and 'wife', then ignores his dream of a terrible
beast, as well as his natural antipathy for the beast when one appears in the yard, and
allows himself to be seduced into a disastrous conversation. Russell's success with
Chauntecleer rests on his ability to offer the rooster a self-image that flatters by suggesting his courtliness. In assuring Chauntecleer that he has not come upon him to
do him harm or to spy on him, but to hear him sing, he also implies that the type of
singing Chauntecleer can provide is genteel, or courtly. Russell addresses the rooster
as 'Gentil sire' (3284), as 'My lorde' (3295), and speaks also of the 'gentillesse' of
Chauntecleer's mother (3296). A rooster as regal as Chauntecleer, with red comb, black
bill, azure legs and toes, white nails, and feathers like burnished gold, might well
merit such an elevated mode of address, but the sight of Chauntecleer swelling with
pride at his high lineage reminds us of more than barnyard fowls. When Chauntecleer rises to the occasion and stands high on his toes, stretches his neck, and closes
his eyes (3341–2), Russell grabs him and makes for the woods. However, what appears
to be merely another episode in a series of 'tragic' falls, whereby Chauntecleer follows
his father and mother in 'easing' daun Russell, becomes another sort of tale altogether.
In the previous tale, the Monk had told a series of tragedies, defining tragedy as a
state for which 'ther is no remedie'; Chaucer uses Chauntecleer to suggest there is
more to tragedy than a series of repeated mistakes, passed down relentlessly from
father to son. Chauntecleer evades his fate by coming to his wits, by addressing the
fox in language that recalls Russell's approach a few moments previously, 'Sire, if that
I were as ye', advising the fox he should yell back at those following them. As
Chauntecleer apparently comes to understand, courtly address is all too often a
medium for false-seeming. In ignoring the manipulative thrust of the very mode of
address he had employed, the fox falls into his own trap, a trap Chauntecleer can now
work with ease. Russell opens his mouth, and Chauntecleer flies into a tree, from
which Russell, in the above passage, tries to woo him down again. Chauntecleer's
response substitutes self-regard for vanity. His adroit use of 'Sire' when speaking to
the fox also suggests that he has arrived at a place of creative self-irony.

Though we cannot in fairness to Chaucer's mastery of chicken-talk and -lore say that Chauntecleer's words come from his experience of inwardness, we can none the less think about what such a speech might mean if a person, rather than a rooster, said it. We could begin by thinking about what Chauntecleer was in the beginning of the tale. Chaucer describes him as gorgeous, as proud, as devoted to his own very public image of himself. He speaks to Pertolete, his favourite hen, in the elevated language of the courtier, calling her 'Madame'. He lectures her in a way that seems to echo Chaucer's own sense of what male pomposity might sound like. When he tells her about the terrible and fearful beast he saw in his dream, he is sensitive to her taunt of cowardice. He acts out his importance in his procession through the yard with his seven hens. In contrast, his speech from the tree to Russell is self-descriptive in another way. He describes himself as 'beguiled' by flattery and as potentially blind. In the final sentence, in which he casts his perception in the form of a proverb, 'He that winks when he should see, all wilfully, God let him never thrive', he offers another way of thinking about the self, even a rooster's self.

At the risk of sounding as absurd as one of Chauntecleer's dress lectures, I would like to take this sentence seriously for what it can tell us about one aspect of Chaucer's understanding of the emergence of the self. First, by applying proverb lore to himself, Chauntecleer admits that he fits into a category of those who close their eyes, wilfully or voluntarily, in situations when they should see. In being able to apply such a saying to himself, Chauntecleer demonstrates a certain self-reflexiveness that he did not have at the beginning of the tale. The community to which he rhetorically admits himself is a community of gulls, of those who are wilfully blind to the realities of dangerous situations. He no longer speaks of his genteel mother or shows interest in being addressed as *sire*, but seems intent on this act by which he escapes history while, at the same time, fitting into it. In this case, Chaucer links selfhood both to an awareness of continuity over time and to a sudden assumption of agency. By this I do not necessarily mean the ability to act, but the ability and willingness to consider the relationship between action and self-understanding. What for a rooster can be worked out in a quick interchange with a fox and stated in a simple proverb must naturally take a more complicated form for a person. Moreover, Chauntecleer's 'insight' re-establishes him within his community, the barnyard thrown into chaos by his capture. As the Nun's Priest tells his audience at the beginning of the tale, Chauntecleer is the timekeeper of the widow's yard; his crowing is more certain 'than is a clokke or an abbey orlogge' (2854). The narrator does not moralize about the effect of Chauntecleer's loss, although the crowd following Russell – the widow and her two daughters, giving the hue and cry, men carrying staves, dogs, cows and pigs – and the noise of ducks, geese and bees capture the chaos into which the barnyard is thrown by the rooster's own folly.

What Chauntecleer has at the end of his experience is experience. He also has a more fully developed memory, one that can incorporate his own story into the stories of the past that he told Pertelote and that the fox told him. What do we have? We have what we wish – either simply a tale of a fox, a cock and a hen or something meatier, as the Nun's Priest implies in his closing words when he tells us to let the chaff (the story itself) blow free and take the wheat, the nourishing kernel. And Chaucer? In depicting barnyard folly, he has described folly in courtly terms, in the habits of self-regard that, like all attempts at public self-creation, are carried out through language as empty as Chauntecleer's claims to gentility. To turn elsewhere is a 'wilful' decision to lay one self to rest in favour of another attempt to see the self in relation to another community, this one mortally constituted, limited, but at least knowing (and laughing).

For his entire life as a writer Chaucer scrutinized the idea of authority – his own authority as a poet, the relationship between authority and power, or the degree to which authority is bound up in textuality – in relation to that of identity. In the tale of Chauntecleer he plays out in comic terms the lessons that are explicitly stated and authoritatively bolstered in the Tale of Melibee, the tale he gives to himself. Melibee's wife Prudence urges her distraught and irrational husband towards an assumption of agency, a realization of authority, that allows for creative and intelligent rule by building on past experience. In allowing the Nun's Priest to best his creator with a tale any writer would be proud to own, Chaucer demonstrates his characteristic generosity, and the Nun's Priest emerges as the real star of Fragment VII of the *Canterbury Tales*, which begins with the Shipman's tale of financial chicanery and includes the Nun's bloody tale of Christian revenge, Chaucer's two efforts at tale-telling, and the Monk's endless accounts of tragedies without remedy. Of all the characters presented in this fragment, only Chauntecleer illustrates what authority might be; moreover, his authority as a rooster, which is his value as a rooster to his barnyard, comes directly from his new sense of personal authority or identity. Tragedy, such as it is, is thereby averted.

Troilus and Criseyde V, 1051–71

At about the same time as he was beginning to write some of the tales that would become the Canterbury book, in the mid-1380s, Chaucer was finishing *Troilus and Criseyde*, which he describes as a tragedy, a poem that explores in searching detail the complex relationships between authority, agency, community and identity that also underwrite the *Canterbury Tales*. Where the *Canterbury Tales* contain figures drawn from ecclesiastical, civic and manorial life, *Troilus* is focused upon the court. The sometimes gritty immediacy of the *Tales*, with their rude jokes, farts, admissions of greed and lechery, and overt acts of self-interest, is a radical departure from the world of *Troilus*, where the menials can be numbered on one hand, and the life of an entire city is concentrated in a few elaborately drawn rooms and spaces. The figures upon whom the focus is concentrated (Troilus, Criseyde, Pandarus, Diomede) seem, like the other Trojans and Greeks, like Troy itself, caught within webs of history, figures whose desires finally render identity moot. But, rather than do what his Canterbury pilgrim the Monk does and bemoan a tragedy that has no remedy, Chaucer explores the sources of this tragedy by dramatizing the failure to acknowledge, certainly to understand, the contingencies that enmesh his characters (see Aers 1992; Fleming 1990; Patterson 1991; Robertson 1962; Wetherbee 1984). To Criseyde, Chaucer grants a language about the self that at once fashions an identity and retreats from any assumption of agency into elegy:

> But trewely, the storie telleth us,
> Ther made nevere womman moore wo
> Than she, whan that she falsed Troilus.
> She seyde, 'Allas, for now is clene ago
> My name of trouthe in love, for everemo!
> For I have falsed oon the gentileste
> That evere was, and oon the worthieste!
>
> 'Allas, of me, unto the worldes ende,
> Shal neyther ben ywriten nor ysonge
> No good word, for thise bokes wol me shende.
> O rolled shal I ben on many a tonge!
> Thorughout the world my belle shal be ronge!
> And wommen moost wol haten me of alle.
> Allas, that swich a cas me sholde falle!
>
> 'Thei wol seyn, in as muche as in me is,
> I have hem don dishonour, weylaway!
> Al be I nat the first that dide amys,
> What helpeth that to don my blame awey?
> But syn I se ther is no bettre wey,
> And that to late is now for me to rewe,
> To Diomede algate I wol be trewe.'

This speech is rich in ironies. The narrator, who always describes himself as a translator, tells us that the stories tell us how bitterly Criseyde lamented her 'falsing' of Troilus, particularly because she saw herself as losing her 'name' of truth in love. Though the speech of Criseyde that he recounts sounds as immediate and fresh as any self's lament, it is a selective translation of portions of Briseida's lament in Benoît de Sainte-Maure's *Roman de Troie*.[3] The Criseyde who speaks with such apparent individuality is as enmeshed in an authoritative textuality as the textual tradition she here questions and rejects. But Chaucer also uses Criseyde's description of what her ('false') textual identity will be to describe a failure to take history into account that likewise characterizes the tragedy of Troy. 'They' will say or sing of her no good word, recalling her dishonourable behaviour, even though she is not the first to 'do amiss'. Criseyde here elides history by recounting it as a fall from a primordial place she calls 'truth-in-love'. Further back than the clandestine relationship with Troilus she does not go, certainly not back to any attempt to understand any originary desire or sense of lack, as does, for example, St Augustine in the *Confessions*.

Criseyde is, of course, a Trojan and not a Christian, so the means of thinking about the self that are expressed through the *Confessions* are not available to her; but her use of her own history is none the less self-congratulatory rather than self-searching. At no point does she recall her early motives for entertaining Troilus' suit (see II, 660–5). Nor does she recall that her ultimate practicality here is no different from the earlier 'Nothing ventured, nothing gained' with which she agreed to Troilus' courtship (II, 806–8). She seems to realize that she has stumbled on to a world stage, but, like Troy, she makes no attempt to understand the contingencies that helped shape her own decisions. Personally fearful, in need of security, vain, adept at Troy's language of love, flattery and deceit, Criseyde does not emerge as venal so much as representative of Troy's own misplaced energy.

She is also a woman, and her speech links her future textual identity to her gender. In her 'rolled on many a tonge' and 'thorughout the world my belle shal be ronge' she forecasts a promiscuous relationship between her false textual image and anyone who hears or tells her story. Criseyde distinguishes between the private and the public, but she does little to articulate a private self except to assign it a 'truth' whose out-lines are certainly ambiguously defined throughout the poem. Moreover, 'truth in love', as she and Troilus define it, demands that there be a sharp divide between a public and a private self, a divide that Chaucer emphasizes with his descriptions of the lovers by public daylight and in night's private spaces; with his accounts of their deceptive actions; and with his careful attention to Pandarus, the smooth-tongued courtier and Criseyde's uncle, who serves as their facilitator and go-between. The private space of the femininized self may well be hostage to the masculine courtly and chivalric community of Troy at war, which at once values and trades in women (Aers 1988: ch. 3); but by her actions Criseyde, like Helen, who is the ostensible reason for the war, has become complicit in a devalued economy and language. Through her speech she re-inserts herself into this community that takes false for true, implying that the only framework within which she can be understood is that of the Trojan community. Not only are its limitations her own, but she has no power to envision any other, no ability to break with it in any but the most illusory way. The private world she created with Troilus can hardly be called a 'break' with Troy, nor can her status as Diomede's mistress be seen as a rupture with her lost Trojan past. Finally, she binds herself to what will be the communal experience of reading or singing a history, false but authoritative.

In giving Criseyde this haunting and powerful speech of passivity and protest, Chaucer captures some of the inherent tensions – and feints and dodges – he seems to associate with attempts to articulate selfhood. First, he strongly suggests that individual consciousness cannot be separated from one's consciousness of a community. Criseyde at no point sees herself as a free agent; she never makes the mistake of thinking she might be able to create a new identity for herself apart from communal sanctions. Thus, when Troilus suggests they run away from Troy, she knows all too well how futile a gesture that would be (IV, 1499–1540). On the other hand, she does not attempt to understand that community as anything more than a force ranged against her; thus, 'They will say . . .'. Nor does she see herself as an agent in the truest sense.

She will be sung about, written of, her name rolled on others' tongues; in each case she will be acted upon. The self-ironizing reversal by which Chauntecleer escapes into a tree is not a motion she, by her very nature, can make. To ask why not is to be forced to return to Chaucer and go back over his quizzing of the impulse to make a self, to articulate an identity.

*

To pick three passages from Chaucer's works that illuminate Chaucer's attitude about the concept of personal identity is, of course, an impossible assignment. Chaucer's poetry is a poetry of the voice, of voices creating and re-creating identities for themselves before an audience. To some extent, the audience, Chaucer's imagined or actual audience, provided him with the framework for these voices, the defining community within which articulacy makes sense (Taylor 1989: 36, 45); but, as I suggested in the first section of this chapter, that 'defining community' was not a monolithic whole, but was composed of men and women who felt to greater or lesser degrees the tensions, needs, acts of violence, political machinations, fears and frustrations of a world that in hindsight looks at least as confusing as our own (see also Knight 1986; Knapp 1990). Chaucer's voices thus emerge from the very contingencies that define their limits. If Criseyde can only envisage the two states – truth-in-love or falsity – she at once speaks from within her own limited (and pagan) imagination and underlines the severe historic limitations of Troy itself, where the falsified concept of truth-in-love has become the slogan that will destroy the city in the end. But Criseyde also serves to remind Chaucer's audience that the language we purport to use for communication is, too often, a medium of self-justification, the evidence of how little we choose to know about ourselves. Like Criseyde's speech, each of these passages is confessional. Each speaker attempts to explain a past action or practice to an audience. There is thus a reason for each speech, the need to justify, excuse or excoriate a self in relation to a perceived community.

It is in the juncture between self and community that consciousness happens; but, as Chaucer demonstrates throughout his works, there is no question of breaking the bond between the two. Like his contemporaries, Langland and Julian, he is all too aware of the ways in which communal frameworks can threaten an emergent selfhood. But Chaucer compounds the issues submerged in identity in several ways. He demonstrates the frequently self-interested and destructive sources for acts of 'personal identity'. The pilgrims who jostle one another for preference, who wear distinctive clothing, who proclaim their identities in a kind of verbal imitation of the market index suggest his scepticism about the virtues of self-creation. Yet he was more than an observer of the trends of his day; he was also an author and therefore an outsider who must speak or risk telling his tale 'untrue'. That he chooses to speak through other voices, that he fashions his own half-comic identity as a non-threatening failure of a man, says many things about his understanding of the practice of self-creation. As he himself demonstrates, it is certainly possible to make a self from words. But then, to what purpose do we fashion our images; to whom do we speak; how do we come to understand ourselves? Chauntecleer ends with proverbs, the language of communal morality, communal wisdom. Chaucer ended with the Parson's Tale, which is a translation, and a retraction of all individual practices that might lead others into sin.

See also AUTHORITY; BODIES; CHRISTIAN IDEOLOGIES; CONTEMPORARY ENGLISH WRITERS; CRISIS AND DISSENT; LIFE HISTORIES; LONDON; LOVE; NARRATIVE; OTHER THOUGHT-WORLDS; SOCIAL STRUCTURES; TEXTS; TRANSLATION; VISUALIZING; WOMEN.

NOTES

1 Stephen Greenblatt, *Renaissance Self-fashioning: From More to Shakespeare* (Chicago: University of Chicago Press, 1980).

2 For new considerations about dating the C-Text of *Piers Plowman*, see Anne Middleton, 'Acts of vagrancy: the C version "autobiography", and the statute of 1388', in *Written Work: Langland, Labor and Authorship*, ed. Steven Justice and Kathryn Kerby-Fulton (Philadelphia: University of Pennsylvania Press, 1997), 208–318.

3 See *Troilus and Criseyde*, ed. B. A. Windeatt (London: Longman, 1984), V, 1051–71.

REFERENCES AND FURTHER READING

Aers, David (1988) *Community, Gender, and Individual Identity: English Writing, 1360–1430* (London and New York: Routledge). Contains chapters on *Piers Plowman*, the *Book of Margery Kempe*, *Troilus and Criseyde* and *Sir Gawain and the Green Knight*, each problematizing the relationship between self and community in the late Middle Ages; the chapter on *Troilus* pays particular attention to the issue of gender as a signifier of social power.

——(1992) 'A whisper in the ear of early modernists; or, reflections on literary critics writing the "history of the subject"', in *Culture and History 1350–1600: Essays on English Communities, Identities and Writing*, ed. David Aers (London: Harvester Wheatsheaf; Detroit: Wayne State University Press), 77–202. Argues that an understanding of subjectivity and identity is fundamental to the medieval social experience and deeply engraved in the Augustinian cast of medieval religious thought.

Dobson, R. B., ed. (1970) *The Peasants' Revolt of 1381* (London: Macmillan; 2nd edn 1983). An invaluable collection of translated primary documents describing the rising of 1381.

Fleming, John V. (1990) *Classical Imitation and Interpretation in Chaucer's* Troilus (Lincoln, Nebr.: University of Nebraska Press). Articulates the degree to which the details of character in the poem evince Chaucer's careful reading of classical sources.

Gordon, Dillian (1993) *The Wilton Diptych: Making and Meaning* (London: National Gallery Publications). A collection of essays exploring the historical relevance of the Wilton Diptych and the ways it which it served a discursive function within Ricardian court culture.

Justice, Steven (1994) *Writing and Rebellion: England in 1381*, The New Historicism 27 (Berkeley and Los Angeles: University of California Press). Focuses attention upon the rising in relation to literate culture and upon the rebels' production of a coherent and disciplined ideology.

Knapp, Peggy Ann (1990) *Chaucer and the Social Contest* (New York and London: Routledge). Pays particular attention to Chaucer's use of highly charged language to describe both individual and social stresses.

Knight, Stephen (1986) *Geoffrey Chaucer* (Oxford: Blackwell). Scrutinizes Chaucer's poetry in relation to the social and political tensions of the time.

Macfarlane, Alan (1978) *The Origins of English Individualism: The Family, Property, and Social Transition* (Cambridge: Cambridge University Press). Argues for a socio-economic basis for English individualism, which he suggests has its roots in the increasing flexibility of the late thirteenth-century market economy.

Mann, Jill (1973) *Chaucer and Medieval Estates' Satire: The Literature of Social Classes and the General Prologue to the* Canterbury Tales (Cambridge: Cambridge University Press). The classic study of Chaucer's exploitation of the social language of the late English Middle Ages in his descriptions of the characters within the General Prologue.

Patterson, Lee (1991) *Chaucer and the Subject of History* (London: Routledge; Madison: University of Wisconsin Press). Describes Chaucer's handling of those historical sources that underlie the constructions of identity within his poetry.

Pearsall, Derek (1989) 'Interpretative models for the Peasants' Revolt', in *Hermeneutics and Medieval Culture*, ed. P. J. Gallacher and H. Damico (Albany: State University of New York Press), 63–70. 'Reads' the chronicle descriptions of the leaders of the rising of 1381 as interpretative gestures.

Robertson, D. W., Jr (1962) *A Preface to Chaucer: Studies in Medieval Perspectives* (Princeton: Princeton University Press). A study of those allegorical texts and ways of reading that formed the cultural context for Chaucer's detailing of character.

Saul, Nigel (1997) *Richard II* (New Haven: Yale University Press). This will be the standard work on Richard II and his court for many years to come.

Staley, Lynn (1996) 'Chaucer and the postures of sanctity', in David Aers and Lynn Staley, *The Powers of the Holy: Religion, Politics, and Gender in Late Medieval English Culture* (University Park, Pa.: Pennyslvania State University Press), 179–260. Points up the deliberately ambiguous relationship between Chaucer's works and the political world in which he lived.

Strohm, Paul (1992) *Hochon's Arrow: The Social Imagination of Fourteenth-century Texts* (Princeton: Princeton University Press). Contains essays that address key late medieval English texts as offering perspectives upon issues of dominance, gender, politics and rebellion.

Taylor, Charles (1989) *Sources of the Self: The Making of Modern Identity* (Cambridge, Mass.: Harvard University Press). Surveys ways of thinking about selfhood, from classical times to the present; required reading for anyone interested in the subject of identity.

Thrupp, Sylvia L. (1948) *The Merchant Class of Medieval London, 1300–1500* (Chicago: University of Chicago Press; repr. Ann Arbor: University of Michigan Press, 1989). Thrupp's work on the late medieval merchant and urban culture provides a wealth of information about the material culture that underwrote the process of identity-making.

Wetherbee, Winthrop (1984) *Chaucer and the Poets: An Essay on* Troilus and Criseyde (Ithaca, NY: Cornell University Press). A study of Chaucer's debts to his sources that deepens our understanding of Chaucer's ability to make characters whose verisimilitude is more apparent than real.

23

Science

Irma Taavitsainen

Science may be regarded as a mood in which we consider our world; it is one of the major activities in our minds (*Encyclopedia Britannica*, 1966). Science includes knowledge of the world order, natural phenomena and laws that govern existence and, as a fundamental aspect of culture, it is reflected in literature. In Chaucer's works science is present both explicitly in passages dealing with scientific activities and as an underlying factor, the mood in which the tales are told and the poems written.

The ideas and conceptions of what science is have undergone fundamental changes since the late Middle Ages. In this chapter I shall first outline the socio-historical background of scientific writing in Chaucer's time, when the English language in its scientific register was being created. In the second part I shall analyse some passages of Chaucer's texts reflecting the medieval world order and scientific ideas. I shall indicate some parallel or relevant passages in non-literary scientific writing, texts that Chaucer is likely to have encountered in his reading and texts with which his audience may have been familiar and which would have shaped their experience of science. The passages also illustrate Chaucer's skill in using such sources, and how their transformation into a literary mode took place.

The Paradigm of Science

Defining the concept of science in the late medieval and Renaissance periods is problematic. There are two approaches. The exclusive view includes only those aspects of medieval thought that are similar to the concerns of modern science, so that sciences that have undergone a paradigm change are considered as marginal. The second, more inclusive, view is based on medieval classifications of knowledge. The latter definition includes areas like music and, for example, physiognomy, or the science of telling people's characteristics from their facial features and build. Nowadays such skills belong to the occult and some border on magic.

Rigid distinctions between various branches of science were not made in the Middle Ages as they are today. Astronomy was the main scientific interest of the scholastic age and it cannot be distinguished from astrology. As this example indicates, the medieval scientific world view was very different from ours. Its roots lie in antiquity; the practices of Greek scientists and their principles of argumentation formed the model, and new generations of scientists based their texts on the Greek inheritance. Changes started gradually in the Renaissance, but new ideas were adopted and developed at different times in different branches of science.[1] For instance, the basis of medical treatment started to change as knowledge of human anatomy and physiology grew, with the work of important scientists like Andreas Vesalius (1514–64) and William Harvey (1578–1657) accelerating the process. Their influence was first felt in the forefront of science, but it disseminated into other layers of writing more gradually, while traces of old beliefs still continue in some areas of popular medicine. The decline of alchemy is another case in point, at the other extreme. In the Middle Ages it was at the core of science, although attitudes oscillated (see section on 'Alchemy' below). By modern criteria it cannot be considered a science at all, as its grounds have been proved false; elements cannot be transmuted.

Vernacularization

Another important issue connected with late medieval science is vernacularization. This term means the written application of the vernacular languages instead of Latin. The language of science widened the functions of the vernacular to prestigious fields, a process which was contemporaneous with the increasing use of English in administration and literature. Within science, medicine led the way, this first phase of the vernacularization of learned texts starting in the last quarter of the fourteenth century and thus coinciding with Chaucer's prime. Chaucer created a literary canon, but it is significant that he also wrote an instructive non-literary text in prose, the *Treatise on the Astrolabe* (1391), for 'Lyte Lowys my sone'. This work explains how to use a technical device to determine the positions of the celestial bodies in the sky. It is possible that he also wrote another astronomical work, the *Equatorie of the Planets* (1392), though conclusive evidence is lacking and the issue is debated. The reason for writing the *Astrolabe* in English is discussed in the preface 'This tretis . . . wol I shewe the under full light reules and naked wordes in Englissh, for latyn cast thou yit but small, my litel sone' (25–7). The passage goes on to defend English as an equal among languages, a view that is often expressed in contemporary prefaces: 'But natheles suffise to the these trewe conclusions in Englissh as wel as sufficith to these noble clerkes Grekes these same conclusions in Grek; and to Arabiens Arabik, and to Jewes in Ebrew, and to Latyn folk in Latyn' (28–33).

Most Middle English scientific texts are translated from or, in one way or another, derived from Latin treatises, but there were also new compositions in English. A good number of scientific texts survive in manuscripts from the early period, but generally only parts of them are edited. Scientific writing is the field where most discoveries of new texts are being made. Translators of scientific writings struggled with many difficulties in both syntax and lexicon to find adequate expressions in English, since scientific writing in the vernacular was new and the conventions had to be created. The model was Greco-Roman writing, and translators strove to transfer features of Latin scientific discourse to the vernacular. The field of medical writing comprised both the learned tradition and remedy books. Academic and surgical texts belong to the learned sphere and were new in Chaucer's time. Remedy books had a longer vernacular tradition: early writings of this genre are extant in Old English, and there are also texts from the transition period, the eleventh century. Texts of other branches of science were rendered into English as well; here, John Trevisa's translation of the most important contemporary encyclopedia, *De proprietatibus rerum* by Bartholomaeus Anglicus, was an important achievement. The process of vernacularization was slow and lasted for centuries: Latin continued to dominate scientific writing in England to the middle of the seventeenth century, and was used after that as well. In this period, a pragmatic knowledge of Latin was widespread among literate lay people, although literacy itself was not common.

Scientific Language and Textual Conventions

Genre conventions and features typical of the register of scientific writing were transferred from foreign models, and the underlying traditions can be traced to antiquity. This transfer can be seen in textual forms as well as in individual stylistic features. Present-day scientific writing is characterized by heavy nominal groups with information integrated into pre- and post-modifications, specialized vocabulary and verbs reduced to express relations between the nominal groups. This style register is the outcome of a long development shaped by tradition, with later texts building on earlier ones in a continuum from Chaucer's time to the present day. The underlying thought-styles are reflected in the choice of linguistic expressions.

The influence of Greco-Roman writing is pervasive in the scientific register: it can be seen in lexis and in syntax, as well as in the macroforms of text. Lexical borrowing from Latin is well charted and a great deal of attention has been paid to the first emergence of scientific words in English; there was an influx of new vocabulary at Chaucer's time caused as the demands of translation filled gaps in the vernacular lexicon. Stylistic influence is evident in translated phrases and idioms like *notandum est* ('it is to be noted') and *sciendum est* ('it is to wit'), which were used to elevate the style. The macroforms of discourse were also borrowed in the process of establishing and transferring genre conventions to the vernacular.

Instructional works often used direct address to involve the readers. This device occurs in the *Astrolabe* as well, and its discourse form is typical of the instructional mode. The treatise is divided into five parts with short numbered passages dealing with the uses of the instrument, theoretical background, tables and other relevant material. The text form resembles that of modern manuals and can be traced in instructional texts throughout the history of English. Another macroform frequently used in this register is the dialogue. Chaucer makes use of it in the Canon's Yeoman's Tale, in a passage of imagined conversation between Plato and another philosopher. The tradition is long: the dialogue form dates from the Greek philosophers, was first used by Plato in written form, and developed into a more abstract question-and-answer format in Aristotle's treatises. The tradition continued in the Middle Ages, when debates belonged to the teaching methods of universities. Dialogues are commonly found in scientific and philosophical writing. This text form developed literary modifications in genres like debate poetry, as seen in *The Owl and the Nightingale* (*c.*1200), and from the fifteenth century onwards mimetic dialogues were employed in handbooks and guides to health.

Authorities of Science

Medieval science was scholastic and relied on earlier texts rather than empirical knowledge. Observation as the mode of knowing became important with empiricism, especially in the period of the Royal Society, founded in 1660. Medieval scholars aimed at reconstructing the original meanings of texts, and a typical feature of scholastic science is frequent reference to authorities. Each branch of science had its own list, with Greek philosophers and scientists at the top in all fields and Muslim authors coming next; this reflects the transmission of science from antiquity through Arab culture to the Western world. Aristotle was the master of all sciences, and references to him may be real or spurious, as the undergrowth of pseudo-Aristotelian writings was prolific. The references show different patterns in different layers of writing, so that academic and surgical texts generally have more precise reference systems, as for example in Trevisa's translation of Bartholomaeus, *On the Properties of Things*: '*Aristoteles in libro de animalibus 3° capitulo* [setteþ] oþthir propirtees of blood, and seith . . .' (Seymour et al. 1975: i, 150). Remedy books with recipes and miscellaneous materials are more vague and may give fanciful accounts of the origins of texts. The target audience is also mentioned in some texts: 'A greet astronomyer drowe out þis tretys of astronomye for lewide men schulden knowe hereby whanne it were good tyme to leten blood and good tyme to ȝeue medicyn or take for sore or.'[2]

Readership of Scientific Texts

Prefaces often describe the readers of vernacular texts as *lewid* (ignorant), but this may be a textual convention. The real audience is likely to have consisted of professional practitioners of medicine, for science was the concern of the learned, although its practical applications were more widely known. Medicine, for instance, was both a craft and a science. The classification of medical writings according to the underlying traditions reflects the audience in its broad outline: university medicine was for physicians of the highest class, surgical books for surgeons and barber-surgeons, and remedy books for a large and heterogeneous group including medical practitioners of all classes and lay people. The matter is, however, more complicated. Ownership studies of medieval manuscripts show that besides professional medical practitioners, noble women and gentry owned medical books, and the libraries of professional physicians contained more popular materials as well. Books were expensive. Only a small part of the population was literate, and reading and writing were separate skills. The lowest social rank with writing skills in late medieval England is perhaps represented by John Crophill, a rural empirical practitioner and a bailiff from Wix, Suffolk, who wrote a medical notebook *c.*1446.[3] The ability to read was more widespread. Almanacs with a wide circulation in the fifteenth century included medical and astrological material, such as rules for appropriate times with pictures of the zodiacal man (see section on 'Medicine' below), and other useful information. Interest in alchemy in late medieval England was wide, and extended from the royal family and court circles to gentry, churchmen, lawyers, surgeons, apothecaries, distillers and even common practitioners, although prohibitions against its practice were issued from time to time. The readership of alchemical texts must have been very restricted. Richard II is known to have owned alchemical books, and alchemical commissions were set up by King Henry VI and his council by special permission to rescue the monarch from his financial troubles and to solve his health problems. For obvious reasons, they failed in their tasks.

In the preface of the *Astrolabe* the author claims to have taken his son's age into consideration and made the text suitable for a ten-year-old. This treatise can be considered a textbook, or a handbook, accordingly. The audience of the *Canterbury Tales* and Chaucer's shorter poems consisted of members of the court, construed in its widest sense as including not only the king and his nobility but also members of the administration: knights, officials, diplomats and civil servants. The same audience was certainly familiar with at least some scientific writing and understood some scientific principles. Proof of that claim can be found in the contents of codices including both scientific materials and Chaucer's works; such a combination is found, for example, in a manuscript by John Shirley, a well-known contemporary scribe who ran some kind of a lending library.[4] Scholarship on the sources of Chaucer's texts has shown that Chaucer was familiar with non-literary scientific writings in both Latin and the vernacular: some of the *Canterbury Tales* show the influence of such texts to the extent that parallel passages can be found. It is particularly interesting that Chaucer gained the reputation of an alchemist through his Canon's Yeoman's Tale. As Elias Ashmole put it in the seventeenth century: 'Now as Concerning *Chaucer* (the *Author* of this *Tale*) he is ranked amongst the *Hermetick Philosophers* . . . Besides he that reads the latter part of the *Chanon's Yeoman's Tale*, will easily perceive him to be a *Iudicious Philosopher* and one that fully knew the *Mistery*.'[5] This comment would not have been possible without knowledge of alchemy as it circulated in manuscripts; it is based on the recognition of resemblance. Chaucer and his audience shared common ground, but without special study the scientific principles underlying his compositions escape modern readers. The importance of these principles is explicit in several texts, such as the anonymous *Wise Book of Philosophy and Astronomy*: 'without wyche science and knowynge, no man may come to perfitt wurchinge of astronomye and philosophie, ne surgere, ne of no oþer science' (Krochalis and Peters 1975: 5).

Cosmology

The medieval world view was holistic: everything had its place, with the microcosm of man reflecting the macrocosm of the universe. In the Ptolemaic system, the universe consisted of concentric spheres with the earth at the centre. In each sphere one of the planets moved at an individual speed from west to east; the moon was the nearest to the earth and the swiftest, completing its course in the sidereal month of 27.32 days.[6] Then came the other planets, Mercury, Venus and the sun, which completed its course in a year. Mars and Jupiter were slower. Saturn was furthest from the earth and revolved round its sphere in thirty years. The sphere of the fixed stars and the zodiac came next, and then the *primum mobile*. This revolved daily from east to west, causing the daily motions of the sun, the moon and other heavenly bodies, affecting them all as a group. Below the moon were the spheres of the elements 'in þe myddis of wyche hangyth þe erthe, of a centre of all þe world', as the *Wise Book* put it (ed. Krochalis and Peters 1975: 9).

The structure of the universe is explained in medieval encyclopedias, which range from learned to popular. Trevisa's translation of Bartholomaeus' *De proprietatibus rerum, On the Properties of Things* represents the academic end. The coverage of the work is comprehensive, with the order of the chapters reflecting the medieval hierarchies and correspondences. The first chapter deals with God through the writings of various authorities; angels are next; man is dealt with in several chapters, from different points of view. The treatise proceeds to elements and humours, planets, and natural and unnatural things, of which the latter deals with sicknesses. The astronomical part of the book explains the planets and the signs of the zodiac, seasons and air. After this the text proceeds to lower creatures and miscellaneous matters like birds, fish, the earth and its provinces, stones, plants, animals and colours. The popular end of the scale is represented by the *Wise Book* mentioned above, which shows how encyclopedic texts were understood by the contemporary audience. The book begins with the structure of the universe and the order of the angels and predestination, but the end of the tract is purely astrological and varies in different manuscripts. The text seems to have been flexible and open-ended, with various starting points given for elections, or advice for choosing the right time for the right action. The manuscripts have their own individual combinations – perhaps reflecting what was available at the time, and the location of copying.

The macrocosm–microcosm relationship provided explanations for everything. Elements and humours, seasons, and ages of man, formed grids that could be used for practical applications based on theories of the origin of diseases or astral influences. Planets were associated with mythology and pagan gods, but the influence of the stars was also part of God's working and thus connected with theology. According to the medieval world order, what happened in the world below depended on the positions of the skies: evil planets in unfavourable aspects caused accidents, and actions taken at proper times were guaranteed to succeed. In a simplified form, like favoured like. For example, travel undertaken in the hour of Mercury, the god of merchandise in mythology and a movable planet, should come to a happy end. The issue of predestination was debated in religion, and it is dealt with in some astrological texts. The optimistic solution was briefly expressed in the maxim 'A wise man rules the stars.' The issue is dealt with in the *Wise Book* in a more comprehensive way, and it shows how everything was placed in a religious context: 'it is to knowe þat non of hem [planets] contreyneth a man to good or to evyll, ffor why be a manys owen good wille, and þe grace of God comynge beffor; and by his owen good levynge may do good, thow he were disposide to do evyll after þe nature and inffluence of his planete' (ed. Krochalis and Peters 1975: 8). The line of argumentation indicates the level of the tract, as the text suddenly reverts to the 'dismal' days, which belong to the superstitious category (see section on 'Perilous Mondays', below). A vast literature on elections is extant from the late medieval period in English, though most of it still remains unedited.

Astronomy and Astrology

Astronomy belonged to the quadrivium, together with arithmetic, music and geometry, and formed part of the university curriculum. Knowledge of astrologically propitious moments was important for the right timing of actions, and the importance of elections was generally acknowledged. Special devices, such as the astrolabe, were used for this end. The system was complicated and detailed instructions were needed to master the procedure. The annual pathway of the sun, the ecliptic, was depicted as a belt around the earth and divided into twelve 'houses' through which the planet moved. The first house was called the ascendant because of its location on the eastern horizon. The power of the planet or sign depended on the type of house in which it was located. The ascendant was the most powerful of the angles and the most important single point of any astrological configuration. The course ended after a full circle in the twelfth house just below the horizon, called the 'prison' since the planet's power was impeded in it. The signs of the zodiac were ascribed two planets each, except the sun and the moon which had only one, and the sign enhanced the power of the planet over which it was the 'lord'.

The astrolabe, or some other device like the volvelle, was used to compose a chart and predict appropriate times. Proof of the wide circulation and the importance of such prognostications can be gleaned from the extant literature on elections and from passages that reflect the prevailing system. The starting point could be the sun, as in the model described above, or the moon, which is perhaps the most important planet in astrology, since its phases could be followed without special instruments. Three kinds of moon books are extant. The simplest ones are 'lunaries', based on the thirty days of the moon. 'Zodiacal lunaries' take the moon's passage in the twelve signs of the zodiac into account; predictions according to the twenty-eight 'mansions of the moon' are based on an Arab system and are rarer than the other types. Other points of departure, like the hours of the planets, were also possible.

Besides predicting appropriate times, astronomical details are often given as indications of the precise time at which something happened (e.g. in MLI 1–15 and NPT 2857). It has been suggested that these are humorous touches because such computations are too sophisticated to fit the characters. The references serve as deictic indicators in the stories and reflect the medieval way of defining the course of time before the era of calendars and clocks. Astrological passages may also serve other functions. In the Man of Law's Tale (see section below) a controversy between the determinism of the stars and divine guidance underlies the whole story. The heroine's fate is determined by the positions of the heavens. Her pious character suffers no harm from her hardships and she reaches a happy end by her faith and divine guidance. The story is a blend of a saint's life and a romance, including confrontations with worldly rulers and miracles, as well as adventures at sea and in strange lands. In the Miller's Tale (see section below) the plot is developed around an astrological practical joke on the credulous carpenter, who is made to believe that the second Flood will come. He is tricked to make preparations which, in fact, promote the lecherous aims of the astrologer, 'hende' Nicholas, who has set his eyes on the carpenter's wife. The second Flood is invented by him to promote lechery, whereas the original Flood was a punishment for the same sin.

Medicine

The holistic world view provided explanations for all aspects of human life, outward events as well as mental constitution and physical well-being. Man was the centre of the universe and the influences of the skies were reflected in him. Health was conceived as a balance of humours, described by Trevisa in the following way: 'Good disposicioun of body is iclepid hele, bi þe whiche mannes body in complexioun and composicioun is in suche state þat he may frelich and parfiteliche do his werkes and dedis. And ȝif kynde slidiþ out of þis temperatnes it falleþ into iuel and sikenes' (Seymour et al. 1975: i, 342). Contemporary practices of healing aimed at restoration of the balance, which could be done by bloodletting or taking medicine, often administered in accordance with dietary principles. A hot and dry sickness like fever was treated by cold and moist herbs. Humours were connected with particular elemental qualities, with the seasons of the year and the time of day. Planets and the signs of the zodiac were also part of the system. Thus Aries was considered a fiery hot and dry sign, Mars a hot and dry planet; spring hot and moist, like blood; summer hot and dry, like choler; autumn cold and dry, like melancholy; and winter cold and moist, like phlegm. All these aspects were to be taken into account in medical treatment.

The signs of the zodiac ruled the parts of the body. Pictures of zodiac man (see figure 3.1 above, p. 41) are common in medical manuscripts, often with advice and rules for medication:

> Astronomours sayne þat cirurgione shulde not kutte ne kerue ne opyn no veyne on mannes body whanne þe mone is in þe token þat gouernethe þat membre and therefore he moste knowe þe xij tokens þat arne in þe firmamente. Luna reule *and* gouerne alle bodyes on erth þat lyfe beren as is shewed in þe ymage of man of þe 12 tokens þat is to say ramme in þe hede, a bole in þe necke, a twynlynge in þe armes, a crabbe in þe breste, a lyone in þe stomack, a mayden in þe wombe, a paire of balaunce in þe lyndes, an adder in þe prevy membrys, an archere in þe thyes, a goot in þe kneys, a water tokyn in þe legges as a man with a pott or a tankard on eyþer legge hildynge oute water, ij fysshys in þe fete.[7]

Similar figures were used for other purposes as well, such as depicting which veins to bleed (see figure 23.1). Medicine is not directly discussed in Chaucer's works, but the portrait of the Physician in the General Prologue of the *Canterbury Tales* reflects contemporary practices and cannot be understood without the socio-historical context.

Alchemy

Alchemy was the predecessor of chemistry. The first document in the field is a jeweller's recipe book, in Greek, from Alexandria in AD 300–400. One branch of alchemy developed into iatrochemistry, or medical alchemy, especially with the influence of Paracelsus (1493–1541), the forerunner of pharmacology. Chemistry was an important research area of the Royal Society, and Robert Boyle's *The Sceptical Chymist* (1661) was one of the works that contributed to the gradual development of the modern discipline, which is fairly late – the structure of the atom was discovered only in the early twentieth century.

Chaucer's Canon's Yeoman's Tale (see section below) is a literary text on alchemy and alchemical practice. Chaucer is unquestionably writing in the tradition set by the denunciations and prohibitions,[8] but at the same time his text has a firm grounding in non-literary alchemical texts. Medieval alchemy is still a relatively unknown area as very few texts have been edited. The non-literary materials of the late medieval period fall into two different types. The first covers texts concerning practical chemical experimentation on the 'philosopher's stone' or elixir. Such tracts are mostly recipes, and their aim was to discover a universal remedy. Their interests overlap with medicine even at this early stage, since the elixir would be supreme in all respects: 'to this medicine all the welth in the world cannot be compared'.[9] The second type of text covers the other goal of alchemy, which was to transform baser metals

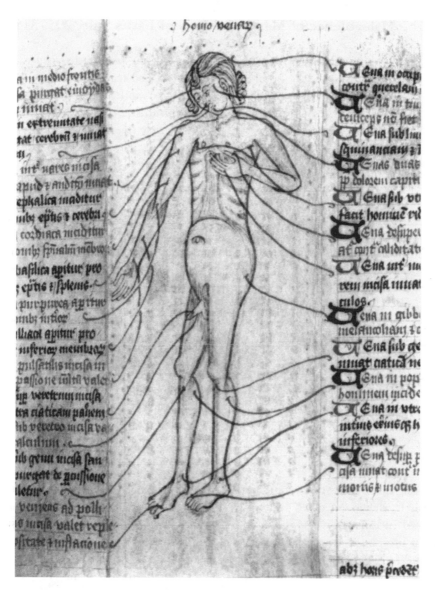

Figure 23.1 Bloodletting man. From a medical practitioner's handbook. London, Wellcome Libary for the History and Understanding of Medicine, Western MS 40, fo. 5 (1463). [Wellcome Trust Medical Photographic Library.]

into gold and increase the alchemist's own or his commissioner's riches; thus alchemists were often employed by courts throughout Europe. A more philosophical and religious trend emerged somewhat later and increased considerably in the Renaissance, especially in poetry, and there are several metaphorical works that deal with alchemical processes from the fifteenth century by authors like Thomas Norton and George Ripley.

The Malevolence of Mars: The Man of Law's Tale, 295–315

In this passage the narrator of the story contemplates the factors that contribute to the grim fate of Custance, the humble, beautiful and god-fearing protagonist of the story, tossed from one worse-than-death situation to another. The lines detail the cosmic influences and present the situation in a deterministic manner, giving the positions of the stars as the cause of her hardships. The first lines of the passage refer to the cosmic order and the two opposite motions of the spheres (see section above on 'Cosmology').

The configuration was particularly unfortunate at the moment of Custance's departure because the dominant planet, 'atazir', was Mars with its evil influence.[10] The malevolence of Mars was increased by its location in Scorpio, associated with death and travail, and the ill fortune was further enhanced by the moon's unfavourable position. The specific astrological configuration presented in this passage does not provide enough information for attempts to reconstruct the real situation; it may be a purely fictional creation to enhance the unhappy astrological indications for Custance and her journey. The evil influence of Mars was common knowledge, and descriptions of its effects and characteristics are found in contemporary literature, as in Trevisa's translation of Bartholomaeus:

> Mars . . . is an hoot planete and drye, male, and a nyȝt planete, and so haþ maistrie ouer colera and fire and colerik complexious, and disposith to boldnesse and hardinesse, and to desire of wreche. þerfore he is iclepid god of bataille and of werre. . . . Also as Ptholomaeus seiþ, vndir Mars . . . is conteyned werre and bataille, prisoun, and ene[m]ie, and he tokeneþ wraþþe and swiftnesse and woodnesse, and is reede, and vntrewe, and gilefulle. (Seymour et al. 1975: i, 481)

The view that one's 'root', or configuration of the heavens at the moment of one's birth, should be taken into account in judicial astrology (lines 313–14) was advocated in learned astrology. Nativities were cast for the wealthy and Custance, being of high birth, would have had one. The rhetorical question about astrologers addressed to the emperor of Rome with the familiar, or contemptuous, second person singular pronoun 'thou', instead of the correct and polite 'ye', enforces the determinism of the stars and the stupidity of not seeking the advice of judicial astrology before an important action. The pronoun 'we' in the last exclamation refers collectively to people, thus emphasizing the shared human folly of not acting in the best possible way.

Perilous Mondays: Miller's Tale, 3515–21

The passage from the Man of Law's Tale referred to above is based on learned astrology and relies on judicial astrology in its more complicated form. In contrast, the

Miller's Tale refers to popular lunar astrology and superstitions. The prediction of the second Flood is based on the moon alone, the mock astrologer's interpretation of its appearance. The moon had dominion over the sea and the waters and all fluids on the earth. This passage also makes use of the popular lore of perilous Mondays that belongs to the literature of 'dismal days'. Various kinds of popular predictions can be counted into this category, such as critical days, Egyptian days, dog days, and lucky and unlucky days. Tracts on perilous Mondays circulated in various forms and are found in calendars and astrological manuscripts of the period. Mondays, dedicated to the moon, were considered unfortunate for all kinds of actions. A Monday was thus an appropriate day for the second Flood. The prognostication is invented by Nicholas to fool the carpenter and his vivid language depicts the second Flood in terms that would scare and convince him.

> 'As I have looked in the moone bright,
> That now a Monday next, at quarter nyght,
> Shal falle a reyn, and that so wilde and wood
> That half so greet was nevere Noes flood.
> This world,' he seyde, 'in lasse than an hour
> Shal al be dreynt, so hidous is the shour.
> Thus shal mankynde drenche, and lese hir lyf.'

A Medical Practitioner of High Rank: The Doctour of Phisik (General Prologue, 411–544)

There were various kinds of medical practitioner in Chaucer's time: lay and clerical, men and women, learned and illiterate, and the training grounds for the profession ranged from formal institutions to private study and shared experience. The Doctour of Phisik represents the highest class, a small elite who had had a university education. According to the records, there were few representatives of this class in the later fourteenth century. Surgeons and physicians had different trainings, but the ethical code of 'a verray, parfit praktisour' was likely to be the same for both groups.[11] Good behaviour and constant study are emphasized, as well as 'vsyng mesure in al thingis', in food and drink especially. In clothing, a doctor should 'shew the manner of clerkes'. Astronomy had an important share in the curriculum of medicine, alongside logic and natural philosophy, and in order to become a 'Doctour of Phisik' the student had to master the science and acquire the practical skills of the craft. Besides appropriate times for treatment, astral knowledge was used to predict the outcome of the sickness in medical practice. The moment the sickness first set in was decisive, and the outcome could be calculated from the positions of the skies and the patient's horoscope. If the humours were out of balance, the physician attempted to determine the nature of the imbalance by various diagnostic means, especially by urinoscopy. The origin of the disease could be deduced from the colour, and medicine was prescribed accordingly. Speculations are found in medical texts, as in a treatise by Henry Daniel, who had a clerical background to the profession:

> And þen it turnith into matere [of] corrupcioun, whiche is cause of diuerse sekenesses and maladyis and passiowns in man, and þat vpon þe kynde and the complexiown of the fode. For *cibus calidus* et *humidus*, fode þat is kyndely hote and moyst, cawsith sekenes of blode; *frigidus et humidus*, cold and moiste, fleumatik; *frigidus et siccus*, colde and drye, melancolik; *calidus et siccus*, hot and drye, colrik. Than yf siche materes makyn dwellyng in þe body, and wykked eyr or grevawnce or colde takyng or myskepyng or swyche oþer poyntis comyn, tho helpin and comfortyn and strenghin þo wikkid humuris, and tha[n] are þay more feruent and more parilous. And þan þey flowyn aboutyn in þe body and in the veynis, and so they arn cawse and matere of dyuerse febris and sekenessis. (Hanna 1994: 208)

Herbs were used for medication, and according to Trevisa the practitioners 'nedith to knowe the qualitees of herbs and of othir medicinal thinges and diversite of degrees, what is hote and drye, what is colde and moiste, in what degree, yif he wil nought erre in his office' (Seymour et al. 1975: i, 435). There were herbals for this purpose, and treatises like *Macer floridus* and *Agnus castus* had wide circulations. They described the qualities of the herbs and their strengths. For example, the latter describes how mandrake was effective against fever: 'þis herbe is wonder cold. þis herbe qwenchit and distroyeth wyld fyȝer. Also it qwenchith and dysstroyeth þe grete hete of brennyng colour. Also it wele hele a man of þe flyx' (Brodin 1950: 83). Drugs and electuaries were made accordingly. The collaboration between the doctor and the apothecary for mutual gain is part of the social satire of the portrait. The last comment is ironical and refers to alchemical practices (see next section).

The Doctour's portrait includes a long list of medical authorities. University curricula systematized the transmission of knowledge and reinforced the authority of books. The list serves to enhance the scholastic learnedness of the Physician. According to a frequency study (Taavitsainen and Pahta 1998), the leading authority in early English medical writing was Galen (*c*.AD 129–99). Ypocras (Hippocrates, about 460 BC) comes next, and then Muslim authors Avicenna (Ibn Sina, 980–1037), Averrois (Averroës, 1126–98), Rhasis (Rhazes, *c*.854–930) and Haly (Ali ibn Abbas, d. 994). In addition, Chaucer's list includes well-known authors like Constantyn (*fl.* 1065–85), Bernard of Gordon (*fl.* 1283–1309) and Gilbertus Anglicus, who was an English physician. It also includes names of Greek founders of medicine, Deyscorides and Damascus, and the legendary Esculapius, who is mentioned in medical lyrics.[12] References to near-contemporary authorities are found in surgeries, and the name of John of Gaddesden, a fellow of Merton College who died *c*.1349, is one such. This gallery does not include alchemical authorities, but such a list is included in the Canon's Yeoman's Tale; Hermes, Albertus Magnus, Roger Bacon, Arnold of Villanova and Raimón Llull are especially important in alchemical texts, and some of them are quoted in medical texts as well.

The Discourse of Alchemy: The Canon's Yeoman's Tale, 720–42

The twofold goal of alchemy is described in the prologue of the Canon's Yeoman's Tale. The narrator boasts by stating that the alchemist could, if he wanted to, transform the whole way to Canterbury into precious metals and thus produce as much riches as he pleased: 'He koude al clene turnen up-so-doun / And pave it al of silver and of gold' (CYP 625–6). This exaggeration provides an ironic contrast to the threadbare looks of the alchemist and his servant, and to their great debts, which are lamented a little later in the tale. The second aim of alchemy, the discovery of the philosopher's stone or elixir, was part of the narrator's dream as well: 'For hadde we hym, thanne were we siker ynow' (CYT 864). The same two goals are described in non-literary alchemical texts of a somewhat later period but with their roots in earlier tracts. Their tone is more matter-of-fact, but they still express the same desires:

In the beginninge you shall vnderstand þat ould philosophers agreed togethers to do by art aboue the ground in short space that nature doth within the ground in longe space, that is to say, to make by craft both perfect gould and siluer.
. . .

And yt is a most soueraigne medycen for the eyesighte without doubte and aboue all this yt restoreth and completeth most specially the nature and geveth semblance to the visage and reviveth the spirites and powers. Blessed be almightye God that hath geven suche a sciencs vnto men. And blessed also be he þat maye come to the knowledge of this precyous stone.[13]

The practice of alchemy was difficult and the goals not attainable. The effects of the elixir are described in detail in a non-literary manuscript in which the author states that he has cured several maladies by the wonderful power of this supreme medicine: 'The dose is very little, but the vertue therof great. With it I have cured the leprosye, French pox, dropsy, collyck, epylepsy, apolexy, the wolfe, cancer, fystula, impetigo, and dyvers inward diseases, more then a man can thynk.'[14]

The Canon's Yeoman's Tale falls into two distinct parts. The first is a warning against alchemical practice. It is given in the form of an autobiography, in the first person singular, and focuses on the changes the practice of this science has caused in the narrator's life. His earlier comfortable life has become constant toil and labour in vain pursuit of riches and eternal health. In his present state, he appears poverty-stricken and utterly exhausted. The tone of lines 720–42 is extremely affective, with contrasting expressions of emotive adjectives and ironic exclamations.

The elusiveness of alchemy and the frustration caused by it are emphasized by phrases like 'slidynge science' and 'cursed craft'. The same despair and frustration can be encountered in non-literary alchemical treatises and warnings against practising alchemy: 'Sith yt is that many men haue perished in laboring abowt the perfeccion and cleere truth of this science to the which as yet wee could neuer come, I shall exhorte yow at this tyme to forsake all.'[15] A typical feature of scientific language is

Figure 23.2 Alchemical processes and receipts. From Raimón Llull, *Ymage de vie*. London, Wellcome Library for the History and Understanding of Medicine, Western MS 446, fo. 14ᵛ (late 15th cent.). [Wellcome Trust Medical Photographic Library.]

specialized vocabulary. Here alchemical texts follow other scientific writing. The jargon is well presented in the Canon's Yeoman's Tale, with long lists of the ingredients of the concoctions and names of alchemical processes (798–818).

Such processes are also enumerated in non-literary texts (see figure 23.2): 'and know that the philosophors have made many chapters of the stone and of sublymatyon distillatyon seperatyon putrefaction ablution or washyng inceratyon calcynation which are all one and operation in one vessel'.[16] Lists of the same ingredients given in Chaucer's text occur in non-literary recipes, including all kinds of strange components, like hair or manure, that according to modern views do not belong to medical use.

Like the science itself, alchemical language has an 'elusive' quality. It is difficult to pinpoint the exact meanings of the referents. One feature that contributes to this effect is the use of negations, as in the definition of the philosopher's stone, widespread in the literature. First the text verifies the existence of 'a stone' and gives some of its qualities in positive terms, but then denies all and continues again with affirmative statements so that at the end the reader does not know what 'the stone' actually is: 'Taake the stone animal, vegetable, and mynerall, the which is no stone, neither hath the nature of a stone. And this stone is like in manner to stones of montaynes, of mynes, and of planetes and animals, and it is founde in euery place, in euery tyme, in euery man.'[17]

The passage on which Chaucer's reputation as an alchemist was based exhibits an elusive quality as well. It contains alchemical metaphors like 'dragon' and 'brother', and the reference to Hermes enforces the veracity of the contents. Animal imagery is often used in alchemical texts for particular reasons, as described in the following passage: 'Some thynk it is to be drawn out of anymalles and seeke it in basylyskes, salamanders, vypers, vades, and other venemous creatures because the philosophers do many tymes apply by symylytude these names to there stone.'[18] Compare Chaucer's argumentation:

> Of philosophres fader was, Hermes;
> He seith how that the dragon, doutelees,
> Ne dyeth nat but if that he be slayn
> With his brother; and that is for to sayn,
> By the dragon, Mercurie, and noon oother
> He understood, and brymstoon by his brother,
> That out of Sol and Luna were ydrawe.
> (CYT 1434–40)

There have been several attempts to explain the meaning of this passage, which has been pointed out as a true alchemical text providing a key to the alchemists' secret. The results have, however, been similar to the attempts to construct the astrological configurations referred to in the passage quoted above of Man of Law's Tale. The text does not provide enough material for a precise interpretation. Perhaps it is enough to state that a fictional creation with resemblance to real-life non-literary texts creates the illusion of being real, thus fulfilling the Aristotelian function of literature.

See also AFTERLIFE; AUTHORITY; BODIES; CHRISTIAN IDEOLOGIES; LANGUAGE; PAGAN SURVIVALS; TEXTS; TRANSLATION.

NOTES

1 Some medieval scientists have been championed as forerunners who developed ideas usually associated with later periods. See e.g. A. C. Crombie, *Robert Grosseteste and the Origins of Experimental Science*, 1100–1700 (Oxford: Clarendon, 1953).

2 British Library, MS Royal 17.A.III, fo. 91.

3 See James K. Mustain, 'A rural medical practitioner in fifteenth-century England', *Bulletin of the History of Medicine* 46 (1972), 469–79.

4 For example, Cambridge, Trinity College, MS R.3.20, John Shirley's autograph manuscript from 1431, contains poetry by Chaucer, Lydgate, Hoccleve and others as well as 'The Thirtry Days of the Moon' under the title 'A Dyetarie for Mans Heele'.

5 Elias Ashmole, *Theatrum Chemicum* (London: 1652), 470.

6 Cf. the synodic month, the time from new moon to new moon, of 29.53 days, which became rounded to the constant of 30 days of the moon's age in astrological texts.

7 British Library, MS Sloane 121, fos 35–6.

8 The church condemned the art of alchemy in a decree of Pope John XXII (1316–34), which contains a denunciation of all alchemists as ignorant tricksters and counterfeiters: 'Poor themselves, the alchemists promise riches which are not forthcoming; wise also in their own conceit, they fall into the ditch which they themselves have digged.' Quoted from Edgar H. Duncan, 'The literature of alchemy and Chaucer's Canon's Yeoman's Tale: framework, theme, and characters', *Speculum* 63 (1968), 633–56 at 636.

9 'Rosarius', Copenhagen, Royal Library, MS GKS [= Old Royal Collection] 240, fo. 231^{v}.

10 For a detailed analysis of the passage, see J. D. North, *Chaucer's Universe* (Oxford: Clarendon, 1988), 488–98.

11 John Arderne, a highly learned surgeon and contemporary of Chaucer, wrote about the ethical code. See *Treatises of Fistula in Ano: Hæmorrhoids, and Clysters by John Arderne*, ed. d'Arcy Power, Early English Text Society, original series 139 (1910), 4.

12 'Esculapius taght the doctryne / To know the qualities of the iiij compliccions, / Of electuaries, drages, pociouns': 'Doctrines of Temperate Diet', in *Secular Lyrids of the XIVth and XVth Centuries*, ed. R. H. Robbins (Oxford: Clarendon, 1952), 76.

13 'Practica Raymundi', Copenhagen, Royal Library, MS GKS 1727, fos 1, 53.

14 'Of the vse of the stone when it is made', Copenhagen, Royal Library, MS GKS 240, fo. 158.

15 Copenhagen, Royal Library, MS GKS 1727, fo. 33.

16 'The physycall chemyck of trythemius', Copenhagen, Royal Library, MS GKS 240, fo. 71.

17 Oxford, Bodleian Library, MS Ashmole 396, fos 22^{v}–23, quoted in Mahmoud A. Manzalaoui, 'Chaucer and science', in *Geoffrey Chaucer*, ed. Derek S. Brewer, 2nd edn, Writers and Their Work (London: Bell, 1974), 226.

18 'Axiomata philosophica', Copenhagen, Royal Library, MS GKS 240, fo. 1.

REFERENCES AND FURTHER READING

Brodin, Gösta, ed. (1950) *Agnus Castus: A Middle English Herbal* (Uppsala: Almqvist & Wiksells). The standard edition of this important text.

Burrow, John (1986) *The Ages of Man: A Study in Medieval Writing and Thought* (Oxford: Clarendon). Gives an outline of the holistic world view

with the grid of correspondences used for explanations in medieval thought.

Chapman, Allan (1979) 'Astrological medicine', in *Health, Medicine and Mortality in the Sixteenth Century*, ed. Charles Webster (Cambridge: Cambridge University Press) 275–300. Explains the principles of medieval astrological medicine as background to the developments in the Renaissance.

Curry, Walter Clyde (1960) *Chaucer and the Medieval Sciences*, rev. and enlarged edn (New York: Barnes & Noble; London: Allen & Unwin). The starting point of several later studies on Chaucer's science.

Duncan, Edgar H. (1968) 'The literature of alchemy and Chaucer's Canon's Yeoman's Tale: framework, theme, and characters', *Speculum* 63, 633–56. Relates Chaucer's work to the literature of alchemy and its contemporary practice.

Eade, J. C. (1984) *The Forgotten Sky: A Guide to Astrology in English Literature* (Oxford: Clarendon). This book explains the principles and key terms of astronomy and astrology, and analyses astrological passages of English literature from Chaucer to Laurence Sterne.

Edwards, A. S. G., ed. (1984) *Middle English Prose: A Critical Guide to Major Authors and Genres* (New Brunswick, NJ: Rutgers University Press). Contains two chapters relevant to scientific writing: Linda Voigts (315–35) writes about medical prose and Laurel Braswell (337–87) about utilitarian and scientific prose. They are useful introductions, although the information about editions and individual texts should be updated.

Getz, Faye M. (1998) *Medicine in the English Middle Ages* (Princeton: Princeton University Press). The most recent general survey of medical practice in late medieval England.

Hanna, Ralph, III, ed. (1994) 'Henry Daniel's *Liber Uricrisiarum*, Book I, Chapters 1–3', in Lister Matheson, ed., *Popular and Practical Science of Medieval England* (East Lansing, Mich.: Colleagues), 185–92. An excerpt from a widespread translation of a treatise on the use of urine in medical diagnosis.

Jones, Peter Murray (1984) *Medieval Medical Miniatures* (London: British Library). Illustrates the transmission of medical practices through images and gives useful background information.

Krochalis, Jeanne and Peters, Edward, eds (1975) 'The Wise Book of Philosophy and Astronomy', in *The World of Piers Plowman* (Philadelphia: University of Pennsylvania Press), 3–17. An anthology of text dealing with the cultural background.

Lewis, C. S. (1964) *The Discarded Image: An Introduction to Medieval and Renaissance Literature* (Cambridge: Cambridge University Press). Explains the medieval world order and the complex system of the universe with its Christian elements and other characteristics.

Manzalaoui, Mahmoud A. (1974) 'Chaucer and science', in *Geoffrey Chaucer*, Writers and Their Work, 2nd edn, ed. Derek S. Brewer (London: Bell), 224–61. Places Chaucer's works in the broad frame of medieval science, including pseudo-sciences and the occult, and gives examples of the various types of influence.

Matheson, Lister, ed. (1994), *Popular and Practical Science of Medieval England* (East Lansing, Mich.: Colleagues). Sections on astrology, prognostication, medicine, horticulture and navigation contain editions of shorter texts or text extracts with introductions.

North, J. D. (1988) *Chaucer's Universe* (Oxford: Clarendon). Gives an introduction to medieval astronomy and demonstrates the application of this science in Chaucer's works in detail. The authoritative work in the field.

Power, d'Arcy, ed. (1910) *Treatises of Fistula in Ano: Hæmorrhoids, and Clysters by John Arderne*, Early English Text Society, original series 139. An early fifteenth-century translation of a work describing surgical techniques for the treatment of anal disorders (illustrated).

Rawcliffe, Carole (1995) *Medicine and Society in Later Medieval England* (Frome: Sutton). A survey of medieval medicine as social practice, with focus on society, the more popular traditions, women and the craft of healing.

Robbins, Rossell Hope, ed. (1952) *Secular Lyrics of the XIVth and XVth Centuries* (Oxford: Clarendon). See sections on the almanac, the body and alchemy.

Seymour, M. C., Liegey, G. M. et al., eds (1975–88) *On the Properties of Things: John Trevisa's Translation of Bartholomaeus Anglicus, De Proprietatibus Rerum*, 3 vols (Oxford: Clarendon). An influential compilation of authoritative material that includes extensive coverage of key scientific topics.

Siraisi, Nancy (1990) *Medieval and Early Renaissance Medicine* (Chicago: University of Chicago Press). A survey of ancient, medieval and Renaissance medicine in its socio-historical context with a focus on the developments of the learned tradition from the twelfth to the fifteenth centuries.

Taavitsainen, Irma and Pahta, Päivi (1998) 'Vernacularisation of medical writing in English: a corpus-based study of scholasticism' *Early Science and Medicine*, special issue, ed. William Crossgrove, Margaret Schleissner and Linda E. Voigts, 157–85. A study made of the 1375–1500 part of the 'Corpus of early English medical writing', a comprehensive computer-readable database of *c.*600,000 words.

Talbot, Charles H. (1967) *Medicine in Medieval England* (London: Oldbourne). A survey of medical practice based on manuscript evidence; references are lacking.

Tester S. J. (1987) *A History of Western Astrology* (Woodbridge, Suffolk: Boydell). An outline of the history of astrology from classical antiquity to the Renaissance.

Thomas, Keith (1973) *Religion and the Decline of Magic: Studies in Popular Beliefs in Sixteenth- and Seventeenth-century England* (Harmondsworth: Penguin). The focus is on the changing world order of the sixteenth and seventeenth centuries from the point of view of common people; the practice of science in all its aspects, including alchemy, astrology and medicine in the late Middle Ages, is given as background.

Ussery, Huling E. (1971) *Chaucer's Physician: Medicine and Literature in Fourteenth-century England*, Tulane Studies in English, 19 (New Orleans: Tulane University). Places Chaucer's Physician in context with the state of the medical profession at the time.

Voigts, Linda E. (1989) 'Scientific and medical books', in *Book Production and Publishing in Britain, 1375–1475*, ed. Jeremy Griffiths and Derek Pearsall (Cambridge: Cambridge University Press) 345–402. Discusses the dissemination of science and medicine through manuscript studies and book production.

Wood, Chauncey (1970) *Chaucer and the Country of the Stars: Poetic Uses of Astrological Imagery* (Princeton: Princeton University Press). Discusses Chaucer's attitude to astrology; explains the contemporary background as well as astrological passages in Chaucer's works.

24
Social Structures
Robert Swanson

No more than any other author can Chaucer be divorced from his contemporary context. To understand him properly requires an appreciation of the world in and for which he produced his works, which in turn necessitates some consideration of contemporary social structures: such is the function of the present chapter. The reality of Chaucer's world must be approached both in its own terms, and as Chaucer depicted it, for that depiction offers insights into his understanding of his society. Moreover, aspects which Chaucer does not discuss or incorporate are perhaps as important as those he does address: the gaps matter. No consideration of Chaucer's reflections of and on social structure can be confined to his portrayal of the lay world; it must also integrate his stance on the social role of the church. Even if we see Chaucer primarily as a secular writer, that secularity is explicitly medieval, and accordingly 'worldly'. His views on the church's place in society can also therefore be considered in terms of contemporary 'worldliness', without bringing in modern notions of secularity as a rejection of religion and spirituality. The demanding agenda makes the following discussion highly compressed; one result is that the texts may be cited less often than elsewhere, as the matter for comment expands beyond Chaucer's own words.

Chaucer as Social Commentator

Whatever else might be said of him, Chaucer was a social commentator, the *Canterbury Tales* being judged 'the shrewdest and most capacious analysis of late-medieval society we possess' (Patterson 1991: 26). The historical background to his writing necessarily affected his perceptions and ideology. He wrote at a time of social change and of resistance to social change; when traditional patterns of social and political organization were being both defended and attacked, supported and subverted. The chief problem his works present when assessed against that background is how to identify the personal tone in the social commentary. Chaucer's perspectives are often hard to elucidate, because of the many voices he uses, or allows to be used. Immediately recognizable contemporary references – such as the list of the Knight's battle honours in the General Prologue to the *Canterbury Tales* (GP 51–63), or a brief allusion in the Nun's Priest's Tale to the Peasants' Revolt of 1381 (NPT 3394–6) – are few and far between.

That Chaucer drew extensively on preceding literary traditions, adapting their contents for his own ends (but without necessarily eradicating all the elements which, while offering social comment, might be extraneous to the realities of late medieval England), also complicates the analyses, for those literary reproductions also lack contemporary reference, and possibly relevance. Yet the texts are all we have to go on to apprehend Chaucer's own view of his society, and that creates problems (leaving aside those which affect the *Canterbury Tales* as a result of the project's unfinished nature, and uncertainties about the ordering and allocation of the tales). Quite simply, commentators cannot agree on what Chaucer's views were. From one standpoint he appears as a staunch supporter of the accepted order, writing for the perfection of society through the proper implementation of current social ideals, making criticisms in order to recall those attacked to their proper social roles and functions (Olson 1986). From the opposing direction, he can be declared inherently subversive, explicitly challenging contemporary mores in order to overthrow false perceptions and align himself with a reformist trend which sought, among other things, to undermine contemporary denigration of women and the misuse of Christianity (Strohm 1989).

Here is not the place to attempt to resolve that polarization; or, indeed, to adopt a partisan stance. It is necessary, though, to try to establish the context for Chaucer's writing, and elucidate contemporary attitudes. That attempt must consider the social structures of the time, both lay and ecclesiastical. In a society supposedly governed by Christian ideals (even if those ideals were constantly interpreted and re-interpreted against a changing background of contemporary demands and understandings, rather than treated as universal timeless givens), the role of the church and its spiritual demands were unavoidable social forces.

The Body Politic

Although late medieval England clearly acknowledged the existence of the individual and the self – and with them individualism and self-interest – positive contemporary interpretations of social structures were essentially holistic, fundamentally based on ideas of community and interdependence. These were perhaps most explicitly set forth in the anthropomorphic or organological conceit of human society as a body politic. Dissecting social and political structures and relationships in terms of the human body (usefully summarized as 'head and members') conferred on each group in society its anatomical analogue. All contributed to the body's efficient functioning; any part's failure to perform its proper function would cause the whole body to suffer, and ultimately to die. This was an old but highly adaptable way of explaining any political or social order. It had been used back in the twelfth century by John of Salisbury, in his *Policraticus*, to exemplify the notion of the commonwealth; it was also invoked in the statutes of Oxbridge colleges to indicate the relationships between the various ranks of their memberships.

Whatever the scale of the body to which it was applied, this anthropomorphic ideal allowed political and spiritual ideologies to coalesce: monarchy went almost without saying. At the higher levels, and despite some realities to the contrary (in some Italian cities, and embryonically in the Swiss cantons), every European country was still technically a monarchy. (Chaucer indeed seems to endorse a monarchist, 'top–down' approach to governance in the envoy to Richard II at the end of 'Lak of Stedfastnesse'.) Lower down the scale, fraternities, religious houses and lay households were all assumed to be monarchical (and, in addition, effectively patriarchal) in governance. Within the church, monarchy also held sway, although from 1378 the papacy's monarchical status was challenged by the practical and theoretical problems generated by the Great Schism. That contest erupted when two popes were elected in quick succession, each asserting his own legitimacy and attracting adherents. The division outlived Chaucer, being settled only in 1417, and even then without conclusive resolution of the problem of ecclesiastical monarchy.

Orders and Estates

Beyond their centrality to the concept of the body politic, ideas of community and interdependence also inhered in the principal model of social structure in the late fourteenth century. This was the notion of the 'three orders', which also went back centuries. This scheme separated society into three groups: those who fought, those who prayed and those who worked. In theory, this was a harmonious and cohesive structure of support, protection and intercession. But ideals and practice differed: when the model is invoked in sermons, it is usually to castigate the separate orders for failing to maintain the theory and live up to their obligations. This need not be a static model, but stasis was clearly one possible aspect of its timelessness and teleology. As a social model, the notion of the three orders was also, obviously, extremely simplistic. With its presupposition of a rigid demarcation within society, based on an idealized trinity of functions, and perhaps assuming the continuance of a structure originally derived from a very different and almost exclusively rural world, it could not easily accept and accommodate social changes which challenged the validity of that trinity. This proved especially problematic as the range of non-agricultural employment expanded and traders and merchants (and money) became increasingly important.

Alongside the idea of orders, and slightly different (although often difficult to disentangle), ran a notion of a society of estates, of ranks rather than functions. This is best reflected in England in parliament, although the elision with the society of orders is there also exemplified, as the three estates of clergy, lords and commons are structurally almost indistinguishable from a society of orders. However, the estates model permitted greater nuancing, by allowing for a multiplicity of estates beyond the parliamentary three. It was also certainly less theorized, more capable of adapting to change and of accommodating new groups as new estates. Such features may also make it a more difficult scheme to appreciate fully in retrospect. The Franklin among the Canterbury pilgrims clearly epitomizes an 'estate'; but just where franklins fitted into the social hierarchy is still unclear (Sembler 1996). Nevertheless, the idea of estates was probably more widely known in England than that of orders: a fairly stand-ard list of estates (more comprehensive but less detailed than that provided in the General Prologue) was recited in the bidding prayers at mass, which were also used in the assemblies of some religious fraternities.[1]

The estates notion was more fluid than the society of orders, less prescriptive. Cat-egories were not absolute: individuals might in fact be members of several estates con-currently, either because they had dual roles (as the Knight's Yeoman is also a forester, the Reeve a carpenter), or because the lists could be constructed using different defin-ing criteria (so that the Man of Law is also a husband, or the Wife of Bath both cloth-worker and widow). Estates might also change, permanently or temporarily. The most significant short-term change precisely affects the *Canterbury Tales*. The estate lists in the bidding-prayers often treat pilgrims as a separate category, suggesting that they were to abandon any other estate identity, to confirm the social liminality of their pilgrim status. Yet this clearly does not apply in reality to the Canterbury group – with one notable exception. The narrator–Chaucer has no estate identity other than as pilgrim. His liminal pilgrim state is perhaps one solution to the problem of fitting Chaucer himself into the estate system, giving no indication of where he comes from, or where he will revert to. (For the uncertainty about Chaucer's personal estate see Patterson 1991: 39.)

These idealizations of society did not focus on 'class', as a recognition of essen-tially economic relationships and divisions within society. Nevertheless, while a 'class-based' analysis of late medieval English society is anachronistic, there was clearly something which can only be labelled as 'class-consciousness', a social awareness which clearly distinguished *churls* from *gentils*. Chaucer acknowledges this, identifying the Miller, Reeve and others as *churls* who introduce harlotry into their tales (MilP 3182–4); occasionally indicating different responses by *churls* and *gentils* to indi-vidual tales (e.g. MilP 3109–13); and most emphatically in the put-down by the manorial lord's wife in the Summoner's Tale: 'I seye a cherl hath doon a cherles dede' (2206).

The estates system had the flexibility to accommodate change, but the social models of the body politic and the three orders were less adaptable. The notion of the body politic could evolve for particular circumstances – being an analogy, the paral-lels could be changed to meet specific needs – but both schemes carried the risk of being insufficiently nuanced to be easily applicable to contemporary society; or of being in practical terms anachronistic (a charge especially relevant to the three orders). Of course, it goes without saying that all the appreciations of social structure were male-oriented: fourteenth-century social and political thought made no real attempt to accommodate female autonomy, even if women in the real world did sometimes, in certain contexts, act independently in practice.

The Impact of Plague and Revolt

In Chaucer's lifetime, the stability presupposed by the inherited ideas of social structure was threatened by the massive social and economic changes resulting from the Black Death of 1348–9 and subsequent plague visitations. Attempts to re-impose traditional patterns, notably in the so-called 'feudal reaction' whereby landlords sought to keep the peasants in their place to defend their own incomes, contributed in 1381 to the outbreak of the Peasants' Revolt. Other attempts to ossify social ranking, by laws to fix wages, or by sumptuary legislation like that of 1363, similarly acknowledged tensions within the system. Further fundamentals were also changing, as the social system became more fluid with the transition to bastard feudalism and the growth of affinities (more fluid and informal connections based on networking, mutual interest and cash), which essentially required manipu-lation of patronage arrangements to maintain personal contacts. This was the world in which Chaucer was himself personally deeply implicated, a position reflected in some of the shorter poems, with their pleas for favours and money (see For 73–9; Purse 22–6).

The radical effects of these social changes became increasingly obvious after 1381, as rural lordship based on manorialism went into decline. The changes in the countryside were of crucial significance, for England was still overwhelmingly a rural society, the towns and town dwellers rarely totally divorced from some rural or agricultural connections. Yet manorialism was certainly not extinct when Chaucer wrote, and reflections of 'feudal' lordship appear in his works, as in the portrayal of the village lord in the Summoner's Tale, or the castigation of extortionate lordship in the Parson's Tale (751–7). Alongside lordship and manorialism, other aspects of a 'feudal' society still showed signs of life: serfdom was among them, and in 1385 Richard II summoned his feudal levies for war against Scotland. That was admittedly an anachronistic action (the process had not been used for a century), and proved to be the last medieval summons; but that could not be known at the time.

The General Prologue

Society's developing tensions spill over into Chaucer's personal history, and into his writings; most vividly into the *Canterbury Tales*. The General Prologue, while arguably presenting models who exemplify the three orders (in the Knight, the Parson and the Plowman), also accommodates a wide range of other characters whose social positions challenge the traditional triad, and who can be more easily placed in a social system through the estates model. Yet the group of pilgrims is also a selective, and selected, company. They quite emphatically do not include representatives of society's highest and lowest levels. The Monk might be fit to be an abbot (167), but he has not yet attained that rank. There are no bishops or abbots on the journey. Nor are there any nobles: the best that can be managed is the Knight, and his social status remains somewhat unclear, probably fitting among the minor gentry. Equally, there are none of the rural or urban poor, and ostensibly no serfs (although serfs need not be poor): the Plowman is at worst a reasonably well-off peasant.

While selected, the Canterbury pilgrims also constitute a somewhat disordered society, as reflected in their jumbled and incomplete presentation – something for which the narrator–Chaucer feels obliged to apologize (GP 743–6). Several of the pilgrims operate within a money-based society, one inherently in opposition at least to the functional division of the three orders. This society also had to acknowledge the existence and activities of women: not just the Wife of Bath and the Prioress and her companions, but also the *éminences grises* of the socially ambitious Guildsmen's wives, the women whose purses (and more) were pillaged by the Friar and Pardoner, and those portrayed in the individual tales.

Despite contemporary theories, among the pilgrims a strict differentiation between orders or estates – perhaps particularly between orders – proves impractical: elision is unavoidable, as was the case in real life. A celibate clergy clearly could (or, rather, should) not reproduce; its ranks always had to be replenished from at least one other order or estate; and the new recruits might retain the characteristics of their original estate, rather than converting fully to those of their newly adopted status. The Parson as brother to the Plowman reveals the links between work and prayer; and if, as a rector, he exercised manorial jurisdiction over tenants, he would also have affinities with at least the lesser lords among the ranks of 'those who fought'. The Monk – that 'fish out of water' – offers a potential bridge between those who prayed and the vestiges of the fighting order. Similarly, in parliament, the presence of abbots and bishops among the lords linked them (whatever their actual social origins) to the theoretical fighters; by contrast, the lower clergy had firmly separated themselves from the commons by evolving their own representative institutions, the Convocations of York and Canterbury (yet clerics were still in certain circumstances taxed among the laity). The role of the 'fighters' was also changing. Whatever is actually to be made of his career as recounted in the Prologue, the Knight appears exotic, somehow extrinsic to the insularities of English society. While crusading abroad still attracted English participants in the later Middle Ages, what, in truth, was the place of the Knight's knightliness in late fourteenth-century England – when the Man of Law had probably also been knighted on attaining the rank of serjeant-at-law? Likewise, as already suggested, the ranks of 'those who work' were evolving, as a money-based economy demanded the recognition of non-agricultural work and the acknowledgement of the existence of artisans, bureaucrats and merchants. The period was characterized by social fluidity, rather than by the formal maintenance of traditional hierarchies.

Chaucer's own life-history exemplifies this social fluidity. Traditionally counted as a brother-in-law of John of Gaunt (the prince in 1396 having married his mistress, Katherine Swynford, usually identified – on very slim evidence – as the sister of Chaucer's wife), and so step-uncle to King Henry IV, Chaucer was nevertheless, within that penumbra of the three orders, a non-landed bureaucrat: non-productive, non-fighting (even making allowances for his capture and ransom in 1359–60), and non-intercessory (except in a private capacity). His wife's nephews would include a bishop (who eventually became a cardinal) and dukes; his own grand-daughter was to be a duchess. Yet he was a vintner's son, and a customs official: someone unavoidably embroiled in a world of cash and commodities.

Caritas and the Common Good

Thus far, social structures and resulting relationships have been approached mainly in practical and pragmatic terms. That tack, however, ignores society's moral imperatives. To some extent, those imperatives are built into the assumptions of collaboration and interdependence, in a concern for 'the common good', which are inherent in the models of the body politic and the three orders (they are perhaps less obvious when dealing with a society of estates); but they are not forcefully articulated. To find explicit invocation of morality as a societal imperative requires the integration of a spiritual dimension, and consideration of Christianity's social message. An underlying ideology of *caritas* – of the mutual responsibility of Christians for each others' salvation – clearly imposed social obligations and social relations.

Christian fellowship and mutual obligations, encapsulated in Christ's two great commandments, and enjoined in the prescriptions and proscriptions of the Ten Commandments and the corporal acts of mercy, were constantly put forward as part of the social bedrock. Christianity's social dimension was forensically delineated in a wide range of catechetical and penitential works, like the lengthy analysis of the Ten Commandments in *Dives and Pauper* (written about 1405), or the more succinct analysis contained in the Parson's Tale. The sense of community and mutuality in Chaucer's writings is at its most profound in that tale, where the universalized inter-relationships of humans as Christians are expounded through the teller's dissection of sin and penitence. (It also appears, pithily, and with an appeal to self-interest, in the *Parliament of Fowls*, 71–84.) The ethereal and decontextualized nature of the Parson's moral exhortation – despite resonances between some of his comments and the specific behaviour of individual pilgrims in the preceding tales – cannot undermine his message. His tale's call for fellowship and mutual aid on the road to heaven seems intended, ultimately, to concentrate the pilgrims' minds on their posthumous goal (and may indeed do so, if the placing of Chaucer's Retraction immediately following is deliberate). However, the Parson's Tale also sends his message beyond that small group en route to Canterbury to the much wider community of readers and hearers which was also assumed to be seeking that celestial Jerusalem.

Fellowship, Community and Pilgrimage

It is primarily as a Christian fellowship, with all its flaws, that the pilgrims of the *Canterbury Tales* come together. For all their bickering and discords, they are a unity of sorts. Even though not fully socially comprehensive, the group still contains representatives of each of the three orders, of a range of estates, even some women. Despite the absence of the highest social ranks, the group can be seen to function as a kind of monarchically governed unity under the direction of Harry Bailly (even if it is an elected monarchy, and the monarchical governance is often contested and insecure). On another level, the pilgrims present a mirror (albeit tarnished, possibly cracked) of a society organized by estates and orders, assuming a unity which indeed may not be there in fact.

For this community must not be made too uniform. Even if the group can be interpreted as having some attributes of a polity, it remains no more than an accidental agglomeration, a short-term and utilitarian association, with its own inner tensions which break through in the personal comments and rivalries of the text. That real pilgrim parties were riven with tensions – including social tensions – is clear from the experience of Margery Kempe a few decades later, ostracized for her excessive piety, abandoned for being a pain or for being simply an inappropriate travelling companion for one perhaps of higher rank: her experiences need to be set alongside those of Chaucer's fictional group.

That the Canterbury pilgrims are only superficially a community is clear from the way they are introduced and described in the General Prologue. At first the narrator–Chaucer knows them (and presents them) only from their own words and appearances, not from long-term acquaintance. Hence, perhaps, many of the ambiguities which have been found in the portraits. Within the group as a whole there are sub-groups, each with its own unity and cohesions. The Knight with his Squire and Yeoman constitute a household (but perhaps one less impressive than might be expected), or alternatively a military unit. The Prioress and her associates have their own identity, and their own group dynamic. The Parson and his Plowman brother act as a mutually supportive family pairing; the Summoner and Pardoner likewise offer a pairing, but one rather less congenial. The Guildsmen, somewhat aloof, aggressively assert their shared experience and own community through their livery, and their separateness with their own Cook. Stand-offish at the start, they take no discernible part in the pilgrims' progress. The fragility of a pilgrim community is epitomized in the appearance and disappearance en route of the Canon: superficial acquaintance is acceptable, but once skins start to be penetrated and secrets revealed the Canon 'fledde awey for verray sorwe and shame' (CYP 702), leaving his Yeoman-assistant behind to add to the storytellers. But then, the narrator–Chaucer is also an added extra: he was already at the Tabard when the other twenty-nine pilgrims arrived, all together, and already a 'compaignye' (GP 20–7).

Looking more generally to the social picture reflected in that company, integrative ideas of community are further challenged by the presence and behaviour of some of its members, notably the Monk, and the peripatetic Friar, Summoner and Pardoner. The first has abandoned his own community responsibilities for individual satisfaction; the others (in reality, or in tales) threaten established communities – village, family, household – by intruding and then departing: they take without giving, despite appearances (or subterfuges) to the contrary. And throughout the progress to Canterbury, Harry Bailly's precise status remains unclear: another late addition to the party, he remains always in a sense extraneous, not assuredly a pilgrim.

During the journey, the group's unity is threatened by individual actions, like the Miller's interruption of the intended ordering of the storytelling (MilP 3109–35: the *Canterbury Tales'* own equivalent of a Peasants' Revolt), or the Pardoner's attempts to ply his trade (PardT 925–59). The pattern of quitting and counter-quitting makes the trip to Canterbury a time of contest rather than spiritual preparation, until the Parson has his say. Although the cracks may be papered over by traditional rituals, notably the kiss of peace to reconcile the Pardoner and the Host after the former's tale (PardT 960–8), the tensions simmer away.

The Social Influence of the Church

While Chaucer casts his eye, and his comments, across a broad swathe of late medieval English experience, the personnel of the General Prologue, and the tales themselves, often draw attention to the church and its social influence. Even where the institution is not highly visible, the church's presence is signalled by references to spirituality, or in the debates over marriage. Yet despite the ubiquity, Chaucer's commentary is highly selective. Given the tensions of his time – the latter days of the Avignon papacy and the outbreak of the Great Schism; the early manifestations of Wycliffite heresy; the institutional and spiritual traumas initiated by the Black Death – his treatment of the church is in fact remarkably low-key. Low-key, but accessible; for the clerical personnel Chaucer deals with are those with whom most of his contemporaries would have most dealings: parish priests, pardoners, summoners and friars. The Pope was too distant for most, even if regularly prayed for. Crusades were chivalrous endeavours, yet despite their lingering relevance for the Knight and a few of the real nobility, for the populace at large their main function was merely to generate indulgences. Heresy was patchily distributed, mainly (in its Wycliffite guise) an academic exercise, and in any case hard to recognize. (The Host might scent a whiff of Lollardy around the Parson (MLE 1170–7), but this is misguided and perhaps misleading, as was the aroma similarly detected around Margery Kempe.) For most people the key point when dealing with the church was the immediate interface, the point of contact with the low-level and local personnel: it is again worth stressing that there are no prelates among the Canterbury pilgrims, or in the tales.

This makes some consideration of the roles of the lesser ecclesiastical personnel worthwhile, for the reality of the contacts and their social implications need to be assessed. Here, again, an ethical issue arises; for the *caritas* which ideally underpinned social relations was merely an extension of that which was to guide the church as a whole. Arguably, Chaucer's main criticism of the ecclesiastical personnel who are attacked is that they threaten, indeed subvert, the working of *caritas* as social cement. Thus, the Friar of the Summoner's Tale may announce that his preaching to the people 'taught hem to be charitable'; but this is immediately followed by the injunction 'And spende hir good ther it is resonable' (SumT 1795–6). This immediately undermines the *caritas*, replacing the carelessness of its true form by the commercial valorization and commodification of spiritual acts. The friar urges donations to his order because its prayers are more effective and more effectively produced.

The Pardoner can likewise gull his dupes by playing on the commodification of indulgences which developed in the fourteenth century, and was to become a topos of literary depictions of pardoners through to the sixteenth century. (His offers are nevertheless less questionable than some of the spurious indulgences associated with devotional activity of this period.) The Summoner, who can legitimately be considered among this group, buys and sells justice and thereby negates the operation of charity. By contrast, the Parson is good because he withdraws from this process – allegedly. Placing his duties above his pockets, he does not over-tithe, nor put his benefice to hire and dash off to gain extra income from a chantry. Indeed, in his own tale the Parson rails against profiteering and commodification as disruptive of charity. Such disruption also upsets the whole social order which, while validly hierarchical, nevertheless ultimately constitutes one family through humanity's common descent from Adam: 'of swich seed as cherles spryngen, of swich seed spryngen lordes. As wel may the cherl be saved as the lord. The same deeth that taketh the cherl, swich deeth taketh the lord' (ParsT 760–1).

Christianity's social demands, as expressed in the Parson's Tale, clearly negate any rigid division between 'church' and 'society'. The church's integration into secular structures accordingly exposed it to worldly influences, readily apparent in some of the Canterbury portraits. Beyond worldly influence, the church lay open to lay exploitation, for both social and private purposes. Much is naturally made of the Wife of Bath, thrusting herself forward against all comers to lead the parish offertory (WBP 449–52), and exploiting the pilgrimage for questionable purposes. She is not alone. The Guildsmen were likewise using the church for social ends, through their membership of a fraternity. Despite frequent attempts to tie them in with London politics and craft guilds, their fraternity was clearly not a craft or trading guild: their occupations are too disparate for that to apply. (Moreover, suggestions of links with London and city politics are actually imposed by commentators; Chaucer never says where the Guildsmen come from.) Their guild must, therefore, be one of those religious fraternities – recently neatly labelled as 'guilds of *homo prudens*' (Hanawalt and McRee 1992) – for which considerable evidence survives from the late fourteenth century, especially in the returns to the nationwide inquest of 1389: it is the status of alderman of such a group which their wives want them to attain. The seeming aloofness of the Guilds-men might even be explained by their fraternity membership: the behaviour of many of the pilgrims is precisely the sort which guild members were required by oath to eschew, if they wished to remain members and preserve their social status. Chaucer says nothing about the religious side of their activities: for all practical purposes the guild is a lay assembly, publicly asserting its status through a livery, with its own hierarchy of aldermen and members. Whether the men's wives are also members is not clear; but it is not impossible that they were. However, in the patriarchal world of the late fourteenth century, even if the wives were members, they could not aspire to governance. They therefore sought to push their husbands forward, concerned like the Wife of Bath with their own status. After all,

> It is ful fair to been ycleped 'madame',
> And goon to vigilies al bifore,
> And have a mantel roialliche ybore.
> (WBP 376–8).

(See also the hen-pecking of Harry Bailly when his wife feels herself snubbed in church: MkP 1901–7.)

The Parson

The lower ranks of the ecclesiastical hierarchy provide some of the liveliest portraits in Chaucer's gallery: roguery, not saintliness, makes good poetry. Yet this layer also provides one of the most striking nonentities, in the Parson. He lacks a physical description, and has only a muted personal voice (his lengthy tale is essentially deriv-ative: he becomes a ventriloquist's dummy). Nevertheless, the Parson is the main rep-resentative of the clerical order, precisely because he runs a parish. Monasteries, for all the attention they receive from historians, were scattered, their inmates only a small fraction of the total clerical population. Friars, although more mobile, were relatively few in number, and tended to be urban-based rather than rural. Nunneries were generally small, poor, and even more scattered communities, and again not places of general resort. A parish priest was in a different category. Everywhere was part of a parish, everywhere would (or should) have had a priest. Chaucer's Parson, a com-posite character from the General Prologue, his tale and occasional interjections, is one of his most complex creations; yet because the Parson's Tale is so rarely included in translations, he is also one of the most remote.

The Parson's portrait is easily, possibly rightly, read as positive: a good priest set in implicit or explicit contrast to those whose faults – absenteeism, extortionate tithing, neglect of pastoral care – he does not share. Here we have a hard-working and conscientious pastor of souls; someone perhaps a touch priggish (at least in his opposition to swearing). He appreciates the need to inculcate Christian morality and social expectations, as he attempts in his tale. If the Parson is to be fitted into an argument for estates satire, those being satirized are the clergy who fail to meet the demands which he fulfils. However, the Parson is also somewhat dry in his delivery – his tale is not exactly a riveting read, his sermonizing dull and (to modern perceptions) unattractive. Modestly, he knows his intellectual limitations (ParsP 55–60, ParsT 955–6, although some of this reads like an academic commonplace), and appears more concerned with Christianity's practicalities than with theological niceties.

However, the Parson is also an abnormal priest. Despite working at parish level, he is probably not the type of cleric that most of late fourteenth-century England's populace would have regularly encountered. He is the rector of a predominantly rural parish, not a hired parochial assistant; but a rector who insists on meeting his pastoral obligations. He was entitled to all the tithes, and therefore was potentially well off – a priest who perhaps could afford not to tithe to extremes, unlike many of his colleagues in the period's uncertain economy. Perhaps, then, Chaucer hints that the Parson is not quite what he appears or makes himself out to be. He has worked the system, secured patronage and, seemingly against all the odds, acquired a relatively good benefice, just when complaints about abuses of the patronage system alleged that patrons were using their control of appointments to reward kitchen clerks rather than theologians. As an exemplary cleric, Chaucer's Parson had real-life counterparts, like Richard Caistor, vicar of St Stephen's in Norwich, who died in 1420 and was considered a saint.[2] Such, however, appear rarely in the records: the only other late medieval English parish priest who attracted a cult – one more enduring than Caistor's – was John Schorn of North Marston in Buckinghamshire, famed primarily for having conjured the devil into a boot.

In treating Chaucer's Parson, his link with the Plowman also merits attention, for they are brothers, and clearly travelling companions. It is possible that they are from a servile family (but if so the Parson should have been granted freedom before taking his orders). Even if they were serfs or former serfs, they were presumably from the wealthier ranks of the peasantry, given the theoretical demands for financial safety-nets for clergy seeking ordination. It may be pushing possibilities too far, given the Plowman's lowly status and apparent lack of wealth, but could these brothers reflect a phenomenon of the late middle ages, the local family which by controlling both church and manor gained a tight grip on a parish economy?

Chaucer's Parson clearly contrasts with the clergy portrayed in critical reformist texts written in this period (most of which were actually written by clergy, and so cannot legitimately be cited as evidence of popular hostility). Other records also provide considerable evidence of clerical immorality and misbehaviour, from visitation reports (like those from Hereford diocese in 1397), court records and private complaints. The Parson is the antithesis of contemporary corrupt clerics like John Crukhorne, rector of Saltash in Devon, who was condemned by his parishioners in the early fifteenth century for a multitude of faults.[3]

The satire of specific ranks within the church shows that Chaucer was aware of criticism of the church, and the Parson vehemently castigates unchaste clerics (ParsT

892–902). Yet his stance is not 'anticlerical'. The Parson's portrait in the Prologue is at many points idealistic, being of a man who 'Cristes loore and his apostles twelve / He taughte; but first he folwed it hymselve' (GP 527–8). Chaucer is well aware of the difference between appearance and reality, and a 'preest that haunteth deedly synne . . . semeth aungel of light, but for sothe he is aungel of derknesse' (ParsT 895). Yet despite the invective of the Parson's Tale – crucially, delivered by a priest – the only 'bad priest' actually depicted is a background character in the Reeve's Tale. He suggests a direct contrast with the Parson, being an equally wealthy rector who used his church-derived wealth to educate his bastard daughter and dower his grand-daughter (RvT 3942–5, 3977–86). Clerical immorality was a persistent problem through to the Reformation; numerous dispensations provide instances of priests as more than merely spiritual fathers. This, though, is skewed evidence, for these records reveal priests as fathers of would-be priests, and therefore of sons; the fate of clerical daughters is rarely revealed. The silence of the sources means that the claim that ecclesiastical wealth was exploited for such daughters' endowment cannot be tested. If priests were acting as shown in the Reeve's Tale, such behaviour seemingly provoked no comment, and was apparently undertaken without undermining the financial standing of the benefice.

The pilgrim Parson in the end appears to be an exemplary priest because he can afford to be one: he has the security of tenure and income which allows him to live up to the ideal – or, at least, to proclaim himself as one who lives up to it. When all is said and done, the fact remains that he is actually on pilgrimage, away from his parish, and in April, a month which, usually containing Easter, should have been one of the busiest for a conscientious shepherd of souls.

Summoner, Pardoner and Friar

The great problem with the portrait of the Parson is that it is virtually untestable against solid historical evidence. Comparable cases of real clergy, at least of real clergy who were not misbehaving, are rare. Similar problems of testing text against reality arise with Chaucer's other clerical portraits, since the lower ranks of the church's personnel are largely absent from the available records, leaving plenty of room for debate, and perhaps scope to ignore historical reality in favour of literary and psychological interpretations. The summoners of the time are particularly elusive. Despite being the link between the church courts and those subject to them, they leave little trace. Perhaps that obscurity is attested by the fact that the extortionate summoner in the Friar's Tale derives from a model of an oppressive bailiff in secular manor courts. While summoners clearly had opportunities to abuse their office, the evidence for corruption on the scale suggested by Chaucer is scant – although here no argument can be based on relative silence, even if the stereotypical reputation of summoners remained poor throughout the later Middle Ages. On the other hand, a summoner's job was neither easy nor carefree; indeed, it could be positively dangerous. People did not like to receive a summons, justly or not; there are plenty of tales of real summoners facing violence in the course of their duties, and sometimes being forced to eat the citation, seal and all. (This was perhaps not as horrific as it sounds: citation documents were usually thin strips of parchment, a mere mouthful if crammed in at one go.)

With Chaucer's depictions of the Pardoner and the Friar, the ground is firmer; but not much more. Traditionally, the Pardoner and the Summoner are seen as a couple; but, in terms of their activities, the Pardoner and the Friar make a better pairing, for they were both engaged in essentially the same business. The Pardoner's indulgences were more probably letters of confraternity, especially if he was acting on behalf of Ronceval hospital at Charing Cross. That clearly aligns him with the Friar, who similarly sought confrères and consorors for his order (although the commitment, and the resulting spiritual privileges, may have been different in degree). It is also likely that the Pardoner was a lessee, having rented a collecting area from the hospital – or from an intermediary – and was therefore working hard to recoup his investment, and turn a profit. Whether the Friar was also a lessee is unclear: an allusion suggesting so is not supported by all the manuscripts (GP 252a–b). Moreover, when an opponent of the mendicants, building on Wycliffite hostility, alleged that the friars did farm out their collectorates, the charges were vigorously refuted. This particular debate is clouded by the activities of the Trinitarians, who were sometimes treated as a fifth order of friars. They too joined in the confraternity or indulgence business, and did lease out some collectorates. Yet in the early sixteenth century one publicity document sought to distance their representatives from the ordinary pardoners, insisting that the collectors 'be no questers [i.e. pardoners] but religious men approved'.[4]

All of this of course assumes that Chaucer's Pardoner was legitimate, a point which has been much debated. There are certainly grounds for challenging his status, and for dismissing him as a fraud, as one of the many false pardoners noted in the period. While his job in some ways forced the Pardoner to over-sell the product, as the ecclesiastical authorities constantly complained, it was not as despised an occupation as Chaucer's stereotype might suggest. In the late fourteenth century the occupation was sufficiently respectable to be used as the job description for entrants to the freedom of York; and pardoners had their own place in the tax tables for the 1379 poll tax. On the other hand, the propensity to fraud was unavoidable, and accusations that pardoners abused their powers or exploited the buyers were common from the late thirteenth to the early sixteenth centuries. The popular craving for the spiritual benefits of indulgences and confraternity created a niche which invited invasion by spivs relying on forged documents and relics. A recent scandal might explain why Chaucer's Pardoner is allocated to Ronceval, for scandal haunted the trade. Beverley Minster sought the arrest of *questors* fraudulently claiming to act on its behalf, and seizure of their false documents and relics; more serious were the (unfortunately undated) charges, probably dating from the 1380s, against the principal proctor for the hospital of St James of Altopascio (one of the international collecting bodies) which suggest the existence of a veritable ring of forgers and fraudulent pardoners operating out of Essex and into Kent, whose activities perhaps put even Chaucer's Pardoner in the shade.[5]

*

The uncertainties surrounding the validity of the portraits of the minor clerical personnel whom Chaucer places among his pilgrims give extra force to the points made right at the start of this chapter. Chaucer is clearly a commentator, but precisely how his commentary should be read – as valid reflection of historical reality, as an essentially conservative call for the restoration of an ideal past, or as a radical challenge to existing social stereotypes – remains an unresolved enigma. He certainly depicts a society: one where poor widows are victims of extortion, where lords lord it over churls and make fun of friars, where marriage is a battleground. He depicts a church apparently undermined at its lower levels by the influence of money and lack of vocation. He apologizes for offering a disordered list of pilgrims in the General Prologue to the *Canterbury Tales*, yet is nevertheless responsible, as author, for that very disorderliness, and for bringing together a group whose community, while based on practical self-protection, remains tense and fragile. The *Canterbury Tales* clearly say something about late fourteenth-century England. It is a reasonable assumption that Chaucer expected them to have immediate resonances, and they can accordingly be accepted as relevant comment on his world. Yet, despite an unending torrent of criticism and analysis, just how he reflects that world and its society, and the views which should be teased out of his works to reflect his own opinions, are questions still unresolved, and perhaps unresolvable.

See also AUTHORITY; BODIES; CHIVALRY; CHRISTIAN IDEOLOGIES; CRISIS AND DISSENT; GEOGRAPHY AND TRAVEL; ITALY; LIFE HISTORIES; MODES OF REPRESENTATION; PERSONAL IDENTITY; WOMEN.

NOTES

1 The prayer discussed in David Wallace, *Chaucerian Polity: Absolutist Lineages and Associational Forms in England and Italy*, Figurae: Readings in Medieval Culture (Stanford: Stanford University Press, 1997), 87–8 is one such bidding prayer, transposed to a guild setting.

2 For Caistor, see N. P. Tanner, *The Church in Late-medieval Norwich, 1370–1532* (Toronto:

Pontifical Institute of Mediaeval Studies, 1984), 231–3.

3 For the charges against Crukhorne, see *Catholic England: Faith, Religion, and Observance before the Reformation*, ed. R. N. Swanson (Manchester: Manchester University Press, 1993), 261.

4 Lichfield Joint Record Office, B/A/1/14i, fo. 69ᵛ.

5 London, Public Record Office, C270/36/9.

References and Further Reading

Hahn, Thomas and Kaeuper, Richard W. (1983) 'Text and context: Chaucer's Friar's Tale', *Studies in the Age of Chaucer* 5, 67–101. A forceful analysis of attitudes to summoners and church courts in late medieval England, asserting the validity of the characterization in the Friar's Tale. However, some of its assumptions are questionable (especially that summoners as victims were attacked for being victimizers), and the essay cannot avoid a certain circularity in the argument.

Hanawalt, Barbara A. and McRee, Ben R. (1992) 'The guilds of *homo prudens* in late-medieval England', *Continuity and Change* 7, 163–79. This article provides a succinct introduction to the type of religious fraternity of which the Guildsmen may well have been members, setting their social function in context.

Horrox, Rosemary (1994) 'Service', in *Fifteenth Century Attitudes: Perceptions of Society in Late-medieval England*, ed. Rosemary Horrox (Cambridge: Cambridge University Press), 61–78. A neat survey of the role of service and the connections it created in the social and political life of the upper levels of late medieval English society, offering a less militaristic analysis than McFarlane's of the influence and concept of 'bastard feudalism' (see below).

Keen, Maurice (1990) *English Society in the Later Middle Ages, 1348–1500* (Harmondsworth: Penguin). A wide-ranging discussion of the social history of late medieval England, structured on the basis of the three 'estates' (but more properly orders) of clerks, chivalry and commons.

McFarlane, Kenneth B. (1981) 'Bastard feudalism', in his *England in the Fifteenth Century: Collected Essays* (London: Hambledon), 23–43; first publ. in *Bulletin of the Institute of Historical Research* 20 (1945), 161–80. The classic brief statement defining the phenomenon of bastard feudalism in the fourteenth and fifteenth centuries, with an emphasis on the military aspect.

Mann, Jill (1973) *Chaucer and Medieval Estates Satire: The Literature of Social Classes and the General Prologue to the* Canterbury Tales (Cambridge: Cambridge University Press). The most influential interpretation of the *Canterbury Tales* as social comment, within the literary tradition of estates.

Olson, Paul A. (1986) *The* Canterbury Tales *and the Good Society* (Princeton: Princeton University Press). A significant book, interpreting Chaucer's work as offering a positive view of society.

Patterson, Lee (1991) *Chaucer and the Subject of History* (London: Routledge; Madison: University of Wisconsin Press). A major work, giving a series of complex but appealing readings of some of the *Canterbury Tales* and other Chaucerian poems, arguing mainly for the selfhood of the tale-tellers, but setting the issues their tales raise against the perceptions and realities of late fourteenth-century society.

Rigby, Stephen H. (1995) *English Society in the Later Middle Ages: Class, Status and Gender* (Basingstoke: Macmillan). A much more theorized analysis of late medieval England than Keen's, firmly tied to the reality of the history. The discussion is both challenging and demanding, and also highly stimulating and rewarding.

—— (1996) *Chaucer in Context: Society, Allegory and Gender* (Manchester and New York: Manchester University Press). The author seeks to break through the literary encrustations and set Chaucer in a firm historical context, while balancing the polarizations of literary interpretations like those of Strohm and Olson.

Rubin, Miri (1991) 'Small groups, identity and solidarity in the late Middle Ages', in *Enterprise and Individuals in Fifteenth-century England*, ed. Jennifer Kermode (Stroud and Wolfeboro Falls, NH: Sutton), 132–50. A stimulating article which vigorously challenges historians' over-use of ideas of 'community', and emphasizes the tensions which operated among individuals seeking to create identity. Rubin writes mainly of guilds and fraternities, but the ideas are also applicable to the 'community' of Canterbury pilgrims.

Sembler, Elizabeth Mauer (1996) 'A Frankeleyn was in his compaignye', *Chaucer's Pilgrims: An Historical Guide to the Pilgrims in the* Canterbury Tales, ed. Laura C. Lambdin and Robert T. Lambdin (Westport, Conn. and London: Greenwood Press), 135–44. An effective summary of the historiographical debates about the Franklin's social position. (Unfortunately, many of the other contributions to this volume are extremely disappointing, if not actually misleading.)

Strohm, Paul (1989) *Social Chaucer* (Cambridge, Mass.: Harvard University Press). A stimulating book which provides trenchant argument interpreting Chaucer's work as a statement of social radicalism and reformism.

Swanson, Robert N. (1991) 'Chaucer's Parson and other priests', *Studies in the Age of Chaucer* 13, 41–80. An argument for a more cynical under-standing of the Parson than has usually been adopted, testing the portrait in the Prologue against the reality of clerical lives in late medieval England.

Wallace, David (1997) *Chaucerian Polity: Absolutist Lineages and Associational Forms in England and Italy*, Figurae: Readings in Medieval Culture (Stanford: Stanford University Press). A major work for many reasons. Wallace locates Chaucer and his works (especially the *Canterbury Tales*) in a contrast and debate between monarchical/tyrannical governance and more voluntaristic/associational social systems. Chapters 2 3 are especially relevant for the present chapter.

25

Style

John F. Plummer

'Style' is a notoriously slippery concept, having been used in different periods and by different writers in different ways. In literary criticism style usually means what we feel distinguishes one text or writer from another, even if we have difficulty describing it. The term appears to have its origins in the *stylus* used in antiquity to write on wax tablets; presumably, each writer would handle the stylus in a slightly different way. The combination of the many idiosyncratic characteristics of stylus movement came to be seen as a writer's 'style'. As this metaphor suggests, style so understood may be regarded as largely beyond the conscious control of the writer; but more often, style is understood to be an expression of at least semi-conscious artistic intent, and one finds in discussions of style a high density of such terms as '*manner* of expression,' '*how* a writer says what he says', '*characteristic* expressions', which bespeak an understanding of style as intimately connected with the individuality of the writer. The kinds of phenomena examined in studies of a writer's style include such items as diction, syntax, versification (in the case of poets), kinds of metaphor, and rhetorical devices.

Form, Decorum and Gothic Style

At the very general level of style as form, Chaucer ranges widely. The iambic pentameter couplets of much of the *Canterbury Tales* and the *Legend of Good Women* are his most familiar form, but the *Canterbury Tales* also include two prose tales (Melibee and the Parson's Tale), a tail-rhymed stanza romance (Sir Thopas), and a tale in eight-line stanzas (the Monk's Tale). *Troilus and Criseyde*, the *Parliament of Fowls*, *Anelida and Arcite*, the Man of Law's Tale, the Prioress's Tale and the Second Nun's Tale are written in rhyme royal, a seven-line stanza rhyming *ababbcc*. The *House of Fame* and *Book of the Duchess* are in octasyllabic couplets. While none of these forms carries with it an intrinsic meaningfulness, Chaucer does seem to have developed the pentameter couplet as a kind of 'base-line' form for narrative which comes to be his 'natural' or artless storytelling mode. It is far from artless, of course, seeming so only in contrast to the more complex forms like rhyme royal. Alan Gaylord (1994) makes this point tellingly in his analysis of Chaucer's comic juxtaposition of the tail-rhymed stanzas of Sir Thopas, what Harry Bailly calls 'rhyme doggerel', and the rhymed couplets in which Harry complains. Rhyme royal can also serve a variety of uses, but critics have frequently observed that Chaucer uses it in relatively formal ways. Barbara Nolan, for example, has studied its use in four of the *Canterbury Tales* and concluded that 'the rhyme-royal stanza, like the theme of transcendence to which Chaucer attached it, implies completion and finality in a way that his "riding rime" in most of the other Canterbury tales patently cannot' (Nolan 1990: 23).

At a more global level, one of the most alien features confronting the modern student of medieval literary style is the prominence its theoreticians gave to the issue of *decorum*, the set of correspondences between style and subject matter. In the standard formulations, serious subjects call for a high or tragic style and low subjects a common style. Chaucer alludes to the idea of decorum in the Clerk's Prologue, when Harry Bailly demands a tale of the Clerk but warns him against excesses of learned rhetorical language:

> Telle us som murie thyng of aventures.
> Youre termes, youre colours, and youre figures,
> Keepe hem in stoor til so be ye endite
> *Heigh style*, as whan that men to kynges write.
> (18–21, emphasis added)

Chaucer uses the word 'style' only four times in his entire corpus, and interestingly enough three of these are found in the Clerk's Prologue and Tale. In the other two passages, the Clerk refers not to his own but to Petrarch's 'heigh stile' (ClP 41, ClT 1148).

In the Squire's Tale, the importance of fit between subject, audience and style arises again as the Squire tells of the coming to Cambyuskan's court of a stranger knight who delivers a formal message in an appropriate manner:

> He with manly voys seide his message,
> After the forme used in his langage,
> Withouten vice of silable or of lettre;
> And for his tale sholde seme the bettre,
> Accordant to his wordes was his cheere,
> As techeth art of speche hem that it leere.
> Al be that I kan nat sowne his stile,
> Ne kan nat clymben over so heigh a style . . .
> (99–106)

Like the Clerk, the Squire thus draws a distinction between the high style and his own, making a little joke out of his inability to ascend to a lofty style or cross over too high a stile. Harry's warning to the Clerk, coupled with the Clerk's identification of Petrarch's style as 'high' and the Squire's mention of the messenger's high style, is not enough to tell us much about Chaucer's attitude towards decorum and stylistic levels, but it is certainly enough to demonstrate his awareness of the issue.

For the *Canterbury Tales*, critics have often addressed decorum and other stylistic issues by focusing on the fit between tellers and their tales, as in the examples of the gentle Knight whose nobly expressed aristocratic romance contrasts with the fabliaux of the Miller, Reeve and Cook, churls' tales told by churls. Although in real life we know aristocrats enjoyed fabliaux as well as romances, with the paired tales of the Knight and Miller Chaucer is arguably displaying his knowledge of and ability to perform at both ends of the medieval rhetorical stylistic spectrum. Many modern readers have found an examination of the appropriateness of the tale to the teller's motivations, temperament, learning or other personal qualities to be fundamental in Chaucer's work. If the style is the man (or woman), then we may seek the combativeness and desires of the Wife of Bath in the contrastive styles of her prologue and her tale, or the motivations of the Pardoner in the rhetorical flourishes of his tale, and we may note with pleasure the disruptive *éclat* of the style of the Miller's Prologue. But we must also admit there are limits to such readings. The Miller is surely not able, especially when drunk, to produce the sophisticated effects of his tale, nor is the Summoner's anger (he quakes like an aspen leaf as he begins) likely to have produced the urbanely eviscerating parody of fraternal hypocrisy featured in his tale.

Late medieval artistic practice, including Chaucer's, frequently considered as 'decorous' combinations of style and subject which we might find surprising or jarring, a quality often referred to as 'Gothic'. Gothic style often combines modes modern writers would not, and may seem disjointed, misshapen, rambling or fragmentary. It is worth remembering how many of Chaucer's texts are fragments: the Cook's Tale, the *House of Fame*, the Squire's Tale and, of course, the *Canterbury Tales* as a whole are all incomplete. We cannot be certain which were left unfinished deliberately and which accidentally, but the interruption (and enforced termination) of the Tale of Sir Thopas and the Monk's Tale dramatize and highlight their fragmentary nature. Chaucer also famously enjoys joining 'high' style, flights of rhetorical virtuosity, with 'low' subject matter, as in the mock-heroic of the Nun's Priest's Tale. There are, further, many instances in which Chaucer seems to mix styles, subjects and our expectations of narrators' voices and abilities without such straightforward comical intent, as in the morally complex mixing of rhetorical powers with ethical bankruptcy in the well-known example of the Pardoner, and the multiple combinations of stylistic registers, speaking characters and ambiguous narrative stance in *Troilus and Criseyde*.

Ideas of Authorship

To return briefly to the present: because style study attributes considerable importance to the uniqueness of the author and the importance of that uniqueness to his or her writing, it is not surprising that studies of style have come under attack in some critical circles. Post-modernist critics such as Michel Foucault and Roland Barthes have argued that criticism has historically attached too much importance to 'the author', his or her uniqueness and imagined 'authority' over, and ownership of, the meaning of the text. For these critics the literary text is not produced by a unique and uniquely creative genius, but rather by a combination of language which speaks through the writer and the responses to the writing of the readership. If the author, then, is demoted in contemporary reading strategies ('dead' in some theories), his intentions no longer regarded as the source of meaning in a literary text, then it follows that we will be less interested in style, the revelation in the text of those unique habits of thought and expression. Interestingly, Chaucer and other medieval writers might have found such 'post-authorial' ideas rather less alarming than some modern readers. As scholars like A. J. Minnis (1984) have shown in recent years, medieval conceptions about authors, authority and their relation to their texts were more complex than is often realized, and certainly different from those of readers accustomed to reading novels in print, with the novelist's name unambiguously announced on the cover.

This is not the place to pursue these issues in depth, but it is important to recognize some ways in which the twin ideas of 'style' and 'author' will probably remain important to Chaucerians. In *Troilus and Criseyde* Book V, as Chaucer bade farewell to his completed book, he sent it forth with the hope that, 'for ther is so gret diversite / In Englissh and in writyng of oure tonge, / So prey I God that non *myswrite* the, / Ne the *mysmetre* for defaute of tonge' (1793–6, emphasis added). On this evidence it seems indisputable that Chaucer felt he had written and 'metered' his verse in a particular way, that he had a sense of his own style, that he quite naturally wanted it preserved intact and feared that it could well be reproduced wrongly. He makes the same point, comically, in his complaint to his scribe Adam about the 'negligence and rape' with which he had copied Chaucer's texts, demanding that in future he 'wryte more trewe'.

Despite the theoretical problems raised about identifying a writer by and through his or her style, Chaucerians are faced with the practical need for a sense of what kind of language is 'Chaucerian'. Long before the modern student opens her volume of 'Chaucer', generations of textual critics have worked over the evidence presented by the many manuscripts and early printed editions of Chaucer's work to settle two crucial questions: What texts did and did not Chaucer write? And, within each text, exactly what words did he write? The answers to those questions must rely in part upon the scholar's trained ability to distinguish the Chaucerian voice or style from a scribal or editorial one, and to identify spurious lines, or in some cases whole texts;

and, within texts agreed upon as actually written by Chaucer, to establish the particular words Chaucer wrote. Despite the theoretical and practical problems and contemporary suspicions about such trans-historical notions as 'genius', most students and scholars will prefer the textual critic to carry on with establishing, as well as possible, what Chaucer wrote, text by text and line by line.

Rhetoric

The Middle Ages had inherited a theory of rhetoric from antiquity. However, classical rhetoric had focused on oral delivery of speeches in political or legal venues, while the medieval practice of rhetoric was more concerned with effective communication in written contexts (though rhetorical handbooks were also written for preaching); and whereas classical rhetoric had developed a tripartite division of styles – high, middle and low – medieval rhetorical practice appears to have collapsed the classical three levels into two. It is not at all clear how much influence such handbooks of rhetoric as John of Garland's *De arte prosayca, metrica et rithmica* or Geoffrey of Vinsauf's *Poetria nova* had on secular writers. These texts were principally concerned to catalogue the different kinds of figures of speech, and their impulse to compile lists in preference to analysing the figures leads us to believe their practical influence on writers like Chaucer was small. We do know that Chaucer was aware of Geoffrey, for he refers to him in the Nun's Priest's Tale, but Murphy (1964) makes a compelling case for Chaucer's knowledge of Geoffrey of Vinsauf deriving from Nicholas Trivet's *Annales*, and his general (and it is only general) knowledge of rhetorical terms and figures probably deriving from grammatical books he would have studied if he attended grammar school, or (if he was educated at court) from French rhetorical poets of the day.

Even if Geoffrey's book would have had little to teach Chaucer in practical terms, it is important to remember that Chaucer's model of the relationship between author, text, subject and audience was probably considerably more rhetorical than ours. As a number of Chaucerians have pointed out in recent years, medieval literary culture anticipated many of the insights of post-modernism on the subject of authors. Robert Jordan's rhetorical study of Chaucerian poetics has argued that much twentieth-century Chaucerian criticism has operated out of unexamined novelistic, even Jamesian assumptions about narrative, 'the assumptions that language is virtually transparent and that life is univalent and accurately perceptible through it' (Jordan 1987: 10). Indeed, the remarks of Harry Bailly, the Clerk and the Squire concerning style, quoted earlier, suggest strongly that Chaucer, like his contemporaries, thought of style not as something inadvertent, beneath the threshold of conscious control, nor as something unique to himself as a poetic genius, but rather as a subject that could be thought about and written about in the abstract, something which could be studied, especially in the writings of the poets whom Chaucer admired most (as his remarks about Petrarch demonstrate). That is, he would have taken it for granted that writing was a skill, that writers studied a craft, that the skills could be complemented by tools and devices which existed prior to and exterior to their own genius or imagination, and that rhetorical strategies varied according to context: who is speaking or writing, to whom, about what?

It is precisely because Chaucer's work is rhetorical – does not pretend to be an open window upon reality, but rather insists that we be aware of the presence and intervention of a speaking voice between us and reality – that so much discussion of Chaucer's style has concerned itself with his speakers: the dreamers in his dream visions, the narrator of *Troilus*, the 'Chaucer' who tells us about his pilgrimage to Canterbury and the many pilgrims who tell their own tales. For many critics, the multiple, complex and shifting relationships among the tellers of tales, their tales and both the fictive and real audiences, this complex rhetorical 'space', has been the most important stylistic feature of Chaucer's work as a whole. The two passages chosen here for closer analysis, from *Troilus* and the Pardoner's Tale, have been selected to illustrate something of Chaucer's formal, visibly rhetorical achievement and his vigorous, colloquial, dramatic style respectively. That said, it will emerge that the formal/colloquial distinction does not hold in any rigorous way; in fact, what is remarkable is the way Chaucer, in both passages, plays stylistic registers off against one another.

The Pardoner's Tale, 895–957

One cannot imagine a more complete violation of rhetorical expectations of decorum or fit between subject, speaker and audience than the Pardoner's famous statement that 'For though myself be a ful vicious man, / A moral tale yet I yow telle kan' (PardP 459–60). A great deal of interesting argument has been produced over the years about *why* the Pardoner believes he can manipulate the pilgrims into purchasing his pardons when he has already exposed their falsity, but here I would like to examine more closely *how* he nearly succeeds in doing so. His confidence game, moving an audience to contrition for sins and motivating them to give him money in expiation of that sin, depends not only upon his own motives and skills as rhetor but on our motivations and investment as audience. After all, we read or listen to the Pardoner's tale even though he has told us he is vicious. To underline the role of the audience in the rhetorical moment, Chaucer constructs a discourse which encourages us, through the power and compelling force of the story, to forget the teller, to be seduced entirely by the teller's tale, so that we can experience more fully the shock as, in the end, we are brought back to a shuddering realization of the teller, and are forced to consider how to evaluate a text, and the pleasure we took in it, that has no ethical core (in the Aristotelean sense of *ethos*).

The passage follows the conclusion to the tale proper, which ends in the 'ends' of the 'wrecches': 'Thus ended been thise homycides two, / And eek the false empoysonere also' (893–4). The lines are spoken by a relatively neutral narrative voice that details, with some relish, the agonies of the poisoned men and dutifully reminds us that the poisoner himself is also already dead. But in this relatively neutral narrative register we hear a voice say 'I suppose' (889); so even here, where we are focused almost entirely on the story – the events we regard through the narrative window – we are dimly aware that its glass is not transparent, that someone mediates between us and the 'facts' of the story. Next the passage shifts into an apostrophe naming the sins the story has illustrated – homicide, gluttony, lechery and gambling – and at first appears to be addressed to those sins. But with 'Thou blasphemour of Crist with vileynye / And othes grete' the addressee can no longer be blasphemy, but must be a blasphemer, and with 'Allas, mankynde' (900) the addressee seems to be mankind as well. We notice, however, how the shift is complicated, vexed: the address to the sins themselves seems to be continued in line 898, because 'glotonye, luxurie, and hasardrye' runs so easily into 'thou blasphemour'. We have to stop to realize that 'blasphemour' is the sinner, a person, not the sin. And who is this sinner? Not until line 900 is that made clear: 'Mankind'.

So the addressee of this new apostrophe is not named until he has been characterized by three highly wrought lines of condemnation parallel to the condemnations hurled at the rioters (one set of sinners), the sins themselves, and then Mankind (another set of sinners). Syntactically, 'Mankind' is not even in the same sentence as 'Thou blasphemour', so we are left to make the connections, and disconnections, as necessary. Next comes 'Thou art so fals' in 903, completing the question begun ('how may it bitide?' [*that* understood]) in 900. Finally we arrive in 904 at 'Now, goode men, God foryeve yow.' Now, who are these 'good men'? Presumably not the dead rioters. Are 'good men' and 'Mankind' coterminous? Or is 'good men' addressed to us? To the pilgrims? Certainly we would wish to be forgiven our sins, and we will beware (905) of avarice. So it seems reasonable if not inevitable that we should accept the pronominal reference in the following line to apply to us as well. But with '*Myn* hooly pardoun may *yow* alle warice' we jump back as if we had stepped into a trap, or on a snake. Our desire to be the 'good men' and to be forgiven our sins leads us to this pass. Having accepted that we are the referent of 'yow' and desiring pardon, we are shocked to remember that the pardon is tied, like all discourse, to a speaker. The pardons are, in the Pardoner's word, 'myn'.

Line 915, 'And lo, sires, thus I preche' is a complex gesture. It identifies – or appears to seek to identify – the preceding passage (904–15) as *not* directed at the pilgrims (sires) by the speaker (the 'I' who preaches), to distinguish between the 'you's of 905–15 and the presently listening pilgrim-audience. But if we look back to the passage we analysed earlier, we see that the term 'mankind' includes us all, however apostrophically and theatrically it was used. Accordingly, there is no firm logical line we can draw between the 'fictional' audience the Pardoner tells the pilgrims he dupes and the pilgrims themselves, and by extension ourselves, to whom he is also speaking. The Pardoner uses 'you', 'ye' or 'yow' fourteen times in the twelve-line passage from 904 to 915. He uses 'I' three times, including the conclusion 'thus I preche'. The referent of such an 'I' is always problematic: who is it that speaks? And is there a natural and necessary relation between the words we hear and their speaker? Can any reliable sense of the 'I' be back-derived from the words we hear? Further, if we say the Pardoner performs or constructs a self for himself in this discourse, is this not done in relationship to an audience, to us? If so, both the 'I' and the 'you' are problematic, provisional and under construction as we listen. Because we are unsure who is included within the 'you', we cannot pin down who 'I' is. If we include ourselves in this 'you', it is because we have been told a story and have assented to membership in its audience. It becomes difficult, once this is done, for us to remove ourselves from the 'you', to stand aside when the sales pitch comes.

Lines 917–19 summarize our whole dilemma with great concentration: 'And Jhesu Crist, that is *oure* soules leche / So graunte *yow* his pardoun to receyve, / For that is best; *I* wol *yow* nat deceyve' (emphasis added). The third party here is Christ, whose salvific healing is offered to all *our* souls. Frighteningly, then, Christ makes possible a union between us and the Pardoner, even if only a grammatical one, in being '*oure* soules leche'. In line 919 the problem is concentrated even further, into an indissoluble paradox: the pardon of Christ *is* 'for the best', unquestionably. But the Pardoner's added reassurance that he will not deceive us, linking the 'I' and 'you' in question with the verb 'to deceive', has the opposite effect to the words' literal meaning (if words can be said to have literal meaning by this point). So far are we from being reassured by the Pardoner's promise not to deceive us, the promise (like the pardon itself a speech act) undercuts our sense of the otherwise sure efficacy of Christ's pardon.

As the Pardoner narrows his focus from the group to the individual, from all the pilgrims to the Host in particular, he who is 'moost envoluped in synne', he switches from the more inclusive second-person plural 'you' to the more intimate, singular 'thee': '*thou* shalt kisse the relikes everychon', he says, adding the injunction, 'Unbokele anon *thy* purs'. The Host responds in the same vein, the same second-person singular '*Thou* woldest', '*thyn* olde breech', '*thy* fundement', '*thy* coillons'. The Host's outburst has frequently been characterized as violent, and that characterization reminds us that speech is never merely a neutral exchange of information but, especially in its spoken form, involves action as well. 'Speech acts', as they are called, are the things language does in addition to referencing. Examples of performatives, or speech acts, include promises, threats, oaths, requests, commands, apologies, and official or sacred linguistic acts like those which effect baptism, marriage and, of course, pardon. Looking at this passage as a whole, from the 'story' told as part of a pitch for money, to the *invitation* from the Pardoner to pilgrims to *confess* and purchase pardon, to his *warning* that they might fall from their horses and die suddenly, we can see that there are many actions in play beyond storytelling. The violence of the Host's response, in other words, reminds us that speech is often action.

We may note that Harry's violent verbal (re)action to the Pardoner consists of a set of largely negative speech acts which underline the Pardoner's illocutionary manipulations and seek to counter them. 'Lat be', he begins, a negative command which blocks, or attempts to, the entire preceding speech with its idea that he will buy a pardon. 'It shal not be' is a negative commissive, promising that he will not allow any such thing. He then 'reads' what the Pardoner has said, interprets it, correctly, as speech acts leading to sin: 'You would,' he says, '*make* me kiss', and 'you would *swear*'. To negate this agenda Harry brings forth a true relic to oppose the false. He swears 'by the croys which that Seint Eleyne fond' that he wishes he had the Pardoner's testicles in his hand. The phrase 'by the cross' is equivalent to 'I swear by the cross that what I say is true', an oath in which something sacred to the speaker and presumably to the listener is called upon to guarantee the truth of what is sworn. Harry thus simultaneously compels the Pardoner to assent to the force of the genuinely sacred and drives home the sincerity of his threat.

Harry concludes then with a triple speech act in lines 954–5, an imperative and two promises. 'Cut them off,' he says, 'and I'll help you carry them; we'll enshrine them in a hog's turd.' The Pardoner's false claim, or pretence, to perform an act of grace, a pardon, through words ('I yow assoile'), is rebuffed by Harry's violent speech acts, and the result of this collision between pretence and violence is, perhaps fittingly, silence. In his *Expression and Meaning*, John Searle suggests that the logical status of fictional discourse is that the author of fictions *pretends* to make assertions and refer. Whereas ordinarily the speech act of reference requires that there must exist an object that the act refers to, in fictions, 'to the extent that we share in the pretense', we the audience also pretend that, for example, the pilgrims of the *Canterbury Tales* exist (Searle 1979: 71).

Is Chaucer perhaps asking us to consider whether, in assenting to the pretences of fiction, especially those of an avowedly vicious narrator, we as audience are logically compelled to assent to his other pretences as well? Chaucer does not leave us in angry silence, of course, concluding rather with the soothing words of the Knight and a kiss of reconciliation. But the Host's violent outburst and the Pardoner's rhetorical legerdemain have led us to consider, however briefly, our own implication as readers in the ethical issues of fiction.

Troilus and Criseyde III, 1415–98

This passage from *Troilus and Criseyde* falls essentially halfway through the whole poem; it is 'central' in that and several other senses. Troilus and Criseyde have spent their first night together; as this passage opens the sun is rising and both recognize that they must separate before they are discovered. Their interchange, in which they take turns condemning the overly hasty night, day, dawn and sun, lamenting the necessity of their parting, and promising to be true to one another, is based upon but highly developed from Boccaccio's *Il Filostrato*. Poems that dramatize the separation of two lovers by the coming of dawn are called *alba*, *aubades* or simply dawn songs. They are found in many languages and times, from classical antiquity down to the twentieth century. In sum, many of Chaucer's readers now and in the fourteenth century might recognize in this interchange a familiar dramatic scene. The combination of an intensely personal interchange between the lovers and the audience's (possible) recognition of the artifice of the *aubade* yields a very interesting mixture of stylistic effects.

There are a number of remarkable qualities about the style of this passage, but I want to focus particularly on its combination of intense rhetorical density (repetitive figures, the formality of the stanza structure, elevated diction and periodic syntax, for example) with its ample balancing measure of naturalistic feel, arising largely from a sense of intimacy. Another way to put this is that we are accustomed to see such intensity of rhetoric deployed on public occasions for large audiences, whereas the occasion here is as personal and intimate as can be imagined.

Before getting into details, let us make a few general remarks about the rhyme scheme or structure of the rhyme royal stanza. Because it is seven lines long it is asymmetrical by nature. The *ababbcc* scheme may map on to the syntax of the stanza in a variety of ways, and Chaucer exploits these possibilities. Viewed abstractly, the *abab* section can be handled as two couplets forming a quatrain; or it can be seen as a structure that expands into five lines to include the final *b* rhyme, followed by a couplet with a new rhyme. In other words, the stanza can operate as a quintain followed by a couplet. In the former case, if the thought-syntax ends with the fourth line, the stanza can be seen as a quatrain followed by a triplet. Of the twelve stanzas in the passage under consideration, one of these two structures (4–3 or 5–2) is used in eight. The tenth stanza (1478–84) has a 3–3–1 structure, and three stanzas, the first and the last two, carry the thought and syntax across the full seven-line length of the stanza.

Note, first, the balance of the opening pair of lines (1415–16) with the second pair (1417–18). In the first line of each pair, the principal actor is identified ('the cok', 'Lucifer') and then amplified by renaming ('comune astrologer', 'dayes messager'). The end of the second line in each pair contains the verb, the action performed by each of these agents in turn (beat his breast 'and after crowe', and 'out hire bemes throwe'). Lines 1420–1 continue the course of the stanza in terms of thought, but reverse the syntax: first we are given the verb, 'estward roos' (followed by the parenthetical remark about whoever might be watching), and then the actor, *Fortuna major*. Next we read 'that anoon Criseyde'. The reading 'that', where we would expect a 'than', might indeed be an error for 'than' (meaning 'then'), but the manuscripts are unanimous in favour of 'that', so editors have understood it to be an extreme condensation (an *anacoluthon* or ellipsis) expandable to 'it was then that'.

However exactly we expand it, the line takes on a great gravity from such condensation, so that we are intensely eager to hear what follows upon such elaborate and stately preparation. And here we see Chaucer risking a reader's impatience in order to respect the integrity of his stanzas, for we learn that the anticipated action will be Criseyde speaking to Troilus, with sore heart, but what she says must await the next stanza. My point is that Chaucer could have begun the substance of Criseyde's speech here. It would have been more naturalistic to do so; but this is not a naturalistic poem. However 'genuine' are the emotions of the lovers in this scene – and there is no reason why we cannot regard them as just as genuine as the emotions of any fictional lovers

– Chaucer is at this point intent more upon the architecture of his poem than upon any 'realistic' haste Criseyde might feel to express herself.

The second stanza is also marked by balance, though of a different kind. The first line names and then renames Troilus in terms of his relation to Criseyde, her 'trust' and her 'pleasure'. The second line turns then fully to her, adducing her sorrow to have been born, so is she filled with woe. Line 1424 concludes the movement from Troilus to Criseyde to 'us', the two together, who are then 'dissevered' within that same line. These lines serve as a rhetorical microcosm of the night they have enjoyed and mark its end. The reader's imaginative focus is moved from Troilus (though Troilus evoked exclusively as he relates to Criseyde) to Criseyde (evoked through her sorrow) and thence to the couple, 'us', only to find the union severed by 'that day' which ends the night and will be the focus of the following dialogue. This stanza nicely illustrates the error in believing that rhetorical effects necessarily dilate action, for the whole story of Troilus and Criseyde is condensed into these three lines.

Of considerable interest to Chaucer, on the evidence of his performance, is the stanza's potential for resonant and meaningful use of rhyme sounds. Chaucer is the master of comic ironic rhymes in the couplets of the *Canterbury Tales*; in *Troilus*, when he draws our attention to the rhyming sounds, he tends to use this extra attention to underline dramatic and seriously, even tragically, ironic rhymes. In the second stanza he uses the triple rhyme on the long 'o' in 'me is wo', 'hennes go', and the finality of 'for evere mo' to bracket and give structure to the expression of pain at parting noted above.

In lines 1427–8 and the third and fourth stanzas (1429–42), Criseyde addresses the night and accuses it of failing to perform its proper duty of providing a time of rest for mankind, or rather performing the duty too hastily. In asking night to hover over them as it did when it stood still for Jove on the night he made love to Alcmene, Criseyde is asking for something contrary to nature. In rhetorical terms this is called an *adynaton*. Troilus will take up this trope in his address to the 'cruel day', demanding that the sun return to its bed. Another form of this figure is found in the last stanza (1492–8), where Criseyde claims that Phoebus will fall from its sphere and eagles and doves will be companions before he (Troilus) leaves her heart. These metaphors are not in the comparable section of Boccaccio's *Filostrato*; Chaucer appears to be developing an idea he found in Ovid's *Amores* (I, Elegy 13). The concentration of these *adynata*, these pleas and promises for the suspension of natural laws and time, here in the very centre of the book, increase dramatically our sense of the star-crossed quality of their love. Unlike Jove, who as a god can compel the night to stand still for his pleasure, Troilus and Criseyde are mortal inhabitants of a doomed city which is hurrying, like the night, along a course towards inevitable destruction.

Again, the rhetorical density of the passage is remarkable, as in for example the fourth stanza, where Criseyde addresses the night in a very complex combination of accusation and imprecation. She uses the intimate (and thus not respectful) second-person singular 'Thow' (four times), 'thyn' (twice) and 'thee' to punctuate her speech. Not surprisingly, with all these pronominals, the speech moves slowly, held back in its progress by the phrases which name the night, God ('maker of kynde') and night's errors ('haste' and 'unkynde vice'), and the speech shifts in its second line from accusation to the wish that God will bind night to their hemisphere so that it can never go beneath the horizon again. This wish 'contrary to nature' is echoed in Criseyde's double use of 'kynde', first (1437) meaning the Nature that God made, and then, with 'unkynde vice' (1438) to mean 'unnatural' and of course 'unkind' in the modern sense.

In the final couplet of the fourth stanza, Criseyde's speech concludes with contrasting speed and simplicity: because night 'hies' (hurries) out of Troy, she has lost thus 'hastily' her joy. The final rhyme 'Troie' and 'joie' here resonates ironically, anticipates the repetition of the rhyme in the sixth stanza, and echoes the same rhyme (now viewable as prophetic) in the opening stanza of the poem.

Troilus next responds (in the next three stanzas) with his own set of accusations and complaints against the day and the sun. He echoes Criseyde in his peremptory use of pronouns to address the day and sun – 'thi' (six times), 'thou', 'thee' (twice), 'thine' – and in wishing for the sun to return to his bed, and even echoes her use of the densely eliptical *anacoluthon*: 'Ther god thy lyght so quench' (1456). In the ninth stanza Troilus turns (metaphorically) to address Criseyde herself. The address is introduced by the alliterating sequence 'sore', 'sighte' and 'seyde', emphasizing the pain he feels. But even in this expression of pain his language is palpably shaped, even stately. He addresses her as 'my lady', the root and well of his well being or woe, his 'goodly [one]', 'Criseyde'. This quadruple nomination of his lover has the initial effect of slowing the movement of the speech and its implied action. The style seeks not verisimilitude or expedition but resonance. We also note the *chiasmus*, or 'crossing' of 'my lady . . . my wele . . . the welle . . . Criseyde' (1472–3). The pun on 'well' meaning 'well-being' and 'welle' meaning 'source' is augmented in its effect by the inclusion of 'wo', the alternative to 'wel'. In line 1474 Troilus gives voice to what he sees as his unacceptable choices, and again, the language is unhurried: the necessity that he must leave is broken into two parts. 'Shall I rise?' and 'shall I go?'; it is as if his speech drags its feet and resists movement in sympathy with his desire to stay. As he continues, his words suggest that he is separated from himself, certainly from any control of himself. In 1475 he separates 'myn herte' from 'fele I', and his heart is separated from itself, 'a-two'. Similarly in the next line, 'I' and 'my lif' are separate, and in the final line of the stanza this trope of separation is completed by the assertion that 'his life' is not 'his' but rests 'with yow'.

Criseyde's answer in the final stanza to Troilus' plea that she be true to him is of course terribly important to the overall sense of the poem. Her multiple promises actually take up another three stanzas after this one, and there is no hint in what she says that she is not sincere. Stylistically the final stanza is interesting in part because it is one of the few in which the syntactic structure, the unit of thought, occupies the entire seven lines of the stanza. The first line announces that Criseyde answered (the second line adding that she did so with a sigh), and her answer occupies the remaining lines. The third to the sixth lines form a list: *first* shall Phoebus fall, / *And* every eagle be friends with the doves, / *And* every rock start from its place, before Troilus will fade from Criseyde's heart. Once again we hear the *adynaton*, as she promises to be faithful until the list of impossibilities comes about.

One stylistic feature of the passage that is striking is the quasi-passive quality of the first element: 'the game . . . so ferforth now *is gon*'. This is an image of actions and events beyond the speaker's control, and indeed the images of the sun and eagle are of things suffering action (falling, feeling affection) and, since rocks cannot 'start' of their own accord, being thrown. On the one hand, then, Criseyde's list of *impossibilia* seems varied enough to cover all contingencies; there seems no chance whatever of these things coming to pass. On the other hand, the passive quality of the expression hints at what Criseyde cannot yet know or guess, that she will be taken against her will from Troy to the Greek camp, out of her 'sphere', out of her 'natural' place. Chaucer's language again reinforces the sense pervading the whole poem that, whatever the lovers' sincerity or intentions, they are not in a position to guarantee a future to or for one another.

See also AUTHORITY; GENRE; LANGUAGE; MODES OF REPRESENTATION; TEXTS; TRANSLATION; WOMEN.

REFERENCES AND FURTHER READING

Baum, Paul (1961) *Chaucer's Verse* (Durham, NC: Duke University Press). A careful study of interrelations of style and versification in Chaucer.

Benson, C. David (1986) *Chaucer's Drama of Style: Poetic Variety and Contrast in the* Canterbury Tales (Chapel Hill, NC: University of North Carolina Press). Argues that the stylistic drama in the *Canterbury Tales* is not between teller and tale but between tales.

Burnley, David (1983) *A Guide to Chaucer's Language* (Basingstoke: Macmillan). A thorough exploration of Chaucer's style in the context of the English of fourteenth-century London. Historically oriented discussion of levels of style.

Cannon, Christopher (1998) *The Making of Chaucer's English: A Study of Words*, Cambridge Studies in Medieval Literature 39 (Cambridge and New York: Cambridge University Press). Critically examines the common claim that Chaucer invented English as a literary language, and explores his vocabulary and stylistic registers.

Copeland, Rita (1994) 'The Pardoner's body and the disciplining of rhetoric', in *Framing Medieval Bodies*, ed. Sarah Kay and Miri Ruben (Manchester and New York: Manchester University Press), 138–59. Sees in the Pardoner a staging of the excesses of personal and academic rhetoric and their potential control.

Elliott, Ralph, W. V. (1986) 'Chaucer's clerical voices', in *Medieval English Religion and Ethical Literature: Essays in Honour of G. H. Russell*, ed. Gregory Kratzmann and James Simpson (Cambridge: Brewer), 146–55. A nuanced reading of the techniques of Chaucer's clerical narrators.

Fisher, John, H. (1985) 'Chaucer and the written language', in *The Popular Literature of Medieval England*, ed. Thomas J. Heffernan, Tennessee Studies in Literature 28 (Knoxville, Tenn.: University of Tennessee Press), 237–51. Argues that Chaucer's language, though often taken as written for oral delivery, shows unmistakable signs of being directed at a literate, solitary reader.

Gaylord, Alan (1994) 'Chaucer's dainty "doggerel": the "elvyssh" prosody of *Sir Thopas*', in *Chaucer's Humor: Critical Essays*, ed. Jean E. Jost (New York and London: Garland), 271–94. Explores the complexity of Chaucer's playfulness with versification.

Hanks, D. Thomas, Jr, Kamphausen, Arminda; and Wheeler, James (1996) 'Circling back in

Chaucer's *Canterbury Tales*: on punctuation, mis-reading, and reader response', *Chaucer Yearbook* 3, 35–53. Demonstrates that, because Chaucer wrote for manuscript books, and without punctuation, his style affords the reader clues for navigation obscured by modern punctuation and reading habits.

Jordan, Robert M. (1987) *Chaucer's Poetics and the Modern Reader* (Berkeley, Los Angeles and London: University of California Press). Uses post-modernist and medieval rhetorical ideas together to argue for a Chaucerian aesthetics marked by a 'problematic outlook, an uncertainty about fundamental truths'.

Knight, Stephen (1973) *Rymyng Craftily: Meaning in Chaucer's Poetry* (Sydney and London: Angus & Robertson). A careful examination of style and meaning in seven Chaucerian poems, couched in medieval stylistic terms. Includes examples of rhetorical figures as listed in medieval treatises found in Chaucer.

Manly, John M. (1926) *Chaucer and the Rhetoricians*, Warton Lecture on English Poetry 17, *Publications of the British Academy* 12, 95–113; repr. in *Chaucer Criticism: The* Canterbury Tales, ed. Richard J. Schoeck and Jerome Taylor (Notre Dame, Ind.: Notre Dame University Press, 1960), 268–90. Makes the case for the influence of the rhetoricians on Chaucer.

Minnis, Alastair J. (1984) *Medieval Theory of Authorship: Scholastic Literary Attitudes in the Later Middle Ages* (London: Scolar; Philadelphia: University of Pennsylvania Press; 2nd rev. edn 1988). A detailed study of medieval conceptions of authority, authors and literary theory.

Murphy, James J. (1964) 'A new look at Chaucer and the rhetoricians', *Review of English Studies*, new series 15, 1–20. Discounts the influence of medieval rhetorical writers on Chaucer.

——(1971) *Medieval Rhetoric: A Select Bibliography* (Toronto: University of Toronto Press). An annotated guide to the primary and most important secondary materials for the study of medieval rhetoric.

——(1974) *Rhetoric in the Middle Ages: A History of Rhetorical Theory from Saint Augustine to the Renaissance* (Berkeley, Los Angeles and London: University of California Press). The complete history of the subject for the Middle Ages.

Muscatine, Charles (1957) *Chaucer and the French Tradition: A Study in Style and Meaning* (Berkeley, Los Angeles and London: University of California Press). A magisterial exploration of the French 'courtly' and 'bourgeois' styles in Chaucer.

Nolan, Barbara (1990) 'Chaucer's tales of transcendence: rhyme royal and Christian prayer in the *Canterbury Tales*', in *Chaucer's Religious Tales*, ed. C. David Benson and Elizabeth Robertson (Cambridge: Brewer), 21–38. A detailed look at Chaucer's exploitation of the potentials of this stanza in four spiritual tales.

Payne, Robert O. (1963) *The Key of Remembrance: A Study of Chaucer's Poetics* (New Haven and London: Yale University Press). Provides an overview of rhetorical tradition and studies Chaucer's attitude towards that tradition and literary tradition as a whole.

——(1978) 'Chaucer's realization of himself as rhetor', in *Medieval Eloquence: Studies in the Theory and Practice of Medieval Rhetoric*, ed. James J. Murphy (Berkeley, Los Angeles and London: University of California Press), 270–87. The antique model of rhetoric based on speaker–language–audience, shifted by medieval writers to an idea–language model, is reborn in Chaucer's first-person narrators.

Roscow, G. H. (1981) *Syntax and Style in Chaucer's Poetry* (Cambridge: Brewer). A thorough and detailed analysis of Chaucer's syntax, especially in reference to that found in other Middle English texts.

Searle, John (1979) *Expression and Meaning: Studies in the Theory of Speech Acts* (Cambridge: Cambridge University Press). An excellent overview of speech-act theory to its date of publication.

26

Texts

Tim William Machan

The experiences of someone sitting down to write and publish a book in the modern world differ considerably from those of Chaucer or any other late medieval English writer. Today, whether beginning with a longhand draft or composing directly on a word processor, writers exercise immediate control over the texts of their books, worrying over commas, words and phrases as they revise them for submission. When writers are satisfied with their own efforts, they may simply submit them to a publishing house or hire a literary agent, who will work on their behalf. In either case, once at a publisher books are reviewed by editors, who may reject or accept them outright or who may make publication conditional on stipulated revisions. If a book is accepted for publication, its author signs a legal contract that typically specifies a production date, a press run, the author's compensation and, perhaps, provisions for future reprints or film versions. Once the book is in production, copy-editors work with the author on stylistic changes, while other individuals attend to layout and design, advertising, printing and binding, and distribution. Eventually, perhaps years later, the book appears in shops with the author's copyright stated on the converse of the title page and the cost of the book stamped on its cover.

To some extent, I have idealized the production and reception of books in the modern world, for I have omitted many of the complicating details that have ramifications for our conception of literary works and that are currently of great interest to textual scholars. The process of composition is often collaborative, for example, with friends and spouses effectively co-authoring some works; and the process of production may materially affect the integrity and meaning of literary works, sometimes in ways that authors would resist. Whatever these complications, certain general features of contemporary book production and reception stand out, not only because they differentiate the modern era from the medieval but also because they have become so naturalized for us that they are easy to overlook. Modern literary texts and authors, for instance, are legal entitities. Particular sequences of words and punctutation literally belong to particular individuals, with the result that anyone who appropriates those sequences without attribution or permission has committed plagiarism and copyright infringement and is therefore subject to legal prosecution. Writers may allow others to adapt their texts, as in films, but expressed permission is needed, and it will come, typically, only in exchange for financial compensation, which points again to the legal status of the written text in the modern world. Further, the format of the documents in which these texts appear is itself a legal entity; one cannot simply adopt the layout, design and cover of an already published book, for production and advertising efforts effectively belong to publishers as much as a text belongs to a writer.

In the nexus between text and document lies one other significant but easily under-appreciated aspect of modern book production. With the exception of some popular novels and memoirs, which may have more than one cover design, modern published documents of the same text – that is, different copies of the same book – are, for all intents and purposes, identical when they appear from the same press run. Subsequent press runs may of course change layout or illustrations, and glitches in printing may result in copies with unique omissions or transpositions of pages, but writer, reader and publisher alike characteristically anticipate that all copies of the same book, in whatever bookshop or library they may be, have exactly the same text and appear in virtually the same document.

Producing a Medieval Text

Things were otherwise for Chaucer and his readers. When Chaucer sat down to write the *Parliament of Fowls* or the *House of Fame*, his task was more time-consuming, physi-cally demanding and unpredictable than a modern counterpart's. He would have begun with either a wax tablet or a quire, which is a stack of perhaps four parchment sheets folded in half to make eight leaves and sixteen writing pages. By pricking a series of holes down the side margins of the quire's top leaf and then using a heavy object like a straight edge to score the space between these holes, Chaucer or the parchment maker would have produced indentations that ran through all eight leaves of the quire and that constituted the lines on which text could be written. Mistakes in these kinds of text could not simply be deleted with a keystroke. Rather, the surface of wax tablets had to be smoothed over, while that of a parchment leaf had to be laboriously scraped with a knife, as Chaucer whimsically suggests in a poem to his allegedly personal scribe, Adam:

> Adam scriveyn, if ever it thee bifalle
> Boece or Troylus for to wryten newe,
> Under thy long lokkes thou most have the scalle,
> But after my makyng thow wryte more trewe;
> So ofte aday I mot thy werk renewe,
> It to correcte and eke to rubbe and scrape,
> And al is thorugh thy negligence and rape.

Longer poems, like *Troilus and Criseyde* or the *Legend of Good Women*, would have required several quires, which would have been joined with thread or leather. In the absence of regularized pagination conventions, the order of these quires was fixed by catchwords; the opening few words of a given quire, that is, were also written at the conclusion of the succeeding quire, and in this way Chaucer could easily arrange a stack of many quires in the appropriate sequence.

Publication in a Manuscript Culture

Up to this point in the composition of a literary work, Chaucer's methods differed from a modern counterpart's primarily in the amount and kind of labour involved, for both methods result, at some point after the completion of all drafting and revising, in a text that a writer might regard as finished. But while a modern writer's text maintains its integrity throughout the production process that it enters – with the qualifications I noted above – Chaucer's works participated in a manuscript culture that characteristically transformed them physically and textually. If modern writers can explicitly choose to publish their works, for example, by securing agents or by sending the works to publishing houses, medieval writers could simply make their works available to patrons or friends, who in turn might make their own copies available to still other readers, and so forth. Unable to register a copyright claim, further, Chaucer had no legal claim to his texts and no right or opportunity to make any money from their sale, aside from whatever recompense a work's initial patron might choose to give him.

When the parchment on which Chaucer had written became available to others, whether directly or through the hands of a scribe like Adam, it entered a world that offered none of the legal, production or cultural processes that stabilize the integrity of modern literary works. Chaucer might well have resented this situation, and in an address to what he calls his 'litel bok' at the end of *Troilus* he does indeed express his frustration with the manuscript culture that allowed and even sanctioned the transformations of his 'makyng':

> And for ther is so gret diversite
> In Englissh and in writyng of oure tonge,
> So prey I God that non wyswrite the,
> Ne the mysmetre for defaute of tonge.
> (V, 1793–6)

None the less, with a small handful of exceptions, perhaps most notably John Capgrave, medieval vernacular writers had no opportunity to supervise the production and distribution of their works once they entered this diversity of writing. Chaucer and others might have wished for a kind of authorial control tantamount to that available to a modern writer, but they had no way to acquire or retain it.

Much of the miswriting and mismetring that Chaucer laments was rooted in the simple fact that the medieval manuscript trade was a bespoke trade. When modern publishing houses print books, they do so not with the assurance that every copy already has a purchaser but on speculation – on the belief, derived from market studies, that a given book is likely to sell a given number of copies at a given price. As a speculative practice, modern publishing succeeds when the house has enough capital to underwrite what is effectively an investment and to withstand the loss of time and money if a book should sell poorly and this investment should fail. The production of medieval books, as will become clear, represented a comparatively much greater involvement of time and money, leaving little incentive for Chaucer or anyone else (at least until well into the fifteenth century) to arrange for manuscript production on speculation. Books were produced, rather, on demand, on an individual request for a particular sequence of texts, and this characteristic has consequences for both the texts and the appearances of Chaucerian manuscripts.

The Book Trade

In the popular imagination, the topic of medieval manuscripts may evoke images of lavish, illuminated codices produced in large monastic scriptoria, but such was not the typical case for vernacular manuscripts of the late fourteenth and fifteenth centuries. As the demand for English manuscripts increased in the later Middle Ages, it led to the professionalization of book production alongside the continued production of religious books in scriptoria and at universities. In the secular, professionalized sphere, book artisans came to specialize as text-writers, binders or illuminators. Grouped into guilds, many of these artisans congregated in London in the environs of St Paul's Cathedral, where they worked independently in small shops, each often involving only one artisan. As independent craftsmen, these artisans took commissions from stationers, who themselves took their commissions directly from customers, who might specify not only the kinds of texts they wanted but also their sequence and layout.

This is what makes late medieval vernacular book production a bespoke trade: setting aside books that individuals might copy just for themselves, most English manuscripts were produced only when requested and only according to the specifics of the request. What customers requested obviously depended on their literary taste, their familiarity with vernacular literature and the amount of money they had to spend. In light of both the absence of legal or cultural aids to textual fixity and the variability in any kind of human (as opposed to mechanical) reproduction, this bespoke trade allowed purchasers and book artisans as much if not more control over the character of their manuscripts and texts as the writer – like Chaucer – whose efforts originally attracted them. A purchaser generally interested in lyric poetry and without much disposable cash or property might order a casual anthology of poems, while another, wealthier reader with more defined tastes might specify certain poems in a layout replete with rubricated titles, multi-coloured, floriated decorations down the margins (*demivinets*) and illustrations of scenes in the poems. The stationer, in turn, passed on these specifics by lending out exemplars of the requested texts to one or more book artisans, who would collectively write, illustrate and compile the manuscript that the stationer, perhaps several months after the original order, would assemble and deliver to the customer.

These methods of production entailed risks and advantages. Some risks were inherent in the amount of manual labour involved, for at any point between the author's original draft and the bespoke copy quires might become displaced and, their catchwords omitted or overlooked, reassembled in a new order. Furthermore, different scribes understood their task differently. Some strove to reproduce exactly what was in front of them, while others performed 'dialect translation' by rendering a poem originally composed in a southern dialect, for example, in a northern one. Working against a theoretical backdrop that conceived of vernacular literature and its makers as inferior and even inconsequential in comparison to the great *auctores* of Roman literature and patristic commentary, still other scribes participated in the composition of the poems they transmitted by deleting or adding passages. Scribes of the *Canterbury Tales*, we shall see, sometimes added their own links and tales, while one scribe in particular truncates the *Squire's Tale* with the comment 'Iste fabula est valde absurda' – 'This story is really stupid.' Even more extreme textual transformations occurred when one vernacular writer simply appropriated lines or stanzas written by another (as Henry Scogan did with Chaucer's 'Gentillesse') or when extracts from long compositions circulated as short lyrics (as frequently happened with John Lydgate's poems).

At least from a medieval perspective, however, the prevailing methods of vernacular manuscript production also had distinct advantages. Often, small groupings of texts were combined into booklets, a stage intermediate between a quire and a complete manuscript. Whether organized by theme, style or topic, these booklets could contain several distinct works and could themselves be combined into larger units according to the desires of a purchaser. On a fundamental level, then, medieval book production was an open-ended process, one that always allowed for the expansion or contraction of books and, in the process, that always kept vernacular literature vital and responsive to the interests of its audiences. It should here be recalled that well into the early modern period English was generally excluded from the intellectual, academic, religious and legal domains that validate any literary tradition. In the absence of such validation, appropriation of another's words and the rearrangement of another's texts were useful ways for writers to propagate vernacular culture. What Chaucer laments as miswriting, then, many medieval writers and readers embraced as opportunities for literary production.

The Work of Scribes

From this conflux of the processes of book production and the versatility of vernacular traditions flowed an ever-growing stream of English manuscripts in the fourteenth and fifteenth centuries. Many medieval lyrics and romances are extant in only one copy, in which case the transformations effected by manuscript culture are not always easy to identify. But for some works, including most of Chaucer's, the survival of multiple copies can reveal how distinctively the processes of manuscript production shaped the character of medieval literature. A useful way to approach this issue is through a modern edition's critical apparatus, as in the case of this brief excerpt from the Miller's words in the prologue to his tale:

> It is a synne and eek a greet folye
> To apeyren any man, or hym defame,
> And eek to bryngen wyves in swich fame
> (3146–8)

If one consults the textual notes for this passage, one finds a record something like the following:

3148 swich fame] s. name Ad^{3}DdPw; ylle name Ha^{4}WR; s. shame He; s. a name FiCx; s. blame Bo^{1}TH; swyh f. Gg

Reading from left to right, there are here a line number, a lemma and a list of variants, meaning (in this case) that at line 3148 of the Miller's Tale scholarship indicates that Chaucer wrote 'swich fame' but that in its manuscript transmission this phrase was replaced by 'swich name', 'ylle name', 'swich shame', 'swich a name', 'swich blame', and 'swyh fame' in various manuscripts, each of which is represented with a siglum, or abbreviation.

By themselves, however, such collations obscure two important issues. The first is that Chaucer's putatively original reading (represented by the lemma) is a matter of speculation – informed speculation, to be sure, but speculation none the less. No manuscripts that were unambiguously written by Chaucer himself survive and, as this brief example indicates, the extant texts sometimes vary considerably from one another. Out of this variation an original Chaucerian reading can be advocated on several textual-critical criteria including, most simply, the agreement of a majority of manuscripts. But even unanimous agreement does not guarantee that the word in question was the one Chaucer wrote, for a copying error early in a work's transmission history might easily be reproduced in all subsequent manuscripts, in which case the original wording would be recoverable only by conjecture. What this means for readers of Chaucer today is that the texts in front of them must always be regarded with a kind of suspicion typically excluded from the reading of modern novels: they always represent hypotheses about Chaucer's work, and as such they are always subject to scrutiny, objection and replacement. By no means are these idle exercises, for it is on the wording of a work that we base interpretative conclusions about that work, Chaucer and even the Middle Ages. In the example above, it matters a great deal whether one brings women into defame, fame, shame, blame or a name.

The second important issue that collation banks can obscure involves the witness they provide to the character of medieval manuscript culture. Variants certainly can be simply copying mistakes; but they can also be intentional editorializations that, even if they are errors in relation to what Chaucer wrote, testify to the vitality of his works, the peculiarities of manuscript culture and the evolving status of vernacular writers and their compositions in the still largely latinate culture of the late Middle Ages. The second part of this chapter further explores both of these topics.

Reception and Audience

Before turning to these topics, however, a few words need to be said about the medieval reception of Chaucer's works. Since we seem to have no manuscripts in Chaucer's own hand, the extant manuscripts of all his compositions are at least one copy removed from whatever text Chaucer originally wrote. None the less, cross-references in other medieval works suggest that copies of at least some of Chaucer's poetry and prose circulated while he was alive, at which time his primary audience was likely to have been courtly. The *Book of the Duchess*, for example, seems to have been composed for John of Gaunt, the uncle of King Richard II, and Chaucer's works are everywhere imbued with the scenes and conventions that figure in other courtly works, including the reading of refined literature. Episodes in both the *Book of the Duchess* (44–61) and the *Parliament of Fowls* (15–21) describe such reading as a private exercise, as it typically is for modern readers; but because medieval England was still largely pre-literate, and also because social custom encouraged communal activities, group approaches to Chaucer's works occurred as well. On some occasions, that is, Chaucer may have recited his poems before a court gathering, as is fancifully depicted in one manuscript of *Troilus* (Cambridge, Corpus Christi College MS 61), and on many others one member of the court probably read aloud to several others. This is the kind of siutation in which Pandarus first finds Criseyde when he comes to tell her of Troilus' love:

> When he was come unto his neces place,
> 'Wher is my lady?' to hire folk quod he;
> And they hym tolde, and he forth in gan pace,
> And fond two othere ladys sete and she,
> Withinne a paved parlour, and they thre
> Herden a mayden reden hem the geste
> Of the siege of Thebes, while hem leste.
>   (II, 78–84)

Already by 1400, however, this original courtly audience was expanding to include both individuals who sympathized with the dissident Lollards and, increasingly, members of a growing literate merchant class that had disposable income to buy manuscripts and a particular interest in the evolving traditions of vernacular literature. This was the audience that was responsible for a spectacular increase in the quantity and quality of Chaucerian manuscripts in the first half of the fifteenth century. Indeed, measured in terms of the number of surviving manuscripts, Chaucer ranks as one of the most popular authors of the English Middle Ages. While we have one manuscript copy each of *Havelok the Dane*, *Sir Gawain and the Green Knight* and Thomas Malory's *Morte d'Arthur*, for instance, we have sixteen manuscripts of *Troilus and Criseyde*, fourteen of the *Parliament of Fowls*, twelve of the *Legend of Good Women*, thirty-one of the *Treatise on the Astrolabe* and eighty-two of the *Canterbury Tales*. Many of these copies are casual productions reflective of the diminished status of English literature *vis-à-vis* Latin and French, but others point to Chaucer's growing popularity and a sense that his works marked him as a unique figure in the vernacular literary tradition.

When the early fifteenth-century poet Thomas Hoccleve (among others) described Chaucer as 'firste fyndere of oure faire langage', he corroborated the prestige physically suggested by San Marino, Huntington Library MS Ellesmere 26 C 9 (figure 26.1). One of the most famous of all medieval manuscripts, Ellesmere contains a carefully edited and arranged copy of the *Canterbury Tales* that is lavishly laid out and illuminated with *demivinets* and portraits of each of the Canterbury pilgrims. The manuscript must have cost an extraordinary amount of money early in the fifteenth century, and so whoever ordered it evidently held Chaucer in very high esteem indeed. By the same token, the luxurious design of Ellesmere – its *ordinatio*, in medieval terms, or bibliographic codes, in modern ones – would have invited among its users a kind of reverent response that the small, casual manuscript containing *Sir Gawain* does not. In this way Ellesmere, and other manuscripts throughout the fifteenth century, both *reflected* Chaucer's evolving prestige and *conditioned* readers to attribute this same prestige to him.

As the century progresses, we see continued attention to the physical appearance of Chaucer's works and to the identification and collection of an authentic Chaucerian canon. A bibliophile named John Shirley was especially important in the latter enterprise, for some of the most important Chaucerian manuscripts and attributions come from his hand. Also indicative of a desire to fix the Chaucerian canon almost in despite of the character of medieval manuscript production are three manuscripts collectively known as the Oxford group; produced at the middle and end of the century and sometimes evidently drawing on the same exemplars, these manuscripts offer anthologies of Chaucer's poetry, making them among the first author-centred collections in English. Yet another way in which manuscript evidence reflects Chaucer's growing reputation is the editing that the *Canterbury Tales* in particular experienced. In addition to developing varying arrangements for this collection of stories that Chaucer never finished, scribes and editors strove to complete and polish Chaucer's composition by developing their own links between tales and also, in the cases of the Tale of Gamelyn, the Ploughman's Tale and the Tale of Beryn, by supplementing it with other tales. Given the evidently wide audience and cultural status that had accrued to Chaucer by the 1470s, it comes as no surprise that when William Caxton

Figure 26.1   The Franklin's Prologue. From the *Canterbury Tales* by Geoffrey Chaucer. San Marino, California, Huntington Library, MS EL 26 C9, fo. 123ᵛ (*c*.1410). [This item is reproduced by permission of The Huntington Library, San Marino, California.]

established England's first printing press in 1476, Chaucer's works were among the first and most frequently issued.

Editing Chaucer: The *Legend of Good Women*

The specifics of the production and reception of medieval manuscripts affect the reading and interpretation of Chaucer's works in several ways since, as I noted earlier, authentic readings are always matters of speculation and sometimes reveal less about medieval manuscript culture than do inauthentic ones. The clean reading-texts of editions like the *Riverside Chaucer* should therefore always be understood as acts of editorial interpretation on which any subsequent acts of literary interpretation depend. Further, editorial interpretations are themselves informed by literary considerations, for a sensibility about Chaucer, his writings and the period in which he wrote is one heuristic an editor uses to make sense of the divergent materials produced by medieval manuscript culture. In making decisions based on this sensibility, editors necessarily foreclose certain interpretative possibilities and open up others in ways that sometimes remain obscure, even to the scholarly reader.

The Prologue to the *Legend of Good Women* offers a relatively simple illustration of this point. Eleven of the twelve extant manuscripts of the *Legend* begin with more or less the same prologue, differing among themselves only in ways obviously indicative of scribal transmission. Cambridge University Library MS Gg.4.27, however, contains a substantially different version, including adjustments of readings found in the other version, reorderings of some of its episodes, and lines and passages absent from it. For example, while in the more common version (known as the F Prologue) it is the dreamer who recites the famous *balade* 'Hyd, Absalon' in praise of Queen Alceste, in the Cambridge manuscript version – the G Prologue – the *balade* is sung by a multitude of courtly women as they dance a carol around the queen. Thinking the G treatment of this and other passages more dramatically and artistically successful than the F version, and assuming that authors typically improve as they mature, many critics conclude that G must represent Chaucer's final treatment of the matter. Yet although some details in G do suggest composition later than F, the manuscript containing G is in fact the earliest of the twelve authorities. Other critics argue, moreover, that many if not all of the differences between F and G can be attributed to the usual processes of scribal transmission, so that F may in fact be the only authorial version.

Before readers open their copy of the *Legend*, therefore, several critical interpretative decisions will have been made for them. In order to print a prologue with the nine legends, an editor will need to make judgements on the literary meaning and merits of G and F, on the nature of Chaucer's style, on the character of authors' careers and on the typical features of scribal transmission. When, as in the case of the *Riverside Chaucer*, both G and F are printed side-by-side, editors make still another kind of pre-interpretative decision for their readers: that the transmission history of the prologue is so profoundly different from those of the rest of Chaucer's works that it alone merits recognition of the possibility of revision and an indeterminate final form, since it alone is printed with parallel texts, even though the transmission of other works displays a good deal of variation and possible revision.

By comparison, the link between the Monk's Tale and the Nun's Priest's Tale similarly survives in two versions often regarded as equally Chaucerian. Yet typically only the longer, presumptively later and better version is printed, again reflecting critical suppositions about how literary artists mature but also obscuring traces of the patently unfinished character of a work (the *Canterbury Tales*) whose pre-eminence and aesthetic accomplishment have become givens for much modern critical activity in ways that the achievement of the *Legend of Good Women*, at least until quite recently, has not. Presentation of only one prologue to the Nun's Priest's Tale attributes literary polish to that poem and invites certain kinds of critical expectations and responses that are foreclosed by the appearance of two prologues to the *Legend* and the implications they have about the poem's apparently *un*polished character. In this way, the prologue to the *Legend* appears both aberrant in the Chaucerian canon and resistant to the textual certitude on which critical interpretation often rests.

Editing Chaucer: The *Parliament of Fowls*, 680–92

More complex issues must be resolved with perhaps greater consequences in the *Parliament of Fowls*, which Chaucer composed around 1380 or 1381. Surviving in fourteen manuscripts and one early printed edition based on a manuscript no longer extant, the *Parliament* is one of the liveliest and most intriguing dream visions of the Middle Ages. Though probably inspired by negotiations to arrange a marriage between Richard II of England and Anne of Bohemia, and though everywhere concerned with the love and marriage of the birds mentioned in the poem's title, the *Parliament* also touches on strictly political issues of Chaucer's day. The birds seat themselves, for instance, in a hierarchical fashion that recalls the stratification of English medieval society, with the raptors occupying the highest positions followed, in order, by the worm fowl, the water fowl and the seed fowl. Further, Nature decrees that the birds shall choose their mates in an order beginning with the worthiest ones and moving through the other groups 'by ordre . . . After youre kynde' (400–1). She recalls this same stratification when she allows a representative of each group to advocate a solution to the impasse reached in the attempt to find a mate for the formel eagle, as do the birds themselves when fowls of one group verbally assault those advocating the views of another. The conclusion of the *Parliament* restores order to love and politics. Once Nature reasserts her authority and grants the formel eagle the space of a year to chose among her three suitors, the other birds quickly find their mates before the poem concludes with the gathered birds singing a roundel in praise of summer, love and Nature:

'Now welcome, somer, with thy sonne softe,
That hast thes wintres wedres overshake,
And driven away the longe nyghtes blake!

'Saynt Valentyn, that art ful hy on-lofte,
Thus syngen smale foules for thy sake:
[Now welcome somer, with thy sonne softe,
That hast thes wintres wedres overshake.]

'Wel han they cause for to gladen ofte,
Sith ech of hem recovered hath hys make,
Ful blissful mowe they synge when they wake:
[Now welcome, somer, with thy sonne softe,
That hast thes wintres wedres overshake,
And driven away the longe nyghtes blake!']

The *Parliament* thereby ends with rhetoric of closure, rhetoric that underscores the necessity of Nature's authority and the submission to it of the diverse groups of birds – as of the diverse groups of human beings.

Or at least, that's how the poem ends in modern editions. As the bracketed, conjectured lines imply, in the medieval materials the status of the roundel as such a rhetorically and thematically powerful gesture of closure is complex and ambiguous. Some of the manuscripts are fragmentary, breaking off long before this passage, but of those that contain a conclusion to the *Parliament*, only one has a proper roundel in its proper place in the text; and in this one manuscript, the roundel was copied at least half a century after the original scribe copied the poem, leaving a blank space for text that he presumably thought should be there but did not have. One manuscript has nearly all of this material but reorders and reconfigures the lines from the metrical structure of a roundel into a rhyme-royal stanza, making it like the rest of the poem. Two authorities leave ample blank space, as if for the roundel, but offer no indication of what text ought to be there, while others that omit the material leave only enough space for the customary stanza break, into which they insert the title of a popular French song. Still other authorities simply omit the roundel without any indication of doing so – they simply adjoin the rhyme-royal stanza after the absent roundel to the one that would have preceded it.

The roundel is thus textually suspect in various ways: present in no manuscript before the middle of the fifteenth century, absent altogether from some manuscripts and stylistically problematic in any case, since in it the birds refer to themselves in the third person. It is entirely possible that the roundel is authentically Chaucerian – it certainly sounds like him – but entered the manuscript history of the *Parliament* only a half-century after his death when an early scribe was puzzled by a reference to a 'nexte vers' that was absent in Chaucer's original version. Without the roundel, in any case, the *Parliament* would be a very different poem, one that exposed the force and even violence that stratified medieval society and kept it functioning but that did so without affirming in its conclusion that its members joyfully recognized the need for such a system. A much darker poem than that printed in the *Riverside Chaucer*, a roundel-less *Parliament* would foreground but not resolve questions about the structure of society, the character of what is considered natural and the unprotesting acceptance of an authority that maintains – perhaps at the advent of the Peasants' Revolt – advantages for a group less organized and effective than the groups economically and socially subject to it. For readers familiar with the poem's textual history and with the distinct possibility that if the roundel powerfully resolves the conflicts of Chaucer's poem in modern printed versions, it does so because of an early scribe, the conclusion of the *Parliament* takes on new meanings. Like Nature herself, scribes and editors have perhaps commanded 'pes' to the poem and the notions it raises, complicitly defusing some of Chaucer's most provocative ideas by unquestioningly accepting the very passage whose transmission history reveals the tensions and opportunities of his manuscript culture with particular clarity.

Editing Chaucer: *Boece*

As *Boece* suggests, such issues of transmission and interpretation are not simply localized to textual cruces but fundamental to the character of Chaucer's writings as medieval literature, pervading his works and the various witnesses that preserve them. Probably written about 1380, *Boece* is a translation of Boethius' early sixth-century *De consolatione Philosophiae*, though in composing his translation Chaucer also drew on Jean de Meun's early fourteenth-century French translation (*Li Livres de confort de Philosophie*) as well as on some commentary traditions that had accrued to the *Consolatio* throughout the Middle Ages. Surviving in twelve authorities, *Boece* evidently circulated widely and was received enthusiastically in the fifteenth century, its variants demonstrating several kinds of characteristic ways by which medieval manuscript production processes could inform and shape Chaucer's works.

The Latin *Consolatio* consists of five books, each of which has alternating passages of prose and verse; but Chaucer, following the lead of Jean de Meun, rendered the whole work in prose. While he did keep the original prose and verse sections distinct from one another, Chaucer utilized only brief extracts from the corresponding Latin to demarcate where each began. One way scribes participated in and even improved on the structure of *Boece*, then, was by inserting a variety of rubrication systems. Some manuscripts simply lengthen the original extracts, but others include the rubrics for individual *prosae* and *metra* that occur in Latin manuscripts (e.g. *prosa prima*, *metrum primum*), while one manuscript sequentially numbers all the proses and metres together for each book. Other manuscripts transform the presentation of *Boece* in still other ways: much of the work is given over to a dialogue between Boethius and Lady Philosophy, and these manuscripts clarify the structure of the dialogue by prefacing sentences with a 'B' or 'P' to indicate who is speaking.

The *Boece* scribes intruded more than simply rubrics and dialogue markers, however. Where Chaucer apparently wrote 'than hastow thyng in thi powere', for example, one scribe produced the syntactically easier but semantically different 'than hastow power of thinge'; and where Chaucer wrote 'mortel', another scribe developed his sense by substituting 'worldely and mortal'. But many other variants seem inspired less by a desire to clarify Chaucer's intention than by a preference for different intentions altogether. When confronted by 'whilom', a word that Chaucer uses frequently and that would become archaic by the sixteenth century, two scribes invariably substituted 'sometime'. The scribe of another manuscript evidently felt that much of Chaucer's language was antiquated, for he regularly replaced words or usages that were dying out in the fifteenth century with their current synonyms. For 'maugre hem', thus, this manuscript reads 'aӡen þer will'; for 'his thankes', 'willingly'; and for 'to-hepe', 'to þe peple'. More dramatically, some scribes supplemented the Middle English in front of them with readings they drew from their own consultation of the Latin original, the French translation or the commentaries, while others developed an elaborate tradition of interlinear glosses to difficult words and concepts in the *Boece*; like the commentary tradition to the Latin *Consolatio*, this gloss tradition was transmitted along with the Middle English text, sometimes even appearing incorporated in it. Where Chaucer wrote 'place' and the interlinear tradition specified 'prison', for instance, one scribe combined text and gloss as 'place or prison.'

At any point in any Chaucerian work, then, a cleanly edited reading text can obscure and transform the manuscript culture that everywhere informed Chaucer as a late medieval vernacular writer. To get behind this text and explore the evidence of this culture is to open up new approaches to his works, which, paradoxically, may well reintroduce us to their old, medieval meanings. In the *Parliament of Fowls*, Chaucer states that 'out of olde bokes . . . Cometh al this newe science that men lere' (24–5). But equally, out of new books on manuscript culture or new editions of Chaucer's work will come the old knowledge of his day.

See also AFTERLIFE; CONTEMPORARY ENGLISH WRITERS; CRISIS AND DISSENT; LANGUAGE; LONDON; PERSONAL IDENTITY; SCIENCE; STYLE; TRANSLATION.

REFERENCES AND FURTHER READING

Benson, Larry D. (1981) 'The order of the *Canterbury Tales*', *Studies in the Age of Chaucer* 3, 77–120. An argument for the authenticity of the Ellesmere order of the *Canterbury Tales*.

Blake, N. F. (1985) *The Textual Tradition of the Canterbury Tales* (London: Edward Arnold). An account of how the *Canterbury Tales* manuscripts were transmitted after Chaucer's death.

Boffey, Julia (1993) 'The reputation and circulation of Chaucer's lyrics in the fifteenth century', *Chaucer Review* 28, 23–40. An examination of how Chaucer's lyrics circulated and influenced other poets.

Brusendorff, Aage (1925) *The Chaucer Tradition* (Oxford: Clarendon). A dated but still useful overview of the textual transmission of Chaucer's works.

Doyle, A. I. and Parkes, M. B. (1978) 'The production of copies of the *Canterbury Tales* and the *Confessio Amantis* in the early fifteenth century', in *Medieval Scribes, Manuscripts and Libraries: Essays Presented to N. R. Ker*, ed. M. B. Parkes and Andrew G. Watson (London: Scolar), 163–210. A seminal article on independent scribal activity in vernacular book production.

Fisher, John H. (1992) 'A language policy for Lancastrian England'. *Proceedings of the Modern Language Association* 107, 1168–80. An argument that the early fifteenth-century increase in Chaucerian manuscripts reflected a concerted nationalistic policy by Henry V.

Greetham, D. C. (1992) *Textual Scholarship: An Introduction* (New York: Garland). A survey of the history and procedures of editing and textual criticism.

Griffiths, Jeremy and Pearsall, Derek, eds (1989) *Book Production and Publishing in Britain 1375–1475* (Cambridge: Cambridge University Press). An essential anthology of articles relating to the production and dissemination of manuscripts in the late medieval period.

Hanna, Ralph, III (1991) 'Presenting Chaucer as author', in *Medieval Literature: Texts and Interpretation*, ed. Tim William Machan (Binghamton, NY: Medieval and Renaissance Texts and Studies), 17–39. A discussion of the manuscript evidence for the roundel in the *Parliament of Fowls*.

—— (1996) *Pursuing History: Middle English Manuscripts and their Texts* (Stanford: Stanford University Press). A collection of articles on late medieval book production, many specifically on Chaucer.

Kane, George (1983) 'The text of *The Legend of Good Women* in CUL MS Gg.4.27', in *Middle English Studies Presented to Norman Davis in Honour of His Seventieth Birthday*, ed. E. G. Stanley (Oxford: Clarendon), 39–58. A discussion of the *Legend* manuscript evidence.

Machan, Tim William (1994) *Textual Criticism and Middle English Texts* (Charlottesville, Va.: University Press of Virginia). A theoretical consideration of medieval vernacular conceptions of authors, works and texts.

—— (1997) 'The *Consolation* tradition and the text

of Chaucer's *Boece*', *Papers of the Bibliographical Society of America* 91, 31–50. A discussion of the *Boece* manuscript evidence.

McGann, Jerome J. (1992) *A Critique of Modern Textual Criticism* (Chicago: University of Chicago Press). A theoretical analysis of textual criticism that inspired a school of socialized textual studies.

Manly, John M. and Rickert, Edith, eds (1940) *The Text of the* Canterbury Tales, *Studied on the Basis of All Known Manuscripts*, 8 vols (Chicago: University of Chicago Press). A flawed but still valuable edition that aspires to record all of the poem's manuscript variants.

Parkes, M. B. (1976) 'The influence of the concepts of *ordinatio* and *compilatio* on the development of the book', in *Medieval Learning and Literature: Essays Presented to Richard William Hunt*, ed. J. J. G. Alexander and M. T. Gibson (Oxford: Clarendon), 115–41. An account of the nexus between bibliographic and literary codes in the late medieval period.

Pearsall, Derek, ed. (1987) *Manuscripts and Texts: Editorial Problems in Later Middle English Literature* (Cambridge: Brewer). An anthology of essential papers on late medieval book production.

Ruggiers, Paul G., ed. (1984) *Editing Chaucer: The Great Tradition* (Norman, Okla.: Pilgrim Books). A collection of essays surveying the theories and practices of Chaucerian editors from the advent of print to the modern era.

Stevens, Martin and Woodward, Daniel, eds (1995) *The Ellesmere Chaucer: Essays in Interpretation* (San Marino, Ca.: Huntington Library). An anthology of essays on perhaps the most famous of the Chaucerian manuscripts.

Strohm, Paul (1989) *Social Chaucer* (Cambridge, Mass.: Harvard University Press). An account of the historical circumstances of Chaucer and his audience.

27

Translation

Roger Ellis

Some sense of the distance that Chaucer studies have travelled in respect of the question of translation, even since the early 1980s, can be gained by looking at the bibliography provided by John H. Fisher to accompany his revised edition of Chaucer's works in 1989, and then by reading Glending Olson's contribution ('Geoffrey Chaucer') to the new *Cambridge History of Medieval English Literature*. Olson writes that 'thinking of Chaucer's achievement as a range of different kinds of translation is perhaps as valid as any single approach to the entirety of his work' (1999: 576) – an approach which I hope the present article will instantiate.

The contrast with Fisher is telling. Translation is clearly implicit in two subdivisions of Fisher's bibliography, 'Sources and Analogues' and 'Classical and Continental Associations'; yet it appears as a category in its own right, along with 'Rhetoric', only as a subheading of 'Language', where it receives just five entries. In the main these refer to early translations, including the *Romaunt of the Rose* (Eckhardt 1984), or to prose translations on the fringes of the canon like the *Boece* (Machan 1985) and the *Treatise on the Astrolabe* (Lipson 1983). The translations which get a subdivision all to themselves in the bibliography – 'Translations' – are all *modern* translations of Chaucer's works. And one book, several of whose chapters study Chaucer's translations from French, classical Latin and Italian (the last tellingly described as 'transformations'), does not figure there at all (Brewer 1974).

Translation and Originality

Fisher's linkage of translation with rhetoric as related aspects of language makes an important point, which Roman theoreticians writing about translation, like Cicero, Horace and Quintilian (Copeland 1991: ch. 1), were quick to grasp: that translation is not the carbon copy of an original text in another language, but rather the *performance* of one text in a new language. But only since the mid-1980s or thereabouts has this understanding of translation come to the fore.[1] The layout of Fisher's bibliography tacitly suggests, in fact, that readers are interested in the original works of the creative artist, not in his workaday translations. Likewise, they are interested in Chaucer's reading only in so far as he made from its chaff the building blocks of his own creative work. Chaucer's *Boece*, for instance, will be of interest principally as cannibalized in *Troilus and Criseyde*, alongside Chaucer's principal source, Boccaccio's *Il Filostrato* (modern translation in Havely 1980). More straightforward Chaucerian translations, like the Second Nun's Tale, a translation of the life of St Cecilia from the *Legenda aurea* of James of Varaggio (modern translation in Miller 1977), or the Tale of Melibee, from the *Liber consolationis et consilii* of Albertano of Brescia (Bryan and Dempster 1941), both of them in the *Canterbury Tales*, will then need to be rescued from charges of dullness by invoking Chaucerian irony; Chaucer *couldn't* have meant us to take such dull writing straight.

At their simple-minded worst, such formulations straightforwardly read medieval texts in the light of post-Romantic preferences for original work at the expense of translation. (Religious understandings, current throughout the Middle Ages, of the sacred nature of foundational texts like the Bible, reinforce this preference from a very different angle, and to very different ends.) More recent studies, like those of Shoaf (1979), Machan (1989), Copeland (1991) and Olson (1999), however, are showing us a very different Chaucer, one more in keeping with the diversity of medieval understandings of translation. This new interest helps us to position Chaucer's translations relative to the ferment of translation activity in the last twenty or so years of the fourteenth century (for fuller discussion see Hanna 1989, 1990, 1999; Watson 1995). It is more attentive, overall, to the politics of translation.

Late Medieval Translation

Copeland presents medieval translation as the ambiguous outgrowth of ambiguous classical and patristic pronouncements on the subject, many of which had, by Chaucer's time, acquired the status of rhetorical commonplaces. Chaucer does not directly invoke many of them, except perhaps the problem of translating 'word by word' (Ven 81; cf. Wogan-Browne et al. 1999: 26–8), and the envy formula practised to perfection by the argumentative St Jerome (cf. *Astr* 64 and n.; *LGWP* F 358–61). The movement that Copeland charts from translation-as-rhetorical-accomplishment, in the classical period, to translation-as-interpretation, in the high Middle Ages, makes it possible for writers like Chaucer to use translation as a tool to assist in their creation of themselves as vernacular authors which, as we shall see, was a contentious issue for medieval vernacular writers.

Olson uses the *ballade* by Chaucer's French contemporary Eustache Deschamps to frame his discussion (full text and modern translation in Fisher 1989: 952–3; and see Shoaf 1979: 58). Much as Chaucer himself does in *LGWP*, Deschamps, who praises Chaucer repeatedly as a 'grant translateur' [great translator], identifies him as the translator of the *Roman de la rose* and (so Patterson 1991: 103–4) of the story of Troilus and Criseyde. He praises Chaucer's work both for its teaching and for its rhetorical accomplishment: Chaucer philosophizes like Socrates, moralizes like Seneca, writes poetry like Ovid, and combines wisdom and brevity in enlightening the ignorant. He also, possibly, presents Chaucer the translator as a sort of go-between, like the Pandarus figure of *Troilus*, whose task is to bring source text and target readerships, so to speak, into the one bed.[2] Granted, Deschamps' comments do not provide much of a frame for talking in detail about Chaucer as a translator, though they do show how insistently medieval writers evaluated their own achievements in relation to the benchmark of classical Latin culture.

Machan (1989) draws on earlier writing of Copeland to argue that a generous understanding of the term 'translation' will allow us to see virtually all of Chaucer's works as translations, either in the familiar and narrow sense that Chaucer was translating into English a text written in another language, or in the wider sense that a text like the Miller's Tale, which lacks a specific 'source' in a foreign language, though it has plenty of analogues (modern translations in Benson and Andersson 1971), 'translates' several elements of fabliau narratives into its own accomplished comment on them.

Chaucer as Translator

Chaucer himself shows plenty of interest in the status of his translations. In the three passages in which he publicizes his own work, he gives them an important place, though several may have been merely projected, or at all events have not survived. His list in the Prologue to the *Legend of Good Women* (*c.*1386–8) includes Boethius, the *Rose*, a homily of Origen on St Mary Magdalene, the life of St Cecilia, and Boccaccio's *Teseida* and *Il Filostrato*; these latter are described as 'the love of Palamon and Arcite' (F 420) and 'the bok / How that Crisseyde Troylus forsok' (G 264–5). Other named early works, the three early dream visions, may also function as translations if we take a broad view of the subject, since material in all of them is derived from other texts (modern translations in Windeatt 1982). The list (*c.*1390) in the Prologue to the Man of Law's Tale names two works with Ovidian connections, the *Legend of Good Women* and the *Book of the Duchess*, the latter for its version of the story of Ceyx and Alcyone from Ovid's *Metamorphoses*. To these lists, that in the Retraction, at the end of the *Canterbury Tales*, adds a 'book of the Leoun', which might be a version of either of two poems with the same name by, respectively, Deschamps and a French writer of an earlier generation, Guillaume de Machaut (Chaucer translated other material by both writers); those Canterbury tales, unspecified, 'that sownen into synne'; and 'othere bookes of legends of seintes and omelies and moralitee and devocioun', likewise unspecified (Ret 1086–8), though possibly including works like the Parson's Tale (Patterson 1976).

Chaucer does not always speak of his works as 'translacions' (Ret 1085, 1088; *LGWP* F 329, 370, 425, G 341); sometimes he speaks of them as 'enditynges' (Ret

1085; *LGWP* F 370–1, both times in combination with translating or translations); more often, he speaks of them as things he 'made' or 'seyd' or 'toold' or 'wroot'. The flexibility of these terms, as relating now to writing, now to speech and now to translation, now to something closer to original composition ('enditing', 'making'), points to the very grey area that is medieval translation in general, and Chaucerian translation in particular.

One translation surprisingly absent from all three lists – an absence this chapter hopes to make good – is Chaucer's astronomical work for Lewis Chaucer, his ten-year-old son, the *Treatise on the Astrolabe* (1391). This text survives in more copies than any of Chaucer's other works, except for the *Canterbury Tales*, and is a further marker of Chaucer's determination to be up-to-date in his writing since, according to Hanna (1999: 499), scientific translation in English starts only 'rather fitfully in the 1370s'. Added to the more obviously literary translations noted by Chaucer in his three lists, the *Astrolabe* helps to fill out our picture of Chaucer's range of translational interests: classical literature, contemporary French and Italian writing, religious and secular narratives, romance and epic, science. Indeed, there is even the possibility that another scientific translation, the *Equatorie of the Planets* (1392) was by Chaucer, and that the single manuscript in which it survives, 'full of corrections, incomplete, and still in the process of composition when its author laid it aside' (Fisher 1989: 936), was written by him. Machan (1985) has argued similarly that distinctive elements of the translation in the *Boece* point to its status as work-still-in-progress.

Chaucer's interest in translation leads him at a number of points in his work to offer what we might almost see as a theory, or theories, of translation. Texts of particular relevance in this connection include the envoy to the 'Complaint of Venus'; *TC* I, 393–8, II, Proem, III, 1324–36, V, 1786–98; *LGWP* F 328–35, 362–72, 425–8; ClP 31–55; Th 940–64; SNP 78–84; and *Astr* 1–64.

Characteristically, Chaucer presents himself as humbly dependent upon an authoritative original which he is proposing to make more widely available, under correction from the learned, to readers who would otherwise have no access to it. He thus appears to conform to the religious model of translation associated with Sts Jerome and Augustine, one which, in Eagleton's phrase, makes a fetish of the original text: the translator as faithful interpreter (*fidus interpres*), a concept first found in Horace as something to be avoided at all costs, and taken up by St Jerome as a translational ideal. Chaucer's understanding of his own works as 'translations' – an understanding shared with writers like Thomas Hoccleve and John Lydgate – is a partial reflex of the ambiguous and limited status which a living vernacular author could claim (cf. Minnis 1988; Copeland 1991; Wogan-Browne et al. 1999). Given that authorship presupposed texts written in Latin by long-dead figures – and given, additionally, the dangers of rocking the intellectual and religious boat – Chaucer is careful, for the most part, *not* to make any very elevated claims for himself.

But at a number of places he is significantly more radical in his theorizings, and makes common cause, while nowhere acknowledging them, with the already-noted Roman authors for whom translation from Greek into Latin was a matter of national pride and self-aggrandizement. Twice he uses the proverb that all roads lead to Rome as a way of arguing that differences between translations and, by implication, between a translation and its source, are no barrier to their communication of the same truth (*TC* II, 36–7; *Astr* 39–40); then, as St Jerome had done, in his *Epistula ad Pammachium* (modern translation in Robinson 1997), he appeals to variations in the text of holy Scripture, specifically in the Gospel accounts of the Passion, to assert that the truth of a text may well survive its very different telling in translation (Th 943–52). This emphasis on the translator's answerability for the truth of his *matere* clearly witnesses to the long shadows cast by medieval religious understandings of translation, but it also allows for the translation to vary from its original at least on the level of style.

A more important understanding is provided by the prologue to Chaucer's translation of Messahala's work on the astrolabe. This text is literally a working translation, since it is intended as an elementary textbook in astronomy and therefore, if it is to be of any use to its first reader, will need to be tailored precisely to the location in which Lewis will be using it ('the latitude of Oxenforde', *Astr* 10). This leads Chaucer to the perfectly straightforward – but thoroughly modern and, for his time, radical – conclusion that an original text exists only as realized in different versions: the *Treatise*, in Greek, Latin, Arab and Hebrew. Latin, from which Chaucer is proposing to translate the work, is not the origin and ultimate point of reference of the work; the 'Latyn folk had hem [astronomical treatises] first out of othere dyverse langages, and writen hem in her owne tunge, that is to seyn, in Latyn' (*Astr* 33–6).

The Politics of Translation

This awareness of linguistic and cultural relativity is not unique to Chaucer. It also occurs in other prologues at much the same time, by John Trevisa to his translation (1387) of Higden's *Polychronicon* and by an anonymous Wycliffite who produced a prologue to accompany the so-called late version of the Wycliffite Bible (1395–7): modern translations of both are in Robinson (1997); a more reliable edition of the former, and other relevant material, is in Wogan-Browne et al. (1999). For that matter, this understanding has echoes in England as far back as King Alfred's *Preface to the Pastoral Care*. And it has clear precedent in the writings of the Italian Renaissance: in Boccaccio's *Teseida*, for example, used by Chaucer as the source of his Knight's Tale, Boccaccio offers a spoof commentary on his own Italian text, and claims to have translated it not from Latin but directly from Greek, so reducing Latin, as in Chaucer, to the penultimate link in a translational chain whose real origins lie elsewhere.

The origin of Chaucer's comments in what amounts to an instruction manual goes some way, perhaps, to neutralizing any challenge they might present. In this context they prove much less contentious than others, particularly those produced to accompany the Wycliffite Bible translation project. But in the increasingly dangerous closing years of the fourteenth century, when Chaucer was writing, and when the Wycliffites were mounting their determined but ultimately futile challenge to ecclesiastical authority – one focused by the question of the adequacy of the vernacular to translate sacred *Latin* texts – support for the vernacular was far from self-evidently the best cause for a writer to embrace. This may, indeed, be one reason why Chaucer includes in his prologue a reference to King Richard II as 'lord of this langage' (*Astr* 56–7). A royal patron might provide a bulwark against any rising tides of ecclesiastical reaction. Trevisa's patron, the Duke of Berkeley, for example, may well have afforded him scope and security to theorize more boldly about his work: in his prologue, Trevisa is much more relaxed than either Chaucer or the author of the Wycliffite Prologue had been about the possibility – rather, the certainty – of error in their translations (Wogan-Browne et al. 1999: 117–19, 134). Unfortunately for any hopes Chaucer might have had, though, Richard II was deposed even before Chaucer died, and his successors understood their lordship over the language in ways that brought firmly to heel the various experiments that had marked the closing years of Richard's reign (Watson 1995).

Previous remarks have clearly implied the important role accorded to royalty in the promotion of a vernacular literary culture which, for practical purposes, means a culture founded on translations. An awareness of that important role is to hand in another of Chaucer's works, the Prologue to the *Legend of Good Women*. Here the poet finds himself hauled over the coals by an irate royal reader, the God of Love (a lightly fictionalized version of Richard II?) for translating works, the *Roman de la rose* and *Il Filostrato*, which have given women a bad press and turned men off love (F 322–33). We are in very familiar antifeminist territory here. In his defence, the god's consort, a possible surrogate for Queen Anne, to whom, when finished, the work is to be presented (F 496–7), describes Chaucer as a humble and half-witted translator – *fidus interpres* indeed – who translates whatever is set before him without attending to its meaning, in response to commissions which he dare not refuse (F 364–7). In any case, as Chaucer urges in his own defence, whatever his originals *meant*, his intention in translating them was 'to forthren trouthe in love . . . / And to ben war fro falsnesse and fro vice' (F 472–3). A translator, that is to say, may be marching to the beat of another drum than that of simple fidelity to the truth of his originals. A patron may provide not only protection, but also a set of demands of his own; a translator cannot work disinterestedly.

But the God of Love has not yet finished with Chaucer. In the revised (G) version of the prologue (1395–6), he faults Chaucer not only for sins of commission but also for sins of omission: Chaucer *must* have known, from his reading, of 'som story of wemen that were goode and trewe' (G 272). The God knows of numerous writers, including 'Valerye, Titus, or Claudyan . . . / [and] Jerome agayns Jovynyan' (G 280–1), on whom Chaucer could have drawn. Jerome, in particular, tells of virgins, wives and widows, upwards of 'an hundred on a rewe' (G 285), who endured suffering and death rather than prove false. The god shares this understanding of Jerome's work with Dorigen, the courtly heroine of the Franklin's Tale, who finds herself on the horns of an adulterous dilemma because of her love for her husband, and who similarly invokes the example of St Jerome's virtuous women to encourage herself (1367ff).

Of course, the added passage in the G version provides a fictional explanation for the literary commission which it prefaces, and which Chaucer has already written, as an act of penance, to put himself back in the god's good books: the *Seintes Legende of Cupide*, a series of tales commending women for faithfulness in love and generally depicting men as faithless seducers. But it does more. It focuses for us the politics of literary production. The light and characteristic comic touch with which Chaucer handles this question may suggest that he wants to see his actual, as opposed to his fictional, situation – that of a vernacular writer–translator – as, still, relatively uncontentious. Even so, his self-presentation in the prologue shows that interpretation is never a neutral or self-evident business, however much single- or simple-minded critics like to pretend it is.

The Bias of Gender: The Wife of Bath

This understanding is brought clearly to the fore by considering another use Chaucer makes of St Jerome, in a work produced some time in the 1390s, the celebrated prologue to the Wife of Bath's Tale. Here too antifeminism is rampant. The text shamelessly recycles the pronouncements of the antifeminist lobby (modern translations in Miller 1977), from one of the very earliest writers (a Theophrastus known to us only as quoted by St Jerome in his *Adversus Jovinianum*) possibly to one of the most recent (the *Miroir de mariage* of Eustache Deschamps), and produces an extremely literal translation of their pronouncements by giving the Wife to say exactly what the sources claimed such a woman would say. It makes her as argumentative, repetitious and ignorant as they had said she would be; as little able to follow the thread of an argument or to lift her sights from the particular to the general; a *fida interpres*, so to say, who in her own person translates truthfully even the sources' assertion that she will be a liar (WBP 382). In so translating, she cannot help but, back-handedly, confirm the subordinate and dependent status of the translation (or the translated), and the absolute authority of the original.

Possibly contemporary anxieties that translation might enable women to trespass on the male preserves of Latin literacy inform this presentation: hence, perhaps, the Pardoner's ironic praise, in this context, of the Wife as a 'noble prechour' (165); hence too, perhaps, the readiness of modern scholars to set the Wife alongside historical figures like the orthodox Margery Kempe. Women as translators are far more likely to fall foul of authority when they belong to the lower classes, as Margery Kempe did, though Margery's translations are a rather different business from the Wife's (for general comment on women as translators and readers of translation, and detailed comment on Kempe, see Wogan-Browne et al. 1999).

But our noisy Mrs Punch suddenly, and unexpectedly, turns the tables on her opponents, and their arguments on their head, with her invocation of the Aesopian fable of the lion:

> Who peyntede the leon, tel me who?
> By God, if wommen hadde writen stories,
> As clerkes han within hire oratories,
> They wolde han writen of men moore wikkednesse
> Than al the mark of Adam may redresse.
>
> (692–6)

Translation, that is, depends on who is doing the translating, and for what purpose; on how translators and readers interpret what they are translating. Hence, she tells us, her fifth husband, the clerical Jankyn, reads, both for his own pleasure and to put her back in her box, the antifeminist literature which has given her all her words. The 'book of wikked wyves' (685), from which he reads, includes the very text, 'Jerome . . . agayn Jovinian' (675) which we have seen the God of Love use to precisely opposite effect, for its praise of virtuous women.

As it turns out, both readings, Jankyn's and Cupid's, are, at least partly, right. St Jerome was writing in support of virginity against Jovinian's criticism of that state, which required him both to savage worldly women and to eulogize chaste women, whether virgin, married or widowed (cf. *LGWP* G 282–3). Even a cursory reading of the *Adversus Jovinianum* will suggest that Jankyn was closer to Jerome's mark than either Dorigen or the God of Love. But that isn't the point. In the first place, the point is simply the pleasurable sense of unreality that reading the text either way, as simple-minded praise or simple-minded blame of women, produces. More important, though, is the awareness of the multitude of possible meanings which the text – any text – turns out to have: meanings which it realizes only according to the interests and purposes of its readers. A *locus classicus* of medieval literary theory (cf. Minnis 1988), the *accessus ad auctores* which introduced texts to readers, used a number of different headings to categorize literary works, including particularly the intention of the author (*intencio auctoris*), so far as that could be deduced from the broad thrust of his or her work. As we have seen from Chaucer's self-defence in the Prologue to the *Legend*, medieval practice more generally, and more systematically, addressed the situation of the reader: what one might call *intencio lectoris*. This view of the reader as ultimate arbiter of a work's meaning makes common cause with much (post)modern theorizing about literature.

From Scribe to Translator

So far, so good, if also so general. In order to analyse Chaucer's translations rather more narrowly, though, we need a different frame, which translators' prefaces do not very well provide. Since the whole thrust of this chapter has been to blur the accepted line between translation and original writing, my next step should not come as a surprise: models devised in the Middle Ages to account for the production of original literature in Latin can be adapted to discuss the production of translated texts.

For my money the best such model, though Chaucer need not have known it directly, or at all, is that formulated by St Bonaventura in 1250–2 (modern translation and discussion in Minnis 1988: 94, Wogan-Browne et al. 1999: 3–5). For St Bonaventura, literature is the product of a number of linked activities of increasing sophistication: from the scribe, who copies a text without altering it in any way; to the compiler, who joins texts together, but without adding anything of his own; to the commentator, who accompanies the text he is copying with words of his own by way of explication and gloss, though still according formal priority and authority to the text being so treated; and to the author, who blends words from other writers with his own words, using theirs so as to confer authority on his.

This model must not be taken literally as suggesting that any one of these literary functions ever exists in isolation from the others. I am doubtful, for instance, of the offered distinction between the roles of compiler and commentator. The only difference between them that I can see is that the former uses the voice of an existing text, whereas the latter uses the translator's own voice, so that Bonaventura seems to be making the distinction as a way of attempting to maintain, what his final category will emphatically deconstruct, the difference between authentic, authorized – above all, ancient – writing, and that practised by the moderns.

Nor is it a simple business in practice to set 'material composed by other people' (an 'original' text) against material copied by a scribe (a 'translated' text) so as to decide on the precise relation of those texts to each other. Since the interventions of the scribes continually change the works they are engaged upon, sometimes in subtle, sometimes in major ways, scribal activity hugely complicates the study of Chaucerian, and other medieval, translations. The generous medieval understanding of a text as a kind of constant work-in-progress entails regular scribal revisions as a logical consequence.

The translator-as-scribe, in the narrowly formal sense of the role that Bonaventura implies, is clearly, and easily, identified in several of Chaucer's more literal translations, like the *Romaunt* and the Tale of Melibee. This may also be true of the Second Nun's Tale. Present understandings (Reames 1978) suggest that Chaucer laid two versions of this story end-to-end to produce his own, but arguably the copy from which he was translating had itself created this new version.

Chaucer's *Boece* could be argued to belong to this kind of translation, too. Admittedly, it incorporates material from medieval commentators on Boethius, and also material from the French translation of Jean de Meun, so that it might appear better to exemplify the second of the Bonaventuran roles, that of the translator-as-compiler; but since, as earlier noted, the medieval understanding of text was more generous than ours, and allowed for a framing commentary and sometimes even a translation alongside the original – and since the various supplements to the Boethian text were subordinate in principle to it, designed to facilitate its exposition – the *Boece* can still be thought of as belonging to the first level of translation practice. Here, too, in principle, we may locate the Clerk's Tale, Chaucer's version of Petrarch's retelling of the last of the tales in Boccaccio's *Decameron*, for all that it uses an anonymous French version of the Petrarch text as a supplement (Severs 1942; for modern translation of Petrarch, see Miller 1977). Two versions of the same story, even in different languages, do not necessarily signal a departure from this first translational role.

The Translator as Compiler and Commentator: *Troilus and Criseyde*

Of course, supplementary texts inevitably modify the text which they accompany, and their use signals a move to the more complex functions of translator-as-compiler and translator-as-commentator. The more obviously the supplementary text modifies or contradicts the main text, the easier it is to see Chaucer abandoning the scribal role which he professes so regularly, and starting to assume the functions of compiler or commentator. This is especially evident in the Clerk's Tale, where the anonymous French version is more sceptical of the exemplary colours in which Petrarch was attempting to paint the openly secular narrative of Boccaccio. Chaucer's version, by incorporating this critical reading of the Petrarchan original, and moving jerkily between them, leaves the relation of the two versions in a state of unresolved tension.

Chaucer's exercise of this second translational function is still more clearly seen in his major translation, *Troilus and Criseyde*. As earlier noted, Chaucer uses Boethian material to complicate radically the relatively straightforward Boccaccian narrative of erotic passion and betrayal which he was principally translating. This new material was, in various ways, suggested by Boccaccio's own text, since Troiolo's pursuit of sexual fulfilment places him inevitably under the realm, and subject to the vicissitudes, of Fortune; even as it also, during the brief period of his love's consummation, grants him an awareness of the cosmic principles to which sexual love, however imperfectly, approximates. Both elements – the role of Fortune, and the overarching cosmic ordering of earthly affairs – figure prominently in Boethius. But Boccaccio's text, designed, in the fictional scheme of things, to get his own mistress to make him some return for his devotion, has its eyes firmly set not on eternal values but on the values of this world. By contrast, Boethius aims to lead his readers from the realm of Fortune to the higher sphere of divine order. For him, therefore, the love which refuses to lift its eyes above its own 'dull sublunary' preoccupations is its own judgement.

Chaucer's strategic use of Boethius at a number of points in *Troilus* thus goes further than ever his use of the French version of Petrarch did to undermine the main thrust of his Boccaccian original. The ironies have partly to do with the parts of the *Consolatio* that he assigns to his principal characters. They have all, as it were, read the *Consolatio* only for confirmation of their own limited understandings of themselves.

The time-serving Pandarus gets an awareness of the uses of mutability ('That, as hir [Fortune's] joies moten overgon / So mote hir sorwes passen everechon', I, 846–7; cf. *Bo* II, prosa 3, 75–9); Criseyde finds a perfect correlative for her experience of the uncertainties of worldly happiness ('O brotel wele of mannes joie unstable!', III, 820; cf. *Bo* II, prosa 4).

Troilus goes further than either of the others in his drive to realize a transcendent love, and, after he has consummated his relationship with Criseyde, Chaucer gives him a hymn to Love from the *Consolatio* (III, 1744–71; cf. *Bo* II, metrum 8) which necessitates the displacement to the start of that book of the hymn which Boccaccio had given his hero at the same point in his narrative. This hymn, interestingly, occurs near the middle of both source and translated texts, but the differences are more striking. In the *Consolatio*, as sung by the authoritative figure of Lady Philosophy, it marks for the narrator–protagonist the beginning of the serious mental journey from error to truth that is the real point of the work, and the beginning of a process of identification between himself and Philosophy which will leave him silent at the end of the work, having by then made her understandings his own. In *Troilus*, by contrast, just as the whole work has consistently divided its actual readers – some finding the Boethian material a completely adequate tool for the interpretation of the work, others disagreeing – the Boethian hymn divides its fictional readers. For Troilus, it marks a hoped-for narrative *point final* (what more is there to hope for, except more of the same?); for the narrator, it marks the beginning of an irreversible downward turn to the very tragic outcome which the benighted protagonist of the *Consolatio* had predicted for himself at the outset.

In similar fashion when, in Book IV, Troilus, having heard that Criseyde is to be swapped for Antenor, meditates gloomily on the inevitability of events, he uses the *Consolatio* to shape his reflections on the relation of free will to divine foreknowledge (IV, 960–1078; cf. *Bo* V, prosae 2–3). Once again he goes further than either of his fellow actors; the material comes from near the very end of the *Consolatio*. But, like the simple-minded protagonist of the *Consolatio* – and like Dorigen near the start of the Franklin's Tale, contemplating a similar separation from her loved husband (865–7) – he is unable to find a satisfactory resolution to the problem. Such a solution is, of course, the point to which the whole of the *Consolatio* has been leading, and Lady Philosophy begins her demonstration with a comment to which the actions of the characters in *Troilus* have borne constant witness: 'al that evere is iknowe, it is rather comprehendid and knowen, nat aftir his strengthe and his nature, but aftir the faculte (that is to seyn, the power and the nature) of hem that knowen' (*Bo* V, prosa 4, 137–41). Objective and absolute truth may exist – the *Consolatio* is certain of it – but humans can never know it unmediated: separate, that is, from their own perspective upon it. The *Consolatio* provides another telling figure for this understanding: when first he sees her, the narrator observes that Philosophy's clothes have been 'korve [cut] . . . by violence and by strengthe, and everich man . . . had boren [carried] away swiche peces as he mighte geten' (*Bo* I, prosa 1, 38–41). In this catch-as-catch-can world that we inhabit, nobody gets the whole meaning.

The Reader as Translator and *Auctor*: The Merchant's Tale

This awareness of the unavoidable provisionality that attaches to human understandings can be seen as the informing principle of everything that Chaucer wrote, and Philosophy's words, and depiction, offer a clear pointer to the preoccupations of this chapter. They implicate not just Chaucer, or his fictional characters, as readers and translators of their sources, but medieval and modern readers too, who are also 'translating' even as they read.

The scribes of Chaucer's works often function in just this way (Windeatt 1979). Thus, de facto, they confer the status of authority upon the texts they annotate. Most obviously, they annotate passages of apostrophe and other heightened writing or sententious moralizing with the word 'auctor'. Or they offer as marginal glosses the Latin originals of texts which Chaucer has been translating at that point, and so paradoxically confirm his publicly professed status of *fidus interpres*, in that they allow the knowledgeable reader to check the translations against their originals, and at the same time claim for this *fidus interpres* the status of *auctor*, since only an established author requires, and receives, marginal glosses to explain his text. Comparison of the glosses in Chaucer manuscripts with those in the margins of the *Confessio Amantis* of Chaucer's older contemporary Gower shows, though, how ambiguous the authorship is to which the scribes lay claim on Chaucer's behalf. Gower's Latin material (cf. Wogan-Browne et al. 1999: 173–81) functions in two ways: to show his mastery of that language whose fluent use confers the status of author on a writer; and to suggest the inadequacy of the Latin material as an interpretation of the vernacular text which follows. Either way, and notwithstanding the formal primacy accorded to Latin by the larger liturgical script used for it in the manuscript copies, Gower can lay claim to the status of authorship. Chaucer, by contrast, is never able to break free from the role of translator–scribe: it's always somebody else's Latin that his scribes are copying out.

Nevertheless, as previous remarks have, I hope, repeatedly implied, Chaucer's practice, as opposed to his theorizing, is regularly radical, and points to his assumption of authorial roles even when he professes to be functioning as a *fidus interpres*. The most striking instance of this comes when several of his pilgrim–narrators presume to contest the issue with the sources from which they are translating. We have already seen this happen in the prologue to the Wife of Bath's Tale. It also happens in the prologue to the Clerk's Tale, whose narrator casts a coolly critical eye over the Petrarch text he is proposing to translate and cuts most of its prologue as 'impertinent' (54): cutting a text as a way of claiming authorship over it has a parallel in Caxton's version of the *Dictes and Sayengis of the Philosophres* (1477). There is also the double ending of the *Clerk's Tale*, the first translated faithfully from Petrarch and enjoining obedience to the will of God, the second added by the pilgrim–narrator and urging the women in the audience to reject the impossibly idealized heroine who has been offered to them as a model.

Most striking of all, in this connection, is the Merchant's Tale. At the start of that work, the Merchant–narrator translates a number of sources, several in praise of marriage and the virtuous wife – in particular, two texts by Albertano of Brescia: the already-noted *Liber consolationis*, and a *Liber de amore Dei* – and one clearly opposed to it, the already-noted work of Theophrastus, as preserved in Jerome's *Adversus Jovinianum*. Similar translations of conflicting material, I have argued, characterized Chaucer's assumption elsewhere of the role of compiler–commentator. In the Merchant's Tale, something much more complicated is happening. The narrator primly dismisses the Theophrastan counter-arguments as lies and 'vanytee' (1295, 1309), and invites the reader to share his enthusiasm for the idealizing frames of Albertano's texts. Yet the tale as a whole refuses to accept this neat opposition, and ends by playing both sides off against each other.

Theophrastus urges the reader to prefer a loyal servant (1298, 1302) or a friend to a wife: a servant is cheaper to maintain and less interested in getting his hands on the property, while with a friend there is more likelihood of disinterested help should the reader fall sick; with a wife, a much greater likelihood arises of being cuckolded. Neither wife nor servant, though, comes out of the actual tale with any credit. The tale obviously, and easily, undercuts the simple-minded Theophrastan view of the loyal servant. It is the servant, Damian, not the master, January, who takes to his bed, sick with love for May his master's wife, and, more importantly, the servant who cuckolds his master. Just as obviously, though the tale's presentation of May does not directly confirm the Theophrastan view of a wife's mercenary instincts, it confirms her propensity for adultery.

The tale's playing of the two sides off against each other is most clearly revealed, though, in its attention to the figure they both take for granted as normative in their discussions: the husband. The woman exists as a helpmeet (so Albertano) or distraction (so Theophrastus) for her husband. It is his money and goods that she will help him either to keep (Albertano, 1343) or to waste (Theophrastus, 1296–7). The protagonist of the tale confirms their shared understanding of the centrality of the husband. January makes a marriage for himself without reference to the wants of his bride; though he enfeoffs May with property when he marries her (1698), he is still holding on to the purse strings at the end, and stringing her along with promises of owning all his property (2172). To the very end he oscillates between sexual fantasies and a clear grasp of economic realities. So much for norms.

The figure of January, then, functions as the clearest possible critique of two translated texts, both equally unsatisfactory in their understanding and presentation of human relations. Here, if anywhere, we can see Chaucer exercising the fourth of Bonaventura's literary functions: 'Another writes both his own materials and those composed by others, but his own are the most important materials and the materials of others are included in order to confirm his own; and this person must be called the author.' Interestingly, medieval readers did not annotate the Theophrastus material in the margins of the tale, perhaps because Chaucer had already identified him as the author of that material in the body of the text (1294, 1310); but they did provide marginal glosses for the material by Albertano. They also wrote 'auctor' against the opening line of a Chaucerian apostrophe (1783). All of which shows us, I suppose, that authorship, like translation, exists only as the moving point on a line that has neither beginning nor end.

See also AUTHORITY; CHRISTIAN IDEOLOGIES; COMEDY; CRISIS AND DISSENT; FRANCE; ITALY; LANGUAGE; MODES OF REPRESENTATION; PERSONAL IDENTITY; SCIENCE; STYLE; TEXTS; WOMEN.

NOTES

1   For information about these recent developments, mainly the product of studies in comparative literature and modern language departments, see the bibliography in *Western Translation Theory from Herodotus to Nietzsche*, ed. and trans. D. Robinson (Manchester: St Jerome, 1997), particularly entries for Bassnett-McGuire, Cheyfitz, Louis Kelly, Lefevere, Steiner, Venuti.

2   Translation is often described as warfare, and sometimes as a laborious service, in which the original is gendered male and the translator and translation are gendered female; translation as seduction occurs much less often as a metaphor, though readers of Chaucer will readily perceive its appropriateness.

REFERENCES AND FURTHER READING

Benson, L. D. and Andersson, T. M., eds and trans (1971) *The Literary Context of Chaucer's Fabliaux* (Indianapolis, Ind. and New York: Bobbs-Merrill). Provides a very useful set of analogues for Chaucer's fabliaux; supplements Bryan and Dempster (see below).

Brewer, Derek S., ed. (1974) *Geoffrey Chaucer*, rev. edn, Writers and Their Background (London: Bell). Series of essays on different aspects of Chaucer: of most relevance in the present context are articles on Chaucer's translations from French, Italian and Latin.

Bryan, W. R. and Dempster, G., eds (1941) *Sources and Analogues of Chaucer's* Canterbury Tales (Chicago: University of Chicago Press; repr. New York: Humanities, 1958). Standard edition of the sources and analogues of Chaucer's *Canterbury Tales*, which regrettably provides only running summaries of those sources: supplement with Benson and Andersson (above) and Miller (below).

Cooper, Helen (1989) *The Canterbury Tales*, Oxford Guides to Chaucer (Oxford: Oxford University Press). Thorough account of the *Canterbury Tales*

with judicious interpretations of its own and (when published) an up-to-date account of critical responses; still a good place to start.

Copeland, Rita (1991) *Rhetoric, Hermeneutics and Translation in the Middle Ages* (Cambridge: Cambridge University Press). Magisterial and difficult, but should be attempted: relates Chaucer, to whose *Legend of Good Women* it devotes half a chapter, to developments in medieval translation theory, which it traces to its very different origins in patristic and classical writers.

Eckhardt, C. D. (1984) 'The art of translation in *The Romaunt of the Rose*', *Studies in the Age of Chaucer* 6, 41–63. Describes Chaucer's translation of Fragment A of the *Romaunt* as faithful but more intimate and 'English'; recognizes the need to position such translations more generally in the context of translation in Middle English.

Fisher, J., ed. (1989) *The Complete Poetry and Prose of Geoffrey Chaucer*, rev. edn (New York: Holt, Rinehart & Winston). Includes an edition of the *Equatorie of the Planets*, possibly by Chaucer, not available in the *Riverside Chaucer*, and has other interesting material in accompanying essays; useful bibliography up to 1989.

Hanna, Ralph, III (1989) 'Sir Thomas Berkeley and his patronage', *Speculum* 64, 878–916. Comprehensive account of the career and literary interests of the patron of translator John Trevisa, a contemporary of Chaucer, in support of the theme that 'Ricardian provincial magnates were substantially involved in the creation of medieval English literary culture'.

—— (1990) 'The difficulty of Ricardian prose translation: the case of the Lollards', *Modern Language Quarterly* 51, 319–40. Admirable account of Wycliffite and other contributions to late fourteenth- and early fifteenth-century debates about translation; overlaps with Watson (see below), and makes incidental reference to Chaucer's *Astrolabe* and Trevisa.

—— (1999) 'Alliterative poetry', in *The Cambridge History of Medieval English Literature*, ed. D. Wallace (Cambridge: Cambridge University Press), 488–512. Argues for the period 1370–1413 as crucial in respect of developments in translation; the bulk of the article is less immediately relevant.

Havely, Nicholas R., ed. and trans. (1980) *Chaucer's Boccaccio* (Cambridge: Brewer). Translates the Boccaccian sources of Chaucer's Knight's Tale, *Troilus and Criseyde* and Franklin's Tale, the second in full; informative introduction and commentary.

Lipson, C. (1983). '"I n'am but a lewd compilator": Chaucer's *Treatise on the Astrolabe* as translation', *Neuphilologische Mitteilungen* 84, 192–200. Refers the *Astrolabe* to its source, by Messahala, and claims to have found in an Oxford manuscript a version of Messahala close to Chaucer's in respect of significant detail.

Machan, Tim William (1985) *Techniques of Translation: Chaucer's* Boece (Norman, Okla.: Pilgrim Books). Detailed account of Chaucer's translation in the *Boece* of the vocabulary, syntax and style of the *Consolatio* of Boethius, as supplemented by Jean de Meun's French translation and medieval commentaries and glosses.

—— (1989) 'Chaucer as translator', in *The Medieval Translator*, ed. R. M. Ellis, J. Wogan-Browne, S. Medcalf and P. Meredith (Cambridge: Brewer), 55–67. A generous understanding of the term 'translation' allows for the whole of Chaucer's work to be seen as

translation of one sort or another: 'posing as a translator . . . enabled Chaucer to act as [a vernacular] author'; similar material in Olson (see below).

Miller, R. P. (1977) *Chaucer: Sources and Backgrounds* (Oxford: Oxford University Press). Offers translations of a number of relevant texts, including (complete) sources of the Clerk's and Second Nun's Tales; elsewhere, accompanies its selections of material – for example, from the *Roman de la rose*, Deschamps' *Miroir de mariage* or Jerome's *Adversus Jovinianum* – with footnotes, helpfully indicating places where Chaucer draws on the material.

Minnis, Alastair J. (1988) *Medieval Theory of Authorship: Scholastic Literary Attitudes in the Later Middle Ages*, 2nd rev. edn (London: Scolar; Philadelphia: University of Pennsylvania Press). Key work on medieval literary theory which, though not addressing directly questions of translation, overlaps with them at numerous points.

Olson, Glending (1999) 'Geoffrey Chaucer', in *The Cambridge History of Medieval English Literature*, ed. David Wallace (Cambridge: Cambridge University Press), 566–88. Excellent account of Chaucer as a translator, though it takes a fair bit for granted: supplement with Cooper and Machan (see above).

Patterson, L. (1976) 'The Parson's Tale and the quitting of the *Canterbury Tales*', *Traditio* 34, 331–80. Magisterial account of the religious context of the Parson's Tale, and convincing literary analysis of the way in which it *quites* (pays back) as well as *quits* (ends) the *Canterbury Tales*.

—— (1991) *Chaucer and the Subject of History* (London: Routledge; Madison: University of Wisconsin Press). A thoroughly historicized account of Chaucer's work, which sees 'translation', by implication, like literary production, as an intensely political act.

Reames, S. L. (1978) 'The sources of Chaucer's Second Nun's Tale', *Modern Philology* 76, 111–35. Argues that changes between the first and second halves of the tale result from a change to the Latin source Chaucer was translating.

Robinson, D., ed. and trans. (1997) *Western Translation Theory from Herodotus to Nietzsche* (Manchester: St Jerome). Extremely full and interesting selection of translators' prefaces;

some surprising gaps in the section on Middle English: supplement with Wogan-Browne et al. (see below).

Severs, J. B. (1942) *The Literary Relationships of Chaucer's Clerk's Tale*, Yale Studies in English 96 (New Haven: Yale University Press). Standard work on Chaucer's uses, in his Clerk's Tale, of Petrarch's version of the last tale of the *Dec-ameron* and of an anonymous French reworking of Petrarch.

Shoaf, A. (1979) 'Notes towards Chaucer's poetics of translation', *Studies in the Age of Chaucer* 1, 55–66. Uses metaphor of old fields and new corn, from the *Parliament of Fowls*, to organize its reading of Chaucer 'making new' even as he purports to be translating faithfully.

Watson, Nicholas (1995) 'Censorship and cultural change in late-medieval England: vernacular theology, the Oxford translation debate, and Arundel's Constitutions of 1409', *Speculum* 70, 822–64. Important account of the stifling of experimentation in religious writing in the aftermath of the Constitutions promulgated by Archbishop Arundel in 1409, readily extend-able to other literary developments in the fif-teenth century.

Windeatt, Barry (1979) 'The scribes as Chaucer's early critics', *Studies in the Age of Chaucer* 1, 119–41. On scribal responses to *Troilus*, as revealed in their modifications, especially stylis-tic ones, to the text; relevant as offering intra-lingual instances of interlingual practices conventionally associated with translation.

——, ed. and trans. (1982) *Chaucer's Dream Poetry: Sources and Analogues* (Cambridge: Brewer). Col-lection of major sources for Chaucer's early dream poetry; good introductory essay.

——(1992) *Troilus and Criseyde*, Oxford Guides to Chaucer (Oxford: Clarendon). In the words of the publisher's blurb, 'the most comprehensive introduction to *Troilus and Criseyde* yet produced . . . [with] the fullest and most convenient account of Chaucer's use of sources'; also offers a comprehensive account of secondary literature up to 1992.

Wogan-Browne, Jocelyn; Watson, Nicholas; Taylor, Andrew; and Evans, Ruth, eds (1999) *The Idea of the Vernacular: An Anthology of Middle English Literary Theory 1280–1520* (University Park, Pa.: Penn State University Press; Exeter: University of Exeter Press). Huge range of texts, practically all of them relevant to the study of translation, though Chaucer is largely absent; magisterial essays on the politics and mechanics of literary production and 'the notion of vernac-ular theory'.

28

Visualizing

Sarah Stanbury

In *Voir Dit*, Guillaume de Machaut's *Book of the True Poem*, the lover Machaut is revived from his love-sickness by the arrival of a long-awaited gift. Trembling in heart and limb, he unwraps the kerchiefs to find the gift that the Lady has promised: an image of her 'fait au vif', made from life (Leech-Wilkinson 1998: 110–111, Letter 9). He studies the image, pleased with its beauty. He names it Toute Bele, 'All Beautiful'. Later he places it on the wall high above his bed, where he can gaze on it and touch it when rising in the morning and turning in at night.

Machaut's account of the image of his beloved, 'made from a living study', owned by a lay individual and placed for viewing within a private chamber, appears to offer us an extraordinary early account of a secular portrait – 1360s France is long before the development of portraiture as a popular genre. It quickly presents some ambiguities, however. Is it a painted panel or a sculpted image in a niche? In medieval texts the term 'image' almost always refers to a sculpted figure,[1] an equivalence supported by the first miniature depicting the image in the manuscript, where Toute Bele appears to be a piece of framed statuary, evidenced by the messenger's beard peeking around the backside of the frame (figure 28.1). In later miniatures, however, Toute Bele appears more like a painting or stained-glass picture in a Gothic niche-shaped frame. Even more puzzling, if Machaut's term *ymage* is meant to refer to a likeness or portrait, we would expect it to have the representational promise of the surrogate: the value of a portrait lies at least partly in its successful imitation of physiognomy. Rather like a photograph of a pen pal, which takes at least part of its value from mimesis, the fact that it 'looks like' someone, a portrait should be simultaneously authenticated and trumped later by the arrival of the prototype, the real thing. ('You look just like/are even prettier than your picture.') In *Voir Dit*, however, the image of Toute Bele does not participate in a neoplatonic drama of this type. When Toute Bele finally appears in the flesh long after sending the lover her image, he registers no confirmation or surprise, and in fact says nothing to indicate any connection between her person and her portrait. He is pleased with her face, her manner, her body; but whether or

Figure 28.1   A messenger hands an image of the lady to Machaut. From *Le Livre dou voir dit* by Guillaume de Machaut. Paris, Bibliothèque Nationale, MS fonds français 1584, fo. 235ᵛ (between 1370 and 1377, probably Reims) [Cliché Bibliothèque nationale de France.]

not she looks like the image to which he has performed reverent oblations and services of devotion, he says not a word.

Image or Portrait?

This curious disjunction between the image and the lady, the representation and the real, suggests that this story about the gift of a lover's portrait may not be as familiar or prosaic as it first appears, in spite of its remarkable apparent humanism. The economy or value of this image, this is to say, does not appear to reside in its likeness or verisimilitide to a living body, and its function as 'image' is structured within a rather different set of conventions. It is *not* a portrait. Portraiture as we understand it today was, in fact, rarely practised in northern Europe in the fourteenth century. While some images were judged acceptable for display in private homes, it is clear from letters and manuals of domestic advice that they were almost exclusively devotional; images for domestic display would have been understood to be models for behaviour and would be drawn from biblical and apocryphal stories – the life of the holy family, the saints (Belting 1990: 232, n. 45; Freedburg 1989: 4). For a woman to have sat for her portrait, commissioning her image to be made 'au vif', describes an astonishing act of artistic self-representation for its time and place – so astonishing, in fact, that we should be careful how we read this artful fiction.[2] It is within a humanist project, many years after Machaut's long epistolary romance, that we find fully developed conventions for portraits 'made from life', with subjects that singly command the frame and occupy the picture space.[3]

If it is not a portrait, then what is it? Toute Bele invites us to consider her image as a performative in a relationship – an image that is not simply an object, but an object whose meaning *occurs* through its relationship with the viewer who looks at it. With the image of Toute Bele, this relationship clearly exceeds aesthetic appreciation. Kneeling before it, dressing it in expensive robes, the lover treats the image in ways that mime Christian devotional practices in the 1360s. At the same time, however, he worships the image not just as an icon but as a pagan idol; and figures such as this almost always take the form of outlaw 'others' in medieval art, appearing in dialectical contrast to Christian images (Camille 1989). Making sacrifice, not with bull nor calf but with his own body, hands, mouth and heart, the lover kneels before the image and worships her as his sovereign goddess, 'ma souvereinne deesse', a Venus, better than the saints because of her power to heal (Leech-Wilkinson 1998: 112–16, lines 1536–1627).

The Image Debate

The likeness of Toute Bele that the Lady sends her lover in *Voir Dit* condenses a number of attitudes, some of them the subjects of increasing public debate, towards images in pre-Reformation Europe. It also offers a graphic context for considering Chaucer's description of devotional or 'artistic' images as well as his accounts of visual responses to those images in his poetry. The *Voir Dit*, it has been suggested, may even have been a source for Chaucer, as he reshaped Boccaccio for *Troilus and Criseyde* with Machaut's text in mind (Leech-Wilkinson 1998: p. lxxxiii). Yet we should be alerted to a difference. Though the trope of the lady's image, adored by the courtier/lover, is a common feature in French courtly poetry in the fourteenth century, and earlier, the motif of the 'lover's portrait' makes few appearances in English poetry of the same period. Even Chaucer, widely read in the poetry circulating in French courtly circles, pictures fealty to the beloved's portrait chiefly in metaphoric ways: Troilus, in love with Criseyde, makes an image of her – but only an image in his mind.

In the years following the writing of *Voir Dit*, the relationship, or fine line, between idol and icon, between idolatry and orthodox uses of devotional images, became the subject of focused and increasingly heated debate. Many of the positions in this debate were set and sharpened between the 1370s and the 1390s in England, the period in which Chaucer was most productive as a writer. In a wide variety of literate circles, some of which would almost certainly have included Chaucer, the uses of devotional images were debated, and with increasing tensions as the critique of images, or icono-machy, became identified with the Lollard heresy, a widespread reformist movement. Do we worship the idea behind the object? Or is it the beautiful object itself – the carved saint on a pedestal, the exquisite stained-glass image of the Virgin – that we are coveting? How do we position the self in relation to a devotional image and still heed the second commandment forbidding worship of graven images?

Less clearly articulated but also central to what we might call the 'image debate' were social and economic anxieties: where do we put ourselves in a material field in which images are proliferating, the technologies of production and display are rapidly transforming, and the liquid capital for endowing and even purchasing images is becoming increasingly (if unequally) available? In *Piers Plowman*, Langland's brilliant satire of fourteenth-century English mores, donations of stained-glass windows as forms of self-aggrandizement are the focus of a biting critique.[4] Fundamental to the debate about images was an ethical discourse about the relationship between the self and the other, with the image as both surrogate and agent in the social field of operations. The image in its late medieval form demands a relationship: what is the nature of my sacrifice, and what will be the terms of my reward?

In Chaucer's England the most vocal challenges to the uses of devotional images came from the Lollards, a religious reform group that increasingly argued for a non-visual textuality – *verbum*, the word, over *res*, the thing – and inveighed against devo-tional images as 'blind stocks and stones': that is, lifeless wood and stone from which images are carved. John Wyclif, the important reformer and founder of the Lollard movement, was moderate on the question of images, at least in his early works, noting their value for devotional practice while pointing to the dangers of idolatry when we worship the image itself and not the idea behind it (Jones 1973: 29). In his *Treatise on the Decalogue* from 1375–6 Wyclif writes:

It is evident that images may be made both well and ill: well in order to rouse, assist and kindle the minds of the faithful to love God more devoutly; and ill when by reason of images there is deviation from the true faith, as when the image is worshipped with *latria* or *dulia*, or unduly delighted in for its beauty, costliness, or attachment to irrel-evant circumstances. (Aston 1984: 138)

As Margaret Aston points out, however, Wyclif's contemporaries and followers, 'ready to hang a great deal on every magisterial hint and parenthesis' (142), were quick to take up and promulgate Wyclif's general critique; and there is evidence to suggest that in the years just before his death in 1384 Wyclif's own writings became increasingly forthright in their condemnation of images as agents of idolatry.[5] Within a short time, therefore, the Lollard movement became identified with the attack on images, a critique claiming that worship of images of the saints and especially of the Trinity, particularly of the kind represented in increasingly common Nottingham alabasters (figure 28.2), was tantamount to idolatry (Aston 1984: 165).

Of particular interest for Chaucer's uses of images in his poetry are documents from the 1380s and 1390s that indicate the extent and complexity of the debate as it developed in these decades. In an Easter sermon of 1383 Thomas Brinton, Bishop of Rochester, wrote that heretics 'newly preach and assert that the cross of Christ and images should not be worshipped' (Aston 1984: 143, Hudson 1978: 179–81), a comment that points to the contemporaneity of the Lollard challenges ('newly preach') even as it implies that these challenges were common knowledge.[6] Responses to the Lollard attack on devotional images appear from across a wide spectrum of discourses. Some of these are direct, orthodox and Latinate, such as the treatise by Walter Hilton, *De adoracione ymaginum*, generally dated in the 1380s, that systematically outlines Lollard arguments attacking images and then, in scholastic form, refutes them. The rhetorical and ecclesiological intent is clearly stated from the outset: 'against heretics who claim that the image of the crucifix and of other saints in the church of God are idolatrous' ('contra hereticos qui asseruerunt ymaginem crucifixi ceterorumque sanctorum ymagines in ecclesia Dei statuere ydolatriam esse').[7]

Responding from an entirely different locale, the anchorite's cell, and from within a different kind of discourse, a vernacular spiritual autobiography, Julian of Norwich also appears keenly aware of the controversy, as Nicholas Watson has argued, voicing in the early short text of her *Revelations* a brief but pointed description of her uses of an image, a move that appears carefully calculated to defend herself from any suggestion of heresy (Watson 1993: 661). Even closer to Chaucer, John Gower – the 'moral Gower' to whom, with Ralph Strode, Chaucer dedicated *Troilus and Criseyde* (V, 1856) – included in his *Vox clamantis*, a long moral and political treatise begun after 1378 and continued into the 1380s, a discussion of images that takes up many of the central issues of the debate: whether the viewer worships the image or the idea behind the image; whether richly decorated images deceive worshippers into giving false offerings. Although Gower does not mention Lollards directly, the argument itself seems clearly inflected by the image debate, and walks a reformist though carefully orthodox path, critiquing images while also defending their utility to the faithful, condemning rich images yet locating blame in the producers and stage-managers rather than in the lay worshipper (Stockton 1965: 109–11, II, ch. 10).

Gower's contribution to the image debate is noteworthy for its sustained critique of images, even as it simultaneously defends the uses of devotional objects, particularly the cross. Gower was by no means alone in mounting a critique of images from within an orthodox position. One of the key features of the image debate is its wide

Figure 28.2   The Holy Trinity. Polychromed alabaster, probably made in Nottingham (1400–50). Boston, Museum of Fine Arts. [Decorative Arts Special Fund. Courtesy, and © 1999 Museum of Fine Arts, Boston (Mass.). Reproduced with permission. All rights reserved.]

reach, with invective on the abuses of image and image worship voiced from within orthodox circles as well as from heterodox ones, as the ethical and disciplinary anxieties about uses of images in *Dives and Pauper*, an early fifteenth-century treatise on the Ten Commandments, articulate (Barnum 1976: 81–109). The energy of this debate certainly underscores the ubiquity of devotional images in late medieval material culture; the parishes and cathedrals of Chaucer's world were saturated with images, their walls painted with life-sized sequences from the lives of the saints, choir screens and pulpits decorated with images of saints and apostles, and windows glazed with scenes from both Old and New Testaments. The debate over images also bespeaks their powerful hold over popular imagination and desire, a hold that gave them tremendous symbolizing value. In some respects the ethical discourse over images in the late fourteenth century was not unlike the current debate waged perennially and futilely over television, in broadsides that acknowledge its seductive appeals, its powers of mind-control over social ethics and communal will. In both debates over the 'society of the spectacle', to borrow a term from Guy Debord, much of the passion rises from a recognition of our entanglement in complex nets of visual pleasure, as well as our powerlessness to have an impact on the technologies of the spectacle or to control our own response.

What the debate about images records, above all, is a pervasive recognition of their apotropaic and mesmeric powers. Images have agency. An incident recorded in Henry Knighton's Leicester Chronicle for 1382, in which Lollards burned an image of St Catherine, offers a fascinating snapshot of orthodox response to an incident of image-breaking long before the mass destruction of saints' images in the Reformation. In this anecdote, which Knighton tells with great detail and journalistic relish in the midst of an account of activities of Lollards in and around Leicester, he records how two Lollards, William Smith and Richard Waythestathe, burned an image of St Catherine as cooking fuel to make a cabbage soup. The burning of the statue occurs as a kind of evidentiary sacrifice; as the Lollards prepare to cut off the statue's head, one says to the other that if it bleeds they will worship it as a saint, if it doesn't they will burn it and their bodily hunger will be appeased. The statue, of course, does not bleed. Knighton concludes the account with the statement: 'The numbers believing in those doctrines increased, and as it were bred and multiplied greatly,'[8] as if to say that the Lollards have performed a loaves and fishes trick, turning an image into food that in turn converts the multitudes. Yet the very telling of this story, which Knighton splices with a vitriolic aside to tell us about 'that sect of Lollards' which 'hated and inveighed against images', takes as its given the power of images, and makes a powerful case for the orthodox position. The two Lollards burn the image as a deliberate act of investigative blasphemy. The fact that the image burns rather than bleeds, far from supporting the Lollard position, reinforces the folkloric trick (powers never lie where the blasphemers think) even as it supports the conventional and orthodox justification for devotional images: worship the idea behind the image, not the image itself. In burning the image for evidence of its miracle-working powers, the Lollards demonstrate the very literalism and carnality that they fault.

The Affective Gaze

Although Knighton's story appears from one perspective as an account of a kind of scientific experiment, the narrative is fraught with the eroticism of desire and sacrifice, played through even as a mini-martyrdom, the burning of the statue at the stake. The discourse about images in the late fourteenth century, both reformist/orthodox and Lollard/heterodox, sought to discipline or control the transactional powers of the image; yet in performance and in representation images resist the stasis and disembodiment with which even the reformers would endow them. In clerical ritual as Chaucer would have experienced it as a late fourteenth-century parishioner, images consistently take on life and demand a full mobilization of affective responses. Even the most familiar of daily sacred rituals, the elevation of the host by the priest during the mass, involved a collective gaze on a devotional image – Christ's body condensed into the eucharistic wafer (Rubin 1991: 49–63; Beckwith 1993: 34–7; Duffy 1992: 91–130). Witnessing this object, an image of Christ, is powerful, magical, even apotropaic. As John Mirk's *Instructions for Parish Priests* describes the transaction, the parishioner is even a bodily beneficiary whose gains from seeing the host include food and reprieve on that day from blindness or sudden death.[9] Witnessing promulgates itself; through this daily act of gazing we gain insurance that we will be able to do it again.

In Mirk's instructions, as in Machaut's *Voir Dit*, seeing, the act of gazing, is the crucial action that mobilizes the image, or more precisely transforms the self before it. One strand of optical theory as understood in the Middle Ages even underwrites this interactive drama, providing a mechanistic foundation for the psychic experience of visual agency, the double sense that the very act of gazing has power over others and that the image or object we desire has power over us. The physicality of the visual process, a physicality that could be said to animate dead space, was understood through the theory of visible 'species', rays emanating from the eye (extramission) to meet with the rays emitted by the object. While the existence of visual rays was the subject of university debate, directly refuted by Ockham in the early fourteenth century, a number of influential theorists accepted a model of extramission. As Grosseteste argued in the thirteenth century, vision operates through the double action of visual rays: 'but it should be understood that the visual species [issuing from the eye] is a substance, shining and radiating like the sun, the radiation of which, when coupled with the radiation from the exterior shining body, entirely completes vision'.[10] The dynamism of this process, and the close link between optics and metaphysics and even ethics, are further reinforced by the theory of the multiplication of species, developed by Grosseteste, in which the visible species is self-replicating (Klassen 1995: 49). It is not a long step from the animating model of vision to the mortifying, from a metaphysics crediting vision with productive agency to one crediting vision with powers to harm. The eye of the basilisk, a mythical beast, was believed to emit a fatal ray. *We* might say, disavowing the agency of the gaze, 'if looks could kill . . .' In medieval folklore, they can.

Visualizing

It is impossible to measure with any precision what effect popular understanding of the mechanics of vision and the public debates on the uses of devotional images might have exerted on descriptive conventions in medieval literature or on Chaucer's poetry. We might expect, however, a belief in the affective powers of devotional images, coupled with an increasingly fraught public discourse over how religious carvings and paintings should be used, to exert an influence on the representation of the human body in non-religious poetry. Descriptions of devotional bodies in medieval texts consistently denature the aesthetic and renature the body in ways that seem fully responsive to the demands of devotional practice. The quickstep to a passionate presentism in devotional writing effectively dissolves the aesthetic screen: in fourteenth- and fifteenth-century poems of the Passion the crucifix speaks to the passer-by; in Julian's meditation the literal sight of a crucifix quickly leads to her first revelation, animate and immediate: the 'rede blode trekelyn downe fro under the garlande hote and freisly and ryth plenteously, as it were in the time of His passion'.[11] Indeed, notably absent from late medieval English writings are descriptive or ekphrastic accounts of devotional images, except as transformed, as in Julian's text, into visions. This lacuna, a peculiarly yawning absence that is seldom remarked, may represent a careful, if unconscious, dodge of the temptation to worship the image, a temptation whose confusing material seductions are voiced in *Dives and Pauper*, 'Me thynky3t qhanne meen knelyn aforn þe ymage and makyn here preyere aforn þe ymage þat þey doon it to þe ymage and so wurshepyn þe ymage' (Barnum 1976: 85). The absence might even be explained as strategic avoidance of a dangerous subject. To describe a devotional image is to risk coveting it for the pleasure of the object.

For a striking contrast we can look at Roger Martin's account of Long Melford Church, dating from the 1580s, a nostalgic description in which he recalls the images of his parish before their removal in the Reformation. A fascinating exercise in devotional ekphrasis, Martin's account is valuable for its documentation of church holdings but perhaps even more for its voicing of a transformed valuation of ritual objects, in which the devotional now blends with a new aestheticized consciousness of the object in ways that would have been impossible two hundred years earlier. Speaking of an altarpiece once in his family's chapel and now in his home, Martin writes: 'There was also in my ile [aisle] called Jesus Ile, at the back of the altar, a table with a crucifix in it, with the two thieves hanging, on every side one, which is in my house decayed, and the same I hope my heires will repaire, and restore again, one day.' And later in the same document, an ekphrasis of a carved pietà: 'And, in the tabernacle at the south end, there was a faire image of our Blessed Lady, having the afflicted body of her dear son, as he was taken down, off the Cross, lying along in her lapp, the tears, as it were, running down pittyfully upon her beautiful cheekes, as it seemed, bedewing the said sweet body of her son, and therefore named the image of our Lady of Pitty.'[12] 'As it were,' 'as it seemed', 'the said sweet body': in terms that differ markedly from Julian's focused animism, Martin is speaking of an object from the world of likenesses.

Chaucer's Imaging

For Chaucer, the controversy over images in his own time provides a fascinating discursive backdrop against which to look at his construction of textual bodies – his arts of describing the human form. Chaucer's descriptive practice may be contoured by a contemporary culture of visual affective piety, and even inflected by a certain anxiety about the line demarcating the point at which a person slips into image and image into idol. Although Chaucer, unlike Gower, does not engage directly in the controversy nor take up the uses of images as the subject for overt polemic or defence, he doubtless would have been familiar with the image debate. Recent historical research on Chaucer's social networks offers tantalizing evidence of his affiliation with a circle of 'Lollard knights',[13] one of whom, Sir John Montague, took aggressive action on the images in his own chapel by packing them up and stowing them away – a story that, as grist for a chronicler, would probably have been familiar to Chaucer.[14] And although Chaucer does not engage in the image debate in his poetry, he clearly indicates familiarity with some of its key terms. Chaucer's most directed use of terms that are voiced in the image debate appears in the Second Nun's Tale, first when Cecile shows Tiburce that idols are deaf and dumb (286), and again later when she rebukes Almachius for worshipping stones (e.g. carvings of images from stone). A critique of images as blind 'stocks [blocks of wood] and stones' became a commonplace of Lollard polemic, transposed into heterodox rhetoric from traditional/orthodox condemnations of idolatry that can be traced to Aelfric. Chaucer's Pandarus also uses the same phrase in *Troilus and Criseyde*, and in terms that support a transparent falsification. Promising to Criseyde that all will be well when she comes to his house for dinner, an asseveration that promises both that Troilus will not be there and also that if he is there no one will know it, Pandarus swears 'by stokes and by stones' (III, 589), an oath whose pagan logic is simultaneously vitiated by its resonance within the discourses on idolatry. Pandarus is a Trojan and hence should swear by pagan images; but to swear by stocks or stones is to swear by idols with no power at all.

In techniques of description of person, of human imaging, of course, Chaucer exhibits formidable, even unparalleled talents. The *Canterbury Tales* has been described as a cross-section and gallery of late fourteenth-century English society, laying out a series of descriptions that seem very much like portraits – and in fact the descriptions of the General Prologue are usually called just that. Yet, as we have seen with Machaut, an image made from life in the fourteenth century would not necessarily portray a likeness in a mimetic or photographic sense; the very concept of portraiture was intricated with devotional schemata, and image and viewing subject were closely bound by a system of intersubjective 'rays'. Chaucer's techniques of 'portraiture' have long been a subject of interest, with most readers agreeing that the aesthetic principles framing his descriptions of persons are not consistently sensory and unifocal; neither are his descriptions meant to be 'au vif', from life, as portraits of living individuals. Chaucer 'gives a detailed account of what is before him, but does not refer to his mind and senses as organizers of the descriptive pattern'; Chaucer's descriptions are characterized by 'spatial incoherence' and a subordination of visual detail to idea.[15]

The nature of the 'idea' governing Chaucer's representation of form has been addressed in depth by D. W. Robertson Jr and V. A. Kolve. Chaucer's view of the person was limned, Robertson argues, from Gothic principles of hierarchy and ordering, and his interest lies in 'the reality of the idea; details are arranged, just as they are in Romanesque and Gothic art, with a view to developing the idea and not with a view to rendering a photographic image' (Robertson 1962: 248). With less attention to portraiture and more to what he calls 'narrative images', 'symbolic images integral to the action that encloses them' (Kolve 1984: 72), Kolve examines the pressure of the symbolic on the mimetic, developing a set of iconographic readings that demonstrate how Chaucer's representation of exterior form often operates according to the psychic and intellectual logic of the ideogram, even as 'the image remains rooted in the mimetic surfaces of his art' (364). In a study that turns to reception or the textual record of visual experience, Norman Klassen more recently has surveyed the philosophical and optical history of sight to argue that Chaucer uses sight to explore the often polarized boundaries of love and knowledge: 'The eye operates on both sides of this spiritual battle: it can contribute to spiritual progress, with the implied goal of mystical union with God; or it can work destructively, in contexts where it subverts any mystical system of love and knowledge' (Klassen 1995: 23).

The outline I have sketched of the image debate in late medieval England departs from these approaches by framing Chaucer's arts of portraiture within a discourse specific to his time and place, localizing 'idea' in ritual practice and the pressures of a culture saturated with images but publicly anxious about their use. The vast majority of representations of the human body, and certainly the most expensive and beautiful, took the form of devotional likenesses: Christ, the saints, the holy family, biblical patriarchs. To what extent, this chapter asks, is Chaucer's descriptive practice contoured by a contemporary culture of visual affective piety – and specifically by public discourse with increasingly high ethical and political stakes about how we are to see and use the ubiquitous images decorating public buildings? Chaucer consistently invests the act of gazing with potently, often dramatically affective agency; the act of gazing as an eye-witness risks the seductions of both icon and idol.

When Chaucer describes the gaze on another, it is either to repress description as untellable, as in the Squire's Tale (34ff) or the *Book of the Duchess* (895ff), or – far more frequently – to locate it elsewhere, legitimizing or perhaps de-institutionalizing the gaze by express transposition to loci of exotic otherness: the pagan locales of the Knight's Tale and of *Troilus and Criseyde*; the fictive and atemporalized locations of the dream visions. Paradoxically, the disengagement of description from a textual eye-witness dramatically licenses 'portraiture' as a practice of a kind of photorealism, a record of both the appealing and the grotesque side by side with the messy and often comic details of human bodies and actions. While Chaucer is perhaps best known to many for techniques of description, the dazzling arts of synaesthetic concreteness that fabricate the portraits in the General Prologue or of Alisoun in the Miller's Tale, those portraits are also independent from a recording gaze within the narrative, or what we might call a focalizer (Stanbury 1991: 4). We see them, but not through the responsive screen of a textual eye of the beholder. Chaucer's most 'visual' descriptions, that is to say, are also his most virtual.

In the readings that follow, I have selected passages from Chaucer's poetry that locate a focalizer recording an encounter with a human body, either as image of a body or as the living being itself. The first of these will be the descriptions in the temples in the Knight's Tale, in particular that of the statue of Venus. In these graphic descriptions of images, with a textual witness in a gallery of sculpted and painted human figures, Chaucer reveals both a connoisseur's appreciation of the aesthetic object and also an uneasiness about those very pleasures, a subjection of the viewer to images that appear to come to life through the action of a gaze. A second reading will consider one of Chaucer's most brilliantly evoked accounts of visual intersubjectivity, the scene at the temple in Book I of *Troilus and Criseyde*, Chaucer's long Troy romance. In this scene Chaucer crafts a detailed account of a would-be lover's gaze on a living human body – the experience of falling in love at first sight.

Ekphrasis: The Knight's Tale

In Chaucer's poetry, the experience of eye-witness recording is detailed most flexibly and easily in ekphrasis, the literary description of a work of art. Ekphrastic description in Chaucer is almost entirely reserved for classical materials, and practised with close attention to reception, the placement of a focalizer within the gallery. Defamiliarizing the representational gallery as quite literally a *locus classicus*, as if the pleasure of viewing pictures at an exhibition can only be told when the gallery is neither here nor now, pagan images appear to allow Chaucer legitimate or safe objects for the pleasures of connoisseurship, fully exploited in the lengthy descriptive accounts. The narrator can take the position of recording agent ('ther saugh I') who wanders through the temple describing its ornament. At the same time, however, in the Knight's Tale, as in the similar descriptive programme in the *House of Fame*, pagan images tend to come to life, transforming repeatedly from sculpted images into living or at least lifelike beings under the gaze of an observer, a surprising animation that may itself reflect attitudes towards devotional images as things of power.

The cover of antiquity gives the fourteenth-century poet licence to pay close attention to form, the pleasure of the image, an immersion we can see in the description of the statue of Venus in the Knight's Tale. A striking feature of this description is its three-dimensionality, a particular attention to extremities, supports and attachments that pulls the eye away from the centre to the margins; a technique that allows the statue to take up space as a carved and painted sculpture. Rhetorical manuals in the Middle Ages offered prescriptions for describing the human body, the most common of which were the top-to-toe catalogues, beginning first with the eyes and moving downwards in a list of idealized attributes. In the description of Venus, Chaucer expressly articulates an appreciation of three-dimensional sculpted form. He begins with the support and moves briefly downwards and then up, but not through the centre; rather, through the margins:

> The statue of Venus, glorious for to se,
> Was naked, fletynge in the large see,
> And fro the navele doun al covered was
> With wawes grene, and brighte as any glas.
> A citole in hir right hand hadde she
> And on hir heed, ful semely for to se,
> A rose gerland, fressh and wel smellynge;
> Above hir heed hir dowves flikerynge.
> Biforn hire stood hir sone Cupido;
> Upon his shuldres wynges hadde he two,
> And blynd he was, as it is often seene;
> A bowe he bar and arwes brighte and kene.
>
> (1955–66)

For shape and dimensionality, the statue grows in a sense from its centre or foundation on a painted and sculpted sea, its contours defined by its props – the right hand carrying a stringed instrument, the head circled by first a rose garland and then a grouping of doves. For depth of field, Chaucer describes Cupido, standing before Venus, also defined by borders and edges: the wings on his shoulders, his bow and arrows.

Repeated references to the action of sight in this ekphrasis also switch on the sensory. With the line of sight located in the double position as that which can simply record and as that which can record with delight, the action of a gaze also appears to bring the statue almost to life. 'Glorious for to se' in the first line of the description interrupts the declarative statement on the statue's nudity, a Janus-faced splicing that looks not only backwards to the statue but forwards to the next line, the pleasures of the nudity, though the poet quickly moves on to cover the exposure. When he describes Venus' head, the parenthetical 'ful semely for to se' leads to the rose garland, 'fressh and wel smellynge', as if the action of the gaze or attention to one sense activated another, breathing life into the garland; metaphorical slips into virtual, beyond an 'as if' odour of real flowers into fragrance itself.

In the descriptions of the temples that follow, the boundaries between art or image and reality increasingly blur, as the imagined eye that constructs the ekphrasis of Venus becomes a literal eye-witness ('saugh I ther') and as the images described increasingly seem to take on animation and dimensionality. Within the temples, images and 'portreyture' repeatedly slip out of the representational into a textual real, a kind of virtualizing that plays out as a struggle for control between the maker and the artefact, the artist as fabricator and the text (or image) that takes on a life of its own. Lee Patterson has noted this shift, pointing to the inexplicable intrusion of the Knight into the text as if he were there as a character in the story, and also the shift whereby images and paintings seem to take on life.[16] Patterson explains this forfeiture of control as emblematic of the tale's general commentary on the seductions and paralysis of chivalry, an institution that 'submerges the self in a surface pattern of ritual and replication' (227–8) – and in this text, a giving over of the individual or collective will to Theseus, who not only builds the amphitheatre, but purports to stage-manage the events of the tale in general.

I would want to nuance Patterson's reading by pointing to the close relationship between these images and devotional figures in a culture where all images were to some extent iconic. Readers have understood the ekphrases of the images and paintings in the Knight's Tale to represent various forms of entrapment: of the self by the fictions of chivalry, as Patterson argues; of the individual will by transforming images of imprisonment, as Kolve argues (1984: 113–30); of the free choice to Christian charity by the seductions of pagan idols, and specifically Venus, the 'mother of all fornication', as D. W. Robertson argues (1962: 371); or even of the visual field by *le regard*, a socially constructed desire that endows the object of the gaze, however harmful, with an illusory will and wholeness, as Marshall Leicester argues (1990: 268). Both Patterson and Leicester, rightly I think, understand Chaucer as a disenchanted maker whose Knight's Tale critiques the chivalric institutions it memorializes: the Knight, recorder of aristocratic spectacle, acts as a nostalgic spokesman for an anachronistic social form. The complex commentary on art, spectacle, images and subjectivity generated through the temple ekphrases suggests we should also include Chaucer among the voices of the subject; and that voice, I believe, also takes the occasion to play out both the pleasures of 'art for art's sake' and the complex entanglements of a gaze on devotional objects. If Chaucer details the images and paintings in the temples to comment on the Knight's willing subjection of judgement to the institutions of an outmoded chivalric order, that drama also illustrates the pleasures of the gallery – on the one hand a love of images, their three-dimensionality, their sensuality; and on the other a distrust that may echo the voices of the image debate, critiquing images as dead 'stocks and stones'.

The description of the temples also represents the seductions of images as a developing process, a drama of sorts that increasingly entangles its viewer. Following the description of Venus, recounted with an attempt to capture the pleasures of three-dimensional form, the lines between art and reality blur, and images and murals take on increasingly malevolent agency. The final lines of the description of the temples brilliantly focus this set of tensions around an image whose verisimilitude troubles the boundaries not only between art and narrative, but between life and death. In front of the statue of Diana is an image of a woman in childbirth – whose pain is even imagined as speech:

> A womman travaillynge was hire biforn;
> But for hir child so longe was unborn,

Ful pitously Lucyna gan she calle
And seyde, 'Help, for thou mayst best of alle!'
Wel koude he peynten lifly that it wroghte;
With many a floryn he the hewes boghte.

(2083–8)

The image is so lifelike it appears to speak. Or is it that the image is so lifelike it *does* speak? The image might be said to illustrate the drama of lifelikeness, but also, in the picture of the woman trapped in childbirth, a terrible stasis, the place of the undead, the inability to bring to life. This final ekphrasis bespeaks a number of very different responses, highly ambivalent, towards images, but condenses to an image as lodged between life and death, as death-dealing nascent life. In the final two lines of the account of the temples, the narrator retreats suddenly and entirely to disavow the drama he has just enabled, turning from the plea for help to change the subject, speaking at the end about art and the production of the image. If the image is painted 'lifly', in a lifelike manner, it is done so with purchased pigments, 'many a floryn'. It is just a picture.

In the description of the temples in the Knight's Tale the ekphrastic mode thus seems not only to engage techniques of the observer but also to license them. In this long descriptive piece, the engagement of the subject ('ther saugh I', 140), organizes the frame in an oscillation between detachment and engagement, although, as we have seen, detachment is always tenuous. When Chaucer describes the gaze on another person, rather than an image from pagan antiquity, the image brought to life in a human form through visual intersubjectivity, it is often to record that act as one of extraordinary potency – so much so, in fact, that the object is even indescribable. In the Squire's Tale, the Squire begs to be excused from describing Canacee on the grounds of rhetorical inadequacy. A similar excuse also appears, and with direct reference to a textual eye-witness, in a complex discussion of White's gaze intercalated with his own, in the *Book of the Duchess*, when the man in black says he is incapable of describing White's beauty, except to say that she 'was whit, rody, fressh, and lyvely hewed' (905). In the *Legend of Good Women*, the dynamism engaged in the act of looking renders the God of Love even expressly unseeable: the narrator is so blinded by his face, 'But of his face I can not seyn the hewe, / For sikerly his face shon so bryghte / That with the glem astoned was the syghte' (G 162–5). In the Knight's Tale, the non-description of Emelye may also be reflex of a visual animism that evacuates its target. The gaze on Emelye is of course the action that sets this story going: Palamon and Arcite spot Emelye out of their prison window as she is walking in the garden, and both are stung to the heart with amorous rays. Readers have noted that Emelye is peculiarly absent from the story, even though it purports to be about, or at least for her; she is also graphically absent, as she is described entirely in formulaic terms. The only distinctive attribute we see about Emelye, in fact, is her long, blonde braid. The single detail recorded about Emelye sees her from behind.

The Drama of the Gaze: *Troilus and Criseyde*

For Chaucer's most complex story of the visual, we have to turn to *Troilus and Criseyde*, a poem that, like the Knight's Tale, was written in the 1380s and is thus temporally and culturally similarly situated within new public dialogue on the uses and abuses of devotional images. In Book I of *Troilus*, Chaucer details the process by which Troilus falls in love with Criseyde in explicitly visual terms, even as a drama of 'the look', *le regard*, that exploits the language and terminology of devotional worship and optics to forfeit agency to the object of the gaze. Like Machaut before the image of Toute Bele in *Voir Dit*, Troilus is given over with remarkable suddenness to a woman-as-image. Following the decisive or fateful instant when Troilus' glance falls on Criseyde at the festival of the Palladion, one of the terms repeated most often is 'look' or 'lokynge'. With Troilus' gaze Chaucer takes up the familiar trope of the lover's gaze that pierces the eye to wound the heart, but reverses it to exploit the illusion that Troilus' gaze has agency over its object, piercing Criseyde rather than himself. Looking over the ladies at the festival, Troilus spots Criseyde, and his self-wounding is imagined as an action of violence on Criseyde's body:

> And upon cas bifel that thorugh a route
> His eye percede, and so depe it wente,
> Til on Criseyde it smot, and ther it stent.
>   (271–3)

He is suddenly conscious of her, and of 'looks' which refer variously to her demeanour and her gaze, and also to his gaze on her:

> To Troilus right wonder wel with alle
> Gan for to like hire mevynge and hire chere,
> Which somdel deignous was, for she let falle
> Hire *look* a lit aside in swich manere
> Ascaunces, 'What, may I nat stonden here?'
> And after that hir *lokynge* gan she lighte,
> That nevere thoughte hym seen so good a syghte.
>
> And of hire *look* in him ther gan to quyken
> So gret desir . . .
>   (288–96, emphasis added)

'Look', in this passage and beyond, participates in the doubled register of the word in modern use: we look at; we also bear a look (an attitude) that is the record of someone else's look on us. The way I look, or my looks, register my face and demeanour in the gaze of another. The coupling of the term in Troilus with the metaphor of love-through-the-eyes exploits this elision of the transitive with the intransitive – to the extent that Troilus' own gaze on Criseyde fictively mobilizes her gaze. He imagines its agency on him:

> Lo, he that leet hymselven so konnynge,
> And scorned hem that Loves peynes dryen
> Was ful unwar that Love hadde his dwellynge
> Withinne the subtile stremes of hire yen;
> That sodeynly hym thoughte he felte dyen,
> Right with hire look, the spirit in his herte.
>
> (I, 302–7)

Although he feels himself struck dead 'with hire look', there is no indication that she looks at him. Troilus controls the gaze in this account, and her gaze has only been invoked to indicate her sense of entitlement, the look aside that claims her right to be there: 'What, may I nat stonden here?' (292). The look or *le regard* is dramatized as a metphysical ligature, the 'subtile stremes of hire yen', not tears but affective visual 'species'. Love through the eyes electrifies this temple with visual rays. Dynamically phallic, piercing the crowd and then Criseyde, Troilus' gaze blurs the lines between voyeurism and exhibitionism as it turns around to slay the messenger. To look at with desire is to imagine being seen.

In his use of the language of optics and of visual rays in Book I, Chaucer thus performs a brilliant sleight of hand, reproducing agency as victimization, action as passivity, Troilus who looks and desires as Troilus a captive.[17] Through this illusionistic shift Chaucer establishes some of the central issues of his romance: Is Troilus a victim or a maker of his fate? Do we shape our fortunes or are we acted upon? By drawing on visual tropes that ground, as we have seen, the science of optics and the language of affective devotion in Christian ritual, Chaucer not only plays out a convincing psychological drama ('this is what it feels like to fall in love') but also valorizes the erotic story with evidence from anatomy and metaphor from religion.

The spatial representation of Criseyde also contributes to a system of resonances and an overlay in modes or even genres. Standing within the temple, Criseyde is located in a place clearly exotic (a pagan temple) but also curiously familiar – as indeed the city of Troy, as readers have remarked, seems very much like a fourteenth-century town and its buildings remarkably similar to late medieval English palaces.[18] Within the temple on a high holiday, the place she occupies is not unlike a church; she even seems framed within it, occupying space as an image in a niche, but also sequestered among the laity at the back near the porch: 'And yet she stood ful lowe and stille allone, / Byhynden other folk, in litel brede, / And neigh the dore, ay undre shames drede' (178–80). She is among them but separate from them, still and curiously detached, as if framed, 'in litel brede', a little space – a space that later she appears to claim with her 'look a lite aside' (291). As object of Troilus' gaze, she is iconized within this temple rather like an image in a niche, but within a space she also appears to claim as her own.

Seeing Criseyde in Book I is thus a process of seeing Troilus – and in fact later we are told that when he goes home he makes a 'mirour of his mynde' in which he can recall 'hire figure'. She is only described in the most general terms, more as a body that occupies a still space in the temple than as a detailed physiognomic portrait. She is first in beauty; she wears a black widow's habit; she is 'simple of atir and debonaire of chere' (181). Unlike the statue of Venus in the Knight's Tale, given shape through attention to form and surfaces, Criseyde takes up space through her gaze as much as through her body. Seeing Criseyde, introducing as it does the beginnings of a love affair in terms that introduce as well a rich set of questions about agency and determinism, is an action that exploits familiar terminology and habits of the visual. By describing her only generally, the text iconizes her; she is visible but untellable, or perhaps fetishized in attributes of her own power and sexual status, her 'look' or her gaze and her widows' weeds. The action of the gaze, operating as it does within a theatre whose structure suggests not only temple but also church, however light the touch, focuses attention on the votive structure of vision itself.

But if temple, does the spatial framing of Criseyde as a kind of image suggest she stands in relation to Troilus as pagan idol? Readers of *Troilus* have often commented on the text's highly ambiguous treatment of love and its shift from the apparently benign and domestic to an increasingly public and destructive sphere, in which the very cultural formations, such as chivalry and courtly love, that construct the subject and give him or her over to desire, also vitiate will to give the subject over to betrayal and death.[19] The moment of apprehension of Criseyde, brilliantly recreating the press of real bodies and human energies, also recalls or evokes, taking its meaning in part from its likeness to ritual forms of worship, either of pagan goddesses or of Christian devotional images. Whether as idol, icon or bodily woman, or all in one, as I believe, Criseyde in Book I mobilizes an extraordinary excitation of the air; she stands still in her little space as the temple seems to reverberate with visual rays. In *Troilus* as elsewhere in Chaucer's poetry, vision is an act of agency and potency, a performative that transforms the self, subjecting the will in dramatic acts of fealty. And in *Troilus*, as in the Knight's Tale, the very act of visual apprehension tends to iconize its object; recorded in the action of the gaze, images become people and people become images.

The position of the subject before the objects it sees and desires, ethically charged, seems to echo the terms of the image debate in the late fourteenth century, or at least reverberate within it. Characters in Chaucer repeatedly submit to the pleasures of images as if to a seduction, as in *Dives and Pauper*, where Dives anxiously records the difficulty of knowing how to position himself before images in ritual spaces where the gestures of most worshippers suggests they love the object itself like a living god (Barnum 1976: 85–6). For Chaucer, the pleasures of vision repeatedly entangle the subject in a similar ethical and passional dilemma, conditioning the apprehension of form in terms that may well be inflected by the anxieties of the object. The gaze on the body demands a sacrifice, the giving over of self to what is seen. In *Troilus* this sacrifice is direct, dramatic and immediate: he is an instant victim. With descriptive accounts of images from antiquity, descriptions in which Chaucer clearly seems to take a good deal of pleasure, Chaucer allows a recording eye to roam more freely, but even there detachment repeatedly slips into entanglement and objects transform into living bodies. Like the stocks and stones of the image debate, whose trouble lies in the worshipper's unwillingness to see them in their essences, Chaucer's images never stay fully in the gallery.

See also CHIVALRY; CHRISTIAN IDEOLOGIES; CONTEMPORARY ENGLISH WRITERS; CRISIS AND DISSENT; FRANCE; GEOGRAPHY AND TRAVEL; LIFE HISTORIES; LOVE; MODES OF REPRESENTATION; NARRATIVE; PAGAN SURVIVALS; PERSONAL IDENTITY; WOMEN.

NOTES

1 Elert Dahl, 'Heavenly images: the statue of St Foy of Conques and the signification of the medieval "cult-image" in the West', *Acta ad Archaeologiam et Artium Historiam Pertinentia* 8 (1978), 175–91.

2 According to Michael Camille, a fourteenth-century illustration from a French version of Bartholomeus Anglicus is 'one of the earliest examples of what we would call a modern framed painting'; the image of Toute Bele may offer an equally early example. See 'The image and the self: unwriting late medieval bodies', in *Framing Medieval Bodies*, ed. Sarah Kay and Miri Rubin (Manchester and New York: Manchester University Press, 1994), 66.

3 Norbert Schneider, *The Art of the Portrait* (Cologne: Taschen, 1994), 6–9; Joanna Woodall, *Portraiture: Facing the Subject* (Manchester: Manchester University Press, 1997), 1.

4 William Langland, *Piers Plowman: The Prologue and Passus I–VII of the B Text*, ed. J. A. W. Bennett (Oxford: Clarendon, 1972), 22, ll. 48–50, 59–63.

5 Joy M. Russell-Smith, 'Walter Hilton and a tract in defence of the veneration of images', *Dominican Studies* 7 (1954), 200, n. 78.

6 As Russell-Smith notes (ibid.), the lines preceding and following this sentence echo a sermon delivered a year earlier, so the sentence appears to have been added to reflect a new development. Sermons of Wyclif's advocating removal of images from churches have been dated to the same year, 1383; see also

Margaret Aston, *Lollards and Reformers: Images and Literacy in Late Medieval Religion* (London: Hambledon, 1984), 142.

7 *Walter Hilton's Latin Writings*, ed. John P. H. Clark and Cheryl Taylor, Analecta Cartusiana (Salzburg: Institut für Anglistik und Amerikanistik, 1987), 179.

8 *Knighton's Chronicle, 1337–1396*, ed. and trans. G. H. Martin (Oxford: Clarendon, 1995), 299; for the story as a whole see 292–9.

9 John Mirk, *Instructions for Parish Priests*, ed. Edward Peacock, Early English Text Society, original series 31 (1868), 312–17.

10 Grosseteste, *De iride*, cited from Edward Grant, *A Source Book in Medieval Science* (Cambridge, Mass.: Harvard University Press, 1974), 389.

11 *The Shewings of Julian of Norwich*, ed. Georgia Ronan Crampton, TEAMS Middle English Series (Kalamazoo, Mich.: Medieval Institute, 1993), 42, lines 114–15.

12 David Dymond and Clive Paine, *The Spoil of Melford Church: The Reformation in a Suffolk Parish* (Ipswich: Salient Press, 1992), 2.

13 Glending Olson, 'Geoffrey Chaucer', in *The Cambridge History of Medieval English Literature*, ed. David Wallace (Cambridge: Cambridge University Press, 1999), 570–4; Steven Justice, 'Lollardy', ibid., 670–3.

14 The Montague story is related in Thomas Walsingham's *Chronicon Angliae*, ed. E. M. Thompson, Rolls Series 64 (1875), 377.

15 Claes Schaar, *The Golden Mirror: Studies in Chaucer's Descriptive Technique and Its Literary*

Background (Lund: Gleerup, 1955); John Bender, *Spenser and Literary Pictorialism* (Princeton: Princeton University Press, 1972), 46–53; Sarah Stanbury, *Seeing the Gawain-Poet: Description and the Act of Perception* (Philadelphia: University of Pennsylvania Press, 1991), 118–23.

16 Lee Patterson, *Chaucer and the Subject of History* (Madison and London: University of Wisconsin Press, 1991), 225.

17 Sarah Stanbury, 'The lover's gaze in *Troilus and Criseyde*', in *Chaucer's* Troilus and Criseyde, *'Subgit to Alle Poesye': Essays in Criticism*, ed. R. A. Shoaf (Binghamton, NY: Medieval and Renaissance Texts and Studies, 1992), 225–38, and the companion essay,

'The voyeur and the private life in *Troilus and Criseyde*', *Studies in the Age of Chaucer* 13 (1991), 141–58.

18 H. M. Smyser, 'The domestic background of *Troilus and Criseyde*', *Speculum* 31 (1956), 297–315; Saul N. Brody, 'Making a play for Criseyde: the staging of Pandarus's house in Chaucer's *Troilus and Criseyde*', *Speculum* 73 (1998), 115–40.

19 See e.g. Louise O. Fradenburg, '"Our owen wo to drynke": loss, gender, and chivalry in *Troilus and Criseyde*', in *Chaucer's* Troilus and Criseyde, ed. Shoaf, 88–106; Sheila Delany, 'Techniques of alienation in *Troilus and Criseyde*', ibid., 29–46.

References and Further Reading

Aston, Margaret (1984) *Lollards and Reformers: Images and Literacy in Late Medieval Religion*. London: Hambledon. Essays on the Lollard movement from the fourteenth to the sixteenth centuries; long chapter on images.

Barnum, Priscilla Heath, ed. (1976) *Dives and Pauper*, i, part 1, Early English Text Society, original series 275. Long prose treatise on the commandments, in dialogue form, written between *c.*1405 and 1410. Contains debate on the uses of images in which Dives, the worldly bourgeois, is instructed on their uses by Pauper, the voice of the good cleric.

Beckwith, Sarah (1993) *Christ's Body: Identity, Culture and Society in Late Medieval Writings* (New York: Routledge). Materialist and social examination of the image at the centre of medieval representation, Christ's suffering body.

Belting, Hans (1990) *The Image and its Public in the Middle Ages: Form and Function of Early Paintings of the Passion* (New Rochelle, NY: Carodzas). Studies development of Passion paintings in Europe with close attention to ownership and patronage; traces shift in use of images from public to private worship.

Camille, Michael (1989) *The Gothic Idol: Ideology and Image-making in Medieval Art* (Cambridge: Cambridge University Press). Broad overview of idolatry in Gothic art and the uses of idolatry as a trope signifying multiple forms of cultural

'otherness' in medieval social critique. Many illustrations.

Duffy, Eamon (1992) *The Stripping of the Altars: Traditional Religion in England c.1400–1580* (New Haven: Yale University Press). Study of popular attitudes toward images and ritual in pre-Reformation English parish culture. Many illustrations.

Freedberg, David (1989) *The Power of Images: Studies in the History and Theory of Response* (Chicago: University of Chicago Press). Wide-ranging study of social and psychological uses of images, with focus on the cultic and erotic, chiefly (though not exclusively) from the classical era through to the late Renaissance in the European West.

Holley, Linda Tarte (1986) 'Medieval optics and the framed narrative in Chaucer's *Troilus and Criseyde*', *Chaucer Review* 21, 26–44. Study of sight, optics and perspective in *Troilus*.

Hudson, Anne (1978) *Selections from English Wycliffite Writings* (Cambridge: Cambridge University Press). Useful selections, with glossary, covering general Wycliffite belief and orthodox response; biblical translation and commentary; and selections from Lollard polemic and doctrine. Detailed annotations.

Jones, W. R. (1973) 'Lollards and images: the defence of religious art in later medieval England', *Journal of the History of Ideas* 34,

27–50. Well-documented introduction to the image controversy in fourteenth- and fifteenth-century England.

Klassen, Norman (1995) *Chaucer on Love, Knowledge and Sight* (Cambridge: Brewer). Survey of medieval optical theory; uses of medieval optics in Chrétien de Troyes, Dante, Guillaume de Lorris and Chaucer.

Kolve, V. A. (1984) *Chaucer and the Imagery of Narrative: The First Five Canterbury Tales* (Stanford: Stanford University Press). Extensive general examination of aesthetic and philosophical idea of images in medieval thought and application to first five Canterbury tales. Richly illustrated.

Leech-Wilkinson, Daniel, ed. (1998) *Guillaume de Machaut: Le Livre dou voir dit (The Book of the True Poem)*, trans. R. Barton Palmer (New York: Garland). Courtly epistolary love narrative, with alternating prose and poetry. Early 1360s.

Leicester, H. Marshall, Jr (1990) *The Disenchanted Self: Representing the Subject in the Canterbury Tales* (Berkeley, Los Angeles and London: University of California Press). Close readings, nuanced by deconstruction and Lacanian psychoanalysis, of Chaucer's Knight's Tale, Wife of Bath's Tale and Pardoner's Tale. Long analysis of representation of the gaze in the scenes in the temples in the Knight's Tale.

Robertson, D. W., Jr (1962) *A Preface to Chaucer: Studies in Medieval Perspectives* (Princeton: Princeton University Press). Study of Chaucer as contextualized by Christian exegesis and iconography. Many illustrations.

Rubin, Miri (1991) *Corpus Christi: The Eucharist in Late Medieval Culture* (Cambridge: Cambridge University Press). History of the uses of the eucharist in later medieval culture and church ritual as central image and sacrament of the church.

Spearing, A. C. (1993) *The Medieval Poet as Voyeur: Looking and Listening in Medieval Love-narratives* (Cambridge: Cambridge University Press). Close readings of voyeurism and visuality in a wide range of continental and especially Middle English love narratives, including Chaucer's Knight's Tale, Manciple's Tale and Merchant's Tale, the *Parliament of Fowls* and *Troilus and Criseyde*.

Stanbury, Sarah (1991) *Seeing the* Gawain-*poet: Description and the Act of Perception* (Philadelphia: University of Pennsylvania Press). Close readings of techniques of description and a focalized subject in *Pearl*, *Cleanness*, *Patience* and *Sir Gawain and the Green Knight*.

Stockton, Eric, W., ed. (1965) *The Major Latin Works of John Gower – The Voice of One Crying and the Tripartite Chronicle: An Annotated Translation into English with an Introductory Essay on the Author's Non-English Works* (Seattle: University of Washington Press). One of the longest Anglo-Latin works, the *Vox clamantis* critiques the three estates of the clergy, knighthood and peasantry. It is most often read for its account, in Book One, of the Peasants' Revolt of 1381. Critique of the abuses of images.

Watson, Nicholas (1993) 'The composition of Julian of Norwich's *Revelation of Love*', *Speculum* 68, 637–83. Consideration of Julian within contemporary social and cultural controversies; survey of image controversy.

29

Women

Nicky Hallett

'fayre wordes brake neuer bone'

Imagine this. Rolf and Liesl in the conservatory as the storm rages against its windows, archetypal love's young dream, sixteen, going on seventeen. He sings (is it a threat, a promise, a mere description?): 'You wait, little girl on an empty stage / for fate to turn the light on; / Your life, little girl, is an empty page / that men will want to write on.' She compliantly, admiringly (is it ever ironically?) underscores this, echoes singingly, 'to write on'. Femininity here is a type of mimicry; her language is shaped by his. It might be asserted that *The Sound of Music* (1959) reiterates in this way a pattern of women's representation within Western culture, where man writes woman and thus determines by his writing the bounds of her identity. She has no substance without him, and there is no prospect of a language of autonomous female desire.

Yet an historian easily might reply to such an assertion that context is all, that film as a genre has its own critical traditions, that lyrics are not life, that the earlier book on which this film is based had its own peculiar inception – that, in other words, extrapolations based on generalized ideas of oppression are misleading unless historically and culturally contingent. Having grounded observations in such specifics, we might then more legitimately ask whether patterns *can* be delineated, having been explained (and not away) by geography and history, space and time. Does Rodgers and Hammerstein's reworking of the tale, even with its particular conditions, reveal wider preconceptions some of which also occupied Chaucer some six hundred years before? Are there shapes to be seen of stylized repetition that are both in, and beyond, their immediate genre or time-frame? Does examination of the historical process reveal not only truths but also reasons for representing things in certain ways? Can we, then, infer that the depiction of women, like that of men (but probably differently) has its motives?

Speech Acts: Medieval and Modern

If materialist historicism can help to explain literary and life conditions, speech-act theory may help penetrate (or at least stage) the paradox of what is 'new' and what is reiterative in a tradition of representation. Words do not only neutrally describe, after all, they also create: in speech-act theory words do what they say, at that moment, and effects follow. Originating in the ideas of J. L. Austin (1962), notions of language being 'performative' challenge the assumption that speech, or writing, consists only of true or false statements. Instead, a statement performs with language the deed to which it refers: those discussing the theory often use the example of a cheque, that has no worth as a piece of paper, but the signing of which transforms it into the value inscribed on it. Language in this philosophy is perlocutory, it has an effect on actions and that, sometimes, may be different from the one(s) intended by the speaker's inter-locution. The effect, too, may be larger in scope than the moment of speaking and writing, since users of language do not necessarily originate it, but often restate prior performative exercises: 'responsibility is thus linked with speech as repetition, not as origination' (Butler 1997: 39). How far, then, is Chaucer (ir)responsible for his representation of women? Can we hold him to account for starting or merely subscribing to a line of depiction that has a fourteenth-century style to it but a source that precedes him?

Empty Pages

Imagine, then, the empty page. And Chaucer does continually ask us to pretend that something is unwritten, is in the process of appearing before us as we speak, like the Canterbury pilgrims' tales unfolding. Yet, even as we most dramatically engage with that fiction, the narrator invokes his own pre-written text and urges his reader 'whoso list it nat yheare, / Turne ove the leef and chese another tale' (MilP 3176–7). The non-written is always illusory even in the act of pretence. Just so the 'empty page' of Woman: Chaucer's women come with a history, bag ladies who carry their own wardrobe from literary place to place. Someone has written them. Authors might be sources whom Chaucer claims simply to translate 'in no malyce' (*LGWP* G 341), or whose words he artlessly repeats (as he continually states, hence making happen what he says he does). For Chaucer operates, and knowingly, in the performative arena of language.

Although formulated in modern theoretical terms, such ideas are not unfamiliar in medieval philosophy: 'In the beginning was the Word' (John 1: 1); this, perhaps the greatest speech act in/of the Judeo-Christian world, underlined, even originated, most ideas of (re)creation and authorship. Typology, too, functions as repetition when characters are both themselves and represent previous 'types', commonly drawn from religious sources (such as Isaac or Adam being a type of Christ, Eve being a type of

Mary, where New Testament characters both echo and develop the significance of the Old). Accordingly, literary characters frequently come with past histories that extend their significance beyond the literary moment of the text in front of us. If male characters are constructed in sight of ideas of masculinity, for a character to be made a 'woman' is to imbue her (un)wittingly with a set of histories and reputations, not necessarily her own. To name her, for example, Delilah (or Criseyde, May, Philomela: the subjects of the studies in this chapter) is to baptize her in fire: there is, of course, a politics to naming.

Naked Texts

There is, then, no such thing as a 'naked text' (*LGW* G 86): if sources are not cited as such, 'there is tradition at large, literary tracts as a source of information' (Delany 1994: 43). Chaucer often toys with the very idea of this, makes it his subject. On those occasions, there is sometimes a ceremonial, even jokey, laying bare of sources, a rhetorical reclothing. In the Clerk's Tale this is enacted before our readerly eyes. Grisilde arrives at her new spouse's home, as she later says of herself, 'Naked out of my fadres hous' (871). There is a typology at play here, and, as ever, some Chaucerian complication of it. Grisilde's long-suffering saintliness is inferred by this reference to Job (1: 21): yet Job says 'Naked came I out of my *mother's womb*, and naked shall I return thither.' Grisilde is told by her husband to bring 'no thyng of hire olde geere' to the marital home and she is, at his order, 'clothed . . . al newe' (372, 378). Stripping and reinscription are literal and literary. Chaucer, like Walter, is well aware that words are ceremony. 'This is my wyf' says Walter (369) and, with that, so she is.

Individuals do not come to their writer naked, as here they need to be *re*dressed even as they are *ad*dressed: 'To understand this, one must imagine an impossible scene, that of a body that has not yet been given social definition, a body that is, strictly speaking, not accessible to us, that nevertheless becomes accessible on the occasion of an address' (Butler 1997: 5). Individuals are thus reconstituted as they are spoken of and to, but not created at that point. When the Merchant's January addresses May as 'wyf', the subject is relative. When Criseyde says 'Now nece' to Antigone (*TC* II. 877), the latter is put in her place, and replies in the form of 'Madame' (880). The scene is one where they negotiate for authority, skirt around the power to interpret, in a dialogue of said and unsaid. Forms of address constitute a figure and their relationship to the speaker, yet it is not a constitution in a vacuum. Criseyde's reputation runs behind and ahead: she arrived with it before Chaucer wrote her or we read, and she knows all too well that, of her, 'Shal neyther ben ywriten nor ysonge / No good word' (V, 1059–60).

The poet, too, can act helpless with some truth: there is nothing he can do, mere cipher, for 'Hire name, allas, is publysshed so wide' (V, 1095), 'Ye may hire gilt in other bokes se' (1776). Thus the fictivity of blame(lessness) is writ. Chaucer's women come to their medieval readers ready-clad, as to their hapless writer, ready-written. Woman is an inscribed representational body, bearing the mark of Eve (who already wore it before she was herself engraved): there is (was) no empty page.

The Condition of Women

It is so, too, for any writer on the very topic itself. Chaucer's women have already been much written about. Gender has long been a subject within medieval, as other, literary studies. Early amazed recognitions, at the time radical acts, which drew attention to the very existence of women at all, have given way to more sophisticated probings of women's places within culture. In this, we have moved beyond ideas that medieval antifeminism versus idealism gave women the choice of being only Eve or Mary; and other conceptions of fixed stereotypes are also being modified by research (discussed in Evans and Johnson 1994: 112, 180). There have been many possible approaches to take. If we accept that there is no 'empty page', then we might wish to go behind the written, either to oral traditions or to the earliest representations of women, to look for sources, equating here, perhaps spuriously, earliest with origination. At best, this may result in a sense of the formation of women's voices, of women not simply as passive, but active in both oral and early written culture (Meale 1993). Historical research has greatly contributed to the sense of the conditions within which women, as well as men, structured their lives and the ways that this was manifested in literature. Mary Carruthers, for example, has established the milieu of the Wife of Bath within a capitalistic wool trade (in Evans and Johnson 1994: 24). Scrutiny of property law of the fourteenth century can reveal that other women were less materially fortunate, were themselves regarded as property and formed in the face of an idealized subservience. The Wife's railing against authority can thus be seen in a wider context of literary and material pressures.

Other aspects of women's life and its representation can be revealed when we are told that unmarried daughters lived in their parental home, whereas many married women were absorbed into their husband's family (Goldberg 1992: pp. x, 122). This can enlighten us about the family set up at the miller's home in the Reeve's Tale, Custance's dilemma with her mother-in-law (in the Man of Law's Tale) and Criseyde's isolation and precarious autonomy in her widowhood. Conduct texts, such as the mid fourteenth-century *The Good Wife Taught Her Daughter*, from which the epigraph to this chapter is taken (Mustanoja 1948), can be set alongside the behaviour of Chaucer's women, to see how they measure up. This text, purporting to be notes of guidance of mother to daughter, was probably written by a male cleric. We might ask whether the daughters (motherless and otherwise) of Chaucer's narratives – and there are many – formed their behaviour against such codes, whether indeed their action in the literary text is 'typical' or aberrant, how far the *Good Wife* was effective in controlling daughters or was itself a product of a struggle to control already lost as family and patterns of authority shifted from such a posited ideal? Do they represent fourteenth-century women as they truly were, or are they barring stable doors too late, nostalgic for a lost (or never existing) social order?

Masculinity and the Limits of Gender

The relationship between history and literature has bearings in both directions. Reconstruction of historical moments from literary texts has allowed space in women's studies for deconstruction of the complexities of masculinity as well as femininity: Troilus was made as well as Criseyde by the pressures on gender, the need to act out his biology and masculine identity in the laddish face of his pals (Aers 1988: 117–52). Other studies have shown how women, like men, are constructed in particular ways by the political situation. Elaine Tuttle Hansen (1992) has described 'rules of the game', arguing that they are different for male and female figures: Criseyde is thus condemned for being the person that men want her to be, for indeed coming up to the scratch of the conduct manuals. Ideology is not neutral, and realities of history have a literary bearing (Delany 1990). Among such studies of the conditions that affect responses as well as actions is Carolyn Dinshaw's influential study of the genderization of Chaucer's reader (1989). She considers what narrattee is constituted by Chaucer's narrators and poetics, what it means to 'read like a man'. Writing, she contends, is a male act, performed on a body, construed as female (9). The male author and the reader he constructs are inclined to closure as a narrative device, so *Troilus and Criseyde* ends by rejecting 'the troubling feminine' (65). In a sense, Dinshaw's approach relates to performatives too, for readers, like characters, are formed by the utterance of writing. Discourse is itself gendered. Dinshaw, especially in her claim that the Pardoner's Tale challenges heterosexual hermeneutics, has queered the medieval pitch, unsettled ideas that texts, like people, operate as if only 'masculine' and 'feminine' sexualities were available at any given time. The issue is thus highlighted of wider ramifications within and beyond Chaucer's texts (and see Dinshaw 1999).

Writers have accordingly deconstructed, and historically reconstructed, ideas of gender, with a sense of the cultural circumstances within which characters operated in a fourteenth-century social set-up. Consequently, they have been able to ask supposedly modern questions, derived from supposedly real life, of a medieval fiction. By this means we can ask women's questions, feminist questions, of the texts, can pose and self-consciously stage the maleness of other questions, to probe the (self-)construction of characters in the fourteenth century. There is a paradox here. Writers have, in a sense, assumed a fixedness to gender at a certain time, in order to write about it: this may appear antithetical to moves such as Dinshaw's to suggest a permeability to boundaries, while still seeing a genderization in the stance readers take. For a moment, ideas of masculinity and of femininity are held as if still, in stasis, in order to observe their flux. Other post-modern issues are likewise inferred: can we consider, as well as women's questions, questions of 'Woman'? Within post-modernism, the category itself has been potentially dissolved in a meltdown of the knowable. Can we probe the idea of Woman, then, in the fourteenth century, ask whether it was an established, or movable, category within this period?

If, as we shall do, we look at Criseyde's (self-)formation, in view of Troilus even when she is hidden from his eyes, we can see her moving about, shifting and trying on identities to please him and herself. She is socially constructed as she mediates between what she wants and needs, what she infers of his desire. Though she is undoubtedly a woman throughout, Woman moves, even as we watch. In the fourteenth century, then, feminisms of the post-modern can be observed: 'Woman' is not essentially created by biology alone, but (self-)constructed by discourses, some of them antagonistic, which she adopts or adapts. Becoming a woman may be seen as a process, not a destination; literary, like 'real' women, are always by way of becoming, or resisting becoming, either before our eyes, or off-stage (both of which arenas are subjects for discussion). Not all women are the same. Some are less mobile than others, less able to escape their social circumstances, and their individuation poses issues of class, sexuality, location, as differing oppressions shape or hinder resistance in time and in space. We might ask of Chaucer's women, then, a range of questions for which we seek literary–historical evidence: if our model within a Judeo-Christian framework is one where individuals are generated by something outside, in a creation paradigm, who made Chaucer's women (and men)? How far *can* Criseyde say 'I am myn owene womman'? The idea that the Cartesian 'cogito ergo sum' was the first magically performative sign of a subject, that no medieval figure therefore can show subjectivity, is now seriously in doubt (Dollimore 1991). Writers have demonstrated that Chaucer's women, as other subjects, can, indeed, be distinguished, to probe 'those aspects of experience to which someone is subject . . . a position in a larger structure, a site through which various forces pass' (Leicester 1990: 14).

The Language of Women

If such an idea makes the subject-woman (and also man) seem like an empty space, the empty page we wanted to begin with, then we might probe the historical circumstances of construction. We might ask, to what are Chaucer's women subject? If forces have bearings, what effects do they have? Are women, even if they are individuated, really free to 'be themselves' if so being is itself constituted by ideas of what is possible at a given time? The act of becoming a woman might be pretty well prescribed; a choice of roads to a destination is itself mapped, a choice of scripts is not necessarily a choice of how to write them. We might, then, ask the kind of question that Gayatri Chakravorty Spivak (1988) posed within post-colonial criticism: Can the subaltern speak? She queried the capacity of a member of a marginalized group to use anything but her master's voice, to be an agent as well as a (potentially resisting) subordinate. She probed the 'subject-effects', the ways by which the subaltern can organize narrative resistance. Elaine Showalter, too, has argued that a 'double-voiced discourse' can be heard in which a member of a less powerful group is both passive and active, both shares the language of the determining and engages in her own formation of reality: 'Both muted and dominant groups generate beliefs or ordering ideas of social reality at the unconscious level, but dominant groups control the forms or structures in which consciousness can be articulated. Thus muted groups must mediate their beliefs through the allowable forms of dominant structures' (quoted Rose 1986: 249).

In considering the language of Chaucer's women, we might recognize a situation of power, not peculiar to the fourteenth century, but with particular historical and social ramifications. In considering Chaucer's women, then, we might recognize what Judith Butler has observed of language sites in general, that 'no simple inspection of words will suffice'; that there is, rather, a need to analyse 'the position of dominance' within which words operate for/against their subjects (1997: 13, 19). Analysis of the performative within which Chaucer, and his subjects, operate, may provide insight into this enslaved subject, one who operates within, and uses, a language of thrall. If a subject is constituted when addressed, we raise issues of injurious speech, posing, like Butler, the conundrum: 'When we claim to have been injured by language, what kind of claim do we make?' (1). Several new directions are thus offered in raising postmodern queries of Chaucer's women: and the analysis that follows will consider chosen passages to examine the subjectivity of Criseyde, her (self-)formulation within language; the injurious language around and shaping May in the 'Merchant's Tale'; and the double-voiced discourse of Procne and Philomele in the *Legend of Good Women*.

Subjectivity: *Troilus and Criseyde* II, 771–805

The passage has a widespread context. Criseyde, widowed and alone in Thebes after the defection of her traitorous father, has been persuaded of Troilus' affection by her uncle Pandarus. Alone in her 'closet', 'stylle as any ston' (600), she 'has aspien' Troilus riding past, back home victorious from battle. Her stillness and location should alert our readerly ears: such words often presage a scene of rape (MerT 1818; *LGW* 1818, 2322). As Criseyde mulls over Pandarus' words, the narrator tells us what she thought, knew, said (701–3). Her acts of (non-)agency are manifold and complex. Knowledge of Troilus enters via her eyes as she looks at him, 'And leet it so softe in hire herte synke, / That to hireself she seyde, "Who yaf me drynke?" ' (650–1). Internally debating, she tacitly recalls the biblical association of drunkenness and nakedness (Genesis 9: 20–4), yet 'He naught forbet that every creature / Be drynkeles for alwey' (717–18). A little later she, to herself, laments 'Oure wreche is this, oure owen wo to drynke' (784). Thus she moves through various stages of (non-)resistance, acts as if she is forbidden, then able to choose (not to) 'drink', yet sees actions as self-damaging.

Socially vulnerable, Criseyde undergoes traditional female temptation. Like many women within Chaucer's narratives, she is alone, in motherless fracture. Characters with influential mothers are a rarity in this literature. Women are traded, and not only during times of war. Criseyde, as a widow, may have had a relative economic independence, but it came with a concomitant isolation, exacerbated by the shame of her father's treason. The women with whom she is in contact do not present an alternative to her isolation, only inadequately compensate for male protection, and are situated, for the most part, squarely in the heterosexual domain of the ancillary. Though she does her best, the name alone of Criseyde's niece, Antigone, suggests that she has her own typological troubles to bear. Her soothing song (827–75) offers cold comfort, and leads Criseyde, indeed, into a troubling dream where a white eagle 'Under hire brest his long clawes sette, / And dide his herte into hire brest to gon' (927–8). Other women, nameless, faceless, gather with the callousness of crowds, and misunderstand Criseyde crucially when most she needs their wisdom: they read about the siege of Thebes as Pandarus arrives to besiege his niece (84), they chatter about 'wommanysshe thynges' whilst Criseyde is in anguish (681–707), and they misinterpret her grief (715–28). Motherless and sisterless, then, Criseyde has no recourse to nurturing female figures. The temptations offered by Troilus are indeed great.

With Criseyde as she sits in the seeming safety of her 'closet' (a place of frequent danger, III, 681–91), the narrator is able to tell us what she is thinking. The poet is within Criseyde's most secret spaces, making public her mind. She has already said what she thinks (aloud, to herself, 703–63). Like all manifestations of the confession, this adumbrates a listener, and infers the lie of the genre that it attains a closure, for something has been said but has not been lain to rest, as Criseyde continues to mull over her choices. Speaking aloud, to herself and, unwittingly, to the eavesdropping voyeur narrator, Criseyde expresses self-disjunction, 'who yaf me drynke?' This confession has been a de-subjectifying moment, as she recognizes her own non-agency, even as, from it, she attains an eloquence over several stanzas (703–63), significantly ending with the word 'shame'. At this point, she is again consigned to the realm of the non-verbal, and thinks silently, but aloud because of the presence of the narrator. In the circularity of narrative, she arrives back where she began, and is returned to a pre-confession stage, wherein she re-enacts her own indecision, which again takes her to the brink of utterance, at the end of this passage: 'He which that nothing undertaketh, / Nothyng n'acheveth' (807–8). This is a cliché of which uncle Pandarus might have been proud: she does not, even having found words via trauma, use her own, but iterates through a familiar saying, a proverb, by definition a hollow truth.

Within her thinking, Criseyde visits many of the dilemmas affecting women subjects. Having just stated aloud 'I am myn owene womman, wel at ese / . . . Right yong, and stonde unteyd in lusty leese' (750, 752), she now asks of herself 'Syn I am free, / Sholde I now love, and put in jupartie / My sikernesse, and thrallen libertee?' (771–3). This is a language of enslavement, within which her own sense of autonomy is tested. She tries out various possibilities of action in the face of Troilus' desire. And she moves back and forth, expressing indecision, 'cloude over that sonne' (781). This echoes, unwittingly of course, the narrator's own description of her: she is not, though she does not know it, even here using her own words. Criseyde's thinking, then, cross-refs to her own, and others', earlier, spoken-aloud thinking, and to a wider textuality. She situates herself within a tradition of the spoken and the written: 'we wrecched wommen nothing konne, / Whan us is wo, but wepe and sitte and thinke . . . Also, thise wikked tonges be so prest / To speke us harm; ek men ben so untrewe' (781–2, 785–6).

Bodily harm is inflicted by language: 'The threat prefigures or, indeed, promises a bodily act, and yet is already a bodily act' (Butler 1997: 11). Criseyde, within the stream of language that contains her, is sufficiently self-aware to know she is part of a larger narrative. She refers to the 'jangle of love' (800), a word of, and sounding like, language's chatter. It is a word that was used several lines earlier, when the narrator says 'Now myghte som envious jangle thus' (666). Criseyde is enmeshed in a web of language with its capacity to harm her, and not only in the narrative present. Gossip echoes on, and before her, contained in her traitorous reputation. Hers is a sin of language: she breaks her word 'whan she falsed Troilus' (V, 1053) and with its shards is punished. Language occupies at best a place of temporary reprieve. That which can smooth things over, pacify ('coye'), please ('quemen', 803), can also do endless harm. The positive performative of language's miracle is reversible.

Criseyde asks the rhetorical question, 'And who may stoppen every wikked tonge, / Or sown of belles whil that thei ben ronge?' (804–5). No one, came the loud reply. This is one of those marvellous medieval moments when the past and future rock together, poised on the elegance of typology. Criseyde has gone into her own future, recognized a subjectivity beyond her immediate subject-status, and become her own prophet of doom. By the fifteenth century, in Robert Henryson's version of her story, Cresseid has become a leper: it is for her that this bell tolls. And for Shakepeare she was to be the embodiment of fickleness, 'Let all constant men be Troiluses, all false women Cressids' (*Troilus and Cressida* III. ii. 202–3). Chaucer's Criseyde could not possibly really know this, but knows all too well the death-knell of her own reputation. Hers is a tragedy of understanding. She is in, and beyond, history:

> She seyde, 'Allas, for now is clene ago
> My name of trouthe in love, for everemo!
> . . .
> Allas, of me unto the worldes ende,
> Shal neyther ben ywriten nor ysonge
> No good word, for thise bokes wol me shende.
> O, rolled shal I ben on many a tonge!
> Thorughout the world my belle shal be ronge!
> (V, 1054–5, 1058–62)

Criseyde's is a fate of women in books, one of language. In resorting to it, she plays, and dies, by the (s)word. Other women suffer similarly.

Injurious Language: The Merchant's Tale, 2132–59

May has married old January: their names hint at the mistake that this is, and soon May is lusting after January's squire, the youthful Damyan. January is suddenly 'woxen blynd' (2071) as metaphor is made flesh, just as, physically, he builds an enclosed garden to contain his bride. May, with Freudian panache, 'in warm wex hath emprented the clyket / That January bar of the smale wyket' (2117–18) and gives the duplicate key to Damyan, the satisfying rhyme underlining the neatness of her ploy. The poet invokes Ovid and refers, twice in six lines, to 'sleighte', once significantly at the line's end that precedes this passage: trickery is far-reaching, beyond even the perpetrators.

Chaucer does not repeat words lightly, even for the sake of good rhymes. The 'sleighte' here is manifold. It is January's, May's, and it is textual, as protagonists are enfolded in words. January eggs on his wife 'for to pleye' – often a sign that there is no fun ahead – in his garden (2135–6). He uses then, to seduce *his* wife into *his* garden, words from the Song of Songs (chs 2–4), though in somewhat bowdlerized form. This has a number of effects: an immediate, narrative one of repulsion as the smoothie seeks to lure his 'innocent' (we know she is not) spouse into sexual-like plea-sure; and a series of wider effects arising from complex textual responses. For all its high comedy, this is one of the most sinister moments in the whole of Chaucer's works. January's speech produces effects, initiates a set of consequences. Here, they are literal (the couple, and Damyan, go into the garden) and consequential, setting in train a number of actions, some of them non-physical and unintended. January's use of the *hortus conclusus* links the Old Testament to the new covenant. The Virgin and her immaculate conception are often referred to as an enclosed garden in medieval literature and art. Conventions are drawn upon that operate in the narrative present, the textual past and the figurative, and actual, future. The speech act makes things, as well as events, happen, and the effects are not always, as here, those that the speaker intended: 'Interpellation is an address that regularly misses its mark' (Butler 1997: 33).

Readers are invited to respond by recognizing the Song of Songs, operating in effect as co-writers by interpreting ahead to see the consequences of the garden routine. All sorts of possible actions can happen and unsettling potential denouements present themselves in the fabliau-like scenario the narrator offers. Here 'the text is not a line of words releasing a single "theological" meaning (the "message" of the Author–God) but a multi-dimensional space in which a variety of meanings, none of them origi-nal, blend and clash' (Culler [quoting Barthes] 1983: 32–3). Yet not everything is possible, as we can see for ourselves. The action to which May is called by her croon-ing husband is enclosed in a male plot (literally January's garden and literarily a wider Garden) and operates within a theological tradition where the text has the authority of the Father (God–husband). The woman enters into the realm of language not yet her own.

Hence, though she seems to take charge of the situation (and part of her tragedy is the gap that emerges between the possible and the real: what *might* have been), May is particularly lost within the garden innuendo that is not of her own making, encased within several texts (biblical, the Canterbury tale within a tale, January's). For women the mind and body are accordingly fractured, and it is May who is 'groping blind and wordless toward an Other who should provide meaning but does not, only leads her back to the real of her body' (de Lauretis 1994: 210).

When January addresses May 'Rys up, my wyf, my love, my lady free' (2138), this '*constitutes* its addressee at the moment of its utterance'; though 'lady free' infers an autonomy, 'wyf' animates the ancillary, 'the subject in subordinate position' (Butler 1997: 18). January, and his author, invoke a formula established by source texts, their 'inherited set of voices' (25). Within this cacophony, women subjects struggle. Some, like Criseyde ('Who made this song . . . ?', *TC* II, 876), or the Wyf of Bath ('Who peyntede the leon, tel me who?', WBP 692), articulate their bewilderment or anger. May is slighter in her understanding than Criseyde, hence does not intellectually know her own tragedy. She does not (does he?) realize the signification of January's words and their weightiness in the scheme of things, but she experiences their force, albeit while wantonly seeking to appropriate the space they create for her own sexual enterprise. Hers is a tragedy of misunderstanding.

Yet May, like Criseyde, has constructed her sexual identity and desire in male sites/sights; she is contained by them, and her alternative to an old man is only a younger replica, not female company or independence. 'She' is a subject constituted, yet she attempts to be insubordinate, within the alien and male realm of language: 'Swiche olde lewed wordes used he. / On Damyan a signe made she' (2149–50). Words and signs are not accidentally juxtaposed here, just as they are not several lines later (2207, 2209, 2214). The blind author is led (as the Wife of Bath inverted leadership by 'sowe's nose' or 'bridel', WBP 785, 813) by the silent woman, who has the power accorded to sign but cannot speak because her husband will hear. Though May, partially at least, evades passivity, both husband and wife are, if only temporarily, incapacitated by the dissimulation of language (not) of their own making: 'no wight myghte it se neither yheere' (2154). Knowledge, entering through the doors of the senses, is barred by misunderstanding, misapplication, misappropriation. The comedy is a tragedy of errors, beyond, within, words.

There is here, as elsewhere within Chaucer's work, a poetics of space. This is January's garden, just as Criseyde, with her women, roams in her 'yerd . . . rayled alle th'aleynes . . . And benched newe' (*TC* II, 820–2). Someone else, and male, has constructed this private place, the sphere of women. In the Merchant's Tale, May tries to subvert the space for her own game, and all are trapped as 'clapte to the wyket sodenly' (2159), the word again not used casually, but echoing the suddenness of chance, of blindness, of lust (2056, 2071, 2094). The scene of utterance is the 'fresshe gardyn', the site of all sexual action before, during, since the Fall. Here, Damyan waits, 'stille he sit under a bussh anon. / This January, as blynd as is a stoon' (2154–5): the adjectives, again, should give us a clue to the action that will ensue. Elsewhere in Chaucer's narratives it is women who are described thus, before they are about to be, or are being, literally or literarily, raped. We should anticipate that shaftings of all sorts, sexual/textual, will occur. The Merchant's Tale is unsettling, then, in many senses, invokes, to dismantle, authority, exposes the performatives and the destructiveness of language as words turn against their user(s). There is a complexity of genderized poetics here.

Double-voiced Discourse: The *Legend of Good Women*, 2349–82

Many of the women in the *Legend* know, and feel, their tragedies. Subtitled 'The Seintes Legende of Cupide' after its designation in the prologue of the Man of Law's Tale, this is a series of tales about 'good' women, ostensibly written by the poet to make amends for the *Romaunt of the Rose* and *Troilus and Criseyde* (G 344). The stories are composed in 'penaunce' (1485, 489), in the dramatized context of previous tales 'reneyed' and a poet who will 'repente' (G 314, 316). Here, as often, the 're-' itself suggests both closure and incompleteness: returning suggests going back to something that will be surely different, yet the fiction is one of recovery.

Such juxtaposition of certainty and its difference is the subject and the process of the *Legend of Good Women*. Chaucer uses Ovid as his ostensible source, and 'translates' tales. In the legend of Philomela, Tereus, sovereign of Thrace, marries Procne, daughter of King Pandiones, and takes her far away to his own land. Procne misses her sister, Philomela, so the good husband sets off to fetch her, persuades her father to 'vouche-sauf' her into his custody for a while, then himself 'saw hire beaute' and 'He caste his fyry herte upon hyre so / That he wol have hir' (2292–3). Accordingly, he transports her 'to a cave pryvely' (2311) where he 'kepte hire to his usage and his store' (2337). When she protests, he cuts out her tongue with his sword. Procne is told that her sister is dead, and her 'herte brak a-two' (2347). Female subjectivity emerges thus in both sisters from their sense of trauma.

The speechless Philomela, deprived physically of access to words by the fledgling Lacanian male, embroiders her story, 'As it of wemen hath be woned yore' (2352); 'with a penne coude she nat wryte. / But letters she can weve to and fro' (2357–8). She draws upon female traditions to self-express. Like May, and other Chaucer women, she is deprived of direct access to *logos*, and invokes the language of 'signes' (repeated 2367, 2369), and so 'wrot the storye above'. This 'storye' is not just her immediate own, that which we have been (re)told by the poet; it is the story contained within a male literary tradition, that Ovid himself re-rehearsed. Translation occurs at several locations, and Philomela is part of the fabric she weaves, her own imaginative thread yet within someone else's far-reaching story. She communicates with the messenger-knave 'by signes', just as May, (self-)confined and kicking in her husband's plot, secretly motioned Damyan. The male 'listener' conveys messages between agents, this time both female. Procne duly arrives. 'No word she spak, for sorwe and ek for rage'

(2374). Both sisters are rendered speechless subjects by the male effect. She 'feyned', and pretends to go on pilgrimage, so that she can reach her sister: the ritual quest is thus subverted by the woman in support of her 'dombe sister'. On reunion, what 'wo . . . compleynt . . . mone / That Progne upon her doumbe sysster maketh!' (2379–80). Speech, though born of anguish, is returned. Here the women are thwarted, and enabled, by a double-voiced discourse: they need to use the language of their oppressor in order to communicate with each other, and to resort to signs beyond sound. The subaltern speaks, from the space she is allocated within discourse. Her sounds are horrible, a travesty of language, all that is left by her oppressor.

However, the nuance of that speech might be queried, along with Chaucer's use of his sources. In Ovid, when Tereus tears out Philomela's tongue, it offers resistance:

> The stump recoiled, silenced,
> Into the back of her throat.
> But the tongue squirmed in the dust, babbling on –
> Shaping words that were now soundless.
> It writhed like a snake's tail freshly cut off,
> Striving to reach her feet in its death-struggle.
>   (Hughes 1997: 237)

Chaucer has none of Ovid's revenge. In the *Legend*, the tongue goes quietly (2334), and the sisters are suspended, mid-story, where he leaves them 'Wepyng . . . In armes everych of hem other taketh, / And thus I late hem sorwe dwelle' (2378, 2381–2). He has chosen to leave them unavenged, though his ostensible source offered an alternative. His stance as hapless translator, repenting for his own misuse of women, is thus exposed. Female grief, like Emelye's in the Knight's Tale, is consigned to speechless flopping and non-action.

In the *Legend*, Chaucer invites his knowing reader to interpolate beyond his text. The writing finger, having writ, stops short, and asks its reader to take up the story. Ostensibly closing, the narrator states 'The remenaunt is no charge for to telle' (2383). And Chaucer leaves the tale 'unended', averring 'Ye may be war of men, if that yow liste' (2387). If we have knowledge of Ovid, which a medieval reader well might from *Ovide moralisé*, then we know the story continues.

It has often been said that the structure of the *Legend* is unsatisfactory, that the poet, indeed, became bored with the monotony of his retelling and simply gave up (see e.g. Dinshaw 1989: 87). It is more complex than this. Behind the legends are complicated inter-relationships both with other legends and with tales beyond. Cleopatra, for example, dies by her own hand in a pit of serpents (prefiguring Procne's cave, Ovid's snake-tongue, Eve's thrall); Medea's revenge is, like Philomela's, child-murder; Lucrece, when raped, 'for fer of sclaundre and drede of deth / She lost bothe at ones wit and breth . . . She feleth no thyng' (1814–15, 1819), recalling other 'raped' women in Chaucer, those who suffer both physically and are 'rapen' by the text, their future reputation carried forward by injurious words.

Chaucer writes, then, with a full consciousness of language as a site of power. His texts exemplify, and contain experts in, speech-act theory that structures dominance with a medieval edge. Women are represented with fourteenth-century familial frameworks that isolate or commodify them, construct them as objects of thrall. Their sense of themselves thus emerges from a struggle for some autonomy in a male, and heterosexually, determined discourse. While male figures likewise struggle for self-meaning in a bewildering universe, they at least have the upper hand of history, of naming, of theology. Chaucer's women, meanwhile, know, but do not often learn, the lesson uttered by their successor, *The Sound of Music*'s Liesl: 'Totally unprepared am I, to face a world of men. / Timid and shy and scared am I, of things beyond my ken'. So, like Criseyde, wary, canny, careful, she places her trust in the one man.

See also AUTHORITY; CHIVALRY; CRISIS AND DISSENT; LIFE HISTORIES; LOVE; NARRATIVE; OTHER THOUGHT-WORLDS; PERSONAL IDENTITY; SOCIAL STRUCTURES; STYLE; TRANSLATION; VISUALIZING.

REFERENCES AND FURTHER READING

Aers, David (1988) *Community, Gender, and Individual Identity: English Writing 1360–1430* (London and New York: Routledge). An analysis of gender and other facets of identity formation in the context of social history.

Austin, John L. (1962) *How To Do Things With Words* (Cambridge, Mass.: Harvard University Press; rev. edn 1975). A text that has formed the basis of many of the ideas of performance and performativity, including those by Jacques Derrida and Judith Butler.

Butler, Judith (1997) *Excitable Speech: A Politics of the Performative* (New York and London: Routledge). An application of speech-act theory, particularly of aspects of hate speech and the nature of injurious language.

Culler, Jonathan (1983) *Barthes* (Glasgow: Fontana). Discusses Barthes' ideas, including the effects of *plaisir*, a state of reassurance of existing values, and that of *jouissance*, an action derived from unsettling features in a text.

de Lauretis, Teresa (1994) *The Practice of Love: Lesbian Sexuality and Perverse Desire* (Bloomington and Indianapolis: Indiana University Press). A feminist discussion of woman's relationship with language, and with philosophies of body and mind.

Delany, Sheila (1990) *Medieval Literary Politics: Shapes of Ideology* (Manchester and New York: Manchester University Press). A Marxist discussion of ideology and its effects on literature.

——(1994) *The Naked Text: Chaucer's* Legend of Good Women (Berkeley, Los Angeles and London: University of California Press). A focus on one work, using Chaucer's own phrase for its thesis (*LGWP* G 85–8), from which she describes medieval intertextual poetic production.

Dinshaw, Carolyn L. (1989) *Chaucer's Sexual Poetics* (Madison and London: University of Wisconsin Press). An influential text, credited with introducing the idea of gendered reading and exploring how Chaucer constructs the reader in his poetry.

——(1999) *Getting Medieval: Sexualities and Communities, Pre- and Postmodern* (Durham, NC and London: Duke University Press). An exanimation of medieval communities in the light of queer and other theory.

Dollimore, Jonathan (1991) *Sexual Dissidence: Augustine to Wilde, Freud to Foucault* (Oxford: Clarendon). Challenges the idea of the birth of the modern subject in the Renaissance by investigating the complex formation of subjectivity from Augustine – 'Si enim fallor sum' (If I am deceived, then I exist) – onwards.

Evans, Ruth and Johnson, Lesley, eds (1994) *Feminist Readings in Middle English Literature: The Wyf of Bath and All Her Sect* (London and New York: Routledge). A set of key essays by feminist scholars, including Mary Carruthers' essay on the Wife of Bath, with a useful bibliography.

Goldberg, Jeremy P., ed. (1992) *Women in Medieval English Society* (Stroud: Sutton; repr. 1997). A collection of essays by historians which casts light on conditions of women in marriage, family, work and piety.

Hallissy, Margaret (1993) *Clean Maids, True Wives, Steadfast Widows: Chaucer's Women and Medieval Codes of Conduct* (Westport, Conn. and London: Greenwood). Contends that women's lives were divided into three stages of virgin, wife, widow, each stage having its own norms.

Hansen, Elaine T. (1992) *Chaucer and the Fictions of Gender* (Berkeley, Los Angeles and Oxford: University of California Press). Considers the ways in which women and men operate by different codes, how feminization (of both sexes) occurs as a fictional failure of manliness.

Hughes, Ted (1997) *Tales from Ovid: Twenty-four Passages from the Metamorphoses* (London: Faber). A highly acclaimed translation by another poet.

Leicester, H. Marshall, Jr (1990) *The Disenchanted Self: Representing the Subject in the* Canterbury Tales (Berkeley, Los Angeles and London: University of California Press). Questions ideas of the poet as a source of meaning, contends that the subject originates in aspects of experience s/he may not fully control yet which contribute to her/his individuation.

Martin, Priscilla (1990) *Chaucer's Women: Nuns, Wives and Amazons* (Basingstoke and London: Macmillan; repr. 1996). An early, and sound, full-length study of Chaucer's women, raising the main issues of authority, ideals, roles and sexual discourse.

Meale, Carol M., ed. (1993) *Women and Literature in Britain 1150–1500* (Cambridge: Cambridge University Press). A collection of essays on women's access to, and formation of, written culture in various genres.

Mustanoja, Tauno-F., ed. (1948) *The Good Wife Taught Her Daughter* (Helsinki: Kirjapainon). Editions of various versions of this text, with commentary and manuscript details.

Rose, Mary B., ed. (1986) *Women in the Middle Ages and the Renaissance* (Syracuse, NY: Syracuse University Press). Quotes Elaine Showalter's ideas of the 'double voiced discourse'; the collection of essays as a whole relates to women's situations in the period.

Spivak, Gayatri C. (1988) 'Can the subaltern speak?' in *Marxism and the Interpretation of Culture*, ed. Cary Nelson and Lawrence Grossberg (New York: New York Literary Forum), 271–313. A key text in post-colonial theory which asks how far the subordinated or marginalized can develop their own language.

Index

A COMPANION TO
CHAUCER